Women, Men, & Gender

Seattle Therapy Alliance
200 1st Avenue W. #400
Seattle, WA 98119

Seattle Therapy Alliance
200 1st Avenue W. #400
Seattle, WA 98119
206.660.4395

Women, Men, & Gender

ONGOING DEBATES

EDITED BY

Mary Roth Walsh

YALE UNIVERSITY PRESS   NEW HAVEN & LONDON

Set in Minion with Copperplate Gothic display type
by Northeastern Graphic Services, Inc., Hackensack,
New Jersey.
Printed in the United States of America by
Hamilton Printing Company,
Rensselaer, New York.

Library of Congress Cataloging-in-Publication Data
Women, men, and gender : ongoing debates / edited by Mary Roth Walsh.
   p.   cm.
  Includes bibliographical references and index.
  ISBN 0–300–06896–4 (cloth : alk. paper)—
  ISBN 0–300–06938–3 (pbk. : alk. paper)
  1. Women—Psychology. 2. Men—Psychology. 3. Sex differences
(Psychology) 4. Gender identity. I. Walsh, Mary Roth.
HQ1206.W8748 1996
305.3—dc20 96–16540
          CIP

A catalogue record for this book is available from the
British Library.

The paper in this book meets the guidelines for perma-
nence and durability of the Committee on Production
Guidelines for Book Longevity of the Council on Library
Resources.

10 9 8 7 6 5 4 3 2 1

CONTENTS

Preface x

Acknowledgments xiii

Publication Information xvi

List of Contributors xix

Introduction 1

PART I: FUNDAMENTAL QUESTIONS

Question 1. Research Priorities: Should We Continue to Study Gender Differences? 15

> **No:** Bernice Lott, "Cataloging Gender Differences: Science or Politics?" 19

> **Yes:** Alice H. Eagly, "Comparing Women and Men: Methods, Findings, and Politics" 24

Question 2. Biological Causation: Are Gender Differences Wired into Our Biology? 33

> **Yes:** June M. Reinisch, Leonard A. Rosenblum, Donald B. Rubin, and M. Fini Schulsinger, "Sex Differences Emerge during the First Year of Life" 37

> **No:** Linda L. Carli, "Biology Does Not Create Gender Differences in Personality" 44

Question 3. Diversity Issues: Are Race, Class, and Gender of Comparable Importance in Producing Inequality? 55

> **Yes:** Candace West and Sarah Fenstermaker, "Doing Difference" 58

> **No:** Patricia Hill Collins, "On West and Fenstermaker's 'Doing Difference' " 73

PART II: POWER AND INFLUENCE STRATEGIES

Question 4. Conversational Style: Do Women and Men Speak Different Languages? 79

> **YES:** Deborah Tannen, "Women and Men Talking: An Interactional Sociolinguistic Approach" 82

> **NO:** Elizabeth Aries, "Women and Men Talking: Are They Worlds Apart?" 91

Question 5. Nonverbal Behavior: Are Women's Superior Skills Caused by Their Oppression? 101

> **YES:** Marianne LaFrance and Nancy M. Henley, "On Oppressing Hypotheses: Or, Differences in Nonverbal Sensitivity Revisited" 104

> **NO:** Judith A. Hall and Amy G. Halberstadt, "Subordination and Nonverbal Sensitivity: A Hypothesis in Search of Support" 120

Question 6. Negotiation Strategies: Do Women and Men Have Different Styles? 135

> **YES:** Deborah M. Kolb, "Her Place at the Table: Gender and Negotiation" 138

> **NO:** Carol Watson, "Gender versus Power as a Predictor of Negotiation Behavior and Outcomes" 145

PART III: SEXUALITY

Question 7. Pornography: Is It Harmful to Women? 155

> **YES:** Diana E. H. Russell, "Pornography Causes Harm to Women" 158

> **NO:** Nadine Strossen, "Why Censoring Pornography Would Not Reduce Discrimination or Violence against Women" 170

Question 8. Sexual Orientation: Is It Determined by Biology? 181

> **YES:** J. Michael Bailey and Richard C. Pillard, "The Innateness of Homosexuality" 184

> **NO:** Celia Kitzinger and Sue Wilkinson, "Transitions from Heterosexuality to Lesbianism: The Discursive Production of Lesbian Identities" 188

PART IV: VIOLENCE

Question 9. Domestic Violence: Are Women as Likely as Men to Initiate Physical Assaults in Partner Relationships? 207

> **YES:** Murray A. Straus, "Physical Assaults by Women Partners: A Major Social Problem" 210
>
> **NO:** Demie Kurz, "Physical Assaults by Male Partners: A Major Social Problem" 222

Question 10. Rape: Are Rape Statistics Exaggerated? 233

> **YES:** Neil Gilbert, "Advocacy Research Exaggerates Rape Statistics" 236
>
> **NO:** Charlene L. Muehlenhard, Barrie J. Highby, Joi L. Phelps, and Susie C. Sympson, "Rape Statistics Are Not Exaggerated" 243

PART V: KNOWING AND LEARNING

Question 11. Ways of Knowing: Do Women and Men Have Different Ways of Knowing? 249

> **YES:** Nancy Goldberger, "Ways of Knowing: Does Gender Matter?" 252
>
> **NO:** Mary M. Brabeck and Ann G. Larned, "What We Do Not Know about Women's Ways of Knowing" 261

Question 12. Mathematics: Is Biology the Cause of Gender Differences in Performance? 271

> **YES:** Camilla Persson Benbow and David Lubinski, "Psychological Profiles of the Mathematically Talented: Some Sex Differences and Evidence Supporting Their Biological Basis" 274
>
> **NO:** Janet Shibley Hyde, "Gender Differences in Math Performance: Not Big, Not Biological" 283

PART VI: THE WORKPLACE

Question 13. Leadership: Do Women and Men Have Different Ways of Leading? 291

> **YES:** Judy B. Rosener, "Leadership and the Paradox of Gender" 294
>
> **NO:** Gary N. Powell, "Leadership and Gender: *Vive la Différence?*" 298

Question 14. Discrimination: Is Sex Stereotyping the Cause of Workplace Discrimination? 307

No: Gerald V. Barrett and Scott B. Morris, "The American Psychological Association's Amicus Curiae Brief in *Price Waterhouse v. Hopkins*" 310

YES: Susan T. Fiske, Donald N. Bersoff, Eugene Borgida, Kay Deaux, and Madeline E. Heilman, "What Constitutes a Scientific Review? A Majority Retort to Barrett and Morris" 321

PART VII: PSYCHOTHERAPY

Question 15. Diagnosis: Is There Gender Bias in the 1994 *Diagnostic and Statistical Manual* (DSM-IV)? 337

YES: Terry A. Kupers, "The Politics of Psychiatry: Gender and Sexual Preference in DSM-IV" 340

No: Ruth Ross, Allen Frances, and Thomas A. Widiger, "Gender Issues in DSM-IV" 348

Question 16. Relational Therapy: Is the Stone Center's Relational Theory a Source of Empowerment for Women? 359

No: Marcia C. Westkott, "On the New Psychology of Women: A Cautionary View" 362

YES: Judith V. Jordan, "The Relational Model Is a Source of Empowerment for Women" 373

PART VIII: SOCIAL CHANGE

Question 17. Women's Behavior: Do Mothers Harm Their Children When They Work Outside the Home? 383

YES: Penelope Leach, "Nurseries and Daycare Centers Do Not Meet Infant Needs" 386

No: Diane E. Eyer, "There Is No Evidence That Mothers Harm Their Infants and Toddlers by Working Outside the Home" 391

Question 18. Men's Behavior: Is the Mythopoetic Men's Movement Creating New Obstacles for Women? 399

No: Marvin Allen, "We've Come a Long Way, Too, Baby. And We've Still Got a Ways to Go. So Give Us a Break!" 402

YES: Michael S. Kimmel and Michael Kaufman, "Weekend Warriors: The New Men's Movement" 406

Index 421

PREFACE

This book is designed to introduce the reader to some of the major debates in the field of gender studies. Although most of the debates that follow can be characterized as "mutually respectful conversations" (Stimpson, 1996, p. 70), several involve heated exchanges. But this is to be expected, for as Harvard University President Neil Rudenstine points out, "Discussion and debate are not purely intellectual processes. They involve emotion and conviction as well as reason and argument" (1996, p. 52).

Each of the eighteen controversies in this book offers two opposing points of view. Further, all of the debates were chosen with the conviction that the research on women that emerged in the 1970s transformed the field of psychology from a profession that, in Naomi Weisstein's words, had "nothing to say about women" (1968, p. 208) to one that now has a great deal to say. The new psychology of women, in turn, has served as a model for the study of men's roles. Where once only women seemed to have "gender" (Kimmel, 1995), the new psychology of men discusses gender, not as a biological given, but as a social construct capable of change (Levant & Pollack, 1995).

I am aware that a few feminist scholars oppose using a debate format. As they point out, by participating in certain arguments—for example, whether or not the Holocaust occurred—one may be tacitly agreeing that the question is worth asking in the first place. The gender debates in this book, however, involve legitimate questions that have persisted over time. Meredith Kimball has provided a superb rationale for gender debates when she argues, "Feminist theories and politics will be richer and stronger, and . . . each of us will provide a better criticism of our own work if we engage in practicing double visions" (1995, p. 11). My goal in editing this book of debates is to encourage a vigorous exchange of ideas among both scholars and other readers to gain a better understanding of gender issues.

There is, of course, nothing new in employing debates as a learning device. The Socratic method is some 2,400 years old. Nevertheless, the debate approach is especially appropriate at the present time. Charges of political correctness to the contrary, the following chapters demonstrate that there is no monolithic feminist viewpoint. Debates are no longer only between feminists and nonfeminists, nor are all the feminists female, as illustrated by several chapters.

The debate format also encourages critical thinking and engages the reader more actively. We live in a psychological society in which we are bombarded with information, much of it misleading, about gender issues. I believe that by being forced to evaluate conflicting viewpoints, readers will become more discriminating about psychological data, whether presented in the media or in the scientific literature. Lisa Elliot (1993), who used my previous book *The Psychology of Women: Ongoing Debates* (Walsh, 1987) in her classes, reported that the debate format empowered her students by enhancing their critical thinking skills.

WHO SHOULD READ THIS BOOK

This book is intended for the general reader as well as for students and scholars. Many of the questions explored here are regularly debated in the popular media: "Is pornography harmful to women?" "Is one's sexual orientation determined by biology?" and "Do mothers harm their children when they work outside the home?" At the same time, the topics represent some of the most crucial issues in the field of gender studies. Although my own research area is the psychology of women, the contributors to this book represent many academic disciplines, including sociology, law, linguistics, management science, and psychiatry. Research on gender is constantly breaking new ground, and it depends on conflict and debate for the energy to grow. I hope that some scholars who read this book will want to expand (or refute) the arguments presented here and add to the published literature in the field, as many did after the publication of my earlier book.

CHOOSING THE DEBATE TOPICS

After the publication of my first book of debates (Walsh, 1987), I was often asked how I selected the topics. I discovered the questions, in part, by drawing on my twenty years of teaching and consulting with colleagues in the field of gender studies. Equally valuable for this book were the new debate suggestions from a survey of 113 fellows of the American Psychological Association's Division of the Psychology of Women conducted by Yale University Press. I made my final choice of topics after additional research, including a systematic study of the literature and a careful analysis of textbooks in the field. In order to include as much new material as possible, I had to move beyond the published literature. Of the thirty-six chapters that follow, ten are original contributions and nineteen are revised versions of earlier publications.

Clearly not every controversy within the field found its way into this book. Space limitations forced me to choose from a number of possibilities. In making those difficult decisions, I used four criteria: (1) the controversy should deal with a significant question; (2) the controversy should be an ongoing one; (3) it should be relevant to some larger social issue, and (4) most important, the debate should involve strongly divergent points of view. The growing literature on diversity issues is impressive, and whenever possible, I made a special effort to bring this new multicultural research into my introductions to the debate topics.

FEATURES OF THE BOOK

I hope that this book will provide some understanding of how we arrive at what is defined as psychological knowledge. My goal as a scholar has always been to make material accessible. In order to place each question in context, I have written a brief introduction outlining the important issues. Because all the debates represent ongoing controversies, I have also included suggestions for further reading for each topic. In all, there are more than 1,800 recent bibliographical citations in this book.

I do not claim that the two selections for each question always represent the definitive answers to a given issue. In some cases, both points of view will appear unsatisfactory. One of the underlying assumptions of this book is that research is a continuous dialogue in which dissent and difference of opinion are essential. As Virginia Woolf noted, "When a subject is highly controversial—and any question about sex is that—one cannot hope to tell the truth. One can only show how one came to hold whatever opinion one does hold. One can only give one's audience a chance of drawing their own conclusions as they observe the limitations, the prejudices, the idiosyncracies of the speaker" (1929, p. 4).

I hope, however, that the debate format provides some sense of the complexity of these issues: this would be the most valuable outcome. As historian C. Vann Woodward has pointed out: "Questions have to be asked before they can be even wrongly answered. Answers have to be ventured even before we are sure that they are addressed to the right questions. Errors have to be made before they can be corrected and contrary answers provoked. All of which leads to controversy, to be sure; but controversy is one of the ways we have of arriving at what we assign the dignity of truth" (1986, p. 33).

REFERENCES

Elliot, L. B. (1993). Using debates to teach the psychology of women. *Teaching of Psychology, 20,* 35–38.

Kimball, M. M. (1995). *Feminist visions of gender similarities and differences.* New York: Harrington Park Press.

Kimmel, M. S. (1996). *Manhood in America: A cultural history.* New York: Free Press.

Levant, R. F., & Pollack, W. S. (1995). Introduction. In R. F. Levant & W. S. Pollack (Eds.), *A new psychology of men.* New York: Basic Books.

Rudenstine, N. (1996). The uses of diversity. *Harvard Magazine,* (March-April), pp. 48–62.

Stimpson, C. R. (1996, Winter). Women's studies and its discontents. *Dissent,* pp. 67–75.

Walsh, M. R. (Ed.). (1987). *The psychology of women: Ongoing debates.* New Haven: Yale University Press.

Weisstein, N. (1968). "Kinder, Küche, Kirche" as scientific law: Psychology constructs the female. In R. Morgan (Ed.), *Sisterhood is powerful: An anthology of writings from the women's liberation movement* (pp. 205–220). New York: Vintage Books.

Woodward, C. V. (1986, Feb. 3). Between Little Rock and a hard place. *New Republic,* pp. 29–33.

Woolf, V. (1929). *A room of one's own.* New York: Harcourt, Brace, & World, 1957.

ACKNOWLEDGMENTS

I would like to begin by thanking Gladys Topkis, senior editor at Yale University Press, whose enthusiasm for my work made both of my debates books possible. When I first met Gladys in the fall of 1985 at an American Educational Research Association conference in Boston, I could see she was a very special person. That first impression has been confirmed time after time through my own experience as well as by the numerous scholars who sing her praises.

Thomas Edison is said to have coined the phrase that genius is 1 percent inspiration and 99 percent perspiration. If Gladys is right about the genius in my original idea for a gender debates book, then Edison's comment about perspiration explains why it has taken me so long to complete this second volume. I long ago lost count of the sheer number of discussions, letters, telephone calls, faxes, and e-mail messages used to research the individual debate topics in this book. The amount of aid I received from generous colleagues overwhelmed my filing system, and I apologize to those whose names I may be omitting. I hope they will not hesitate to remind me so I can properly acknowledge them in subsequent printings of this book.

Margaret Matlin's friendship has meant much to me over the years. Since I first met Margaret in 1980, she has enriched both my professional and personal life in numerous ways. I am glad to be able to thank her publicly for her ideas, her constant encouragement, and her "care packages" of articles and citations that I might otherwise have missed. I am also grateful to Laurel Furumoto for her help and friendship for over sixteen years. She has always been there when I needed her.

More than 113 Fellows in the American Psychological Association's Division 35, The Psychology of Women, contributed to this book through their detailed responses to a survey about gender debates initiated by Gladys Topkis at Yale University Press. I am also grateful to Meg Elise Wirth, a 1991 graduate of Harvard University, who volunteered her time to make meaning of these voluminous responses. Sometimes an individual's research did not appear to fit into the topics finally selected for this book, and I welcome correspondence from those who may disagree with my selections and who have another point of view.

I also want to thank colleagues who have worked with me in developing Division 35's pre-convention teaching workshop on women and gender beginning in the early 1980s. This workshop is now in its ninth year, and several hundred faculty have attended our workshops helping to create a national network of scholars and teachers who serve as mentors for one another in this important area. I am grateful for the gentle prodding I felt, year after year, as workshop participants asked me when a new debates book would be published. I hope they like this book. I am also indebted to several wonderful workshop colleagues with whom I have worked over the years: Margaret Matlin, Janet Shibley Hyde, Pamela Trotman Reid, Beverly Daniel Tatum, and Bernice Lott.

The fifty-four authors whose work was selected for this book contributed to my knowledge on specific debate topics in ways that are not easily acknowledged by the usual scholarly attributions. I hope I have done justice to the complexity of their arguments. Judith V. Jordan, one of the authors in this book, and I also had extensive dialogues about the debates in the field when I was just beginning my research. At various times she and I had joint meetings with Carol Gilligan, Frances Conley, Robin Ely, Janet Shibley Hyde, and Pamela Trotman Reid. This is also a good place to thank Linda Carli, Michelle Wittig, and Kat Quina for their friendship and support over many years. Gwen Puryear Keita is director of the Women's Program Office at the American Psychological Association but her expertise goes far beyond this. Whenever I have contacted her, she always found answers to my questions or she knew where I could go to get more information.

Brendan Maher, professor of psychology at Harvard University, generously sponsored me as a visiting scholar in the psychology department at Harvard, and this appointment made it possible for me to expand my scholarly resources in unexpected ways. For example, the Radcliffe College Research Scholars program introduced me to several very enthusiastic undergraduate research partners at Harvard, and I am grateful to each of these students, though I know that they will be surprised to find that the topics in this book bear little resemblance to the topics we worked on in those early days of excavation in this rapidly exploding field. Research often means abandoning cherished theories so one can move forward in one's thinking, and that is precisely what happened, time after time, as this book developed in the years since I first worked with those eager students who scoured the Harvard University libraries for debate topics.

While this book was in gestation, I also spent a considerable amount of time working at the Harvard Law School, first as a participant in a month-long Negotiation Workshop, then in a variety of programs sponsored by the Harvard Law School's Program on Negotiation, and more recently as a co-sponsor of two conferences at the Law School on issues relating to women in the workplace. I am very grateful to many colleagues in this exciting field for what they have taught me about the magic of conflict, and to four new colleagues, Rhona Mahony, Elizabeth Kopelman, Andrea Kupfer Schneider, and Melanie Greenberg, for working so hard to make women's voices heard in the field of negotiation and conflict management.

The Henry A. Murray Research Center of Radcliffe College and its acting director, Jacquelyn B. James, organized a conference on "Beyond Difference As a Model for Studying Gender: In Search of New Stories to Tell" in May 1995, at just the right moment in time for me. I participated in the conference's small research groups, listened to knowledgeable colleagues as they talked about their work, and observed live debates about gender and difference. I am especially grateful to Elizabeth Aries, Rosalind C. Barnett, Leslie R. Brody, Penelope Eckert, Cynthia Fuchs Epstein, Nancy Rule Goldberger, Aida Hurtado, Anne Fausto-Sterling, Deborah K. King, Rose Olver, Elizabeth Paul, Stephanie Riger, Althea Smith, Deborah Tolman, and Rhoda Unger for their contributions to my learning. Rosemary Krawczyk, a very gifted and dynamic teacher, has been using my 1987 debates book in her classes for the past eight years at Mankato State University in Minnesota. I am grateful to her for the detailed feedback she gave me on her students' reaction to the debates in the book.

Whenever I have visited the University of California at Los Angeles, Anne Peplau and Jacqueline Goodchilds have been generous in sharing their time and hospitality. Their individual kindnesses to me, the delightful meetings in local restaurants and get-togethers at the UCLA faculty club, including a meeting with Carol Tavris, have created wonderful memories for me. Shortly after the publication of *The Psychology of Women: Ongoing Debates* in 1987, Anne Peplau sent me detailed responses, written by the students in her psychology of gender class, and I am extremely appreciative of the way she has supported my work. Sherri Matteo, deputy director of the Institute for Research on Women and Gender at Stanford University, also provided me with a wonderful reception when I visited her in the spring of 1996. I appreciate the time we spent together and our discussions about factors affecting research in the field.

Two authors in this book, Alice Eagly and Bernice Lott, deserve special praise. Both are my friends, and their chapters in this book testify to the power of their own feminism and the intellectual breadth of their knowledge. That they can be in such diametric disagreement with each other in this book and, at the same time, remain such wonderful colleagues, creates a model for intellectual exchange.

Researchers Pat Rieker, Shulamith Reinharz, and Sharlene Hess-Biber have been generous scholars and each has contributed, in different ways, to my ability to work on this book. I appreciate the speedy responses sent by Judith Lorber and my colleagues in other social science areas when I have sent out e-mail requests for help. My thank-you to Mary Beth Norton for her early support of my work is belated but very heartfelt.

Catherine Madsen, who served as a research assistant for this book, did prodigious work to ensure that I covered all the databases. Throughout the research process she provided a constant flow of information about new scholarship and in the process she has provided skillful computer searches, located important and strategic articles, and found the energy to search for books in more libraries than we dreamed existed. I thank her for her hard work and also for her constant support as we ran several marathons to find material for the topics in this book.

My manuscript editors at Yale University Press—Laura Dooley, Heidi Downey, Dan Heaton, Larry Kenney, Noreen O'Connor, Mary Pasti, and Jenya Weinreb—carefully read every word of the manuscript. Noreen O'Connor, who coordinated the editing process, was unfazed by each new development in this manuscript, and her dedication helped make this book what it has become. Linda Webster did a superb job in preparing the index.

My husband, Frank Walsh, helped me to laugh through several snowstorms this past winter, and he read every page of this book. As he has pointed out on numerous occasions, he would not do this kind of work for money, but his love is evident throughout this book. I am particularly grateful to him for planning two wonderful trips while this book was going through its final stages of production. Without those interludes, I am sure it could never have been completed, and certainly not with such happy moments. Now that it is finished, I look forward to many other adventures.

PUBLICATION INFORMATION

Articles in their current form by the following authors are original to this volume: **Elizabeth Aries**, **Mary M. Brabeck** and **Ann G. Larned**, **Linda L. Carli**, **Alice H. Eagly**, **Diane E. Eyer**, **Nancy Goldberger**, **Judith A. Hall** and **Amy G. Halberstadt**, **Janet Shibley Hyde**, **Judith V. Jordan**, and **Bernice Lott**.

Articles by the following authors have appeared elsewhere in a different form, and many have been updated for this volume.

J. Michael Bailey and **Richard C. Pillard**, "The Innateness of Homosexuality," was originally published in the *Harvard Mental Health Letter*, 10 (7), 1995. In consultation with the authors, text references have been added. Adapted with permission of the Harvard Mental Health Letter, 164 Longwood Avenue, Boston, Mass. 02115.

Gerald V. Barrett and **Scott B. Morris**, "The American Psychological Association's Amicus Curiae Brief in *Price Waterhouse v. Hopkins*," was originally published in *Law and Human Behavior*, 17 (2), 1993. Copyright © 1993 by Plenum Publishing Corporation. Adapted with permission.

Camilla Persson Benbow and **David Lubinski**, "Psychological Profiles of the Mathematically Talented: Some Sex Differences and Evidence Supporting Their Biological Basis," was originally published in *The Origins and Development of High Ability*, edited by Kate Ackrill and Gregory Bock, Chichester, England: John Wiley and Sons Ltd., 1993. Adapted with permission.

Susan T. Fiske, **Donald N. Bersoff**, **Eugene Borgida**, **Kay Deaux**, and **Madeline E. Heilman**, "What Constitutes a Scientific Review? A Majority Retort to Barrett and Morris," was originally published in *Law and Human Behavior*, 17 (2), 1993. Copyright © 1993 by Plenum Publishing Corporation. Adapted with permission.

Neil Gilbert, "Advocacy Research Exaggerates Rape Statistics," is excerpted from *Welfare Justice: Restoring Social Equity* by Neil Gilbert, New Haven: Yale University Press, 1995. Adapted with permission.

Michael S. Kimmel and **Michael Kaufman**, "Weekend Warriors: The New Men's Movement," was published in *The Politics of Manhood: Profeminist Men Respond to the Mythopoetic Men's Movement (And the Mythopoetic Leaders Answer)*, edited by Michael S. Kimmel, Philadelphia: Temple University Press, 1995. Copyright © by Michael S. Kimmel and Michael Kaufman. Adapted with permission.

Terry A. Kupers, "The Politics of Psychiatry: Gender and Sexual Preference in DSM-IV," was originally published in *masculinities*, 3 (2), 1995. Text and citations have been updated by the author. Adapted with the permission of Guilford Press, Inc.

Demie Kurz, "Physical Assaults by Male Partners: A Major Social Problem," was originally published under a different title in *Current Controversies in Family Violence*, edited by Richard Gelles and Donileen Loseke, pp. 88–103, Newbury Park, Calif.: Sage Publications, Inc., 1993. Text and citations have been updated by the author. Adapted with permission.

Charlene L. Muehlenhard, **Barrie J. Highby**, **Joi L. Phelps**, and **Susie C. Sympson**, "Rape Statistics Are Not Exaggerated," was originally published under a different title in *the Journal of Sex Research (1994)*, *31*, 144–146. Updated with the permission of the authors and reprinted with the permission of the Society for the Scientific Study of Sexuality.

Gary N. Powell, "Leadership and Gender: *Vive la Différence?*" is an expanded and revised version of "One more time: Do female and male managers differ?" *Academy of Management Executive* (1990), *4*, 68–75. Adapted with permission. Copyright © Gary N. Powell.

June M. Reinisch, **Leonard A. Rosenblum**, **Donald B. Rubin**, and **M. Fini Schulsinger**, "Sex Differences Emerge during the First Year of Life," was originally published under a different title in the *Journal of Psychology and Human Sexuality*, *4* (2), 1991, pp. 19–36. Copyright © 1991 by The Haworth Press, Inc. (Binghamton, N.Y.). Adapted with permission.

Judy B. Rosener, "Leadership and the Paradox of Gender," is excerpted from *America's Competitive Secret: Using Women as a Management Strategy* by Judy B. Rosener. Copyright © 1995 by Oxford University Press, Inc. Adapted with permission.

Ruth Ross, **Allen Frances**, and **Thomas A. Widiger**, "Gender Issues in DSM-IV," was originally published in the *Annual Review of Psychiatry, Vol. 14*, edited by John M. Oldham and Michelle B. Riba, Washington, D.C.: American Psychiatric Press, 1995. Adapted with permission.

Diana E. H. Russell, "Pornography Causes Harm to Women," is excerpted from *Against Pornography: The Evidence of Harm* by Diana E. H. Russell, Berkeley, Calif.: Russell Publications, 1994. Adapted with permission.

Murray A. Straus, "Physical Assaults by Women Partners: A Major Social Problem," was originally published under a different title in *Current Controversies in Family Violence*, edited by Richard Gelles and Donileen Loseke, pp. 67–87, Newbury Park, Calif.: Sage Publications, Inc., 1993. Text and citations have been updated by the author. Adapted with permission.

Nadine Strossen, "Why Censoring Pornography Would Not Reduce Discrimination or Violence Against Women," was originally published in *Defending Pornography: Free Speech, Sex, and the Fight for Women's Rights* by Nadine Strossen. Copyright © 1995 by Nadine Strossen. Adapted with permission.

Deborah Tannen, "Women and Men Talking: An Interactional Sociolinguistic Approach," is excerpted from *You Just Don't Understand: Women and Men in Conversation* by Deborah Tannen, New York: William Morrow, copyright © 1990 by Deborah Tannen, and

CONTRIBUTORS

Marvin Allen, M.A., is director of the Texas Men's Institute, which sponsors Men's Wilderness Gatherings across the country. He is also a psychotherapist in private practice, specializing in men's issues and romantic relationships. He is the author of *Angry Men, Passive Men: Understanding the Roots of Men's Anger and How to Move Beyond It* (1993).

Elizabeth Aries, Ph.D., is professor of psychology at Amherst College. Her work has appeared in such journals as *Small Group Behavior, Psychological Reports, Journal of Personality and Social Psychology, Sex Roles*, and *Psychology of Women Quarterly*. She is also the author of a book, *Men and Women in Conversational Interaction: Reconsidering the Differences* (1996).

J. Michael Bailey, Ph.D., is a member of the psychology department at Northwestern University. His work has appeared in such journals as *Behavior Genetics, Personality and Individual Differences, Journal of Consulting and Clinical Psychology, International Journal of Sociology and Social Policy, Psychological Medicine*, and *American Journal of Psychiatry*.

Gerald V. Barrett, Ph.D., J.D., is an attorney and professor of psychology at the University of Akron. His work has appeared in such journals as *American Psychologist, Law and Human Behavior, Journal of Business and Psychology, Journal of Applied Psychology*, and *Human Performance*. His books include *Man, Work, and Organizations: An Introduction to Industrial and Organizational Psychology* (1972); *Assessment of Managers: An International Comparison* (1979); and *People, Work and Organizations: An Introduction to Industrial and Organizational Psychology* (1981).

Camilla Persson Benbow, Ph.D., is chair of the psychology department, Distinguished Professor of Liberal Arts and Sciences, and professor of psychology at Iowa State University. Her work has appeared in such journals as *Science, Gifted Child Quarterly, Behavior and Brain Sciences, Journal of Personality and Social Psychology, Developmental Psychology*, and *Cognitive Neuropsychology*. Her latest book, *Psychometric and Social Issues Concerning Intellectual Talent*, is in press.

Donald N. Bersoff, Ph.D., J.D., is an attorney and professor at Villanova University School of Law and the Medical College of Pennsylvania—Hahnemann University. His work has appeared in such journals as *Professional Psychology, American Psychologist, Ethics and Behavior, Journal of Consulting and Clinical Psychology*, and *Law and Human Behavior*, and in a book, *Ethical Conflicts in Psychology* (1995).

Eugene Borgida, Ph.D., is professor of psychology and adjunct professor of law and political science at the University of Minnesota. His work has appeared in such journals as *Basic and Applied Social Psychology, American Psychologist, Journal of Applied Social Psychology, Law and Human Behavior*, and *Journal of Social Issues*.

Mary M. Brabeck, Ph.D., is professor of counseling and developmental psychology at Boston College. Her work has appeared in such journals as *Journal of Moral Education, Psychology of Women Quarterly, Journal of Early Adolescence, New Ideas in Psychology, Brain and Cognition*, and *Sex Roles* and in a book, *Who Cares? Theory, Research, and Educational Implications of the Ethic of Care* (1989).

Linda L. Carli, Ph.D., is visiting associate professor of psychology at Wellesley College. Her work has appeared in such journals as *Journal of Personality and Social Psychology, Advances in Group Process, Theory and Research, Personality and Social Psychology Bulletin, Journal of Experimental Social Psychology*, and *Journal of Social and Clinical Psychology*.

Patricia Hill Collins, Ph.D., is professor of African-American studies at the University of Cincinnati. Her work has appeared in such journals as *Journal of Comparative Family Studies, Gender and Society, The Black Scholar, Signs: Journal of Women in Culture and Society, Feminist Studies*, and *Sage: A Scholarly Journal on Black Women*. Her books include *Black Feminist Thought: Knowledge, Consciousness, and the Politics of Empowerment* (1990) and *Race, Class, and Gender* (co-edited with Margaret Andersen) (2nd edition, 1995).

Kay Deaux, Ph.D., is Distinguished Professor of Psychology at the City University of New York Graduate School and University Center. Her work appears in such journals as *Journal of Personality and Social Psychology, Sex Roles, Law and Human Behavior, American Psychologist, Psychology of Women Quarterly*, and *Psychological Review*. Her books include *The Behavior of Women and Men* (1976); *Social Psychology in the 80s* (1981); *Women of Steel: Female Blue-Collar Workers in the Basic Steel Industry* (1983); *Social Psychology* (5th edition, 1988); and *Social Psychology in the 90s* (6th edition, 1993).

Alice H. Eagly, Ph.D., is professor of psychology at Northwestern University. Her work has appeared in such journals as *American Psychologist, Psychological Bulletin, Journal of Personality and Social Psychology, Journal of Experimental Social Psychology*, and *Feminism and Psychology*. Her books include *Readings in Attitude Change* (1974), *Sex Differences in Social Behavior: A Social-Role Interpretation* (1987), and *The Psychology of Attitudes* (1993).

Diane E. Eyer, Ph.D., is a writer, an independent scholar, and a consultant at the National Center on Fathers and Families at the University of Pennsylvania. Her books include *Mother-Infant Bonding: A Scientific Fiction* (1992) and *Motherguilt and the Psychology of Motherblame* (1996).

Sarah Fenstermaker, Ph.D., is associate dean, graduate division, and professor of women's studies and sociology at the University of California, Santa Barbara. Her work has appeared in such journals as *Gender and Society, Journal of Marriage and the Family, Law and Society Review, Social Science Research*, and *Victimology*. Her books include *The Gender Factory: The Apportionment of Work in American Households* (1985) and *Individual Voices, Collective Visions: Fifty Years of Women in Sociology* (1995).

Susan T. Fiske, Ph.D., is Distinguished University Professor, department of psychology, University of Massachusetts, Amherst. Her work has appeared in such journals as *Journal of Personality and Social Psychology, Small Group Research, Basic and Applied Social Psychology, Journal of Social Issues*, and *American Psychologist*. Her books include *Social Cognition*

(2nd edition, 1991) and *Personality Research, Methods, and Theory: A Festschrift Honoring Donald W. Fiske* (1995).

Allen Frances, M.D., is professor and chair, department of psychiatry at Duke University Medical Center. His work has appeared in such journals as *American Journal of Psychiatry, Journal of Abnormal Psychology, Journal of Personality Disorders,* and *Psychiatric Research.* He was a member of the DSM Task Force for *Diagnostic and Statistical Manual of Mental Disorders: DSM-IV* (4th edition, 1994) and the *Diagnostic and Statistical Manual of Mental Disorders—DSM-IV: International Version with ICD-10 Codes* (1995). He is coauthor of the *DSM-IV Handbook of Differential Diagnosis* (1995).

Neil Gilbert, Ph.D., is Milton and Gertrude Chernin Professor of Social Welfare and Social Services at the University of California, Berkeley. His work has appeared in such journals as *Society, Social Service Review, Journal of Social Policy, Social Work,* and *Transaction/Society.* His books include *Capitalism and the Welfare State: Dilemmas of Social Benevolence* (1983); *The Enabling State: Modern Welfare Capitalism in America* (1989); and *Welfare Justice: Restoring Social Equity* (1995).

Nancy Goldberger, Ph.D., is a member of the psychology faculty at the Fielding Institute, Santa Barbara, California. Her work has appeared in such journals as *Journal of Experimental Research in Personality, Psychosomatic Medicine, Perceptual Motor Skills, Liberal Education,* and *Journal of Education.* Her books include *Women's Ways of Knowing: The Development of Self, Voice, and Mind* (1986); *The Culture and Psychology Reader* (1995); and *Knowledge, Difference, and Power: Essays Inspired by Women's Ways of Knowing* (1996).

Amy G. Halberstadt, Ph.D., is associate professor of psychology at North Carolina State University. Her work has appeared in such journals as *Psychological Assessment, Sex Roles, Journal of Nonverbal Behavior, Motivation and Emotion,* and *Journal of Personality and Social Psychology.* Her books include *Social Psychology Readings* (1990) and *Explorations in Social Psychology* (1995).

Judith A. Hall, Ph.D., is professor of psychology at Northeastern University. Her work has appeared in such journals as *Journal of Personality and Social Psychology, Social Science and Medicine, Journal of Occupational Medicine, Journal of General Internal Medicine,* and *Applied and Preventive Psychology.* Her books include *Sensitivity to Nonverbal Communication: The PONS Test* (1979); *Nonverbal Sex Differences: Communication Accuracy and Expressive Style* (1984); *Nonverbal Communication in Human Interaction* (3rd edition, 1992); and *Doctors Talking with Patients / Patients Talking with Doctors: Improving Communication in Medical Visits* (1993).

Madeline E. Heilman, Ph.D., is professor of psychology at New York University. Her work has appeared in such journals as *Journal of Business Ethics, Law and Human Behavior, Journal of Applied Psychology, American Psychologist,* and *Organizational Behavior and Human Decision Processes.*

Nancy M. Henley, Ph.D., is professor emerita of psychology at the University of California, Los Angeles. Her work has appeared in such journals as *Journal of Language and Social Psychology, Women's Studies Quarterly, Journal of Sex Research, Journal of Social Issues,* and

Psychology of Women Quarterly. Her books include *Language and Sex: Difference and Dominance* (1975); *Body Politics: Power, Sex, and Nonverbal Communication* (1977); *Gender and Nonverbal Behavior* (1981); and *Language, Gender and Society* (1983).

Barrie J. Highby is a doctoral student in the clinical psychology graduate program at the University of Kansas in Lawrence.

Janet Shibley Hyde, Ph.D., is professor of psychology and women's studies at the University of Wisconsin, Madison. Her work has appeared in such journals as *American Psychologist, Psychology of Women Quarterly, Psychological Bulletin, Feminism and Psychology,* and *Sex Roles.* Her books include *Psychology of Gender: Advances Through Meta-Analysis* (1986); *Psychology of Adjustment* (1989); *Parental Leave and Child Care: Setting a Research and Policy Agenda* (1991); *Understanding Human Sexuality* (5th edition, 1994); and *Half the Human Experience: The Psychology of Women* (5th edition, 1996).

Judith V. Jordan, Ph.D., is director of training at the Stone Center, Wellesley College, assistant professor of psychology at Harvard Medical School, and Founding Scholar of the Jean Baker Miller Institute. Her work has appeared in such journals as *Adolescent Psychiatry, Psychotherapy Bulletin, Advance Development Journal,* and *Contemporary Psychotherapy;* in a series of working papers published by the Stone Center at Wellesley College; and in her book, *Women's Growth in Connection* (1991).

Michael Kaufman, Ph.D., is a writer and speaker. His books include *Beyond Patriarchy: Essays by Men on Pleasure, Power and Change* (1988) and *Cracking the Armour: Power, Pain and the Lives of Men* (1993).

Michael S. Kimmel, Ph.D., is professor of sociology at State University of New York at Stony Brook. He has published articles in such journals as *Journal of Psychology and Human Sexuality, Feminist Issues, masculinities, Harvard Business Review, Society,* and *University of Miami Law Review.* His books include *Directions in the Study of Men and Masculinity* (1987); *Men Confront Pornography* (1990); *Against the Tide: ProFeminist Men in the United States, 1776–1990* (1992); *The Politics of Manhood: Profeminist Men Respond to the Mythopoetic Men's Movement (And the Mythopoetic Leaders Answer)* (1995); *Men's Lives* (3rd edition, 1995); and *Manhood in America: A Cultural History* (1995).

Celia Kitzinger, Ph.D., is senior lecturer in social psychology and women's studies at Loughborough University of Technology in England. Her work has appeared in such journals as *Feminism and Psychology, Contemporary Social Psychology, European Journal of Social Psychology, Developmental Psychology,* and *The Psychologist.* Her books include *The Social Construction of Lesbianism* (1987); *Changing Our Minds: Lesbian Feminism and Psychology* (1993); *Heterosexuality: A "Feminism and Psychology" Reader* (1993); and *Feminism and Discourse: Psychological Perspectives* (1995).

Deborah M. Kolb, Ph.D., is professor of management at the Graduate School of Management and director of the Institute on Leadership and Change at Simmons College, and senior fellow at the Program on Negotiation at the Harvard Law School. Her work has appeared in such journals as *Negotiation Journal, Journal of Social Issues, Journal of Management Inquiry, Journal of Organizational Behavior,* and *Journal of Conflict Resolution.* Her books include *The Mediators* (1983); *Hidden Conflict in Organizations: Uncovering Behind-the-Scenes Disputes* (1992); and *Making Talk Work: Profiles of Mediators* (1994).

Terry A. Kupers, M.D., M.S.P., is a professor in the Graduate School of Psychology, the Wright Institute, Berkeley, California, and is in private practice. His work has appeared in such journals as *American Journal of Orthopsychiatry, Journal of Couples Therapy, Community Mental Health, Urban Health*, and *Journal of Pediatrics*. His books include *Public Therapy: The Practice of Psychotherapy in the Public Mental Health Clinic* (1981); *Ending Therapy: The Meaning of Termination* (1988); *Using Psychodynamic Principles in Public Mental Health* (1990); and *Revisioning Men's Lives: Gender, Intimacy and Power* (1993).

Demie Kurz, Ph.D., is co-director of women's studies and is also affiliated with the sociology department at the University of Pennsylvania. Her work has appeared in such journals as *Health Policy and Education, Program Planning and Evaluation, Social Problems, Social Interaction*, and *Victims and Violence* and in her book, *For Richer, For Poorer: Mothers Confront Divorce* (1995).

Marianne LaFrance, Ph.D., is professor of psychology at Boston College. Her work has appeared in such journals as *Psychology of Women Quarterly, Journal of Applied Social Psychology, Gender and Education, Journal of Nonverbal Behavior*, and *Journal of Personality and Social Psychology*. Her books include *Evaluating Research in Social Psychology: A Guide to the Consumer* (1977); *Moving Bodies: Nonverbal Communication in Social Relationships* (1978); and *Guide to Knowledge Acquisition for Expert Systems* (1986).

Ann G. Larned is a doctoral student in the counseling psychology graduate program at Boston College.

Penelope Leach, Ph.D., is a psychologist, child development expert, writer, and educator. Her books include *Who Cares? A New Deal for Mothers and Their Small Children* (1979); *Babyhood: Infant Development from Birth to Two Years* (1983); *Your Growing Child: From Babyhood through Adolescence* (1986); *The First Six Months: Coming to Terms with Your Baby* (1987); *Baby and Child: From Birth to Age Five* (1989); and *Children First* (1994). She also writes a syndicated column, "Your Baby and Child," and scripts for television programs on child development.

Bernice Lott, Ph.D., is professor of psychology at the University of Rhode Island. Her work has appeared in such journals as *American Psychologist, Sex Roles, Journal of Psychology, Psychology of Women Quarterly, Journal of Social Issues*, and *Journal of Personality and Social Psychology*. Her books include *Women's Lives: Themes and Variations in Gender Learning* (2nd edition, 1994); *Combatting Harassment in Higher Education* (1995); and *The Social Psychology of Interpersonal Discrimination* (1995).

David Lubinski, Ph.D., is associate professor of psychology at Iowa State University. His work has appeared in such journals as *Journal of Personality and Social Psychology, Journal of Counseling Psychology, Journal of the Experimental Analysis of Behavior, Psychological Bulletin*, and *Behavioral and Brain Sciences*. His books include *Assessing Individual Differences in Human Behavior: New Methods, Concepts, and Findings* (1995) and *Intellectual Talent: Psychometric and Social Issues*, which is in press.

Scott B. Morris, Ph.D., is assistant professor of psychology at the Illinois Institute of Technology's Institute of Psychology in Chicago. He has published articles in such journals as *American Psychologist, Law and Human Behavior, Human Performance*, and *Educational and Psychological Measurement*.

Charlene L. Muehlenhard, Ph.D., is associate professor of psychology and women's studies at the University of Kansas, Lawrence. Her work has appeared in such journals as *Psychology of Women Quarterly, Journal of Social and Clinical Psychology, Journal of Consulting Psychology, Journal of Personality and Social Psychology*, and *Journal of Psychology and Human Sexuality*.

Joi L. Phelps is a doctoral student in the clinical psychology graduate program at the University of Kansas, Lawrence.

Richard C. Pillard, M.D., is professor of psychiatry and director of the Family Studies Laboratory at the Boston University School of Medicine, and medical director and associate superintendent for clinical services at the Dr. Solomon Carter Fuller Mental Health Center. His work has appeared in such journals as *Archives of Sexual Behavior, Psychosomatic Medicine, Journal of Gay and Lesbian Psychotherapy, American Journal of Psychiatry*, and *Archives of General Psychiatry* and in a book, *The Wild Boy of Burundi* (1978).

Gary N. Powell, Ph.D., is professor of management in the School of Business Administration at the University of Connecticut. His work has appeared in such journals as *Personnel Psychology, Academy of Management Journal, Academy of Management Executive, Human Relations*, and *Psychological Reports*. His books include *Women and Men in Management* (2nd edition, 1993) and *Gender and Diversity in the Workplace: Learning Activities and Exercises* (1994).

June M. Reinisch, Ph.D., is director emerita and senior research fellow, the Kinsey Institute for Research in Sex, Gender, and Reproduction, and director and principal investigator of prenatal development projects. Her work has appeared in such journals as *Journal of the American Medical Association, Family Planning Perspectives, Hormones and Behavior, American Psychologist*, and *Science*. Her books include *Masculinity/Femininity: Basic Perspectives* (1987); *Adolescence and Puberty* (1990); *Homosexuality/Heterosexuality: Concepts of Sexual Orientation* (1990); *AIDS and Sex: An Integrated Biomedical and Biobehavioral Approach* (1990); and *The Kinsey Institute New Report on Sex: What You Must Know to be Sexually Literate* (1994).

Leonard A. Rosenblum, Ph.D., is professor in the department of psychiatry and director, Primate Behavior Laboratory, at the State University of New York Health Science Center at Brooklyn (Downstate Medical Center). His work has appeared in such journals as *American Journal of Psychiatry, Learning and Motivation, Developmental Psychobiology, Journal of Psychology and Human Sexuality*, and *Biological Psychiatry*. His books include *The Genesis of Behavior: The Uncommon Child* (1981); *Normal and Abnormal Social Development in Primates* (1982); and *Masculinity/Femininity: Concepts and Definitions* (1987).

Judy B. Rosener, Ph.D., is professor and former assistant dean in the Graduate School of Management at the University of California, Irvine. Her books include *Workforce America!*

Managing Employee Diversity as a Vital Resource (1991) and *America's Competitive Secret: Utilizing Women as a Management Strategy* (1995).

Ruth Ross, M.A., is managing editor of the *Journal of Practical Psychiatry and Behavioral Health* and a science writer for the DSM-IV project of the American Psychiatric Association. Her work has appeared in such journals as *Journal of Medicine and Psychiatry*, *Journal of Practical Psychiatry and Behavioral Health*, and *Review of Psychiatry*.

Donald B. Rubin, Ph.D., is professor in the department of statistics at Harvard University. His work has appeared in such journals as *Sociological Methodology*, *Journal of the American Statistical Association*, *Journal of the American Medical Association*, *Biometrika*, and *Psychological Science*. His books include *Multiple Imputation for Nonresponse in Surveys* (1987); *Statistical Analysis with Missing Data* (1991); and *Bayesian Data Analysis* (1995).

Diana E. H. Russell, Ph.D., is professor emerita of sociology at Mills College. Her work has appeared in such journals as *Signs: Journal of Women in Culture and Society* and *The Sciences*. Her books include *Rape in Marriage* (1990); *Femicide: The Politics of Woman Killing* (1992); *Making Violence Sexy: Feminist Views on Pornography* (1993); *Against Pornography: The Evidence of Harm* (1994); and *Incestuous Abuse: Its Long-Term Effects* (1995).

M. Fini Schulsinger, M.D., is professor emeritus and senior researcher at the Institute of Preventive Medicine, Copenhagen Health Services, Denmark. His work has appeared in such journals as *Schizophrenia Research*, *Archives of General Psychiatry*, *International Journal of Mental Health*, *Neuropsychobiology*, and *Psychophysiology*.

Murray A. Straus, Ph.D., is professor of sociology and co-director of the Family Research Laboratory at the University of New Hampshire. His books include *The Social Causes of Husband-Wife Violence* (1980); *Behind Closed Doors: Violence in the American Family* (1980); *Physical Violence in American Families: Risk Factors and Adaptations to Violence in 8,145 Families* (1990); and *Beating the Devil Out of Them: Corporal Punishment by Parents* (1994).

Nadine Strossen, J.D., is professor of law at New York Law School; associate professor of clinical law, New York University School of Law; and president of the American Civil Liberties Union. Her work has appeared in such journals as *Cornell Journal of Law and Public Policy*, *Harvard Civil Rights—Civil Liberties Law Journal*, *Virginia Law Review*, *Harvard Journal of Law and Public Policy*, and *Cornell Law Review*. Her books include *Defending Pornography: Free Speech, Sex, and the Fight for Women's Rights* (1995) and *Speaking of Race, Speaking of Sex: Hate Speech, Civil Rights, and Civil Liberties* (1995).

Susie C. Sympson is a doctoral student in the clinical psychology graduate program at the University of Kansas, Lawrence.

Deborah Tannen, Ph.D., is a University Professor and professor of linguistics at Georgetown University. Her work has appeared in such journals as *Discourse Processes*, *Text*, *Language*, *International Journal of the Sociology of Language*, and *Anthropological Linguistics*. Her books include *That's Not What I Meant! How Conversational Style Makes or Breaks Relationships* (1986); *You Just Don't Understand: Women and Men in Conversation* (1990); *Framing in Discourse* (1993); *Gender and Conversational Interaction* (1993); *Gender and Discourse*

(1994); and *Talking from 9 to 5: How Women's and Men's Conversational Styles Affect Who Gets Heard, Who Gets Credit, and What Gets Done at Work* (1994).

Mary Roth Walsh, Ph.D., is a University Professor and professor of psychology at the University of Massachusetts, Lowell, where she is also the director of the Women in the Workplace Research Center. Her work has appeared in such journals as the *Journal of Social Issues, Harvard Educational Review, Journal of the American Medical Women's Association, Signs: A Journal of Women and Culture, Teaching of Psychology*, and the *Annals of the New York Academy of Sciences*. Her books, all published by Yale University Press, are *"Doctors Wanted: No Women Need Apply"* (1977); *The Psychology of Women: Ongoing Debates* (1987); and *Women, Men, and Gender: Ongoing Debates* (1997).

Carol Watson, Ph.D., is associate professor and chair of the department of management and human resources at Rider University College of Business Administration in Lawrenceville, N.J. Her work has appeared in such journals as *Negotiation Journal, Sex Roles, Group and Organization Studies, Journal of Personality and Social Psychology*, and *Journal of Management Systems*.

Candace West, Ph.D., is professor of sociology at the University of California, Santa Cruz. Her work has appeared in such journals as *Social Problems, Sociological Perspectives, Gender and Society, Discourse and Society*, and *Social Science and Medicine*.

Marcia C. Westkott, Ph.D., is professor of women's studies and sociology at the University of Colorado, Boulder. Her work has appeared in such journals as *Philosophy of the Social Sciences, Frontiers: A Journal of Women's Studies, Harvard Educational Review, National Women's Studies Journal*, and *American Journal of Psychoanalysis* and in a book, *The Feminist Legacy of Karen Horney* (1986).

Thomas A. Widiger, Ph.D., is a professor of psychology at the University of Kentucky. His work has appeared in such journals as *American Journal of Psychiatry, Journal of Psychopathology and Behavioral Assessment, Clinical Psychology: Science and Practice*, and *Journal of Abnormal Psychology*. His books include *DSM-IV Sourcebook*, Vol. 1 (1994); *Understanding the DSM-IV* (1994); *Personality Disorder Interview-IV, A Semistructured Interview for the Assessment of Personality Disorders* (1995); and *DSM-IV Sourcebook, Vol. 2*, which is in press.

Sue Wilkinson, B.Sc., C.Psychol., FBPsS., is a lecturer in social psychology and women's studies at Loughborough University of Technology in England. Her work has appeared in such journals as *Self and Society, Developmental Psychology, Gender and Society, Journal of Gender Studies*, and *Feminism and Psychology*. Her books include *Heterosexuality: A "Feminism and Psychology" Reader* (1993); *Women and Health: Feminist Perspectives* (1994); and *Feminism and Discourse: Psychological Perspectives* (1995).

Introduction

MARY ROTH WALSH

A BRIEF HISTORY OF THE SCIENTIFIC STUDY OF GENDER

The study of gender has a long and checkered history. Many of the early "scientific" studies on the subject sought to prove that women, along with people of Color and the poor, "occupy their subordinate roles by the harsh dictates of nature" (Gould, 1981, p. 74). I discovered this for myself when I began researching my first book, *"Doctors Wanted: No Women Need Apply"* (Walsh, 1977). Much to my surprise, male physicians, who surely should have known better, were quick to seize upon scientific arguments whenever they could to oppose the advancement of women in the medical profession.

For example, Dr. Horatio Storer, vice president of the American Medical Association in 1866, opposed female physicians on the grounds that menstruation, which he characterized as "periodical infirmity" and "temporary insanity," left women more in need of medical aid than able to furnish it (Storer, 1866, p. 191). Storer's view of women's limited capabilities coincided with those of another widely quoted physician of the era, Dr. Charles Meigs, who wrote in his textbook on obstetrics that woman "has a head almost too small for intellect but just big enough for love" (Meigs, 1847, p. 67).

Perhaps no other nineteenth-century book on the limitations of female biology evoked more controversy than Dr. Edward Clarke's *Sex and Education; Or, A Fair Chance for the Girls* (1873). Clarke's status as a former professor at Harvard Medical School and member of the Harvard Board of Overseers made him a national spokesman for the antifeminists in the United States. Within thirteen years, his book had gone through seventeen printings. Years later, M. Carey Thomas, an early president of Bryn Mawr College, recalled being haunted by Clarke's book when she was growing up because "we did not know when we began whether women's health could stand the strain of education" (1908, p. 68).

Clarke argued that unlike the male, whose development into manhood he viewed as a continuous process of growth, the female at puberty experienced a sudden and unique spurt during which the development of her reproductive system took place. If this did not occur at puberty, or if some outside force interfered, the result would be devastating. The most dangerous threat to normal female development, Clarke believed, stemmed from the mistake of educating females as if they were males. The results, he declared, were "monstrous

1

brains and puny bodies; abnormally active cerebration and abnormally weak digestion; flowing thought and constipated bowels" (Clarke, 1873, p. 41).

Dr. Mary Putnam Jacobi (1877) was one of the first scientists to challenge Clarke's theory that women were physically and intellectually weaker than men. On the basis of a survey of young women, she demonstrated that menstruation was not an impediment to women's mental or work activities. Jacobi's prize-winning monograph was followed by a number of other studies indicating that higher education was not injurious to women's health. In fact, Louise Marvel (1883) found that college life, far from being deleterious to women's physical development, "has resulted in a stronger physique and a more perfect womanhood" (p. 501).

Beginning in the 1890s and spurred on by psychology's new emphasis on empirical research, a few female psychologists launched an attack on the Victorian notion of gender differences. In the process, they succeeded in narrowing the scientific definition of the differences between men and women. Helen Thompson Woolley's 1903 study, the first experimental laboratory research on gender differences in mental abilities, demonstrated that the intellectual similarities between the two sexes far outweighed the differences. The noted sociologist William Isaac Thomas, who had earlier defended the idea that there were significant differences between women and men, hailed her findings as "probably the most important contribution to this field" (quoted in Rosenberg, 1982, p. 81). Her own research made Woolley contemptuous of what passed for scientific research when it came to gender comparisons. "There is perhaps no field aspiring to be scientific," she wrote, "where flagrant personal bias, logic martyred in the cause of supporting a prejudice, unfounded assertions, and even sentimental rot and drivel, have run riot to such an extent as here" (Woolley, 1910, p. 340).

Leta Stetter Hollingworth, another brilliant pioneer, established a remarkable record of scholarship in gender research, turning out nine scientific papers and one book before she received her Ph.D. from Columbia University in 1916. Her research and writing have a strikingly modern flavor. In one of her articles, for example, she criticized the social forces that pressured women into becoming mothers, a situation that later feminists would label "the motherhood mandate" (Hollingworth, 1916; Russo, 1979, p. 7). Hollingworth also rejected the notion, widely accepted by leading psychologists of her time, that men tended to have a wider range of intellectual abilities than women, an idea known as "the variability thesis." In addition, she attacked the popular view that women's cognitive abilities declined during menstruation (Hollingworth, 1914a, 1914b). Although Hollingworth shifted the focus of her research when she took a teaching position in child psychology at Columbia University, her interest in the psychology of women continued. Hollingworth hoped to see the time when a psychology of women would be written "based on truth, not opinion; on precise, not on anecdotal evidence; on accurate data, rather than on remnants of magic" (1914b, p. 99). She also had a plan (which she never realized) to write a book on the psychology of women entitled "Mrs. Pilgrim's Progress," reflecting her emphasis on women's self-determination (Shields, 1975, p. 857).

Meanwhile, a new controversy over gender issues had begun to take shape, arising out of Freud's work on female psychosexual development (Fliegel, 1986). Three of the five protagonists involved in the debate were women. Helene Deutsch and Jeanne Lampl-de Groot supported Freud's position while Karen Horney dissented. In her critique of Freud's views, Horney struck a note to which feminists of the 1970s would resonate: she insisted that psychoanalytic theories about women evolved from a male point of view and reflected male bias (Horney, 1926; Westkott, 1986).

Positions on both sides of the debate quickly hardened. At one point, Freud dismissed criticism of his work on women as the "denials of the feminists, who are anxious to force us to regard the two sexes as completely equal in position and worth" (1925, p. 258). As Zenia Odes Fliegel (1986) has noted, after Horney's break with Freud in the 1920s, criticism of his views on women disappeared almost entirely from the mainstream of psychoanalytic literature. So powerful was Freud's influence that what Betty Friedan called the "feminine mystique" could just as easily be called the "Freudian mystique" (Donovan, 1985, p. 105).

Women psychologists experienced great difficulty in making their voices heard within the profession. Helen Thompson Woolley never obtained an academic position that would have enabled her to continue her research. Other women also found themselves marginalized by the profession (Scarborough & Furumoto, 1987). Although women made up one-third of the membership of the American Psychological Association by the 1930s, they were largely relegated to clinical and counseling work, then considered lower in status than teaching and research positions. Consequently, women remained outside the academic circles, where most of the research and theory building was taking place (Furumoto, 1987, 1988).

In 1941, in an effort to improve their standing within the profession, a number of women psychologists banded together to form the National Council of Women Psychologists (later the International Council of Women Psychologists). Although the council sponsored a number of projects, including a newsletter and efforts to expand job opportunities that prefigured the efforts of women psychologists in the 1970s, its leaders were able to effect only minimal changes in the profession's treatment of women (Walsh, 1985).

When the council voted to eliminate the word *women* from the title of the organization in 1959, its role as an advocate for women within the profession came to a close. Cynthia Deutsch, who had once unsuccessfully attempted to persuade the council to sponsor a study of sex discrimination, later described the forces working against women psychologists in those years. Deutsch claimed that a good deal of the blame for the dearth of professional training and career opportunities could be traced to psychoanalytic theory, which assigned women a dependent and passive role vis-à-vis men. She claimed that the psychoanalytic movement identified women with the concept of "mom," thus confirming the attitudes of male psychologists who continued to treat women colleagues as "dependent and subordinately nurturing, rather than as fully equal scientists" (Deutsch, 1986, p. 187).

CREATING A CLIMATE FOR CHANGE

Ironically, within a decade of the disappearance of the International Council of Women Psychologists as a women's interest group, a feminist effort to improve the standing of women in American psychology began to take shape. Spurred on by the civil rights and social reform movements of the late 1960s, women psychologists demanded a larger role within the profession and a new approach to the study of women. In 1969, a group of women formed the Association for Women in Psychology (AWP). The following year, at the annual meeting of the American Psychological Association (APA), they presented their demands, including $50,000 for research on the psychology of women. Charging that "modern psychotherapy has perpetuated male supremacy and contributed to mental illness among women," they also called for $1 million in reparations from the association (Tiefer, 1991, p. 639).

The APA recognized the scholarship in psychology of women by establishing it as an official division in 1973. Today, the 6,033 members of Division 35 make it the fourth largest APA division (personal communication, 1996). A number of other divisions, including counseling and clinical psychology, have separate women's interests sections. The APA has also established an office for women's programs and a committee on women in psychology, which continue to the present day. Special task forces have issued reports on a number of topics ranging from women and depression (McGrath et al., 1991) to male violence against women (Koss et al., 1994).

Another sign of progress is the number of specialized journals on gender that have appeared since 1975, both in the United States and abroad, including *Sex Roles*, *Psychology of Women Quarterly*, *Gender and Society*, and *Feminism and Psychology*. New concepts, theories, and research methods have led to an explosion of knowledge about the psychology of gender that can easily be measured by the shift in focus at the annual APA conference. Whereas the 1969 program contained only one symposium and seven papers that specifically pertained to women (Denmark & Fernandez, 1993, p. 17), in 1995 women and gender issues were included in ninety-six symposia, 263 poster sessions, twenty-seven paper sessions, ten film programs, three presidential addresses, and eight workshops (Walsh, 1996).

Further evidence of the proliferation of research on gender can be found in the rapidly expanding number of specialized textbooks on this topic. In psychology alone, there are currently at least fourteen texts[1] sold for classroom use and countless anthologies and readers designed for supplementary use. Judith Bardwick's *Psychology of Women* (1971), the

---

1. The 14 gender textbooks currently in print are: Susan A. Basow (1992), *Gender Stereotypes and Roles* (3rd ed.), Pacific Grove, Calif.: Brooks/Cole; Linda Brannon (1996), *Gender: Psychological Perspectives*, Boston: Allyn & Bacon; Sharon Meghan Burn (1996), *The Social Psychology of Gender*, New York: McGraw-Hill; James A. Doyle (1995), *The Male Experience* (3rd ed.), Madison,Wisc.: WCB Brown & Benchmark; James A. Doyle & Michele A. Paludi (1995), *Sex and Gender: The Human Experience* (3rd ed.), Madison, Wisc.: WCB Brown & Benchmark; Katharine Hoyenga and Kermit Hoyenga (1993), *Gender-Related Differences: Origins and Outcomes*, Boston: Allyn & Bacon; Janet Shibley Hyde (1996), *Half the Human Experience* (5th ed.), Lexington, Mass.: D. C. Heath; Christopher T. Kilmartin (1994), *The Masculine Self*, New York: Macmillan; Hilary M. Lips (1993), *Sex and Gender: An Introduction* (2nd ed.), Mountain View, Calif.: Mayfield; Bernice Lott (1994), *Women's Lives: Themes and Variation in Gender Learning* (2nd ed.), Pacific Grove, Calif.: Brooks/Cole; Margaret W. Matlin (1996), *The Psychology of Women* (3rd ed.), Ft. Worth, Tex.: Harcourt Brace; Michele A. Paludi (1992), *The Psychology of Women*, Madison, Wisc.: WCB Brown & Benchmark; Joan H. Rollins (1996), *Women's Minds Women's Bodies: The Psychology of Women in a Biosocial Context*, Upper Saddle River, N.J.: Prentice-Hall; Rhoda Unger & Mary Crawford (1996), *Women and Gender: A Feminist Psychology* (2nd ed.), New York: McGraw-Hill.

first textbook on the subject, contained 368 references; Margaret Matlin's third edition of her textbook, also entitled *The Psychology of Women* (1996), has 2,343 citations, 1,167 of which were published since 1990 (M. Matlin, personal communication, 1996). In preparing her book, Matlin collected a stack of reprints more than seven feet tall in addition to citations from more than 400 books, all of them published in the previous four years. Similarly, Janet Hyde (1996) notes in the preface to the fifth edition of her textbook that twenty years earlier, when she began work on the first edition, her problem was that "the field was too new" and the research was "too thin" (p. ix). Now she finds more information than could possibly be included in one textbook, forcing her to be highly selective in her choice of material.

One area that has expanded considerably since the first edition of Hyde's book is research on women of Color. The first edition (Hyde & Rosenberg, 1976) included a separate chapter on Black women. In her fourth edition (1990), the scholarship on ethnic women had increased to the point that her chapter on women of Color included four major groups: African Americans, American Indians, Asian Americans, and Latinas. Psychologists in recent years have also begun to integrate research on cultural diversity into a number of areas, including teaching (Graham & Henley, 1994), psychotherapy (Comas-Diaz & Greene, 1994), and theory (Landrine, 1995).

Nevertheless, there is still much to be done. Much of the research on the psychology of women is still based on White middle-class women. However, as Elaine Pinderhughes points out, "Whether a woman of Color is considered a member of an oppressed cultural group and it is her subordinate sex-role status that must be understood, or whether she is considered a member of an oppressed sex group and it is her subordinate cultural identity that must be understood, her circumstances are unique" (1994, p. xi). Furthermore, researchers have a tendency to treat racism and sexism as discrete, but parallel forces. The effects of racism are typically assumed to apply to men and women equally, just as sexism is thought to affect White women and women of Color in the same way (Reid, 1993). Consequently, feminist research often ignores women of Color, while studies of ethnic and race discrimination omit gender differences. A case in point is socialization, where little work has been done on the effects of ethnicity and social class on gender-role development. For example, researchers have largely ignored the Chinese-American family's expectation for girls. Chinese-Americans hold a conservative attitude toward women, yet somehow Asian-American women's rate of participation in the work force is greater than that of any other group of women (Reid et al., 1995). Latinos also hold traditional attitudes toward women's roles, but these views become less restrictive with acculturation, education, and work outside the home, among other factors. Consequently, the commonly accepted view of Latinos as endorsing a confining conception of women's roles represents the attitude of only a subgroup within the larger population (Ginorio et al., 1995).

The study of the relationship between gender and ethnicity is further complicated by a debate over how researchers should proceed (see question 3). One school believes that gender, race, and economic class should be studied separately and then the findings combined to measure an individual's experience with oppression. Others argue that the study of all three factors should be combined to get an accurate picture of the psychology of women of Color.

THE EMERGENCE OF A NEW PSYCHOLOGY OF MEN

Janet Hyde was the first author of a textbook on the psychology of women to include a chapter on the psychology of men. As she pointed out in the third edition of her book (1985), there is now a "self-aware psychology of men" rooted in feminism and conscious of the power of gender roles, particularly how the male role influences the lives of men. Margaret Matlin (1996) also includes material on the new psychology of men and makes the point that just as there has been no unitary "women's movement," so there is no single focus in the new "men's movement." She cites the work of James Doyle (1995) and other leading men's studies scholars and identifies the three most visible strands within the current men's movement: the profeminist belief that the traditional male role is harmful to men and women; the men's rights position that men are the victims of discrimination, particularly in divorce courts and child-custody battles; and, finally, the spiritual or mythopoetic men's movement, which maintains that modern men have become soft and lost their connection with the "deep masculine" inner self (Bly, 1990). The solution, the mythopoetic view argues, is for men to come together in all-male gatherings so that they can work through their psychological difficulties and gain a mature masculine quality (Matlin, 1996; Kimmel, 1995).

A number of organizations are now involved in expanding the scholarship on men, including the American Men's Studies Association, the Men's Studies Association of the National Organization for Men Against Sexism, and the Society for the Psychological Study of Men and Masculinity (Division 51 of the APA). Two journals were established in the 1990s: *masculinities*, featuring profeminist scholarship, and the *Journal of Men's Studies*, which offers a variety of perspectives. Two psychology textbooks, the latest edition of James Doyle's *Male Experience* (1995) and Christopher Kilmartin's *Masculine Self* (1994), as well as a number of valuable collections like Ronald Levant and William Pollack's *A New Psychology of Men* (1995b) attest to the growing scholarship in this field.

Some feminists object to devoting energy to studies showing that men also are negatively impacted by gender stereotypes. "What troubles me," declared Letty Cottin Pogrebin, "is the overeagerness to weigh in with the male side of every women's issue, and the suggestion that the existence of male victims, no matter how few, balances the suffering of the overwhelming numbers of women" (1993, p. 96). Moreover, having heard for so long the feminist criticism that all psychology in the past was a psychology of men, some might ask, "Why do we need a new psychology of men?"

But as Kilmartin (1994) and others have pointed out, traditional psychology rarely focused on the experience of being male. Joseph Pleck, whose pioneering study *The Myth of Masculinity* (1981) has been acclaimed a "milestone" in the new psychology of men (Hyde, 1985, p. 106), has demonstrated, for example, how contradictory and inconsistent gender roles lead to low self-esteem, gender-role trauma, and dysfunction in men (Pleck, 1995). Researchers also point out that the traditional values attached to the male role, such as competitiveness, concern with status, stoicism, and toughness, can negatively impact women when expressed as violence, misogyny, and detached fathering (Levant & Pollack, 1995a).

THE STUDY OF GENDER DIFFERENCES AND SIMILARITIES

Researchers generally distinguish between the concepts of sex and gender. Sex refers to the biological differences between women and men; gender relates to the normative expectations attached to each sex. Gender is viewed, therefore, not as a trait inherent in an individual but as something that is socially constructed. This is what psychologists mean when they declare that individuals "do not have gender . . . they do gender" (Kimball, 1995, p. 6).

Much of the early work by feminist psychologists in the 1970s revolved around correcting what Crawford and Marecek have characterized as a "womanless psychology," one that not only ignored the female experience but assumed that male behavior was the prototype of all human behavior (1989, p. 149). John Atkinson's (1958) study of achievement motivation is a case in point. Although Atkinson devoted more than 800 pages to his subject, all the research on women can be found in a single footnote (Horner, 1972). In the absence of substantive studies on the female life experience, employers and admissions officers have often relied on stereotypic sex differences to discriminate against women. Dr. Alfred Ingegno, for example, writing in *Medical Economics* in the 1960s, declared that because male doctors were more productive, it would be "socially logical" to deny women entrance to medical schools (1961, p. 48). This is precisely what happened to most female applicants in that era.

Little wonder that one of the first objectives of feminist psychologists in the 1970s was to demonstrate that gender differences were either groundless or too small to explain the privileges men enjoyed in society. Many believed that research demonstrating that women were "as good as men" would play a key role in overthrowing patriarchy. Eleanor Maccoby and Carol Jacklin's *Psychology of Sex Differences* (1974), which found few significant gender differences, was hailed as a powerful argument for equality. As Naomi Weisstein noted, "we really believed that pretty soon we would change the world" (quoted in Kitzinger, 1993, p. 190).

Not all feminist psychologists are interested in pursuing research devoted to minimizing gender differences. As Meredith Kimball (1995) points out, feminist social scientists working within the concept of gender differences, including Nancy Chodorow (1978) and Carol Gilligan (1982), began to celebrate what were considered such special qualities of women as empathy, caring, and consensus building. Consequently, while one school of feminist psychologists would enhance the status of women by minimizing gender differences, others argued that the goal should be the creation of a better world built on traditional feminine values rather than equality within the existing social system (Kimball, 1995).

Some feminists are troubled by the notion of women's special aptitude for care and relationships, an idea that has often been used in the past to restrict women's activities (Crawford & Marecek, 1989). Rachel Hare-Mustin and Jeanne Marecek (1990) have also raised the possibility that these special qualities may stem from women's subordinate position in society rather than from some special trait in women's nature. Furthermore, thinking in opposites is a mistake even when it seems to elevate women, Carol Tavris argues, as it emphasizes difference and opposition rather than similarity and reciprocity. "That is why," she concludes, "the woman-is-better school is ultimately as self-defeating as the woman-is-deficient school it hopes to replace" (1992, p. 92).

In fact, when it comes to the question of similarities versus differences, a number of feminist psychologists in recent years have come close to invoking a plague on both houses. Several writers have argued that simple gender comparisons are no longer a "relevant feminist concern" (Unger, 1992, p. 231). The implied question in this research, as Marecek notes, is always "Are women as good as men?" (1995, p. 106). Moreover, by focusing on gender differences, feminists run the risk of ignoring the social forces that caused them. Sandra Bem (1996), for example, believes that it would be more profitable to investigate how society converts gender differences into female disadvantage. Moreover, many researchers reject the idea that we can ever know the true nature of gender, which is constantly being reconstructed (Kahn & Yoder, 1989).

Furthermore, research findings that gender stereotypes have changed very little in the past twenty years might make one wonder about the practical value of continuing the study of gender differences and similarities. Yet gender continues to be one of the "primary categories that people use to understand and think about their social world" (Cross & Markus, 1993, p. 58). Certainly the media seem to approach any new finding about gender differences with a magnifying glass. Magazines like *Newsweek* regularly report on differences between the sexes while ignoring the vast literature showing how much the sexes have in common. Some writers, in fact, seem to revel in the notion of gender differences. Michael Norman, writing for the *New York Times*, defended the gender gap, convinced that his androgens send him in one direction while his wife's estrogens send her in the other. Nevertheless, he happily notes, it is those very differences that he values: "her maternalism—her woman's sensibility perhaps, her woman's physiology for certain" (1994, p. 55).

GENDER RESEARCH AND SOCIAL CHANGE

If it were merely an academic question one might be tempted to put the entire issue of gender differences aside. But, as Meredith Kimball argues, "If feminist theorists abandon gender, gender will not disappear. Rather, male-dominated theories of gender will dominate the field" (1995, p. 12). Research on gender differences and similarities can play an important role in social change. Maccoby and Jacklin's *Psychology of Sex Differences* (1974), for example, has been cited as often in equal rights litigation as in psychological studies (Kimball, 1995). On the other hand, feminist research on gender differences can have unintended consequences. Feminist psychologists have to be on guard to ensure that their findings are not distorted in court, as has happened in two recent cases.

In the first instance, the Equal Employment Opportunity Commission investigated complaints that female employees at Sears Roebuck & Company in the 1970s were relegated to lower-paying salaried jobs while men held better-paying jobs in the so-called big ticket departments, like fencing, auto parts, and washers and dryers. Sears's response was that women didn't want to sell on commission. Ironically, the company's key witness in the case, which was decided in favor of Sears in 1986, was Rosalind Rosenberg, a historian whose 1982 book, *Beyond Separate Spheres*, recounted the work of feminist social scientists in combating the Victorian belief that gender differences were biologically determined. Rosenberg testified that Sears's distribution of men and women in its work force reflected not discrimination but rather women's preference for more traditional, noncompetitive positions. In her written testimony, she cited Nancy Chodorow's *Reproduction of Mothering* (1978) and Carol Gilligan's *In a Different Voice* (1982) in support of her argument that whereas men tend to focus on their work, women are inclined to be more "relationship centered" and to derive their sense of self-worth from their roles as wife and mother rather than from a big paycheck. As a consequence, she claimed, women are less willing to work evenings and weekends than men are (Faludi, 1991; Wiener, 1985; Offer of proof, 1985).

Feminist scholarship on gender differences was also cited in the U.S. Supreme Court briefs involving the state-supported Virginia Military Institute's ongoing effort to defend itself against the charge that it had violated the equal protection clause of the Fourteenth Amendment by refusing to admit women. VMI had successfully argued in the U.S. Fourth Circuit Court of Appeals that its "adversative" program, which stresses character building by requiring students to withstand harassment and humiliation, would be destroyed if women were admitted. The court's only requirement was that Virginia offer a comparable program for women, which the state met by creating a parallel "leadership" program especially designed for women at Mary Baldwin College, a private women's institution (Jaschik, 1995).

In oral arguments before the Supreme Court, the Justice Department summarized its written briefs and charged that VMI's admissions policy, with its implied message that only men can meet the institution's exacting requirements, reaffirms the notion that "biology is truly destiny" (U.S. Department of Justice brief, 1995, pp. 39–40). As one of Virginia's expert witnesses explained in defending the school's single-sex system, women "could not shed their gender" (U.S. Department of Justice brief, 1995, p. 58). The dean of students at Mary Baldwin College agreed, testifying that women would not benefit from the VMI program because they are different from men. As proof, she noted that fraternity members at VMI paddled their pledges, whereas the sorority members at her college gave flowers and wrote poems to each other (U.S. Department of Justice brief, 1995).

Among the briefs that have been filed in support of the Justice Department is one from the American Association of University Professors (AAUP) and a group of women scholars charging that VMI has distorted the existing research on gender. Joan Bertin, director of the Program on Gender, Science, and Law at Columbia University, who compiled the AAUP brief, charged that VMI's testimony was replete with "classic, time-worn generalizations picturing women as passive, men as aggressive; women as peaceful, men as violent; women as cooperative, men as competitive; women as insecure, men as confident" (AAUP et al. brief, 1995, p. 9).

Specifically, the AAUP brief accused VMI's expert witnesses of misrepresenting the work of a number of scholars, including Carol Gilligan. Among other things, these witnesses had claimed that women were more emotional than men and less able to cope with stress. Moreover, they continued, women did not have the same incentive as men to achieve success in an adversarial educational system like VMI's (U.S. Department of Justice brief, 1995). They also enumerated a number of alleged psychological and developmental gender differences such as women's "different ways of knowing" (AAUP et al. brief, 1995, p. 4). One witness summed up the school's case by stating that VMI's educational system was unsuitable because women "respond more naturally to an ethic of care," based on the notion that "no one should be hurt," rather than adhering to a male or egalitarian "ethic of justice" (U.S. Department of Justice brief, 1995, pp. 55–56).

The brief, signed by Gilligan along with other feminists, rejected VMI's contention that her research supported its position. It also pointed out that attempts to generalize about female and male characteristics only reinforced stereotypes. Citing Unger and Crawford (1996), the AAUP brief argued that there was a great deal of overlap between women and men in psychological, behavioral, and cognitive traits and that the area of overlap was usually larger than the area of difference (AAUP et al. brief, 1995). In the end, the VMI case illustrates that although one may be frustrated occasionally by the uses to which gender comparison research is put, the continued scientific study of gender similarities and differences is the only way to eliminate stereotypes.

REFERENCES

AAUP. (1995). Brief *Amici curiae* in support of petitioner by the American Association of University Professors et al., Nov. 27, 1995.

Atkinson, J. W. (Ed.). (1958). *Motives in fantasy, action and society: A method of assessment and study.* New York: Van Nostrand.

Bardwick, J. M. (1971). *Psychology of women: A study of bio-cultural conflicts.* New York: Harper & Row.

Bem, S. (1996). Transforming the debate on sexual inequality: From biological difference to institutionalized androcentrism. In J. C. Chrisler, C. Golden, & P. D. Rozee (Eds.), *Lectures on the psychology of women* (pp. 9–21). New York: McGraw-Hill.

Bly, R. (1990). *Iron John.* Reading, Mass.: Addison-Wesley.

Chodorow, N. (1978). *The reproduction of mothering: Psychoanalysis and the sociology of gender.* Berkeley: University of California Press.

Clarke, E. H. (1873). *Sex in education; Or, a fair chance for the girls.* Boston: Osgood & Company.

Comas-Diaz, L., & Greene, B. (1994). *Women of Color: Integrating ethnic and gender identities in psychotherapy.* New York: Guilford Press.

Crawford, M., & Marecek, J. (1989). Psychology reconstructs the female. *Psychology of Women Quarterly, 13,* 147–166.

Cross, S., & Markus, H. (1993). Gender in thought, belief, and action: A cognitive approach. In A. Beall & R. Sternberg (Eds.), *The psychology of gender* (pp. 55–98). New York: Guilford Press.

Denmark, F. L., & Fernandez, L. C. (1993). Historical development of the psychology of women. In F. L. Denmark & M. A. Paludi (Eds.), *Psychology of women: A handbook of issues and theories* (pp. 3–22). Westport, Conn.: Greenwood Press.

Deutsch, C. (1986). Gender discrimination as an intergroup issue: Comment on Capshew and Laszlo. *Journal of Social Issues, 42,* 181–184.

Donovan, J. (1985). *Feminist theory.* New York: Frederick Ungar.

Doyle, J. A. (1995). *The male experience* (3rd ed.). Madison, Wisc.: WCB Brown & Benchmark.

Faludi, S. (1991). *Backlash: The undeclared war against American women.* New York: Crown.

Fliegel, Z. O. (1986). Women's development in analytic theory. In J. L. Alpert (Ed.), *Psychoanalysis and women: Contemporary reappraisals* (pp. 3–31). Hillsdale, N.J.: The Analytic Press.

Freud, S. (1925). *Some psychological consequences of the anatomical distinction between the sexes. Standard Edition,* 19 (pp. 248–258). London: Hogarth Press, 1961.

Furumoto, L. (1987). On the margins: Women and the professionalization of psychology in the United States, 1890–1940. In M. G. Asch & W. R. Woodward (Eds.), *Psychology in twentieth-century thought and society* (pp. 93–114). Cambridge: Cambridge University Press.

Furumoto, L. (1988). Shared knowledge: The experimentalists, 1904–1929. In J. G. Morawski (Ed.), *The rise of experimentation in American psychology* (pp. 94–113). New Haven: Yale University Press.

Gilligan, C. (1982). *In a different voice: Psychological theory and women's development.* Cambridge, Mass.: Harvard University Press.

Ginorio, A. B., Gutierrez, L., Cauce, A. M., & Acosta, M. (1995). Psychological issues for Latinas. In H. Landrine (Ed.), *Bringing cultural diversity to feminist psychology: Theory, research, and practice* (pp. 241–263). Washington, D.C.: American Psychological Association.

Gould, S. J. (1981). *The mismeasure of man.* New York: Norton.

Graham, S., & Henley, N. (1994). Psychology and cognate fields. In L. Fiol-Matta & M. K. Chamberlain (Eds.), *Women of Color and the multicultural curriculum: Transforming the college classroom* (pp. 75–85). New York: Feminist Press.

Hare-Mustin, R. T., & Marecek, J. (1990). Gender and the meaning of difference. In R. T. Hare-Mustin & J. Marecek, *Making a difference* (pp. 22–64). New Haven: Yale University Press.

Hollingworth, L. S. (1914a). Variability related to sex differences in achievement. *American Journal of Sociology, 19,* 510–530.

Hollingworth, L. S. (1914b). *Functional periodicity: An experimental study of the mental and motor abilities of women during menstruation.* New York: Teachers College Press.

Hollingworth, L. S. (1916). Social devices for impelling women to bear and raise children. *American Journal of Sociology, 22,* 19–29.

Horner, M. S. (1972). Toward an understanding of achievement-related conflicts in women. *Journal of Social Issues, 28,* 157–176.

Horney, K. (1926). The flight from womanhood. In H. Kelman (Ed.), *Feminine psychology* (pp. 54–70). New York: Norton, 1967.

Hyde, J. S. (1985). *Half the human experience* (3rd ed.). Lexington, Mass.: D. C. Heath.

Hyde, J. S. (1990). *Half the human experience* (4th ed.). Lexington, Mass.: D. C. Heath.

Hyde, J. S. (1996). *Half the human experience* (5th ed.). Lexington, Mass.: D. C. Heath.

Hyde, J. S., & Rosenberg, B. G. (1976). *Half the human experience.* Lexington, Mass.: D. C. Heath.

Ingegno, A. (1961). Editorial. *Medical Economics* (Dec. 4), 41–48.

Jacobi, M. P. (1877). *The question of rest for women during menstruation.* New York: Putnam.

Jaschik, S. (1995). Divisions over VMI: Women's colleges disagree on whether institute should remain all male. *Chronicle of Higher Education* (Dec. 1), A37, A39.

Kahn, A. S., & Yoder, J. D. (1989). The psychology of women and conservatism: Rediscovering social change. *Psychology of Women Quarterly, 13,* 417–432.

Kilmartin, C. T. (1994). *The masculine self.* New York: Macmillan.

Kimball, M. M. (1995). *Feminist visions of gender similarities and differences.* New York: Harrington Park Press.

Kimmel, M. S. (1995). *The politics of manhood: Profeminist men respond to the mythopoetic men's movement (and the mythopoetic leaders answer).* Philadelphia: Temple University Press.

Kitzinger, C. (1993). "Psychology constructs the female": A reappraisal. *Feminism and Psychology, 3,* 189–193.

Koss, M. P., Goodman, L. A., Browne, A., Fitzgerald, L. F., Keita, G. P., & Russo, N. F. (1994). *No safe haven: Male violence against women at home, at work and in the community.* Washington, D.C.: American Psychological Association.

Landrine, H. (Ed.). (1995). *Bringing cultural diversity to feminist psychology: Theory, research, and practice.* Washington, D.C.: American Psychological Association.

Levant, R. F., & Pollack, W. S. (1995a). Introduction. In R. F. Levant & W. S. Pollack (Eds.), *A new psychology of men* (pp. 1–8). New York: Basic Books.

Levant, R. F., & Pollack, W. S. (Eds.). (1995b). *A new psychology of men.* New York: Basic Books.

Maccoby, E. E., & Jacklin, C. N. (1974). *The psychology of sex differences.* Stanford, Calif.: Stanford University Press.

Marecek, J. (1995). Psychology and feminism: Can this relationship be saved? In D. C. Stanton & A. J. Stewart (Eds.), *Feminisms in the academy* (pp. 101–132). Ann Arbor: University of Michigan Press.

Marvel, L. H. (1883). How does college life affect the health of women? *Education, 3,* 501–512.

Matlin, M. W. (1996). *The psychology of women* (3rd ed.). Fort Worth, Tex.: Harcourt Brace.

McGrath, E., Keita, G. P., Strickland, B. R., & Russo, N. F. (1991). *Women and depression: Risk factors and treatment issues (Final report of the American Psychological Association's national task force on women and depression).* Washington, D.C.: American Psychological Association.

Meigs, C. D. (1847). Lecture. Philadelphia: Jefferson Medical College.

Norman, M. (1994, Dec. 11). Against androgyny: The gender gap shouldn't be bridged, it should be cherished. *New York Times Magazine,* pp. 54–55.

Offer of proof concerning the testimony of Dr. Rosalind Rosenberg. 1985. *Equal Employment Opportunity Commission v. Sears, Roebuck and Co.* U.S. District Court for the Northern District of Illinois Eastern Division.

Pinderhughes, E. (1994). Foreword. In L. Comas-Diaz & B. Greene (Eds.), *Women of Color: Integrating ethnic and gender identities in psychotherapy* (pp. xii-xiii). New York: Guilford Press.

Pleck, J. H. (1981). *The myth of masculinity.* Cambridge, Mass.: MIT Press.

Pleck, J. H. (1995). The gender role strain paradigm: An update. In R. F. Levant & W. S. Pollack (Eds.), *A new psychology of men* (pp. 11–32). New York: Basic Books.

Pogrebin, L. C. (1993, November-December). The stolen spotlight syndrome: You can always count on a male "me too." *Ms. Magazine*, p. 96.

Reid, P. T. (1993). Women of color have no "place." *Focus: Newsletter of the Psychological Study of Ethnic Minority Issues, Division 45 of the American Psychological Association, 7*, 1–2.

Reid, P. T., Calliope, H., Kelly, E., & Holland, N. E. (1995). In H. Landrine (Ed.), *Bringing cultural diversity to feminist psychology: Theory, research, and practice* (pp. 241–263). Washington, D.C.: American Psychological Association.

Rosenberg, R. (1982). *Beyond separate spheres: Intellectual roots of modern feminism.* New Haven: Yale University Press.

Russo, N. F. (1979). Overview: Sex roles, fertility, and the motherhood mandate. *Psychology of Women Quarterly, 4*, 7–15.

Scarborough, E., & Furumoto, L. (1987). *Untold lives: The first generation of American women psychologists.* New York: Columbia University Press.

Shields, A. A. (1975). Ms. Pilgrim's progress: The contributions of Leta Stetter Hollingworth to the psychology of women. *American Psychologist, 30*, 852–857.

Storer, H. R. (1866). *Boston Medical Surgical Journal,* 191–192.

Tavris, C. (1992). *The mismeasure of women.* New York: Simon & Schuster.

Thomas, M. C. (1908). Present tendencies in women's college and university education. *Education Review, 25*, 68.

Tiefer, L. (1991). A brief history of the association for women in psychology: 1969–1991. *Psychology of Women Quarterly, 15*, 635–649.

Unger, R. (1992). Will the real sex difference please stand up? *Feminism and Psychology, 2*, 231–238.

Unger, R., & Crawford, M. (1996). *Women and gender: A feminist psychology.* New York: McGraw-Hill.

U.S. Department of Justice Brief. (1995). *United States of America, Petitioner, v. Commonwealth of Virginia, et al.* On writ of certiorari to the United States Court of Appeals for the Fourth Circuit, Nov. 27, 1995. Academe Today, Electronic Document Archive, *Chronicle of Higher Education.*

Walsh, M. R. (1977). *"Doctors Wanted: No Women Need Apply."* New Haven: Yale University Press.

Walsh, M. R. (1985). Academic professional women organizing for change: The struggle in psychology. *Journal of Social Issues, 41*, 17–28.

Walsh, M. R. (1996). Division 35-sponsored presentations at the APA annual conference, 1995. Unpublished raw data.

Westkott, M. (1986). *The feminist legacy of Karen Horney.* New Haven: Yale University Press.

Wiener, J. (1985). The Sears case: Women's history on trial. *Nation* (Sept. 7), 161, 176.

Woolley, H. T. (1903). *The mental traits of sex: An experimental investigation of the normal mind in men and women.* Chicago: University of Chicago Press.

Woolley, H. T. (1910). Psychological literature: A review of the recent literature on the psychology of sex. *Psychological Bulletin, 7*, 335–342.

PART I

Fundamental
Questions

Research Priorities: Should We Continue to Study Gender Differences?

Gender comparisons have had a long and controversial history. At first their major objective was to keep women in a subordinate position. According to the *Boston Medical and Surgical Journal*, whose nineteenth-century editors were opposed to the education of female physicians, women could not become doctors because the strain of constant house calls would be more than their system could bear. But the same journal hailed the work of nurses who regularly went into "the slums of our city, through the dark alleys, among the ash barrels and swill, up the dark and dirty staircases of the tenements" (1897, p. 214).

In the early twentieth century, feminist psychologists like Leta Stetter Hollingworth and Helen Thompson Woolley objected to the distortions and misuse of the research, which invariably reinforced popular views of women's inferiority, but they could only chip away at the distortions that dominated scientific views of women's capabilities. The publication of Maccoby and Jacklin's *Psychology of Sex Differences* in 1974 marked a major breakthrough in research on gender differences because, on the one hand, the two authors synthesized more than 2,000 studies and concluded that gender differences had been demonstrated to exist only in aggression and in spatial, verbal, and mathematical aptitude. On the other hand, they found that a number of ideas were unfounded, including the beliefs that boys are better at higher-level cognitive tasks and that girls are more suggestible.

Maccoby and Jacklin's finding that there were few significant gender differences was widely hailed as a major contribution to psychology. It was also welcome news to feminist social scientists, who viewed it as ammunition in their battle to shatter existing sex stereotypes. As Rabinowitz and Sechzer noted, Maccoby and Jacklin's work "has gone far to dispel many popular myths about gender that have permeated bodies of literatures in psychology and to warn psychologists about the dangers of overgeneralizing gender differences" (1993, p. 54).

Feminist inquiries into gender differences, according to Alice Eagly (1995), were fired by the expectation that findings demonstrating that women were not different from men would open new opportunities for women. Thus fueled by a feminist perspective, the study of sex differences, which sociologist Jessie Bernard had once characterized as "battle weapons against women" (quoted in Eagly, 1995, p. 149), would be transformed into battering rams to break down the walls of discrimination.

Interest in gender differences remains high both in the popular press and in scholarly research. The media, of course, is much more interested in news about differences than similarities. The cover of *Time*, for example, asked "Why Are Men and Women Different?" (Gorman, 1992), while *Newsweek* focused on "Guns and Dolls: Scientists Explore the Differences Between Girls and Boys" (Shapiro, 1990). Psychologists have maintained their interest in the topic, albeit in more measured tones, as a glance at Janet Hyde's 1996 textbook on the psychology of women demonstrates. Hyde lists fifty-three separate subheadings under "gender differences" in her index, ranging from achievement to work turnover rates. In fact, Diane Halpern argues that gender differences are at the heart of women's studies courses. "If there were no differences," she maintains, "then there would be no need for a psychology of women" (1994, p. 527).

Nevertheless, the question as to whether psychologists should continue to study gender differences has become a matter of serious debate. Many social scientists believe we have no choice but to go forward. They view scientific research on gender differences as the only way to demolish stereotypes and to recognize legitimate differences (Halpern, 1994). However, Eagly (1995), who identified a significant number of "nontrivial" gender differences in such areas as quantitative problem solving, visuospatial ability, verbal fluency, and nonverbal behavior, believes that there is a growing feminist opposition to research on gender differences. She ascribes much of this antipathy to feminist fears that the increasing body of evidence showing a considerable number of gender differences will undermine women's social and political agenda.

Janet Hyde and Elizabeth Plant (1995) do not find the monolithic feminist agenda Eagly identified in her article. A number of feminist psychologists, they point out, have found significant gender differences in their research, including Carol Gilligan (1982) in moral reasoning, Nancy Henley (1973) in patterns of interpersonal touching, and Diane Halpern (1992) in verbal and mathematical ability. Moreover, as Rachel Hare-Mustin and Jeanne Marecek (1994) suggest, a finding that there are no differences between women and men does not always serve the feminist cause. Sex-blind treatment of women in the work force that does not take into consideration pregnancy and women's responsibility for child care, for example, can result in inequitable treatment.

Still, a number of feminist psychologists believe that there are problems associated with gender-difference research. Although Hyde (1994) is not opposed to the continuation of such work, she recommends the adoption of guidelines to remedy problems in gender-difference research, such as refusing to publish reports finding no gender differences. Another concern is that much gender-comparison research has failed to take into consideration the connection between gender, on the one hand, and race, ethnicity, and social class, on the other. Studies of nonverbal behavior (Smith, 1983) and dominance (Adams, 1983), for example, show differences between Black and White women, complicating any attempt to generalize about all women and all men in these areas.

Others argue that it is time for feminist psychologists to put the question of gender differences aside (Hare-Mustin & Marecek, 1994). Carol Tavris notes that this type of research "cannot explain, for instance, why, if women are better than men in verbal ability, so few women are auctioneers or diplomats, or why, if women have the advantage in making rapid judgments, so few women are air-traffic controllers or umpires" (1992, p. 54).

Moreover, some psychologists contend that a preoccupation with gender differences may divert feminist scholars from more fruitful lines of inquiry. "Why is this the question we are always asking?" inquires Sandra Bem. "And even more importantly, is there some other question we should be asking?" (1996, p. 11). Finally, postmodern scholars assert that we can never know what women and men are really like because gender is constantly being reconstructed. Therefore, the attempt to come up with an exact measure of sex differences is ultimately a futile task (Kahn & Yoder, 1989).

In the following essays, Bernice Lott argues that cataloging sex differences and similarities not only obscures the complexities of human behavior but also reinforces the existing political arrangements that maintain those differences. Alice Eagly disagrees; she believes that scientific research on gender differences should be expanded because, as she sees it, the resulting evidence can make a useful contribution to public-policy debates that involve gender issues.

REFERENCES

Adams, K. A. (1983). Aspects of social context as determinants of black women's resistance to challenges. *Journal of Social Issues, 39*, 67–78.

Bem, S. (1996). Transforming the debate on sexual inequality: From biological difference to institutionalized androcentrism. In J. C. Chrisler, C. Golden, & P. D. Rozee (Eds.), *Lectures on the psychology of women* (pp. 9–21). New York: McGraw-Hill.

Boston Medical and Surgical Journal (1896), *136*, 214.

Eagly, A. H. (1995). The science and politics of comparing women and men. *American Psychologist, 50*, 145–158.

Gilligan, C. (1982). *In a different voice: Psychological theory and women's development.* Cambridge, Mass.: Harvard University Press.

Gorman, C. (1992). Sizing up the sexes. *Time* (Jan. 20), pp. 42–51.

Halpern, D. F. (1992). *Sex differences in cognitive abilities.* (2nd ed.). Hillsdale, N.J.: Erlbaum.

Halpern, D. F. (1994). Stereotypes, science, censorship, and the study of sex differences. *Feminism and Psychology, 4*, 523–530.

Hare-Mustin, R. T., & Marecek, J. (1994). Asking the right questions: Feminist psychology and sex differences. *Feminism and Psychology, 4*, 531–537.

Henley, N. (1973). Status and sex: Some touching observations. *Bulletin of the Psychonomic Society, 2*, 92–93.

Hyde, J. S. (1994). Should psychologists study gender differences? Yes, with some guidelines. *Feminism and Psychology, 4*, 507–512.

Hyde, J. S. (1996). *Half the human experience* (5th ed.). Lexington, Mass.: D. C. Heath.

Hyde, J. S., & Plant, E. A. (1995). Magnitude of psychological gender differences: Another side of the story. *American Psychologist, 50*, 159–161.

Kahn, A. S., & Yoder, J. D. (1989). The psychology of women and conservatism: Rediscovering social change. *Psychology of Women Quarterly, 13*, 417–432.

Maccoby, E. E., & Jacklin, C. N. (1974). *The psychology of sex differences.* Stanford, Calif.: Stanford University Press.

Rabinowitz, V. R., & Sechzer, J. A. (1993). Feminist perspectives on research methods. In F. L. Denmark & M. A. Paludi (Eds.), *Psychology of women: A handbook of issues and theories* (pp. 23–66). Westport, Conn.: Greenwood Press.

Shapiro, L. (1990, May 28). Guns and dolls. *Newsweek*, pp. 56–65.

Smith, A. (1983). Nonverbal communication among black female dyads: An assessment of intimacy, gender and race. *Journal of Social Issues, 39*, 55–67.

Tavris, C. (1992). *The mismeasure of women.* New York: Simon & Schuster.

Walsh, M. R. (1977). *"Doctors Wanted: No Women Need Apply."* New Haven: Yale University Press.

ADDITIONAL READING

Buss, D. M. (1995). Psychological differences: Origins through sexual selection. *American Psychologist, 50,* 164–168.

Eagly, A. H. (1987). *Sex differences in social behavior: A social-role interpretation.* Hillsdale, N.J.: Erlbaum.

Epstein, C. F. (1988). *Deceptive distinctions: Sex, gender, and the social order.* New Haven: Yale University Press.

Holloway, W. (1994). Beyond sex differences: A project for feminist psychology. *Feminism and Psychology, 4,* 538–547.

Kitzinger, C. (1994). Sex differences: Feminist perspectives. *Feminism and Psychology, 4,* 501–506.

Marecek, J. (1995). Psychology and feminism: Can this relationship be saved? In D. C. Stanton & A. J. Stewart (Eds.), *Feminisms in the academy* (pp. 101–132). Ann Arbor: University of Michigan Press.

Cataloging Gender Differences: Science or Politics?

BERNICE LOTT

There is little question that U.S. mainstream society, still dominated by European-American mythology, ascribes different behaviors to persons on the basis of their female or male sexual category, and that there are important consequences for behaving or not behaving in these ascribed ways under certain circumstances. The major task for scientific psychology, in my view, is to focus on the culturally selected behaviors and to study the necessary and sufficient conditions under which they are learned and under which they are practiced. This is a different agenda from one which concentrates on cataloging all the ways in which some members of two groups of people sometimes differ from one another. Betancourt and Lopez (1993), in presenting a research agenda on culture, ethnicity, and race, have argued, similarly, that psychologists who simply identify intergroup differences on various measures do not contribute to our knowledge about the specific conditions that influence the behaviors or the phenomena measured.

Cataloging sameness and difference serves a primarily political function as it rationalizes and perpetuates differences in power. Every ruling group justifies its position on the basis of characteristics which are better, stronger, or more appropriate than those of the people in group(s) it dominates. But cataloging sameness and difference does not serve the interests of a science of psychology, first, because we well know that behavior always occurs in a context and that the situation or circumstance makes a significant difference. In addition, a focus on sameness and difference is primarily descriptive and does not provide explanations of behavior that relate what persons do to reliable antecedents and consequences.

The accumulated research on gender indicates that differences between women and men or between girls and boys can certainly be found for some behaviors, at some ages, in some situations, at some times, and in some places. But a conceptualization of human capacities, interests, and behaviors in terms of gender dichotomies obscures the complexities of individual experiences, reinforces existing political arrangements that maintain such dichotomies, and diverts our attention from formulating the more significant questions for psychological research. If a culture arranges the experiences of its children and adults so that gender will be associated with differential expectations, opportunities, and consequences, it is those *arrangements* that we must study in order to understand their outcomes for behavior.

Alice Eagly (1995) tells us, for example, that on the American College Testing program test of math achievement "boys would score higher than girls in 63% of randomly selected pairs of girls and boys" (p. 152). While that may well describe today's general state of affairs and justify expectations, rewards, and patterns of academic and job counseling, the far more important research goal for both science and society is to identify the necessary and sufficient conditions for acquiring skill in mathematics by children and adults of either gender.

Similarly, although many girls and women may be systematically exposed to situations that encourage empathic responses, while such responses are systematically discouraged in boys and men, it is the task of scientific psychology to identify what those conditions are so that, if we value empathy, we can advise parents and teachers about how best to encourage its acquisition. This seems far more sensible and empirically defensible than simply encouraging people to have more girls! And, of course, we need to study the contexts in which this behavior is more or less likely to be manifested. If we want to understand and explain empathy (or any other apparently gender-related response) then we should focus on the *behavior* itself and search for probable antecedents in persons of *both* genders.

An example of this kind of research is a study by Barnett, Howard, King, and Dino (1980), who found in a sample of college students that, although women scored reliably higher than men on a self-report measure of empathy, high empathy scorers of both genders, compared with low empathy scorers of both genders, similarly reported that their parents had spent more time with them, been more affectionate with them, and discussed feelings more often. Thus, similar experiences appear to enhance empathic responses in both genders, although we are not surprised to learn that more women than men reported such empathy-promoting parental interactions. A similar approach has been taken by Melson and Fogel (1988) with respect to children's nurturance behavior. They concluded that children display more nurturance as a result of more practice in caregiving, regardless of gender.

To list behaviors for which selected groups of women and men show some average difference—under the present circumstances of overall differences in status, power, and opportunities for practice—is not too difficult. And it is the differences (not the sameness) that interest the media and make the headlines because it is these that justify that status quo and reinforce the continuing social and political barriers to gender equity. Yet, despite all the conditions in our society that push girls and boys, and then women and men, into different spheres, the differences so painstakingly searched for are small indeed. The extraordinary findings are that gender differences are so minimal, not that they are sometimes demonstrated, and that small average gender differences are always overshadowed by the much larger overlap between genders and by within-gender variability. Eagly (1995) is correct in noting that the extent of gender differences is quite typical of the effect on social be-

havior of most variables studied by social psychologists, but this argument is not convincing because none of the other variables we typically study are, like gender, systematically and relentlessly promoted by all social institutions as being relevant.

In light of the stake of U.S. society in the development and maintenance of gender differences, the consistent finding of "inconsistency" takes on far greater importance than inconsistent findings in other areas of research. Many have shown that it is the moderator variables that make a difference. The gender of the actor is often of no predictive significance when compared with situational or other factors. A good example of such research comes from a laboratory study by Deutsch (1990) of same- and mixed-gender pairs in which one member was assigned the role of interviewer and the other the role of applicant for a part-time job as a news reporter. Unobtrusive observations of pair interactions revealed that in all pairs, regardless of gender, "applicants, who presumably occupied the low-power role, smiled more than interviewers" (p. 537) and that among applicants there was no gender difference in smiling. Similar findings regarding the significance of social role have come from a study by Moskowitz, Suh, and Desaulniers (1994). A sample of employed adults reported every day for twenty days on their interactions with supervisors, coworkers, and supervisees. Dominant behaviors by women and men were found to be self-reported more often in interaction with supervisees than with bosses, and submissive behaviors were found to be reported more with bosses and coworkers. "Gender was not found to influence agentic behavior at work" (p. 758), nor was it significantly related to self-reported agreeable behavior, but men did report more quarrelsomeness than women.

The importance of the situation can also be illustrated by findings reported by Sharps, Walton, and Price (1993), who studied spatial cognitive performance on a number of tasks. The men in their sample were found to outperform the women under instructions that emphasized the spatial or "map character" of the task, but "when the spatial characteristics of the tasks were not made explicit, sex differences in performance were not observed" (p. 79). In this investigation, the instructions made a difference. In a study by Lightdale and Prentice (1994) on aggressive behavior, the important variable was anonymity. A video game was played by groups of six, and the number of "bombs" dropped on others by each player was used as the measure of aggression. Among participants who had provided personal information on themselves, men dropped more bombs than women, but among participants who remained anonymous, there were no significant gender differences in aggression. Bjorkqvist (1994), in a review of recent research on aggression that included studies of physical, verbal, and indirect aggression, concluded that there were no overall significant differences between women and men.

The issue, it seems to me, is not one of difference or sameness but rather that, as members of the human species, girls and boys, and women and men, share a biological nature that makes us superb learners and provides us with similar capacities for acquiring and performing similar behaviors under similar circumstances. Innate and experiential individual differences provide the basis for variability in capacity, circumstances, and outcomes. It is because we have the biological structure that we do, especially our nervous system, that environmental factors are as potent as they are in influencing what we do. In both genders, environmental factors are typically related to where and with whom one lives and grows up, to social class and ethnicity, and to other social categories. For example, Feingold (1994), who examined within-gender variability in verbal, mathematical, and spatial cognitive performance across several countries, found an "absence of any consistent gender difference in variability in the intellectual domains examined. . . . Males were more variable in some countries and females were more variable in other countries" (p. 89).

The often quoted words of Sojourner Truth speak to a fundamental lesson about gender. Sojourner Truth asked, "Ain't I a woman?" (quoted in Lott, 1994). As a slave who "bore the lash" and labored in the fields, she behaved quite differently than the wives and daughters of the White southern plantation owners. What "feminine traits" did slave women and delicate and refined upper-class ladies have in common? "None" was the answer for those who practiced and defended slavery at the time. The common exclusion of women of Color from empirical and theoretical work in psychology results in limitations in conclusions and a lack of appreciation of gender variability. Those excluded because of their ethnicity (or social class or sexual orientation) have made these points most eloquently. Hurtado (1989), for example, has reminded White middle-class women in the United States of their position of privilege. Because White heterosexual women are subordinated through seduction, while women of Color are subordinated through rejection, Hurtado argues, "these groups of women have different political responses and skills" (p. 843). This crucial insight informs her conclusion, and that of others, that "the definition of woman is constructed differently for [W]hite women and women of Color" (p. 845).

An example of the kind of research that expands our understanding of gender as it intersects with other social categories and situational demands is that of Deutsch and Saxon (1994), who studied parenting behavior among twenty-three dual-earner heterosexual couples. In these couples, the wives and husbands worked at different hours and alternated child care. What the investigators found was a "radical difference" between the verbally expressed traditional gender ideology of both mothers and fathers and their actual nontraditional egalitarian behavior in the day-to-day care of their children. These "alternating shift fathers . . . perform[ed] all the tasks that mothers have traditionally done: feeding children, bathing them, comforting them, and putting them to bed" (pp. 4ff.), thus functioning as nurturers.

Deutsch and Saxon's study illustrates how gender socialization, which is a life-long process, is continuously affected by variations in circumstances and by idiosyncratic family and personal history. In a complex heterogeneous society like that of the United States, gender is frequently deconstructed by experiences that contradict typical,

majority culture associations so that both within-gender variability and within-person variability are more the rule than the exception. The reality of within-person variability, while of enormous practical as well as theoretical importance, is typically ignored in discussions of gender differences.
Relevant to this issue are data from a study by Vonk and Ashmore (1993) in which a sample of adults was asked to provide self-ratings on thirty traits, qualified by situation. The investigators found evidence in support of a "general situational flexibility" and within-self variability.

Such findings support the importance of distinguishing between the concepts of trait and habit (Lott, 1990; Lott & Maluso, 1993), and questioning such conclusions as "Donna is a caring person because she is a woman." The question for scientific psychology must be how one becomes a caring person: Under what circumstances is care learned and manifested? Gender research in psychology should focus on the antecedents of the behaviors that culture pairs with gender, and it must pay attention to variations in the definitions of what it means to be a girl or a boy, a woman or a man. At the same time we must continue to study the relationship between gender and status — the ways in which gender functions as a signifier of differential prestige and power and as a salient cue for interpersonal interaction.

The conclusions that human behavior has no gender and that individuals learn responses within particular situations continuously throughout our lives are supported by the accumulated evidence that as conditions and opportunities for practice change, so does our behavior. We need only remember the ease and speed with which women during World War II went from being happy homemakers (if they were White) or domestic servants (if they were Black) to being skilled Rosie-the-Riveters in shipyards and munitions plants. In our own time, we need only note the numbers of young women who go from playing with Barbie dolls in childhood to working in medicine, law, and business management. Consider, for example, the findings of a study by the National Women's Political Caucus that when women run for political office in the United States they win as often as men ("For women . . . ," 1994).

Despite the fact that predictions based solely on gender are often inaccurate, social institutions in the U.S. continue to expend enormous efforts to support stereotypes and to generalize about gender differences in behavior. There is good reason to assume that these efforts are undertaken in order to maintain gender inequities in power and privilege. A culture that encourages belief in gender-related traits (regardless of whether they are said to be learned or innate) more easily supports the continuation and justification of separate spheres for women and men. The question of gender sameness or difference is one that does not do justice to the complexity of human behavior, to the diversity among persons of the same gender, or to intra-individual variability. It obscures the more fundamental scientific questions about relationships between behavior and particular variables, and thus primarily serves an agenda directed toward preserving the political status quo.

REFERENCES

Barnett, M. A., Howard, J. A., King, L. M., & Dino, G. A. (1980). Antecedents of empathy: Retrospective accounts of early socialization. *Personality and Social Psychology Bulletin, 6*, 361–365.

Betancourt, H., & Lopez, S. R. (1993). The study of culture, ethnicity, and race in American psychology. *American Psychologist, 48*, 629–637.

Bjorkqvist, K. (1994). Sex differences in physical, verbal, and indirect aggression: A review of recent research. *Sex Roles, 30*, 177–188.

Deutsch, F. M. (1990). Status, sex, and smiling: The effect of role on smiling in men and women. *Personality and Social Psychology Bulletin, 16*, 531–540.

Deutsch, F. M., & Saxon, S. (1994). Traditional ideologies, nontraditional lives. Paper read at meeting of the Association for Women in Psychology, March, Oakland, Calif.

Eagly, A. H. (1995). The science and politics of comparing women and men. *American Psychologist, 50*, 145–158.

Feingold, A. (1994). Gender differences in variability in intellectual abilities: A cross-cultural perspective. *Sex Roles, 30*, 81–92.

For women, the road to political office is paved with victory. (1994). *Providence Journal-Bulletin*, (Sept. 9) p. A7.

Hurtado, A. (1989). Relating to privilege: Seduction and rejection in the subordination of white women and women of color. *Signs, 14*, 833–855.

Lightdale, J. R., & Prentice, D. A. (1994). Rethinking sex differences in aggression: Aggressive behavior in the absence of social roles. *Personality and Social Psychology Bulletin, 20,* 34–44.

Lott, B. (1990). Dual natures of learned behavior: The challenge to feminist psychology. In R. T. Hare-Mustin & J. Marecek (Eds.), *Making a difference: Psychology and the construction of gender* (pp. 65–101). New Haven: Yale University Press.

Lott, B. (1994). *Women's lives: Themes and variations in gender learning.* Monterey, Calif.: Brooks/Cole.

Lott, B., & Maluso, D. (1993). The social learning of gender. In A. E. Beall & R. J. Sternberg (Eds.), *The psychology of gender* (pp. 99–123). New York: Guilford Press.

Melson, G. F., & Fogel, A. (1988). Learning to care. *Psychology Today* (January), 39–45.

Moskowitz, D. S., Suh, E. J., & Desaulniers, J. (1994). Situational influences on gender differences in agency and communion. *Journal of Personality and Social Psychology, 66,* 753–761.

Sharps, M. J., Walton, A. L., & Price, J. L. (1993). Gender and task in the determination of spatial cognitive performance. *Psychology of Women Quarterly, 17,* 71–83.

Vonk, R., & Ashmore, R. D. (1993). The multifaceted self: Androgyny reassessed by open-ended self-descriptions. *Social Psychology Quarterly, 56,* 278–287.

Comparing Women and Men:
Methods, Findings, and Politics

ALICE H. EAGLY

In her essay, Bernice Lott (this volume) displays profound discomfort about an activity that is common among research psychologists—comparing women and men in research data and then reporting the results of this comparison. In fact, most research psychologists record the sex of their research participants and run at least one analysis to determine whether the females and males behaved differently. Despite the common practice of examining one's research data for sex differences, psychologists do not necessarily publish the results of these analyses. Researchers may omit a report of such analyses when they find no evidence of differences because they find null findings uninteresting. They also may decline to report their comparisons of the sexes because they find differences that they cannot readily interpret or that they believe would reflect unfavorably on women or men. Indeed, Lott expressed the idea that publishing reports of differences is harmful to women, and the fears that she articulated are shared by some other feminist critics (e.g., McHugh, Koeske, & Frieze, 1986; Mednick, 1991). However, in her chapter Lott cited several studies that report sex-related differences (e.g., Barnett, Howard, King, & Dino, 1980; Lightdale & Prentice, 1994), albeit findings congenial to her rhetorical purposes.

Lott's reasons for distrusting the activity of comparing the sexes deserve careful scrutiny, in the context of contemporary research on gender. In this essay I offer counterarguments to a number of

Lott's points and also highlight some areas of agreement. To begin, I will explain the subtleties of the activity that Lott calls "cataloging differences." Then I will discuss Lott's claim that differences between the sexes are small and therefore trivial. Finally, I will consider the political implications of research findings that compare men and women.

HOW DO CONTEMPORARY PSYCHOLOGISTS DRAW CONCLUSIONS FROM RESEARCHERS' COMPARISONS OF WOMEN AND MEN?

Readers of Lott's essay may get the impression that reviewers of psychological research count up (or catalog) reports of sex differences and then announce in simple fashion that the sexes are the same or different in a given domain. That is, a reviewer might announce that men are more aggressive than women or that women are more socially sensitive, because most relevant studies obtained such a finding. Although it was once common practice for psychologists to base their conclusions about sex differences and similarities on a simple count of research findings, or even on their informal impressions of the general trend of results appearing in research literatures, in the late 1970s a revolution occurred in the methods that psychologists use to integrate research findings.

It is important to understand in some detail the much more sophisticated methods that contemporary reviewers use to draw conclusions from groups of studies, in order to appreciate that these methods address exactly the issue that Lott believes is not addressed by cataloging differences—namely, the identification of contexts in which differences do and do not occur. Contrary to Lott's understanding of contemporary reviewing, the analysis of context is the major point of most efforts to survey existing research findings. Gone are the days when psychologists were interested only in simple conclusions about similarity and difference. Rather, when research psychologists synthesize a complex research literature, they are sensitive to understanding the conditions under which findings of sex differences grow larger and smaller and sometimes even reverse their typical direction. Indeed, Lott's understanding of what reviewing is all about seems to be anchored in practices that prevailed in psychology twenty or more years ago, not current practices.

To illustrate how research on sex differences and similarities is synthesized, imagine that a researcher wanted to address a general question, for example, "do women have a different leadership style than men?" This researcher could, of course, conduct a new study to produce an answer to this question, perhaps a study in which male and female managers and their subordinates complete various questionnaire measures that have reasonable validity for assessing leadership style. However, before embarking on such a study, any researcher would be well advised to take a close look at the existing research literature. On the question of differences and similarities in leadership style, for example, anyone with access to such psychology and social science databases as PsycINFO and Social SciSearch would quickly discover that hundreds of researchers have already addressed the question. Therefore, conducting one additional study would add only a pebble to a rather large pile of empirical research and probably would do little to answer the general question of whether women and men differ in their leadership style. After all, no single study, no matter how high its quality, can really answer this question (or any other question of such breadth), because that study is inevitably conducted in a particular environment with specific research participants and a defined set of methods. The answer produced by any such study may or may not generalize to other environments, participants, and methods.

Given the existence of a substantial research literature, the more important and meaningful activity is to try to make sense out of the existing studies. An enormous amount of work by hundreds of researchers has already gone into addressing many questions about sex differences and similarities, such as the question of whether women and men differ in cognitive abilities and performance. Some of these studies were con-

ducted specifically to examine the sex-difference issue. Other studies were mainly concerned with addressing different questions, and the researcher happened to compare the male and female participants on various measures and include this comparison in the research report.

General conclusions based on multiple studies addressing the same question were once quite unreliable because psychologists lacked sound methods for drawing conclusions from large bodies of research literature. The traditional informal methods that prevailed until the late 1970s made it difficult to discern whether there was a consistent pattern in the findings in the many studies that examined some aspect of female and male behavior. To draw a conclusion from multiple studies, traditionally an investigator with expertise in the area of research would merely read through a number of these studies. The studies themselves were usually located haphazardly; there was rarely a systematic effort to find all the relevant research. Then the reviewer would draw conclusions about the research literature as a whole, also using informal methods. Perhaps most of the studies would support a particular conclusion, and often some studies would seem methodologically stronger than others and therefore more worthy of emphasis. Conclusions would be drawn, then, based on a process that psychologists now call *narrative reviewing*. This type of reviewing could be more or less insightful and informative, but it always consisted of a type of qualitative conclusion-drawing based on impressions gleaned from reading selected research literature on a particular question.

During the past twenty years, psychologists have developed more formal techniques for aggregating and integrating research findings. These techniques, popularly known as *meta-analysis*, are more formally described as *quantitative synthesis* because they use various forms of quantification in drawing conclusions from multiple studies (see Cooper & Hedges, 1994). These methods have greatly increased the scientific rigor of the process by which social scientists (and other scientists) draw conclusions from their research literatures. These methods of quantitative synthesis of findings

of studies are analogous to the techniques that research psychologists use within an individual study
to draw conclusions based on multiple observations. For example, 100 people may have participated in a particular study of leadership style. The
researcher's conclusion based on the data provided
by the 100 participants would not be based on an
impression of trends in the data but instead would
be disciplined by applying statistical inference. For
example, a sex difference would not be claimed on
a measure of leadership style unless that difference
was shown to be statistically significant among the
100 participants. In a meta-analysis, analogous statistical criteria must be satisfied before a reviewer is
allowed to conclude that the findings of a group of
studies collectively show that men differ from
women.

The first step that a contemporary reviewer
takes is to find the existing research literature. Considerable effort is devoted to obtaining a copy of all
studies that have ever tested a particular hypothesis
and been written up in some fashion. The published literature is located through examining electronic databases such as PsycINFO and PsycLIT as
well as the reference lists of existing review articles
and published studies. Using these and other methods, reviewers make a concerted effort to find all
the studies that have ever addressed a particular hypothesis, such as the hypothesis that men are more
aggressive than women or that women are verbally
more fluent than men.

With a preliminary group of studies in hand, reviewers must develop systematic rules for including
and excluding studies from the review. For example, some studies may be so methodologically
flawed that they should not be included in the review, and others might differ so fundamentally in
their method from the majority of studies that the
information they yield is not comparable. These
rules for inclusion and exclusion are eventually
published with the review and therefore must be
clear, defensible, and systematically implemented.

After a reviewer has decided on the sample of
studies that she or he regards as providing an adequate test of the hypothesis in question, how does
this individual draw conclusions from these stud-

ies? The reviewer proceeds by calculating a statistic
that represents the outcome of each study. For example, to represent the outcome of a study that
compared women and men on leadership style, a
reviewer would calculate a statistic that expresses
the extent to which women and men differed on
the particular measure or measures of style used in
that study. This statistic is known as an *effect size;*
the reviewer calculates an effect size for every report. In research that compares the sexes, the effect
size ordinarily computed is known as *d.* This
number is the difference between male and female
participants' means in standard deviation units. In
other words, the men in each study obtained a
score on leadership style, as did the women. The effect size is the difference between the male and female mean scores, divided by the standard
deviation (computed within each sex separately
and then averaged). This effect size or *d* is thus an
instance of the type of statistic that statisticians call
a *standard score.* A *d* of 0.5 would indicate that
there is a difference of 0.5 standard deviations between the average behavior of women and men,
and *d* of 1 would indicate a difference of one standard deviation. The reason that findings have to be
expressed in terms of effect sizes is to give them a
common metric or measurement scale so that they
can be averaged and otherwise statistically analyzed.

One of the advantages of calculating effect sizes
is that the results of comparing women and men
are then placed on a continuum. Thus, the sexes
are not described as "the same" or "different" in a
particular study but as different or similar along a
scale that allows for gradations. In order to address
the global question of the extent to which the behavior of men and women differs in general in the
group of studies, the meta-analyst averages the effect sizes from the individual studies and then interprets this average. This average is itself located
somewhere along a continuum that runs from no
difference to large differences and thus does not
provide a simple yes or no answer to the question
of whether in general men differ from women.
Rather, the two groups may differ strongly, moder-
ately, slightly, or not at all. As explained later in
this essay, deciding whether an aggregated differ-

ence is small or large requires careful analysis of the results of a quantitative synthesis.

Meta-analysis does much more than portray difference and similarity in terms of a continuum rather than absolute categories of sameness versus difference. Each quantitative synthesis produces a set of effect sizes, each of which represents a particular study. These individual effect sizes are not merely averaged into an overall mean that addresses the question of whether women and men differ in general. Instead, the individual findings are preserved and are collectively much more important and informative than their average or central tendency because the effect sizes vary in magnitude (and often in direction as well). This set of effect sizes is highly informative to the reviewer, and analysis of variability in these effect sizes is the heart of quantitative synthesis.

In addition to calculating averages, a contemporary reviewer uses the set of effect sizes that represents the findings of all the reviewed studies to determine whether the studies produced consistent results. Although chances are that the answers produced by the studies to the question of whether the sexes differ in leadership style were somewhat different, the reviewer would not address the issue of studies' consistency impressionistically but would run a statistical test that assesses whether the inconsistencies in the effect sizes are within the range of variation that could be accounted for by random error.

If the inconsistencies in the findings of the studies were larger than what would be expected only from error, then the reviewer must try to explain this variability. However, first the reviewer would see if only a very few studies produced different answers from the remainder of the studies. These studies may be "outliers" for reasons of error (e.g., the data may have been miscalculated or misreported by the researchers) or for reasons of very atypical methods. If differences in findings are not due to a few aberrant studies, the reviewer must find out why the findings varied.

It is at this point in the reviewing process when the reviewer who follows Lott's advice ought to take into account the context of sex differences and

similarities. However, modern research synthesis imposes statistical procedures that constrain this aspect of the reviewing process, just as they constrain other aspects. Lott's point that context is important cannot be made convincingly merely by citing some well-chosen examples. Particular examples do not make a general case because readers cannot discern if the examples are typical or atypical of the research literature as a whole. Specific studies may be brought to readers' attention as if they are typical illustrations of phenomena, but they may represent a biased and highly selective choice from the research literature.

To take the contexts of studies into account in a fair and systematic manner, reviewers must first code the many ways that studies differ. This coding of studies' characteristics (including their methodological quality) is carried out by two people who must establish the reliability of their individual work through obtaining high agreement in their independent judgments. Ordinarily within a research area in psychology, studies differ in scores of ways—for example, in their participant populations, measuring instruments, and social context. The reviewer must attempt to discern which of these many differences in studies' methods are responsible for the differences in studies' findings. Figuring out which are the critical features of studies is like putting together a puzzle. The individual studies are the pieces of the puzzle, and the reviewer seeks a pattern that allows the characteristics of the studies to account for the observed variability in the study outcomes.

One way that contemporary reviewers solve the puzzle of inconsistent findings is to consult relevant theories of sex differences and similarities. Theories may suggest why studies would differ in their outcomes. In fact, the variability reviewers observe in effect sizes is an appealing invitation to theory building and theory testing (Eagly & Wood, 1991; Miller & Pollock, 1994). For example, when Johnson and I (Eagly and Johnson, 1990) synthesized research on sex differences in leadership style, our social-role theory suggested that differences would be greater in studies conducted with student groups than with managers, because female and male managers are selected for their positions by the same criteria and then socialized to perform the same role. These factors should produce greater similarity among female and male managers than among female and male students in general. Our prediction was corroborated in our analysis of research on leadership style.

Another way that reviewers sort out why findings differ is to consult their knowledge of methodology. For example, the study of psychometrics (e.g., Cronbach, 1990) suggests to most psychologists that if two variables are related to one another (as sex may be related to aggressiveness), this relation would appear larger in studies that feature measures based on multiple responses rather than a single response. Indeed, in our leadership style review (Eagly and Johnson, 1990) and in many other meta-analyses, this principle has been upheld.

Resolving the question of whether various features of the studies produce different results is disciplined by further statistical analyses. The reviewer thus places the studies into groups—for example, studies conducted in university laboratories with student participants versus those conducted with managers. Then the reviewer uses a statistical test to determine if the two groups of studies had different outcomes, at a statistically significant level. The reviewer may conduct correlational analyses as well—for example, relating the date when studies were conducted to their outcome (possibly tracking the hypothesis that cultural change accounts for differences in findings).

Contemporary reviewers who follow appropriate meta-analytic procedures are thus extremely attentive to the context of studies. However, rather than making the case that context is important by citing a few illustrative research findings, as Lott has done, they address this issue systematically using all the available research findings and appropriate statistical tests. These procedures allow reviewers to assess the broader issue of whether sex-difference comparisons are more inconsistent across studies than research findings relevant to hypotheses having nothing to do with sex or gender. In quite a few quantitative syntheses of studies that compared the sexes, findings have not been particularly inconsistent across the studies, compared with studies testing other hypotheses, despite Lott's view that variability would be unusually high in this research area (see Eagly, 1995).

ARE SEX-RELATED DIFFERENCES SMALL?

One contentious issue among psychologists is whether the differences discovered between women and men are small or large, important or unimportant. Even though there is plenty of room for researchers to disagree about magnitude issues, Lott's extreme view that "the differences so painstakingly searched for are small indeed" (this volume) is not defensible. Lott seems to forget the importance of comparing sex-related differences to other findings in psychology and fails to realize that shared factors constrain the magnitude of almost all research findings. Therefore, any sensible perspective for judging the magnitude of research findings requires that their magnitude be regarded as a relative matter. Factors including unreliability and invalidity of measures lower the magnitude of almost all findings, and the percentage of variability that can be explained by systematic factors is usually far less than 100. Ordinarily in psychology, measures are only somewhat reliable and valid, and the differences due to any single variable appear as overlapping distributions of numbers. The question then becomes whether differences due to the sex of research participants are particularly small, compared with other kinds of findings that are of interest to psychologists.

There are various ways to compare the magnitude of sex-difference findings to the magnitude of other findings in psychology (e.g., comparing average effect sizes across research questions), but, without introducing these methods in detail, suffice it to say that some sex-difference findings truly warrant being described as large relative to typical phenomena examined by psychologists. Such large differences occur with respect to at least one test of cognitive abilities (e.g., the Shepard-Metzler test of mental rotation), some social behaviors (e.g., facial expressiveness, frequency of filled pauses in speech), some sexual behaviors (e.g., incidence of masturbation, attitudes toward casual sexual intercourse), one class of personality traits (tendermindedness and nurturant tendencies), and some physical abilities (e.g., the velocity, distance, and accuracy of throwing a ball). Therefore, any statement that all sex-difference findings are small is manifestly false. However, most aggregated sex-difference findings appear to be in the small-to-moderate range, which appears to be more typical of psychological research. In summary, when research that has compared the sexes is judged in relation to reasonable benchmarks for judging the magnitude of psychological findings, it does not support descriptions of sex-related differences as routinely small or as generally smaller than other types of findings of interest to psychologists.

What about those sex-related differences that most psychologists would label as small? Does small mean inconsequential in terms of everyday life? To evaluate this matter, it is important to know that psychologists often index the magnitude of findings by the percentage of variability in data that is accounted for by a variable—in this case the sex of the research participant. Some researchers believe that findings accounting for less than 5 percent of the variability are small, whereas others may think that findings accounting for less than 1 percent of the variability are small. However, even findings accounting for less than 1 percent of the variability can have important practical implications. To make this point, Martell, Lane, and Willis (1995) carried out a computer simulation to demonstrate the practical importance of sex differences that Lott, along with most psychologists, would surely label as extremely small. This simulation was carried out in an imaginary organization in which there was a difference in performance evaluations favoring men but accounting for only 1 percent of the variability in scores. Martell, Lane, and Willis then assumed that managers were promoted through an organizational hierarchy based only on these performance evaluations. Given a pyramidal structure in which there are relatively fewer people in higher positions than in lower ones, this 1 percent difference in performance evaluations produced an organizational structure in which only 35 percent of the highest-level positions were filled by women. Also dramatic was Abelson's (1985) earlier demonstration that a baseball player's batting skill has a substantial impact on the team's success, despite the fact that the percentage of variance in any single batting performance that is explained by batting skill is approximately 0.3 percent. These simple illustrations of the practical importance of seemingly small effects thus underscore the point that psychologists are generally misled when they look at a sex difference and label it small or trivial based on examining the percentage of variance accounted for by sex. As Martell, Lane, and Willis have shown, examining the consequences of group differences in natural settings provides the best indicator of the importance or unimportance of differences.

Contemporary reviewers also make use of metrics other than percentage of variance to provide more intuitive and useful descriptions of the magnitude of sex differences. One such metric is Rosenthal and Rubin's (1982) *binomial effect size display*, which translates an effect into a comparison of the percentages of cases that exceed some criterion in two groups. For sex-related differences, the binomial effect size display would compare the percentage of women who are above the overall median of the combined female and male distribution with the percentage of men who are above this median. For example, a researcher might be tempted to dismiss the sex difference in social smiling reported in one of Hall's (1984) meta-analyses as unimportant because it accounted for a mere 9 percent of the variability in smiling. However, description in terms of the more intuitively meaningful metric of the binomial effect size display indicates that above-average amounts of smiling occurred for 65 percent of women and 35 percent of men.

Another useful metric, the *common language effect size statistic*, was presented by McGraw and Wong (1992). This metric indexes the percentage of occasions on which a score randomly sampled from one distribution exceeds a score randomly sampled from another distribution. For example, McGraw and Wong reported data from the American College Testing Program's (ACT) test of math achievement showing that sex accounted for 5.4 percent of the variation in performance, with boys scoring higher than girls. Although this percentage may seem small to most psychologists, repeated comparisons of randomly selected boys and girls would show that on 63 percent of the occasions the boy's score would exceed the girl's score. Descriptions of group differences in terms of the common language effect size indicator thus convey the meaning of the findings in everyday terms.

DO REPORTS OF SEX DIFFERENCES PERPETUATE WOMEN'S DISADVANTAGED STATUS?

Lott (this volume) raised the important issue of whether the identification of differences primarily serves a political function of perpetuating differences in power. On the issue of what function is served by identifying sex-correlated differences, I would give far greater weight to such research's scientific function of identifying phenomena that psychologists can then investigate empirically and theoretically. To thus give science a voice does not deny Lott's point that reports of differences convey political meaning. Indeed, there is no doubt that comparisons between women and men have political implications (see Eagly, 1995).

In contrast to Lott's view that scientific evidence of differences necessarily perpetuates power differences that favor men, I see a considerably more varied and complex political landscape. Surely differences between the sexes reflect the social position of women and men, with women manifesting social behaviors that are less agentic and more communal than those of men. Nonetheless, in the context of the feminist social movement, such differences can often be harnessed, with the aid of feminist rhetoric, to help produce social change that is favorable to women. For example, evidence of women's oppression (e.g., statistics showing victimization and discrimination) can be deployed to attract attention to women's plight and to galvanize people into action to raise women's status. In addition, many sex differences in social behavior

can be construed as reflecting poorly on men. For example, men can be described not merely as more aggressive than women, but as more violent and destructive (e.g., Archer, 1994). The resulting critique of male behavior can be used to promote the cause of women. Other differences, such as women's greater friendliness and attentiveness to others in small groups (see Eagly & Wood, 1991), put women in a favorable light. Thus, scientific attention to sex differences and similarities exists in a political environment that offers numerous methods for fostering change in the status of women. Feminist writers and activists are highly skilled in using a wide range of scientific findings to promote their social goals.

Research that compares the sexes attracts attention and can be used in ways that are beneficial or harmful to women or men. Therefore, some discomfort and anxiety about the implications and potential uses of this research is warranted. Some psychologists may allow their analysis of the political implications of such research to determine whether and how they participate in the research area; others will give priority to science over politics and compare men and women in their research data primarily because of the scientific challenge posed by the resulting findings.

The rigor of contemporary quantitative synthesis injects into these political debates a far more reliable and accurate rendering of scientific research that has compared the sexes. Better science can make a more useful contribution to public-policy debates that involve issues of gender. Thoughtful writers of all political persuasions will understand the fundamental scientific advance that has been made in synthesizing research and will build their political arguments on this new science. Less thoughtful writers will continue to use research as pure rhetoric by selectively describing individual studies that happen to suit their political preferences, without taking any responsibility for determining whether the science they cite is of high quality or low quality or is typical or atypical in its outcomes. Let us hope that the thoughtful writers will prevail over the less thoughtful ones.

REFERENCES

Abelson, R. P. (1985). A variance explanation paradox: When a little is a lot. *Psychological Bulletin, 97*, 129–133.

Archer, J. A. (Ed.). (1994). *Male violence.* New York: Routledge.

Barnett, M. A., Howard, J. A., King, L. M., & Dino, G. A. (1980). Antecedents of empathy: Retrospective accounts of early socialization. *Personality and Social Psychology Bulletin, 6*, 361–365.

Cooper, H., & Hedges, L. V. (Eds.). (1994). *The handbook of research synthesis.* New York: Russell Sage Foundation.

Cronbach, L. J. (1990). *Essentials of psychological testing* (5th ed.). New York: HarperCollins.

Eagly, A. H. (1995). The science and politics of comparing women and men. *American Psychologist, 50*, 145–158.

Eagly, A. H., & Johnson, B. T. (1990). Gender and leadership style: A meta-analysis. *Psychological Bulletin, 108*, 233–256.

Eagly, A. H., & Wood, W. (1991). Explaining sex differences in social behavior: A meta-analytic perspective. *Personality and Social Psychology Bulletin, 17*, 306–315.

Hall, J. A. (1984). *Nonverbal sex differences: Communication accuracy and expressive style.* Baltimore: Johns Hopkins University Press.

Lightdale, J. R., & Prentice, D. A. (1994). Rethinking sex differences in aggression: Aggressive behavior in the absence of social roles. *Personality and Social Psychology Bulletin, 20*, 34–44.

Martell, R. F., Lane, D. M., & Willis, C. E. (1995). Male-female differences: A computer simulation. *American Psychologist, 51*, 157–158.

McGraw, K. O., & Wong, S. P. (1992). A common language effect size statistic. *Psychological Bulletin, 111*, 361–365.

McHugh, M. C., Koeske, R. D., & Frieze, I. H. (1986). Issue to consider in conducting nonsexist psychological research: A guide for researchers. *American Psychologist, 41*, 879–890.

Mednick, M. T. (1991). Currents and futures in American feminist psychology: State of the art revisited. *Psychology of Women Quarterly, 15*, 611–621.

Miller, N., & Pollock, V. E. (1994). Meta-analytic synthesis for theory development. In H. Cooper & L. V. Hedges (Eds.), *The handbook of research synthesis* (pp. 457–483). New York. Russell Sage Foundation.

Rosenthal, R., & Rubin, D. B. (1982). A simple, general purpose display of magnitude of experimental effect. *Journal of Educational Psychology, 74*, 166–169.

Biological Causation:

Are Gender Differences

Wired into Our Biology?

Scholars have long debated the origin of gender differences. Although social scientists now agree that men and women are much more alike than they are dissimilar and that differences within each sex are much greater than differences between the sexes, the topic of gender differences continues to fascinate researchers. As Carol Jacklin and Laura Baker point out, in attempting to weigh the influence of nature versus nurture, "much of the research on gender differences has focused on the early years of life, even though it is the differential expectations about adult women and men that we are ultimately interested in understanding" (1993, p. 41).

Unfortunately, the media do not approach the question with the same caution. A *Time* cover story, for example, showing a young girl gazing admiringly at a boy flexing his muscles, confidently proclaimed that men and women are different because they are born that way (Gorman, 1992). A 1995 ABC television special entitled *Boys and Girls Are Different: Men, Women, and the Sex Difference* came to a similar conclusion. According to John Stoessel, the program's narrator, no matter how much conscientious parents like himself try to treat their children equally, boys prefer to play with guns and girls prefer to play with dolls. Why? The answer is simple: "Right after the sperm meets the egg," he asserted, "things start to happen that just make us into different kinds of people."

While not as sweeping in their conclusions as Stoessel, a number of researchers argue that the effects of prenatal hormones on the brain help explain why men and women differ in the ways in which they solve intellectual problems (Kimura, 1992). Some of the best evidence of the influence of sex hormones, they argue, comes from studies of girls who were exposed to prenatal androgens (masculinizing hormones) because of a genetic defect known as congenital adrenal hyperplasia. These girls were more likely to be tomboyish, preferring, for example, to play with "boys' toys" like cars and fire engines (Berenbaum & Snyder, 1995).

Many researchers, however, remain skeptical about the implications of biological studies. Early research findings that women's intellect is inferior to men's owing to their smaller brain size are a constant reminder that theories are more readily accepted when they coincide with our prejudices (Gould, 1981). Moreover, the fact that infants are bombarded with gender-specific messages as soon as they are born is always a confounding factor in attempting to identify the origins of gender differences. Barbara Ehrenreich recounts an episode that occurred when her son, who had long, blond hair, was about two years old. "A waitress came up to us and said, 'Oh, she's so cute. What a sweetie,' and so on. And I said, 'Well, he's actually a boy.' The waitress, without missing a beat, said, 'Tough little guy, huh?'" (cited in Baxter, 1994, p. 52).

The extent to which parental behavior influences gender differences remains a source of contention. Maccoby and Jacklin's (1974) study of sex differences found little evidence to support the hypothesis that parents' treatment shapes the behavior of boys and girls in other than such narrowly defined areas as play activities and toy choices. Lytton and Romney's meta-analysis of 172 studies on the topic similarly concluded that there was little evidence to support the notion that parents treated their sons and daughters differently except in the area of sex-typed activities like encouraging girls to play with dolls and boys with toy cars. Consequently, they argued, "we cannot close our eyes to the possibility of biological predispositions providing a part of the explanation for existing sex differences" (1991, p. 289).

Nevertheless, there is evidence that parents *do* influence gender development. Any number of studies have demonstrated that a parent's perception of a child begins at, and occasionally before, birth. Expectant mothers who found out the sex of the child through amniocentesis reported different levels of prenatal activity depending on whether they were carrying a boy or a girl. The stirrings of a male fetus were described as "vigorous" and "a saga of earthquakes," whereas mothers of girls identified the movements as "very gentle" and "lively but not excessively energetic" (Beal, 1994). It is not a big leap to assume that the mothers' perception of their children will continue to be influenced by gender expectations after the birth.

Similarly, experiments in which the sex of a toddler was manipulated (identified as male for some subjects and female for others) resulted in different characterizations of the child's actions. Those who thought the toddler was male described "his" activities as masculine. Those who thought it was female characterized "her" activities as feminine (Delk et al., 1986). Nevertheless, after reviewing twenty-three gender-labeling studies, Stern and Karraker (1989) cautioned that the researchers did not provide strong evidence for early gender-role socialization.

Play, along with independence training and achievement, is perhaps a better example of parents' differential treatment of their children (Beal, 1994). Parents, especially fathers, purchase different toys for boys and girls and tend to choose the gender-typical toy when playing with them (Smith & Daglish, 1977; Eisenberg et al., 1985). Studies have also demonstrated that young boys have on the average three times as many spatial toys (small vehicles, blocks, and so on) as young girls have, while girls have three times as many dolls as their male peers (Tracy, 1987; Pomerleau et al., 1990). Lytton and Romney (1991), however, warn that parents' choice of toys may reflect the child's existing preferences. One-year-old boys, for example, when given a doll, were less likely to play with it than were girls.

There is also evidence that parents differentiate between boys and girls in encouraging independent activities. Girls are rewarded for remaining close to their parents while boys are encouraged to explore the limits of their play areas. Parents, in addition, "not only expect greater achievements from their sons, they help them get there" (Beal, 1994, p. 77). Alessandri and Lewis (1993) demonstrated that despite the fact that three-year-old boys and girls performed equally well in a series of activities, the boys' parents responded with more positive evaluations than did the girls' parents.

Parents, of course, are not the only factors in children's gender socialization. In fact, boys and girls may be more likely to obtain ideas on what is appropriate gender behavior—what Sandra Bem (1983) describes as a "gender schema"—from other family members, teachers, television, and children's literature. For example, a study of 150 children's picture books indicated that boys are still portrayed as instrumental and independent while girls are characterized as passive and dependent (Kortenhaus & Demarest, 1993).

The topic of early gender development is clearly a complex one. In the following articles, June M. Reinisch, who was featured in the 1995 ABC special on children's sex differences, and her colleagues argue that biology plays an important role in explaining adult gender differences in such areas as agentic and communal behavior. Linda L. Carli, in contrast, disagrees. She claims that there is considerable evidence that early socialization experiences offer a better explanation for these gender differences.

REFERENCES

ABC. (1995). *Boys and Girls Are Different: Men, Women, and the Sex Difference.* Feb. 1.

Alessandri, S. M., & Lewis, M. (1993). Parental evaluation and its relation to shame and pride in young children. *Sex Roles, 29,* 335–343.

Baxter, S. (1994). The last word on gender differences. *Psychology Today* (March-April), 50–53, 85–86.

Beal, C. R. (1994). *Boys and girls: The development of gender roles.* New York: McGraw-Hill.

Bem, S. L. (1983). Gender schema theory and its implications for child development: Raising gender aschematic children in a gender schematic society. *Signs, 8,* 598–616.

Berenbaum, S. A., & Snyder, E. (1995). Early hormonal influences on childhood sex-typed activity and playmate preferences: Implications for the development of sexual orientation. *Developmental Psychology, 31,* 31–42.

Delk, J. L., Madden, R. B., Livingston, M., & Ryan, T. T. (1986). Adult perceptions of the infant as a function of gender labeling and observer gender. *Sex Roles, 15,* 527–534.

Eisenberg, N., Wolchik, S. A., Hernandez, R., & Pasternack, J. F. (1985). Parental socialization of young children's play: A short-term longitudinal study. *Child Development, 56,* 1506–1513.

Gorman, C. (1992). Sizing up the sexes. *Time* (Jan. 20), 42–51.

Gould, S. J. (1981). *The mismeasure of man.* New York: Norton.

Jacklin, C. N., & Baker, L. A. (1993). Early gender development. In S. Oskamp & M. Costanzo (Eds.), *Gender Issues in Contemporary Society* (pp. 41–57). Newbury Park, Calif.: Sage.

Kimura, D. (1992). Sex differences in the brain. *Scientific American* (September), 119–125.

Kortenhaus, C. M., & Demarest, J. (1993). Gender role stereotyping in children's literature: An update. *Sex Roles, 28,* 219–232.

Lytton, H., & Romney, D. M. (1991). Parents' differential socialization of boys and girls: A meta-analysis. *Psychological Bulletin, 109,* 267–296.

Maccoby, E. E., and Jacklin, C. N. (1974). *The psychology of sex differences.* Stanford, Calif.: Stanford University Press.

Pomerleau, A., Bolduc, D., Malcuit, G., & Cossette, L. (1990). Pink or blue: Environmental gender stereotypes in the first two years of life. *Sex Roles, 22,* 359–367.

Smith, P. K., & Daglish, L. (1977). Sex differences in parent and infant behavior in the home. *Child Development, 48,* 1250–1254.

Stern M., & Karraker, M. K. (1989). Sex stereotyping of

infants: A review of gender labeling studies. *Sex Roles,* *20,* 501–522.

Tracy, D. M. (1987). Toys, spatial ability, and science and mathematics achievement: Are they related? *Sex Roles, 17,* 115–138.

ADDITIONAL READING

Bjorkqvist, K., & Niemela, P. (Eds.). (1992). *Of mice and women: Aspects of female aggression.* San Diego: Academic Press.

Fausto-Sterling, A. (1985). *Myths of gender: Biological theories about women and men.* New York: Basic Books.

Jacklin, C. N. (1993). Gender and childhood socialization. In A. E. Beall & R. J. Sternberg (Eds.), *The psychology of gender.* New York: Guilford Press.

Leaper, C. (Ed.). (1994). *Childhood gender segregation: Causes and consequences.* San Francisco: Jossey-Bass.

Lorber, J. (1993). Believing is seeing: Biology as ideology. *Gender and Society, 7,* 568–581.

Thorne, B. (1993). *Gender play: Girls and boys in school.* New Brunswick, N.J.: Rutgers University Press.

Sex Differences Emerge during the First Year of Life

June M. Reinisch,

Leonard A. Rosenblum,

Donald B. Rubin, and

M. Fini Schulsinger

INTRODUCTION

Evidence gathered during the last two decades has established that many sexually differentiated patterns of human behavior have their origins in confluence of genetic, prenatal, and postnatal factors (De Vries, De Bruin, Uylings & Corner, 1984; Glucksmann, 1981; Hall, 1982; Hines, 1982; Maccoby & Jacklin, 1974; Money, 1988; Money & Ehrhardt, 1972; Reinisch, 1981; Rubin, Reinisch & Haskett, 1981). In light of these complex interactions, investigations into the behavioral differentiation of the sexes must begin as early in the life of the individual as possible (Freedman, 1974; Jacklin, Snow & Maccoby, 1981; Maccoby, Doering, Jacklin & Kraemer, 1979; Money & Ehrhardt, 1972; Rosenblum, 1971; Thoman, Leiderman & Olson, 1972). Moreover, because the sexually dimorphic behaviors that emerge during early development initially may be quite subtly expressed, it is often necessary to examine the emergence of these patterns in relatively large groups of both sexes to detect differences. The current data, based on records of nearly 5,000 full-term Caucasian infants, demonstrate that small but clear sex differences in the attainment of fundamental developmental milestones and in the successive intervals between the achievement of progressively more mature behaviors are apparent during the first year of life. An understanding of these early dimorphic patterns may provide insights into the foundations of many childhood and adult sex differences (Korner, 1973; Meaney & Stewart, 1985; Money, 1988; Money & Ehrhardt, 1972).

METHOD

SUBJECTS

The Copenhagen Consecutive Perinatal Cohort consists of all children born from September 1959 to December 1961 in Rigshospitalet, Copenhagen, Denmark (Zachau-Christiansen & Ross, 1975). Rigshospitalet is the university hospital in which the largest number of pregnancies in Denmark were delivered during that period. The cohort consists of 9,006 consecutive pregnancies which produced 9,181 children comprising 8,833 single births, 170 twin births, and three sets of triplets. The 4,653 infants included in the current analyses are those: (1) who survived the first year of life; (2) whose gestation length was in the normal range of 38–41 weeks; and (3) whose mothers provided contemporaneous records of infant attainment of developmental milestones.

DATA COLLECTION

Mothers were instructed to record the day of first occurrence of each of ten developmental milestones. These predefined milestones were: (1) lifts head while lying on stomach; (2) smiles; (3) holds head up; (4) reaches for objects; (5) sits without support; (6) stands with support; (7) crawls independently; (8) walks with support; (9) stands without support; and (10) walks without support. Records were maintained in diaries provided to mothers upon release from the hospital following delivery, and generated milestone data reported to the nearest week or month. These diaries were collected when the infants were between 12 and 18 months of age. For any particular milestone, records were available for 1,006 to 1,916 males and 979 to 1,928 females.

BACKGROUND VARIABLES

Also available for the subjects were nine prospectively collected, developmentally relevant covariates. These nine variables which might have differentially affected attainment of the milestones were: (1) birth weight; (2) birth stage (i.e., length of gestation within 38–41 weeks); (3) socioeconomic status; (4–6) three Pregnancy and Birth Complications Scores: Predisposing Factors, Pregnancy Complications, and Complications of Delivery; and (7–9) three scores reflecting Neonatal Complications: Non-Maturity Score, Neonatal Physical Examination Score, and Neonatal Neurological Examination Score (Mednick, Hocevar, Baker & Teasdale, 1983).

DATA ANALYSES

Maximum likelihood estimates of the means, variances, and correlations among the ten milestones, nine covariates, and sex were obtained by application of the EM algorithm (Dempster, Laird & Rubin, 1977) to all 4,653 subjects. This analysis adjusted for potential biases due to selective reporting that could be explained by the covariates and sex, under the assumption that the conditional expectation of each milestone variable, given the covariates and sex, was a normal linear regression. Standard errors for tests were obtained as follows: maximum likelihood estimates of parameters were inserted in the standard expressions for test statistics, where the sample size (n) employed in each test statistic was the sample size for the variable being tested (i.e., the number of subjects for whom the milestone was recorded when determining the standard error for a particular milestone, and the number of subjects with both milestones recorded when determining the standard error for the difference between two milestones). *This method is adequate given the pattern of missing data in our data set. A more principled, but computationally far more expensive, method is to use the SEM*

algorithm (Meng & Rubin, 1991) to compute standard errors. Another statistical issue concerns the effects of rounding error in the reporting of milestones. We can legitimately report milestone results to the nearest day because the variance of the rounding error is less than 10 percent of the variance of the milestone variables. Thus, the rounding will (1) have essentially no effect on estimates of means, and (2) lead to slight overestimates of variances of the milestones, thereby resulting in consistent effect estimates and accurate tests (Dempster & Rubin, 1983).

RESULTS

In general, the ten developmental milestones studied emerged in the following chronological order: lifts head while lying on stomach (M1); smiles (M2); holds head up (M3); reaches for objects (M4); sits without support (M5); stands with support (M6); crawls independently (M7); walks with support (M8); stands without support (M9); and walks without support (M10). A similar ordering and chronology of the emergence of milestones has been observed in studies in both the United States and western European countries (Bayley, 1935; Brazelton, 1983; Gesell, 1940; Gesell, 1952; Hindley, Filliozat, Klakenberg, Nocolet-Meister & Sand, 1966).

Although the sequence of behaviors was identical for males and females, an analysis of sex differences in the age at which milestones were achieved revealed potentially important differences in timing. Three milestones were reached significantly earlier by boys: "lifts head while lying on stomach" (M1: Diff. = 2.7 days; p < .002); "stands with support" (M6: Diff. = 5.6 days; p < .001); and "crawls independently" (M7: Diff. = 7.4 days; p < .001). Boys also tended to reach "walks with support" somewhat earlier (M8: Diff. = 2.5 days; p < .09). Although there was a trend for girls to achieve "sits without support" before boys (M5: Diff. = 2.5 days; p < .10), none of the milestones appeared significantly earlier in females.

The progress of development during the first year was also examined in a second analysis of the 45 time intervals among the ten milestones. Of these, 19 were significantly (p < .05) different between male and female infants, with seven of the intervals longer in boys and twelve longer in girls. An additional five intervals closely approached significance (p < .10), two longer in girls and three longer in boys.

The period during which the largest sex differences occurred (in terms of both age of attainment and duration of intervals) began with the attainment of "sits without support" (M5) and ended with "walks with support" (M8), that is, between approximately 7 and 11 months of age. During this period, five of the six milestone intervals were significantly different for boys and girls. The complex nature of the differing developmental paths of the two sexes is reflected by the finding that although girls tended to reach "sits without support" (M5) earlier than boys, they attained the next two milestones—"stands with support" (M6) and "crawls independently" (M7)—after significantly longer intervals. Indeed, although they typically sat (M5) nearly three days earlier, girls began crawling independently seven days later than boys. In contrast, the interval between "crawls independently" (M7) and "walks with support" (M8) was significantly longer for boys than girls. The period of marked sex differences which emerged after "sits without support" (M5) concluded when both sexes attained the final milestone, "walks without support" (M10), at virtually identical ages. It should be noted that although these differences in age of attainment and the intervals between the milestones were relatively small in the absolute number of days involved, they reflect important variations in the process of infant development and represent the first such set of coordinated sex differences reported.

In order to determine whether these sex differences could be explained as a secondary consequence of other factors that might be related to biological sex, using the data for both the age of milestone attainment and the intervals between milestones, we used correlation to examine, and multiple regression to adjust for, the potential contribution of nine confounding variables. With this approach, the effect of sex on the timing of milestone attainment and the intervals between them could be examined for hypothetical males and females with identical values for all nine potentially confounding variables.

The importance of the nine variables was first considered in terms of their simple correlations with each milestone attainment. As would be expected, signs of neurological damage showed small but consistently positive correlations with later attainment of milestones (range = .05 to .11; mean correlation = +.06). That is, the more evidence of neurological damage, the later the attainment of milestones. Of the remaining confounding variables, the strongest relationships were to birth weight and birth stage, both of which showed small but consistently negative correlations to milestone attainment (range = −.12 to −.02; mean correlations of −.06 and −.05, respectively). This pattern of correlations reflected the fact that heavier neonates born later during the full-term period of 38–41 weeks reached milestones earlier. The remaining variables each showed mean correlations of only +.01.

The multiple regression analyses, which adjusted for these same covariates, suggested one additional sex difference in milestone attainment, i.e., girls smile (M2) somewhat earlier than boys (p < .10) when all confounding variables have equal values. None of the measures that exhibited significant sex differences in the initial analyses proved nonsignificant after adjustment for the potential confounding variables (i.e., none shifted from significant to nonsignificant as a result of the regression analyses), and the effect estimates are nearly the same before and after adjustment.

DISCUSSION

Data from the large perinatal cohort studied here indicate that consistent sex differences in the ages at which children first achieve important developmental milestones and the relative speed with which they progress from milestone to milestone appear within the first year of life. Importantly, in these full-term infants who survived through the first year of life, these fundamental sex differences were relatively unaffected by a wide variety of background variables.

The ten developmental milestones we studied can be usefully divided into two categories. The first involves those behaviors that can be characterized as potentially facilitating or fostering *en face* interaction between the infant and the caretaker. These include "smiles" (M2), "holds head up" (M3), and "sits without support" (M5). The second category includes behaviors which have the potential to facilitate independent, nonsocial action and separation. These include "stands with support" (M6), "crawls independently" (M7), "walks with support" (M8), and "stands without support" (M9). Viewed from this perspective, the data suggest that girls move more quickly than boys to attain the milestones that may foster social interaction and communication (Korner, 1969; Lewis, Kagan & Kalafat, 1966), and once developed, they spend more time than boys between the attainment of these behaviors and the development of activities that may foster independence. In contrast, after attaining those milestones that may foster social interaction, boys proceed to the next milestone relatively quickly. Thus boys may have relatively less opportunity for face-to-face contact with caretakers. Moving more rapidly to attain those activities that may serve to foster independence, boys then spend longer intervals than girls involved in these activities. The relatively more rapid movement towards independent activity is characteristic of most nonhuman primate males (Meaney & Stewart, 1985; Rosenblum, 1974) and in humans may also reflect the development of greater early physical strength and spatial skills in males (Beatty, 1984; Bell & Darling, 1965; Hobson, 1947; Korner, 1969). It is important to keep in mind, however, that these data indicate that despite these somewhat disparate paths, boys and girls typically reach the last milestone of "walks without support" at almost exactly the same age, i.e., just prior to the thirteenth month.

These sex differences in the chronology of developmental milestone attainment appear to reflect the same distinction embodied in the joint concepts of agentic/instrumental and communal/expressive patterns, which have been used to characterize the categories of dichotomized adult human masculine and feminine traits. Agentic (Baken, 1966)/instrumental (Parsons & Bales, 1955) behavior is defined as including those behavioral traits that relate to advancement of the individual or self-preservation and is considered to be more characteristic of males. Communal (Baken, 1966)/expressive (Parsons & Bales, 1955) behavior refers to traits that relate to interrelationships between the individual and the community and has been suggested to be more characteristic of females.

The sex differences in the age of milestone attainment and duration of intervals between milestones may of course be the product of systematic reporting biases but appear more likely to be: (1) the direct consequence of genetic or prenatal environmental biological differences between the sexes (De Vries, De Bruin, Uylings & Corner, 1984; Glucksmann, 1981; Hall, 1982; Reinisch, 1983); (2) the result of maturational differences between the sexes (Garai & Scheinfeld, 1968); (3) the product of early differences in specific expectations and treatments of the sexes by the postnatal environment; and/or (4) the byproduct of general differences in the pattern of interaction between male and female infants and their caretakers (Lewis, 1972; Meaney & Stewart, 1985; Olley, 1973). Finally, these differences may be interpreted as a product of biological and environmental interactions. In support of at least a partial prenatal biological basis for infant sex differences are data on newborns, which demonstrate significant sex differences in: (1) sensory thresholds, with females showing more responsivity than males to haptic stimulation (Bell & Costello, 1964; Wolff, 1969), electrical stimulation (Lipsett & Levy, 1959), the taste of sweetness (Nisbett & Gurwitz, 1970), and photic stimulation (Engel, Crowell & Nishijima, 1968); (2) several types of oral behavior, with females exhibiting higher frequencies than males (Balint, 1948; Korner, 1969; Korner, 1973); and (3) greater physical strength and vigor of males (Korner, 1969; Rosenblum, 1974). In addition to the sex differences in behavior that have been identified during infancy (Kagan, 1969; Lewis, Kagan & Kalafat, 1966; Moss, 1967; Silverman, 1970; Watson, 1969), recent evidence points to sex differences as early as three months of age in the functional development of the central nervous system (Shucard, Cummins & Campos, 1981). Notwithstanding the nature of the mechanisms that they reflect, these data on the attainment and development of infant behavioral milestones make it clear that human males and females exhibit a range of differences in the expression of behavior beginning early in the first year of life.

We believe that at least some of the identified early sex differences reflect to some extent the divergent prenatal hormonal milieu of males and females. Our view of the influence of exposure to differing prenatal hormone environments by males and females and its role in the development of human behavioral sex differences is derived from the "multiplier effect" concept of E. O. Wilson (1975). This model represents the transactions between the organism and the environment that we believe contribute to the development of sex differences in human behavior.

At the time of conception the only difference between the sexes is chromosomal/genetic. As the testes of a normal male differentiate, androgens are produced, leading to divergent prenatal hormone environments for male and female fetuses. Beginning during the second month of gestation, the presence or absence of virilizing or masculinizing hormones (primarily testosterone in normally developing males) produces morphological (somatic and central nervous system) and physiological differences between the sexes which contribute to the development of behavioral differences.

At birth, the sex differences in appearance and behavior consequent to these differences in gestational milieu may be small but are nonetheless relevant to (1) the manner in which the infant responds to the environment and (2) how the social environment responds to the baby. To begin with, the sexes differ in their perception of environmental stimuli (Gandelman, 1983; Reinisch, Gandelman & Spiegel, 1979). These perceptual differences could be the result of somatic and physiological sex differences in the CNS or in peripheral (sensory) receptors. It is likely that even small perceptual, cognitive, and temperamental differences lead to different interpretations of, and responses to, the environment. Second, most societies treat infants, children, and adults differently, based on the appearance of their external genitalia.

The interactions between the organism and the environment over time are probably responsible for increasingly apparent behavioral sex differences which emerge over the course of postnatal development. We believe that small sex differences in appearance, behavior, and responsiveness at birth of the types reflected in the differences in milestone attainment and their temporal pattern shown in the current study combine with cultural expectations about "appropriate" behavior for each sex and lead to augmentation of the initial behavioral dimorphism. Successive interactions alter the child slightly. The modified organism then perceives and responds to the environment a little differently and, in turn, is perceived and treated in a slightly different fashion following these alterations. Through this dynamic transaction between the organism and its environment involving biological, psychological, and social factors, pronounced sex differences in behavior emerge over time. At puberty, the development of secondary sexual characteristics, prompted by the release of adult levels of reproductive hormones, dramatically increases the physical and perceptual differences between the sexes. These pubertal changes further differentiate societal expectations of how the young man or woman should behave. It is through the coalescence of these processes that overall sex differences are maximized during the reproductive years.

It is through just such a series of transactions that the small sex difference identified in the infant developmental milestone data presented here would be magnified over the years of childhood and early adolescence, providing the foundation for at least some of the differences found between adult males and females.

Although cultures may act to suppress or diminish some forms of sexually differentiated behavior, it appears most commonly the case that the more divergent the sex stereotypes within a culture, the more the biologically based sexual dimorphisms in behavior tend to be magnified by postnatal socioenvironmental influences. In such societies, sex differences which have no basis in biology also may be generated through highly differentiated sex role expectations. However, as the current data and an increasing body of other findings make clear, even if differential treatment of the sexes did not occur, some behavioral differences between males and females would remain, nevertheless.

REFERENCES

Baken, D. (1966). *The Duality of Human Existence.* Chicago: Rand McNally.

Balint, M. (1948). Individual differences of behavior in early infancy and an objective way of recording them. *Journal of Genetic Psychology, 73,* 57–117.

Bayley, N. (1935). The development of motor abilities during the first three years. *Monograph Society for Research in Child Development, 1,* 26–61.

Beatty, W. W. (1984). Hormonal organization of sex differences in play fighting and spatial behavior. In: G. J. De Vries, J. P. C. De Bruin, H. B. M. Uylings & M. A. Corner (Eds.), *Sex Differences in the Brain: Progress in Brain Research, vol. 61* (pp. 315–30). Amsterdam: Elsevier.

Bell, R. Q. & Costello, N. (1964). Three tests for sex differences in tactile sensitivity in the newborn. *Biologia Neonatorum, 7,* 335–47.

Bell, R. Q. & Darling, J. F. (1965). The prone head reaction in the human neonate: Relation with sex and tactile sensitivity. *Child Development, 36,* 943–49.

Brazelton, T. B. (1983). *Infants and Mothers: Differences in Development.* New York: Delacorte Press.

Dempster, A. P., Laird, N. & Rubin, D. B. (1977). Maximum likelihood from incomplete data via the EM algorithm. *Journal of the Royal Statistical Society, Series B 39,* 1–38.

Dempster, A. P. & Rubin, D. B. (1983). Rounding error in regression: The appropriateness of Sheppard's corrections. *Journal of the Royal Statistical Society, Series B 45,* 51–59.

De Vries, G. J., De Bruin, J. P. C., Uylings, H. B. M. & Corner, M. A., Eds. (1984). *Sex Differences in the Brain: Progress in Brain Research, vol. 61.* Amsterdam: Elsevier.

Engel, R., Crowell, D. & Nishijima, S. (1968). Visual and auditory response latencies in neonates. In: B. N. D. Fernando (Ed.), *Felicitation Volume in Honour of C. C. De Silva* (pp. 31–40). Ceylon: Kulartne & Company, Ltd.

Freedman, G. (1974). *Human Infancy: An Evolutionary Perspective.* New York: Halstead.

Gandelman, R. (1983). Gonadal hormones and sensory function. *Neuroscience and Biobehavioral Reviews,* 7:1–17.

Garai, J. E. & Scheinfeld, A. (1968). Sex differences in mental and behavioral traits. *Genetic Psychology Monographs, 77,* 169–299.

Gesell, A. (1940). *The First Five Years of Life: A Guide to the Study of the Preschool Child.* New York: Harper.

Gesell, A. (1952). *Infant Development: The Embryology of Early Human Behavior.* New York: Harper.

Glucksmann, A. (1981). *Sexual Dimorphism in Human and Mammalian Biology and Pathology.* New York: Academic Press.

Hall, R. L. (1982). *Sexual Dimorphism in Homo Sapiens: A Question of Size.* New York: Praeger.

Hindley, C. B., Filliozat, A. M., Klakenberg, G., Nocolet-Meister, D. & Sand, E.A. (1966). Differences in age of walking in five European longitudinal samples. *Human Biology, 38,* 364–79.

Hines, M. (1982). Prenatal gonadal hormones and sex differences in human behavior. *Psychological Bulletin, 92,* 56–80.

Hobson, J. R. (1947). Sex differences in primary mental abilities. *Journal of Educational Research, 41,* 126–32.

Jacklin, C. N., Snow, M. E. & Maccoby, E. E. (1981). Tactile sensitivity and muscle strength in newborn boys and girls. *Infant Behavior and Development, 4,* 261–68.

Kagan, J. (1969). On the meaning of behavior: Illustrations from the infant. *Child Development, 40,* 1121–34.

Korner, A. F. (1969). Neonatal startles, smiles, erections and reflex sucks as related to state, sex and individuality. *Child Development, 40,* 1039–53.

Korner, A. F. (1973). Sex differences in newborns with special reference to differences in the organization of oral behavior. *Journal of Child Psychology and Psychiatry, 14,* 19–29.

Lewis, D. M. (1972). State as an infant-environment interaction: An analysis of mother-infant interaction as a function of sex. *Merrill-Palmer Quarterly, 18,* 95–121.

Lewis, M., Kagan, J. & Kalafat, J. (1966). Patterns of fixation in the young infant. *Child Development, 37,* 331–41.

Lipsett, L. P. & Levy, N. (1959). Electrotactual threshold in the neonate. *Child Development, 30,* 547–54.

Maccoby, E. E., Doering, C. H., Jacklin, C. N. & Kraemer, H. (1979). Concentrations of sex hormones in umbilical-cord blood: their relation to the sex and birth order of infants. *Child Development, 50,* 632–42.

Maccoby, E. E. & Jacklin, C. N. (1974). *The Psychology of Sex Differences.* Stanford, CA: Stanford University Press.

Marecek, J. (1979). Social change, positive mental health, and psychological androgyny. *Psychology of Women Quarterly,* 3:241–247.

Meaney, M. J. & Stewart, J. (1985). Sex differences in social play: The socialization of sex roles. In: J. S. Rosenblatt, C. Beer, M. C. Busnel & P. J. B. Slater (Eds.), *Advances in the Study of Behavior, vol. 15* (pp. 2–58). New York: Academic Press.

Mednick, B. R., Hocevar, D., Baker, R. L. & Teasdale, T. W. (1983). Effects of social, familial, and maternal state variables on neonatal and infant health. *Developmental Psychology, 19,* 752–765.

Meng, X. L. & Rubin, D. B. (in press). Using EM to obtain asymptotic variance-covariance matrices: The SEM algorithm. *Journal of the American Statistical Association.*

Money, J. (1988). *Gay, Straight, and In-between: The Sexology of Erotic Orientation.* New York: Oxford University Press.

Money, J. & Ehrhardt, A. A. (1972). *Man and Woman, Boy and Girl: The Differentiation and Dimorphism of Gender Identity from Conception to Maturity.* Baltimore: Johns Hopkins University Press.

Moss, H. A. (1967). Sex, age, and state as determinants of mother-infant interaction. *Merrill-Palmer Quarterly, 13,* 19–36.

Nisbett, R. E. & Gurwitz, S. B. (1970). Weight, sex and the eating behavior of human newborns. *Journal of Comparative and Physiological Psychology, 73,* 245–53.

Olley, J.G. (1973). Sex differences in human behavior in the first year of life. Major area paper, Department of Psychology, George Peabody College for Teachers, Nashville, TN. Cited in: A. F. Korner, Sex differences in newborns with special reference to differences in the organization of oral behavior. *Journal of Child Psychology and Psychiatry, 14,* 19–29.

Parsons, T. & Bales, R. E. (1955). *Family Socialization and Interaction Process.* Glencoe, IL: Free Press.

Reinisch, J. M. (1981). Prenatal exposure to synthetic progestins increases potential for aggression in humans. *Science, 211,* 1171–73.

Reinisch, J. M. (1983). The influence of early exposure to steroid hormones on behavioral development. In: W. Everaed, C. B. Hindley, A. Bot, J. J. van der Werff ten Bosch (Eds.), *Development in Adolescence: Psychological, Social, and Biological Aspects* (pp. 63–113). Boston: Martinus Nijhoff Publishers.

Reinisch, J. M., Gandelman, R. & Spiegel, F. S. (1979). Prenatal influences on cognitive abilities: Data from experimental animals and human genetic and endocrine syndromes. In M. A. Wittig & A. C. Petersen (Eds.), *Sex-related Differences in Cognitive Functioning* (pp. 215–239). New York: Academic Press.

Rosenblum, L. A. (1971). The ontogeny of mother-infant relations in macaques. In: H. H. Moltz (Ed), *The Ontogeny of Vertebrate Behavior.* New York: Academic Press, pp. 315–67.

Rosenblum, L. A. (1974). Sex differences in mother-infant relations in monkeys. In: R. C. Friedman, R. M. Richart & R. L. Vande Wiele (Eds.), *Sex Differences in Behavior* (pp. 123–45). New York: Wiley.

Rubin, R. T., Reinisch, J. M. & Haskett, R. (1981). Postnatal gonadal steroid effects on human behavior. *Science, 211,* 1318–24.

Shucard, D. W., Cummins, K. R. & Campos, J. J. (1981). Auditory evoked potentials and sex-related differences in brain development. *Brain and Language,* 93–102.

Silverman, J. (1970). Attentional styles and the study of sex differences. In: D. Mostofsky (Ed.), *Attention: Contemporary Theory and Analysis* (pp. 61–98). New York: Appleton-Century-Crofts.

Thoman, E. B., Leiderman, P. H. & Olson, J. P. (1972). Neonate-mother interaction during breast-feeding. *Developmental Psychology, 6,* 110–18.

Watson, J. S. (1969). Operant conditioning of visual fixation in infants under visual and auditory reinforcement. *Developmental Psychology, 1,* 508–16.

Wilson, E. O. (1975). *Sociobiology: The New Synthesis.* Cambridge, MA: The Belknap Press, Harvard University, pp. 11–13.

Wolff, P. H. (1969). The natural history of crying and other vocalizations in early infancy. In: B. M. Foss (Ed.), *Determinants of Infant Behavior, vol. 3* (pp. 113–38). London: Methuen.

Zachau-Christiansen, B. & Ross, E. M. (1975). *Babies: Human Development During the First Year.* London: Wiley.

Biology Does Not
Create Gender Differences
in Personality

Linda L. Carli

June Reinisch and her colleagues argue that the origin of gender differences in personality is biological. They report the results of a study showing that boys lift their heads while on their stomachs, stand with support, and crawl earlier than girls and contend that these differences in maturation predispose boys to be *agentic* or self-promoting, independent, and directive and predispose girls to be *communal* or warm, nurturant, and interested in relationships with others. Although there is evidence that boys and men are more likely to exhibit agentic behaviors and girls and women to exhibit communal behaviors (Eagly, 1987; Maccoby, 1990), there is considerable evidence that these differences are socialized and not based in biology. First I will discuss problems with the arguments presented in the Reinisch et al. chapter, and then I will present evidence in favor of the socialization approach.

ON "SEX DIFFERENCES EMERGE DURING THE FIRST YEAR OF LIFE"

Reinisch et al. base their argument on several assumptions: (1) that the variation in the timing of developmental milestones in the first year of life is biologically determined, (2) that gender differences in the milestones they tested affect gender differences in personality, (3) that parents' records of the

first occurrence of a milestone are unlikely to be gender biased, and (4) that the particular milestones they measured are "fundamental" reflections of early maturation. I disagree with each of these assumptions.

IS THE TIMING OF DEVELOPMENTAL MILESTONES EXCLUSIVELY DETERMINED BY BIOLOGY?

The assumption that the variation in timing of developmental milestones is biologically determined is essential to the argument made by Reinisch and her colleagues. Obviously, there are biological limits as to how early infants can attain milestones. Newborns do not have the strength to stand or crawl. But there is great variation in when milestones are attained (e.g., for walking the range is nine to seventeen months, Rosenblith & Sims-Knight, 1989). If the timing of milestones can be readily altered by manipulating the environment, then it is not possible to argue that the *variation* in the attainment of milestones is biologically based. In fact, the current view in research on motor development is that a wide variety of factors affects when particular developmental milestones emerge, including such situational factors as the amount of friction or gravity experienced by the child and such experiential factors as how much opportunity the child has had to learn the particular behavior and the extent to which parents teach the behavior to the child (Super, 1976; Thelen, 1995). Infants can show signs of developmental milestones long before the milestones are normally attained if the environmental conditions are right. For example, although children usually begin to walk with their body weight supported at around eleven months of age, one-month-old infants will show coordinated stepping with their body supported if their feet are placed on motorized treadmills (Thelen & Ulrich, 1991). Hence, infants possess abilities that only become apparent with the right environmental conditions.

Experience also has a dramatic effect on the attainment of milestones. Children who are raised in certain African cultures sit, stand, and walk, on average, about one month earlier than American infants (Super, 1976). In African cultures in which mothers teach their children to crawl, children typically crawl at five months of age, whereas in African cultures where crawling is not taught, children crawl, on average, at eight months (Super, 1976). Similar cultural variations showing the importance of the child's experience have also been found for sitting and walking. In the United States, research reveals that giving infants specific practice in sitting or stepping *causes* improvements in their abilities (Zelazo, Zelazo, Cohen, & Zelazo, 1993). Moreover, specifically training infants to step *causes* them to walk earlier (Zelazo, Zelazo, & Kolb, 1972).

The timing of milestones can be affected by other environmental factors as well. A study examining the onset of crawling in children living in Denver revealed that crawling is delayed an average of three weeks in those born in the summer or fall compared with those born in the winter or spring (Benson, 1993). This occurs because children born in the winter or spring enter the crawling stage when the weather is warm, and they are therefore more likely to be placed on the floor or ground, where they can learn to crawl, than infants entering the crawling stage when the weather is cold. The relation between monthly temperature and the onset of crawling was unusually large in this study, revealing that the season of birth was as important in determining when children crawled as all other factors combined. Similarly, cross-cultural research showed that the variation in the timing of crawling was almost entirely due to whether the parent taught the child and the opportunities the child had to practice crawling (Super, 1976). Clearly, being given the opportunity to crawl, being placed on the ground in unrestrictive clothing, has a dramatic effect on the timing of this milestone. It does not make sense to talk about milestones as reflections of biological maturity alone; they are very much a product of particular infants' past experience and the current environmental conditions.

The gender difference in timing of milestones reported by Reinisch and her colleagues is a matter of days. Such a difference could easily be the product of small differences in the treatment of male and female infants. If parents dressed boys in less restrictive clothing (for example, in pants instead of dresses), placed them on the floor more than girls, or encouraged them to stand by pulling them to a standing position more than girls, this differential treatment could account for the gender differences in milestone attainment. In fact, given that the data were collected in 1959 through 1961, I would be surprised if parents did not show some of these sex-typed behaviors.

DOES THE TIMING OF MILESTONES AFFECT GENDER DIFFERENCES IN PERSONALITY?

According to Reinisch and her colleagues, the milestones they included in their study can be divided into two categories, those that lead to communal traits and those that lead to agentic traits. The milestones in the former category—smiling, holding the head up, and sitting without support—presumably facilitate "*en face*" or face-to-face interaction between the caretaker and the child, creating opportunities for social interaction and greater concern with relationships. The milestones in the latter category—standing with support, crawling independently, walking with support, and standing without support—presumably facilitate independence and separation. The other milestones—lifting the head, reaching for objects, and walking without support—were not specifically linked to either style. However, given the logic of their argument, that interactions involving orienting the face should facilitate the development of communal traits and interactions which move the body should facilitate the development of agentic traits, then lifting the head should also be considered a social milestone and walking without support should be considered an agentic milestone. If their logic is correct, then boys should exhibit standing with support, crawling, walking with support, standing without support, and walking without support earlier than girls. Girls should lift their heads, smile, hold their heads up, and sit without support earlier than boys. Based on the results of their study, of these nine predictions, two were significant in the predicted direction (i.e., stands with support and crawls), one was significant, but in the opposite direction (i.e., lifts head), and the remaining six milestones showed nonsignificant differences. The results do not provide much support for their predictions.

Past research has not reported gender differences in milestones, either. Of course, past studies have not used such a large sample size. Large samples increase the likelihood that any gender difference, no matter how small, will be significant. For example, imagine that, in reality, boys actually walk one hour earlier than girls. This small and relatively meaningless gender difference could be revealed and found significant if the sample is large enough. The present study had a sample of over 4,500 infants, an unusually large sample. Yet most of the gender differences in milestones were not significant. This leads to the conclusion that any real gender differences in milestones, if they exist at all, are probably small. To measure the size of a difference, researchers compute the effect size, d, a statistical measure of how large a difference is (Cohen, 1977). Indeed, when I compute the effect size of the gender differences for the two milestones that were statistically significant and in the predicted direction, they range from about 0.07 to 0.09. Because effect sizes of 0.20 are considered small, the gender differences in milestones must be considered very small.

In this section, I have so far given Reinisch et al. the benefit of the doubt and assumed that their argument—that face-to-face milestones lead to communal traits and other milestones facilitate agentic traits—was correct. However, there is no evidence to link early attainment of these milestones to either social or agentic traits. Why should the fact that boys stand with support or crawl about a week earlier than girls make much difference in the development of personality? Recall that children who were born in the winter or spring crawled three weeks earlier than other children, that training speeds the attainment of milestones, and that cross-cultural differences of several months in the timing of milestones were almost entirely due to how much training the child had. Given the large variation in timing of milestones (e.g., five to eleven

months for crawling and five to twelve months for standing with support), and the powerful effects of experience on milestone attainment, the sex differences reported in this study seem quite trivial. Reinisch and her colleagues were looking for subtle gender differences. Would they have formed the same conclusions if the results showed that boys attain the milestones one day earlier, an hour earlier, or a minute earlier than girls?

To provide additional support for their arguments, Reinisch and her colleagues examined the forty-five time intervals among the ten milestones, finding that nineteen of the forty-five showed significant gender differences. They argued that many of the significant differences revealed that boys move more quickly from the face-to-face milestones to the milestones fostering independence; therefore, boys are naturally more agentic in personality than girls. Unfortunately, these tests are redundant and tend to exaggerate the number of gender differences. For example, they tested whether the time interval between milestones 1 and 2 showed gender differences, whether the interval between milestones 1 and 3 showed gender differences, whether the interval between milestones 1 and 4 showed gender differences, and so on. It took girls about fourteen days from milestone 1 to reach milestone 2, whereas it took boys seventeen days; this was reported as a significant gender difference. It took girls an additional sixty-eight days to reach milestone 3 from milestone 2, whereas boys took an additional sixty-nine days; this difference wasn't significant. Yet, Reinisch et al. also report that the interval between milestones 1 and 3 was larger for boys (17 + 69 = 86 days) than girls (14 + 68 = 82 days). But obviously this difference is entirely due to the interval between milestones 1 and 2. No information is gained by comparing each interval with every other interval, but the many redundant comparisons create the impression of numerous gender differences. In fact, when comparing the intervals between consecutive milestones in order (milestone 1 with 2, 2 with 3, 3 with 4, etc.), five of the nine intervals were significant, three for the males and two for the females. One of these five did show that boys moved more quickly than girls from the so-called "face-to-face" milestone of sitting to the milestone for standing, which, according to Reinisch et al., presumably fosters independence. Reinisch and her colleagues argue that because of the gender difference in this interval and the gender differences in timing of standing and crawling, boys have less face-to-face interactions with their caretakers, showing a biological predisposition to agentic traits. Yet these milestones were attained in the tenth and the eleventh months, long after considerable face-to-face encounters with caretakers had undoubtedly taken place.

ARE PARENTS' SELF-REPORTS OF MILESTONES
GENDER-BIASED?

A fundamental assumption of the study by Reinisch et al. is that parents are unbiased in their reporting of the timing of milestones. If parents had systematically underestimated the timing of milestone attainment for boys and overestimated it for girls, then parental bias may have created the gender difference. Unfortunately, no attempt was made to assess how accurate parents were in estimating the timing of milestones, nor was any measure taken to determine whether gender bias may have been operating. In the study, parents were told simply to record the first instance of each milestone to the nearest week or month. What constituted the first instance of a milestone? In research on motor development, researchers precisely define the attainment of milestones. For example, in one study (Zelazo et al., 1972), walking independently was defined as taking two steps without holding on to any support. In Benson's (1993) study, crawling was defined as crawling a distance of four feet in one minute. It is possible that, in the Reinisch et al. study, parents' definitions as to what constituted a milestone could have been somewhat arbitrary and idiosyncratic. Moreover, only half of the parents responded for some of the milestones, suggesting two possibilities: parents were unsure as to how the milestones were defined or, more likely, may not have noticed when a milestone had been reached. Research in the United States and other countries reveals that parents typically prefer male children (Gilroy & Steinbacher, 1991; Williamson, 1976); it is possible that parents' greater interest in their sons resulted in sex-biased reporting of the timing of milestones.

ARE THESE MILESTONES "FUNDAMENTAL"
MEASURES OF MATURATION?

Reinisch and her colleagues view the milestones they included in their study as somehow "fundamental." But they do not explain why these milestones are more fundamental than any other. There are many so-called milestones in development and great variation in how they can be defined: the first word spoken, the ability to track slow-moving objects visually, the ability to track fast-moving objects, the ability to track swinging objects, the ability to grasp objects, holding the head up for several seconds, holding the head up for a minute, holding the head up for several minutes, balancing the head on the trunk, rolling the body from the side to the back, rolling the body from the back to the side, and so on. Any measure of perceptual, cognitive, motor, physical, or emotional development could be considered a milestone; the list of possibilities is extensive. Moreover, the achievement of a milestone is not a discrete event but an ongoing process. That is, there is no one clear moment when a milestone is achieved. For example, the development of smiling in infants changes over a period of weeks from a movement of the corners of the mouth to a movement involving the whole mouth, then movements involving the mouth and eyes, then active movements of the mouth, eyes, and face, and all the subtle variations in between these stages (see Rosenblith & Sims-Knight, 1989). At which point has the infant smiled? It depends on how smiling is defined. Consequently, the milestones measured in the Reinisch et al. study are not at all "fundamental." With somewhat different, but equally valid, measures of development, very different results may have been obtained.

I conclude from the Reinisch et al. study that the gender differences in the two milestones that they report could easily have occurred as a result of the different experiences of male and female infants. Boys may have been placed on the floor or ground more often or dressed in less restrictive clothing. They may have been encouraged to stand or crawl more than girls. The gender differences may also have been the result of biases in the reports by their parents, perhaps due to expecting the boys to stand or crawl earlier than the girls. Reinisch and her colleagues' research provides no evidence that gender differences in crawling or standing (or any of the other eight milestones that were measured) are biologically based, no evidence that gender differences in milestones are associated with agentic or communal traits, no controls to ensure that parental reports of milestone attainment are not biased, and no explanation as to why their measurement of development was in any way fundamental. Yet research on gender differences has revealed that boys do exhibit more agentic behavior than girls and that girls do exhibit more communal behavior than boys. How are these differences manifested in children and what could cause them?

The Socialization Explanation for Gender Differences

Research on gender differences in children reveals that boys in all-boy groups are more agentic. They are more direct in exerting influence; they interrupt more, issue more directives, provide more opinions, and are generally more competitive, argumentative, threatening, and publicly resistant to influence. Girls in all-girl groups are more communal. They express more agreement, warmth, and mutual affirmation; give others more opportunity to speak; and are more cooperative, polite, and pleasant (Hendrick & Stange, 1991; Miller, Danaher, & Forbes, 1986; Sachs, 1987; Sheldon, 1990). Reinisch and her colleagues view these differences as biologically based, a function of gender differences in personality. I view them as a product of gender differences in life experiences and status and power. I will provide evidence that gender differences in behavior emerge as a result of the (1)

differences in the way boys and girls are socialized, (2) different reactions that boys and girls elicit in their parents and other caretakers, and (3) higher status of males in Western cultures.

DIFFERENT SOCIALIZATION OF BOYS AND GIRLS

Observational research on parents' and teachers' actual communications with young children reveals differential treatment of boys and girls beginning at an early age. Mothers are more emotionally expressive (Malatesta, Culver, Tesman, & Shepard, 1989) and make more references to emotions when interacting with girls than with boys (Dunn, Bretherton, & Munn, 1987; Zahn-Waxler, Ridgeway, Denham, Usher, & Cole, 1993). They also exhibit more anger when talking to their sons and sadness when talking to their daughters (Fivush, 1989; Kuebli & Fivush, 1992). When speaking to girls, parents typically use what is considered a more feminine style of speech, asking for or eliciting responses from the child or repeating the child's utterances; with boys, they are more likely to use what is considered to be a masculine style, including using physical restraints, verbal prohibitions, disparaging comments, threats, and directives (Cherry & Lewis, 1976; Gleason, 1987). Teachers show a similar pattern. In response to the communication attempts of infants, teachers provide more positive responses to girls and more negative responses to boys (Fagot, Hagan, Leinbach, & Kronsberg, 1985). Even one- and two-year-old children imitate a wide variety of their parents' behaviors, including affective, task, and disciplinary behaviors (Kuczynski, Zahn-Waxler, & Radke-Yarrow, 1987). Consequently, parents and teachers, and their sex-typed interactions with male and female infants and preschoolers, are a likely source of gender differences in agentic and communal behaviors.

Are any other parental behaviors likely to increase the gender differences in children's interaction? A recent meta-analytic review of twenty studies revealed that mothers and fathers encourage sex-typed activities in their children (Lytton and Romney, 1991). For example, parents encourage girls to play with dolls and boys to play with toy cars. The mere act of playing with girls' toys or engaging in girls' sex-typed activities leads children to express positive emotions and exhibit social and nurturant behavior; children show higher levels of activity, aggression, rough-and-tumble play, and task orientation when playing with boys' toys or engaging in boys' sex-typed activities (Block, 1984; Hughes, 1991; O'Brien and Huston, 1985). In addition, when parents interact with their child during play, they further encourage sex-typed behavior patterns. For example, they are more likely to ask questions and verbalize extensively with their toddler, regardless of his or her gender, when the child is playing with dolls than with toy cars (O'Brien and Nagle, 1987). Parents who ask many questions are modeling a collaborative behavior to their child. Consequently, encouraging doll play in girls teaches girls to be nurturant, other-directed, and collaborative. Encouraging sex-typed activities undoubtedly has wide-ranging effects on the development of gender differences in behavior.

Once gender differences in behavior emerge, they tend to be further reinforced by children's peers. At around age three, boys and girls begin to play in sex-segregated groups; it appears that this may occur initially because girls find boys' behavior to be pushy and unpleasant (Maccoby, 1990). As a result, both boys and girls end up interacting with same-sex peers, peers whose behavior is already sex-typed. These peer groups further reinforce the gender differences in behavior.

BOYS AND GIRLS ELICIT DIFFERENT REACTIONS
FROM TEACHERS AND PARENTS

The child's gender is not the only factor that influences parents' and teachers' communication style. Boys, compared with girls, are generally more difficult and challenging to parents and teachers. Male infants and toddlers are more active, particularly in large body movements (Block, 1984; Eaton and Enns, 1986). There is some evidence that boys are more emotional or irritable than girls (Bezirganian and Cohen, 1991; Prior, Sanson, and Oberklaid, 1989). Research does not reveal the origin of these differences. However, both irritability and ac-

tivity can challenge parents and can affect how they treat children.

Parents and teachers tend to restrain active, irritable children and to speak to them in a negative, controlling, or directive manner; whereas children who are less challenging are more likely to receive encouragement and positive responses from parents and teachers (Green, Gustafson, and West, 1980; Hinde, Stevenson-Hinde, and Tamplin, 1985). A review of the literature on children's externalizing behavior, which involves hostility, negativism, and noncompliance, shows that parents of difficult children are more likely to use higher levels of control, commands, and threats and to show less approval and warmth than parents of easier children (Rothbaum and Weisz, 1994). In effect, when children are active, irritable, and difficult, parents and teachers interact with them in a stereotypically masculine manner. In contrast, parents and teachers interact with easy children in a more feminine manner. Clearly, the gender difference in how active, and possibly how irritable, children are should result in boys being exposed to a more masculine behavioral style and girls to a more feminine style, which would encourage sex-differences in agentic and communal behavior.

Even if there were no overall gender difference in children's behavior, parents' and teachers' responses to difficult children would probably create gender differences in children's interaction because parents communicate somewhat differently with difficult boys than with difficult girls. For example, teachers respond more often to the assertive and negative behaviors of boys than girls and to the positive behaviors of girls than boys (Fagot, Hagan, Leinbach, and Kronsberg, 1985), and parents respond more strongly to their sons' negative behaviors than to their daughters' (Radke-Yarrow, Richters, and Wilson, 1988; Snow, Jacklin, and Maccoby, 1983). In addition, parental behavior is more strongly related to externalizing among boys than among girls (Rothbaum and Weisz, 1994). This means that the cycle of child difficulty and parental unresponsiveness is more robust for boys.

Research on differences between securely and insecurely attached children provides additional evidence that boys and girls elicit different responses from adults and that these responses may contribute to gender differences in interaction. Children who are insecurely attached to their parents, whose early child-parent relationships have been unsupportive and difficult, show more pronounced gender differences than securely attached children, who have had a more supportive and responsive parent-child relationship (Turner, 1991). Insecurely attached boys show high levels of externalizing behavior, controlling behavior, and assertiveness, and insecurely attached girls show low levels of assertiveness and high levels of dependency and compliance; secure boys and girls do not differ from one another and fall somewhere between the two extremes (Lewis, Feiring, McGuffog, & Jaskir, 1984; Turner, 1991). Again, the pattern suggests that when children and parent-child relationships are difficult, boys are more likely than girls to display stereotypically masculine behavior. Insecure girls show more stereotypically feminine behavior. Although the cause of these effects is not known, there is evidence that parents' and teachers' different treatment of boys and girls may again be the cause. For example, teachers respond more to dependency in insecure girls than in insecure boys, ignoring the boys (Turner, 1993). Parents provide more instruction to insecure girls than insecure boys (Fagot & Kavanagh, 1993). Given the absence of gender differences in secure children, it may be that the gender differences in children's behavior are due, in large part, to the subset of children who are insecurely attached (Turner, 1991). In any case, it is clear that parents and teachers respond differently to difficultness and insecurity in boys and girls and that these differences contribute to gender differences in the children's behavior.

GENDER DIFFERENCES IN STATUS

In Western culture, most women and girls have lower status than men and boys; females are expected to be pleasant and agreeable and not expected to exert leadership, make direct demands, or appear overly confident, whereas males are expected to be status-asserting, confident, and direc-

tive; females who violate these status expectations are penalized (Carli, 1990; 1991). The gender differences in agentic and communal behaviors reflect these expectations and status demands. High-status individuals view themselves and are viewed by others as being competent and leaderlike (see Carli, 1990; 1991). As a result of the status difference, boys have higher expectations for success and evaluate their performance more favorably than do girls—even when females perform as well as or better than males (American Association of University Women, 1992; Frey & Ruble, 1987). Moreover, whereas males tend to attribute their successes to their abilities and their failures to external factors, such as bad luck or an unfair situation, females are more likely than males to attribute their successes to external factors and their failures to their lack of ability (AAUW, 1992; Brown, Fulkerson, Furr, Ware, & Voight, 1984).

A 1992 study indicates that this difference probably originates in early childhood. In the study, parents were videotaped while administering puzzles to their three-year-olds. Analyses of the tapes revealed that although the boys and girls were equally likely to express pride in their successes, girls were more likely to express shame after failure (Lewis, Alessandri, & Sullivan, 1992). To determine whether parents contribute to this gender difference, the videotapes were transcribed and the parents' comments to their children were coded. Results showed that parents gave more positive feedback to boys than to girls, even though there were no gender differences in the children's performances, and that the less positive feedback they gave, the more shame the children expressed (Alessandri & Lewis, 1993). Apparently, interactions between parents and children may create gender differences in self-evaluation.

This gender difference in shame among three-year-olds may be an early reflection of the lower status of females. Peer reinforcement of sex-typed activities occurs in both boys and girls but is particularly powerful among boys (Feiring & Lewis, 1987; Maccoby & Jacklin, 1987). By the age of one and a half to three and a half, boys are already avoiding cross-sex toys and activities more than girls are (Lloyd & Smith, 1985; Lloyd, Duveen, & Smith, 1988). The sanctions for cross-sex behavior are also much more severe for boys than for girls (Fagot, 1977). Further evidence that this effect is status-based comes from cross-cultural data. Boys' avoidance of feminine activities is higher in cultures where the status inequality between the sexes is greater; higher status groups typically denigrate and avoid the behaviors and characteristics of lower status groups (Archer, 1992). In children, boys' lower tolerance for cross-sex behavior, and the more serious consequences of such behavior, underscore the higher status of boys relative to girls.

By thirty-three months boys are more likely to ignore the verbal prohibitions or directives of girls than those of boys (Jacklin & Maccoby, 1978), a pattern that holds up in both older preschoolers (Powlishta & Maccoby, 1990) and in men and women and which reflects the male status advantage (Carli, 1991, 1995). Because lower-status individuals are less able to influence those of high status, they must use an approach that is less contradictory, more social, and more collaborative—in effect, the very approach that girls and women use. As it turns out, this collaborative style is also more effective than the more confrontational and dominant approach, even for males interacting with other males (Carli, 1989; 1995). Why then are males more likely to exhibit a dominant agentic style? Perhaps this occurs because the more masculine style is perceived as powerful, even though it is not (Carli, 1995). Another possibility is that males are more likely than females to evaluate their performance and effectiveness favorably, independent of actual performance. For example, Fagot (1994) has reported that boys who are negatively evaluated by their peers rate themselves as having the highest levels of peer acceptance, whereas girls receiving negative peer evaluations more accurately rate themselves as having low peer acceptance. Insecure boys are especially likely to exaggerate their standing among their peers. In fact, the more preschool boys are domineering, aggressive, and intrusive, the more highly (and inaccurately) they rate themselves and their peer standing (Cramer & Skidd, 1992). Given peer pressure on boys to avoid

feminine behavior and their tendency to exaggerate their social standing, it is not surprising that they maintain agentic behavior patterns and avoid communal behaviors.

CONCLUSION

The socialization approach is far better able to account for gender differences in agentic and communal behavior than the timing-of-milestones argument proposed by Reinisch and her colleagues. First, there is an extensive literature demonstrating that parents and teachers treat boys and girls differently, interacting with boys and girls in a sex-typed manner and encouraging sex-typed activities in children. Second, adults are more forceful, controlling, and negative with difficult children than with easy ones, and boys tend to be slightly more difficult. Children exposed to controlling, negative adults are more controlling and negative themselves; consequently, adults' attempts to limit boys' difficultness are likely to increase gender differences in behavior. Moreover, even in the absence of gender differences in children's activity and irritability, adults respond more strongly to the negative behaviors of difficult boys than difficult girls, further encouraging gender differences in the children's behavior. This difference in the treatment of boys and girls results in the traditional pattern of gender differences in behavior. Boys are more self-asserting, direct, argumentative, forceful, and detached, and girls are more collaborative, agreeable, pleasant, polite, and other-directed; these are the very differences that define agentic and communal behavior. It is clear that these differences are not intrinsic or based on biological differences in personality. They are very much a product of a gender-biased world.

Finally, gender differences in agentic and social behaviors reflect the higher status of males, status differences which appear even in young children. Agentic behavior is expected from and tolerated in high-status individuals, but not in low-status individuals. Consequently, the higher status of boys not only encourages the gender differences in behavior, it justifies them. Boys' perceptions of themselves tend to be self-serving and to legitimate their higher status and their more assertive, confident, and controlling behavior. Boys avoid girls and feminine behavior; to show signs of femininity would lead to a loss of status among their male peers. Girls, on the other hand, appraise themselves more modestly and display warmth, openness, and collaboration. They are expected to behave in a sextyped manner. Immodesty and forcefulness are not acceptable in girls.

These factors combine to create behavioral differences in boys and girls that may appear intrinsic, a function of biological differences in personality. In fact, they are a product of the very different life experiences of boys and girls.

REFERENCES

Alessandri, S. M., & Lewis, M. (1993). Parental evaluation and its relation to shame and pride in young children. *Sex Roles, 29*, 335–343.

American Association of University Women. (1992). *How schools shortchange girls.* Washington, D.C.: AAUW Educational Foundation.

Archer, J. (1992). Childhood gender roles: Social context and organization. In H. McGurk (Ed.), *Childhood social development: Contemporary perspectives.* Hillsdale, N.J.: Erlbaum.

Benson, J. B. (1993). Season of birth and onset of locomotion: Theoretical and methodological implications. *Infant Behavior and Development, 16*, 69–81.

Bezirganian, S., & Cohen, P. (1991). Sex differences in the interaction between temperament and parenting. *Journal of the American Academy of Child and Adolescent Psychiatry, 31*, 790–801.

Block, J. H. (1984). *Sex role identity and ego development.* San Francisco: Jossey-Bass.

Brown, D., Fulkerson, K. F., Furr, S., Ware, W. B., & Voight, N. L. (1984). Locus of control, sex role orientation, and self-concept in black and white third- and sixth-grade male and female leaders. *Developmental Psychology, 20*, 717–721.

Carli, L. L. (1989). Gender differences in interaction style and influence. *Journal of Personality and Social Psychology, 56*, 565–576.

Carli, L. L. (1990). Gender, language, and influence. *Journal of Personality and Social Psychology, 59*, 941–951.

Carli, L. L. (1991). Gender, status, and influence. In E. Lawler, B. Markovsky, C. Ridgeway, & H. Walker (Eds.), *Advances in group processes* (Vol. 8, pp. 89–113). Greenwich, Conn.: JAI Press.

Carli, L. L. (1995). Gender, nonverbal behavior and influence. *Journal of Personality and Social Psychology, 68*, 1030–1041.

Cherry, L., & Lewis, M. (1976). Mothers and two-year-olds: A study of sex-differentiated aspects of verbal interaction. *Developmental Psychology, 12*, 278–282.

Cohen, J. 1977. *Statistical power analysis for the behavioral sciences.* New York: Academic Press.

Cramer, P., & Skidd, J. E. (1992). Correlates of self-worth in preschoolers: The role of gender-stereotyped style of behavior. *Sex Roles, 26*, 369–391.

Dunn, J., Bretherton, I., & Munn, P. (1987). Conversations about feeling states between mothers and their young children. *Developmental Psychology, 23*, 132–139.

Eagly, A. H. (1987). *Sex differences in social behavior: A social-role interpretation.* Hillsdale, N.J.: Erlbaum.

Eaton, W. O., & Enns, L. R. (1986). Sex differences in human motor activity level. *Psychological Bulletin, 100*, 19–28.

Fagot, B. I. (1977). Consequences of moderate cross-gender behavior in preschool children. *Child Development, 48*, 902–907.

Fagot, B. I. (1994). Peer relations and the development of competence in boys and girls. In C. Leaper (Ed.), *Childhood gender segregation: Causes and consequences* (pp. 53–65). San Francisco: Jossey-Bass.

Fagot, B. I., Hagan, R., Leinbach, M. D., & Kronsberg, S. (1985). Differential reactions to assertive and communicative acts of toddler boys and girls. *Child Development, 56*, 1499–1505.

Fagot, B. I., & Kavanagh, K. (1993). Parenting during the second year: Effects of children's age, sex, and attachment classification. *Child Development, 64*, 258–271.

Feiring, C., & Lewis, M. (1987). The child's social network: Sex differences from three to six years. *Sex Roles, 17*, 621–636.

Fivush, R. (1989). Exploring sex differences in the emotional content of mother-child conversations about the past. *Sex Roles, 20*, 675–691.

Frey, K. S., & Ruble, D. N. (1987). What children say about classroom performance: Sex and grade differences in perceived competence. *Child Development, 58*, 1066–1078.

Gilroy, F. D., & Steinbacher, R. (1991). Sex selection technology utilization: Further implications for sex ratio imbalance. *Social Biology, 38*, 285–288.

Gleason, J. B. (1987). Sex differences in parent-child interaction. In S. U. Philips, S. Steele, & C. Tanz (Eds.), *Language, gender, and sex in comparative perspective* (pp. 189–199). New York: Cambridge University Press.

Green, J. A., Gustafson, G. E., & West, M. J. (1980). Effects of infant development on mother-infant interactions. *Child Development, 51*, 199–207.

Hendrick, J., & Stange, T. (1991). Do actions speak louder than words? An effect of the functional use of language on dominant sex role behavior in boys and girls. *Early Childhood Research Quarterly, 6*, 565–576.

Hinde, R. A., Stevenson-Hinde, J., & Tamplin, A. (1985). Characteristics of 3-to 4-year-olds assessed at home and their interactions in preschool. *Developmental Psychology, 21*, 130–140.

Hughes, F. P. (1991). *Children, play, and development*. Boston: Allyn & Bacon.

Jacklin, C. N., & Maccoby, E. E. (1978). Social behavior at 33 months in same-sex and mixed-sex dyads. *Child Development, 49*, 557–569.

Kuczynski, L., Zahn-Waxler, C., & Radke-Yarrow, M. (1987). Development and content of imitation in the second and third years of life: A socialization perspective. *Developmental Psychology, 23*, 276–282.

Kuebli, J., & Fivush, R. (1992). Gender differences in parent-child conversations about past emotions. *Sex Roles, 27*, 683–698.

Lewis, M., Alessandri, S. M., & Sullivan, M. W. (1992). Differences in shame and pride as a function of children's gender and task difficulty. *Child Development, 63*, 630–638.

Lewis, M., Feiring, C., McGuffog, C., & Jaskir, J. (1984). Predicting psychopathology in six-year-olds from early social relations. *Child Development, 55*, 123–136.

Lloyd, B. B., Duveen, G., & Smith, C. (1988) Social representations of gender and young children's play: A replication. *British Journal of Developmental Psychology, 6*, 83–88.

Lloyd, B. B., & Smith, C. (1985). The social representation of gender and young children's play. *British Journal of Developmental Psychology, 3*, 65–73.

Lytton, H., & Romney, D. M. (1991). Parents' differential socialization of boys and girls: A meta-analysis. *Psychological Bulletin, 109*, 267–296.

Maccoby, E. E. (1990). Gender and relationships: A developmental account. *American Psychologist, 45*, 513–520.

Maccoby, E. E., & Jacklin, C. N. (1987). Gender segregation in childhood. In H. W. Reese (Ed.), *Advances in child development and behavior* (Vol. 22, pp. 239–288). New York: Academic Press.

Malatesta, C. Z., Culver, C., Tesman, J. R., & Shepard, B. (1989). The development of emotion expression during the first two years of life. *Monographs of the Society for Research in Child Development, 54*, 1–2.

Miller, P., Danaher, D., & Forbes, D. (1986). Sex related strategies for coping with interpersonal conflict in children aged five to seven. *Developmental Psychology, 22*, 543–548.

O'Brien, M., & Huston, A. (1985). Activity level and sex-stereotyped toy choice in toddler boys and girls. *Journal of Genetic Psychology, 146*, 527–533.

O'Brien, M., & Nagle, K. J. (1987). Parents' speech to toddlers: The effect of play context. *Journal of Child Language, 14*, 269–279.

Powlishta, K. K., & Maccoby, E. E. (1990). Resource utilization in mixed-sex dyads: The influence of adult presence and task type. *Sex Roles, 23*, 223–240.

Prior, M. R., Sanson, A. V., & Oberklaid, F. (1989). The Australian temperament project. In G. A. Kohnstamm, J. E. Bates, & M. K. Rothbart (Eds.), *Temperament in childhood* (pp. 537–554). New York: Wiley.

Radke-Yarrow, M., Richters, J., & Wilson, W. E. (1988). Child development in a network of relationships. In R. Hinde & J. Stevenson-Hinde (Eds.), *Relationships within families* (pp. 48–67). Oxford: Clarendon.

Rosenblith, J. F., & Sims-Knight, J. E. (1989). *In the beginning: Development in the first two years*. Newbury Park, Calif.: Sage.

Rothbaum, F., & Weisz, J. R. (1994). Parental caregiving and child externalizing behavior in nonclinical samples: A meta-analysis. *Psychological Bulletin, 116*, 55–74.

Sachs, J. (1987). Preschool boys' and girls' language in pretend play. In S. U. Phillips, S. Steele, & C. Tanz (Eds.), *Language, gender, and sex in comparative perspective* (pp. 178–188). New York: Cambridge University Press.

Sheldon, A. (1990). Pickle fights: Gendered talk in preschool disputes. *Discourse Processes, 13*, 5–31.

Snow, M. E., Jacklin, C. N., & Maccoby, E. E. (1983). Sex-of-child differences in father-child interaction at one year of age. *Child Development, 54*, 227–232.

Super, C. M. (1976). Environmental effects on motor development. *Developmental Medicine and Child Neurology, 18*, 561–567.

Thelen, E. (1995). Motor development: A new synthesis. *American Psychologist, 50*, 75–95.

Thelen, E., & Ulrich, B. D. (1991). Hidden skills: A dynamic systems analysis of treadmill stepping during the first year. *Monographs of the Society for Research in Child Development, 56* (1, Serial No. 223).

Turner, P. J. (1991). Relations between attachment, gender, and behavior with peers in preschool. *Child Development, 62*, 1475–1488.

Turner, P. J. (1993). Attachment to mother and behavior with adults in preschool. *British Journal of Developmental Psychology, 11*, 75–89.

Williamson, N. E. (1976). *Sons and daughters: A cross-cultural survey of parental preferences*. Beverly Hills, Calif.: Sage.

Zahn-Waxler, C., Ridgeway, D., Denham, S., Usher, B., & Cole, P. M. (1993). Pictures of infants' emotions: A task for assessing mothers' and children's verbal communications about affect. In R. Emde, J. Osofsky, & P. Butterfield (Eds.), *The IFEEL pictures: A new instrument for interpreting emotions* (pp. 217–236). Madison, Conn.: International Universities Press.

Zelazo, N. A., Zelazo, P. R., Cohen, K. M., & Zelazo, P. D. (1993). Specificity of practice effects on elementary neuromotor patterns. *Developmental Psychology, 29*, 686–691.

Zelazo, P. R., Zelazo, N. A., & Kolb, S. (1972). "Walking" in the newborn. *Science, 176*, 14–15.

Diversity Issues:
Are Race, Class, and Gender
of Comparable Importance
in Producing Inequality?

One of the feminist psychologists' earliest criticisms of mainstream psychology was that male behavior was used as the standard for all human behavior. Ironically, since the 1980s, a growing number of critics have charged that the psychology of women has similarly erred by basing its findings largely on studies that only include White women. Jean Baker Miller warns that White middle-class women should not presume to speak for all women. "Indeed, if they do," she writes, "they are liable to fall into the same position for which they have criticized men—that is, generalizing about all people when they really only speak from their own experience" (1994, p. ix). Just as mainstream psychology was once accused of having nothing to say about women (Weisstein, 1968), so one could fault the field of the psychology of women today for having little to say about ethnicity or economic class. As Michele Wittig notes in an otherwise laudatory review of a new handbook on the psychology of women, the work "reflects the lamentable and longstanding paucity of research on issues of racial, ethnic, cultural, sexual and class diversity within the United States and Canada" (1995, p. 428).

When Pamela Reid (1993) used the word *woman* in her search of a database for the years 1984–1991, she found 14,517 abstracts, only twelve of which touched on "feminist" and "poverty," or "feminist" and "working class." Reid and Kelly (1994) claim that feminist researchers accept the notion of a common women's experience. This blinds them to issues of heterogeneity, they argue, and results in a ghettoization of subject pools. As they point out, when researchers are focusing on similar experiences like sexual harassment and self-esteem, they select homogeneous samples of White middle-class women. However, when they turn to deviations from mainstream behavior, such as welfare mothers or teenage pregnancy, they tend to study African-American women or Latinas. Judith Lorber notes that it is simplistic for researchers to think in terms of male and female when race and class create a number of categories of men and women that form a hierarchical social system, a stratified arrangement in which "race, class and gender intersect to produce domination by White upper-class men *and* women and subordination of lower-class women *and* men of Color" (Lorber, 1994, p. 4).

Laura S. Brown (1990) asserts that the problem of using White middle-class women as the norm is also prevalent in feminist therapy and feminist therapy theory. She singles out such landmark studies as Chodorow (1978) and Gilligan (1982), which are based on research with White, Northern European and North American women. Feminist psychologists insist on the importance of context in female socialization, Brown contends, "and then seem to forget that . . . socialization to be a White, middle-class Jewish woman is not socialization to be a Black, middle-class Southern Baptist" (p. 6).

Efforts are being made to identify what connects women of Color and different classes to other women and what separates them. Some therapists are trying to navigate this dilemma (Comas-Diaz & Greene, 1994). Sandra Lewis, for example, interweaves cognitive behavioral therapy with the belief in a higher supernatural power, "which is most often an integral part of the cultural experience of African-American women" (1994, p. 234).

The question remains: how do we treat the relationship of race, class, and gender? Social scientists have typically followed an additive approach, studying the independent effects of race, class, and gender on human behavior, on the assumption that these effects can then be combined. The result is the use of terms like *double* and *triple jeopardy* to describe the oppression of women of Color by gender and class as well as race (Anderson & Collins, 1995). Too often, however, White middle-class women remain the norm, and data on non-middle-class women and women of Color are added to preexisting theories (Morawski & Bayer, 1995).

Taking a different tack, Orlando Patterson (1995, p. 63) challenges the notion that Black women are uniquely oppressed, noting that they have higher college enrollments and lower suicide rates than African-American men. Although he prefers to speak of different gendered burdens, he declares that the lot of poor African-American men has "always been oppressive, dispiriting, demoralizing, and soul-killing," in contrast to Black women's role, which has "always been at least partly generative, empowering, and humanizing." Consequently, he believes that Black men have experienced greater burdens than Black women (p. 63).

In the following articles, Candace West and Sarah Fenstermaker propose a reconceptualization of the relationship of race, class, and gender in which all three are viewed as comparable mechanisms for producing inequality. Patricia Hill Collins disagrees. She argues that despite West and Fenstermaker's critique of "additive" approaches, they end up doing exactly what they criticize in other researchers: "treating gender as the most fundamental, theoretical category and then 'adding' on race and class."

REFERENCES

Anderson, M. L., & Collins, P. H. (Eds.). (1995). *Race, class and gender*. Belmont, Calif. Wadsworth.

Brown, L. S. (1990). The meaning of a multicultural perspective for theory-building in feminist therapy. In L. S. Brown & M. P. P. Root (Eds.), *Diversity and complexity in feminist therapy* (pp. 1–21). New York: Harrington Park Press.

Chodorow, N. (1978). *The reproduction of mothering.* Berkeley: University of California Press.

Comas-Diaz, L., & Greene, B. (1994). Overview: Connections and disconnections. In L. Comas-Diaz & B. Greene (Eds.), *Women of Color: Integrating ethnic and gender identities in psychotherapy* (pp. 341–346). New York: Guilford Press.

Gilligan, C. (1982). *In a different voice: Psychological theory and women's development.* Cambridge, Mass.: Harvard University Press.

Lewis, S. (1994). Cognitive-behavioral therapy. In L. Comas-Diaz & B. Greene (Eds.), *Women of Color: Integrating ethnic and gender identities in psychotherapy* (pp. 223–238). New York: Guilford Press.

Lorber, J. (1994). *Paradoxes of gender.* New Haven: Yale University Press.

Miller, J. B. (1994). Foreword. In L. Comas-Diaz & B. Greene (Eds.), *Women of Color: Integrating ethnic and gender identities in psychotherapy* (pp. ix–x). New York: Guilford Press.

Morawski, J., & Bayer, B. M. (1995). Stirring trouble and making theory. In H. Landrine (Ed.), *Bringing cultural diversity to feminist psychology: Theory, research, and practice* (pp. 113–137). Washington, D.C.: American Psychological Association.

Patterson, O. (1995). The crisis of gender relations among African Americans. In A. F. Hill & E. C. Jordan (Eds.), *Race, gender, and power in America: The legacy of the Hill-Thomas hearings* (pp. 56–104). New York: Oxford University Press.

Reid, P. T. (1993). Poor women in psychological research: Shut up and shut out. *Psychology of Women Quarterly, 17,* 133–150.

Reid, P. T., & Kelly, E. (1994). Research on women of Color: From ignorance to awareness. *Psychology of Women Quarterly, 18,* 477–486.

Weisstein, N. (1968). "Kinder, Kirche, Kuche" as scientific law: Psychology constructs the female. In R. Morgan (Ed.), *Sisterhood is powerful: An anthology of writings from the women's liberation movement* (pp. 205–220). New York: Vintage Books.

Wittig, M. A. (1995). An American psychology of women: Retrospect and prospect. (Review of *Psychology of women: Handbook of issues and theories.*) *Psychology of Women Quarterly, 19,* 427–428.

ADDITIONAL READING

Adelman, J., & Enguidanos, G. M. (Eds.). (1995). *Racism in the lives of women: Testimony, theory, and guides to antiracist practice.* New York: Haworth Press.

Betancourt, H., & Lopez, S. R. (1993). The study of culture, ethnicity, and race in American psychology. *American Psychologist, 48,* 629–637.

Cole, J. B. (1986). Commonalities and differences. In J. B. Cole (Ed.), *All American women: Lines that divide, ties that bind* (pp. 1–30). New York: Free Press.

Donald, J., & Rattansi, A. (Eds.). (1992). *"Race," culture and difference.* London: Sage and Open University Press.

Espin, O. M., & Gawelek, M. A. (1992). Women's diversity: Ethnicity, race, class, and gender in theories of feminist psychology. In L. S. Brown & M. Ballou (Eds.), *Personality and psychopathology: Feminist reappraisals.* New York: Guilford Press.

Goldberger, N. R., & Veroff, J. B. (Eds.). (1995). *The culture and psychology reader.* New York: New York University Press.

Graham, S. (1992). "Most of the subjects were White and middle class": Trends in published research on African Americans in selected APA journals, 1970–1989. *American Psychologist, 47,* 629–639.

Henwood, K. (1994). Resisting racism and sexism in academic psychology: A personal/political view. *Feminism and Psychology, 4,* 41–62.

James, S. M., & Busia, A. P. A. (Eds.). (1993). *Theorizing Black feminisms: The visionary pragmatism of Black women.* New York: Routledge.

Taylor, J. M., Gilligan, C., and Sullivan, A. M. (1996). *Between voice and silence: Women and girls, race and relationship.* Cambridge, Mass.: Harvard University Press.

Willie, C. V., Rieker, P. P., Kramer, B. M., & Brown, B. S. (Eds.). (1995). *Mental health, racism and sexism.* Pittsburgh: University of Pittsburgh Press.

Young, I. M. (1994). Gender as seriality: Thinking about women as a social collective. *Signs, 19,* 713–738.

Zinn, M. B., & Dill, B. T. (Eds.). (1994). *Women of Color in U.S. society.* Philadelphia: Temple University Press.

Doing Difference

Candace West and

Sarah Fenstermaker

Few persons think of math as a particularly feminine pursuit. Girls are not supposed to be good at it, and women are not supposed to enjoy it. It is interesting, then, that we who do feminist scholarship have relied so heavily on mathematical metaphors to describe the relationships among gender, race, and class. For example, some of us have drawn on basic arithmetic, adding, subtracting, and dividing what we know about race and class to what we already know about gender. Some have relied on multiplication, seeming to calculate the effects of the whole from the combination of different parts. And others have employed geometry, drawing on images of "interlocking" or "intersecting" planes and axes.

To be sure, the sophistication of our mathematical metaphors often varies with the apparent complexity of our own experiences. Those of us who, at one point, were able to "forget" race and class in our analyses of gender relations may be more likely to "add" these at a later point. By contrast, those of us who could never forget these dimensions of social life may be more likely to draw on complex geometrical imagery all along. Nonetheless, the existence of so many different approaches to the topic seems indicative of the difficulties all of us have experienced in coming to terms with it.

Not surprisingly, the proliferation of these approaches has caused considerable confusion in the existing literature. In the same book or article, we may find references to gender, race, and class as "intersecting systems," as "interlocking categories" and as "multiple bases" for oppression. In the same anthology, we may find some chapters that conceive of gender, race, and class as distinct axes and others that conceive of them as concentric ones. The problem is that these alternative formulations have very distinctive, yet unarticulated, theoretical implications. For instance, if we think about gender, race, and class as additive categories, the whole will never be greater (or lesser) than the sum of its parts. By contrast, if we conceive of these as multiples, the result could be larger or smaller than their added sum, depending on where we place the signs. Geometric metaphors further complicate things, since we still need to know where those planes and axes go *after* they cross the point of intersection (and, if they are *parallel* planes and axes, they will never intersect at all).

Our purpose in this chapter is not to advance yet another new math, but to propose a new way of thinking about the workings of these relations: to consider explicitly the relationships among gender, race, and class, and to reconceptualize *difference* as an ongoing interactional accomplishment. We start by summarizing the prevailing critique of much feminist thought, and next, we consider how existing conceptualizations of gender have contributed to the problem, rendering mathematical metaphors the only alternatives. Then, calling upon our earlier ethnomethodological conceptualization of gender (Fenstermaker Berk 1985; Fenstermaker, West, and Zimmerman 1991; West and Fenstermaker 1993; West and Zimmerman 1987), we develop the further implications of this perspective for our understanding of race and class. We assert that while gender, race, and class—what people come to experience as organizing categories of social difference—exhibit vastly different descriptive characteristics and outcomes, they are nonetheless comparable as *mechanisms* for producing social inequality.

WHITE MIDDLE-CLASS BIAS
IN FEMINIST THOUGHT

What is it about feminist thinking that makes race and class such difficult concepts to articulate within its own parameters? The most widely agreed upon and disturbing answer to this question is that feminist thought suffers from a White middle-class bias. The privileging of White and middle-class sensibilities in feminist thought results both from who did the theorizing and how they did it. For example, Adrienne Rich contends that although White (middle-class) feminists may not consciously believe that their race is superior to any other, they are often plagued by a form of "White solipsism"—thinking, imagining, and speaking "as if Whiteness described the world," resulting in "tunnel-vision which simply does not see nonwhite experience or existence as precious or significant, unless in spasmodic, impotent guilt reflexes, which have little or no long-term, continuing usefulness" (1979, p. 306). Patricia Hill Collins (1990) argues that the suppression of Black feminist thought stems from both the White feminists' racist and classist concerns and from Black female intellectuals' consequent lack of participation in White feminist organizations. Similarly, Cherríe Moraga (1981) argues that the "denial of difference" in feminist organizations derives not only from White middle-class women's failure to "see" it, but also from the reluctance of women of Color and working-class women to challenge such blindness. Alone and in combination with one another, these sources of bias do much to explain why there has been a general failure to articulate race and class within the parameters of feminist scholarship. However, they do not explain the attraction of mathematical metaphors to right the balance. To understand this development, we must look further at the logic of feminist thought itself.

MATHEMATICAL METAPHORS AND FEMINIST THOUGHT

Following the earlier suggestion of bell hooks (1981), Elizabeth Spelman (1988) criticizes the presumption that we can effectively and usefully isolate gender from race and class. To illustrate this point, she draws on many White feminists who develop their analyses of sexism by comparing and contrasting it with "other" forms of oppression. Herein she finds the basis for additive models of gender, race, and class, and "the ampersand problem": "De Beauvoir tends to talk about comparisons between sex and race, or between sex and class, or between sex and culture . . . comparisons between sexism and racism, between sexism and classism, between sexism and anti-Semitism. In the work of Chodorow and others influenced by her, we observe a readiness to look for links between sexism and other forms of oppression as distinct from sexism" (1988, 115).

Spelman notes that in both cases, attempts to *add* "other" elements of identity to gender, or "other" forms of oppression to sexism, disguise the race (White) and class identities (middle) of those seen as "women" in the first place. Rich's "White solipsism" comes into play again, and it is impossible to envision how women who are not White and middle-class fit into the picture. Spelman's (1988) analysis highlights the following problem: if we conceive of gender as coherently isolatable from race and class, then there is every reason to assume that the effects of the three variables can be multiplied, with results dependent on the valence (positive or negative) of those multiplied variables. Yet if we grant that gender *cannot* be coherently isolated from race and class in the way we conceptualize it, then multiplicative metaphors make little sense.

If the effects of "multiple oppression" are not merely additive nor simply multiplicative, what are they? Some scholars have described them as the products of "simultaneous and intersecting systems of relationship and meaning" (Andersen and Collins 1992, xiii; see also Almquist 1989; Collins 1990; Glenn 1985). This description is useful insofar as it offers an accurate characterization of persons who are simultaneously oppressed on the basis of gender, race, and class, in other words, those "at the intersection" of all three systems of domination. However, if we conceive of the basis of oppression as more than membership in a category, the theoretical implications of this formulation are troubling. For instance, what conclusions shall we draw from potential comparisons between persons who experience oppression on the basis of their race and class (e.g., working-class men of Color) and those who are oppressed on the basis of their gender and class (e.g., White working-class women)? Would the "intersection of two systems of meaning in each case be sufficient to predict common bonds among them"? Clearly not, says June Jordan: "When these factors of race, class and gender absolutely collapse is whenever you try to use them as automatic concepts of connection." She goes on to say that while these concepts may work very well as indices of "commonly felt conflict," when they are used as "elements of connection," their predictive value is "about as reliable as precipitation probability for the day after the night before the day" (1985, 46).

What conclusions shall we draw from comparisons between persons who are said to suffer oppression "at the intersection" of all three systems and those who suffer in the nexus of only two? Presumably, we will conclude that the latter are "less oppressed" than the former (assuming that each categorical identity set amasses a specific quantity of oppression). However, Moraga warns that "the danger lies in ranking the oppressions. *The danger lies in failing to acknowledge the specificity of the oppression*" (1981, 29).

Spelman (1988, 123–125) attempts to resolve this difficulty by characterizing sexism, racism, and classism as "interlocking" with one another. Along similar lines, Margaret Andersen and Patricia Hill Collins (1992, xii) describe gender, race, and class as "interlocking categories of experience." An image of interlocking rings comes to mind, with the rings linked in such a way that the motion of any one of them is constrained by the others. Certainly this image is more dynamic than those conveyed by additive, multiplicative, or geometric models: we can imagine where the rings would be joined (and where they would not), as well as how the movement of any one of them would restrict the others. But note that this image would still depict the rings as *separate parts.*

If we try to imagine situating particular persons within this image, the problem with it becomes

clear. We could, of course, conceive of the whole as "oppressed people," and of the rings as "those oppressed by gender," "those oppressed by race," and "those oppressed by class." This would allow us to situate women and men of all races and classes within the areas covered by the circles, save for White middle- and upper-class men, who fall outside them. However, what if we conceived of the whole as "experience," and of the rings as gender, race, and class?

Then, we would face an illuminating possibility and leave arithmetic behind: no person can experience gender *without simultaneously* experiencing race and class. As Andersen and Collins (1992, xxi) put it, "While race, class and gender can be seen as different axes of social structure, individual persons experience them simultaneously." It is this simultaneity that has eluded our theoretical treatments and is so difficult to build into our empirical descriptions (for an admirable effort, see Segura 1992). How do forms of inequality, which we now see are more than the periodic collision of categories, operate *together?* How do we see that all social exchanges, regardless of the participants or the outcome, are simultaneously "gendered," "raced," and "classed"?

To address these questions, we first present some earlier attempts to conceptualize gender. Appreciation for the limitations of these efforts, we believe, affords us a way to the second task: reconceptualizing the dynamics of gender, race, and class as they figure simultaneously in human institutions and interaction.

TRADITIONAL CONCEPTUALIZATIONS OF GENDER

To begin, we turn to Arlie Russell Hochschild's "Review of Sex Role Research," published in 1973. At that time, there were four distinct ways of conceptualizing gender within the burgeoning literature on the topic: (1) as sex differences, (2) as sex roles, (3) in relation to the minority status of women, and (4) in relation to the caste/class statuses of women. Hochschild observed that each of these conceptualizations led to a different perspective on the behaviors of women and men: "What to type 1 is a feminine trait such as passivity is to type 2 a role element, to type 3 is a minority characteristic, and to type 4 is a response to powerlessness. Social change might also look somewhat different to each perspective; differences disappear, deviance becomes normal, the minority group assimilates, or power is equalized" (1973, 1013).

Feminist scholars have largely abandoned the effort to describe women "as a caste," "as a class," or "as a minority group" as a project in its own right (see, for example, Aptheker 1989; Hull et al. 1982). What we have been left with, however, are two prevailing conceptualizations: (1) the sex differences approach and (2) the sex roles approach. And note that, while the minority group and caste/class approaches were concerned with factors external to the individual (e.g., the structure of social institutions and the impact of historical events), the approaches that remain emphasize factors that characterize the individual (Glazer 1977).

Arguably, some might call this picture oversimplified. Given the exciting new scholarship that focuses on gender as something that is socially constructed, and something that converges with other inequalities to produce difference among women, haven't we moved well beyond "sex differences" and "sex roles"? A close examination of this literature suggests that we have not. New conceptualizations of the bases of gender inequality still rest on old conceptualizations of gender (West and Fenstermaker 1993, 151). For example, those who rely on a sex differences approach conceive of gender as inhering in the individual, in other words, as the masculinity or femininity of *a person*. Elsewhere (Fenstermaker et al. 1991; West and Fenstermaker 1993; West and Zimmerman 1987), we note that this conceptualization obscures our understanding of how gender can structure distinctive domains of social experience (see also Stacey and Thorne 1985). "Sex differences" are treated as the explanation, instead of the analytic point of departure.

Although many scholars who take this approach draw on socialization to account for the internalization of femininity and masculinity, they imply that by about five years of age, these differences have be-

come stable characteristics of individuals—much like sex (West and Zimmerman 1987, 126). Thus, the careful distinction between sex and gender is obliterated, as gender is reduced effectively to sex (Gerson 1985). When the social meanings of sex are re-rooted in biology, it becomes virtually impossible to explain variation in gender relations in the context of race and class. We must assume, for example, that the effects of inherent sex differences are either added to or subtracted from those of race and class. Moreover, we are led to assume that sex differences are more fundamental than any other differences that might interest us (see Spelman 1988, 116–119, for a critical examination of this assumption)—unless we also assume that "race differences" and "class differences" are biologically based (see Gossett 1965, Montagu 1975, Omi and Winant 1986, and Stephans 1982 for refutations of this assumption).

Those who take a sex-roles approach are confounded by similar difficulties, although these may be less apparent at the outset. What is deceptive is role theory's emphasis on the specific social locations that result in particular expectations and actions (Komarovsky 1946/1992; Linton 1936; Parsons 1951; Parsons and Bales 1955). In this view, the actual enactment of an individual's "sex role" (or, more recently, "gender role") is contingent on his or her social structural position and the expectations associated with that position. The focus is on gender as a role or status, as it is learned and enacted. In earlier work (Fenstermaker et al. 1991; West and Fenstermaker 1993; West and Zimmerman 1987), we have noted several problems with this approach, including its inability to specify actions appropriate to particular "sex roles" in advance of their occurrence, and the fact that sex roles are not situated in any particular setting or organizational context (Lopata and Thorne 1978; Thorne 1980). The fact that "sex roles" often serve as "master statuses" (Hughes 1945) makes it hard to account for how variations in situations produce variations in their enactment. Given that gender is potentially omni-relevant to how we organize social life, almost any action could count as an instance of sex role enactment.

The most serious problem with this approach, however, is its inability to address issues of power and inequality (Connell 1985; Lopata and Thorne 1978; Thorne 1980). Conceiving of gender as made up of the "male role" and the "female role" implies a "separate but equal" relationship between the two; one characterized by complementary relations rather than conflict. Elsewhere (Fenstermaker et al. 1991; West and Fenstermaker 1993; West and Zimmerman 1987), we illustrate this problem with Barrie Thorne and her colleagues' observation that social scientists have not made much use of role theory in their analyses of race and class relations. Concepts such as "race roles" and "class roles" have seemed patently inadequate to account for the dynamics of power and inequality operating in those contexts.

As many scholars have observed, empirical studies of the "female role" and "male role" have generally treated the experiences of White middle-class persons as prototypes, dismissing departures from the prototypical as instances of deviance. This is in large part what has contributed to the charges of White middle-class bias we discussed earlier. It is also what has rendered the "sex-role" approach nearly useless in accounting for the diversity of gender relations across different groups.

Seeking a solution to these difficulties, Joan Acker (1992a, 1992b) has advanced the view that gender consists of something else altogether, namely, "patterned, socially produced distinctions between female and male, feminine and masculine . . . [that occur] in the course of participation in work organizations as well as in many other locations and relations" (Acker 1992a, 250). The object here is to document the "gendered processes" that sustain "the pervasive ordering of human activities, practices and social structures in terms of differentiations between women and men" (1992b, 567).

We agree fully with the object of this view and note its utility in capturing the persistence and ubiquity of gender inequality. Its emphasis on organizational practices restores the concern with "the structure of social institutions and with the impact of historical events" that characterized earlier class and caste approaches, and facilitates the simultaneous documentation of gender, race, and class as basic principles of social organization. However, we suggest that the popular distinction between "macro" and "micro" levels of analysis reflected in this view makes it possible to describe and explain inequality empirically without fully apprehending the common elements of its daily unfolding. For example, "processes of interaction" are conceptualized *apart* from the "production of gender divisions," that is, "the overt decisions and procedures that control, segregate, exclude, and construct hierarchies based on gender, and often race" (Acker 1992b, 568). The analytic "missing link," as we see it, is the mechanism that ties these seemingly diverse processes together: one that could "take into account the constraining impact of entrenched ideas and practices on human agency, but [could] also acknowledge that the system is continually construed in everyday life and that, under certain conditions, individuals resist pressures to conform to the needs of the system" (Essed 1991, 38).

In sum, if we conceive of gender as a matter of biological differences or differential roles, we will be forced to think of it as standing apart from and outside other socially relevant organizing experiences. This will prevent us from understanding how gender, race, and class operate simultaneously with one another. It will also prevent us from seeing how the particular salience of these experiences might vary across interactions. Most important, it will give us virtually no way of adequately addressing the mechanisms that produce power and inequality in social life. Instead, we propose a conceptual mechanism for perceiving the relations between individual and institutional practice, and among forms of domination.

AN ETHNOMETHODOLOGICAL PERSPECTIVE

Don Zimmerman concisely describes ethnomethodological inquiry as proposing "that the properties of social life which seem objective, factual, and transsituational, are actually managed accomplishments or achievements of local processes" (1978, 11). In brief, the "objective" and "factual" properties of social life attain such status through the situated conduct of societal members. The aim of ethnomethodology is to analyze situated conduct in order to understand how "objective" properties of social life achieve their status as such.

The goal of this paper is not to analyze situated conduct per se, but to understand the workings of inequality. We should note that our interest here is not to separate gender, race, and class as social categories, but to build a coherent argument for understanding how they work simultaneously. How might an ethnomethodological perspective help with this task? As Marilyn Frye observes, "For efficient subordination, what's wanted is that the structure not appear to be a cultural artifact kept in place by human decision or custom, but that it appear natural—that it appear to be quite a direct consequence of facts about the beast which are beyond the scope of human manipulation" (1983, 34).

GENDER

For example, within Western societies, in everyday life, we take for granted that there are two and only two sexes (Garfinkel 1967). We see this state of affairs as "only natural" insofar as we see persons as "essentially, originally and in the final analysis either 'male' or 'female' " (Garfinkel 1967, 122). When we interact with others, we take for granted that each of us has an "essential" manly or womanly nature—one that derives from our sex and one that can be detected from the "natural signs" we give off (Goffman 1976, 75).

These beliefs constitute the *normative conceptions* of our culture with respect to the properties of normally sexed persons. Such beliefs support the seemingly "objective," "factual," and "transsituational" character of gender in social affairs, and in this sense, we experience them as exogenous (i.e., as outside of us and the particular situation we find ourselves in). But simultaneously, the meaning of these beliefs is dependent on the context in which they are invoked—rather than transsituational, as implied by the popular concept of "cognitive consensus" (Zimmerman 1978, 8–9). What is more,

because these properties of normally sexed persons are regarded as "only natural," questioning them is tantamount to calling ourselves into question as competent members of society.

Consider how these beliefs operate in the process of *sex assignment:* the initial classification of persons as either females or males (West and Zimmerman 1987, 131–132). We generally regard this process as a biological determination, requiring only a straightforward examination of the "facts of the matter" (compare the description of sex as an "ascribed status" in many introductory sociology texts). Yet the criteria for sex assignment can vary across cases (e.g., chromosome type before birth or genitalia after birth); they sometimes do and sometimes don't agree with one another (e.g., hermaphrodites); and they show considerable variation across cultures (Kessler and McKenna 1978). It is our moral conviction that there are two and only two sexes (Garfinkel 1967, 116–118), which explains the comparative ease of achieving initial sex assignment. This conviction accords females and males the status of unequivocal and "natural" entities, whose social and psychological tendencies can be predicted from their reproductive functions (West and Zimmerman 1987, 127–128). From an ethnomethodological viewpoint, sex is socially and culturally constructed, rather than a straightforward statement of the biological "facts."

Now, consider the process of *sex categorization:* the ongoing identification of persons as girls or boys or women or men in everyday life (West and Zimmerman 1987, 132–134). Sex categorization involves no well-defined set of criteria that must be satisfied in order to identify someone. Rather, it involves treating appearances (e.g., deportment, dress, and bearing) as if they were indicative of underlying states of affairs (e.g., anatomical, hormonal, and chromosomal arrangements). The point worth stressing here is that while sex category serves as an indicator of sex, it does not depend on it. Societal members will "see" a world populated by two and only two sexes, even in public situations that preclude inspection of the physiological "facts." From this perspective, it is important to distinguish sex category from sex assignment, and to distinguish both from the "doing" of gender.

Gender, we argue, is a situated accomplishment of societal members: the local management of conduct in relation to normative conceptions of appropriate attitudes and activities for particular sex categories (West and Zimmerman 1987, 134–135). From this perspective, gender is not merely an individual attribute but something that is accomplished in interaction with others. Here, as in our earlier work (Fenstermaker et al. 1991; West and Fenstermaker 1993; West and Zimmerman 1987), we rely on John Heritage's (1984, 136–137) formulation of accountability: the possibility of describing actions, circumstances, and even descriptions themselves in both serious and consequential ways (e.g., as "unwomanly" or "unmanly"). Heritage points out that members of society routinely characterize activities in ways that take notice of those activities (e.g., naming, describing, blaming, excusing, or merely acknowledging them) and place them in a social framework (i.e., situating them in the context of other activities that are similar or different).

The fact that activities can be described in such ways is what leads to the possibility of conducting them with an eye to how they might be assessed (e.g., as "womanly" or "manly" behaviors). Three important but subtle points are worth emphasizing here. One is that the notion of accountability is relevant not only to activities that conform to prevailing normative conceptions (and thus do not warrant more than a passing glance), but also to those activities that deviate. The issue is not deviance or conformity: rather, it is the possible *evaluation* of action in relation to normative conceptions, and the likely consequence of that evaluation for subsequent interaction. The second point worth emphasizing is that the process of rendering some action accountable is an interactional accomplishment. As Heritage (1984, 179) explains, accountability permits persons to conduct their activities in relation to their circumstances—in ways that permit others to take those circumstances into account and see those activities for what they are. Hence, "the intersubjectivity of actions ultimately

rests on a symmetry between the *production* of those actions on the one hand and their *recognition* on the other"—both in the context of their circumstances. That persons *may be* held accountable does not mean that they necessarily *will be* held accountable in every interaction. Particular interactional outcomes are not the point here, but rather the possibility of accountability in any interaction.

The third point we must stress is that, while individuals are the ones who do gender, the process of rendering something accountable is both interactional and institutional in character: it is a feature of social relationships and its idiom derives from the institutional arena in which those relationships come to life. In the United States, for example, when the behaviors of children or teenagers have become the focus of public concern, the Family and Motherhood (as well as individual mothers) have been held accountable to normative conceptions of "essential" femininity (including qualities like nurturance and caring). Gender is obviously much more than role or an individual characteristic: it is a mechanism whereby situated social action contributes to the reproduction of social structure (West and Fenstermaker 1993, 158).

Thus, womanly and manly natures achieve the status of objective properties of social life (West and Zimmerman 1987). They are rendered natural, normal characteristics of individuals and, at the same time, furnish the tacit legitimation of the distinctive and unequal fates of women and men within the social order. If sex categories are potentially omni-relevant to social life, then persons engaged in virtually any activity may be held accountable for their performance of that activity *as women* or *as men* and their category membership can be used to validate or discredit their other activities. This arrangement provides for countless situations in which persons in a particular sex category can "see" that they are out of place and that if they were not there, their current problems would not exist. It also allows for seeing various features of the existing social order as "natural" responses, for example, the division of labor (Fenstermaker Berk 1985), the development of gender identities (Cahill 1986), and the subordination of women by men (Fenstermaker et al. 1991). These things "are the way they are" by virtue of the fact that men are men and women are women—a distinction seen as "natural," as rooted in biology, and as producing fundamental psychological, behavioral, and social consequences.

Through this formulation, we resituate gender, an attribute without clear social origin or referent, in social interaction. This makes it possible to study how gender takes on social import, how it varies in its salience and consequence, and how it operates to *produce* and *maintain* power and inequality in social life. Below, we extend this reformulation to race and then to class. Through this extension, we are not proposing an equivalence of oppressions. Race is not class, and neither is gender. Nevertheless, we suggest that although in any given social situation race, class, and gender will likely take on different import, and will often carry vastly different social consequences, *how they operate* may be productively compared. Here, our focus is on the *social mechanics* of gender, race, and class, for that is the way we may perceive their simultaneous workings in human affairs.

RACE

Within the United States, virtually any social activity presents the possibility of categorizing the participants on the basis of race. Attempts to establish race as a scientific concept have met with little success (Gossett 1965; Montagu 1975; Omi and Winant 1986; Stephans 1982). There are, for example, no biological criteria (e.g., hormonal, chromosomal, or anatomical) that allow physicians to pronounce race assignment at birth, thereby sorting human beings into distinctive races. Moreover, since racial categories and their meanings change over time and place, they are arbitrary. Nevertheless, in everyday life, people can and do sort themselves and others out on the basis of membership in racial categories.

Michael Omi and Howard Winant argue that the "seemingly obvious, 'natural' and 'common sense' qualities" of the existing racial order "themselves testify to the effectiveness of the racial forma-

tion process in constructing racial meanings and identities" (1986, 62). For instance, any scientific theory of race would be hard pressed to explain the relatively recent emergence of the category *Asian-American*, in the absence of a well-defined set of criteria for assigning individuals to the category. Furthermore, in relation to ethnicity, it makes no sense to aggregate in a single category the distinctive histories, geographic origins, and cultures of Cambodian, Chinese, Filipino, Japanese, Korean, Laotian, Thai, and Vietnamese Americans. But, Omi and Winant contend, despite important distinctions among these groups, "the majority of Americans cannot tell the difference" among their members (1986, 24). Thus, "Asian-American" affords a means of *achieving* racial categorization in everyday life. Notions like this one are not supported by any scientific criteria for reliably distinguishing members of different "racial" groups. What is more, even state-mandated criteria (e.g., the proportion of "mixed blood" necessary to legally classify someone as *Black*) are distinctly different in other Western cultures, and have little relevance to the way racial categorization occurs in everyday life. As in the case of sex categorization, we treat appearances as if they were indicative of some underlying state.

Beyond preconceived notions of what members of particular groups *look* like, Omi and Winant suggest that we share preconceived notions of what members of these groups *are* like. They note, for example, that we are likely to become disoriented "when people do not act 'Black,' 'Latino,' or indeed 'White' " (1986, 62). From our ethnomethodological perspective, what Omi and Winant are describing is the *accountability of persons to race* category. If we accept their contention that there are prevailing normative conceptions of appropriate attitudes and activities for particular race categories, and if we grant Heritage's (1984, 179) claim that accountability allows persons to conduct their activities in relation to their circumstances (in ways that allow others to take those circumstances into account and see those activities for what they are), we can see race also as a *situated accomplishment of societal members*. From this perspective, race is not simply an individual characteristic or trait, but something that is accomplished in interaction with others.

Now, to the extent that race category is omnirelevant (or even verges on this), it follows that a person involved in virtually *any* action may be held accountable for their performance of that action as a member of their race category. As in the case of sex category, race category can be used to justify or discredit other actions; accordingly, virtually any action can be assessed in relation to its race categorical nature. The accomplishment of race (like gender) does not necessarily mean "living up" to normative conceptions of attitudes and activities appropriate to a particular race category. Rather, it means engaging in action at the *risk* of race assessment. Thus, even though individuals are the ones who accomplish race, "the enterprise is fundamentally interactional and institutional in character, for accountability is a feature of social relationships and its idiom is drawn from the institutional arena in which those relationships are enacted" (West and Zimmerman 1987, 137).

The accomplishment of race renders the social arrangements based on race categories as normal and natural, that is, legitimate ways of organizing social life. Although the distinction between "macro" and "micro" levels of analysis is popular in the race relations literature, too (e.g., in distinguishing "institutional" from "individual" racism or "macro-level" analyses of racialized social structures from "micro-level" analyses of identity formation), we contend that it is ultimately a false distinction. These "levels" not only operate continually and reciprocally in "our lived experience, in politics, in culture [and] in economic life" (Omi and Winant 1986, 67), but distinguishing between them "places the individual outside the institutional, thereby severing rules, regulations and procedures from the people who make and enact them" (Essed 1991, 36). We contend that the accountability of persons to race categories is the key to understanding the maintenance of the existing racial order.

Note that there is nothing in this formulation to suggest that race is necessarily accomplished in isolation from gender. To the contrary, if we conceive of both race and gender as situated accomplishments, we can see how individual persons may experience them simultaneously. For instance, Spelman observes that "Insofar as she is oppressed by racism in a sexist context and sexism in a racist context, the Black woman's struggle cannot be compartmentalized into two struggles—one as a Black and one as a woman. Indeed, it is difficult to imagine why a Black woman would think of her struggles this way except in the face of demands by White women or by Black men that she do so" (1988, 124). To the extent that an individual Black woman is held accountable in one situation, to her race category, and in another, to her sex category, we can see these as "oppositional" demands for accountability. But note, it is a *Black woman* who is held accountable in both situations.

Despite many important differences in the histories, traditions, and varying impacts of racial and sexual oppression across particular situations, the mechanism underlying them is the same. To the extent that members of society know that their actions are accountable, they will design their actions in relation to how they might be seen and described by others. And to the extent that race category (like sex category) is omni-relevant to social life, it provides others with an ever available resource for interpreting those actions. In short, inasmuch as our society is divided by "essential" differences between members of different race categories and categorization by race is both relevant and mandated, the accomplishment of race is unavoidable (compare West and Zimmerman 1987, 137).

In sum, the accomplishment of race consists of creating differences among members of different race categories—differences that are neither natural nor biological (cf. West and Zimmerman 1987, 137). Once created, these differences are used to maintain the "essential" distinctiveness of "racial identities," and the institutional arrangements that they support. From this perspective, racial identities are not invariant idealizations of our human natures that are uniformly distributed in society. Nor are normative conceptions of attitudes and activities for one's race category templates for "racial" behaviors. Rather, what is invariant is the notion that members of different "races" have essentially different natures, which explain their very unequal positions in our society.

CLASS

This, too, we propose, is the case with class. Here, we know that even sympathetic readers are apt to balk: gender, yes, is "done," and race, too, is "accomplished," but class? How can we reduce a system that "differentially structures group access to material resources, including economic, political and social resources" (Andersen and Collins 1992, 50) to "a situated accomplishment"? We do not mean to deny the material realities of poverty and privilege imposed by differing relations under capital. However, we suggest that these realities have little to do with class categorization—and, ultimately, with the accountability of persons to class categories—in everyday life.

For example, consider Shellee Colen's description of the significance of maids' uniforms to White middle-class women who employ West Indian immigrant women as child-care workers and domestics in New York City. In the words of "Judith Thomas," one of the West Indian women Colen interviewed, "She [the employer] wanted me to wear the uniform. She was really prejudiced. She just wanted that the maid must be identified. . . . She used to go to the beach every day with the children. So going to the beach in the sand and the sun and she would have the kids eat ice cream and all that sort of thing. . . . I tell you one day when I look at myself, I was so dirty . . . just like I came out from a garbage can" (1986, 57). At the end of that day, says Colen, Thomas asked her employer's permission to wear jeans to the beach next time they went, and the employer gave her permission to do so. But when she did, and the employer's brother came to the beach for a visit. Thomas noted, "I really believe they had a talk about it, because in the evening, driving back from the beach, she said, 'Well, Judith, I said you could wear something else to the beach other than the uniform [but] I think you

will have to wear the uniform because they're very informal on this beach and they don't know who is guests from who isn't guests' " (57).

Of the women Colen interviewed (in 1985), none was making more than $225 a week, and Thomas was the only one whose employer was paying for medical insurance. All (including Thomas) were supporting at least two households: their own in New York, and that of their kin in the West Indies. By any objective social scientific criteria, all would be regarded as members of the working-class poor. Yet in the eyes of Thomas's employer (and, apparently, the eyes of others at the beach), Thomas's low wages, long hours, and miserable conditions of employment were insufficient to establish her class category: without a uniform, she could be mistaken for "one of the guests" and hence not be held accountable "as a maid."

There is more to this example, of course, than meets the eye. The employer's claim notwithstanding, it is unlikely that Thomas would be mistaken for "one of the guests" at the beach, tending to White middle-class children who were clearly not her own. However, the blue jeans might be seen as indicating her failure to comply with normative expectations of attitudes and behaviors appropriate to "a maid," and, worse yet, as belying the competence of her employer. Thomas displaying herself as a maid affirms the authority of her employer. And, as Evelyn Nakano Glenn notes in another context (Glenn 1992, 34), "the higher standard of living of one woman is made possible by, and also helps to perpetuate, the other's lower standard of living."

Admittedly, the normative conceptions that sustain the accountability of persons to class category are somewhat different from those that sustain accountability to sex category and race category. For example, despite earlier attempts to link pauperism with heredity and thereby justify the forced sterilization of poor women in the United States (Rafter 1992), scientists today do not conceive of class in relation to the biological characteristics of a person. Moreover, there is no scientific basis for popular notions of what persons in particular class categories "look like" or "act like." But even though the dominant ideology within the United States is no longer based explicitly on social Darwinism (see, for example, Gossett 1965, 144–175), and even though we believe that, in theory, "anyone can make it," as a society we still hold certain truths to be self-evident. As Donna Langston (1991, 146) observes: "If hard work were the sole determinant of your ability to support yourself and your family, surely we'd have a different outcome for many in our society. We also, however, believe in luck, and on closer examination, it certainly is quite a coincidence that the 'unlucky' come from certain race, gender and class backgrounds. In order to perpetuate racist, sexist and classist outcomes, we also have to believe that the current economic distribution is unchangeable, has always existed, and probably exists in this form throughout the known universe, i.e., it's 'natural.' " Here, Langston pinpoints the underlying assumptions that sustain our notions about persons in relation to poverty and privilege—assumptions that compete with our contradictory declarations of a meritocratic society with its ever-invocable Horatio Algers. For example, if someone is poor, we assume it is due to something *they* did or didn't do: they lacked initiative, they weren't industrious, they had no ambition, etcetera. If someone is rich, or merely "well off," it must be by virtue of their own efforts, talents, and initiative. While these beliefs certainly *look* more mutable than our views of women's and men's "essential" natures, or deep-seated convictions regarding the characteristics of persons in particular race categories, they still rest on the assumption that one's economic fortunes derive from *qualities of the person*. Thus, "initiative" is treated as inherent in those who "have," and "laziness" is seen as inherent in those who "have not." Given that "initiative" is a prerequisite for employment in jobs leading to upward mobility in American society, it is hardly surprising that "the rich get richer and the poor get poorer." As in the case of gender and race, the profound historical effects of entrenched institutional practice result, but they unfold one accomplishment at a time.

As Benjamin DeMott (1990) observes, Americans operate on the basis of a most unusual assumption, namely, that we live in a classless society. On the one hand, our everyday discourse is replete with categorizations of persons by class. Thus, DeMott (1990, 1–27) offers numerous examples of television shows, newspaper articles, cartoons, and movies that illustrate how class will tell in the most mundane of social doings. On the other hand, we believe that we in the United States are truly unique "in escaping the hierarchies that burden the rest of the developed world" (p. 29). Thus, we cannot *see* the system of distribution that structures our unequal access to resources. Because we cannot see this, the *accomplishment of class* in everyday life rests on the presumption that everyone is endowed with equal opportunity and, therefore, that real differences in the outcomes we observe must result from individual differences in attributes like intelligence and character.

The accomplishment of class renders the unequal institutional arrangements based on class category accountable as normal and natural, that is, legitimate ways of organizing social life (compare West and Zimmerman 1987). Differences between members of particular class categories that are created by this process can then be depicted as fundamental and enduring dispositions. In this light, the institutional arrangements of our society can be seen as responsive to the differences—the social order being merely an accommodation to the natural order.

In any given situation (whether that situation is characterizable as face-to-face interaction or the more "macro" workings of institutions), the simultaneous accomplishments of class, gender, and race will differ in content and outcome. Moreover, from situation to situation, the salience of the observables relevant to categorization (e.g., dress, interpersonal style, skin color) may seem to eclipse the interactional impact of the simultaneous accomplishment of all three. Nevertheless, we maintain that just as the mechanism for accomplishment is shared, so too is their simultaneous accomplishment ensured.

CONCLUSION: THE PROBLEM OF DIFFERENCE

As we have indicated, mathematical metaphors describing the relations among gender, race, and class have led to considerable confusion in feminist scholarship. The conceptualizations of gender that support mathematical metaphors (sex differences and sex roles) have forced scholars to think of it as something that stands apart from and outside of race and class in people's lives.

In putting forth this perspective, we hope to advance a new way of thinking about gender, race, and class—namely, as ongoing, methodical, and situated accomplishments. We have tried to demonstrate the utility of this perspective for understanding how people experience gender, race, and class simultaneously. We have also tried to illustrate the implications of this perspective for reconceptualizing "the problem of difference" in feminist theory. What are the implications of our ethnomethodological perspective for an understanding of relations among gender, race, and class? First, and perhaps most important, conceiving of these as ongoing accomplishments means that we cannot determine their relevance to social action apart from the context in which they are accomplished (Fenstermaker et al. 1991; West and Fenstermaker 1993). While sex category, race category, and class category are potentially omni-relevant to social life, individuals inhabit many different identities and these may be stressed or muted, depending on the situation.

A second implication of our perspective is that the accomplishment of race, class, and gender does not require categorical diversity among the participants. To paraphrase Erving Goffman, social situations "do not so much allow for the expression of natural differences as for the production of [those] difference[s themselves]" (1977, 32). Thus, some of the most extreme displays of "essential" womanly and manly natures may occur in settings that are usually reserved for members of a single sex category, such as locker rooms or beauty salons (Gerson 1985). Some of the most dramatic expressions of "definitive" class characteristics may emerge in class-specific contexts (e.g., debutante balls). Situations that involve more than one sex category, race category, and class category may highlight categorical membership and make the accomplishment of gender, race, and class more salient, but they are not necessary to produce these accomplishments in the first place. This point is worth stressing, because existing formulations of relations among gender, race, and class might lead one to conclude that "difference" must be present for categorical membership, and thus dominance, to matter.

A third implication is that, dependent on how race, gender, and class are accomplished, what looks to be the same activity may have different meanings for those engaged in it. Consider the long-standing debates among feminists (e.g., Collins 1990; Davis 1971; Dill 1988; Firestone 1970; Friedan 1963; hooks 1984; Hurtado 1989; Zavella 1987) over the significance of mothering and child care in women's lives. For White middle-class women, these activities have often been seen as *constitutive* of oppression, in that they are taken as expressions of their "essential" womanly natures and used to discredit their participation in other activities (e.g., Friedan 1963). But for many women of Color (and White working-class women), mothering and child care have had (and continue to have) very different meanings. Angela Davis (1971, 7) points out that in the context of slavery, African American women's efforts to tend to the needs of African American children (not necessarily their own) represented the only labor they performed that could not be directly appropriated by White slave owners. Moreover, bell hooks observes that throughout U.S. history, "Black women have identified work in the context of the family as humanizing labor, work that affirms their identity as women, as human beings showing love and care, the very gestures of humanity White supremacist ideology claimed Black people were incapable of expressing" (1984, 133–134). And, looking specifically at American family life in the nineteenth century, Bonnie Thornton Dill (1988) suggests that being a poor or working-class African American woman, a Chinese American woman, or a Mexican American woman meant something very different from being a Euro-American woman. Normative, class-bound conceptions of "woman's" nature at that time included tenderness, piety, and nurturance—qualities that legitimated the confinement of middle-class Euro-American women to the domestic sphere and that promoted such confinement as the goal of working-class and poor immigrant Euro-American families' efforts. "For racial-ethnic women, however, the notion of separate spheres served to reinforce their subordinate status and became, in effect, another assault. As they increased their work outside the home, they were forced into a productive sphere that was organized for men and 'desperate' women who were so unfortunate or immoral that they could not confine their work to the domestic sphere. In the productive sphere, however, they were denied the opportunity to embrace the dominant ideological definition of 'good' wife and mother" (Dill 1988, 429).

Fourth and finally, our perspective affords an understanding of the accomplishment of race, gender, or class as constituted in the context of the differential "doings" of the others. Consider, for example, the dramatic case of the U.S. Senate hearings on Clarence Thomas's nomination to the Supreme Court. Wherever we turned, whether to visual images on a television screen or the justificatory discourse of print media, we were overwhelmed by the dynamics of gender, race, and class operating in concert with one another. It made a difference to us as viewers (and certainly to his testimony) that Clarence Thomas was a Black *man* and that he was a *Black* man. It also made a difference, particularly to the African American community, that he was a Black man who had been raised in *poverty* (Bickel 1992). Each categorical dimension played off the others, and off the comparable but quite different categorizations of Anita Hill (a self-made Black woman law professor, who had grown up as one of thirteen children). Most White women who watched the hearings identified gender and men's dominance as the most salient aspects, whether in making sense of the Judiciary Committee's handling of witnesses, or understanding the relationship between Hill and Thomas (Bickel 1992). By contrast, most African American

viewers saw racism as the most salient aspect of the hearings, including White men's prurient interest in Black sexuality, and the exposure of troubling divisions between Black women and men (Bickel 1992; Morrison 1992). The point is that how we *label* such dynamics does not necessarily capture their complex quality. Foreground and background, context, salience, and center shift from interaction to interaction, but all operate interdependently.

Of course, this is only the beginning. Gender, race, and class are only three means (though certainly very powerful ones) of generating difference and dominance in social life. Much more must be done to distinguish other forms of inequality and their workings. Empirical evidence must be brought to bear on the question of variation in the salience of categorical memberships, while still allowing for the simultaneous influence of these memberships on interaction. We suggest that the analysis of situated conduct affords the best prospect for understanding how these "objective" properties of social life achieve their ongoing status as such and, hence, how the most fundamental divisions of our society are legitimated and maintained.

REFERENCES

Acker, Joan. 1992a. Gendering organizational theory. In *Gendering Organizational Theory*, edited by Albert J. Mills and Peta Tancred. London: Sage.

Acker, Joan. 1992b. Gendered institutions: From sex roles to gendered institutions. *Contemporary Sociology* 21:565–569.

Almquist, Elizabeth. 1989. The experiences of minority women in the United States: Intersections of race, gender, and class. In *Women: A feminist perspective*, edited by Jo Freeman. Mountain View, Calif.: Mayfield.

Andersen, Margaret L., and Patricia Hill Collins. 1992. Preface. In *Race, class and gender*, edited by Margaret L. Andersen and Patricia Hill Collins. Belmont, Calif.: Wadsworth.

Aptheker, Bettina. 1989. *Tapestries of Life: Women's work, women's consciousness, and the meaning of daily experience*. Amherst: University of Massachusetts Press.

Bickel, Ofra. 1992. *Frontline*. PBS, Oct. 14, 1992.

Cahill, Spencer E. 1986. Childhood socialization as recruitment process: Some lessons from the study of gender development. In *Sociological studies of child development*, edited by Patricia Adler and Peter Adler. Greenwich, Conn.: JAI Press.

Colen, Shellee. 1986. "With respect and feelings": Voices of

West Indian child care and domestic workers in New York city. In *All American women*, edited by Johnetta B. Cole. New York: Free Press.

Collins, Patricia Hill. 1990. *Black feminist thought*. New York: Routledge.

Connell, R. W. 1985. Theorizing gender. *Sociology* 19:260–272.

Davis, Angela. 1971. The Black woman's role in the community of slaves. *Black Scholar* 3:3–15.

DeMott, Benjamin. 1990. *The imperial middle: Why Americans can't think straight about class*. New Haven: Yale University Press.

Dill, Bonnie Thornton. 1988. Our mother's grief: Racial ethnic women and the maintenance of families. *Journal of Family History* 13:415–431.

Essed, Philomena. (1991). *Understanding everyday racism: An interdisciplinary theory*. Newbury Park, Calif.: Sage.

Fenstermaker, Sarah, Candace West, and Don H. Zimmerman. 1991. Gender inequality: New conceptual terrain. In *Gender, family and economy: The triple overlap*, edited by Rae Lesser Blumberg. Newbury Park, Calif.: Sage.

Fenstermaker Berk, Sarah. 1985. *The gender factory: The apportionment of work in American households*. New York: Plenum.

Firestone, Shulamith. 1970. *The dialectic of sex*. New York: Morrow.

Friedan, Betty. 1963. *The feminine mystique*. New York: Dell.

Frye, Marilyn. 1983. *The politics of reality: Essays in feminist theory*. Trumansburg, N.Y.: Crossing Press.

Garfinkel, Harold. 1967. Studies in ethnomethodology. Englewood Cliffs, N.J.: Prentice-Hall.

Gerson, Judith. 1985. The variability and salience of gender: Issues of conceptualization and measurement. Paper presented at the annual meeting of the American Sociological Association, Washington, D.C., August.

Glazer, Nona. 1977. A sociological perspective: Introduction. In *Woman in a man-made world*, edited by Nona Glazer and Helen Youngelson Waehrer. Chicago: Rand McNally.

Glenn, Evelyn Nakano. 1985. Racial ethnic women's labor: The intersection of race, gender and class oppression. *Review of Radical Political Economics* 17:86–108.

Glenn, Evelyn Nakano. 1992. From servitude to service work: Historical continuities in the racial division of paid reproductive labor. *Signs* 18:1–43.

Goffman, Erving. 1976. Gender display. *Studies in the Anthropology of Visual Communication* 3:69–77.

Goffman, Erving. 1977. The arrangement between the sexes. *Theory and Society* 4:301–331.

Gossett, Thomas. 1965. *Race: The history of an idea in America*. New York: Schocken Books.

Heritage, John. 1984. *Garfinkel and ethnomethodology*. Cambridge, England: Polity Press.

Hochschild, Arlie Russell. 1973. A review of sex role research. *American Journal of Sociology* 78:1011–1029.

hooks, bell. 1981. *Ain't I a woman: Black women and feminism*. Boston: South End Press.

hooks, bell. 1984. *From margin to center*. Boston: South End Press.

Hughes, Everett C. 1945. Dilemmas and contradictions of status. *American Journal of Sociology* 50:353–359.

Hull, Gloria T., Patricia Bell Scott, and Barbara Smith (eds.). 1982. *All the women are White, all the Blacks are men, but some of us are brave*. Old Westbury, N.Y.: Feminist Press.

Hurtado, Aída. 1989. Relating to privilege: Seduction and rejection in the subordination of White women and women of Color. *Signs* 14:833–855.

Jordan, June. 1985. Report from the Bahamas. In *On call: Political essays*. Boston: South End Press.

Kessler, Suzanne J., and Wendy McKenna. 1978. *Gender: An ethnomethodological approach*. New York: Wiley.

Komarovsky, Mirra. 1946/1992. The concept of social role revisited. *Gender and Society* 6:301–312.

Langston, Donna. 1991. Tired of playing monopoly? In *Changing our power: An introduction to women's studies*, edited by Jo Whitehorse Cochran, Donna Langston, and Carolyn Woodward, 2nd ed. Dubuque, Iowa: Kendall-Hunt.

Linton, Ralph. 1936. *The study of man*. New York: Appleton-Century.

Lopata, Helen Z., and Barrie Thorne. 1978. On the term "sex roles." *Signs* 3:718–721.

Montagu, Ashley (ed.) 1975. *Race & I. Q.* London: Oxford University Press.

Moraga, Cherríe. 1981. La güera. In *This bridge called my back: Radical writing by women of Color*, edited by Cherríe Moraga and Gloria Anzaldúa. New York: Kitchen Table Press.

Morrison, Toni (ed.). 1992. *Race-ing justice, engender-ing power: Essays on Anita Hill, Clarence Thomas, and the construction of social reality*. New York: Pantheon.

Omi, Michael, and Howard Winant. 1986. *Racial formation in the United States from the 1960s to the 1980s*. New York: Routledge and Kegan Paul.

Parsons, Talcott. 1951. *The social system*. New York: Free Press.

Parsons, Talcott, and Robert F. Bales. 1955. *Family, socialization and interaction process*. New York: Free Press.

Rafter, Nichole H. 1992. Claims-making and socio-cultural context in the first U.S. eugenics campaign. *Social Problems* 39:17–34.

Rich, Adrienne. 1979. Disloyal to civilization: Feminism, racism, gynephobia. In *On lies, secrets, and silence*, by Adrienne Rich. New York: Norton.

Segura, Denise A. 1992. Chicanas in white collar jobs: "You have to prove yourself more." *Sociological Perspectives* 35:163–182.

Spelman, Elizabeth V. 1988. *Inessential woman: Problems of exclusion in feminist thought*. Boston: Beacon Press.

Stacey, Judith, and Barrie Thorne. 1985. The missing feminist revolution in sociology. *Social Problems* 32:301–316.

Stephans, Nancy. 1982. *The idea of race in science*. Hamden, Conn.: Archon.

Thorne, Barrie. 1980. Gender . . . how is it best conceptualized? Unpublished manuscript. East Lansing: Department of Sociology, Michigan State University.

West, Candace, and Sarah Fenstermaker. 1993. Power, inequality and the accomplishment of gender: An ethnomethodological view. In *Theory on gender/feminism on theory*, edited by Paula England. New York: Aldine.

West, Candace, and Don H. Zimmerman. 1987. Doing gender. *Gender and Society* 1:125–151.

Zavella, Patricia. 1987. *Women's work and Chicano families: Cannery workers of the Santa Clara Valley.* Ithaca, N.Y.: Cornell University Press.

Zimmerman, Don H. 1978. Ethnomethodology. *American Sociologist* 13:6–15.

NO

On West and Fenstermaker's "Doing Difference"

PATRICIA HILL COLLINS

How wonderful it would be to possess the insight to see beyond the messy, contemporary politics of race, class, and gender in order to propose "a new way of thinking about the workings of these relations" (West and Fenstermaker, this volume). The area of race, class, and gender studies struggles with the complex question of how to think about intersections of systems of oppression of race, class, and gender. We clearly need new models that will assist us in seeing how structures of power organized around intersecting relations of race, class, and gender frame the social positions occupied by individuals; work explaining how interlocking systems of oppression produce social locations for us all, where Black men are routinely stopped by the police for no apparent reason, or African American women like Patricia Williams are denied entry to stores where they could spend their hard-earned law professor salaries.

Despite West and Fenstermaker's initial promises to retheorize the intersections of race, class, and gender in a way that transcends the limitations of existing models, a surprising thing happened on the way to the end of their chapter. One by one, race, gender, and even class were erased. As a result, an article that claims to retheorize the interconnections of race, class, and gender said remarkably little about racism, patriarchy, and capitalism as systems of power. How this happened was impressive. Race and class appeared as gender in drag, each arriving in analytical forms virtually unrecognizable to practitioners of these respective fields. Each made brief appearances, before returning to the safe haven of social constructionist arguments about difference. In the place of the race, class, and gender came a rehashing of social constructionist views of society, a technique of ethnomethodology masquerading as new theory, and —most amazing—the concept of difference used as proxy for the interconnectedness of race, class, and gender itself. The very things the article claimed to reveal it curiously erased, all the while talking about them.

Perhaps articles like "Doing Difference" wouldn't bother me so much if the stakes weren't so high. Since I have long worked in the field of race, class, and gender studies, a quick summary of the field provides a context for evaluating the contributions of this article. For years, scholars in the separate areas of race or class or gender struggled for the primacy of each as an analytical category explaining inequality. To do this, they diligently chipped away at a social science logic that constructed race, class, and gender as benign attributes that were useful for describing human subjects in research designs, but treated racism, sexism, and class exploitation as variations of other more fundamental processes. More important, race, class, and gender studies each emerged, not in the rarefied atmosphere of academia, but in conjunction with social movements populated by people who had a real stake in understanding and changing inequalities of power resulting from systems of oppression called racism, patriarchy, and class exploitation.

These links between theory and politics meant that, despite their historical differences, all three areas shared certain fundamentals. Each aimed to explain the links between micro level experiences structured along axes of race, class, and gender with the larger, overarching macro systems. Each reasoned that, if individuals could link their own experiences with oppression on a micro level with the larger macro forces constructing their social position, they could address some of the major social problems of our day.

This commitment to theorizing oppression via these distinctive emphases eventually encountered the limitations of privileging any one system of oppression over others—of patriarchy over class, for example, or White supremacy over homophobia. The very notion of the intersections of race, class, and gender as an area worthy of study emerged from the recognition of practitioners of each distinctive theoretical tradition that inequality could not be explained, let alone challenged, via a race-only, class-only, or gender-only framework. No one had all the answers and no one was going to get all of the answers without attention to two things. First, the notion of interlocking oppressions refers to the macro level connections linking systems of oppression such as race, class, and gender. This is the model describing the social structures that create social positions. Second, the notion of intersectionality describes micro level processes —namely, how each individual and group occupies a social position within interlocking structures of oppression described by the metaphor of intersectionality. Together they shape oppression.

At this historical moment we have something very momentous happening—the linking of three historically distinct areas of inquiry with a renewed commitment to theorize connections on multiple levels of social structure. To accomplish this goal, all must support a working hypothesis of equivalency between oppressions that allows us to explore the interconnections among the systems and to extract ourselves from the internecine battles of whose oppression is more fundamental. The intent of race, class, and gender studies is to push to understand oppression (or in the more polite language of academia, "inequality" or "stratification").

"Doing Difference" claims the language of inclusivity, but decontextualizes it from the history of race, class, and gender studies. It strips the very categories of race, class, and gender of meaning and then recasts the problems of institutional power in the apolitical framework of how we might "do difference."

The authors achieve this intellectual sleight of hand impressively. Consider the order in which they construct the individual discussions of gender, race, and class. Despite criticizing others who use "additive" approaches, in constructing their argument, the authors use this same approach of treating gender as the most fundamental theoretical category and then "adding" on race and class. They lay out their theoretical argument within a gender-only framework and then generalize this argument to race and class. Note that there are no "experience" examples within the gender category; apparently gender speaks for itself and needs no examples. In contrast, the discussion of race has more "experiences" included, thus providing the unintended but nonetheless unfortunate outcome of constructing people of Color as less theoretical and more embodied. Amazingly, the discussion of social class opens with an "experience," foreshadowing an unusual approach to social class. Their treatment of social class remains distinctive because the literature of social class, much more so than that of gender and race, has long been grounded in questions of institutional power. After all, it is hard to discuss global capitalist markets as performances and representations.

By the end of the chapter, I found little evidence that the authors had really proposed a new way of thinking. Instead, they managed to transform the interlocking systems of oppression of race, class, and gender that produce positions characterized by intersectionality into, as British cultural critic Stuart Hall puts it, "a difference that didn't make any difference at all" (1992, 23).

To recast race, class, gender politics as an issue of postmodernist difference is indicative of some problems of the politics of postmodernist discourse overall. The construct of difference emerges from social constructionist views of self/other where the self is constructed against the difference of the other, but this is not the use of difference we encounter in this chapter. Social institutions, especially analyses of the institutional bases of power shaping race, class, and gender, are dropped from the analysis, leaving a plethora of postmodernist representations in their wake. Recasting racism, patriarchy, and class exploitation solely in social constructionist terms reduces race, class, and gender to performances, interactions between people embedded in a never ending string of equivalent relations, all containing race, class, and gender in some form, but a chain of equivalences devoid of power relations.

This all leads to the puzzling question of why this is happening. It is one thing to say that manipulating "difference" comprises one effective tactic used by dominant groups to maintain control —this insight is closer to the actual meanings of Williams, Spelman, and myself. It's quite another to wring one's hands about the "problem of difference," laying the groundwork for handling difference as the real problem, instead of the power relations that construct difference.

Because not all social groups appear to find difference to be such a meaningful concept, I'm left wondering who is worried about it? Thinking through the meaning of difference hasn't much concerned people of Color, poor people, and all the other people deemed "different" who disappear from this chapter. Attention by oppressed groups to the meaning of difference remains firmly rooted in the question of the use to which differences are put in defending unequal power arrangements.

Despite the well-intentioned goal of the authors, "Doing Difference" and similar efforts to infuse race, class, and gender studies with postmodernist notions of difference leave us on dangerously thin ice. What type of oppositional politics emerge from a focus on difference devoid of power? What types of directions emerge from theories stressing representations over institutional structures and social policies as central to race, class, and gender relations? Already, I see far too many students who see resistance to oppression as occurring only in the area of representation, as if thinking about resistance and analyzing representations can substitute for active resistance against institutional power. Quite simply, difference is less a problem for me than racism, class exploitation, and gender oppression. Conceptualizing these systems of oppression as difference obfuscates the power relations and material inequalities that constitute oppression. Doing away with thinking about difference will clarify the real problem.

REFERENCE

Hall, Stuart. 1992. What is this "Black" in Black popular culture? In *Black popular culture*, edited by Gina Dent and Michele Wallace. Seattle: Bay Press.

PART II

Power and Influence Strategies

Conversational Style:

Do Women and Men Speak

Different Languages?

The publication of Robin Lakoff's *Language and Woman's Place* in 1975 marked a turning point in the study of gender-communication differences. Lakoff argued that "women's language" differed from "men's language" in a number of ways, including the use of a more uncertain and deferential style, which might explain women's relative lack of success in the corporate world. *Language and Woman's Place* was one of those rare books that touched a chord in both popular and academic circles. The need to overcome women's language "deficiencies" became a major objective of the assertiveness-training programs that flourished in the 1970s, providing women with tips on how to survive, succeed, and grow on the job (Baer, 1976).

In the years following the publication of Lakoff's book, a series of studies appeared that identified differences in women's and men's language styles. Researchers found, among other things, that men tend to talk more than women in mixed-gender groups (Hall, 1984), interrupt women considerably more than women interrupt men (Stewart et al., 1986), and use fewer supportive words than females do (Haas, 1979). One investigator demonstrated the dilemma many women face in public life. Linda Carli (1990) found that a woman who spoke tentatively exerted a greater influence on a male audience than a woman who spoke assertively but that female listeners viewed the woman who spoke tentatively as less competent or knowledgeable than an assertive woman. Since women are usually trying to communicate in a mixed-sex environment, whichever style they adopt is bound to alienate part of their audience.

Unfortunately, much of the research on language and gender has focused on White middle-class women. Nancy Henley has pointed out the need for more research on the relation of ethnicity to gender issues in language, noting: "Gender manifests itself differently in different cultures, but understanding it is crucial to the creation of an equal world for men and women" (1995, p. 387). Progress has been made in recent years. Research shows that Black women are more outspoken and assertive than White women and are able to expand their verbal repertoire through the use of the Black English vernacular. Other studies indicate that Mexican-American girls use English more than their male peers do. Conversely, a separate research project found that Puerto Rican women are more likely to use Spanish than men (Henley, 1995).

Popular interest in the topic of gender and communication was dramatically revived with the publication of Deborah Tannen's *You Just Don't Understand* (1990), which was on the *New York Times* best-seller list for four years. Tannen, a professor of linguistics at Georgetown University and the author of fifteen books, including the equally popular *Talking from Nine to Five* (1994) and *Gender and Discourse* (1994, 1996), maintains that the two sexes don't understand each other because they have distinctly different conversational styles. According to Tannen, these differences stem from the fact that women and men grow up in different worlds of words, starting with the single-sex groups they play in as children. The girls, whose groups are structured around pairs of friends who share secrets, grow up to become women who strive in their conversations to make connections, to be supportive, and to focus on details. Conversely, the nature of boys' play turns out men who develop a competitive conversational style, who are reluctant to talk about their problems, prefer abstractions, and feel uncomfortable seeking advice. The result is that women talk more in private ("rapport-talk"), whereas men are more at ease speaking in public ("report-talk"). Unlike Lakoff (1975), who found women's conversational style self-defeating, Tannen takes a nonjudgmental position. The solution to the gender language gap, she asserts, is for each side to strive to understand the other's conversational styles and objectives.

Some feminist psychologists have criticized Tannen for failing to recognize that women and men's linguistic differences reflect a power imbalance rather than merely asymmetric communication styles. Tannen's failure to focus on men's reluctance to relinquish power, they argue, can lead her readers to conclude that much of what we think of as sex discrimination stems from a failure to communicate. Mary Crawford (1995), for example, contends that the differences in male-female conversational styles should be viewed as male displays and exercises of dominance. "Men's tendency to interpret questions as requests for information and problem-sharing as an opportunity to give expert advice," she writes, "can be viewed as prerogatives of power. In choosing these speech strategies, men take to themselves the voice of authority" (1995, p. 96). Some critics have gone so far as to label Tannen's lack of interest in men's insensitive and dominant behavior as "anti-feminist" (Cameron, 1992; Troemel-Ploetz, 1991).

Tannen has responded to her critics, pointing out that their objections stem from a desire for a different book than the one she wrote. The issues of dominance and the politics of gender, she claims, "are important areas of research . . . [but] they are not the field in which I work. I wrote a book about the role of what I call 'conversational style' in everyday conversation, especially in the context of close relationships, because that has been the subject of my research throughout my academic career" (1992, p. 249).

The question remains, "Do women and men speak different languages?" Tannen argues that there are gender differences in ways of speaking and that we need to identify and understand them. Elizabeth Aries, however, disagrees; she insists that Tannen has polarized the differences between men and women, failing to pay attention to the considerable overlap that exists in men's and women's styles of communication.

REFERENCES

Baer, J. L. (1976). *How to Be an Assertive, Not Aggressive, Woman in Life, in Love, and on the Job: A Total Guide to Self-Assertiveness.* New York: New American Library.

Cameron, D. (1992). Review of Deborah Tannen's *You Just Don't Understand. Feminism and Psychology, 2,* 465–468.

Carli, L. L. (1990). Gender, language, and influence. *Journal of Personality and Social Psychology, 59,* 941–951.

Crawford, M. (1995). *Talking difference: On gender and language.* London: Sage.

Haas, A. (1979). Male and female spoken language differences: Stereotypes and evidence. *Psychological Bulletin, 86,* 616–626.

Hall, J. A. (1984). *Nonverbal sex differences: Communication accuracy and expressive style.* Baltimore: Johns Hopkins University Press.

Henley, N. M. (1995). Ethnicity and gender issues in language. In H. Landrine (Ed.), *Bringing cultural diversity to feminist psychology* (pp. 361–395). Washington, D.C.: American Psychological Association.

Lakoff, R. (1975). *Language and woman's place.* New York: Harper and Row.

Stewart, L. P., Cooper, P. J., & Friedley, S. A. (1986). *Communication between the sexes: Sex differences and sex-role stereotypes.* Scottsdale, Ariz.: Gorsuch Scarisbrick.

Tannen, D. (1986). *That's not what I meant: How conversational style makes or breaks relationships.* New York: Ballantine.

Tannen, D. (1990). *You just don't understand: Women and men in conversation.* New York: William Morrow.

Tannen, D. (1992). Response to Senta Troemel-Ploetz's "Selling the apolitical" (1991). *Discourse and Society, 3,* 249–254.

Tannen, D. (1994). *Talking from nine to five: How women's and men's conversational styles affect who gets heard, who gets credit, and what gets done at work.* New York: William Morrow.

Tannen, D. (1994, 1996). *Gender and discourse.* New York: Oxford University Press.

Troemel-Ploetz, S. (1991). Review essay: Selling the apolitical. *Discourse and Society, 2,* 489–502.

ADDITIONAL READING

Coates, J. (1993). *Women, men and language: A sociolinguistic account of gender differences in language.* 2d ed. New York: Longman.

Kalbfleisch, P. J., & Cody, M. J. (1995). *Gender, power, and communication in human relationships.* Hillsdale, N.J.: Erlbaum.

Mindell, P. (1995) *A woman's guide to the language of success.* Englewood Cliffs, N.J.: Prentice-Hall.

Pearson, J. (1994). *Gender and communication.* Madison, Wis.: Brown and Benchmark.

Tannen, D. (Ed.) (1993). *Framing in discourse.* New York: Oxford University Press.

Wood, J. T. (1994). *Gendered lives: Communication, gender, and culture.* Belmont, Calif.: Wadsworth.

Women and Men Talking:
An Interactional Sociolinguistic
Approach

DEBORAH TANNEN

Each person's life is lived as a series of conversations. Analyzing everyday conversations and their effects on relationships has been the focus of my career as a sociolinguist. As I listen to the voices of women and men, I make sense of seemingly senseless misunderstandings that haunt our relationships and show that a man and a woman can interpret the same conversation differently, even when there is no apparent misunderstanding. I explain why sincere attempts to communicate are so often confounded and how we can prevent or relieve some of the frustration.

My book *That's Not What I Meant!* showed that people have different conversational styles. So when speakers from different parts of the country, or of different ethnic or class backgrounds, talk to each other, it is likely that their words will not be understood exactly as they were meant. But we are not required to pair off for life with people from different parts of the country or members of different ethnic groups, though many choose to. We *are* expected to pair off with people of the other gender, and many do, for long periods of time if not for life. And whereas many of us (though fewer and fewer) can spend large portions of our lives without coming into close contact with people of vastly different cultural backgrounds, few people—not even those who have no partners in life or whose primary relationships are with same-sex partners—can avoid close contact with people of the other gender, as relatives and co-workers if not as friends.

That Not What I Meant! had ten chapters, of which one dealt with gender differences in conversational style. But when I received requests for interviews, articles, and lectures, 90 percent wanted me to focus on 10 percent of the book—the chapter on male-female differences. Everyone wanted to know more about gender and conversational style.

I, too, wanted to find out more. Indeed, I had decided to become a linguist largely because of a course taught by Robin Lakoff that included her research on gender and language. My first major linguistic study was of gender and cultural differences in indirectness, and I was fairly familiar with others' research on the topic.[1] But although I had always inhabited the outskirts of gender research, I had not leaped into its inner circle, partly because the field is so controversial.

Whenever I write or speak about conversational style differences between women and men, sparks fly. Most people exclaim that what I say is true, that it explains their own experience. They are relieved to learn that what has caused them trouble is a common condition and that there is nothing terribly wrong with them, their partners, or their relationships. Their partners' ways of talking, which they had ascribed to personal failings, could be reframed as reflecting a different system. And their own ways of talking, which their partners had been hounding them about for years, could be defended as logical and reasonable.

But although most people find that my explanation of gender differences in ways of talking accounts for their own experience—and they are eager to offer examples to prove it—some people become agitated as soon as they hear a reference to gender. A few become angry at the mere suggestion

1. My study of indirectness in conversation is "Ethnic style in male-female conversation," originally published in 1982 and reprinted in D. Tannen, *Gender and Discourse* (New York: Oxford University Press, 1994), pp. 175–194.

that women and men are different. And this reaction can come from either women or men.

Some men hear any statement about women and men, coming from a woman, as an accusation—a fancy way of throwing up her hands, as if to say, "You men!" They feel they are being objectified, if not slandered, by being talked about at all.

But it is not only men who bridle at statements about women and men. Some women fear, with justification, that any observation of gender differences will be heard as implying that it is women who are different—different from the standard, which is whatever men are. The male is seen as normative, the female as departing from the norm. And it is only a short step—maybe an inevitable one—from "different" to "worse."[2]

Furthermore, if women's and men's styles are shown to be different, it is usually women who are told to change. I have seen this happen in response to my own work. In an article I wrote for the *Washington Post*, I presented a conversation that had taken place between a couple in their car. The woman had asked, "Would you like to stop for a drink?" Her husband had answered, truthfully, "No," and they hadn't stopped. He was later frustrated to learn that his wife was annoyed because she had wanted to stop for a drink. He wondered, "Why didn't she just say what she wanted? Why did she play games with me?" The wife, I explained, was annoyed not because she had not gotten her way but because her preference hadn't been considered. From her point of view, she had shown

concern for her husband's wishes, but he had shown no concern for hers.

My analysis emphasized that the husband and wife in this example had different *but equally valid* styles. This point was lost in a heavily edited version of my article that appeared in the *Toronto Star*, which had me advising: "The woman must realize that when he answers 'yes' or 'no' he is not making a non-negotiable demand." The *Star* editor had deleted the immediately preceding text, which read: "In understanding what went wrong, the man must realize that when she asks what he would like, she is not asking an information question but rather starting a negotiation about what both would like. For her part, however, the woman must realize that. . . ." Deft wielding of the editorial knife had transformed my claim that women and men should *both* make adjustments into a claim that women must make a unilateral effort to understand men. Informing women of what they alone must "realize" implies that the man's way is right and the woman's is wrong. This edited version was reprinted in a textbook, and the error proliferated.[3]

THE USES AND DANGERS OF GENERALIZING

We all know we are unique individuals, but we tend to see others as representatives of groups. It's a natural tendency, since we must see the world in patterns in order to make sense of it; we wouldn't be able to deal with the daily onslaught of people and objects if we couldn't predict a lot about them and feel that we know who and what they are. But this natural and useful ability to see patterns of similarity has unfortunate consequences. It is offen-

---

2. A similar reticence accompanies research on style differences involving minorities. For example, Andrew Hacker ("Affirmative Action: The New Look," *New York Review of Books*, October 12, 1989, p. 68) discusses an incident in which Black organizations demanded the withdrawal of a New York State Department of Education handbook explaining that Blacks and Whites have different learning styles. Even though the research had been done by a Black scholar, Janice Hale-Benson, the protesters branded the findings racist. Hacker explains, "The question, of course, is whether the tendencies Hale-Benson analyzed will be construed not simply as different, but also inferior." The key word here is "construed." Readers' reactions may be very different from researchers' intentions.

3. My article "Did You Say What I Just Heard?" appeared in the *Washington Post* on October 12, 1986, p. D3. The *Toronto Star* version appeared (without my knowledge) under the title "Why We Should Also Listen Between the Lines" on November 16, 1989, p. D1. The textbook that includes excerpts from this edited version is *People in Perspective*, 2d ed., ed. Wayne Sproule (Scarborough, Ont.: Prentice-Hall Canada, 1988). The material appeared as edited by the *Toronto Star*, even though I granted permission on condition that the deleted sentence be restored.

sive to reduce an individual to a category, and it is also misleading. Dividing women and men into categories risks reinforcing this reductionism.

Generalizations, while capturing similarities, obscure differences. Everyone is shaped by innumerable influences—ethnicity, religion, class, race, age, profession, the geographical regions they and their relatives have lived in, and many other group identities—all mingled with individual personality and predilection. People are apt to sum up others by reference to one category or a few, such as "Southern belle," "New York Jewish intellectual," "Boston Brahmin," or "hot-tempered Italian." Although these categories might predict some of the behaviors of the people so described, they miss far more about them than they capture. In innumerable ways, every person is utterly unlike anyone else—including anyone else from many of the same categories.

In spite of these dangers, I am joining the growing dialogue on gender and language because the risk of ignoring differences is greater than the danger of naming them. Sweeping something big under the rug doesn't make it go away; it trips you up and sends you sprawling when you venture across the room.[4] Denying real differences can only compound the confusion that is already widespread in this era of shifting and re-forming relationships between women and men.

Pretending that women and men are the same hurts women, because how they are treated is based on norms for men. It also hurts men who, with good intentions, speak to women as they would to men and are nonplussed when their words don't work as they expected or even spark resentment and anger.

This paradox is expressed by an American Indian woman, Abby Abinanti, describing why she found law school a difficult and alienating experience: "People did not like or accept the idea of Indians or women being lawyers. Some people could not decide which idea they hated more. Some pretended that it didn't make any difference, that we were all the same. I, too, could be 'one of the boys,' 'one of the white boys.' Not likely. Both of these approaches created problems for me."[5] It is easy to see how people who hate the idea of women or Indians being lawyers would create problems for an Indian woman in law school. It is harder to see how those who wanted to accept her as an equal also created problems for her. Assuming she was the same was destructive, because she was not the same; the assumptions, values, and styles that reflected and validated their identities undercut hers.

The desire to affirm that women are equal has made some scholars reluctant to show that they are different, because differences can be used to justify unequal treatment and opportunity. Much as I understand and am in sympathy with those who wish there were no differences between women and men—only reparable social injustice—my research, the work of others, and my own and others' experience tell me it simply isn't so. There *are* gender differences in ways of speaking, and we need to identify and understand them. Without such understanding, we are doomed to blame others or ourselves—or the relationship—for the otherwise mystifying and damaging effects of our contrasting conversational styles.

Recognizing gender differences frees individuals from the burden of individual pathology. Many women and men feel dissatisfied with their close relationships and become even more frustrated when they try to talk things out. Taking a *sociolinguistic* approach to relationships makes it possible to explain these dissatisfactions without accusing anyone of being crazy or wrong and without blaming—or discarding—the relationship. If we recognize and understand our differences, we can take them into account, adjust to, and learn from each other's styles.

4. I have borrowed the metaphor of sweeping things under the rug from Robin Lakoff. I first heard her use it in her course at the Linguistic Institute of 1973 at the University of Michigan.

5. Abby Abinanti, "Lawyer," in *Women and work: Photographs and personal writings*, text edited by Maureen R. Michelson, photographs edited by Michael R. Dressler and Maureen R. Michelson (Pasadena, Calif.: NewSage Press, 1986), p. 52.

A Sociolinguistic Approach

The sociolinguistic approach I take in my work shows that many frictions arise because boys and girls grow up in what are essentially different cultures, so talk between women and men is cross-cultural communication. A cross-cultural approach to gender differences in conversational style differs from the work on gender and language which claims that conversations between men and women break down because men seek to dominate women. No one could deny that men as a class are dominant in our society and that many individual men seek to dominate women in their lives. And yet male dominance is not the whole story. It is not sufficient to account for everything that happens to women and men in conversations—especially conversations in which both are genuinely trying to relate to each other with attention and respect. The effect of dominance is not always the result of an intention to dominate. This is the news that my work brings.

In this era of opening opportunity, women are beginning to move into positions of authority. At first we assumed they could simply talk the way they always had, but this often doesn't work. Another logical step is that they should change their styles and talk like men. Apart from the repugnance of women's having to do all the changing, this doesn't work either, because women who talk like men are judged differently—and harshly. We have no choice but to examine our choices and their effects. Only by understanding each other's styles and our options can we begin to realize our opportunities and escape the prison of a monolithic conversational style.

Conversational style differences do not explain all the problems that arise in relationships between women and men. Relationships are sometimes threatened by psychological problems, true failures of love and caring, genuine selfishness—and real effects of political and economic inequity. But there are also innumerable situations in which groundless allegations of these failings are made, simply because partners are expressing their thoughts and feelings, and their assumptions about how to communicate, in different ways. If we can sort out differences based on conversational style, we will be in a better position to confront real conflicts of interest—and to find a shared language in which to negotiate them.

The Ritual Nature of Talk

Perhaps it is because our sense of gender is so deeply rooted that people are inclined to hear descriptions of gender *patterns* as statements about gender *identity*—in other words, as absolute differences rather than a matter of degree and percentages, and as universal rather than culturally mediated. The patterns I describe are based on observations of particular speakers in a particular place and time: mostly (but not exclusively) middle-class Americans of European background. Other cultures evince very different patterns of talk associated with gender—and correspondingly different assumptions about the "natures" of women and men. I don't put much store in talk about "natures" or what is "natural." People in every culture will tell you that the behaviors common in their culture are "natural." I also don't put much store in people's explanations that their way of talking is a natural response to their environment, as there is always an equally natural and opposite way of responding to the same environment.[6] We all tend to regard the way things are as the way things have to be—as only natural.

The reason that ways of talking, like other ways of conducting our daily lives, come to seem natural is

6. For example, I have been told, "The reason I learned to interrupt and talk along with others is that I grew up in a large family, so if you didn't talk over someone, you never got a chance to talk at all." Yet others have told me, "The reason I learned never to interrupt or talk when someone else is talking is that I grew up in a large family, so if everyone didn't wait their turn, no one would ever have been heard—it would have been pandemonium." The same environment—a large family—seemed obviously to lead to opposite attitudes toward interruption. In a similar spirit, I have heard people suggest that the reason New Yorkers tend to talk over each other, evidencing their great discomfort with silence in a friendly conversation, is that New York City is so crowded. My response is to point out that New York City is not more crowded than Tokyo, where long silences are expected and appreciated in conversation.

that the behaviors that make up our lives are ritualized. Indeed, the "ritual" character of interaction is at the heart of my approach to analyzing conversation. Having grown up in a particular culture, we learn to do things as the people we encounter do them, so the vast majority of our decisions about how to speak become automatic. You see someone you know, you ask "How are you?" chat, then take your leave, never pausing to ponder the many ways you could handle this interaction differently—and would, if you lived in a different culture. Just as an American automatically extends a hand for a handshake while a Japanese automatically bows, what the American and Japanese find it natural to say is a matter of convention learned throughout a lifetime.

No one understood the ritual nature of everyday life better than sociologist Erving Goffman, who also understood the fundamental role gender played in organizing our daily rituals. In his article "The Arrangement Between the Sexes," Goffman pointed out that we tend to say "sex-linked" when what we mean is "sex-class-linked."[7] When hearing that a behavior is "sex-linked," people often conclude that the behavior is to be found in every individual of that group and that it is somehow inherent in their sex, as if it came hooked to a chromosome. Goffman suggests the term *genderism* (on the model, I assume, of "mannerism," not of "sexism") for "a sex-class-linked individual behavioral practice." This is the spirit in which I intend references to gendered patterns of behavior: not to imply that there is anything inherently male or female about particular ways of talking, nor to claim that every individual man or woman adheres to the pattern, but rather to observe that a larger percentage of women or men *as a group* talk in a particular way, or individual women and men *are more likely* to talk one way or the other.

That individuals do not always fit the pattern associated with their gender does not mean that the pattern is not typical. Because more women or men speak in a particular way, that way of speaking becomes associated with women or men—or,

rather, it is the other way around: more women or men learn to speak particular ways *because* those ways are associated with their gender. And individual men or women who speak in ways associated with the other gender will pay a price for departing from cultural expectations.

WHO TALKS MORE

One way that cultural expectations express themselves is in stereotyping—for example, with regard to the question "who talks more, women or men?" According to the stereotype, women talk too much. Linguist Jennifer Coates notes some proverbs:

> A woman's tongue wags like a lamb's tail.
> Foxes are all tail and women are all tongue.
> The North Sea will sooner be found wanting in water than a woman be at a loss for a word.[8]

Throughout history, women have been punished for talking too much or in the wrong way. Linguist Connie Eble lists a variety of physical punishments used in colonial North America: women were strapped to ducking stools and held underwater until they nearly drowned, put into the stocks with signs pinned to them, gagged, and silenced by a cleft stick applied to their tongues.[9]

Though such institutionalized corporal punishments have given way to informal, often psychologi-

7. Erving Goffman, "The arrangement between the sexes," *Theory and Society* 4, 3 (1977): 301–331.

8. Jennifer Coates, *Women, men, and language* (London: Longman, 1986).

9. Connie C. Eble ("Etiquette books as linguistic authority," in *The second LACUS forum, 1975*, ed. Peter A. Reich, 468-475 [Columbia, S.C.: Hornbeam, 1976]) cites Gerald Carson (*The polite Americans: A wide-angle view of our more or less good manners over three hundred years* [New York: William Morrow, 1966], p. 55) for the "cleft stick" reference. In Carson's words, "In East Hampton, New York, cleft sticks were slipped over too-busy tongues" (p. 469).

Authors who discuss the historical attitude that women talk too much include Dennis Baron, Connie Eble, Alette Hill, and Cheris Kramarae. Deborah James and Janice Drakich have written an article ("Understanding gender differences in amount of talk," in *Gender and Conversational Interaction*, ed. Deborah Tannen [New York: Oxford University Press, 1993], pp. 281-312) reviewing research that aims to determine who talks more, women or men.

cal ones, modern stereotypes are little different from those expressed in the old proverbs. Women are believed to talk too much. Yet study after study finds that it is men who talk more—at meetings, in mixed-group discussions, and in classrooms where girls or young women sit next to boys or young men. For example, communication researchers Barbara and Gene Eakins tape-recorded and studied seven university faculty meetings.[10] They found that, with one exception, men spoke more often and, without exception, spoke for a longer time. The men's turns ranged from 10.66 to 17.07 seconds, whereas the women's turns ranged from 3 to 10 seconds. In other words, the women's longest turns were still shorter than the men's shortest turns.

When a public lecture is followed by questions from the floor or a talk show host opens the phones, the first voice to be heard asking a question is almost always a man's. And when they ask questions or offer comments from the audience, men tend to talk longer. Linguist Marjorie Swacker has recorded question-and-answer sessions at academic conferences.[11] Women were highly visible as speakers at these conferences; they presented 40.7 percent of the papers at the conferences studied and made up 42 percent of the audiences. But when it came to volunteering and being called on to ask questions, women contributed only 27.4 percent. Furthermore, the women's questions, on average, took less than half as much time as the men's. (The mean was 23.1 seconds for women, 52.7 for men.) This happened, Swacker shows, because men (but not women) tended to preface their questions with statements, ask more than one question, and follow up the speaker's answer with another question or comment.

I have observed this pattern at my own lectures, which concern issues of direct relevance to women. Regardless of the proportion of women and men in

the audience, men almost invariably ask the first question, more questions, and longer questions. In these situations, women often feel that men are talking too much. I recall one discussion period following a lecture I gave to a group assembled in a bookstore. The group was composed mostly of women, but most of the discussion was being conducted by men in the audience. At one point, a man sitting in the middle was talking at such great length that several women in the front rows began shifting in their seats and rolling their eyes at me. Ironically, what he was going on about was how frustrated he feels when he has to listen to women going on and on about topics he finds boring and unimportant.

Who talks more, then, women or men? The answer was crystallized for me in the following experience. I was sitting in a suburban living room, speaking to a women's group that had invited men to join them for the occasion of my talk about communication between women and men. During the discussion, one man was particularly talkative, full of lengthy comments and explanations. When I made the observation that women often complain that their husbands don't talk to them enough, this man volunteered that he heartily agreed. He gestured toward his wife, who sat silently beside him on the couch throughout the evening, and said, "She's the talker in our family."

Everyone in the room burst into laughter. The man looked puzzled and hurt. "It's true," he explained. "When I come home from work, I usually have nothing to say, but she never runs out. If it weren't for her, we'd spend the whole evening in silence." Another woman expressed a similar paradox about her husband: "When we go out, he's the life of the party. If I happen to be in another room, I can always hear his voice above the others. But when we're home, he doesn't have that much to say. I do most of the talking."

The seemingly contradictory evidence is reconciled by the difference between what I call *public* and *private speaking*. More men feel comfortable doing "public speaking," whereas more women feel comfortable doing "private" speaking. Another way of capturing these differences is by using the terms *report-talk* and *rapport-talk*.

10. Barbara Westbrook Eakins and R. Gene Eakins, *Sex differences in communication* (Boston: Houghton Mifflin, 1978).

11. Marjorie Swacker, "Women's verbal behavior at learned and professional conferences," in *The sociology of the languages of American women*, ed. Betty Lou Dubois and Isabel Crouch (San Antonio: Trinity University, 1976), pp. 155–160.

For most women, the language of conversation is primarily a language of rapport: a way of establishing connections and negotiating relationships. Emphasis is placed on displaying similarities and matching experiences. From childhood, girls criticize peers who try to stand out or appear better than others. People feel their closest connections at home or in settings where they *feel* at home—with one or a few people they feel close to and comfortable with—in other words, during private speaking. But even the most public situations can be approached like private speaking.

For most men, talk is primarily a means to preserve independence and negotiate and maintain status in a hierarchical social order. This is done by exhibiting knowledge or skill and by holding center stage through such verbal performance as storytelling, jokes, or imparting information. From childhood, men learn to use talking as a way to get and keep attention. So they are more comfortable speaking in larger groups made up of people they know less well—in the broadest sense, "public speaking." But even the most private situations can be approached like public speaking, more like giving a report than establishing rapport.

What is the source of the stereotype that women talk a lot? Dale Spender suggests that most people feel instinctively (if not consciously) that women, like children, should be seen and not heard, so any amount of talk from them seems like too much. Studies have shown that if women and men talk equally in a group, people think the women talked more. So there is truth to Spender's view.[12] But an-

other explanation is that men think women talk a lot because they hear women talking in situations where men would not: on the telephone, or in social situations with friends, when they are not discussing topics that men find inherently interesting, or, like the couple at the women's group, at home alone—in other words, in private speaking.

DIFFERENT CONCEPTIONS OF THE COMFORTS OF HOME

Home is the setting for an American icon that features the silent man and talkative woman. And this icon, which grows out of the different goals and habits I have been describing, explains why the complaint most often voiced by women about the men with whom they are intimate is "He doesn't talk to me"—and the second most frequent is "He doesn't listen to me."[13]

A woman who wrote to Ann Landers is typical:

My husband never speaks to me when he comes home from work. When I ask, "How did everything go today?" he says, "Rough . . ." or "It's a jungle out there." (We live in Jersey and he works in New York City.)

It's a different story when we have guests or go visiting. Paul is the gabbiest guy in the crowd—a real spellbinder. He comes up with the most interesting stories. People hang on every word. I think to myself, "Why doesn't he ever tell *me* these things?"

This has been going on for 38 years. Paul started to go quiet on me after 10 years of marriage. I could never figure out why. Can you solve the mystery?

—The Invisible Woman

Ann Landers suggests that the husband may not want to talk because he is tired when he comes

12. The observation that women are thought to talk more if they talk equally has been made by many, including Dale Spender (*Man made language* [London: Routledge and Kegan Paul, 1980]) and Carole Edelsky ("Who's got the floor?" *Language in Society* 10 [1981]: 383–421, reprinted in *Gender and Conversational Interaction*, ed. Deborah Tannen [New York: Oxford University Press, 1993], pp. 189–227). Myra Sadker and David Sadker ("Sexism in the schoolroom of the eighties," *Psychology Today* (March 1995), pp. 54–57; see also *Failing at fairness: How America's schools cheat girls* [New York: Charles Scribner's Sons, 1994]) report that teachers who were shown a film of classroom discussion overwhelmingly thought the girls were talking more when in fact the boys were talking three times more.

13. Andrew Hacker, reviewing *Husbands and wives: A nationwide study of marriage*, by Anthony Pietropinto and Jacqueline Simenauer (New York: Times Books, 1979), has also observed that women frequently give lack of communication as a reason for divorce, whereas men who were parties to the same marriages rarely do (Hacker, "Divorce à la Mode," *New York Review of Books*, May 3, 1979, p. 24).

home from work. Yet women who work come home tired, too, and they are nonetheless eager to tell their partners or friends everything that happened to them during the day and what these fleeting, daily dramas made them think and feel.

Sources as lofty as studies conducted by psychologists, as down-to-earth as letters written to advice columnists, and as sophisticated as movies and plays come up with the same insight: men's silence at home is a disappointment to women. Again and again, women complain, "He seems to have everything to say to everyone else and nothing to say to me."

The film *Divorce American Style* opens with a conversation in which Debbie Reynolds is claiming that she and Dick Van Dyke don't communicate, and he is protesting that he tells her everything that's on his mind. The doorbell interrupts their quarrel, and husband and wife compose themselves before opening the door to greet their guests with cheerful smiles.

Behind closed doors, many couples are having conversations like this. Like the character played by Debbie Reynolds, women feel men don't communicate. Like the husband played by Dick Van Dyke, men feel wrongly accused. How can she be convinced that he doesn't tell her anything when he is equally convinced that he tells her everything that's on his mind? How can women and men have such different ideas about the same conversations?

STATUS AND CONNECTION

The difference between public and private speaking, or report-talk and rapport-talk, can be understood in terms of status and connection. It is not surprising that women are most comfortable talking when they feel safe and close, among friends and equals, whereas men feel comfortable talking when there is a need to establish and maintain their status in a group. But the situation is complex, because status and connection are bought with the same currency. What seems like a bid for status could be intended as a display of closeness, and what seems like distancing may have been intended to avoid the appearance of pulling rank.

Hurtful and unjustified misinterpretations can be avoided by understanding the conversational styles of the other gender.

When men do all the talking at meetings, many women—including researchers—see them as "dominating" the meeting, intentionally preventing women from participating, publicly flexing their higher-status muscles. But the *result* that men do most of the talking does not necessarily mean that men *intend* to prevent women from speaking. Those who readily speak up assume that others are as free as they are to take the floor. In this sense, men's speaking out freely can be seen as evidence that they assume women are at the same level of status: "We are all equals." The metamessage of their behavior could be, "competing for the floor." If this is indeed the intention (and I believe it often, though not always, is), a woman can recognize women's lack of participation at meetings and take measures to redress the imbalance, without blaming men for intentionally locking them out.

The culprit, then, is not an individual man or even men's styles alone but the difference between women's and men's styles. If that is the case, then both can make adjustments. A woman can push herself to speak up without being invited or begin to speak without waiting for what seems a polite pause. But the adjustment should not be one-sided. A man can learn that a woman who is not accustomed to speaking up in groups is *not* as free as he is to do so. Someone who is waiting for a nice long pause before asking her question does *not* find the stage set for her appearance, as do those who are not awaiting a pause, the moment after (or before) another speaker stops talking. Someone who expects to be invited to speak ("You haven't said much, Millie. What do you think?") is not accustomed to leaping in and claiming the floor for herself. As in so many areas, being admitted as an equal is not in itself assurance of equal opportunity, if one is not accustomed to playing the game in the way it is being played. Being admitted to a dance does not ensure the participation of someone who has learned to dance to a different rhythm.

When something goes wrong, people look around for a source to blame: either the person they are trying to communicate with ("You're demanding, stubborn, self-centered") or the group that the other person belongs to ("All women are demanding"; "All men are self-centered"). Some generous-minded people blame the relationship ("We just can't communicate"). But underneath or overlaid on these types of blame cast outward, most people believe that something is wrong with them.

If individual people or particular relationships were to blame, there wouldn't be so many different people having the same problems. The real problem is conversational style. Women and men have different ways of talking. Even with the best intentions, trying to settle the problem through talk can only make things worse if it is ways of talking that are causing trouble in the first place.

NO

Women and Men Talking:

Are They Worlds Apart?

Elizabeth Aries

Differences in the ways women and men communicate have recently been of great interest to the general public, as evidenced by the popularity of such best-sellers as Deborah Tannen's *You Just Don't Understand: Women and Men in Conversation* (1990), which promote a polarized depiction of men's and women's styles of interaction. Tannen argues that men approach conversation with a focus on status and independence, whereas women approach conversation with a focus on intimacy and connection, making communication between the sexes problematic.

Tannen fails, however, to give serious consideration to the large body of research on gender and conversational interaction carried out over the past twenty-five years in psychology, sociology, linguistics, sociolinguistics, communication studies, women's studies, and organizational behavior. As I argue elsewhere (Aries, 1996), my review of this literature suggests a different story, particularly when we address the following questions:

1. How different are the styles of interaction of men and women? Is it accurate to say that most men use a different style of interaction from most women?

2. Do the differences we perceive between men and women result from gender, or are they caused by such other variables as social roles or status?

3. Do sex-related differences in conversational style emerge consistently across different contexts, or are they only found in selected contexts?

4. How do gender stereotypes shape our perceptions of and responses to speakers? How do we perceive and treat men and women differently even when they display the same behavior?

The Magnitude of the Differences

Tannen makes generalizations that contrast men and women. She claims, for example, that women "speak and hear a language of connection and intimacy" (1990, p. 42), that for women, conversations are "negotiations for closeness in which people try to seek and give confirmation and support, and to reach consensus" (p. 25). Men, in contrast, "speak and hear a language of status and independence" (p. 42). Men engage the world "as individuals in a hierarchical social order" (p. 24) in which they try to maintain the upper hand and exhibit their knowledge and skill. We need to ask for how many men and women are these claims true.

Tannen argues that "a larger percentage of women or men *as a group* talk in a particular way, or individual women and men *are more likely* to talk one way or the other" (1994, p. 15). In her attempt to describe group differences between men and women, she acknowledges only briefly how much members of the same sex differ from one another. People of the same sex have a range of values, attributes, and styles, not one style. Many individuals do not find themselves described by the polarized characteristics that have been put forth of men and women. The variability that exists within members of the same sex gets overshadowed by a focus on group differences.

If we are concerned only with statistically significant differences, then gender differences abound. However, a statistically "significant" finding can result even when there is a very small average difference between men and women. A statistically significant difference is not necessarily a sizable or meaningful difference. A 5 percent difference between men and women can be distorted to suggest that all men are alike and all women are alike, and that men differ from women. A different picture emerges of gender differences in interaction if we pay attention to effect sizes (the magnitude of the difference between men and women) rather than to statistical significance.

The question usually posed is: do men as a group differ from women as a group? We can reframe that question and ask how big that difference is, or we might further ask how good a prediction we can make about how a person will behave based only on knowledge of gender. Research shows that gender generally accounts for less than 10 percent of the variability in social behavior and more typically accounts for less than 5 percent (Eagly, 1987; Hyde and Linn, 1986). The remaining 90 percent of the variability in how people interact can not be accounted for without knowledge of many other aspects of the individuals involved and the situation in which they are embedded.

The data reveal that the behavior of most men and women is much more similar than it is different. The men and women whose behavior falls at opposite ends of the distributions for their sex may display contrasting styles of interaction. When we speak of gender differences we often take a minority of men and women as characteristic of their sex. Let me take an example from the literature on self-disclosure. It is generally held that men share less personal information about themselves with their close friends than women do, that men reveal less about themselves, their close relationships, their doubts and fears. In a study of adolescent friendship, which included more than one thousand adolescents, James Youniss and Jacqueline Smollar (1985) found that females were more intimately disclosing with their same-sex friends than males were. However, this difference was produced by a third of males reporting that their friendships lacked intimacy and that they were guarded or defensive with their friends. Although the majority of male friendships involved mutual intimacy, the minority of men whose friendships lacked intimacy were taken as typical. Our stereotypes of men and women do not necessarily characterize most men or women.

STATUS AND SOCIAL ROLES

Are the differences we perceive between men and women really caused by gender or could they be caused by other variables like social roles or status, which co-vary with gender? Tannen draws conclusions about the role of gender in shaping people's behavior without considering the current roles and social contexts that shape those behaviors.

A division of labor in contemporary society allocates different work and responsibilities to men and women. Although there certainly is variability within gender, overall men and women are situated differently in society. Overall, men are allocated to roles with greater power and status and requiring more instrumental competence, leading to the perception that men are more agentic and task-oriented than women (e.g., Eagly, 1987). Likewise, women are believed to be communal and emotionally expressive because they are assigned to domestic roles and occupations that require these traits. Men and women use different social skills because of their disproportionate representation of various social roles.

According to a phenomenon called the "fundamental attribution error" (Ross, 1977), people have a pervasive tendency to attribute behavior to individual dispositions and to underestimate the importance of the situational context in shaping that behavior. We see men in social roles and statuses that differ from those held by women and attribute the differences in their behavior to their gender rather than to their status or role. People who hold positions of superior power and status behave differently than subordinates, and more men than women hold positions of power and status. Variables other than gender serve equally well to explain the differences between men's and women's styles of interaction.

Many gender differences in social behavior may be attributed to differences in the status of men and women. For example, in the study by Eakins and Eakins (1983) of mixed-sex university faculty meetings in a university department, men took more turns and interrupted more than women. This study is often cited as evidence that men are more dominant than women. However, turn-taking and interruptions followed a hierarchy of status based on rank and length of time in the department. The two lowest-ranking women were interrupted during half of their turns at talk. The woman who was interrupted most frequently held no Ph.D., and the woman interrupted least frequently had the greatest seniority. Did gender or status produce the differences in interruptions and speaking time?

Gender differences in language use have been found to vary with social roles. William O'Barr and Bowman Atkins (1980) recorded 150 hours of trials in a North Carolina superior criminal court involving witnesses of both sexes. They looked at a variety of speech features taken to be characteristic of "women's language," such as hedges (e.g., "kind of," "I guess," "perhaps"), super-polite forms ("I'd really appreciate it if"), tag questions (e.g., a statement with a short question tagged onto the end), intensifiers (e.g., "very," "so"), and question intonation in declarative form. They found considerable variability in how much women used "women's language." Those women who used "women's language" frequently were housewives, whereas women who were well educated and professional used this language less frequently. Likewise, those men who used "women's language" most frequently held subordinate, lower-status jobs or were unemployed. O'Barr and Atkins argued that "women's language" may have more to do with social powerlessness than with gender.

Research in the laboratory by Cathryn Johnson (1994) shows that when men and women are assigned to a managerial role and given the same formal legitimate authority, they are quite similar in their patterns of conversation. Cathryn Johnson looked at length of time talking, interruptions, back-channel responses (e.g., "um-hum," "yeah"), and disclaimers. The demands of the managerial role provided the overriding influence on conversational behavior: managers spoke differently from subordinates, but there were no gender differences.

When men and women are placed in the same social roles, their behavior is quite similar. Research by Barbara Risman (1987) shows single fathers who have sole responsibility for raising children to be more similar to mothers, single or married, than to married fathers. Research by Sara Snodgrass (1985, 1992) shows that the interpersonal sensitivity often attributed to women may have more to do with their subordinate role than with their gender. Snodgrass assigned subjects to dyads in which one member was the leader. Subordinates showed more sensitivity to leaders' feelings than leaders did to subordinates' feelings, but there were no gender differences.

How much we express dominance and submissiveness may have more to do with the roles we play than to our gender. D. S. Moskowitz and colleagues (1994) asked 181 adults who worked at least thirty hours a week to monitor their social interactions for twenty days, filling out a form for every interaction that lasted at least five minutes. How much people displayed dominance at work could not be predicted by their gender, but it could be predicted by their social role. People showed more dominance and less submissiveness toward people they supervised than toward bosses or coworkers. Supervisory roles called forth more dominance behavior, whereas subordinate roles called forth more submissive behavior. Lillian Rubin (1994) reports that when women entered the workforce, they entered family decision-making more forcefully than they did when they were not employed outside the home. Having entered the workforce, women felt that they had the right to have their say, to contradict their husbands, and to make demands on husbands for childcare and housework. The difference in their conversational style came from a change in their social roles.

Although we are likely to perceive many differences between the behavior of men and women in our daily lives, gender may not account for the differences; they may result from differences in power and social roles held by men and women. Research shows that men and women act quite similarly when we place them in identical roles and give them equal access to power.

THE SITUATIONAL CONTEXT OF INTERACTION

Do gender differences in conversational style emerge consistently regardless of context, or do they only appear in selected contexts? Gender is only one of many determinants of behavior in interaction. The characteristics of the participants (e.g., sex, age, race, class, ethnicity, sexual orientation) in an encounter, the setting of the interaction, the topic of conversation, and the sex composition of the group all influence the way people behave in an interaction and thereby influence the degree to which gender differences are manifested.

Our cultural stereotypes of men and women are based on White middle- to upper-middle-class samples. Caution must be exercised in extending this portrayal to "men" and "women" in general. We must be wary of talking about "men" differing from "women" when our findings pertain only to selective groups of men and women. In the preface to *Talking from Nine to Five*, Tannen carefully notes that the patterns she describes pertain to "mostly (but not exclusively) middle-class Americans of European background working in offices at the present time" (1994, p. 14).

Racial differences, for example, have been found in the expression of directness and concerns about politeness (Tracy & Eisenberg, 1990/1991). In a series of interviews with Black and White women about their styles of communication with close friends of the same race, Black women used words like "confrontive" and "quick tempered" to characterize themselves and others, whereas White women used words like "non-confrontive," "withdrawn," and "tactful" (McCollough, 1987, cited in Kramarae, 1990). What have been taken to be characteristic of men and women may in fact characterize certain types of men and women in certain contexts.

Tannen argues that if men do all the talking at a meeting, they are not trying to dominate it. Men assume that women are equal competitors for the floor, she writes, and gender troubles result because women are not accustomed to speaking up and tend to wait for a polite pause. But the issue is more complex. Women compete equally for the floor in some situations and do not in others. Let us consider first the situational norms that govern behavior in an interaction.

Leadership is associated with masculinity, and the behavior of men and women is shaped by sex-role norms for behavior. Edwin Megargee (1969) tested subjects on the Dominance Scale of the California Psychological Inventory, forming single-sex and mixed-sex pairs that consisted of one high-dominance and one low-dominance individual. Partners were asked to pick a leader to do a task. Seventy percent of high-dominance women assumed leadership over low-dominance women, but only 20 percent of high-dominance women assumed leadership over low-dominance men. Although personality was a powerful predictor of leadership for women in all-female groups, the study shows the greater power of sex-role norms over personality in shaping behavior in this mixed-sex encounter.

When dominance behavior is legitimized for women, women display it just as men do. Christopher Stitt and his colleagues (1983) studied six-person groups with a leader and five subordinates. Leaders were instructed how to lead their group and were told to display either an autocratic or a democratic style. Male and female leaders displayed comparable leadership behavior in both democratic and autocratic leadership conditions. Thus, when autocratic behavior was legitimized, women made decisions without considering opinions of other group members, were aggressive, and gave orders.

Let us consider the sex composition of the group in which interaction takes place. Men place greater emphasis on dominance and hierarchy in all-male groups than females do in all-female groups, but this gender difference is reduced in mixed groups. I conducted a study of the interaction patterns and thematic content of all-male, all-female, and mixed-sex groups that met for 7.5 hours to get to know one another (Aries, 1976). Females in all-female groups talked about themselves and their feelings, families, and other close relationships, whereas males in all-male groups had a greater focus on competition and status, showing more concern with where they stood in relation to one another. All-male groups established a more stable rank order of speaking, with the same males being high speakers in every meeting. In all-female groups, females who were absent or quiet in one session were encouraged to speak in another session, producing more flexibility in the rank order of speaking.

These findings match the conversational styles of men and women Tannen describes. However, in mixed-sex groups, men talked more personally and showed less of an orientation toward status and dominance than they did with other men. Other studies also report that men talk more personally and show more of an interpersonal orientation with females than with males (Dindia & Allen, 1992; Reis, Senchak, & Solomon, 1985).

Let us consider the length of interaction. In a meta-analysis of fifty-eight data sets examining gender and leadership emergence in initially leaderless groups, Alice Eagly and Steven Karau (1991) found that men are more likely to emerge as leaders in groups formed for fewer than twenty minutes (effect size d=.58). Nevertheless, the magnitude of the difference between men and women decreases as the length of the group's duration increases: for single-session meetings lasting more than twenty minutes the effect size drops to .38, and for studies of interaction that last more than a single session the effect size drops to .09. Thus, the overall finding that men are more likely to emerge as leaders than women is based primarily on interaction in very brief or one-time encounters.

Gender is much less salient in the determination of patterns of communication when groups meet over time. Susan Wheelan and Anthony Verdi (1992) studied a four-day group-relations conference attended by twenty-seven adults. Sessions ran for 4.5 to 7.5 hours. During the first nine thirty-minute periods, men were more task-oriented than women, whereas women were more expressive (i.e., showing expression of warmth, friendship, and support) than men, but this gender difference disappeared in the later sessions. Tannen's claim that men are comfortable with "report-talk" and women are at ease with "rapport-talk" characterizes the early sessions, but over time in groups men and women engaged equally in both forms of talk.

Tannen argues that "women feel men don't communicate" (1990, p. 79) and attributes the problem to conversational style. She cites the case of a woman, married for thirty-eight years, who claimed that her husband had gone quiet on her after ten years of marriage (1990, p. 78). Tannen takes this husband as typical of men's failure to talk to their wives, overlooking the fact that this man *did* talk to his wife for the first ten years of his marriage. The problem could not, then, have arisen from gender differences in style but must have resulted from other changes in the context of their marriage.

Men are capable of sharing intimately and can do so when the situation demands it. When Harry Reis and his colleagues (1985) asked men and women to come to the laboratory and to have an intimate conversation with their same-sex best friend—to discuss something important and to reveal thoughts, feelings, and emotions—they found no gender differences in self-disclosure.

In summary, these studies demonstrate that men and women do not show a single style of behavior; rather, they display different styles depending on the demands of the situation, the characteristics of their conversational partners, the length of their interaction, or the setting of the interaction. Men and women select a style depending on the context in which they find themselves. In some contexts the styles of men and women will be different; in others they will be similar.

GENDER STEREOTYPES AND THE PERCEPTION OF SPEECH

How do gender stereotypes shape our perceptions and evaluations of speakers? Since the 1970s feminists have argued that gender differences reside less in the individual than in the eye of the beholder (e.g., Grady, 1979). The sex of an individual acts as a stimulus variable. We immediately recognize each participant in conversational interaction as a male or a female. To the extent that we hold stereotyped beliefs about men and women, these beliefs can lead us to form different expectations about what male and female participants are like and how they will behave and can cause us to perceive speakers to conform to stereotyped conceptions even when they do not.

Decades of research has shown widespread agreement among people about the characteristics of men and women (Broverman, Vogel, Broverman, Clarkson, & Rosenkrantz, 1972). Men are characterized by a cluster of instrumental traits: they are seen to be leaders, to be dominant, aggressive, independent, objective, and competitive. Women, in contrast, are characterized by a cluster of affective traits: they are seen to be emotional, subjective, tactful, and aware of the feelings of others. Gender stereotypes have changed relatively little over the past twenty years despite considerable changes in women's status in society (Bergen & Williams, 1991; Werner & LaRussa, 1985).

Stereotypes have the power to cause us to bend our perceptions in the direction of expectations. Nora Newcombe and Dianne Arnkoff (1979) had subjects listen to tape recordings of conversations in which males and females used tag questions and qualifiers equally. Females were perceived to use tag questions and qualifiers more frequently than men. The same speech can be perceived differently depending on whether it is attributed to a male or to a female speaker. Philip Smith (1985) had subjects listen to tape recordings of either males or females reading the identical prose passage and give their impressions of what the speaker was like as a person. Male speakers were judged to be more competent, arrogant, aggressive, and dominant, whereas female speakers were judged to be more expressive of emotions, sensitive, and feminine.

Evidence suggests that men display more dominance and assertiveness because they are assumed to possess greater competency in performing group tasks. Wendy Wood and Stephen Karten (1986) studied four-person mixed-sex groups. When no expectations were given about the competency of group members, subjects perceived men to be more competent than women, and men were found to speak more and engage in more active task behavior. When experimenters led subjects to believe that women were more competent at the task than men, behavior was based on perceptions of competency rather than gender, and there were no gender differences in task behavior. Other studies have similarly found that when expectations are altered and women in mixed-sex groups are believed to have greater task competency than men, gender differences in leadership and influence are reduced (Pugh & Wahrman, 1983, 1985; Wagner, Ford, & Ford, 1986).

When men and women behave in an identical fashion they may still be evaluated differently in accordance with gender-role stereotypes, causing women to be evaluated more negatively on the dimension of competency. In a study of interaction in groups Patricia Bradley (1981) had male or female confederates argue a position contrary to other group members. Half the confederates advanced arguments with support, giving evidence and factual data; the other half used no supportive arguments. Half the confederates in each condition used tag questions and disclaimers, whereas the other half did not. Bradley found that male confederates who advanced arguments without support were viewed as more intelligent, knowledgeable, and influential than female confederates who advanced arguments without support. Females who used tag questions and disclaimers were seen as less intelligent, knowledgeable, and dynamic than males who used them. Although responses to males varied only slightly if they used tag questions and disclaimers, women were perceived as less dynamic, knowledgeable, and intelligent when using them. Bradley's study provides evidence to suggest that when men adopt women's language they do not suffer the same negative evaluation in the realm of competence that women do and that when women display the same behavior as men they are viewed as less intelligent and knowledgeable.

When women use language, enter into roles, or exhibit behaviors stereotypically associated with men, they are evaluated more negatively than men in performing those roles or exhibiting those behaviors. When a woman is dominant and forceful she violates the stereotype of femininity, whereas a male displaying the same behavior fulfills expectations of masculinity. Women who interrupted conversation were rated as more aggressive, competitive, and ambitious than men who interrupt (Wiley & Wooley, 1988). Female applicants who used powerful speech were seen as more aggressive than similar male applicants (Wiley & Eskilson, 1985).

Women are caught in a double bind. When women exhibit behavior that goes against expectations for femininity, they are evaluated more negatively than men who perform the identical behavior; they are seen as aggressive and competitive, violating norms for femininity. When women use language stereotypically associated with women, they are viewed as lacking in instrumental competency.

The differing attributions and evaluations we make of women and men can become self-fulfilling prophecies for behavior. In a study of West Point cadets, Robert Rice and his associates (1980) demonstrated that the attitudes group members hold toward women can manifest themselves in group behavior that in turn affects the behavior of female leaders. They studied all-male groups with female leaders. Some groups were composed of men who held liberal attitudes toward women's roles in society, whereas other groups were composed of men who held traditional attitudes toward women's roles. When group members held liberal attitudes toward women's roles, female leaders in those groups initiated more structure and played a more important role. In groups of male followers with traditional attitudes, female leaders were impeded in their potential to lead. Thus, men's attitudes toward women were manifested in their behavior, which in turn affected the behavior of female leaders. Women became less effective leaders when men believed that women should not be leaders.

Gender stereotypes should concern us for several reasons. First, they may dictate what we notice and bias our perceptions in the direction of expectation. Deborah Tannen elucidates gender differences with the goal of helping women and men understand and respond to one another better. In the process, however, her work encourages people to notice and attend to differences rather than to similarities, to perceive men and women in accordance with stereotypes that may not accurately depict their behavior or intentions.

A second cause for concern is that gender stereotypes shape behavior. They not only describe behavior but prescribe it, dictating how men and women "should" behave. People behave in ways that are not internalized but that are prescribed for them because those who deviate from traditional sex-role norms pay a price. Punishment for deviation helps to maintain gender distinctions. Women who violate feminine norms and talk in a masculine way or display masculine behavior in male roles are evaluated more negatively than men who display the same behaviors or speech.

Stereotypes also shape behavior by serving as self-fulfilling prophecies. People begin to act in ways that support other people's gender-role expectations about them. Finally, stereotypes have a critical effect on the evaluation of speakers. A bias favors male speakers on the dimension of instrumental competency; men are evaluated more positively than women on this dimension even when men and women display the same behavior.

RETHINKING GENDER

It is time to rethink our understanding of gender, to move away from the notion that men and women have two contrasting styles of interaction that are acquired during socialization, a notion that is widely being promoted by Tannen in the popular press. We need to move from a conceptualization of gender as an attribute or style of behavior to an understanding of gender as something people do in social interaction, as the performance of gender-related behaviors in certain contexts (West & Zimmerman, 1987). As Janis Bohan proposes, "None of us is feminine or is masculine or fails to be either of those. In particular contexts people do feminine, in others, they do masculine" (1993, p. 13). Muriel Dimen (1991) suggests that we should not associate autonomy with men and dependence with women or activity with men and passivity with women. These polarities are "but different moments of the self" (p. 348) that are activated in different contexts. People display contradictory behaviors as they encounter different social norms and pressures.

Although both sexes perform behaviors labeled masculine and feminine, it is problematic to use these labels for behaviors. Whereas behavior oriented toward achieving status is associated with men and behavior oriented toward establishing intimacy and connection is linked with women, both types of behavior are displayed by men and women; they are not sex-specific. Support work in conversation is not carried out solely by women. Teachers, group facilitators, clinicians, and hosts—male and female—all use support work to draw other people into conversation (e.g., Holmes, 1984; Cameron, McAlinden, & O'Leary, 1988).

The problems in communication that Tannen describes are widespread, but they are neither unique to men and women nor accounted for by gender. Many of these differences appear in other relationships. For example, Tannen claims that when women have troubles they want empathy, "the gift of understanding" (1990, p. 50), whereas men take the role of problem-solver and offer solutions. This problem commonly arises between parents and children. A mother, made anxious by her child's troubles, may rush in to offer solutions when what the child most needs and desires is empathy, not advice. Thus, a woman in the role of mother may show precisely the conversational style Tannen claims is characteristic of men in the role of husband.

Tannen views male-female conversation as cross-cultural communication. She draws on the argument put forth by Daniel Maltz and Ruth Borker (1982) that boys and girls interact in childhood primarily in single-sex groups and thus grow up in two separate sociolinguistic subcultures that have different rules for speaking and different norms for interpreting conversation. The two-cultures approach postulates that difficulties in communication between men and women arise when men and women attempt to talk together as friends and equals in conversation because of a clash of conversational styles.

The two-cultures approach to understanding gender differences in conversational style has a number of limitations. First, the coherence of male and female subcultures in childhood has been exaggerated. In a study of children's play in elementary school, Barrie Thorne (1993) notes that we arrive at a contrasting picture of the cultures of boys and girls only by singling out those children who are most visible and dominant and marginalizing others. We fail to notice the children who do not fit the norm—for example, the children who are not White and privileged by their class or the boys who are shy and who don't like sports.

Second, although children may choose same-sex playmates as preferred partners, they interact daily inside and outside school with the opposite sex. Boys and girls grow up in families and in neighborhoods populated by males and females. Children have countless experiences communicating with people of both sexes; they do not learn to communicate in gender-segregated worlds. They learn to display different styles of interaction in different contexts; they do not learn a single gender-related style. A girl may display dominance, be bossy, and give orders to a younger sibling but show deference and follow orders from an older friend.

The two-cultures approach fails to recognize the importance of sexual inequalities at the societal level. It does not address the fact that men are accorded greater power, status, and privilege than women. Men and women do not simply come together as "friends and equals" (Maltz & Borker, 1982, p. 212). Cheris Kramarae (1990) argues that the unequal status of men and women shapes not only mixed-sex interaction but single-sex interaction as well. "Men are *men* because of their insistence upon the subordinate category *women*; much of their understanding of their behaviors and power (whether they are together in the corporate boardroom or on the street corner) comes from their consistently reiterated *otherness* from women" (p. 350).

Knowledge of people's gender alone will not lead to an accurate prediction of how they will behave. Behavior depends on more than the internalization into personality of unique styles associated with masculinity and femininity. People's behavior can be accounted for by race, class, ethnicity, and sexual orientation; by how they are situated in the social hierarchy; by differences in social roles and the normative expectations of particular settings; by cultural norms about how men and women should behave toward each other; and by the consequences of deviating from expectations. When the norms, roles, and expectations change, so do men's and women's behavior. Gender is not the primary determinant of behavior. In many settings other explanatory variables, such as race, class, and social position, are much more powerful predictors of behavior than gender. Gender is sometimes central and definitive, sometimes marginal and contingent. The fostering of gender stereotypes by books such as Deborah Tannen's sustains current realities, justifies current social inequalities, and keeps those inequalities in place. We must think carefully about the difference we choose to make out of gender differences.

REFERENCES

Aries, E. (1976). Interaction patterns and themes of male, female, and mixed groups. *Small Group Behavior, 7* (1), 7–18.

Aries, E. (1996). *Men and women in interaction: Reconsidering the differences.* New York: Oxford University Press.

Bergen, D. J., & Williams, J. E. (1991). Sex stereotypes in the United States revisited, 1972–1988. *Sex Roles, 24* (7/8), 413–423.

Bohan, J. S. (1993). Regarding gender: Essentialism, constructionism, and feminist psychology. *Psychology of Women Quarterly, 17,* 5–21.

Bradley, P. H. (1981). The folk-linguistics of women's speech: An empirical examination. *Communication Monographs, 48,* 73–90.

Broverman, I. K., Vogel, S. R., Broverman, D. M., Clarkson, F. E., & Rosenkrantz, P. S. (1972). Sex-role stereotypes: A current appraisal. *Journal of Social Issues, 28,* 59–78.

Cameron, D., McAlinden, F., & O'Leary, K. (1988). Lakoff in context: The social and linguistic functions of tag questions. In J. Coates & D. Cameron (Eds.), *Women in their speech communities: New perspectives on language and sex* (pp. 74–93). New York: Longman.

Dimen, M. (1991). Deconstructing difference: Gender, splitting, and transitional space. *Psychoanalytic Dialogues, 1* (3), 335–352.

Dindia, K., & Allen, M. (1992). Sex differences in self-disclosure: A meta-analysis. *Psychological Bulletin, 112* (1), 106–124.

Eagly, A. H. (1987). *Sex differences in social behavior: A social-role interpretation.* Hillsdale, N.J.: Erlbaum.

Eagly, A. H., & Johnson, B. T. (1990). Gender and leadership style: A meta-analysis. *Psychological Bulletin, 108* (2), 233–256.

Eagly, A. H., & Karau, S. J. (1991). Gender and the emergence of leaders: A meta-analysis. *Journal of Personality and Social Psychology, 60* (5), 685–710.

Eakins, B., & Eakins, R. G. (1983). Verbal turn-taking and exchanges in faculty dialogue. In B. L. Dubois and I. Crouch (Eds.), *Proceedings of the conference on the Sociology of the Languages of American Women* (pp. 53–62). San Antonio, Tex.: Trinity University.

Grady, K. E. (1979). Androgyny reconsidered. In J. H. Williams (Ed.), *Psychology of women: Selected readings* (pp. 172–177). New York: Norton.

Holmes, J. (1984). "Women's language": A functional approach. *General Linguistics, 24* (3), 149–178.

Hyde, J. S., & Linn, M. C. (Eds.). (1986). *The psychology of gender: Advances through meta-analysis.* Baltimore: Johns Hopkins University Press.

Johnson, C. (1994). Gender, legitimate authority, and leader-subordinate conversations. *American Sociological Review, 59,* 122–135.

Kramarae, C. (1990). Changing the complexion of gender in language research. In H. Giles & W. P. Robinson (Eds.), *Handbook of language and social psychology* (pp. 345–361). Chichester: John Wiley and Sons.

Maltz, D. N., & Borker, R. A. (1982). A cultural approach to male-female miscommunication. In J. J. Gumperz (Ed.), *Language and social identity* (pp. 196–216). Cambridge: Cambridge University Press.

Megargee, E. I. (1969). Influence of sex roles on the manifestation of leadership. *Journal of Applied Psychology, 53* (5), 377–382.

Moskowitz, D. S., Jung Suh, E., & Desaulniers, J. (1994). Situational influences on gender differences in agency and communion. *Journal of Personality and Social Psychology, 66* (4), 753–761.

Newcombe, N., & Arnkoff, D. B. (1979). Effects of speech style and sex of speaker on person perception. *Journal of Personality and Social Psychology, 37* (8), 1293–1303.

O'Barr, W., & Atkins, B. (1980). "Women's language" or "powerless language"? In S. McConnell-Ginet, R. Borker, & N. Furman (Eds.), *Women and language in literature and society* (pp. 93–110). New York: Praeger.

Pugh, M. D., & Wahrman, R. (1983). Neutralizing sexism in mixed-sex groups: Do women have to be better than men? *American Journal of Sociology, 88* (4), 746–762.

Pugh, M. D., & Wahrman, R. (1985). Inequality of influence in mixed-sex groups. In J. Berger & M. Zelditch (Eds.), *Status, rewards, and influence* (pp. 142–162). San Francisco: Jossey-Bass.

Reis, H. T., Senchak, M., & Solomon, B. (1985). Sex differences in the intimacy of social interaction: Further examination of potential explanations. *Journal of Personality and Social Psychology, 48* (5), 1204–1217.

Rice, R. W., Bender, L. R., & Vitters, A. G. (1980). Leader sex, follower attitudes toward women, and leadership effectiveness: A laboratory experiment. *Organizational Behavior and Human Performance, 25,* 46–78.

Risman, B. J. (1987). Intimate relationships from a microstructural perspective: Men who mother. *Gender and Society, 1,* 6–32.

Ross, L. (1977). The intuitive psychologist and his shortcomings: Distortions in the attribution process. In L. Berkowitz (Ed.), *Advances in experimental social psychology,* vol. 10 (pp. 174–221). New York: Academic Press.

Rubin, L. (1994). *Families on the fault line.* New York: HarperCollins.

Smith, P. M. (1985). *Language, the sexes and society.* Oxford: Basil Blackwell.

Snodgrass, S. E. (1985). Women's intuition: The effect of subordinate role on interpersonal sensitivity. *Journal of Personality and Social Psychology, 49* (1), 146–155.

Snodgrass, S. E. (1992). Further effects of role versus gender on interpersonal sensitivity. *Journal of Personality and Social Psychology, 62* (1), 154–158.

Stitt, C., Schmidt, S., Price, K., & Kipnis, D. (1983). Sex of leader, leader behavior and subordinate satisfaction. *Sex Roles, 9* (1), 31–42.

Tannen, D. (1990). *You just don't understand: Women and men in conversation.* New York: William Morrow.

Tannen, D. (1994). *Talking from nine to five: How women's and men's conversational styles affect who gets heard, who gets credit, and what gets done at work.* New York: William Morrow.

Thorne, B. (1993). *Gender play: Girls and boys in school.* New Brunswick, N.J.: Rutgers University Press.

Tracy, K., & Eisenberg, E. (1990/1991). Giving criticism: A multiple goals case study. *Research on Language and Social Interaction, 24,* 37–70.

Wagner, D. G., Ford, R. S., & Ford, T. W. (1986). Can gender inequalities be reduced? *American Sociological Review, 51,* 47–61.

Werner, P. D., & LaRussa, G. W. (1985). Persistence and change in sex role stereotypes. *Sex Roles, 12,* 1089–1100.

West, C., & Zimmerman, D. H. (1987). Doing gender. *Gender and Society, 1* (2), 125–151.

Wheelan, S. A., & Verdi, A. F. (1992). Differences in male and female patterns of communication in groups: A methodological artifact? *Sex Roles, 27* (1/2), 1–15.

Wiley, M. G., & Eskilson, A. (1985). Speech style, gender stereotypes and corporate success: What if women talk more like men? *Sex Roles, 12* (8/9), 993–1007.

Wiley, M. G., & Wooley, D. E. (1988). Interruptions among equals: Power plays that fail. *Gender and Society, 2* (1), 90–102.

Wood, W., & Karten, S. J. (1986). Sex differences in interaction style as a product of perceived sex differences in competence. *Journal of Personality and Social Psychology, 50* (2), 341–347.

Youniss, J., & Smollar, J. (1985). *Adolescent relations with mothers, fathers, and friends.* Chicago: University of Chicago Press.

Nonverbal Behavior:

Are Women's Superior Skills

Caused by Their Oppression?

Nonverbal behavior plays an important part in the way we communicate with one another. Some researchers claim that as much as 90 percent of our emotions and 65 percent of all information are transmitted through body language rather than verbal exchange (Elgin, 1993). For example, Monica Moore (1985) studied courtship patterns. Observing more than two hundred women in singles bars, she identified fifty-two different "nonverbal solicitation" behaviors. In fact, body language is so powerful that when someone's facial expression, voice inflection, posture, or gestures conflict with the verbal message, we tend to believe the nonverbal message (Mehrabian & Ferris, 1967; Mehrabian & Wiener, 1967).

Researchers generally agree that nonverbal communication differences between women and men are greater than other types of gender differences. Women use more body movements, such as touching, and they engage in interpersonal exchanges more often than men. They also gaze at their partners more than men do and are more likely to favor a closer distance between themselves and their conversational partners (Hall, 1984). Studies show, however, that racial and ethnic differences must be considered in this area of research. For example, White women interacting in a same-sex dyad gaze at each other more often than do African-American women (Smith, 1983).

A good deal of research has focused on gender differences in smiling. Although little or no difference has been found between boys and girls in this respect, women are more likely to smile than men, suggesting the influence of socialization. Evidence indicates that women often feel pressured to smile because of social anxiety (Hall and Halberstadt, 1986). Therefore, their smiling behavior does not always reflect their emotions. For example, Bugental, Love, and Gianetto (1971), in a study of interactions between parents and children, found that mothers smiled more when they thought they were being watched than when they thought they were unobserved, indicating an effort to comply with gender-role expectations. An experiment conducted by Deutsch, LeBaron, and Fryer (1987) shows that women's anxiety is grounded in reality: participants rated unsmiling women as less happy, less warm, less relaxed, and less carefree than the average woman. A man's failure to smile, however, did not lead to a correspondingly negative evaluation. This is another example of the importance of considering the interaction of gender and ethnicity, because smiling behavior is more typical of White women than of African-American women (Halberstadt & Saitta, 1987).

Women are also better than men in decoding nonverbal cues. Their superiority in interpreting others' emotions is greatest in evaluating facial expressions, less in evaluating body posture, and least in evaluating body cues (Brody & Hall, 1993; Hall, 1984). Interestingly, this superiority shows up as early as elementary school in the United States as well as in other cultures, including Australia, Israel, Mexico, and Hong Kong (Hall, 1984). Yet care must be taken in interpreting the behavior of other ethnic groups. In American Indians, for example, avoidance of direct eye contact is a sign of respect, not evidence of guilt or shame (LaFromboise et al., 1995).

Although psychologists agree that gender differences in nonverbal behavior exist, they disagree about the cause. Nancy Henley (1977) pioneered the study of the relation between women's nonverbal skills and their social status. She and Marianne LaFrance argue that these differences stem from women's subordinate role in society: because women are less powerful than men, they are forced to learn to interpret the cues of others in order to survive. Judith A. Hall and Amy G. Halberstadt disagree, contending that the subordination-power hypothesis is simplistic and lacks supporting empirical evidence.

REFERENCES

Brody, L. R., & Hall, J. A. (1993). Gender and emotion. In M. Lewis & J. M. Haviland (Eds.), *Handbook of emotions* (pp. 447–460). New York: Guilford Press.

Bugental, D. E., Love, L. R., & Gianetto, R. M. (1971). Perfidious feminine faces. *Journal of Personality and Social Psychology, 17,* 314–318.

Deutsch, F. M., LeBaron, D., & Fryer, M. M. (1987). What is in a smile? *Psychology of Women Quarterly, 11,* 341–352.

Elgin, S. H. (1993). *Genderspeak: Men, women and the gentle art of verbal self-defense.* New York: John Wiley and Sons.

Halberstadt, A. G., & Saitta, M. B. (1987). Gender, nonverbal behavior, and perceived dominance: A test of the theory. *Journal of Personality and Social Psychology, 53,* 257–272.

Hall, J. A. (1984). *Nonverbal sex differences: Communication accuracy and expressive style.* Baltimore: Johns Hopkins University Press.

Hall, J. A., & Halberstadt, A. G. (1986). Smiling and gazing. In J. S. Hyde & M. C. Linn (Eds.), *The psychology of gender: Advances through meta-analysis* (pp. 136–158). Baltimore: Johns Hopkins University Press.

Henley, N. M. (1977). *Body politics: Power, sex and nonverbal communication.* Englewood Cliffs, N.J.: Prentice-Hall.

LaFromboise, T. D., Choney, S. B., James, A., & Running Wolf, P. R. (1995). American Indian women and psychology. In H. Landrine (Ed.), *Bringing cultural diversity to feminist psychology: Theory, research, and practice* (pp. 197–239). Washington, D.C.: American Psychological Association.

Mehrabian, A., & Ferris, S. R. (1967). Inference of attitudes from nonverbal communication in two channels. *Journal of Consulting Psychology, 31,* 248–252.

Mehrabian, A., & Wiener, M. (1967). Decoding of inconsistent communication. *Journal of Personality and Social Psychology, 6,* 109–114.

Moore, M. M. (1985). Nonverbal courtship patterns in women: Context and consequences. *Ethology and Sociobiology, 6,* 237–247.

Smith, A. (1983). Nonverbal communication among Black female dyads: An assessment of intimacy, gender, and race. *Journal of Social Issues, 39,* 55–67.

ADDITIONAL READING

Brennan-Parks, K., Goddard, M., Wilson, A. E., & Kinnear, L. (1991). Sex differences in smiling as measured in a picture-taking task. *Sex Roles, 24,* 375–382.

Ellyson, S. L., Dovidio, J. F., & Brown, C. E. (1992). The look of power: Gender differences and similarities in visual dominance behavior. In C. L. Ridgeway (Ed.),

Gender, interaction, and inequality (pp. 50–80). New York: Springer-Verlag.

Knapp, M. L., & Hall, J. A. (1996). *Nonverbal Communication in Human Interaction*, 4th ed. Fort Worth, Tex.: Harcourt Brace.

Major, B., Schmidlin, A. M., & Williams, L. (1990). Gender patterns in social touch: The impact of setting and age. *Journal of Personality and Social Psychology, 58*, 634–643.

Segerstrale, U., & Molnar, P. (Eds.). (1996). *Communication in social interaction*. Hillsdale, N.J.: Erlbaum.

Stoppard, J. M., & Gruchy, C. D. G. (1993). Gender, context, and expression of positive emotion. *Personality and Social Psychology Bulletin, 19*, 143–150.

Willson, A., & Lloyd, B. (1990). Gender vs. power: Self-posed behavior revisited. *Sex Roles, 23*, 91–98.

Wood, J. T. (1994). *Gendered Lives: Communication, gender, and culture*. Belmont, Calif.: Wadsworth.

On Oppressing Hypotheses: Or, Differences in Nonverbal Sensitivity Revisited

MARIANNE LAFRANCE AND

NANCY M. HENLEY

Power has figured prominently in debates surrounding why women and men differ on a host of nonverbal behaviors, including how they respond to the nonverbal behavior of other people. For example, research has shown that women are better than men at deciphering the meaning of another person's facial expressions or vocal intonation. This superior ability of women to read accurately others' subtle communication behavior has engendered controversy not over whether it exists but why it exists. One thesis, sometimes labeled the "oppression hypothesis," is that women's superior nonverbal sensitivity or decoding skill originates in their subordinate standing in society. In short, the argument is that people possessing relatively little power need to be able to discern the meaning of others' expressions and especially the expressions of those possessing higher power. Despite its surface cogency, the hypothesis for gender differences in decoding skill based on differential power has been found wanting, or at least, one conspicuous program of research has apparently shown that it has no empirical support. In what follows, we provide a detailed study of the evidence against and for this power-based interpretation. Our conclusion is that power is clearly implicated in why women are better decoders and

that its rejection as a viable explanation is both uninformed and incorrect.

THE POWER OF NONVERBAL BEHAVIOR

Nonverbal behavior has long been a topic of the social and behavioral sciences (Darwin, 1872), and empirical research on it began in earnest nearly three decades ago. Anthropologists like Birdwhistell (1970) and E. T. Hall (1959, 1966) proposed that becoming enculturated involved learning not only the verbal language of one's group but the nonverbal language as well. Sociologists like Goffman (1959, 1967) demonstrated that everyday face-to-face encounters were actually made possible by an elaborate system of subtle yet well-understood nonverbal signs. Ethologists like Eibl-Eibesfeldt (1972) and psychologists like Ekman et al. (1972) have established that the face is capable of registering the full range of human emotions, and social psychologists like Sommer (1969) and Exline (1972) have examined how and when people manage interpersonal distances and employ eye contact. Today, many academic and popular books dealing with political, business, and interpersonal transactions include information stemming from research on nonverbal communication; professional meetings in psychology frequently address the role that nonverbal behavior plays in the management of emotions, in the development of personality, in effecting change in relationships, and in the monitoring of therapeutic progress. The field even has its own journal, the *Journal of Nonverbal Behavior*.

The aspects of behavior called "nonverbal" are rather extensive, but most accounts include messages conveyed by the face, such as facial expression and gaze behavior; messages communicated through body movement (kinesics), such as gesture, posture, and orientation; messages reflected by people's use of space (proxemics); an array of messages carried by the act of touch; and a large set of messages conveyed by vocal intonation and voice quality (paralinguistics). Dress, body type, smell, and use of physical objects are examples of nonverbal cues less often studied.

Research in all these areas has confirmed long-standing intuitions that nonverbal behavior is a significant human activity and that its import is neither redundant nor extraneous to words. But what empirical research has added to intuition is the delineation and depiction of the various functions that nonverbal behavior plays. For example, the expression of feeling is more typically conveyed nonverbally than verbally; one's standing in one's community may be revealed quite literally by how one carries oneself; turn-taking in conversations is negotiated nonverbally, as is evidence of listening; development, maintenance, and change in personal relationships are often handled nonverbally; and nonverbal channels are regularly called upon when there is need to decipher whether a verbal statement is meant to be taken as fact or fabrication. The present chapter addresses another significant face of nonverbal behavior—namely, its role as a marker of power.

Women and men do different things with their eyes, faces, voices, and bodies. In fact, it has been alleged that to be recognizably female or male requires being able to perform a complicated nonverbal script. Our focus here involves taking a close look at one aspect of this extensive nonverbal script. The particular effect is a controversial one and has to do with accounting for why women show greater ability to "read" the nonverbal behavior of other people than do men. A recurring question is whether this well-documented gender difference in nonverbal sensitivity is best understood as stemming from deep-seated differences between the sexes or whether it is due to structures that create power inequities between women and men. As will become apparent, the resolution of this dispute is handled in the social science literature not primarily by recourse to reflection or argument or illustration (although all can be compelling) but rather through a painstaking process that involves methodological critique, valid measurement, and objective scrutiny of reliable data. We follow this latter course not only because we are social scientists but also because we believe that close examination of the processes behind the "facts" often allows us to grasp what is really going on.

ACCOUNTING FOR NONVERBAL SEX DIFFERENCES

Interestingly, there is little controversy in the literature concerning whether there are gendered aspects of nonverbal behavior. Differences in the nonverbal behavior of women and men are now well established (Aries, 1987; Frieze & Ramsey, 1976; Henley, 1977; Hyde, 1990; LaFrance & Mayo, 1979). Although varying with the nature of the situation, the differences sometimes being quite substantial and other times nonexistent, nevertheless the data tend to indicate that women and men display different kinds and degrees of nonverbal behavior. For example, females engage in more mutual and nonmutual gaze at others than males, and they smile more than males. Early on, the favored explanation was that such differences reflected basic gender-stereotypic personality variables. That is, women's greater eye contact was due to their greater affiliative need or more pronounced field dependence (Exline, 1963; Exline et al., 1965), and their tendency to smile more than men was the result of their greater propensity toward social affiliation. Other researchers, however, looked at these same results and saw different forces operating. For example, Henley (1977) noted that the tendency to gaze and smile was also shown by the lower-power person in status-discrepant relationships. Thus a substantial number of nonverbal gender differences might be attributable to power inequities rather than personality differences. In other words, instead of seeing a person's facial expression or body gesture as solely indicative of some underlying trait, such as sociability or emotionality, the conjecture based on a power analysis was that many expressions and gestures are also called for by one's social position or lack thereof. Their role is to signal one's compliance with the social order rather than to reflect one's individuality.

The hypothesis that men and women demonstrate different nonverbal behaviors because they possess unequal power grew out of work in the early 1970s that started to document other inequalities in the small stuff of everyday life, including dynamics within familial and close relationships (Gillespie, 1971; Safilios-Rothschild, 1970), in language used by women and men (Kramer, 1977; Lakoff, 1975; Thorne & Henley, 1975), and in other microsocial domains. More specifically, feminist scholarship had begun to identify power as a significant component of male-female relationships, and so scrutinizing the subtle realm of nonverbal behavior between women and men for the workings of power was a natural outcome. Among those who looked at nonverbal sex differences in the 1970s and considered a power explanation were Frieze and Ramsey (1976), Goffman (1979), J. A. Hall (1979), Henley (1973a, 1973b, 1977), La-France & Mayo (1979), Weitz (1976), and Wex (1979).

Thus another function was added to those already identified with nonverbal behavior. Nonverbal cues could act in such a way not only to embody hierarchical relations but, perhaps more important, to uphold and to justify them. Men's greater social power relative to women is reflected again and again in portrayed interactions seen in the media. Goffman (1979) has provided numerous illustrations of this in a book appropriately entitled *Gender Advertisements*. When men are shown in home settings engaged in stereotypically "feminine" activities, advertisements use nonverbal cues to convey a "clowning" or frivolous flavor. So even if men are shown as doing at home "what women do," and women at work doing "what men do," the accompanying nonverbal messages indicate that the basic gender arrangements are intact.

Men's greater social power relative to women is also substantiated in the subtle yet pervasive nonverbal cues given and received between the sexes in actual everyday interactions. There is now evidence that males are less facially expressive than females (LaFrance & Banaji, 1992). Moreover, males report greater satisfaction with their dating relationship when the exchange has the male disclosing less about himself relative to his female partner than she to him (Millar & Millar, 1988), and males re-

port being more attracted to a high-expressive female than a low-expressive female, especially if she is described as physically attractive (Sprecher, 1989). So the norms call for women to be revelatory even while the men they associate with adopt a nondisclosing stance. In a related study among married couples, husbands' marital complaints were found to increase as their wives' expressive abilities decreased (Sabatelli et al., 1982). No such relation was found for wives.

A particularly interesting difference between the sexes has been the noted superior ability of females accurately to decode the nonverbal behaviors of others (Rosenthal et al., 1979). Here, too, power has been used to interpret the differences (Henley, 1977; Henley & LaFrance, 1984; Snodgrass, 1985). The basic thesis is that it falls to persons of lower power to be able to read the cues of someone possessing higher power, because their ability to respond appropriately, if not their very survival, may depend upon it. But despite the intuitive appeal of a power explanation to account for the observed tendency for females to be more nonverbally sensitive than males, some published work reports failure to find corroborating evidence. Specifically, one often-cited program of research concludes that a power explanation of gender differences in decoding ability is without merit. In what follows, we provide a detailed review of the empirical evidence for and against a power explanation for nonverbal sensitivity.

Our rationale for scrutinizing this issue is based on several considerations. Just as literary and historical scholars see advantage in conducting extremely close textual readings, social scientists believe that intense examination of the data bearing on a particular behavioral phenomenon can reveal something essential about why there are differences. If God is not exactly in the details, then at least valid interpretation may be. Second, we examine this particular nonverbal behavior because it illustrates more generally how psychologists have and have not dealt with power as a key dynamic in human relationships. We expect to show that some researchers have been too quick to dismiss a power explanation of gender differences in nonverbal behavior in part because they have been insufficiently apprised of what a power explanation consists of. Hence we will elaborate its key aspects, especially as they pertain to nonverbal relationships between the sexes. Finally, we tackle this issue because it is interesting on its own terms. It appears that people differ substantially in their ability accurately to read and understand what others are not saying but are nonetheless clearly communicating. It would be fascinating to understand why a lot of the people who are better happen to be women.

POWER AND NONVERBAL BEHAVIOR

As noted, the gender aspects of nonverbal behavior are multiple. So, in tackling why there are sex differences in nonverbal decoding skill, we are necessarily being selective. Nevertheless, this particular issue is in many ways representative of work going on in other areas of nonverbal communication research. The attempt to account for women's greater nonverbal sensitivity taps into a more basic issue—namely, whether the appearance of sex differences is rooted in power inequities.

A power analysis applied to nonverbal sex differences proceeds from two sets of ideas. First, there is the recognition that power constitutes a pervasive dynamic in social relationships whether those relationships take place in public or in private spheres. Second, in the nonverbal communication literature, there are clear indications that power differences between people are expressed via an array of nonverbal cues, whose meaning, though tacit, is nevertheless transparent. For example, Ellyson and his colleagues have consistently found that high-power people (assessed by such measures as higher social rank or greater expertise) look at their conversational partner more when they are speaking than when they are listening but that the reverse is true for lower-power people, who look more at the other when they are listening than when they are talking (Ellyson et al., 1981). Moreover, differences in visual dominance can be perceived by observers such that when individuals exhibit high ratios of look-speak to look-listen behavior, they are rated

as more powerful than when they demonstrate moderate ratios (Ellyson et al., 1981).

Visual behavior thus appears to serve an important function in establishing and conveying social power. But visual behavior is not the sole nonverbal behavior that acts in this way. Other nonverbal cues, such as facial expressivity, postural arrangements, license to touch, and admissible space are also modalities through which power is exercised in the context of personal relationships. Context is important to keep in mind for it is a reminder that power thus conceived is not something that someone invariably possesses but rather an attribute of relations. As such, its concrete manifestations in one or more nonverbal behaviors will vary depending on the nature of a particular relationship. One can have more power with respect to a specific other but have less with respect to someone else even in the same context. Thus, in talking to a subordinate I may adopt the visual dominance pattern described above but would likely cease that pattern when communicating with my superior.

This relational nature also means that in a power-discrepant relationship, each party will display different nonverbal behavior relative to the other, in contrast to equal-power relationships, in which both parties are likely to engage in reciprocal or symmetrical patterns of nonverbal behavior (Henley, 1977). It is also the case that the nonverbal concomitants of power are not entirely arbitrary but are associated with psychological attributes that not only signal difference between individuals but also convey disparities in control. We hypothesized in an earlier chapter that these disparities would be manifest in four separate and significant interpersonal domains (Henley & LaFrance, 1984). The specific domains are as follows:

1. *Readability.* The hypothesis is that power inequity will show itself in how differentially "readable" or nonverbally communicative individuals in a relationship are. Specifically, we predict that lower-power people will be more nonverbally readable, that is, be more nonverbally expressive than higher-power people. The basic idea is that power is sustained, in part, through the exercise of appar-

ent composure and concealment. In contrast, lower-power people are expected to be more disclosing, which has the effect of making them more accountable and vulnerable.

2. *Accommodativeness.* We also predicted that power differentials would be manifest in the degree to which individuals show the tendency to modify their behavior so as to accommodate the other party in an interaction. The specific prediction is that members of a lower-power group will be more nonverbally accommodating, in that they are more likely to adjust their nonverbal behaviors to fit with the behaviors of the higher-power group than the higher-power group will adjust in response to them. Having control means that others will have to adjust.

3. *Submissiveness.* A third prediction stemming from a power analysis of nonverbal behavior is that members of a lower-power group will show more nonverbal signs that convey an attitude of submissiveness than will members of a higher-power group. For example, the submissiveness hypothesis proposes that females' greater smiling, gazing (and gaze aversion, such as eyelid-lowering), head canting and head lowering, lower or "after" spatial positioning, smaller personal spaces, contracted postures, and higher rates of being spatially invaded and being touched are due to their subordinate status (Henley, 1977; Henley & LaFrance, 1984).

4. *Sensitivity.* Finally, a power analysis suggests that members of lower-power groups will need to be more attentive to those possessing higher power than the reverse. As indicated previously, the specific prediction is that the lower-power group will show more nonverbal decoding skills, that is, will be better at reading the expressions of the higher-power group than vice versa.

The argument that certain nonverbal differences stem from power inequities means that situations of status differences other than sex would create similar differences in nonverbal behavior. For example, there is parallel evidence of nonverbal behavior differences in situations involving intercultural inequality (Henley and LaFrance,

1984) or experimentally created hierarchies (Leffler et al., 1982; Snodgrass, 1985).

Finally, it is important to note that the relationship between lower-power and higher-power groups is basic to the theory; the lower-power group's greater readability, accommodation, submissiveness, and sensitivity are expected to be most manifest relative to the higher-power group. However, because of gender-based socialization, they may be manifested in other situations as well.

DECODING SKILL AND THE "OPPRESSION HYPOTHESIS" CONTROVERSY

Each of the hypotheses described above has received some empirical attention, but as we observed earlier, the hypothesis that greater sensitivity by women occurs *because* of their lower status remains controversial. In fact, Judith Hall and her colleagues (Hall, 1984, 1985, 1987; Hall & Halberstadt, 1981, 1986; Stier & Hall, 1984) have been at continued pains to refute a power explanation for gender differences in nonverbal decoding skill, an explanation that Hall has labeled "the oppression hypothesis" (1984, p. 39). In what follows we undertake an extended examination of the theory and research that bear on it. Our reasons for probing Hall's conclusions are several. First, although there already exist reasons to question Hall's rejection of a power analysis (see, e.g., the critiques offered by Henley & LaFrance, 1984; Kramarae, 1985; LaFrance, 1986, 1987), the more typical response, especially within the field of the psychology of women, has been to accept Hall's assessment (e.g., Eagly, 1987b, pp. 103ff; Matlin, 1987, pp. 216–18; Wallston, 1987, p. 1035). Second, we take a close look at this work because for many psychologists Hall's conclusions seem to be the result of having employed a sophisticated and objective research methodology. We suggest, however, that there are flaws in that methodology which if left unearthed might lead others to conclude erroneously that Hall is on the right track. Finally, we undertake this critique in order to clarify the continued viability of a power analysis to account for nonverbal gender differences.

In the following section we begin our examination by attempting to track the origins of what has come to be called "the oppression hypothesis" within the psychology of nonverbal behavior. We consider the appropriateness of the term and then describe the empirical research that bears on it.

THE SOURCE AND APPROPRIATENESS OF THE TERM "OPPRESSION HYPOTHESIS"

The origin of the "oppression hypothesis" to explain nonverbal sex differences has been variously attributed by Hall in her different writings:

1. Hall (1978) cites English (1972) and Weitz (1974);

2. Hall and Halberstadt (1981) cite both these references as well as Thomas et al. (1972);

3. Stier and Hall (1984) cite Henley (1973b);

4. Hall (1984) cites all these (changing the Henley reference to 1977) and adds Frieze and Ramsey (1976);

5. Hall (1985) cites Henley (1973b, 1977) as "the major theorist" of this "one prevalent interpretation"; and

6. Hall and Halberstadt (1986) cite Henley (1977) as the author of the only hypothesis that "has received any serious development" (1986, p. 138).

Henley in turn derived her (1973a, 1977) explanations of power-related nonverbal behavior from the work of Goffman (1967) and Brown (1965) and her explanations of nonverbal decoding sensitivity as related to subordinate status from several sources, including Gitter et al. (1972), Rubin (1970), and Weitz (1974). Snodgrass (1985) attributes the "subordinate role" explanation of interpersonal sensitivity to Hall (in Rosenthal et al., 1979), Miller (1976), Thomas et al. (1972), and Weitz (1974).

The interpretation of women's position as subordinate hardly needs justification, enshrined as it is in law, language, and custom. In what is known as the first wave of feminism, writers like Virginia Woolf (1929) and Elizabeth Cady Stanton, Susan B. Anthony, and Matilda Joslyn (1889) noted a correlation between the subordination of women and how they behaved, as did writers like Friedan (1963), Millett (1969), and Firestone (1970) early in the second wave. This power-based analysis is now widely discussed among feminist scholars.

As indicated, Hall named the idea that women's greater sensitivity might derive from their unequal status the "oppression hypothesis." Although this label has achieved some currency owing to repetition, it is probably not the best choice for the phenomena it describes. The term "subordination hypothesis" is preferable because gender variability is seen to stem from differences in power variously conceived. For example, subordination could result from possessing less social power (defined as influence based on control of resources), lower social status (defined as attributed esteem or importance), or restricted interpersonal dominance (defined as control over another individual's behavior). Because a power-based analysis, while including oppression, also applies to a broader set of phenomena, we find the terms *subordination hypothesis* or *subordination theory* preferable.

Although Hall appears to accept the idea that women's lower standing might play some part in accounting for why they are more nonverbally sensitive than men, her basic argument rejects the notion that women's subordinate status is directly implicated. She writes:

> Girls and women could learn that as females they ought to be good decoders, not because they are actually oppressed in any sense of the word, but because society prescribes certain roles and behaviours for them. . . . Though women's oppression may play a part in such sex-role expectations, in that such expectations reflect the earlier extreme circumscription of women's activities . . . it would nevertheless be an overstatement to claim that women's nonverbal skill stems from their oppression in any direct sense. (1984, p. 42)

Subordination theory also takes account of sex-role expectations and gender socialization, but in a more contiguous and continual way. Patriarchal societies shape, establish, and maintain gender roles that support male dominance. Moreover, patriarchal societies bring about and maintain gender roles drawing on several agencies such as religion, the media, education, public policy, and the legal system. Because socialized roles constitute a significant part of the mechanism that supports inequities, pointing to their part in nonverbal gender differentiation does not diminish the power of subordination theory, as Hall (1984) implies, but rather supports its finer points.

TESTING THE SUBORDINATION HYPOTHESIS OF NONVERBAL DECODING ABILITY

A good deal of evidence apparently refuting a power-based explanation of sex differences in decoding ability has used a test of decoding skill called the Profile of Nonverbal Sensitivity (PONS) (Rosenthal et al., 1979). The PONS was initially designed to measure individual differences in the ability accurately to "read" someone else's communicative cues coming from the face, body, and voice. Although various subtests have been spun off from the original test, the full PONS consists of 220 very brief (two-second duration) visual and/or vocal segments (without verbal content) enacted by one young Caucasian woman. The segments are presented in a regular order on a movie screen or television monitor to one or more test takers who have a few seconds after each segment to decide what each segment conveyed. Specifically, test takers must decide which of two possible situations presented in multiple choice format on a standard rating sheet best describes the presented segment. One's score on the PONS is a tally of how many choices correspond to what the test takers had initially established were correct responses.

In studies involving more than 10,000 people, varying in age and nationality, the original investigators noted a small but consistent sex difference favoring females—that is, females had higher scores on the PONS than did males (Rosenthal et al., 1979). They reported that of 133 separate samples, 80 percent showed difference in this direction, with a median effect size r of 0.20. It is important to note that the size of difference, though reliable,

is quite modest. In addition, a cross-cultural set of data from 46 samples from ten nations plus 6 from the United States showed an average female-male difference of about 2 percentage points. An r of 0.20 (found in both the total 133 samples and cross-cultural subsamples) indicates that sex differences account for only 4 percent of the total variance in the results (Hall, 1984, p. 18).

Hall herself reviewed 75 studies of nonverbal decoding accuracy and concluded that "the analyses revealed that more studies showed female advantage than would occur by chance" (1978, p. 854). Sixty-eight percent showed female superiority in decoding skill, and 31 percent showed statistically significant differences favoring women. When studies reporting no difference between the sexes were excluded, 84 percent of the remaining studies showed female superiority. In 1984, Hall reported results of 50 additional studies, only one based on the PONS. Among these, 20 percent showed a statistically significant difference favoring females, although 52 percent of the total showed a female advantage. When studies that found no sex difference were excluded, 81 percent of the remaining number showed female superiority.

We thus concur with Hall and others that there is evidence for a small but consistent difference favoring females. The problem then becomes how to account for this effect.

HALL AND HALBERSTADT: REFUTATION OR SUPPORT OF THE SUBORDINATION HYPOTHESIS?

Hall and Halberstadt (1981) purport to provide a test of "the hypothesis that persons with less social power need to be especially alert to the behaviours and moods of more powerful others" (p. 275). The empirical test of the hypothesis necessitated measuring two key components on the same set of female respondents. First, it required a way to measure decoding skill, and second, there was a need to measure individual differences in the degree to which a sample of women were "oppressed." This latter variable was derived from the following reasoning. Based on "the assumption that traditionality on questions of women's rights represents acceptance of an ideology of male domi-nation," Hall and Halberstadt predicted that if the "oppression hypothesis" had merit, then "the more traditional, less egalitarian women would be the best decoders" (p. 282). In other words, they in-ferred that women who espoused more traditional sex-role views were more oppressed and as such should, if lower power caused greater sensitivity, score higher on decoding skill than women who held less traditional sex-role views. In fact, they found the opposite relation—namely, that those women who were *less* traditional had higher decod-ing scores—and therefore concluded that the op-pression hypothesis was unsupported.

However, closer inspection of their method indi-cates that they misinterpreted their own results. In fact, their own data may actually be seen to sup-port the subordination hypothesis (Henley & La-France, 1984; LaFrance, 1986). To understand how we arrive at this conclusion, it is necessary to study closely what Hall and Halberstadt did and what they found.

Hall and Halberstadt define "oppression" at the individual level (as contrasted with a structural level) in terms of traditionality of sex roles and as-sess differences in traditionality in two ways: by measuring both attitudes and behaviors of female respondents. Regarding attitudes, they draw on three studies that used the short Attitude toward Women Scale (AWS) (Spence et al., 1973) or a chil-dren's version of the AWS. Regarding behaviors, they examined the relation of decoding skill to mar-ried women's self-reported preference for tradition-ality in their own marriage and actual traditionality via division of labor in housecleaning and laundry. As they conceived it: "We operationalized the con-cept of 'oppressed status' both in terms of subjects' perceptions and their more objective estimations of their own sex-role-related behavior. Of course, these are not the only criteria of 'oppressed status' that one could employ, but they were reasonable ones to start with" (1981, p. 283).

With respect to the studies that used attitudes as a measure of oppression, Hall and Halberstadt found that females with more egalitarian views were actually better decoders than females who

hold more traditional views—exactly the opposite of what they argued would need to occur if the op-pression hypothesis were to be supported (1981, p. 292). With respect to studies using behavioral measures of oppression, they also found that those who adopted a less traditional marital division of labor showed higher decoding skill. However, it is important to note that their results differed with the sex of the *encoder*—that is, the target person who was being "read." For the two tests that meas-ured sensitivity to a *female* encoder (the original PONS), they write: "the more 'liberated' type of woman—at least as indicated by these meas-ures—was a *better* decoder of a woman's nonverbal cues than was the less 'liberated' woman. This is the opposite of the original prediction, as was the case with attitudes towards women" (1981, p. 284, emphasis in original).

In contrast, with the one test of decoding skill involving audio segments only, which used a *male* encoder, they report: "There was a tendency for a more traditional marriage (both actual and prefer-ence) and for performance of more housecleaning to be *positively* associated with ability to decode a man's voice. If this pattern is reliable, it would sug-gest that those who prefer and have traditional marriages are better at understanding a man's sub-tle messages than are less traditional women" (1981, p. 284, emphasis in original).

In other words, their own data indicate a posi-tive association between the tendency to be in a more traditional marriage and the ability to read a man's voice, results that seem entirely compatible with the subordination hypothesis. Their response to these data was twofold: first they worked to un-dermine the results, specifically: "these correlations should be interpreted very cautiously since they are based on a single small sample" (1981, p. 284). Then they reinterpreted findings involving skill in reading female and male encoders as indicating not support for the subordination hypothesis but sup-port for what they called a salience argument. They argued: "The overall picture . . . would suggest the possibility that women may become better nonver-bal decoders of whichever sex is most salient to them—men in the case of more traditional women, other women in the case of less traditional women" (1981, p. 284).

In other words, the two obtained patterns—greater decoding skill of a female encoder for nontraditional women and greater decoding skill of a male encoder for traditional women—are rejected as reflecting support for the subordination hypothesis. They are construed instead as indicating "salience," which, given its proposed stance as an alternative explanation, means that decoding skill is interpreted as being unrelated to power.

Both results are decidedly compatible with a power-based explanation. Had the authors taken feminist arguments seriously, they might have begun by focusing on the ability of women to read a *man*'s nonverbal cues and hypothesized greater sensitivity in more traditional women and directed their test there. As it is, with most of the evidence bearing on the subordination hypothesis coming from skill measured in response to a female, the results are tangential to the issue of subordination with respect to men. In fact, the original developers of the PONS test wrote in 1979: "From the start, we recognized that our observation of sex differences in nonverbal skill might be confounded by the fact that that PONS sender was a woman. . . . Women and young girls may have special skill only at reading another female. . . . We are also incapable of detecting a sender sex × receiver sex interaction, if one exists" (Rosenthal et al., 1979, p. 162).

Hall and Halberstadt eschewed this interpretive problem and proceeded to correlate scores on the PONS with another measure of oppression. This time, structural oppression was defined as indices of women's educational, occupational, and cultural status relative to men's. Using these measures, they reported no relation between decoding skill and degree of oppression in general, although complex patterns emerged when the test was subdivided into separate channels. For vocal cues, "less ostensible oppression was associated with greater skill in women" but for visual cues, the correlations were negative, although "only a few of these were significant" (Hall, 1984, p. 43).

Hall and Halberstadt's (1981) studies, properly interpreted, do yield relevant information. By finding greater sensitivity to a man's vocal cues in more traditional women, the findings appear to support the subordination hypothesis. By finding greater sensitivity to a woman's nonverbal cues in less traditional women, the findings do not bear directly on the subordination hypothesis because the relevant behavior is not decoding skill in general but decoding of men in particular. Nevertheless, the findings are interesting in feminist terms, which might predict that less traditionally orientated women would be more attuned to other women.

Unfortunately, the procedures followed in the 1981 report were flawed in other ways. First, the authors relied almost exclusively on the PONS, which has been criticized as a limited and artificial measure of nonverbal decoding skill.[1] The authors employed a range of measures of "oppression," but did not call on the same range when measuring sensitivity. Second, using women's attitudes as a measure of oppressedness is problematic. Hall and Halberstadt essentially assessed the strength of a relation between women's attitudes toward *women's roles* and their ability to choose a label for the posed emotions of a female that coincided with the emotion the female was attempting to project. Unfortunately, this ill-considered venture and attendant conclusions have been magnified by repetition by Hall (e.g., 1984, 1985). Moreover, when these interpretative problems were pointed out in an otherwise positive review of Hall's book by LaFrance (1987), a published response defended Hall's general approach rather than considering the particular criticism (Eagly, 1987a).

1. The PONS is artificial in presenting posed displays of emotion and limited in having the poses of only one gender and race, in having one actor of that gender and race, and in allowing subjects to choose from only two alternative responses. For brief critiques of the PONS, see Friedman (1980) and Archer and Akert (1977). Rosenthal et al. also describe some of their test's shortcomings (1979, pp. 17–22). Feldman and Thayer (1980) compared the PONS with two other nonverbal sensitivity measures and found no significant relation among the three raising concerns about what aspect of decoding skill is being assessed.

OTHER TESTS OF THE SUBORDINATION HYPOTHESIS

Lamentably, there have been few other tests of the subordination hypothesis with respect to decoding skill, but two studies are suggestive. Looking at racial/ethnic differences, Gitter et al. (1972) photographed encoders, who were either African-American or White and female or male, as they conveyed seven different emotions. Perceivers of both sexes and races were asked to indicate which emotions were being portrayed. African-American respondents were found to be more accurate at decoding the emotions of both races and sexes than White perceivers, although no significant sex differences were found. In another study, Rollman (1978) tested both African-American and White decoders' abilities to read the nonverbal signals of a prejudiced (anti-Black) or nonprejudiced White. He found that Black perceivers were better judges of racial prejudice than Whites. Given that African-Americans as a group are socially and economically oppressed by Whites, both studies seem to support the subordination hypothesis.

Halberstadt (1985), however, reached a different conclusion after conducting a comprehensive review of studies examining the effect of race and socioeconomic status (SES) on nonverbal decoding skill. Her review found no significant difference in decoding skill in seven studies that compared Black and White decoders. For seven studies that investigated the effect of SES, lower-class decoders were found to be less skilled than middle-class ones, with a moderate effect size, a pattern that at first glance fails to support a subordination explanation. However, the difference in decoding skill favoring middle-class decoders decreased as the decoders got older. Even though the age factor showed a large effect size, Halberstadt reported that it was "non-significant because of the small N" (1985, p. 235). Halberstadt might have noted that limited range might have prevented a better test of the relation, since *none* of the reported seven studies used an adult sample (in only one were the subjects even in high school). In summary, the author reports:

All seven of the studies concur; lower class individuals are not as skilled at decoding as more

privileged individuals. . . . Though using the highly conservative procedure of setting the *z*s for these studies at zero, the effect of an advantageous background on nonverbal decoding skill was apparent. . . . lower class children are less skilled at decoding cues than middle-class children. . . . the 14 studies . . . continue to suggest two clear patterns for race and class differences in nonverbal communication skill: (a) young White and middle-class individuals are better decoders than young Black and lower class individuals and (b) these race and class differences are attenuated and possibly even reversed by adulthood. (1985, pp. 234–235)

Again, a closer examination suggests some need for revision. First, for the race comparisons, the author points out (1985, p. 234) that for four of the studies only White encoders were used, thus replicating the problem noted above with respect to encoder sex—namely, the failure to compare skill across encoders who differ on the relevant dimension. In addition, five of the studies confounded race and SES. For the SES comparisons, Halberstadt notes that "most, if not all, of the studies on skill employed middle-class senders only" (1985, p. 258). Thus we have few, if any, true comparisons of differential abilities across race/ethnicity and class lines any more than we have across gender lines. Although Halberstadt concedes this deficiency, nevertheless she combines them in a meta-analysis that leads her to draw inappropriate conclusions. It is our opinion that researchers who review a field and find studies insufficiently constructed to test a desired hypothesis, besides acknowledging and criticizing them, should not then do a meta-analytic conglomeration of them. To do so gives a false scientific gloss to the collection and leads to insupportable claims.

In spite of these reservations, can anything be concluded from the available data? Because the encoders have tended to be White and middle class, this at least is the group for whom the subordination hypothesis would predict decoding superiority in Black and poor subjects. Contradictory data would thus be damaging to the subordination hypothesis. Analogous to our reinterpretation of Hall and Halberstadt (1981) on gender, we submit that the findings reported by Halberstadt (1985) on race and SES are also not in conflict with a subordination explanation. The increasing skill shown by Blacks and by lower-class children with age suggests gains due to social experience, which would be consistent with the subordination hypothesis. Indeed, the finding of no difference at early ages supports a learned rather than an innate basis for the difference. However, scant study has been made of the older end of the age spectrum, which would be a better test of the subordination hypothesis.

AN APPROPRIATE TEST OF THE SUBORDINATION HYPOTHESIS

What then would be an adequate empirical test of the subordination hypothesis? First, an adequate measure of decoding skill should be used. Such a test of individual differences would do the following:

1. incorporate spontaneous instead of or in addition to posed emotions;
2. employ several as opposed to single encoders;
3. include both female and male targets to be "read"; and
4. allow more rather than two response options.

Some attempts along these lines have been made by Buck (1984) and Costanzo and Archer (1989).

Second, the design should incorporate appropriate contrasts. The subordination hypothesis posits that a subordinate group's ability to decode a superordinate group's nonverbal behavior will be superior to the superordinate group's ability to decode the subordinate group's. Thus both groups, and in the case of gender hierarchy both sexes, must be represented as both senders and receivers of nonverbal signals. The comparison that tests the hypothesis is that of cross-group (cross-sex) decoding abilities. Within-group decoding competencies may be used for control comparisons. The question of whether there is a prediction of differential within-group decoding ability is taken up below.

Third, the operationalization of superior or subordinate status should be consistent with a theory of subordination. This could be done in various ways, such as choosing subjects based on pre-existing differences in relative economic, social, political, or relationship power or by creating asymmetric relationships in experimentally created groups. Using self-reported attitudes regarding gender equality, such as was done by Hall and Halberstadt (1981), is more risky as a measure of subordination because people in low-power positions often hold the attitudes of the dominant group (Tajfel, 1984). Nevertheless, an attitudinal measure could conceivably be appropriate if it was independently shown to be a valid indicator of respondents' beliefs about their *own* status vis-à-vis members of an identified superordinate group.

Fourth, the design should at some point test competing alternative explanations for the nonverbal sensitivity difference empirically and specifically, rather than seeking to refute the subordination hypothesis by integrative review, such as was done by Hall and Halberstadt (1981). Their method essentially amounts to an attempt to confirm the null hypothesis, which is at odds with the preferred strategy of attempting to disconfirm it.

Finally, an ideal test would probably entail an experimental design, in which individuals would be randomly assigned to superior and subordinate groups. By so doing, it would be possible to separate status from pre-existing individual differences. The work of Snodgrass (1985, 1992) represents just such an approach, although she measured sensitivity not as a traitlike ability to decode a stranger's nonverbally expressed emotions but as sensitivity to the feelings of the other within a specific situation. In the first investigation, same-sex and cross-sex dyads interacted in a laboratory context. These research participants were asked four times during an interaction to use rating scales to indicate both their own feelings and the other person's regarding themselves, the other, and the activity. Status asymmetry was established by randomly assigning subjects to be either teacher or student in an instruction situation. Following this session, the dyad engaged in both competitive and cooperative games.

The results supported predictions from subordination theory. First, there was no significant main effect for sex collapsed across context; that is, women were not more sensitive than men overall in judging the other's feelings and reactions when status was not considered. Second, there was a strong main effect for status position, such that lower-status people (learners) were significantly more sensitive to the feelings of the higher-status persons (teachers) than higher-status persons were to the feelings of the lower-status participants. Third, there was a significant effect for gender composition, such that women's sensitivity toward men was greater than women's sensitivity toward women, but the reverse was not true for men (that is, men's sensitivity toward women was not significantly greater than their sensitivity toward men). Snodgrass (1985) also found a significant interaction of role, type of judgment, and activity, and a significant contrast within it that indicated that, in the teaching-learning activity, female subordinates with male superordinates were more sensitive than all other combinations.

Snodgrass (1992) extended her examination of the relations among gender, status, and sensitivity to an experimentally created boss-employee relationship. In this study, subjects were not only randomly assigned but also served in both capacities, twice as leader and twice as subordinate. Again, there was no significant main effect for sex; females were not more nonverbally sensitive than males. Again, there was a significant effect for role, such that "employees" were significantly more sensitive to how the "boss" saw them (the employee) than vice versa. Finally, there was a significant statistical interaction among the three factors of subject sex, type of judgment, and role that showed that the effect was more pronounced with female than with male subjects.

The subordination hypothesis has also to be tested with respect to other sex differences in nonverbal behavior. In those domains, the subordination hypothesis predicts that the subordinate group's nonverbal behavior will be more expressive, submissive, and accommodating than that of the superordinate group. Interestingly, Hall and Halberstadt (1986) have also tackled these behaviors and have again found the oppression hypothesis to be without merit. Again, it is our position that there are clear indications that this rejection is also questionable on scientific grounds. We address these areas of research elsewhere (Henley & LaFrance, 1992).

EXPLANATORY POLITICS IN EXPLAINING SEX DIFFERENCES IN NONVERBAL SENSITIVITY

Hall (1978) put forward three possible explanations for the finding of sex difference in nonverbal sensitivity. They are as follows:

(a) socialization to gender role stereotypes;
(b) women's oppressed status;
(c) genetic predisposition from adaptive evolution: that is, females may be "wired" from birth to be especially sensitive to nonverbal cues or to be especially quick learners of such cues . . . because nonverbal sensitivity on a mother's part might enable her to detect distress in her youngsters or threatening signals from other adults, thus enhancing the survival chances of her offspring (1978, p. 854).

Later, Hall (1984) expanded the possible explanations to include:

1. sex-stereotypical masculinity and femininity, as measured by sex role self-concept scales;
2. greater female empathy (also part of the gender stereotype), as measured by empathy scales;
3. attention and practice focused on nonverbal decoding required by the female role;
4. accommodation by women to politeness norms to attend to more controllable (less "leaky") nonverbal channels;
5. women's adaptation to oppression by special alertness to the behavior and moods of the more powerful (men); and
6. males' greater cerebral hemispheric specialization, which may inhibit processing of nonverbal information.

Hall finds the most promising of these explanations to be those based on practice or attention and accommodation. She also repeats the "interesting suggestion" that "girls are born with a pre-disposition to be responsive to nonverbal cues" as a result of biological adaptation toward "maximizing reproductive success" (1984, p. 47).

As we have remarked earlier, subordination theory is not necessarily at odds with all these explanations; those listed above are not in fact competing explanations but ways in which an explanation based on power inequities may be realized. Socialization to perform certain behaviors is quite likely implicated in these behaviors' association with one or the other gender, but we must ask *why* certain behaviors are associated with being male and some with being female, especially when these same behaviors are associated, respectively, with power and subordination? Why might females have greater empathy, attentiveness, accommodation, and alertness? Why might women get more practice in various nonverbal skills? Taken separately, each factor provides part of the answer, but they beg the question as to their cause. It is our contention that they frequently serve as the mechanisms by which subordination is achieved in face-to-face social interaction.

Finally, Hall offers the possibility of a biological cause, in which the observed sex difference in decoding skill results from males' greater cerebral hemispheric lateralization and females' evolutionary shaping toward nonverbal sensitivity. These processes are, of course, highly speculative.

CONCLUSION

Communication between the sexes is a complex business and that is especially true of nonverbal signals. Although nonverbal communication takes place typically subconsciously, it is nonetheless pervasive and potent. It carries many messages and supports many practices, an important one being the maintenance of power differentials between men and women. In this chapter we have presented the case that sex differences in nonverbal sensitivity derive in good measure from sex-based

power inequities and we have tried to show that a particular program of research aimed at disqualifying this conclusion is itself flawed. The research put forward as refuting the "oppression hypothesis" has asked peripheral questions, employed questionable measures, made inappropriate comparisons, drawn unwarranted conclusions, or reported results in a biased manner (downplaying unsupportive findings, overrating seemingly supportive ones).

In contrast, we have described some recent studies using appropriate and rigorous methods that find support for subordination theory as an explanation for women's greater nonverbal sensitivity. (It should be noted that several of these studies were unavailable to Hall and Halberstadt for their various reviews.)

It may appear to some that we are rejecting the use of meta-analytic techniques much favored by Hall and her colleagues to deal with this issue. We have no quarrel with meta-analysis. When used appropriately, it is a most useful tool for integrating and evaluating the findings on a particular topic of research. But we must repeat the caveats that others (e.g., Unger & Crawford, 1989) have raised about its utility: all the meta-analysis in the world cannot draw correct conclusions from poorly designed or inadequately conducted studies. As evaluators, consumers, and citers of others' research we need to examine studies carefully and thoughtfully, to ask whether the question posed can in fact be answered by the research proffered.

Perhaps more critical in this debate has been the reluctance of psychology in general to address issues of power and status. Hierarchies of all kinds exist and psychological processes are implicated at all levels. Yet as a discipline psychology has slighted consideration of a dominant feature of everyday life—hierarchy. When group differences are found there is the lamentable tendency to attribute them to inherent differences (biological) or socialized differences without mention of power. When power inequities are noted in interpreting research findings, socialization is often presented as the culprit that needs to be changed in order to bring about equality. But we, with others, see socialization as the means for perpetuating society's values, beliefs, behaviors, and power structures. Societal supports of inequality are what is basic and need to be changed. The phenomenon of gender will be more clearly understood in psychology only when power becomes a prominent item of the psychological agenda.

The second author wishes to thank Ann Leffler, undergraduate students Caroline Collins, Brian Doherty and Catherine Lerer and graduate classes at the University of California, both Santa Cruz (1987–1988) and Los Angeles campuses, for their stimulating discussion and investigation of the ideas contained herein, contributions to her thinking, and support.

REFERENCES

Archer, D., & Akert, R. M. (1977). Words and everything else: Verbal and nonverbal cues in social interpretations. *Journal of Personality and Social Psychology, 35,* 443–449.

Aries, E. (1987). Gender and communication. In P. Shaver & C. Hendrick (Eds.), *Sex and gender.* Beverly Hills, Calif.: Sage, pp. 149–176.

Birdwhistell, R. L. (1970). *Kinesics and context.* Philadelphia: University of Pennsylvania Press.

Brown, R. (1965). *Social psychology.* Glencoe, Ill.: Free Press.

Buck, R. (1984). *The communication of emotion.* New York: Guilford Press.

Costanzo, M., & Archer, D. (1989). Interpreting the expressive behavior of others: The Interpersonal Perception Task. *Journal of Nonverbal Behavior, 13,* 225–245.

Darwin, C. (1872). *The expression of the emotions in man and animals.* London: John Murray.

Eagly, A. H. (1987a). On taking research findings seriously [Comment on LaFrance, 1986]. *Contemporary Psychology, 32,* 759–761.

Eagly, A. H. (1987b). *Sex differences in social behavior: A social-role interpretation.* Hillsdale, N.J.: Erlbaum.

Eibl-Eibesfeldt, I. (1972). Similarities and differences between cultures in expressive movements. In R. A. Hinde (Ed.), *Non-verbal communication.* London: Cambridge University Press, pp. 297–314.

Ekman, P., Friesen, W. V., & Ellsworth, P. (1972). *Emotion in the human face.* New York: Pergamon.

Ellyson, S. L., Dovidio, J. F., & Fehr, B. J. (1981). Visual behavior and dominance in women and men. In C. Mayo & N. M. Henley (Eds.), *Gender and nonverbal behavior.* New York: Springer-Verlag.

English, P. W. (1972). Behavioral concomitants of dependent and subservient roles. Unpublished manuscript, Harvard University.

Exline, R. V. (1963). Explorations in the process of person perception: Visual interaction in relation to competition, sex and need for affiliation. *Journal of Personality, 31,* 1–20.

Exline, R. V. (1972). Visual interaction: The glances of power and preference. In J. K. Cole (Ed.), *Nebraska symposium on motivation,* vol. 19. Lincoln: University of Nebraska Press, pp. 163–206.

Exline, R. V., Gray, D., & Schuette, D. (1965). Visual behavior in a dyad as affected by interview content and sex of respondent. *Journal of Personality and Social Psychology, 1,* 201–209.

Feldman, M., & Thayer, S. (1980). A comparison of three measures of nonverbal decoding ability. *Journal of Social Psychology, 112,* 91–97.

Firestone, S. (1970). *The dialectic of sex.* New York: Bantam.

Friedan, B. (1963). *The feminine mystique.* New York: Bantam.

Friedman, H. S. (1980). Scientists snatch body language [Review of Sensitivity to nonverbal communication: The PONS test]. *Contemporary Psychology, 25,* 123–124.

Frieze, I., & Ramsey, S. J. (1976). Nonverbal maintenance of traditional sex roles. *Journal of Social Issues, 32,* 133–141.

Gillespie, D. L. (1971). Who has the power? The marital struggle. *Journal of Marriage and the Family, 33,* 445–458.

Gitter, A. G., Black, H., & Mostofsky, D. (1972). Race and sex in the perception of emotion. *Journal of Social Issues, 28,* 63–78.

Goffman, E. (1959). *The presentation of self in everyday life.* New York: Anchor Books.

Goffman, E. (1967). *Interaction ritual: Essays on face-to-face behavior.* Garden City, N.Y.: Doubleday.

Goffman, E. (1979). *Gender advertisements.* New York: Harper and Row.

Halberstadt, A. G. (1985). Race, socioeconomic status, and nonverbal behavior. In A. Siegman & S. Feldstein (Eds.), *Nonverbal behavior in interpersonal relations.* Hillsdale, N.J.: Erlbaum, pp. 227–266.

Hall, E. T. (1959). *The silent language.* Garden City, N.Y.: Doubleday.

Hall, E. T. (1966). *The hidden dimension.* Garden City, N.Y.: Doubleday.

Hall, J. A. (1978). Gender effects in decoding nonverbal cues. *Psychological Bulletin, 85,* 845–857.

Hall, J. A. (1979). Gender, gender roles and nonverbal communication skills. In R. Rosenthal (Ed.), *Skill in nonverbal communication.* Cambridge, Mass.: Oelgeschlager, Gunn and Hain, pp. 32–67.

Hall, J. A. (1984). *Nonverbal sex differences: Communication accuracy and expressive style.* Baltimore: Johns Hopkins University Press.

Hall, J. A. (1985). Male and female nonverbal behavior. In A. Siegman & S. Feldstein (Eds.), *Nonverbal behavior in interpersonal relations.* Hillsdale, N.J.: Erlbaum, pp. 195–225.

Hall, J. A. (1987). On explaining gender differences: The case of nonverbal communication. In P. Shaver & C. Hendrick (Eds.), *Sex and gender*. Beverly Hills, Calif.: Sage, pp. 177–200.

Hall, J. A., & Halberstadt, A. G. (1981). Sex roles and nonverbal communication skills. *Sex Roles, 7*, 273–287.

Hall, J. A., & Halberstadt, A. G. (1986). Smiling and gazing. In J. S. Hyde & M. C. Linn (Eds.), *The psychology of gender: Advances through meta-analysis*. Baltimore: Johns Hopkins University Press, pp. 136–158.

Henley, N. M. (1973a). Power, sex, and nonverbal communication. *Berkeley Journal of Sociology, 18*, 1–26.

Henley, N. M. (1973b). Status and sex: Some touching observations. *Bulletin of the Psychonomic Society, 2*, 91–93.

Henley, N. M. (1977). *Body politics: Power, sex, and nonverbal communication*. Englewood Cliffs, N.J.: Prentice-Hall.

Henley, N. M. & LaFrance, M. (1984). Gender as culture: Difference and dominance in nonverbal behavior. In A. Wolfgang (Ed.), *Nonverbal behavior: perspectives, applications, intercultural insights*. Lewiston, N.Y.: C. J. Hogrefe, pp. 351–371.

Henley, N. M., & LaFrance, M. (1992). Sex difference in nonverbal behavior: Putting power back into the analyses. Unpublished manuscript.

Hyde, J. S. (1990). Meta-analysis and the psychology of gender differences. *Signs, 16*, 55–73.

Kramarae, C. (1985). Beyond sexist language. *Women's Review of Books, 2* (12), 15–17.

Kramer, C. (1977). Perceptions of female and male speech. *Language and Speech, 20*, 151–161.

LaFrance, M. (1986). Reading between the lines [Review of Hall, *Nonverbal sex differences*], *Contemporary Psychology, 31*, 793–794.

LaFrance, M. (1987). On taking the oppression hypothesis seriously. *Contemporary Psychology, 32*, 760–761.

LaFrance, M., & Banaji, M. (1992). Towards a reconsideration of the gender emotion relationship. In M. Clark (Ed.), *Emotion and social behavior. Review of personality and social psychology*, vol. 14. Beverly Hills, Calif.: Sage.

LaFrance, M., & Mayo, C. (1979). A review of nonverbal communication of women and men. *Western Journal of Speech Communication, 43*, 96–107.

Lakoff, R. (1975). *Language and woman's place*. New York: Harper and Row.

Leffler, A., Gillespie, D. L., & Conaty, J. C. (1982). The effects of status differentiation on nonverbal behavior. *Social Psychology Quarterly, 45*, 153–161.

Matlin, M. W. (1987). *The psychology of women*. New York: Holt, Rinehart and Winston.

Millar, K. U., & Millar, M. G. (1988). Sex difference in perceived self- and other-disclosure: A case where inequity increases satisfaction. *Social Behavior and Personality, 16*, 59–64.

Miller, J. B. (1976). *Towards a new psychology of women*. Boston, Mass.: Beacon Press.

Millett, K. (1969). *Sexual politics*. Garden City, N.Y.: Doubleday.

Rollman, S. A. (1978). The sensitivity of black and white Americans to nonverbal cues of prejudice. *Journal of Social Psychology, 105*, 73–77.

Rosenthal, R., Hall, J. A., DiMatteo, M. R., Rogers, P. L., & Archer, D. (1979). *Sensitivity to nonverbal communication: The PONS test*. Baltimore: Johns Hopkins University Press.

Rubin, Z. (1970). Measurement of romantic love. *Journal of Personality and Social Psychology, 16*, 265–273.

Sabatelli, R., Buck, R., & Dreyer, A. (1982). Nonverbal communication accuracy in married couples: Relationship with marital complaints. *Journal of Personality and Social Psychology, 43*, 1088–1097.

Safilios-Rothschild, C. (1970). The study of family power structure: A review 1960–1969. *Journal of Marriage and the Family, 32*, 539–552.

Snodgrass, S. E. (1985). Women's intuition: The effect of subordinate role on interpersonal sensitivity. *Journal of Personality and Social Psychology, 49*, 146–155.

Snodgrass, S. E. (1992). Further effects of role versus gender on interpersonal sensitivity. *Journal of Personality and Social Psychology, 62*, 154–158.

Sommer, R. (1969). *Personal space*. Englewood Cliffs, N.J.: Prentice-Hall.

Spence, J. T., Helmreich, R. L., & Stapp, J. (1973). A short version of the Attitudes toward Women Scale (AWS). *Bulletin of the Psychonomic Society, 2*, 219–220.

Sprecher, S. (1989). The importance to males and females of physical attractiveness, earning potential and expressiveness. *Sex Roles, 21*, 591–607.

Stanton, E. C., Anthony, S. B., & Joslyn, M. (1889). *The history of woman suffrage*, 2d ed. Rochester, N.Y.: Charles Mann.

Stier, D. S., & Hall, J. A. (1984). Gender differences in touch: An empirical and theoretical review. *Journal of Personality and Social Psychology, 47*, 440–459.

Tajfel, H. (1984). Intergroup relations, social myths, and social justice in social psychology. In H. Tajfel (Ed.), *The social dimension*. Cambridge: Cambridge University Press.

Thomas, D. L., Franks, D. D., & Calonico, J. M. (1972). Role-taking and power in social psychology, *American Sociological Review, 37*, 605–614.

Thorne, B., & Henley, N. (1975). Difference and dominance: An overview of language, gender and society. In B. Thorne & N. Henley (Eds.), *Language and sex: Difference and dominance*. Rowley, Mass.: Newbury House, pp. 5–42.

Unger, R. K., & Crawford, M. (1989). Methods and values in decisions about gender differences [Review of Eagly, *Sex differences in social behavior*], *Contemporary Psychology, 34*, 122–123.

Wallston, B. (1987). Social psychology of women and gender. *Journal of Applied Social Psychology, 17*, 1025–1050.

Weitz, S. (Ed.). (1974). *Nonverbal communication: Readings with commentary*. New York: Oxford University Press.

Weitz, S. (1976). Sex differences in nonverbal communication. *Sex Roles, 2*, 175–184.

Wex, M. (1979). *Let's take back our space: "Female" and "Male" body language as a result of patriarchal structures.* Hamburg: Frauenliteraturverlag Hermaine Fees [first published in German].

Woolf, V. (1929). *A room of one's own.* New York: Harcourt, Brace and World.

NO

Subordination and Nonverbal Sensitivity: A Hypothesis in Search of Support

JUDITH A. HALL AND

AMY G. HALBERSTADT

Two decades ago, groundbreaking ideas were proposed that linked gender, power, and nonverbal behavior (Henley, 1973, 1977). Henley's general thesis was that gender (and race and class) differences in nonverbal behavior parallel the power differences in nonverbal behavior in American society. Specifically, Henley (1977) argued that the behavioral styles and communication skills of women and other subordinated groups were the (often adaptive) product of their subordination and that the nonverbal cues of superior and subordinate both expressed and helped to maintain the power differences between them. Other writers have also made this argument (e.g., Frieze & Ramsey, 1976; Goffman, 1976, 1979; J. B. Miller, 1986; Weitz, 1974, 1979), but Henley's formulation and her influential book are probably best known and most instrumental in generating research on this topic.

The hypothesis that subordinate people behave differently from those with more power or status has gained support with respect to some nonverbal behaviors. For example, people higher in power, expertise, or status gaze at others in conversation relatively more while speaking than while listening (Dovidio & Ellyson, 1985). Finding links between power or status and nonverbal behavior gives

added appeal to Henley's hypothesis that power or status can account for gender differences in nonverbal behavior, of which quite a few have been identified (Hall, 1984, 1987). For this reason, Henley's hypothesis was welcomed by nonverbal communication researchers for its potentially sweeping explanatory power in a field criticized for being too descriptive and not theoretical enough. On the other hand, the power or status explanation of gender differences (hereafter called the subordination theory or hypothesis, following LaFrance & Henley, 1994) has become controversial on both theoretical and empirical grounds (e.g., Halberstadt & Saitta, 1987; Hall, 1984, 1987; Hall & Halberstadt, 1981, 1994; Vrugt & Kerkstra, 1984).

In this chapter, we evaluate the subordination hypothesis as an explanation for gender differences in sensitivity to nonverbal cues.[1] The topic of nonverbal sensitivity is particularly interesting because the gender difference in nonverbal sensitivity, though small to moderate in magnitude, is highly persistent across a broad range of testing instruments. More than 80 percent of all studies of school-aged children, adolescents, and adults show females to score higher on tests of understanding nondeceptive nonverbal cues (Hall, 1978, 1984; Rosenthal, Hall, DiMatteo, Rogers, & Archer, 1979). Studies more recent than those covered in the cited reviews still show a female advantage (e.g., Costanzo & Archer, 1989). The subordination hypothesis holds that women's advantage in nonverbal sensitivity is due to their oppressed or subordinate status (Henley, 1977; Henley & LaFrance, 1984; LaFrance & Henley, 1994) and, further, that other individuals of similarly oppressed or subordinate status will be more nonverbally sen-

---

1. Subordination has been suggested as an explanation of other nonverbal gender differences as well. The empirical evidence is, however, debatable. For example, although studies show that women tend to smile more than men, studies do not often show that low-status individuals smile more than higher status individuals (Deutsch, 1990; Dovidio, Brown, Heltman, Ellyson, & Keating, 1988; Halberstadt, Dovidio, & Davidson, 1988; Hall, Carter, Friedman, & Irish, 1996; Hecht, 1995; Johnson, 1994).

sitive compared to their superiors. Because of this logic, an obvious step is to ask, as we do here, whether oppressed or subordinate people are indeed more nonverbally sensitive, regardless of gender.

It is easy to think of everyday examples of subordinate people having a heightened motivation to read the cues and expressions of those higher up. Consider the low-ranking member of a peer group who attends to the "top dog's" every behavior in order to emulate those cues and win more acceptance, the secretary who needs to read his or her boss's every mood or whim in order to stay in favor, the wife who is able to circumvent her tyrannical husband only by "reading" him with extreme accuracy, or the slave whose very life might depend on accuracy at decoding the slave master's moods and wishes.

But to establish the theory's plausibility, it is not sufficient just to list supporting examples. One must also demonstrate a *lack of nonsupporting examples.* Interestingly, nonsupporting examples come to mind easily. Consider managers who are strongly motivated to be sensitive to their subordinates' concerns at an early stage, before bigger problems develop; military leaders who avert disaster by reading signs of distrust or impending panic in their soldiers; parents who (if our own experience is any guide) pay much more attention to their children's nonverbal cues than the children pay to theirs; and politicians or charismatic preachers who gain their power through their ability to "read" the mood of a crowd with great accuracy.

If more powerful or higher-ranking individuals ever do possess superior judgment abilities, the explanation might lie in the instrumental value of interpersonal skill in attaining rank and influence. Possessing good judgment skills might contribute to the good impressions needed to earn promotions or might be an actual requirement for increasingly complex and demanding roles within an organization. A similar situation may exist among monkeys, where rank appears to be attained more by social skill than by brute force (Mitchell & Maple, 1985). It is equally possible that the sensitivity of the more powerful or high-status person might

result from the requirements of the role once he or she is in it. For example, managers probably have to engage in more complex and more "high stakes" interpersonal interactions than stock clerks, cashiers, or assembly-line workers do, and as a consequence the interpersonal judgment skills of managers might develop accordingly.

The ease with which examples contrary to the subordination hypothesis come to mind makes us believe that theorizing about the relation of power, status, and dominance to interpersonal sensitivity may have become fixated prematurely on the notion that only persons lower on these dimensions have a reason to be nonverbally sensitive. Common sense alone should lead theorists to explore the motives of both higher-status and lower-status individuals with regard to interpersonal sensitivity.

In our view the subordination hypothesis is still in its infancy. Therefore our chapter has two main goals. First, we review the studies that have already examined subordination and nonverbal sensitivity to assess the current support for the hypothesis. Second, we attempt to advance theory and research in this area by examining a variety of important theoretical issues, for example, what is meant by power or status, what circumstances should or should not promote enhanced sensitivity, and what motivational and perceptual states or other conditions might enhance (or inhibit) nonverbal sensitivity in people who vary in power, status, or dominance. Theory development should depend closely on the accumulating research literature. For that reason, we next review studies that have examined subordination and nonverbal sensitivity.

THE EMPIRICAL RECORD

Most studies have operationalized subordination as a *trait* concept—that is, as an enduring quality of the person such as personality or social class. In these studies subordination may also be described as having lower status or being less dominant or less powerful than other people. Similarly, this research has mainly operationalized nonverbal sensitivity also as a *trait*, measuring it using such standard psychometric tests as the Profile of Nonverbal Sensitivity (PONS), which tests an individual's ability to judge the meanings of affective cues conveyed in different channels, such as face or voice (Rosenthal et al., 1979). This trait approach asks, therefore, whether people who are more subordinate, measured as an enduring characteristic, are more nonverbally sensitive, also measured as an enduring skill or trait.

The *state* approach, in contrast, asks whether a person who is more subordinate *than the person he or she is currently interacting with* is particularly good at decoding *that particular person*. One might ask whether the low-status person decodes the high-status person better than vice versa, or whether the low-status person decodes the high-status person better than would people who are not in a subordinate relation to the target. In either case, the question is not about generalized status and skill but about one person's ability or motivation to decode another person with whom there is a meaningful status disparity. Only two studies (Snodgrass, 1985, 1992) have attempted to manipulate status roles and then measure encoding and decoding differences between those same individuals. Before considering Snodgrass's studies, however, we review the methods and findings of studies using the *trait* approach.

THE TRAIT APPROACH

Several authors have related personality measures of *submissiveness-dominance* to scores on nonverbal decoding tests. Contrary to what the subordination hypothesis would predict, the literature finds tendencies for more, not less, dominant individuals to be better decoders of nonverbal cues (Kombos & Fournet, 1985; Rosenthal et al., 1979). In the Kombos and Fournet study, personality dominance was not related to men's ability to understand nonverbal cues but was dramatically predictive of women's ability—with more dominant women being the superior decoders. In a recent meta-analysis of these and other studies, personality dominance was shown to be significantly *positively* related to nonverbal sensitivity (Hall, Halberstadt, & O'Brien, 1996).

If status is defined in terms of socioeconomic

class, the evidence again mainly contradicts the subordination hypothesis. Izard (1971) and Pfaff (1954) both found that higher social class was associated with better ability to decode nonverbal cues in children and junior high school students, respectively. Rosenthal et al. (1979) replicated this effect in two samples of high school girls but found that among high school boys the relation was reversed, supporting the subordination hypothesis. Our recent meta-analysis confirmed that the net effect in these and other studies was for higher socioeconomic status to be associated with greater nonverbal sensitivity (Hall et al., 1996).

Research by the present authors measured subordination in terms of women's gender-role ideology as expressed both abstractly (on a gender-role attitudes scale) and concretely (in terms of male-female roles in their own marriages) (Hall & Halberstadt, 1981; Hall & Halberstadt, 1994). We reasoned that a woman could be called "subordinate" in the gender-role domain if she held conservative gender-role attitudes or had a more traditional home. In three studies, married women answered gender-role questions and took vocal nonverbal sensitivity tests (either the original voice clips from the PONS test that had a female encoder or this test plus a male-encoder vocal test modeled after the original PONS test; see Rosenthal et al., 1979, for more detail on these tests).

In the two studies reported in Hall and Halberstadt (1981), the less "subordinate" women were actually the better decoders of the female encoder's nonverbal cues, in apparent contradiction to the subordination hypothesis. In the sample that also took the male-encoder test, however, there was a marginally significant ($p < .10$) tendency for women who said they had a *more* traditional marriage to score higher on decoding the male voice. This raised the possibility that the relation of gender-role subordination to decoding skill was more complex than anticipated; specifically, it now seemed possible that the direction of the relationship depended on the gender whose cues were being judged.

Hall and Halberstadt (1994) used much the same methodology with a much larger sample of married female university employees who were given both the female- and male-encoder PONS tests. Results paralleled the earlier results for the female-encoder test: women who preferred a less traditional marriage, who did less laundry in the home, and who had less traditional gender-role values scored significantly better at decoding the female voice. However, unlike the Hall and Halberstadt (1981) study, there was no suggestion that more traditional women might be better at decoding the male voice.

Hall and Halberstadt (1994) also measured "subordination" in terms of the women's employment situation, using salary grades as an objective measure of status or rank and participants' rated feelings of subordination in their jobs as a more subjective indicator. Results were complex but did not, on balance, support the subordination hypothesis. Women with a significantly higher salary rank were better at decoding cues that were negative-submissive (i.e., sad or regretful) than women with lower salary rank, contrary to the subordination hypothesis. Salary rank had no relation to accuracy at judging other kinds of cues. Subjective ratings of job subordination revealed even more complex findings that on balance gave little support to the hypothesis.

In our most recent study, we measured subordination using yet more definitions, and we used all three of the major tests of nonverbal sensitivity (Hall, Halberstadt, & O'Brien, 1996). In this study of college students, the subordination measures included prior leadership experience; self-rating of social status in high school; gender-role subordination (relevant for female participants), measured as in our earlier studies; socioeconomic background; dominance and capacity for status scales; and a scale to measure the extent to which the subjects believed that their outcomes were controlled by themselves as opposed to powerful other people.

All three nonverbal decoding tests included both male and female nonverbal expressions: (1) vocal tests of judging posed situational or affective cues (PONS test; Rosenthal et al., 1979); (2) a test of ability to judge objectively verifiable facts about people seen and heard on videotape (for example,

which of two adults is the parent of the child with whom they are interacting) (Interpersonal Perception Task, or IPT; Costanzo & Archer, 1989); and (3) a test of ability to decode emotional facial expressions recorded without the encoders' knowledge (Communication of Affect Receiving Ability Test, or CARAT; Buck, 1976).

There were few significant relations between the trait subordination measures and the trait measures of nonverbal sensitivity, and those that did occur provided only mixed support for the subordination hypothesis.

For males, only one correlation supported the subordination hypothesis: lower parental income was significantly associated with higher scores on the CARAT (male encoders and total). However, in contradiction to the hypothesis, higher mother's education was associated with higher scores on the CARAT (male encoders), and higher mother's education was also marginally significantly related ($p < .10$) to higher PONS scores (female encoder). Also in contradiction to the subordination hypothesis, higher scores on the capacity for status scale were associated with higher scores on the PONS (female encoder and total); higher scores on a dominance scale were marginally associated with higher scores on the CARAT (female encoders) and the PONS (female encoder); and stronger feelings of personal control (i.e., not being controlled by powerful others) were associated with higher scores on the PONS (total score). Thus, for men the trends were almost all contradictory to the subordination hypothesis.

For women, two correlations supported the subordination hypothesis: lower ratings of prior leadership effectiveness were associated with higher scores on the CARAT (male encoders), and less traditional gender-role attitudes were associated with higher scores on the CARAT (male encoders). However, in contradiction to the subordination hypothesis, higher scores on a dominance scale were associated with higher scores on the PONS (total score), and higher scores on the capacity for status scale were associated with higher scores on the IPT (total score).

The finding that less liberal gender-role preferences were associated with better decoding of male encoders for one of the tests is intriguing because it is reminiscent of the similar, marginally significant result from Hall and Halberstadt (1981) and could provide some continued viability to the idea that when women's subordination is defined in terms of "oppressed" gender-role values, their nonverbal sensitivity depends on whose cues they are decoding—men for the more "subordinate" woman and other women for the less "subordinate" woman. However, the present study found this result for only one of the three nonverbal tests, and Hall and Halberstadt (1994), as reported above, found no comparable result.

Moreover, our meta-analysis found no overall trend (across the available studies) to suggest that more traditional women are better judges of men's cues, though it did confirm that more liberal women are better at decoding women's cues (Hall et al., 1996). Thus, it seems on balance not to be the case that women who have more subordinate gender-role values and experiences are especially sensitive to men's nonverbal cues.

All in all, the trait approach to testing the subordination hypothesis has produced little support. Considering that repeated null results alone would bring the subordination hypothesis into doubt, it is even more remarkable that so many different studies have found evidence *significantly disconfirming* the predictions of the hypothesis. Thus, it is not simply that trait-subordinate people, by whatever definition, do not have a special advantage in decoding nonverbal cues on standard tests; rather, these individuals are sometimes shown to be *less* sensitive—exactly opposite of what the theory would predict.

THE STATE APPROACH

Only Snodgrass (1985, 1992) has attempted the more difficult test of the subordination hypothesis by assigning people to status roles for a thirty-minute interaction and then measuring their ability to read each other's cues. After assigning students to teacher-learner roles or boss-employee roles, Snodgrass asked both members of the dyad to rate how the other member felt about them as well as about themselves. Snodgrass (1985) found that learners were more aware of how the teachers viewed them than the other way around (i.e., how aware the teachers were of how the learners viewed them). Similarly, in Snodgrass (1992), employees were more aware of how the bosses viewed them than the other way around (i.e., how aware the bosses were of how the employees viewed them). However, the bosses were more aware of how the employees felt about *themselves* than the employees were aware of how the bosses felt about themselves (the bosses); in other words, the boss appeared to have the greater sensitivity, which is not what the hypothesis would predict.

Snodgrass's findings that subordinates were more aware of how the superior felt about them have often been cited as support for the subordination hypothesis (e.g., LaFrance & Henley, 1994). However, as Snodgrass (1992) made clear, in her design the process of sensitivity within the ongoing interaction necessarily confounded decoding and encoding accuracy so that greater accuracy on the part of subordinates could mean either that subordinates were especially motivated to read evaluative cues sent by their superiors or that superiors sent especially clear evaluative cues to their subordinates.

To attempt to separate perceptivity from expressivity in this sensitivity process, Snodgrass, Hecht, and Ploutz-Snyder (1995) played the tapes of the Snodgrass (1992) study to observers and obtained from them ratings of each target on the tape. Based on the pattern of these (unmotivated) observers' ratings, the authors concluded that the sensitivity of the interactants owed more to the clear expressiveness of their partners than to any heightened motivation to read their partners accurately. Thus, the subordinates' superior sensitivity to their bosses' feelings about them was due primarily to the fact that the bosses made those particular cues especially easy to read. It would appear, therefore, that even the most methodologically promising study to date has failed to support a subordination hypothesis that emphasizes the motivation of the subordinate to decode more accurately.

SUMMARY

Given the initially compelling nature of the subordination hypothesis, it is surprising that there is so little evidence to support it. That predicted differences have been difficult to find suggests that they may not be as pervasive as one might surmise. However, it is still possible that the hypothesis is valid for different definitions of subordination, different measures of nonverbal sensitivity, and different circumstances or populations besides those examined to this point. We next suggest areas of needed clarification with regard to theory development.

THEORETICAL DEVELOPMENT

We first discuss definitions of power and related concepts. These terms have often been used in a general way and have not been clarified in the specific context of the subordination hypothesis. Researchers have thus had little guidance regarding which concepts or measures are more promising or relevant than others. In this section we direct readers to various useful sources and then turn to several dimensions that have received little attention but are critical to an understanding of the concepts. Next, we identify several important issues that must be addressed in further development of the subordination hypothesis.

DEFINITIONS

The subordination hypothesis casts a wide net over various terms of power, status, dominance, and oppression. Henley (1977) defines many of the variables she uses in her broad analysis of the hypothesis. However, because power has often been used interchangeably with dominance or status, and lack of power has often been used interchangeably with subordination or oppression, and all of these have been operationalized in the literature in different ways, it is important (1) to note the many different terms used in the field, (2) to call for greater clarity in the empirical usage of these terms, and (3) to open the discussion again

as to which of these many definitions are most relevant to a "subordination" hypothesis.

Regarding terminology, a classic source describing six types of power is French and Raven (1959), and Raven (1992) has recently published a more comprehensive model of these types of power. Continental discussions of power are also of value (e.g., Foucault, 1980), as are feminist analyses (e.g., Starhawk, 1987; and see Griscom, 1992, Radtke & Stam, 1994, and Yoder & Kahn, 1992, for reviews). For empirical usage, Ellyson and Dovidio (1985) provide a comprehensive description of how researchers have defined many of these terms. Rather than summarize these bodies of work we attempt to distinguish three different dimensions that run through the many terms of power and oppression. Although there are more dimensions than these and although these may sometimes overlap, we see these three as the most essential dimensions for understanding and testing the subordination hypothesis. We describe these three dimensions and how they relate to each other and include examples of their implications for the subordination hypothesis.

The first dimension, *process*, describes the degree to which power is conceived of as static, as opposed to dynamic and interactive. When power is conceived of as relatively static, the terms *dominance* and *subordination* suggest that the positions held by individuals are stable and enduring, at least within a given role relationship (e.g., the boss is dominant and the secretary is subordinate). An alternative perspective is of power as dynamic and changing, where power is not so much a stable quality but a juggling act between two people in which power changes hands from moment to moment, or task to task. For example, a boss and a secretary are often highly dependent on each other for achieving a goal, with the secretary sometimes having more expertise and knowledge than the boss or having substantial power to facilitate or impede accomplishment of a goal.

All attempts to test the subordination hypothesis have measured power as a static and stable entity, at least within the limits of the participants' currently defined roles. Indeed, if the hypothesis is intended to explain overall gender differences in nonverbal sensitivity, which is a fairly stable type of skill, then it ought to be the case that the concomitant aspects of power are also fairly stable. However, understanding power as an interactive process leads to some interesting predictions. For example, bosses with the balance of power in their favor may be less motivated to be nonverbally sensitive, and their low-power secretaries may be more motivated to be sensitive to their bosses' cues. However, when the boss is highly dependent on the secretary to complete some work essential to meeting a deadline, the boss may be more motivated to be nonverbally sensitive.

These predictions are not so much about skill, since both individuals would be expected to have a certain amount of skill. Rather the issue is when they might use their skill. Further, if power is dynamic, we cannot assume that positions of low and high power are stable and unchanging. This has two implications for researchers. First, we should base our judgments of participants' relative power on more than their prescribed roles; perhaps we could obtain participants' own judgments of their power at particular points in time. Second, if power and nonverbal sensitivity are linked and power is dynamic, then we need to assess participants' power and nonverbal sensitivity at the same time in order to find the relationship.

The second dimension, *location*, describes where power resides, either in the individuals (who have it or don't have it) or embedded in the relationship itself. This means that power can be seen as located in the individual and static, located in the relationship and static, located in the individual and dynamic, or located in the relationship and dynamic.

Researchers who perceive power as located within the individual and who also see the process as static assume that power is an enduring quality of the person, and they assess power using trait measures. As the section on the empirical record made clear, most of the research conducted to test the subordination hypothesis has been trait-oriented. Thus, the underlying assumptions of those studies is that power is located in the individual and is relatively unchanging.

Researchers who perceive power as relational and see the process as static assume a situational explanation for power. They assess power by finding stable power relationships in the military or in industry (in which cases the positions may also be confounded with such trait or demographic differences as age and education) or by creating power situations in the laboratory, as in Snodgrass (1985, 1992), described earlier. If power is relational and static, then the subordination hypothesis would predict greater sensitivity only in the relationships in which an individual is subordinate. Thus, the subordinate who has an exquisite sense of his or her superior's expressed needs and moods may be merely average when decoding equal-status friends, neighbors, or family.

Researchers who perceive power as located in the individual and see the process as dynamic might still use personality measures, but they would be tailored to answer questions as to power *now*. This perspective envisions power as a ball that is frequently tossed back and forth between partners. And finally, researchers who perceive power as relational and dynamic recognize the constant tension of striving and resistance, that power cannot exist without resistance (e.g., Foucault, 1980), and that power has no individual focus but is located within the relationship. Thus, researchers with this perspective need to study power at the dyadic level or at least need to examine individual responses only in relation to each other (e.g., a time series analysis). We know of no researchers who have pursued these more empirically difficult perspectives.

The third dimension, *quality of power*, describes the degree to which power is coercive versus democratic and cooperative (Starhawk, 1987). *Power-over* is the power wielded by one person on another in an adversarial relationship: who has the power to coerce behavior, either subtly or overtly? This is the form of power that psychologists have most often studied, though it may not be the form of power that laypersons most often think about (C. L. Miller & Cummins, 1992). In terms of location, an individual can have strivings to assert power over another individual; a relationship perspective would note that the ability to have power-over often includes basic acceptance of the hierarchical structures by the oppressed other. *Power-with* is cooperative power; it is a willingness to suggest rather than demand, on the part of one individual, and a willingness to accept, modify, or reject on the part of the other. Power-with is usually the power between equals.[2]

The qualities of power-over and power-with can also be considered in relation to process and location, though the intersections of these three dimensions can be quite complicated. Perhaps more fruitful is to return to the question of how the dimension we call quality of power might help us investigate the subordination hypothesis. In the boss-secretary example, we normally consider such a relationship to be a power-over situation; the boss has the power to evaluate and even fire the secretary, but the secretary rarely if ever has the opportunity to evaluate the boss. Although we can think of the secretary as also having power over the boss (the secretary can quit at a critical time in the work cycle or can comment to the boss's boss, etc.), we can also consider boss-secretary relations that are more oriented toward power-with: secretaries and bosses who work together more collaboratively and with more equivalent respect for each other's ideas and abilities. It seems clear that the subordination hypothesis relates only to power-over, so choosing participants in field settings means screening out relationships that have evolved into power-with and creating experimental tasks that are clearly tapping the power-over dimension. Many studies merely assume status or dominance by virtue of the hierarchical structuring of roles, but this could obscure the difference between power-over and power-with relationships.

It may also be the case that women create more power-with than men do, whereas men may create

more power-over than women, consistent with findings on gender differences in the behavioral styles of managers (Eagly & Johnson, 1990). If women's goals regarding power are different, their nonverbal behaviors and skills may reflect those different goals of collaboration and equality rather than subordination and oppression.

If power-over is the most relevant case for the subordination hypothesis, another question is how extreme the power-over situation must be in order to produce special nonverbal sensitivity in the subordinate. Thus, is the hypothesis valid mainly in extreme circumstances, when powerful others wield almost complete control over less powerful others? Perhaps the reasoning behind the subordination hypothesis is accurate but literal; greater nonverbal sensitivity developed as a survival mechanism, and the difference in nonverbal accuracy will be evident only in cases where survival really is at stake. If so, then researchers need to move out of the laboratory and out of business-type settings into more extreme situations—perhaps studying abusive spousal relations.

A final point to be made with regard to the power-over dimension in male-female relationships is to caution against assuming too glibly the greater status and power of men. An example would be the traditional domestic sphere, where men's higher status may get them certain privileges but where women often have as much or more decision-making power (interior decorating, handling family accounts, choosing and managing child care, planning vacations, orchestrating social life) and often wield power directly over their husbands by telling them when to pick up the children, what to wear, what to pick up at the store, and when to cut the grass.

Paradoxically, it may indeed be relevant to the subordination hypothesis that women wield considerable power by virtue of their responsibility for the socioemotional domain. Although society's association of men with "instrumentality" and women with "expressiveness" may reflect a lower valuation of the expressiveness function, society nevertheless places great power in women's hands by expecting them to be more responsible for the success of social interactions. All this social work

2. A third type of power is *power-within* (Starhawk, 1987): the capacity to act, to use one's energy and potential, to be self-empowered. Power-within is sometimes described as power-to or self-empowerment in the psychological literature and, in at least one sample of 125 women, appears to be the predominant definition of what power ought to be and is in their personal lives (C. L. Miller & Cummins, 1992).

may be a kind of oppression, but it also means that women exercise enormous social power in the microsocial arena. Indeed, a radical thinker might even propose that women's nonverbal skills (and social skills in general) are more meaningfully related to the power they wield in the microsocial arena than to their lack of power in society at large.

These examples raise a question about broad assertions of men's greater status and power compared to women. Although it is true that in many, many situations men are accorded greater prestige, assumed to be more knowledgeable, and so forth (they have "diffuse status"; Berger, Rosenholtz, & Zelditch, 1980), there are also many exceptions to this generalization. To take as a given that men have higher status (power, etc.) renders certain explanations tortured, to say the least. For example, if the female vice president of the company is more nonverbally sensitive than the male high-school dropout who mops the floors, only a rather convoluted chain of reasoning could portray her as oppressed in comparison to him. Such an example raises the complex issue of proximal and distal causation, to which we now turn.

TEMPORAL RELATIONS

We have already discussed the temporal relations that might be studied when employing a dynamic definition of power. But two other temporal issues are also important. The first pertains to events occurring in the life course of an individual. Is the experience of subordination at any time in a person's life sufficient to predict that that individual will have relatively greater decoding skill? Or is it necessary to be experiencing oppression at the time of testing? And how much time must pass in an oppressive state before nonverbal decoding skill increases? J. B. Miller (1986) suggests that nonverbal sensitivity is a skill developed over long practice, whereas laboratory research (Snodgrass, 1985, 1992) seems to rest on the premise that nonverbal sensitivity is motivational and can be activated by transient threats or rewards.

The second issue pertains to events occurring over history and cultural development. LaFrance

and Henley (1994) seem to suggest that oppression at an earlier time in society may have created intervening factors that in turn influence sensitivity. For example, the early subordination of women in Euro-American society may have produced expectancies for their interpersonal sensitivity that could remain in force even if society evolved to a highly egalitarian level. An extreme argument of this sort would hold that the subordinate status of women is the distal cause of *all* psychological gender differences—that is, whatever proximal causes such differences may have are themselves the products of subordination. Thus, by definition, all gender differences are due to subordination. However, such a claim may be unfalsifiable, and therefore more a matter of political rhetoric rather than testable science.

MODIFYING FACTORS

An important part of theory development is to identify what might modify the basic predictions of a theory. Clearly, no broad claims can be universally true, for all people in all times, places, and circumstances. Given what we know about situational influence, blanket statements about differences between men and women are unrealistic (Deaux & Kite, 1987; Deaux & Major, 1987; Eagly, 1987; Forgas, 1979; C. Sherif, 1982; Unger, 1983). Depending on the context, diametrically opposite gender differences sometimes emerge (e.g., Bugental, Love, & Gianetto, 1971; Halberstadt, Hayes, & Pike, 1983). Alternatively, men and women may react differently to similar situations: perhaps men are more nonverbally accurate as subordinates, but not women. Thus, gender itself could modify the predictions of the subordination hypothesis.

Another possible modifying factor stems from the cognitive demands placed on an individual during interpersonal interaction. As pointed out by Patterson (1995), interactants must divide their finite cognitive capacity between *encoding* (choosing their self-presentational goals and behaving in ways consistent with those while sending messages relevant to the topic at hand) and *decoding* (noticing and interpreting the other's messages).

Whether a subordinate has a heightened sensitivity to the other's messages may depend on how much attention he or she is devoting to the encoding task. Heightened attention to one's own performance might lead a subordinate to pay relatively less attention to the superior's cues.

Also relevant here is the phenomenon of cognitive tunnel vision. Easterbrook (1959) demonstrated that "emotional arousal acts consistently to reduce the range of cues that an organism uses" (p. 183). Thus, when anxious, people tend to focus narrowly on immediately pertinent tasks, giving less attention to the field or context. One could make the prediction that an anxious subordinate might focus attention even more on his or her own performance, to the relative exclusion of attending to cues sent by the other person.

If the cognitive demands of being both sender and receiver take a toll on the subordinate's interpersonal judgment accuracy, then one interesting possibility would be that subordinates are more accurate only when they do not have to play both roles at once. Perhaps subordinates are more accurate when they are in the third-party observer role, watching a superior interacting with other subordinates or with the superior's peers.

Another modifying factor is likely to be the *kinds of cues being judged.* If the key to the subordinate's heightened sensitivity is the need to please, then the subordinate may be sensitive primarily to cues that are relevant to his or her own welfare. For example, a subordinate might look carefully for cues of disapproval or approval, or might take pains to notice when the superior wants to terminate the conversation, but might not care at all about whether the superior is enjoying his or her lunch. A similar case for the specificity of certain cues can be suggested in the somewhat analogous case of the nonverbal sensitivities of minority-status individuals; here, one might predict that members of oppressed groups would be particularly skilled at recognizing cues of prejudice (Rollman, 1978) but not necessarily other kinds of nonverbal cues. Alternatively, subordinates might be oversensitive about certain kinds of cues and might read meanings that are not present. This par-

ticular example provides a suitable transition to the next section, in which we take a closer look at the various possible meanings of the term *sensitivity.*

PSYCHOLOGICAL MECHANISMS IMPLICATED IN THE SUBORDINATION HYPOTHESIS

In the remaining section we take up two final issues that a developed theory must address. First, the broad construct of "nonverbal sensitivity" needs to be better defined, and second, the potentially crucial role of the subordinate's (and superior's) motivations for accurate decoding must be clarified.

THE NATURE OF "NONVERBAL SENSITIVITY"

In our own research described earlier and in our hypothetical examples we included several different kinds of "sensitivity." As yet, it is not known which might be most pertinent to the subordination hypothesis, and theory provides no guidance. One kind of sensitivity can be called *perceptual sensitivity* or the tendency to attend to and notice another's cues. Being perceptually sensitive does not necessarily imply accuracy in judging the meanings of another's cues because a person might be oversensitive, reading cues that are not really there, or might chronically give the wrong interpretation to cues that are there. *Inferential accuracy,* or the accurate judgment of the meanings of cues, is a more complex process that involves noticing cues *and* applying a judgment algorithm.

All existing research on subordination and nonverbal sensitivity has used measures of inferential accuracy; even the research of Snodgrass (1985, 1992), in which participants judged each other in an on-line fashion, was based on participants' inferences about each other's moods and attitudes. As far as we know, measures that capture "sensitivity" at a more attentional or perceptual level have not been employed, though many hypothetical examples of special sensitivity in subordinates refer to subordinates' tendencies to *notice* cues rather than to their ability to reach more accurate inferences about cues.

And, to complicate the landscape even more, there is great variability in the kinds of cues that one might be asked to make inferences about. Dimensions include spontaneity (whether the cues were posed by encoders or emitted spontaneously), meaning content of cues (e.g., emotion cues, deception cues, status cues), and cue channels (e.g., face, body, voice). As yet, we do not know which of the many possible kinds of cues might be most relevant to subordinates.

Several subordinate-superior decoding processes can now be enumerated. If sensitivity is defined as attention to cues, then a subordinate's sensitivity could be extremely transient: the subordinate might not be sensitive to the superior in another situation where the motive to attend to cues is not aroused, nor would the subordinate be sensitive to other people's cues (unless, of course, those people aroused the same motivation to attend closely as the original superior did). In a second kind of process, as the result of practice over time (possibly aided by paying extra attention), the subordinate gains skill at reading his or her particular superior's needs, wishes, moods, and intentions (inferential accuracy). Accuracy has now gained a knowledge base and is no longer the simple consequence of heightened attention to cues. In yet a third kind of process, repeated practice with this superior or other superiors produces generalized knowledge of nonverbal cues, such that the subordinate now has an advantage at reading anyone's cues, a skill that might then be picked up with traitlike decoding measures of the sort used in most research. This third process is suggested by Henley and LaFrance (1984) when they suggest that women's greater sensitivity may be due to their greater tendency to attend to others via gaze, a trait they link directly to women's low-dominant group status. Clearly, an understanding of the contribution of subordinate status to "sensitivity" could depend greatly on which definitions of sensitivity are applied.

THE ROLE OF MOTIVATION

Unclear in previous theorizing is the role of the subordinate's motivational states in producing en-

hanced sensitivity. Some aspects of this problem have been raised earlier in this chapter. As mentioned earlier, the assumption seems to be that sensitivity is a survival tactic in subordinates: if you are subordinate, it is in your interests to read the superior's cues in order to avoid criticism, fulfill the superior's needs better, and stay in favor (e.g., Henley & LaFrance, 1984; J. B. Miller, 1986). For convenience we shall call this the *motive to please.*

It is important that the theoretical relevance of the subordinate's motivation be made explicit. If the motive to please were an integral part of the theory, there would be implications for research predictions. Two examples can be provided. First, subordinate status should be related to nonverbal sensitivity only when the motive to please is aroused. An unhappy or resentful subordinate might not be expected to have special sensitivity; indeed, this subordinate might deliberately ignore the superior's cues or notice them and distort their meanings. Second, if a subordinate shows special sensitivity to the superior for *some other motivational reason*, this would not qualify as support for the theory. Let us suppose the fire alarm goes off at work. Subordinates look to their superiors for cues that can define the situation and provide a guide to appropriate action (cf. Latané & Darley, 1970); if the superior does not look troubled and keeps working, the subordinates will probably do the same. Moreover, the superiors do not turn to the subordinates for clues as to what to do. Superficially, the subordinates are manifesting greater "sensitivity" to the superior than vice versa. However, the motive is not to please but rather to *gain information.* Subordinates might be reasoning (with justification in many cases) that the superior is likely to know more about what's going on than they do. Thus, if the motive to please is an explicit part of the subordination hypothesis, the fire alarm example would *not* support it.[3]

Another issue pertaining to motivation is the inadequate discussion of the superior's motives in

3. The motive to please and the motive to gain information correspond to the motivational bases of normative social influence (Asch, 1951) and informational social influence (M. Sherif, 1935), respectively.

the interpersonal decoding process. As we understand previous statements of the subordination hypothesis, superiors' accuracy could be unaffected by their role (i.e., the subordination-sensitivity relationship is due to the subordinates' sensitivity, not the superiors'). Alternatively, superiors may actually be motivated *not* to pay close attention to subordinates' cues, perhaps as a way of saying "I don't need you" to the subordinates. Fiske (1993) has suggested that because superiors have no particular need to monitor the subordinate's cues, they resort to stereotyping as a substitute for direct discernment of individuals' qualities.

But there is more to say about superiors' motives and their decoding of subordinates. First, research paradigms that compare subordinates' to superiors' decoding cannot distinguish one party's *heightened* motivation to attend to cues from the other party's *reduced* motivation. Only a paradigm that, for example, also measures baseline measures of the individuals' sensitivity when not in their respective roles could accomplish this. For example, if people didn't get more sensitive when in subordinate roles but people did get *less* sensitive when in superior roles, it would produce subordinate-superior differences in sensitivity, but *not* because of the subordinate's motive to please or for any other reason located in the subordinate, for that matter. Moreover, reduced sensitivity by superiors in organizational settings could be related not to any invidious motives but rather to the hierarchical structuring that results in few superiors for each subordinate but many subordinates for each superior. Thus, a superior may not be able to attend fully to subordinates' cues even if he or she wants to, because of time and energy constraints.

CONCLUSIONS

The subordination hypothesis is not faring well in empirical tests, but it should not yet be dismissed as unsupportable. In our view, the trait-based measurement approach that has been mainly used is much less likely to produce supportive results than are more dynamic conceptions both of subordination (e.g., as defined by roles) and of nonverbal sensitiv-ity (e.g., as measured between actual interactants as opposed to standard tests). Moreover, an expanded definition of nonverbal sensitivity to include attentional or perceptual measures will also provide more fertile opportunities for testing the hypothesis.

As we have made clear throughout, we believe that a large amount of theoretical work still needs to be done. We have tried to show that both power and sensitivity are highly complex concepts, with a multitude of nuances, underlying assumptions, and theoretical possibilities. Our call is for greater complexity in our thinking about gender, power, and nonverbal sensitivity.

Although LaFrance and Henley (1994) said the recurring question is "whether this well-documented gender difference in nonverbal sensitivity is best understood as stemming from deep-seated differences between the sexes or whether it is due to structures that create power inequities between women and men" (p. 289), we believe the choices are more diverse than this. We can imagine that many possibilities exist as explanations for gender differences besides just these two options. If by "deep-seated differences" the authors mean innate differences, then they seem to be offering "power inequities" as the only possible social explanation. Gender differences in cultural norms, roles, expectancies, and socialization are not synonymous, by definition, with "power inequities between women and men."

Although we have devoted much of our research lives to studying gender differences in nonverbal sensitivity, we recognize that women and men are also quite similar in their nonverbal styles and skills. We do not wish our studies to be used falsely to dichotomize the behavior of women and men, and we do not wish to lose sight of the tremendous variability in people's behavior regardless of their gender.

The preparation of this chapter was supported by grant SBR 9311544 from the National Science Foundation.

REFERENCES

Asch, S. E. (1951). Effects of group pressure upon the modification and distortion of judgments. In H. Guetzkow

(Ed.), *Groups, leadership, and men*. Pittsburgh: Carnegie Press.

Berger, J., Rosenholtz, S. J., & Zelditch, M., Jr. (1980). Status organizing processes. *Annual Review of Sociology, 6,* 479–508.

Buck, R. (1976). A test of nonverbal receiving ability: Preliminary studies. *Human Communication Research, 2,* 162–171.

Bugental, D. E., Love, L. R., & Gianetto, R. M. (1971). Perfidious feminine faces. *Journal of Personality and Social Psychology, 17,* 314–318.

Costanzo, M., & Archer, D. (1989). Interpreting the expressive behavior of others: The Interpersonal Perception Task. *Journal of Nonverbal Behavior, 13,* 225–245.

Deaux, K., & Kite, M. E. (1987). Thinking about gender. In B. B. Hess & M. M. Ferree (Eds.), *Analyzing gender: A handbook of social science research* (pp. 92–117). Newbury Park, Calif.: Sage.

Deaux, K., & Major, B. (1987). Putting gender into context: An interactive model of gender-related behavior. *Psychological Review, 94,* 369–389.

Deutsch, F. M. (1990). Status, sex, and smiling: The effect of role on smiling in men and women. *Personality and Social Psychology Bulletin, 16,* 531–540.

Dovidio, J. F., Brown, C. F., Heltman, K., Ellyson, S. L., & Keating, C. F. (1988). Power displays between women and men in discussions of gender-linked tasks: A multichannel study. *Journal of Personality and Social Psychology, 55,* 580–587.

Dovidio, J. F., Ellyson, S. L., Keating, C. F., Heltman, K., & Brown, C. E. (1988). The relationship of social power to visual displays of dominance between men and women. *Journal of Personality and Social Psychology, 54,* 233–242.

Eagly, A. H. (1987). *Sex differences in social behavior: A social role interpretation.* Hillsdale, N.J.: Erlbaum.

Eagly, A. H., & Johnson, B. T. (1990). Gender and leadership style: A meta-analysis. *Psychological Bulletin, 108,* 233–256.

Easterbrook, J. A. (1959). The effect of emotion on cue utilization and the organization of behavior. *Psychological Review, 66,* 183–201.

Ellyson, S. L., & Dovidio, J. F. (1985). Power, dominance, and nonverbal behavior: Basic concepts and issues. In S. L. Ellyson & J. F. Dovidio (Eds.), *Power, dominance, and nonverbal behavior* (pp. 1–27). New York: Springer-Verlag.

Fiske, S. T. (1993). Controlling other people: The impact of power on stereotyping. *American Psychologist, 48,* 621–628.

Forgas, J. P. (1979). *Social episodes: The study of interaction routines.* New York: Academic Press.

Foucault, M. (1980). *Power/knowledge: Selected interviews and writings, 1972–1977* (Ed. C. Gordon). New York: Pantheon.

French, J. R. P., Jr., & Raven, B. H. (1959). The bases of social power. In D. Cartwright (Ed.), *Studies in social power* (pp. 150–167). Ann Arbor: University of Michigan Press.

Frieze, I. H., & Ramsey, S. J. (1976). Nonverbal maintenance of traditional sex roles. *Journal of Social Issues, 32,* 133–141.

Goffman, E. (1976). Gender advertisements. *Studies in the Anthropology of Visual Communication, 3,* 69–154.

Goffman, E. (1979). *Gender advertisements.* New York: Harper and Row.

Griscom, J. L. (1992). Women and power: Definition, dualism, and difference. *Psychology of Women Quarterly, 16,* 389–414.

Halberstadt, A. G., Dovidio, J. F., & Davidson, L. A. (1988, October). *Power, gender, and smiling.* Paper presented at the Society for Experimental Social Psychology.

Halberstadt, A. G., Hayes, C. W., & Pike, K. M. (1987). Gender and gender-role differences in smiling and communication consistency. *Sex Roles, 19,* 589–604.

Halberstadt, A. G., & Saitta, M. B. (1987). Gender, nonverbal behavior, and perceived dominance: A test of the theory. *Journal of Personality and Social Psychology, 53,* 257–272.

Hall, J. A. (1978). Gender effects in decoding nonverbal cues. *Psychological Bulletin, 85,* 845–857.

Hall, J. A. (1984). *Nonverbal sex differences: Communication accuracy and expressive style.* Baltimore: Johns Hopkins University Press.

Hall, J. A. (1987). On explaining gender differences: The case of nonverbal communication. In P. Shaver & C. Hendrick (Eds.), *Sex and gender* (pp. 177–200). Beverly Hills, Calif.: Sage.

Hall, J. A., Carter, J. D., Friedman, G. B., & Irish, J. T. (1996). Smiling in relation to man's pulsated and acquired status. Manuscript in preparation.

Hall, J. A., & Halberstadt, A. G. (1981). Sex roles and nonverbal communication skills. *Sex Roles, 7,* 273–287.

Hall, J. A., & Halberstadt, A. G. (1994). "Subordination" and sensitivity to nonverbal cues: A study of married working women. *Sex Roles, 31,* 149–165.

Hall, J. A., Halberstadt, A. G., & O'Brien, C. (1996). Nonverbal sensitivity and trait measures of dominance/status. Manuscript submitted for publication.

Hecht, M. A. (1995). The effect of power and gender on smiling. Ph.D. diss., Boston College.

Henley, N. M. (1973). Status and sex: Some touching observations. *Bulletin of the Psychonomic Society, 2,* 91–93.

Henley, N. M. (1977). *Body politics: Power, sex, and nonverbal communication.* Englewood Cliffs, N.J.: Prentice-Hall.

Henley, N., & LaFrance, M. (1984). Gender as culture: Difference and dominance in nonverbal behavior. In A. Wolfgang (Ed.), *Nonverbal behavior: Perspectives, applications, intercultural insights* (pp. 351–371). Lewiston, N.Y.: C. J. Hogrefe.

Izard, C. E. (1971). *The face of emotion.* New York: Appleton-Century-Crofts.

Johnson, C. (1994). Gender, legitimate authority, and leader-subordinate conversations. *American Sociological Review, 59,* 122–135.

Kombos, N. A., & Fournet, G. P. (1985). Effects of dominance-submissiveness and gender on recognition of nonverbal emotional cues. *Educational and Psychological Research, 5,* 19–28.

LaFrance, M., & Henley, N. M. (1994). On oppressing hypothesis: Or differences in nonverbal sensitivity revisited. In L. Radtke & H. Stam (Eds.), *Power/gender: Social relations in theory and practice* (pp. 287–311). London: Sage.

Latané, B., & Darley, J. M. (1970). *The unresponsive bystander: Why doesn't he help?* New York: Appleton-Century-Crofts.

Miller, J. B. (1986). *Toward a new psychology of women*, 2d ed. Boston: Beacon Press.

Miller, C. L., & Cummins, A. G. (1992). An examination of women's perspectives on power. *Psychology of Women Quarterly, 16*, 415–428.

Mitchell, G., & Maple, T. L. (1985). Dominance in nonhuman primates. In S. L. Ellyson & J. F. Dovidio (Eds.), *Power, dominance, and nonverbal behavior* (pp. 49–66). New York: Springer-Verlag.

Patterson, M. L. (1995). A parallel process model of nonverbal communication. *Journal of Nonverbal Behavior, 19*, 3–29.

Pfaff, P. L. (1954). An experimental study of the communication of feeling without contextual material. *Speech Monographs, 21*, 155–156.

Radtke, H. L., & Stam, H. J. (1994). Introduction. In H. L. & H. J. Stam (Eds.), *Power/gender: Social relations in theory and practice* (pp. 1–14). London: Sage.

Raven, B. H. (1992). A power/interaction model of interpersonal influence: French and Raven thirty years later. *Journal of Social Behavior and Personality, 7*, 217–244.

Rollman, S. A. (1978). The sensitivity of black and white Americans to nonverbal cues of prejudice. *Journal of Social Psychology, 105*, 73–77.

Rosenthal, R., Hall, J. A., DiMatteo, M. R., Rogers, P. L., &

Archer, D. (1979). *Sensitivity to nonverbal communication: The PONS test*. Baltimore: Johns Hopkins University Press.

Sherif, C. W. (1982). Needed concepts in the study of gender identity. *Psychology of Women Quarterly, 6*, 375–398.

Sherif, M. (1935). A study of some social factors in perception. *Archives of Psychology, 27*, 1–60.

Snodgrass, S. E. (1985). Women's intuition: The effect of subordinate role on interpersonal sensitivity. *Journal of Personality and Social Psychology, 49*, 146–155.

Snodgrass, S. E. (1992). Further effects of role versus gender on interpersonal sensitivity. *Journal of Personality and Social Psychology, 62*, 154–158.

Snodgrass, S. E., Hecht, M. A., & Ploutz-Synder, R. J. (1995). Interpersonal sensitivity: Expressivity or perceptivity? Manuscript submitted for publication.

Starhawk (1987). *Truth or dare: Encounters with power, authority, and mystery*. San Francisco: Harper and Row.

Unger, R. K. (1983). Through the looking glass: No wonderland yet! The reciprocal relationship between methodology and models of reality. *Psychology of Women Quarterly, 8*, 9–32.

Vrugt, A., & Kerkstra, A. (1984). Sex differences in nonverbal communication. *Semiotica, 50*, 1–41.

Weitz, S. (Ed.). (1974). *Nonverbal communication: Readings with commentary*. New York: Oxford University Press.

Weitz, S. (Ed.). (1979). *Nonverbal communication: Readings with commentary*, 2d ed. New York: Oxford University Press.

Yoder, J. D., & Kahn, A. S. (1992). Toward a feminist understanding of women and power. *Psychology of Women Quarterly, 16*, 381–388.

Negotiation Strategies:

Do Women and Men Have

Different Styles?

Whether at work or in our personal and social relationships, as much as 75 percent of our day is spent in interpersonal negotiations. Interest in this topic can be measured by the popularity and proliferation of negotiation books, ranging from Roger Fisher and William Ury's *Getting to Yes* (1981) and Ury's *Getting Past No* (1991) to such specialized guides for women as Juliet Nierenberg and Irene Ross's *Women and the Art of Negotiating* (1985) and Nicole Schapiro's *Negotiating for Your Life* (1993). Because of the growing importance of international trade, a great deal of attention has also been devoted to the effect of cultural differences on negotiating styles (Griffin & Daggett, 1990; Pye, 1992). Researchers have conducted a series of experiments comparing negotiators from the United States and fifteen other countries, including Japan, China, Canada, Brazil, and Mexico. Their findings indicate that although the negotiators from different countries use different negotiating styles, they secure the same results (Lewicki et al., 1994).

Corporate interest is illustrated by the recent increase of 30–40 percent in training programs in negotiation and how to cope with diversity in the workplace (Filipczak, 1994). Colleges and universities have also entered the field, offering academic courses, certificates, and degree programs. In 1995, Harvard Law School's Program on Negotiation presented its first gender dynamics workshop, focusing on women's concerns in negotiating sexual harassment, leave policy, equal treatment, and "glass ceiling" and "sticky floor" problems.

Much of the early research on gender and negotiation was based on laboratory experiments. These studies found no relation between gender and bargaining behavior (Rubin & Brown, 1975). However, there is considerable evidence that women do not fare as well as men when they engage in real-life negotiating situations. For example, research in which male and female field testers used the same strategy in bargaining for a new car at several Chicago dealerships found that White women were offered markups 40 percent higher than White men and that Black women had to pay more than three times what White male testers paid (Ayres, 1991). Women also appear to be at a disadvantage in negotiating situations of domestic conflict, particularly divorce, where they receive smaller settlements from mediation than from judges. Sexual victimization in work settings presents another problem. Victims of sexual harassment rarely try to negotiate with the harasser to stop (Dunwoody-Miller & Gutek, 1985), and when they do, they commonly experience retaliation (Koss et al., 1994).

The fact that women in the aggregate earn only 70 percent of men's annual salary (U.S. Department of Labor, 1994) has attracted the attention of negotiation researchers. Although male-female salary differences are caused by a number of socioeconomic factors, Cynthia Kay Stevens and her colleagues (1993) believe that the disparity could be reduced if women had better negotiation skills. One inquiry traced 31–34 percent of gender differences in compensation to differences in starting salaries (Gerhart, 1990). In another study, Gerhart and Rynes (1991) found that male MBA students negotiated higher starting salaries than their female counterparts. This suggests that salary inequities could be reduced if women were trained to negotiate starting salaries comparable to those of men. However, Stevens et al. (1993) claim that it is not a matter merely of learning new negotiating skills; women need supplementary training in setting goals and building self-confidence to improve their ability to interact in negotiating situations.

The finding that skill training alone is unrelated to better starting salaries for women suggests that other factors are at work. Bylsma and Major's (1994) experimental study documents that women have lower salary expectations than men and, in turn, that their perceptions of their personal performance are significantly influenced by how much they are paid. This creates a vicious cycle: job discrimination and salary inequality lead women and men to develop different standards for judging whether they have been fairly paid. When women compare their wages with other underpaid women, they may be content with their low salary. This could explain why women seldom complain that their salaries are too low (Clayton & Crosby, 1992). It certainly puts women at a psychological disadvantage in bargaining situations.

The following chapters focus on the question of whether women and men negotiate differently. Deborah M. Kolb identifies a special women's negotiating voice and explores why that voice is not often heard. Carol Watson disagrees and presents the view that the observed differences in negotiating are caused by relative status and power considerations rather than by gender characteristics.

REFERENCES

Ayres, I. (1991). Fair driving: Gender and race discrimination in retail car negotiations. *Harvard Law Review, 104* (4), 817–872.

Bylsma, W. H., & Major, B. (1994). Social comparisons and contentment: Exploring the psychological costs of the gender wage gap. *Psychology of Women Quarterly, 18,* 241–249.

Clayton, S. D., & Crosby, F. J. (1992). *Justice, gender, and affirmative action.* Ann Arbor: University of Michigan Press.

Dunwoody-Miller, V., & Gutek, B. A. (1985). Sexual harassment in the state workforce. Results of a survey.

SHE project report. California State Employees' Association, Sacramento.

Filipczak, B. (1994, October). Looking past the numbers. *Training, 31,* 67–72, 74.

Fisher, R., & Ury, W. (1981) *Getting to yes: Negotiating agreement without giving in.* Boston: Houghton Mifflin.

Gerhart, B. (1990). Gender differences in current and starting salaries: The role of performance, college major, and job title. *Industrial and Labor Relations Review, 43,* 418–433.

Gerhart, B., & Rynes, S. (1991). Determinants and consequences of salary negotiations by male and female MBA graduates. *Journal of Applied Psychology, 76,* 256–262.

Griffin, T. J., & Daggett, W. R. (1990). *The global negotiator: Building strong business relationships anywhere in the world.* New York: Harper Business.

Koss, M. P., Goodman, L. A., Brown, A., Fitzgerald, L. F., Keita, G. P., & Russo, N. F. (1994). *No safe haven: Male violence against women at home, at work, and in the community.* Washington, D.C.: American Psychological Association.

Lewicki, R. J., Litterer, J. A., Minton, J. W., & Saunders, D. M. (1994). *Negotiation,* 2d ed. Burr Ridge, Ill.: Irwin.

Nierenberg, J., & Ross, I. S. (1985). *Women and the art of negotiating.* New York: Simon & Schuster.

Pye, L. W. (1992). *Chinese negotiating style.* New York: Quorum Books.

Rubin, J. Z., & B. R. Brown. (1975). *The social psychology of bargaining and negotiation.* New York: Academic Press.

Schapiro, N. (1993). *Negotiating for your life: New success strategies for women.* New York: Henry Holt.

Stevens, C. K., Bavetta, A. G., & Gist, M.E. (1993). Gender differences in the acquisition of salary negotiation skills: The role of goals, self-efficacy, and perceived control. *Journal of Applied Psychology, 78,* 723–735.

Ury, W. (1991). *Getting past no.* New York: Bantam Books.

U.S. Department of Labor. (1994). *1993 Handbook on women workers: Trends and issues.* Washington, D.C.: U.S. Government Printing Office.

ADDITIONAL READING

Gray, B. (1994). The gender-based foundations of negotiation theory. In R. J. Lewicki, Shephard, B. H., & Bies, R. (Eds.), *Research on Negotiations in Organizations, 4* (pp. 3–36). Greenwich, Conn.: JAI Press.

Gwartney-Gibbs, P. A., & Lach, D. H. (1994). Gender and workplace dispute resolution: A conceptual and theoretical model. *Law & Society Review, 28,* 265–296.

Kaman, V. S., & Hartel, C. E. J. (1994). Gender differences in anticipated pay negotiation strategies and outcomes. *Journal of Business and Psychology, 9,* 183–197.

Taylor, A., & Miller, J. B. (Eds.). (1994). *Conflict and gender.* Cresskill, N.J.: Hampton Press.

Thacker, R. A. (1995). Gender, influence tactics, and job characteristics preferences: New insights into salary determination. *Sex Roles, 32,* 617–638.

Her Place at the Table:

Gender and Negotiation

DEBORAH M. KOLB

"I didn't know it was your table," said Alice at the Mad Hatter's Tea Party.

—Lewis Carroll, *Alice in Wonderland*

A central agenda of recent feminist studies across the social sciences has been to heed the often "unheard" voices of women. They maintain that women's experience is often treated as a variant, typically an inferior variant, of a dominant male model. Recent scholarship has tried to right the record. What has emerged is a conception of an alternative way of making sense of the world and of acting within it.

Existing research and our own experiences suggest that the voices of women are often hushed in formal negotiation. Conflict and competition are important in formal negotiation, and therefore it may not be a comfortable place for many women. In reaction to this unnatural setting, some women may try to emulate (quite successfully) a culturally dominant style. Other women find that their strengths and skills are impaired in this conflict setting. I discuss how women experience conflict as well as how this may affect their behavior and how they are perceived in a negotiation later in this chapter.

There is a certain irony in trying to articulate a woman's voice in negotiation. Negotiation is often put forth as an alternative to violence and adversarial proceedings. Some people argue that it reflects a feminine view of interaction; that it is better to talk than to fight; and, rather than pit parties against one another in a win-lose contest, that all parties' interests and needs should be considered and met. If this is true, why is it necessary to articulate the woman's voice in negotiation?

There are at least three reasons. First, there are significant differences in how men and women approach negotiation and the styles they use in search of an agreement. In every training situation in which I have been engaged, women ask me to talk about gender issues. This leads me to believe that at least some women experience gender as a factor in negotiation. Research on this topic yields contradictory conclusions, but this may be caused by the setting of the research (usually the laboratory) and the questions the researchers pose.

Second, there is evidence in real, as opposed to simulated, negotiations, that women do not fare very well. For example, in divorce mediation, women receive settlements that are economically inferior when compared with the settlements they receive in adjudication. In salary negotiations, men receive higher raises than women. If negotiation were a woman's place, we would expect women to excel and not to be disadvantaged.

There is a third reason to focus on a woman's voice in negotiation. The advice given by principled negotiation advocates is to focus on interests rather than positions and to invent options for mutual gain. This entails separating people from problems and using objective criteria. It emphasizes a rationalized and objective approach to negotiation that may be different from the subjective and embedded feminine approach. Technical and rationalized analysis increasingly dominates negotiation.

Articulating alternative voices has become increasingly important in negotiation. Popular theories of negotiation imply that all conflicts can be formulated in a similar way and that all parties, despite differences in experience and status, can achieve the same results. Although there is much to applaud in this perspective, the prescriptive voice of principled or joint-gain negotiation has a tendency to drown out alternative ways of seeing and doing things. We need to consider the structure and context of negotiations in more nuanced ways.

Four themes are important in understanding how women may frame and conduct negotiations. These themes are a relational view of others, an embedded view of agency, an understanding of control through empowerment, and problem solving through dialogue. Although they suggest some ways women may define their place in negotiated settings, variations in class, race, culture, family makeup, and social setting also affect gender differences.

A RELATIONAL VIEW OF OTHERS

Women view things in terms of relationships, and this fact affects significant aspects of their social lives. They are oriented toward nurturance and affiliation and make meaning through interconnection. Women never had to repudiate identification with a caretaking mother to define their own sexual identity in adolescence. Instead of seeing separation and individuation as a primary motive for action, women conceive of action within the context of affiliation and relatedness to others.

Studies by Miller (1983), Chodorow (1978), and Gilligan (1982) suggest that boys differ from girls in that girls define themselves through their relationships. Gilligan points out that girls consistently show a sensitivity to others' needs and include others' points of view in their judgments on moral dilemmas. Keller (1980) describes women as living "in a domain between one and two" where they are not cast in opposition to others but see themselves in positions of mutual aid and support.

What women expect from interactions is a grounding for emotional connection, empathy, shared experiences and mutual sensitivity, and responsibility. In this two-way interactional model, to understand is as important as to be understood and empowerment is as important as to be empowered.

In negotiation, this relational view is expressed in two major ways. As a negotiating party, a woman conceives of her interests within the context of her responsibilities and commitments. She is always aware of how her actions in one context affect other parts of her life and people who are important to her.

The second way in which this relational view is expressed has to do with relational ordering. Relational ordering means creating a climate in which people can come to know each other, share (or not share) values, and learn of each other's modes of interacting. To women, expressing emotions and feelings and learning how others experience situations are as important as the substance of the discourse. In this context, separating people from the problem *is* the problem. Negotiation conducted in a woman's voice will often start from a different point and run a different course.

EMBEDDED VIEW OF AGENCY

Women understand events contextually, both in terms of their impact on important ongoing relationships and as evolving situations with a past and a future. Men stereotypically focus on individual achievement and activities that are defined in terms of task and structure. This is known as a self-contained concept of agency. Women, in contrast, have an embedded form of agency in which boundaries between themselves and others and between a task and its surroundings are overlapping and blurred. Because women operate from an embedded sense of agency, any negotiation must be understood against the background from which it emerges. It is not experienced as a separate game with its own set of rules but as part of an extended context. Because of this, it is possible that women may be slow to recognize that a negotiation is occurring unless it is specifically separated from the background against which it occurs. An example from one of my students illustrates this point: "When I was working in real estate, there was an occasion when I gave a listing to an associate without a prior agreement as to the split arrangement. I trusted my associate. We had worked together for a long time and I assumed that he would realize my input and include me in the split. He did not and I had to go to management to get my share."

At the same time, background understandings are likely to be imported into a negotiation setting. In a prisoner's dilemma game run with female students, the relationships the women had with each other spilled over into the game and led to coopera-tive outcomes.

CONTROL THROUGH EMPOWERMENT

Power is often conceived as the ability to exert con-trol over others through the use of strength, author-ity, or expertise to obtain an outcome on one's own terms. Conceiving of power in this way leads to a division between those who are powerful and those who are powerless. Power gained at the ex-pense of others may feel alien to some women. Some people see this form of power as being incon-gruent with female roles. Because women may feel that assertiveness can lead away from connection, they tend to emphasize the needs of others so as to allow them to feel powerful. Women's behavior, therefore, often appears to be passive, inactive, or depressed.

Debate about the place of power in negotiation is ongoing. Some, such as Fisher, argue that it is possible to mobilize power in ways that contribute to better outcomes. Others suggest that such a view denies the economic and political context in which negotiation occurs.

Feminist researchers have proposed an alterna-tive model of interaction that stresses *power with* or *power from emerging interaction* rather than domin-ion, mastery, or *power over*. This alternative model emphasizes mutual empowerment rather than com-petition. It overrides the active-passive dichotomy and calls for interaction among all participants in the relationship to build connection and under-standing and enhance everyone's power. It allows all parties to speak their interests and transcend the individualized and personalized notion of acquir-ing, using, and benefiting from power. Mutual em-powerment is often thought of as naive. However, particularly in situations in which there is an ongo-ing and valued relationship, it is often a much pre-ferred model.

PROBLEM SOLVING THROUGH DIALOGUE

Dialogue is central to a woman's model of problem solving. Women frame, consider, and resolve prob-lems through communication and interaction with others. This kind of communication is different from persuasion, argument, and debate. According to Surrey (1987) women seek to engage the other in a joint exploration of ideas whereby under-standing is progressively clarified through interac-tion. There is an expectation that the other will play the part of an active listener and will contrib-ute to the developing movement of ideas.

Women distinguish between two types of talk. One is *really talking*, which requires careful listen-ing and shared interactions. Half-baked or emer-gent ideas grow as both participants draw deeply from their experiences and analytical abilities. In *di-dactic talk* the participants do not share ideas. Stud-ies of women in management roles suggest that women reveal more about their attitudes, beliefs, and concerns than men in similar positions. This can contribute to productive dialogue.

In the strategic-planning model of negotiation, the parties try to analyze and second-guess the possi-ble interests and positions of the other. Although it is possible to plan and strategize about one's role in an interaction, a woman's strength may be in her ability to adapt and grow as she learns more about situ-ations through involvement. Just as conflicts build up over time, women see conflict resolution as evolu-tionary. Problem solving through dialogue entails a special kind of joining and openness in negotiation and leads to newly emerging understanding. The parties learn about the problem together and have a high regard for one anothers' interests.

This framework for negotiation is very different from the "dance" of positions. It is also different in some respects from joint gain negotiation. Joint gain negotiation involves a search for a set of agree-ments that satisfy interests which the parties are seen to value differently. First, there is the identification of differences and then the creative exploration of options that will satisfy them. What is implied in this model is a view that goals and in-terests are relatively fixed and potentially known by the parties. Here, the secret to reaching an agree-ment is to design a process where goals and inter-ests can be discovered and incorporated into an agreement.

In problem solving through dialogue, the process is less structured. Goals emerge from mutual inquiry. Those involved must be flexible and adaptive rather than controlling in response to uncertainty. The process can lead to new understandings of problems and possible solutions.

HER PLACE AT THE TABLE

We rarely hear the woman's voice in formal, public negotiation, and when it is there, it tends to be muted and easily overwhelmed. This may occur because the formal negotiating table may be an alien place for many women. Negotiations are settings for conflict resolution, and conflict runs counter to a woman's qualities and values. Attitude studies consistently show that women are more peaceful and rejecting of violence than men. Conflict is associated with aggressiveness, which is a stereotypical masculine attribute. When women or girls act aggressively it is interpreted differently from aggressive actions of men or boys. Women (similar to other groups who are subordinate) lack the expertise in dealing openly with conflict because this behavior and the feelings associated with it have often been suppressed. Women are socialized to believe that conflict with men or those in authority is wrong, and they feel vulnerable in the face of it. In their private lives, conflict often takes on personal and emotional overtones.

For all these reasons, many women may experience conflict situations as ones in which they have few options and a limited ability to affect outcomes. In bargaining situations, many women may find that their natural problem-solving skills are mitigated by their feelings about place. There are several reasons for this. Some women fear possible hostility or acrimonious relations and tend to emphasize harmony over other interests, including their own. Other women become anxious and find that their presentation style and their ability to communicate are impaired. Some women, through socialization and professional experience, have adopted the dominant negotiating style only to find that others' stereotypes and perceptions of them undermine their behavior and performance.

PRESERVING HARMONY

One of my students recently described herself as "incorrigibly integrative." By *integrative* she meant that it was important to her to ensure that all parties were happy even if it meant downplaying her own interests. Studies of negotiation suggest that a woman's preference for harmony may dominate other interests. Watson and Kasten (1987) have observed that female negotiating pairs can avoid discussing the main point of a conflict and yet still believe that they have negotiated effectively if their interaction was pleasant. In studies of managers, it is clear that women, relative to men, have a lower tolerance for antagonistic situations and do what they can to smooth over differences even if it means making sacrifices.

There is evidence that empathy, considered to be a particular strength of women, leads them to behavior that promotes harmony. Empathy is the capacity to participate in another's experience through shared thought and feeling. Empathy can be advantageous in negotiation because it can enable one to learn about a negotiating partner's interests and intentions. Although research has generally supported the assumption that women are more empathetic than men, there is also some evidence that the opposite is true.

There are several explanations for why women may be less empathetic than men in negotiation. One is that empathy may lead to exploitation. In negotiation, learning of another's interests is carried out to benefit one's own position, sometimes at the expense of the other. If women are highly responsive to how what they do might affect their relationships, they may be reluctant to exploit what information they acquire.

Second, if the negotiating table is not a natural place for women, their ability to empathize may be impaired. I have some evidence from my students that in bilateral negotiating situations, where parties are pitted against each other, women had difficulty in placing themselves in the role of the other. In group decision making female students distinguished themselves in listening to, understanding, and responding to each other. Yet in bilateral negotiation role plays, the students claimed that anxiety interfered with their ability to listen and impaired their performance. Concern over their own next response led them to miss clues that revealed issues of importance to their opponents. They also had difficulty in eliciting information because they were reluctant to probe and persuade. They assessed their opponents' interests based only on information that was volunteered.

Third, it has been suggested that in empathizing with others, women may undervalue their own interests and not develop self-empathy. Studies suggest that in a variety of group settings, women listen more and speak less. This may limit their opportunities to satisfy their own interests. The dilemma is for women to resolve their conflict between compassion for others and their own autonomy. They must overcome a tendency only to be responsive.

Comments from my students support these findings. One of my students gave the following example: "In real life I find it easier to negotiate for others. While supervising two editors this fall, I fought tooth and nail for reasonable schedules, appropriate workloads, and fair performance evaluations. Interestingly enough, I fared better when I represented their interests than when I represented my own!" The ability to take the role of the other in negotiation, to ascertain interests and needs, is an important skill in negotiation. However, it may be a double-edged sword.

STYLES OF TALK

The essence of negotiation is strategic communication. Parties want to learn about the alternatives available to and the interests of the other. At the same time, they want to communicate it in ways that further their own aims, whether they are to clarify their interests or to hide them.

Women speak differently. The distinctive communication style that serves them well in other contexts may be a liability in negotiation. Krieger (1987) notes that the female pattern of communication involves deference, rational thinking in argument, and indirection. The male pattern of communication typically involves linear or legalis-

tic argument, depersonalization, and a more directional style. Whereas women speak with more qualifiers to indicate flexibility and an opportunity for discussion, men use confident, self-enhancing terms. In negotiation, female patterns of communication may be read as weakness or lacking clarity and may get in the way of focusing on the real issues in the conflict. The women in my class had difficulty putting their wants into words and tended, instead, to wait for information that was volunteered.

Because women's speech is more conforming and less powerful, it does not signal influence. Women talk less, are easily interrupted, and are less likely to interrupt others. In mixed groups they adopt a deferential posture and are less likely to advocate their positions openly. At the same time, they tend to be too revealing and to talk too much about their attitudes, beliefs, and concerns.

One student described her deferential efforts to negotiate for AIDS resources with a mayor:

My strategy was to seek incremental progress to ensure that appropriate steps were taken to address the educational and service needs presented by the AIDS epidemic and to eliminate discrimination against gay people. Given the environment of the mayor's office, I believe now that I weakened my position by being too reasonable for too long. My strategy initially had been to demonstrate that I would not waste the mayor's time with trivialities, thereby establishing the understanding that when I pressured him, he should understand that it was a serious issue. I look back now on how polite, calm, and respectful I was with him in communicating the urgency of the AIDS epidemic and in pushing funding and program proposals. It is a horrible and laughable memory, for I failed to make him uncomfortable enough to warrant his attention. My subtlety was a liability when it came to "persuading" the mayor to take action where he was resistant. My negotiation style didn't change, even though I watched the mayor for two years and seldom saw him take action on anything unless he was pinned to the wall. I should have been far less deferential. I would risk approaching him more directly, for I made it too easy for him to dismiss me. I was liked and relatively well respected, but as a negotiator these qualities don't go far. To risk being more of a kick-ass would have served me better, and the mayor as well, by getting things attended to before they reached crisis proportions.

The process of negotiation, as it is customarily enacted, calls for parties to be clear and communicate directly and authoritatively about their goals, feelings, interests, and problems. A deferential, self-effacing, and qualified style may be a significant detriment. Women must become more knowledgeable and experienced with negotiation skills and more adept in an alternative style of communication at the negotiation table.

EXPECTATIONS AT THE TABLE

When men and women come to the table to negotiate, they bring with them expectations and outlooks that shape the way they see the other and the credibility and legitimacy accorded their actions. When women come to the table to negotiate, they often evoke certain stereotypes about feminine behavior that can affect how they are seen by their negotiating partners. The stereotypes are familiar. A woman is expected to act passive, compliant, nonaggressive, noncompetitive, accommodating, and attend to the socioemotional needs of those present. If she displays these characteristics through her behavior, then she reinforces some of these stereotypes and may find her effectiveness impaired. However, and this is often the situation with professional women, she may act in ways that contradict these stereotypes. That is, she is aggressive and competitive in pursuing her interests. The question is: Can she pull it off?

Existing research is not encouraging. It suggests that it is not so easy for women, particularly for those in management, to act forcefully and competitively without inviting criticism and questions about both their femininity and ability. They are seen as a threat to the accustomed social order. When men and women are rated on their performance in decision making and negotiating tasks, women are seen as less influential and receive less credit for what influence they may have exerted. As mediators, they are judged less effective even when the outcomes they achieve are superior.

Women are expected to do the emotional work in a group. In negotiation contexts, they often carry the burden for attending to relationships and the emotional needs of those involved. While such a burden might be consistent with a voice she might like to speak in, these expectations frequently constrain her ability to maneuver for herself or those she represents. Women must learn how to use their strengths and manage the dual impressions of femininity and strategic resolve. These are important negotiating tactics for women.

CONCLUSIONS

I have developed two themes that in some sense stand in contradiction to each other. The first, arguing from existing feminist literature, describes what a woman's voice in negotiation might sound like. If given the opportunity and setting, women might create an alternative structure and process in public negotiation. Women do not always speak in what I have described to be the woman's voice. Variations in class, race, culture, and social setting certainly affect how they approach negotiation. It may, therefore, be more appropriate to speak of alternative voices. An alternative voice can open up possibilities in negotiation, not just to change the kinds of strategies we employ, but to transform our understanding of the process. In situations where trust, openness, and long-term relationships are critical, this voice is likely to be heard and be influential.

The second theme relates to the typical negotiation situation where the voice is not only hushed but the speaker is open to compromise or exploitation. Gender has been a variable in hundreds of negotiating experiments, and yields a picture that is contradictory at best. How a woman acts in a setting has to do with her sense of place and how she defines the situation in which she finds herself. To the degree that negotiation signals conflict and competing interests, a situation often at odds with the voice she speaks, women may experience anxiety and fraudulence in that place. These feelings compounded by her demeanor and style of communication may impact and sometimes impair her efficacy at the bargaining table.

Our dual focus on voice and place suggests some new ways to pursue the gender issue in negotiation as a topic of research and training.

How can we document the fact that an alternative voice—based on a relational view of others, an embedded view of agency, a focus on empowerment, and problem solving through dialogue—is decipherable? Comparisons of homogeneous gender groups is not the best way to study the alternative voice. In such laboratory studies, women may be especially susceptible to cues. Also, most studies take place in a cultural context (professional schools, business and legal negotiations) in which *the* voice dominates. The alternative voice must be studied in a context where it can be heard such as all female organizations (e.g., law firms and consulting practices). We need to learn more about how negotiation in these settings is conducted.

Her place at the table, however, can be studied in more traditional settings. What we want to understand more fully is how men and women experience the process of negotiation. We want to know not just what they do but how they think and feel about what they do, how this is related to outcomes, and how those involved think and feel about the outcomes and process they used to get there. This will form the basis for studying variations among men and women.

Education and training are quite complicated. On the one hand, it is important to know and articulate the voice we, as women, tend to bring to negotiation. It is part of the interpretive lens through which we understand what will happen at the table. What it is and how it is likely to be heard should become part of any analysis we carry out in preparation for negotiation. It is obviously important to realize that speaking the voice has its time and place. We need to help people become better at recognizing it. At the same time, we must be realistic about expectations that are placed on us as women at the table and develop ways to anticipate and manage these expectations. Appreciating some of the ways our style might impede our success, we need to experiment with a variety of presentation modes. There is much we can learn from experience and from those who have successfully managed to find their place at the table and come to speak with a voice that is their own.

REFERENCES

Chodorow, N. (1978). *The reproduction of mothering.* Berkeley: University of California Press.

Gilligan, C. (1982). *In a different voice: Psychological theory and women's development.* Cambridge, Mass.: Harvard University Press.

Keller, E. F. (1980). How gender matters, or why it's so hard for us to count past two. *New Ideas in Psychology.*

Krieger, S. (1987, October). Organizational theory: Implications of recent feminist research (ways women organize). Organizational Behavior and Industrial Relations Colloquium, School of Business Administration, University of California, Berkeley.

Miller, J. B. (1983). The construction of anger in women and men. Work in Progress no. 83–01, Stone Center Working Paper Series, Wellesley, Mass.

Surrey, J. L. (1987). Relationship and empowerment. Work in Progress no. 30, Stone Center Working Paper Series, Wellesley, Mass.

Watson, C., & Kasten, B. (1987). Separate strengths? How women and men negotiate. Working Paper no. 1, Center for Negotiation and Conflict Resolution at Rutgers University, Newark, N.J.

NO

Gender versus Power as a Predictor of Negotiation Behavior and Outcomes

CAROL WATSON

The assumption that women are inferior simply because they are "different" from men has permeated our culture in the United States as it has many other cultures. Women's lot in life has clearly improved dramatically in this country since the 1700s, but equally clearly, there is still significant discrimination against women in our society in the 1990s.

Over the past ten to fifteen years, psychologists and sociologists have mounted a frontal assault on this long-standing "different and inferior" assumption in many domains. Their work has shown that the assumption is frequently inaccurate. Recent literature reviews show, for example, that there are no clear gender differences in verbal ability (Hyde & Linn, 1988), math ability (Hyde, Fennema, & Lamon, 1990), or spatial ability (Caplan, MacPherson, & Tobin, 1985). Nor do there appear to be gender differences in more abstract characteristics or abilities, such as moral reasoning (Friedman, Robinson, & Friedman, 1987) or leadership (Powell, 1990). Nevertheless, the belief in significant, innate gender differences refuses to die.

The probable reason for the durability of this belief is that, on a day-in, day-out basis, men and women *do* differ in countless ways that are apparent to each of us, researchers and members of the general public alike. One response to the dilemmas these differences have posed for women is advanced by the "cultural feminists" who have sought to fight society's inherent sexism by celebrating women as different from but superior to men (e.g., Gilligan, 1982; Rosener, 1990). Although such theories may be appealing because they highlight women's special qualities and help women feel good about themselves (rather than inferior or deficient), the "different-but-superior" argument does not hold up to the rigorous scrutiny of careful empirical investigation any better than does the more prevalent "different-and-inferior" argument (Tavris, 1992).

An alternative perspective, offered in this chapter, is that gender differences do exist but that those of significance relate to contextual rather than to innate personality factors. Contextual factors consist first and most obviously of the immediate situation and its particular demands. More broadly, however, the context of an individual's life includes all aspects in the environment of that individual's life—such as work, family, class, and culture (Tavris, 1992).

Contextual factors have often been found to supplant personality factors in determining behavior, sometimes in highly dramatic demonstrations (e.g., Milgram, 1963). Nevertheless, researchers and the general public continue to make what psychologists have dubbed the "fundamental attribution error" (Jones & Nisbett, 1976). This error consists of assuming that others behave the way they do because of internal personality characteristics rather than because of external situational demands.

COOPERATIVE WOMEN, COMPETITIVE MEN?

Relatively little scholarly attention has been paid to the issue of gender differences in negotiation behavior in recent years. In fact, the question of whether such differences exist and, if so, what they are, has never been satisfactorily resolved. Early research suggested that women are "softer" negotiators than men, that they prefer an accommodating style, are generous, and are more concerned that all parties be treated fairly than they are about gaining positive substantive outcomes for themselves (Terhune, 1970; Vinacke, 1959). These early studies also showed that men are "tough" negotiators who make many demands and few concessions and that they are more concerned about winning positive substantive outcomes for themselves than about how the other party fares (Bartos, 1970; Terhune, 1970). Men were also found to be more flexible negotiators than women in that they seemed to use a tit-for-tat strategy more often and were better at finding rational strategies that allowed them to maximize gains (Terhune, 1970).

Although Rubin and Brown (1975) showed that these supposed gender differences in bargaining and negotiating were not consistently supported by research, there tends to be a continuing expectation that women will negotiate and bargain more cooperatively than men. Nevertheless, a few researchers have reached more negative conclusions. For instance, women have sometimes been found to lock into an unrelenting competitive stance when their partners refuse to cooperate, and this behavior has been construed by some as vindictive (Rapoport & Chammah, 1965; Tedeschi, Schlenker, & Bonoma, 1973). Rubin and Brown (1975) incorporated these findings into their work, but this negative view has been largely ignored by everyone else.

The fact that negotiation researchers have often depicted women as cooperative might be construed to mean that the cultural feminist perspective (i.e., that women are different but superior) has predominated in the negotiation literature. This would be an incorrect assumption, however, because women's cooperativeness has generally been equated with weakness and ineffectiveness. That is, cooperation is generally considered to be a dangerous negotiating tactic because it leaves one open to exploitation by one's opponent (e.g., Gifford, 1989; Pruitt, 1983). Thus, women have frequently been portrayed as "nicer" negotiators than men; and because niceness does not help one to win, men have typically been credited with being more effective negotiators than women. In fact, some researchers have openly questioned women's negotiating competence, claiming that women's behavior in nego-

tiations is similar to that of men who do not understand the rules of the game (Caplow, 1968; Kelley, 1965).

Research on leadership provides a clue as to what might account for the frequent assumption that women are overly soft, ineffective negotiators. Leadership is similar to negotiating and bargaining in that it consists of influencing others. Not surprisingly, women's leadership skills have often been doubted on grounds similar to doubts about their negotiating competence. Many studies have been devoted to examining gender differences in leadership, and the nearly universal consensus that has emerged from reviews of these studies is that, when women earn or are given the leader's role, they behave exactly the way male leaders behave (e.g., Powell, 1990).

The clue this provides to our understanding of the literature on gender differences in negotiating and bargaining behavior is that the leader role typically confers power on the incumbent. Thus, one might argue that it is power rather than gender that determines how leaders behave. Power has been defined as the potential ability to influence others (Mintzberg, 1983; Pfeffer, 1981). It accrues from many sources. Those most commonly recognized by management scholars are legitimate, reward, coercive, expert, and charismatic power (French & Raven, 1960). In this chapter I refer to the number and strength of one's sources of power in a given situation as "situational power."

Similar sources of power are present in negotiating and bargaining encounters. Interestingly, the literature on disputing shows differences in the behavior of high- and low-power negotiators that mirror the most commonly assumed gender differences in negotiator behavior and outcomes (Bartos, 1970). That is, high-power negotiators tend to compete, whereas low-power negotiators tend to cooperate. I am suggesting, then, that because women in American society are more likely to be found in low-power positions and occupations than men, we may have been misled into assuming that observed differences in the way men and women negotiate result from gender when, in fact, they result from status and power differences.

If contextual factors such as situational power are indeed better predictors of negotiation behavior than gender, there are significant implications for both negotiation trainers and policymakers. For instance, women themselves would no longer be viewed as in need of "fixing." Instead, the practices that keep women in low-power and low-status roles in organizations and society at large would become the more legitimate focus of change. The possibility that contextual factors are more important than gender was examined by reviewing the existing literature on gender and power in negotiating and bargaining.

Scholars have offered four explanations for the origin of gender differences in negotiating behavior: gender-role socialization, situational power, gender and power combined, and "expectation states" theory.

The gender-role socialization explanation proposes that men and women will negotiate differently and be differentially successful because of the different behavioral expectations associated with their respective gender roles. The purest description of this perspective would be that, because women in U.S. society are expected to be nurturing and supportive, they should be softer, more cooperative negotiators than men. Because men are expected to be tough and task-oriented in our society, they should be harder, more competitive negotiators than women. Further, since cooperation is generally considered to be a dangerous tactic because it leaves one open to exploitation by one's opponent (e.g., Gifford, 1989; Pruitt, 1983), women should also be less successful negotiators than men. That is, it is assumed that cooperative women will be taken advantage of to a greater extent than competitive men.

As noted earlier, different researchers have drawn contradictory conclusions about the accuracy of the behavioral expectations associated with the gender-role socialization explanation, but most agree with the expectation concerning success.

The situational power explanation suggests that parties who have more power in a given situation, regardless of their gender, should be more competitive and successful negotiators than parties who have less power. This perspective was popularized by Rosabeth Kanter (1977), who argued that women behave the way anyone in a low-power position would behave. Meeker and Weitzel-O'Neill (1977) also argued in the 1970s that women are not any more motivated to help others or to prefer harmony and equality of outcomes than men in conflict situations but that they are forced to behave this way because of their lower status. Almost no one has examined the validity of this hypothesis for negotiation or bargaining situations.

The gender-plus-power explanation is based on the possibility that giving a person power may not eliminate the effects of gender status (i.e., Fagenson, 1990; Powell, Posner, & Schmidt, 1984; Terborg, 1977). According to this perspective, both the gender-role socialization and the situational power explanations are correct. Consequently, males who have a lot of power are expected to be extremely competitive and successful negotiators, whereas women who have little power are expected to be extremely cooperative but weak and unsuccessful. Men who have little power and women who have a lot of power are expected to be equivalent and intermediate in their competitiveness and success.

Finally, expectation states theory proposes that the effects of power and gender combine differently under different circumstances. The specific explanation suggested by this theory is that, when men and women negotiate with each other, gender affects their power and, hence, their behavior and outcomes. In particular, male gender is expected to enhance power and female gender is expected to detract from power in mixed-sex pairs.

This explanation is based on Berger's expectation states theory (Berger, Fisek, Norman, & Zelditch, 1977). Expectation states theory proposes that status characteristics (i.e., gender) establish performance expectations in small group settings; thus, high-status individuals (i.e., men) are expected to be more competent than low-status individuals (i.e., women). Because of these expectations, high-status individuals do in fact initiate more, receive more positive reactions from others, and enjoy more influence. However, the theory argues that gender is activated as a status characteristic only in mixed-sex pairs because it is only in these pairs that gender differentiates the parties. In other words, a powerful woman who must negotiate with a man should have much more difficulty controlling the negotiation than a powerful man who negotiates with a woman. Gender is not expected to have any impact on the power of negotiators in same-sex pairs of negotiators. In other words, being a woman should not diminish one's power when one faces another woman, nor should being a man enhance one's power when one faces another man.

REVIEWING THE LITERATURE

I have examined support for these competing explanations about the origin of gender differences in negotiation behavior by reviewing thirty-four research studies conducted since 1975 that have addressed the topic of gender differences in negotiation, conflict, or power. Only eight of these tested both gender and power and examined actual behavior rather than self-reported behavior, and these eight studies provided the data for this review. Not all of these studies examined standard negotiation or bargaining situations. Nevertheless, each involved some kind of situation in which the parties had conflicting needs and desires and attempted to influence their own and their partner's outcomes.

In four of the eight studies, power emerged as the main explanatory variable. In one of these, gender also emerged as a key explanatory variable. In the remaining four studies, power and gender affected each other, but in ways that differ from any of the four explanations offered earlier. No support was found for either the additive explanation or for the explanation derived from expectation states theory.

Among those studies in which power was the main explanatory factor (Dovidio, Ellyson, Keating, Heltman, & Brown, 1988; Putnam & Jones, 1982; Siderits, Johannsen, & Fadden, 1985; Watson & Hoffman, 1992), some supported the explanation as stated (i.e., that power breeds competitiveness and personally favorable outcomes), but

others showed contradictory results, particularly with respect to the tactics employed by powerful parties. Among the expected results, power led to such behavior as: greater visual dominance; more expressions of overt hostility toward one's opponents; greater feelings of competitiveness, power, and control; greater expectations of cooperation from one's opponents; greater satisfaction with the outcome of negotiation; and a stronger belief that one had been successful.

However, in one of the studies (Putnam & Jones, 1982), powerful parties were found to engage in more defensive than offensive strategies (retractions and accommodations as opposed to threats, rejections, or attacking arguments). In another study (Watson & Hoffman, 1992), powerful parties were found to engage in problem-solving rather than competitive tactics. In this latter instance, the more powerful parties were also less successful than the less powerful parties (according to the experimenters' definition of success) although they believed they had been more successful than their less powerful opponents. Thus, although power generally led to greater dominance, competitiveness, and success, it did not always do so. Perhaps there are circumstances in which strong situational power leads parties to believe that dominant coercive strategies are unnecessary.

Few results were due strictly to gender, as mentioned earlier, and none of the gender effects concerned tactical behaviors or outcomes. However, in one study (Watson & Hoffman, 1992) managerial women reported less self-confidence than managerial men before they took part in a simulated negotiation, less satisfaction with themselves after the negotiation, and the belief that they had been less successful than men, even though this was not true based on the experimenters' definition of success.

Five of the eight studies supported the idea that gender and power affect each other, although the results do not fit any of the explanations that could be derived from existing theory. Among these five studies, two found that having strong situational power leads men, but not women, to behave in what the researchers labeled as more competitive ways (Kravitz & Iwaniszek, 1985; Scudder, 1988).

Competitiveness consisted of winning better pay-offs for oneself in one study and of issuing bottom-line, take-it-or-leave-it statements in the other.

A third study found the reverse effect (Stake & Stake, 1979). That is, power in the form of performance-related self-esteem increased women's dominating behavior (i.e., number of opinions given and disagreements stated) but not men's. The results from this study are questionable, however, because to match men and women, the authors were forced to include a group of women with unusually high self-esteem and a group of men with unusually low self-esteem scores.

The remaining two studies found that powerlessness affected men differently than women (Molm 1986; Watson & Hoffman, 1992). Men in low-power situations were found to adopt an approach that has been labeled "soft competition" by some researchers (i.e., Savage, Blair, & Sorenson, 1989), whereas women did not. Men's approach to dealing with powerlessness consisted of stating their position and then offering logical reasons to support it.

Women's approach to powerlessness depended on the gender of their opponents, according to one study (Watson & Hoffman, 1992). Surprisingly, when low-power women faced a male opponent in this study, they were likely to adopt the highly competitive tactic of threatening. This result is surprising in part because it is completely contrary to the predictions of expectation states theory. The supposedly weakest participants (low-power women facing high-power men) were not expected to use the toughest tactics. Yet they did and they reported feeling somewhat more powerful and satisfied with themselves than other women in that study. Women's threatening behavior is also surprising because such an aggressive approach is generally considered dangerous and unacceptable for low-power parties. Yet it worked for the low-power women in Watson and Hoffman's (1992) study.

Another study (Molm, 1986) also found that gender and power combined in ways that refuted expectation states theory. In this instance, female-female pairs of bargainers were less likely to engage in a tit-for-tat strategy than male-male pairs. Expec-tation states theory predicts no gender differences in same-sex pairs. This finding is noteworthy because the tit-for-tat strategy has been found to be the best one to ensure positive, joint, long-term outcomes in mixed-motive situations. Thus, women may be less likely to settle on a cooperative pattern when they bargain with another woman than will men when they bargain with another man.

CONCLUSIONS AND IMPLICATIONS

This review yields several noteworthy findings about situational power and gender. First, and perhaps most important, situational power appears to be a better predictor of negotiator behavior and outcomes than does gender. Nevertheless, it is also clear that the impact of gender cannot be ignored. Although gender did not affect tactical behavior or outcomes in any of the studies reviewed, it did lead to differences in negotiators' confidence in one study. Further, gender interacted with situational power and other contextual factors in ways that did affect behavior and outcomes.

Power generally leads to greater dominance, competitiveness, and success for both genders. On one hand, this indicates that women are not softer or less effective negotiators than men are, as was suggested in the 1960s and early 1970s. Given a reasonable degree of situational power, women are likely to be just as oriented toward beating their opponents as men are and just as successful at doing so. Thus, there is no reason to mistrust women's negotiation abilities. They are capable of negotiating as competitively and successfully as men.

On the other hand, this finding also implies that women are not nicer negotiators than men are. Women are not necessarily any more fair-minded or compassionate, despite what earlier research and some current feminist writers would have us believe. Thus, if we wish to encourage more humane behavior on the part of the powerful toward the powerless, the answer is not simply to give women a chance to rule but to change the rules that govern how powerful people should behave.

The reader should not construe the assertions of the previous paragraph as an argument against empowering women but rather as an argument against doing so because women will magically change the way those in power behave. It should not be necessary to justify women's empowerment on the grounds that they are somehow in general "better" people than are men. This is an unfair burden to place on women and an implied and equally unfair condemnation of men.

Interestingly, power did not always lead to dominating, selfish behavior in the studies reviewed. In several studies, the more powerful parties to a negotiation chose less threatening approaches than their lower-power opponents. In one of these studies, the subjects were business students playing the role of management in a labor-management negotiation, and in the other, the participants were practicing managers taking part in a simulated negotiation. Although one might conclude that the simulated nature of these negotiations led high-power parties to behave less aggressively, most of the negotiation literature has been based on simulations and role-play exercises, and this literature generally shows that power leads to dominance and aggression.

Another possibility is that being a manager or role-playing a manager leads to different uses of power than typically occur when undergraduates negotiate with other undergraduates as peers. The managerial role carries with it legitimate power that may discourage the use of coercion since subordinates are expected to know that they are supposed to capitulate. In addition, in the studies that used managers or students role-playing managers (Putnam & Jones, 1982; Watson & Hoffman, 1992), the subjects were negotiating with parties from the same organization. Under such circumstances, they may have perceived the conflict within a more cooperative framework and may even have assumed they were responsible for creating such a cooperative framework for the good of the larger organization. These intriguing questions merit further research. Because much of the negotiation and conflict management literature is built on studies of undergraduates, possible limits to the generalizability of this work need to be explored.

As noted earlier, gender by itself had little effect on the behavior or outcomes of negotiators in the studies reviewed, but it did affect participants' feelings about negotiating in one of the studies. Managerial women reported significantly less confidence about negotiating than managerial men, and they disparaged their success as negotiators more than men even though they had behaved no differently and had been no less successful than the men in their negotiations. This is a significant finding, because women's concerns and negative self-evaluations may cause them to shy away from negotiations needlessly and inappropriately. Further, gender interacted with power and with opponent's gender in some unanticipated ways. Several studies showed that men became more aggressive when they had power and more conciliatory when they did not. Women's reactions were more variable and more likely to be dictated by additional contextual factors. In particular, women became highly aggressive when they were powerless against a male opponent. Powerful women were less willing or able to develop a cooperative tit-for-tat strategy when they negotiated with another woman than powerful men were with male opponents. This limited the ability of female-female pairs to achieve cooperative win-win solutions.

In general, the kinds of adjustments men made to power match the recommendations of current normative models of negotiation (e.g., Savage et al. 1989). Women's adjustments to power sometimes contradicted the recommendations of these models even though their unconventional approaches sometimes worked.

Although power accounted for most negotiation behavior previously thought to be gender-related, the effects found for gender alone and in combination with power suggest that women face dilemmas when negotiating that men do not. Assuming positions of power and feeling comfortable about negotiating appear to be more problematic for women than for men. In addition, women appear to be particularly sensitive to the gender of their opponents. When their opponents are high-power males, women seem to engage in risky levels of aggressiveness. When their opponents are low-power women, they seem unable or unwilling to find a co-operative give-and-take approach. Each of these areas needs to be researched more fully so that informed recommendations can be developed for women and for men who negotiate with women.

It is important to bear in mind that the prescriptions for successful negotiating are more ambiguous for women than they are for men. The norms that guide competitive win-lose negotiating were developed by men for men, and they are therefore compatible with stereotypical gender norms for men. These norms, however, are not compatible with gender norms for women. Nor can women be expected simply to adopt behaviors that are considered inappropriate for them. My research (Korabik, Baril, & Watson, 1993; Watson, 1988), as well as that of others, has shown that both men and women are viewed negatively when they behave in ways that are contrary to society's gender role expectations. Thus, even when it might be appropriate for women to behave competitively to protect their own interests in a negotiation, they are likely to incur much greater negative reactions for doing this than men would.

The answer for women may turn out to be that they should learn the skills of principled negotiating (Fisher & Ury, 1981). Fisher and Ury teach negotiators how to understand and protect their interests while maintaining a positive relationship with the other party. Although both men and women would benefit from learning the skills these authors recommend, women may need these skills more than men because of the conflicting expectations they face when negotiating. Whereas men may be able to get away with competitive tactics some of the time, women may not.

Clearly, more research on the issues raised in this review is needed. Although the hypothesis that situational power accounts for assumed gender differences was first proposed nearly twenty years ago, almost no one has sought to test it. Nevertheless, as this review shows, the hypothesis has merit. Furthermore, little thought has been given to the possible interactions between gender and such contextual variables as situational power.

It seems that we have been content to restrict our research to overly simplistic hypotheses and have therefore failed to focus on the factors that are the more powerful determinants of negotiator behavior and outcomes. The interactive effects of gender, power, and opponent's gender that are revealed through this review, though only suggestive given the limited number of studies, point the way toward more meaningful avenues for future research concerning the role of gender in negotiation and bargaining.

REFERENCES

Bartos, O. J. 1970. Determinants and consequences of toughness. *The structure of conflict*, ed. P. Swingle. New York: Academic Press.

Berger, J., M. H. Fisek, R. Z. Norman, & M. Zelditch, Jr. 1977. *Status characteristics and social interaction: An expectation states approach.* New York: Elsevier.

Caplan, P. J., G. M. MacPherson, & P. Tobin. 1985. Do sex-related differences in spatial ability exist? *American Psychologist 40*, 786–799.

Caplow, T. 1968. *Two against one: Coalition in triads.* Englewood Cliffs, N.J.: Prentice-Hall.

Dovidio, J. F., S. L. Ellyson, C. F. Keating, K. Heltman, & C. E. Brown. 1988. The relationship of social power to visual displays of dominance between men and women. *Journal of Personality and Social Psychology 54* (2), 233–242.

Fagenson, E. A. 1990. Perceived masculine and feminine attributes examined as a function of individuals' sex and level in the organizational power hierarchy: A test of four theoretical perspectives. *Journal of Applied Psychology 75* (2), 204–211.

Fisher, R., & W. L. Ury. 1981. *Getting to YES: Negotiating agreement without giving in.* Boston: Houghton Mifflin.

French, J. R. P., Jr., & B. Raven. 1960. The bases of power. In *Group dynamics*, ed. D. Cartwright & A. E. Zander. Evanston, Ill.: Row, Peterson.

Friedman, W. J., A. B. Robinson, & B. L. Friedman. 1987. Sex differences in moral judgment? *Psychology of Women Quarterly 11*, 37–46.

Gifford, D. G. 1989. *Legal negotiation: Theory and practice.* St. Paul, Minn.: West Publishing.

Gilligan, C. 1982. *In a different voice.* Cambridge, Mass.: Harvard University Press.

Hyde, J. S., & M. C. Linn. 1988. Gender differences in verbal ability: A meta-analysis. *Psychological Bulletin 104*, 53–69.

Hyde, J. S., E. Fennema, & S. Lamon. 1990. Gender differences in mathematics performance: A meta-analysis. *Psychological Bulletin 107*, 139–155.

Jones, E. E., & R. E. Nisbett. 1976. The actor and the observer: Divergent perceptions of the causes of behavior. In *Contemporary topics in social psychology*, ed. J. W. Thibaut,

J. T. Spencer, & R. C. Carson. Morristown, N.J.: General Learning Press.

Kanter, R. 1977. *Men and women of the corporation.* New York: Basic Books.

Kelley, H. H. 1965. Experimental studies of threats in interpersonal negotiations. *Journal of Conflict Resolution 9,* 79–105.

Korabik, K., G. Baril, & C. Watson. 1993. Managers' conflict management style and leadership effectiveness: The moderating effects of gender. *Sex Roles 29* (5/6), 407–422.

Kravitz, D. & J. Iwaniszek. 1984. Number of coalitions and resources as sources of power in coalition bargaining. *Journal of Personality and Social Psychology 47* (3), 534–548.

Meeker, B. F., & P. A. Weitzell-O'Neill. 1977. Sex roles and interpersonal behavior in task-oriented groups. *American Sociological Review 42,* 91–105.

Milgram, S. 1963. Behavioral study of obedience. *Journal of Abnormal and Social Psychology 67,* 371–378.

Mintzberg, H. 1983. *Power in and around organizations.* Englewood Cliffs, N.J.: Prentice-Hall.

Molm, L. D. 1986. Gender, power, and legitimation: A test of three theories. *American Journal of Sociology 91* (6), 1356–1386.

Pfeffer, J. 1981. *Power in organizations.* Marshfield, Mass.: Pitman.

Powell, G. N. 1990. One more time: Do female and male managers differ? *Academy of Management Executive 4* (3), 68–76.

Powell, G. N., B. Z. Posner, & W. H. Schmidt. 1984. Sex effects in managerial value systems. *Human Relations 37,* 909–921.

Pruitt, D. 1983. Strategic choice in negotiation. *American Behavioral Scientist 27* (2), 167–194.

Putnam, L. L., & T. S. Jones. 1982. Reciprocity in negotiations: An analysis of bargaining interaction. *Communication Monographs 49* (3), 171–191.

Rapoport, A., & A. M. Chammah. 1965. *Prisoner's dilemma.* Ann Arbor: University of Michigan Press.

Rosener, J. B. 1990. Ways women lead. *Harvard Business Review* (November-December), 119–125.

Rubin, J. Z. & B. R. Brown. 1975. *The social psychology of bargaining and negotiation.* New York: Academic Press.

Savage, G. T., J. D. Blair, & R. L. Sorenson. 1989. Consider both relationships and substance when negotiating strategically. *Academy of Management Executive 3* (1), 37–48.

Scudder, J. N. 1988. The influence of power upon powerful speech: A social exchange perspective. *Communication Research Reports 5* (2), 140–145.

Siderits, M. A., W. J. Johannsen, & T. F. Fadden. 1985. Gender, role, and power: A content analysis of speech. *Psychology of Women Quarterly 9* (4), 439–450.

Stake, J. E., & Stake, M. N. 1979. Performance-self-esteem and dominance behavior in mixed-sex dyads. *Journal of Personality 47,* 71–84.

Tavris, C. 1992. *The mismeasure of woman.* New York: Simon and Schuster.

Tedeschi, J. T., B. R. Schlenker, & T. W. Bonoma. 1973. *Conflict, power, and games: The experimental study of interpersonal relations.* Chicago: Aldine.

Terborg, J. 1977. Women in management: A research review. *Journal of Applied Psychology 62* 647–664.

Watson, C. 1988. When a woman is the boss: Dilemmas in taking charge. *Group and Organization Studies 13* (2), 163–181.

Watson, C., & L. R. Hoffman. 1992. An examination of the impact of gender and power on managers' negotiation behavior and outcomes. Paper presented at the Annual Meeting of the Academy of Management, Las Vegas.

PART III

Sexuality

Pornography:
Is It Harmful to Women?

The question of whether pornography has adverse effects on women usually arouses very strong personal opinions. Nevertheless, until President Lyndon B. Johnson established the Commission on Obscenity and Pornography in January 1968, relatively little was known about the effects of pornography on behavior. The commission's summary report (1970) and the nine volumes containing the studies it sponsored (Committee on Obscenity and Pornography 1971) record the first phase of research in this area (Byrne & Kelley, 1984). The commission concluded that there was no evidence that the easy availability of pornography played a significant role in sexual crimes.

Not surprisingly, those who agreed with the commission's findings hailed the results while critics attacked its research methodology and conclusions. A more conservative political climate in the 1980s led to the formation of a new investigation headed by Edwin Meese (Attorney General's Commission, 1986). In contrast to the 1970 report, the Meese Commission declared that there *is* a causal relationship between exposure to sexually explicit materials and sexual aggression, including unlawful acts.

Conservatives were not the only group to find a direct link between pornography and aggression against women. Some feminists in the mid-1970s also began to raise questions about the harmlessness of pornography. Brownmiller (1975), for example, argued that the open display of pornography, in which women were sometimes portrayed as willing victims, created a climate of tolerance for sexual assault against women. Everywoman (1988) claimed that the link between pornography and sexual violence is "considerably stronger than that for cigarette smoking and cancer" (p. 5). Others view pornography as playing an important role in contributing to sex discrimination and sexual inequality (Itzin, 1993).

Catharine MacKinnon, a professor at the University of Michigan Law School, and the social activist Andrea Dworkin have led the feminist fight in the United States to combat pornography. They coauthored the MacKinnon-Dworkin bill, which allowed victims who believed they had been harmed by sexual material to collect damages from the producers and distributors. Although the bill passed into law in Indianapolis, it was subsequently found unconstitutional (*American Booksellers v. Hudnut*, 1985). However, many feminists, including Marcia Pally (1994), the founder and president of Feminists for Free Expression, have made it clear that MacKinnon and Dworkin do not speak for them.

Those who see a close relationship between pornography and sexual violence draw support from serial killer Ted Bundy's deathbed report that he attributed his behavior to having read pornographic material. Many social scientists, however, believe that an individual's sexual attitudes are determined long before he or she is exposed to sexually explicit material (Becker & Stein, 1991). Interviews with the murderer and his family, for example, reveal that Bundy lived for a time with a sadistic grandfather and that he committed aberrant, violent acts as early as age three (Pally, 1994).

The authors of the 1971 report on obscenity and pornography claimed that 90 percent of pornographic material is produced for male heterosexuals with the remaining 10 percent directed to male homosexuals. Michael Kimmel (1990) estimated that male heterosexuals comprised 80 percent of the market, gay men 15 percent, and women the remaining 5 percent. One aspect of pornography that has only recently begun to receive attention is the connection between gender, ethnicity, and class (Collins, 1993). Gloria Cowan argues that race "exaggerates gender roles in pornography. Women are dominated, but Black women more so than White women. Men are shown as sex machines, but Black men more so than White men" (1995, p. 405).

In spite of the extensive research on pornography, however, there is considerable disagreement among social scientists as to its effect on behavior. The Meese Commission's claim that there was clinical and experimental evidence documenting a causal link between pornography and sexual violence drew heavily on the research of Edward Donnerstein and Daniel Linz. Donnerstein had in fact declared that "there is a direct causal relationship between exposure to aggressive pornography and violence against women" (1984, p. 78). Shortly afterward, however, he joined Linz and Steven Penrod (1987) in criticizing the commission's misuse of research on the subject. They warned that there was little evidence that sexual aggression, as measured by such tests as delivering electric shocks in a laboratory, is representative of real world aggression such as rape. They also pointed out that the antisocial attitudes toward women they discovered in their experiments stemmed from the subjects' exposure to violent material, regardless of whether or not they are also sexually explicit.

In the following articles, Diana E. H. Russell, who has accused experts like Donnerstein of a "cop-out" (1993), presents the view that violent and nonviolent pornography can cause sexual violence such as rape. Nadine Strossen, the first female president of the American Civil Liberties Union, argues that censorship would not reduce violence against women.

REFERENCES

American Booksellers Association v Hudnut, 771 F 2d 323 (1985).

Attorney General's Commission on Pornography. (1986). Final Report of the Commission (Vols. 1 and 2). Washington, D.C.: Government Printing Office.

Becker, J. V., & Stein, R. M. (1991). Is sexual erotica associated with sexual deviance in adolescent males? *International Journal of Law and Psychiatry, 14,* 85–95.

Brownmiller, S. (1975). *Against our will: Men, women and rape.* New York: Simon & Schuster.

Byrne, D., & Kelley, K. (1984). Pornography and sex research. In N. M. Malamuth and E. Donnerstein

(Eds.), *Pornography and sexual aggression* (pp. 1–15). Orlando, Fla.: Academic Press.

Collins, P. H. (1993). The sexual politics of black womanhood. In P. B. Bart & E. G. Moran (Eds.), *Violence against women: The bloody footprints* (pp. 85–104). Newbury Park, Calif.: Sage.

Commission on Obscenity and Pornography. (1970). *The report of the commission on obscenity and pornography.* New York: Bantam Books.

Committee on Obscenity and Pornography. (1971). *Presidential Commission on Obscenity and Pornography.* Washington, D.C.: Government Printing Office.

Cowan, G. (1995). Black and White (and blue): Ethnicity and pornography. In H. Landrine (Ed.), *Bringing cultural diversity to feminist psychology: Theory, research, and practice* (pp. 397–411). Washington, D.C.: American Psychological Association.

Donnerstein, E. (1984). Pornography: Its effect on violence against women. In N. M. Malamuth and E. Donnerstein (Eds.), *Pornography and sexual aggression* (pp. 53–81). Orlando, Fla.: Academic Press.

Everywoman. (1988). *Pornography and sexual violence: Evidence of links*, quoted in Segal, L. (1990). Pornography and violence: What the "experts" really say. *Feminist Review, 36*, 29–41.

Itzin, C. (Ed.) (1993). *Pornography: Women, violence and civil liberties.* Oxford: Oxford University Press.

Kimmel, M. S. (1990). Introduction: Guilty pleasures—pornography in men's lives. In M. S. Kimmel (Ed.), *Men confront pornography* (pp. 1–22). New York: Crown.

Linz, D., Penrod, S. D., & Donnerstein, E. (1987). The Attorney General's Commission on Pornography: The gaps between the "findings" and "facts." *American Bar Foundation Research Journal, 4*, 713–736.

Pally, M. (1994). *Sex and sensibility: Reflections on forbidden mirrors and the will to censor.* Hopewell, N.J.: Ecco Press.

Russell, D. E. H. (1993). The experts cop out. In D. E. H. Russell (Ed.), *Making violence sexy: Feminist views on pornography* (pp. 151–166). New York: Teachers College Press.

ADDITIONAL READING

Carse, A. L. (1995). Pornography: An uncivil liberty? *Hypatia, 10* (1), 155–182.

Cornell, D. (1995). *The imaginary domain: Abortion, pornography and sexual harassment.* New York: Routledge.

Cowan, G. (1992). Feminist attitudes toward pornography control. *Psychology of Women Quarterly, 16*, 165–177.

Cowan, G., & Campbell, R. R. (1994). Racism and sexism in interracial pornography. *Psychology of Women Quarterly, 18*, 323–388.

Linz, D., & Malamuth, N. (1993). *Pornography.* Newbury Park, Calif.: Sage.

MacKinnon, C. A. (1993). *Only Words.* Cambridge, Mass.: Harvard University Press.

McElroy, W. (1995). *A woman's right to pornography.* New York: St. Martin's Press.

Pornography Causes Harm to Women

Diana E. H. Russell

The sociologist David Finkelhor (1984) has developed a very useful multicausal theory to explain the occurrence of child sexual abuse. According to Finkelhor's model, in order for child sexual abuse to occur, four conditions have to be met. First, someone has to *want* to abuse a child sexually. Second, this person's internal inhibitions against acting out this desire have to be undermined. Third, this person's social inhibitions against acting out this desire (e.g., fear of being caught and punished) have to be undermined. Fourth, the would-be perpetrator has to undermine or overcome his or her chosen victim's capacity to avoid or resist the sexual abuse.

According to my theory, these conditions also have to be met in order for rape, battery, and other forms of sexual assault on adult women to occur (Russell, 1984). Although my theory can be applied to other forms of sexual abuse and violence against women besides rape, the following formulation of it will focus on rape because most of the research relevant to my theory is limited to this form of sexual assault.

In *Sexual Exploitation* (1984) I suggest many factors that may predispose a large number of males in the United States to want to rape or assault women sexually. Some examples discussed in this book are (1) biological factors, (2) childhood experiences of sexual abuse, (3) male sex-role socialization, (4) exposure to mass media that encourage rape, and (5) exposure to pornography. Here I will discuss only the role of pornography.

Although women have been known to rape both males and females, males are by far the predominant perpetrators of sexual assault as well as the biggest consumers of pornography. Hence, my theory will focus on male perpetrators.

As previously noted, in order for rape to occur, a man must not only be predisposed to rape, but his internal and social inhibitions against acting out his rape desires must be undermined. My theory, in a nutshell, is that pornography (1) predisposes some males to want to rape women and intensifies the predisposition in other males already so predisposed; (2) undermines some males' internal inhibitions against acting out their desire to rape; and (3) undermines some males' social inhibitions against acting out their desire to rape.

The Meaning of "Cause"

Given the intense debate about whether or not pornography plays a causal role in rape, it is surprising that so few of those engaged in it ever state what they mean by "cause." A definition of the concept of *simple causation* follows:

> An event (or events) that precedes and results in the occurrence of another event. Whenever the first event (the cause) occurs, the second event (the effect) necessarily or inevitably follows. Moreover, in simple causation the second event does not occur unless the first event has occurred. Thus the cause is both the SUFFICIENT CONDITION and the NECESSARY CONDITION for the occurrence of the effect. (Theodorson and Theodorson, 1979)

By this definition, pornography clearly does not cause rape, as it seems safe to assume that some pornography consumers do not rape women and that many rapes are unrelated to pornography. However, the concept of *multiple causation is* applicable to the relationship between pornography and rape.

With the conception of MULTIPLE CAUSA-TION, various possible causes may be seen for a given event, any one of which may be a sufficient but not necessary condition for the occurrence of the effect, or a necessary but not sufficient condition. In the case of multiple causation, then, the given effect may occur in the absence of all but one of the possible sufficient but not necessary causes; and, conversely, the given effect would not follow the occurrence of some but not all of the various necessary but not sufficient causes. (Theodorson and Theodorson, 1979)

As I have already presented the research on males' proclivity to rape, I will next discuss some of the evidence that pornography can be a sufficient (though not *necessary*) condition for males to desire to rape. I will mention when the research findings I describe apply to violent pornography and when to pornography that appears to the viewer to be nonviolent.

THE ROLE OF PORNOGRAPHY IN PREDISPOSING SOME MALES TO WANT TO RAPE

"I went to a porno bookstore, put a quarter in a slot, and saw this porn movie. It was just a guy coming up from behind a girl and attacking her and raping her. That's when I started having rape fantasies. When I seen that movie, it was like somebody lit a fuse from my childhood on up. . . . I just went for it, went out and raped." (Rapist interviewed by Beneke, 1982, pp. 73–74)

According to Factor I in my theoretical model, pornography can induce a desire to rape women in males who previously had no such desire, and it can increase or intensify the desire to rape in males who already have felt this desire. This section will provide the evidence for the four different ways in which pornography can induce this predisposition.

(1) *Pairing sexually arousing/gratifying stimuli with rape.* The laws of social learning (for example, classical conditioning, instrumental conditioning, and social modeling), about which there is now considerable consensus among psychologists, apply

to all the mass media, including pornography. As Donnerstein testified at the hearings in Minneapolis: "If you assume that your child can learn from *Sesame Street* how to count one, two, three, four, five, believe me, they can learn how to pick up a gun" (Donnerstein, 1983, p. 11). Presumably, males can learn equally well how to rape, beat, sexually abuse, and degrade females.

A simple application of the laws of social learning suggests that viewers of pornography can develop arousal responses to depictions of rape, murder, child sexual abuse, or other assaultive behavior. The researcher S. Rachman of the Institute of Psychiatry, Maudsley Hospital, London, has demonstrated that male subjects can learn to become sexually aroused by seeing a picture of a woman's boot after repeatedly seeing women's boots in association with sexually arousing slides of nude females (Rachman and Hodgson, 1968). The laws of learning that operated in the acquisition of the boot fetish can also teach males who were not previously aroused by depictions of rape to become so. All it may take is the repeated association of rape with arousing portrayals of female nudity (or clothed females in provocative poses).

Even for males who are not sexually excited during movie portrayals of rape, masturbation subsequent to the movie reinforces the association. This constitutes what R. J. McGuire, J. M. Carlisle, and B. G. Young refer to as "masturbatory conditioning" (Cline, 1974, p. 210). The pleasurable experience of orgasm—an expected and planned-for activity in many pornography parlours—is an exceptionally potent reinforcer. The fact that pornography is widely used by males as ejaculation material is a major factor that differentiates it from other mass media, intensifying the lessons that male consumers learn from it.

(2) *Increasing males' self-generated rape fantasies.* Further evidence that exposure to pornography can create in males a predisposition to rape where none existed before is provided by an experiment conducted by Malamuth. Malamuth classified twenty-nine male students as sexually force-oriented or non-force-oriented on the basis of their responses to a questionnaire (1981). These students

were then randomly assigned to view either a rape version or a mutually consenting version of a slide-audio presentation. The account of rape and accompanying pictures were based on a story in a popular pornographic magazine, which Malamuth describes as follows:

> The man in this story finds an attractive woman on a deserted road. When he approaches her, she faints with fear. In the rape version, the man ties her up and forcibly undresses her. The accompanying narrative is as follows: "You take her into the car. Though this experience is new to you, there is a temptation too powerful to resist. When she awakens, you tell her she had better do exactly as you say or she'll be sorry. With terrified eyes she agrees. She is undressed and she is willing to succumb to whatever you want. You kiss her and she returns the kiss." Portrayal of the man and woman in sexual acts follows; intercourse is implied rather than explicit. (1981, p. 38)

In the mutually consenting version of the story the victim was not tied up or threatened. Instead, on her awakening in the car, the man told her that "she is safe and that no one will do her any harm. She seems to like you and you begin to kiss." The rest of the story is identical to the rape version (Malamuth, 1981, p. 38).

All subjects were then exposed to the same audio description of a rape read by a female. This rape involved threats with a knife, beatings, and physical restraint. The victim was portrayed as pleading, crying, screaming, and fighting against the rapist (Abel, Barlow, Blanchard, and Guild, 1977, p. 898). Malamuth reports that measures of penile tumescence as well as self-reported arousal "indicated that relatively high levels of sexual arousal were generated by all the experimental stimuli" (1981, p. 33).

After the twenty-nine male students had been exposed to the rape audiotape, they were asked to try to reach as high a level of sexual arousal as possible by fantasizing about whatever they wanted but without any direct stimulation of the penis (1981, p. 40). Self-reported sexual arousal during the fantasy period indicated that those students who had been exposed to the rape version of the first slide-audio presentation created more violent sexual fantasies than those exposed to the mutually consenting version *irrespective of whether they had been classified as force-oriented or non-force-oriented* (1981, p. 33).

As the rape version of the slide-audio presentation is typical of what is seen in pornography, the results of this experiment suggest that similar pornographic depictions are likely to generate rape fantasies even in previously non-force-oriented consumers. As Edna Einsiedel points out, "Current evidence suggests a high correlation between deviant fantasies and deviant behaviors. . . . Some treatment methods are also predicated on the link between fantasies and behavior by attempting to alter fantasy patterns in order to change the deviant behaviors" (1986, p. 60).

Because so many people resist the idea that a desire to rape may develop as a result of viewing pornography, let us focus for a moment on behavior other than rape. There is abundant testimonial evidence that at least some males decide they would like to perform certain sex acts on women after seeing pornography portraying such sex acts. For example, one of the men who answered Shere Hite's question on pornography wrote: "It's great for me. *It gives me new ideas to try and see,* and it's always sexually exciting" (1981, p. 780; emphasis added). Of course, there's nothing wrong with getting new ideas from pornography or anywhere else or with trying them out, as long as they are not actions that subordinate or violate others. Unfortunately, many of the behaviors modeled in pornography *do* subordinate and violate women, sometimes viciously.

The following statements were made by women testifying at the Hearings on Pornography in Minneapolis, Minnesota, in 1983 (Russell, 1993a).

Ms. M testified that

> I agreed to act out in private a lot of the scenarios that my husband read to me. These depicted bondage and different sexual acts that I found very humiliating to do. . . . He read the pornography like a textbook, like a journal. When he finally convinced me to be bound, he read in

the magazine how to tie the knots and bind me in a way that I couldn't escape. Most of the scenes where I had to dress up or go through different fantasies were the exact same scenes that he had read in the magazines.

Ms. O described a case in which a man

brought pornographic magazines, books, and paraphernalia into the bedroom with him and told her [his ex-wife] that if she did not perform the sexual acts in the "dirty" books and magazines, he would beat her and kill her.

Ms. S testified about the experiences of a group of women prostitutes who, she said,

were forced constantly to enact specific scenes that men had witnessed in pornography. . . . These men . . . would set up scenarios, usually with more than one woman, to copy scenes that they had seen portrayed in magazines and books. Then they would make their movies using home video equipment and Polaroid cameras for their own libraries of pornography. [For example, Ms. S. quoted a woman in her group as saying,] "He held up a porn magazine with a picture of a beaten woman and said, 'I want you to look like that. I want you to hurt.' He then began beating me. When I did not cry fast enough, he lit a cigarette and held it right above my breast for a long time before he burned me."

Ms. S also described what three men did to a nude woman prostitute whom they had tied up while she was seated on a chair:

They burned her with cigarettes and attached nipple clips to her breasts. They had many S and M magazines with them and showed her many pictures of women appearing to consent, enjoy, and encourage this abuse. She was held for twelve hours while she was continuously raped and beaten.

Another example cited by Ms. S:

They [several Johns] forced the women to act simultaneously with the movie. In the movie at this point, a group of men were urinating on a naked woman. All the men in the room were able to perform this task, so they all started urinating on the woman who was now naked.

When a male engages in a particularly unusual act that he had previously encountered in pornography, it becomes even more likely that the decision to do so was inspired by the pornography. One woman, for example, testified to the Attorney General's Commission on Pornography about the pornography-related death of her son:

My son, Troy Daniel Dunaway, was murdered on August 6, 1981, by the greed and avarice of the publishers of *Hustler* magazine. My son read the article "Orgasm of Death," set up the sexual experiment depicted therein, followed the explicit instructions of the article, and ended up dead. He would still be alive today were he not enticed and incited into this action by *Hustler* magazine's "How to Do" August 1981 article, an article which was found at his feet and which directly caused his death. (1986, p. 797)

When children do what they see in pornography, it is even more improbable than in the case of adults that their behavior can be attributed entirely to their predispositions.

The psychologist Jennings Bryant testified to the Pornography Commission about a survey he had conducted involving six hundred telephone interviews with males and females who were evenly divided into three age groups: students in junior high school, students in high school, and adults aged nineteen to thirty-nine years (1985, p. 133). Respondents were asked if "exposure to X-rated materials had made them want to try anything they saw" (1985, p. 140). Two-thirds of the males reported "wanting to try some of the behavior depicted" (1985, p. 140). Bryant reports that the desire to imitate what is seen in pornography "progressively increases as age of respondents *decreases*" (1985, p. 140; emphasis added). Among the junior high school students, 72% of the males reported that "they wanted to try some sexual experiment or sexual behavior that they had seen in their initial exposure to X-rated material" (1985, p. 140).

In trying to ascertain if imitation had occurred, the respondents were asked, "Did you actually experiment with or try any of the behaviors depicted [within a few days of seeing the materials]?" (1985, p. 140). A quarter of the males answered that they had. A number of adult men answered no but said that some years later they had experimented with the behaviors portrayed. However, only imitations within a few days of seeing the materials were counted (1985, p. 140). Male high school students were the most likely (31%) to report trying the behaviors portrayed (1985, p. 141).

Unfortunately, no information is available on the behaviors imitated by these males. Imitating pornography is cause for concern only when the behavior imitated is violent or abusive or when the behavior is not wanted by one or more of the participants. Despite the unavailability of this information, Bryant's study is valuable in showing how common it is for males to *want* to imitate what they see in pornography and in revealing that many *do* imitate it within a few days of viewing it. Furthermore, given the degrading and often violent content of pornography, as well as the youthfulness and presumable susceptibility of many of the viewers, how likely is it that these males imitated or wished to imitate only the nonsexist, nondegrading, and nonviolent sexual behavior?

Almost all the research on pornography to date has been conducted on men and women who were at least eighteen years old. But as Malamuth points out, there is "a research basis for expecting that children would be more susceptible to the influences of mass media, including violent pornography if they are exposed to it" than adults (1985, p. 107). Bryant's telephone interviews show that very large numbers of children now have access to both hard-core and soft-core materials. For example:

- The average age at which male respondents saw their first issue of *Playboy* or a similar magazine was 11 years (1985, p. 135).
- All of the high school age males surveyed reported having read or looked at *Playboy, Playgirl,* or some other soft-core magazine (1985, p. 134).

- High school males reported having seen an average of 16.1 issues, and junior high school males said they had seen an average of 2.5 issues.
- In spite of being legally under age, junior high students reported having seen an average of 16.3 "unedited sexy R-rated films" (1985, p. 135). (Although R-rated movies are not usually considered pornographic, many of them meet my definition of pornography.)
- The average age of first exposure to sexually oriented R-rated films for all respondents was 12.5 years (1985, p. 135).
- Nearly 70% of the junior high students surveyed reported that they had seen their first R-rated film before they were 13 (1985, p. 135).
- The vast majority of all the respondents reported exposure to hard-core, X-rated, sexually explicit material (1985, p. 135). Furthermore, "a larger proportion of high school students had seen X-rated films than any other age group, including adults": 84%, with the average age of first exposure being 16 years, 11 months. (1985, p. 136)

In a more recent anonymous survey of 247 Canadian junior high school students whose average age was fourteen years, James Check and Kristin Maxwell (1992) report that 87% of the boys and 61% of the girls said they had viewed video-pornography. The average age at first exposure was just under twelve years.

> 33% of the boys versus only 2% of the girls reported watching pornography once a month or more often. As well, 29% of the boys versus 1% of the girls reported that pornography was the source that had provided them with the most useful information about sex (i.e., more than parents, school, friends, etc.). Finally, boys who were frequent consumers of pornography and/or reported learning a lot from pornography were also more likely to say that it was "OK" to hold a girl down and force her to have intercourse.

Clearly, more research is needed on the effects of pornography on young male viewers, particularly in view of the fact that recent studies suggest that "over 50% of various categories of paraphiliacs [sex offenders] had developed their deviant arousal patterns prior to age 18" (Einsiedel, 1986, p. 53). Einsiedel goes on to say that "it is clear that the age-of-first-exposure variable and the nature of that exposure needs to be examined more carefully. There is also evidence that the longer the duration of the paraphilia, the more significant the association with use of pornography" (Abel, Mittelman, and Becker, 1985).

The first two items listed under Factor I in my theoretical model both relate to the viewing of *violent* pornography. But sexualizing dominance and submission is a way in which nonviolent pornography can also predispose some males to want to rape women.

(3) *Sexualizing dominance and submission*. The Canadian psychologists James Check and Ted Guloien (1989) conducted an experiment in which they distinguished between degrading nonviolent pornography and erotica and compared their effects. Their experiment is rare not only for making this distinction, but also for including nonstudents as subjects; 436 Toronto residents and college students were exposed to one of three types of sexual material over three viewing sessions, or to no material. The sexual materials were constructed from existing commercially available videos and validated by measuring subjects' perceptions of them. The contents of the sexual materials shown to the three groups of subjects were as follows:

1. The *sexual violence* material portrayed scenes of sexual intercourse involving a woman strapped to a table and being penetrated by a large plastic penis.

2. The *sexually explicit*, dehumanizing but *non-violent* material portrayed scenes of sexual activity that included a man sitting on top of a woman and masturbating into her face.

3. The *sexually explicit nondegrading* material portrayed sexual activities leading up to heterosexual intercourse. (Check and Guloien, 1989)

Check and Guloien's experiment revealed that the viewing of both the nonviolent dehumanizing materials as well as the violent materials resulted in

male subjects reporting a significantly greater likelihood of engaging in rape or other coercive sex acts than the control group.

Although self-reported likelihood of raping is not a proper measure of *desire* to rape, as it also indicates that the internal inhibitions against acting out rape desires have been undermined to some extent, Check and Guloien's experiment does offer tentative support for my theoretical model's claim that pornography sexualizes dominance and submission. In addition, it makes theoretical sense that sexualizing dominance and submission would probably be generalized to include eroticizing rape and/or other abusive sexual behavior for some males. For example, Ms. S testified at the Minnesota Hearings that "men constantly witness the abuse of women in pornography and if they can't engage in that behavior with their wives, girlfriends, or children, they force a whore to do it" (Russell, 1993a). And the Rev. Susan Wilhem testified in support of an antipornography ordinance in New York City that "I came across a picture [in pornography] of a position my ex-husband had insisted we try. When we did, I hemorrhaged for three days. My bruised cervix is still a problem after ten years. . . . We should have some place to go to complain about how pornography is part of making our husbands into rapists" (Russell, 1993a).

Further research is needed on this issue, and more researchers need to follow the lead of the Canadian researchers in going beyond the distinction between violent and nonviolent pornography, and distinguishing also between nonviolent degrading pornography and erotica.

(4) *Creating an appetite for increasingly stronger material*. Dolf Zillmann and Jennings Bryant have studied the effects of what they refer to as "massive exposure" to pornography (1984). (In fact, it was not particularly massive: 4 hours and 48 minutes per week over a period of six weeks.) These researchers, unlike Malamuth and Donnerstein, focus on trying to ascertain the effects of *nonviolent* pornography, and, in the study to be described, they use a sample drawn from a nonstudent adult population.

Male subjects in the *massive exposure* condition saw thirty-six nonviolent pornographic films, six per session per week; male subjects in the *intermediate* condition saw eighteen such movies, three per session per week. Male subjects in the control group saw thirty-six nonpornographic movies. Various measures were taken after one week, two weeks, and three weeks of exposure, as well as information about the kind of materials that the subjects were most interested in viewing.

Zillmann and Bryant found that a desire for stronger material was fostered in their subjects. "Consumers graduate from common to less common forms of pornography," Zillmann maintains, that is, to more violent and more degrading materials (1984, p. 127). Zillmann suggests this may be "because familiar material becomes unexciting as a result of habituation" (1984, p. 127).

According to Zillmann and Bryant's research, then, pornography can transform a male who was not previously interested in the more abusive types of pornography into one who *is* turned on by such material. This is consistent with Malamuth's findings that males who did not previously find rape sexually arousing generate such fantasies after being exposed to a typical example of violent pornography.

THE ROLE OF PORNOGRAPHY IN UNDERMINING SOME MALES' INTERNAL INHIBITIONS AGAINST ACTING OUT THE DESIRE TO RAPE

> "The movie was just like a big picture stand with words on it saying 'go out and do it, everybody's doin' it, even the movies.'" (Rapist interviewed by Beneke, 1982, p. 74.)

Evidence has been cited showing that many males would like to rape a woman, but that an unknown percentage of these males have internal inhibitions against doing so. Some males' internal inhibitions are likely to be very weak, others' very strong. Presumably, the strength of internal inhibitions also varies in the same individual from time to time. Research evidence finds seven ways in which pornography undermines some males' internal inhibitions against acting out rape desires.

1. *Objectifying women.* The first way in which pornography undermines some males' internal inhibitions against acting out their desires to rape is by objectifying women. Feminists have been emphasizing the role of objectification in the occurrence of rape for years (e.g., Medea and Thompson, 1974; Russell, 1975). Objectification makes it easier to rape them. "It was difficult for me to admit that I was dealing with a human being when I was talking to a woman," one rapist reported, "because, if you read men's magazines, you hear about your stereo, your car, your chick" (Russell, 1975, pp. 249–250). After this rapist had hit his victim several times in her face, she stopped resisting and begged, "All right, just don't hurt me." "When she said that," he reported, "all of a sudden it came into my head, 'My God, this is a human being!' I came to my senses and saw that I was hurting this person." Another rapist said of his victim, "I wanted this beautiful fine *thing* and I got it" (Russell, 1975, p. 245, emphasis added).

Another example is provided by Ms. N., who testified at the Hearings on Pornography in Minnesota about how her boyfriend treated her as a sexual object after he had watched pornography: "This encounter differed from previous ones. It was much quicker, it was somewhat rougher, and he was not aware of me as a person. There was no foreplay" (Russell, 1993a).

Dehumanizing oppressed groups or enemy nations in times of war is an important mechanism for facilitating brutal behavior toward members of those groups. Ms. U, for example, testified that "A society that sells books, movies, and video games like 'Custer's Last Stand' ['Custer's Revenge'] in its street corners, gives white men permission to do what they did to me. Like they [her rapists] said, I'm scum. It is a game to track me down, rape and torture me" (Russell, 1993a). However, the dehumanization of women that occurs in pornography is often not recognized because of its sexual guise and its pervasiveness. It is important to note that the objectification of women is as common in nonviolent pornography as it is in violent pornography.

Doug McKenzie-Mohr and Mark Zanna conducted an experiment to test whether certain types of males would be more likely to sexually objectify a woman after viewing fifteen minutes of nonviolent pornography. They selected sixty male students whom they classified into one of two categories: masculine sex-typed or gender schematic—individuals who "encode all cross-sex interactions in sexual terms and all members of the opposite sex in terms of sexual attractiveness" (Bem, 1981, p. 361); and androgynous or gender aschematic—males who do not encode cross-sex interactions and women in these ways (McKenzie-Mohr and Zanna, 1990, pp. 297, 299).

McKenzie-Mohr and Zanna found that after exposure to nonviolent pornography, the masculine sex-typed males "treated our female experimenter who was interacting with them in a professional setting, in a manner that was both cognitively and behaviorally sexist" (1990, p. 305). In comparison with the androgynous males, for example, the masculine sex-typed males positioned themselves closer to the female experimenter and had "greater recall for information about her physical appearance" and less about the survey she was conducting (1990, p. 305). The experimenter also rated these males as more sexually motivated based on her answers to questions such as, "How much did you feel he was looking at your body?" "How sexually motivated did you find the subject?" (1990, p. 301).

This experiment confirmed McKenzie-Mohr and Zanna's hypothesis that exposure to nonviolent pornography causes masculine sex-typed males, in contrast to androgynous males, to view and treat a woman as a sex object.

2. *Rape myths.* If males believe that women enjoy rape and find it sexually exciting, this belief is likely to undermine the inhibitions of some of those who would like to rape women. The sociologists Diana Scully and Martha Burt have reported that rapists are particularly apt to believe rape myths (Burt, 1980; Scully, 1985). Scully, for example, found that 65% of the rapists in her study believed that "women cause their own rape by the way they act and the clothes they wear"; and 69% agreed that "most men accused of rape are really innocent." However, as Scully points out, it is not

possible to know if their beliefs preceded their behavior or constitute an attempt to rationalize it. Hence, findings from the experimental data are more telling for our purposes than these interviews with rapists.

As the myth that women enjoy rape is widely held, the argument that consumers of pornography realize that such portrayals are false is totally unconvincing (Brownmiller, 1975; Burt, 1980; Russell, 1975). Indeed, several studies have shown that portrayals of women enjoying rape and other kinds of sexual violence can lead to increased acceptance of rape myths in both males and females. In an experiment conducted by Neil Malamuth and James Check, for example, one group of college students saw a pornographic depiction in which a woman was portrayed as sexually aroused by sexual violence, and a second group was exposed to control materials. Subsequently, all subjects were shown a second rape portrayal. The students who had been exposed to the pornographic depiction of rape were significantly more likely than the students in the control group (1) to perceive the second rape victim as suffering less trauma; (2) to believe that she actually enjoyed it; and (3) to believe that women in general enjoy rape and forced sexual acts (Check and Malamuth, 1985, p. 419).

Other examples of the rape myths that male subjects in these studies are more apt to believe after viewing pornography are as follows: "A woman who goes to the home or the apartment of a man on their first date implies that she is willing to have sex;" "Any healthy woman can successfully resist a rapist if she really wants to;" "Many women have an unconscious wish to be raped, and may then unconsciously set up a situation in which they are likely to be attacked;" "If a girl engages in necking or petting and she lets things get out of hand, it is her own fault if her partner forces sex on her" (Briere, Malamuth, and Check, 1985, p. 400).

In Maxwell and Check's 1992 study of 247 high school students (described above), they found very high rates of what they called "rape supportive beliefs," that is, acceptance of rape myths and violence against women. The boys who were the most frequent consumers of pornography and/or who reported learning a lot from it were more accepting of rape supportive beliefs than their peers who were less frequent consumers and/or who said they had not learned as much from it:

A full 25% of girls and 57% of boys indicated belief that in one or more situations, it was at least "maybe okay" for a boy to hold a girl down and force her to have intercourse. Further, only 21% of the boys and 57% of the girls believed that forced intercourse was "definitely not okay" in any of the situations. The situation in which forced intercourse was most accepted was that in which the girl had sexually excited her date. In this case 43% of the boys and 16% of the girls stated that it was at least "maybe okay" for the boy to force intercourse. (1992)

According to Donnerstein, "After only 10 minutes of exposure to aggressive pornography, particularly material in which women are shown being aggressed against, you find male subjects are much more willing to accept these particular myths" (1983, p. 6). These males are also more inclined to believe that 25% of the women they know would enjoy being raped. (1983, p. 6)

3. *Acceptance of interpersonal violence.* Males' internal inhibitions against acting out their desire to rape can also be undermined if they consider male violence against women to be acceptable behavior. Studies have shown that viewing portrayals of sexual violence as having positive consequences increases male subjects' acceptance of violence against women. Examples of some of the attitudes used to measure acceptance of interpersonal violence include "Being roughed up is sexually stimulating to many women"; "Sometimes the only way a man can get a cold woman turned on is to use force"; "Many times a woman will pretend she doesn't want to have intercourse because she doesn't want to seem loose, but she's really hoping the man will force her" (Briere, Malamuth, and Check, 1985, p. 401).

Malamuth and Check (1981) conducted an experiment of particular interest because the movies shown were part of the regular campus film program. Students were randomly assigned to view either a feature-length film that portrayed violence against women as being justifiable and having positive consequences (*Swept Away* or *The Getaway*) or a film without sexual violence. The experiment showed that exposure to the sexually violent movies increased the male subjects' acceptance of interpersonal violence against women. (This outcome did not occur with the female subjects.) These effects were measured several days after the films had been seen.

Malamuth suggests several processes by which sexual violence in the media "might lead to attitudes that are more accepting of violence against women" (1986, p. 4). Some of these processes also probably facilitate the undermining of pornography consumers' internal inhibitions against acting out rape desires:

1. Labeling sexual violence more as a sexual than a violent act.
2. Adding to perceptions that sexual aggression is normative and culturally acceptable.
3. Changing attributions of responsibility to place more blame on the victim.
4. Elevating the positive value of sexual aggression by associating it with sexual pleasure and a sense of conquest.
5. Reducing negative emotional reactions to sexually aggressive acts (1986, p. 5).

4. *Trivializing rape.* According to Donnerstein, in most studies on the effects of pornography, "subjects have been exposed to only a few minutes of pornographic material" (1985, p. 341). In contrast, Zillmann and Bryant examined the impact on male subjects of what they refer to as "massive exposure" to nonviolent pornography (4 hours and 48 minutes per week over a period of six weeks; for further details about the experimental design, see section 4 above). After three weeks the subjects were told that they were participating in an American Bar Association study that required them to evaluate a trial in which a man was prosecuted for the rape of a female hitchhiker. At the end of this mock trial various measures were taken of the subjects' opinions about

the trial and about rape in general. For example, they were asked to recommend the prison term they thought most fair.

Zillmann and Bryant found that the male subjects who were exposed to the massive amounts of pornography considered rape a less serious crime than they did before they were exposed to it; they thought that prison sentences for rape should be shorter; and they perceived sexual aggression and abuse as causing less suffering for the victims, even in the case of an adult male having sexual intercourse with a twelve-year-old girl (1984, p. 132). They concluded that "heavy exposure to common non-violent pornography trivialized rape as a criminal offense" (1984, p. 117).

5. *Callous attitudes toward female sexuality.* In the same experiment on massive exposure, Zillmann and Bryant also reported that "males' sexual callousness toward women was significantly enhanced" (1984, p. 117). Male subjects, for example, became increasingly accepting of statements such as "A woman doesn't mean 'no' until she slaps you"; "A man should find them, fool them, fuck them, and forget them"; and "If they are old enough to bleed, they are old enough to butcher." However, judging by these items, it is difficult to distinguish sexual callousness from a general hostility to women.

(6) *Acceptance of male dominance in intimate relationships.* A marked increase in males' acceptance of male dominance in intimate relationships was yet another result of massive exposure to pornography (Zillmann and Bryant, 1984, p. 121). The notion that women are, or ought to be, equal in intimate relationships was more likely to be abandoned by these male subjects (1984, p. 122). Finally, their support of the women's liberation movement also declined sharply (1984, p. 134).

These findings demonstrate that pornography increases the acceptability of sexism. As Van White points out, "By using pornography, by looking at other human beings as a lower form of life, they [the pornographers] are perpetuating the same kind of hatred that brings racism to society" (1984).

The greater trivializing of rape by males, the increase in their callous attitudes toward female sexu-

ality, and their greater acceptance of male domination are all likely to contribute to undermining some males' inhibitions against acting out their desires to rape.

For example, Ms. O testified about the ex-husband of a woman friend and next door neighbor: "When he looked at the magazines, he made hateful, obscene, violent remarks about women in general and about me. He told me that because I am female I am here to be used and abused by him, and that because he is a male he is the master and I am his slave" (Russell, 1993a).

(7) *Desensitizing males to rape.* In an experiment specifically designed to study desensitization, Linz, Donnerstein, and Penrod showed ten hours of R-rated or X-rated movies over a period of five days to male subjects (Donnerstein and Linz, 1985, p. 34A). Some students saw X-rated movies depicting sexual assault; others saw X-rated movies depicting only consenting sex; and a third group saw R-rated sexually violent movies—for example, *I Spit on Your Grave*, *Toolbox Murders*, and *Texas Chainsaw Massacre*. Donnerstein (1983) describes *Toolbox Murders* as follows: There is an erotic bathtub scene in which a woman massages herself. A beautiful song is played. Then a psychotic killer enters with a nail gun. The music stops. He chases the woman around the room, then shoots her through the stomach with the nail gun. She falls across a chair. The song comes back on as he puts the nail gun to her forehead and blows her brains out. According to Donnerstein, many young males become sexually aroused by this movie (1983, p. 10).

Donnerstein and Linz point out that "it has always been suggested by critics of media violence research that only those who are *already* predisposed toward violence are influenced by exposure to media violence" (1985, p. 34F). These experimenters, however, actually preselected their subjects to ensure that they were not psychotic, hostile, or anxious.

Donnerstein and Linz described the impact of the R-rated movies on their subjects as follows:

Initially, after the first day of viewing, the men rated themselves as significantly above the norm for depression, anxiety, and annoyance on a mood adjective checklist. After each subsequent day of viewing, these scores dropped until, on the fourth day of viewing, the males' levels of anxiety, depression, and annoyance were indistinguishable from baseline norms. (1985, p. 34F)

By the fifth day, the subjects rated the movies as less graphic and less gory and estimated fewer violent or offensive scenes than after the first day of viewing. They also rated the films as significantly less debasing and degrading to women, more humorous, and more enjoyable, and reported a greater willingness to see this type of film again (1985, p. 34F). However, their sexual arousal by this material did *not* decrease over this five-day period (Donnerstein, 1983, p. 10).

On the last day, the subjects went to a law school where they saw a documentary reenactment of a real rape trial. A control group of subjects who had never seen the films also participated in this part of the experiment. Subjects who had seen the R-rated movies: (1) rated the rape victim as significantly more worthless, (2) rated her injury as significantly less severe, and (3) assigned greater blame to her for being raped than did the subjects who had not seen the film. In contrast, these effects were not observed for the X-rated nonviolent films.[1] However, the results were much the same for the violent X-rated films, despite the fact that the R-rated material was "much more graphically violent" (Donnerstein, 1985, pp. 12–13).

In summary: I have presented only a small portion of the research evidence for seven different effects of pornography, all of which probably contribute to the undermining of some males' internal inhibitions against acting out rape desires. This list is not intended to be comprehensive.

---

1. It is a mystery why Donnerstein finds no effects for nonviolent pornographic movies while Zillmann reports many significant effects. Unfortunately, there is reason to believe that Donnerstein's reporting of his findings that have become unpopular in academia and other segments of the liberal establishment is not entirely accurate. For example, see Page, 1989, 1990a, 1990b; and Russell, "The experts cop out," in Russell, 1993b.

REFERENCES

Abel, Gene, Barlow, David, Blanchard, Edward, & Guild, Donald. (1977). The components of rapists' sexual arousal. *Archives of General Psychiatry, 34,* 895–903.

Abel, Gene, Mittelman, Mary, & Becker, Judith. (1985). Sexual offenders: Results of assessment and recommendations for treatment. In Mark Ben-Aron, Stephen Hucker, & Christopher Webster (Eds.), *Clinical criminology: The assessment and treatment of criminal behavior* (pp. 191–205). Toronto: Clarke Institute of Psychiatry, University of Toronto.

Attorney General's Commission on Pornography: Final Report. (1986). (Vols. 1 and 2). Washington, D.C.: U.S. Department of Justice.

Bem, Sandra. (1981). Gender schema theory: A cognitive account of sex typing. *Psychological Review, 88,* 354–364.

Beneke, Timothy. (1982). *Men on rape.* New York: St. Martin's Press.

Briere, John, Malamuth, Neil, & Check, James. (1985). Sexuality and rape-supportive beliefs. *International Journal of Women's Studies, 8,* 398–403.

Brownmiller, Susan. (1975). *Against our will: Men, women, and rape.* New York: Simon & Schuster.

Bryant, Jennings. (1985). Unpublished transcript of testimony to the Attorney General's Commission on Pornography Hearings, Houston, pp. 128–157.

Burt, Martha. (1980). Cultural myths and supports for rape. *Journal of Personality and Social Psychology, 38* (2), 217–230.

Check, James, & Guloien, Ted. (1989). Reported proclivity for coercive sex following repeated exposure to sexually violent pornography, nonviolent dehumanizing pornography, and erotica. In Dolf Zillmann & Jennings Bryant (Eds.), *Pornography: Recent research, interpretations, and policy considerations* (pp. 159–84). Hillside, N.J.: Lawrence Erlbaum.

Cline, Victor (Ed.). (1974). *Where do you draw the line?* Provo: Brigham Young University Press.

Donnerstein, Edward. (1983). Unpublished transcript of testimony to the Public Hearings on Ordinances to Add Pornography as Discrimination against Women. Committee on Government Operations, City Council, Minneapolis, pp. 4–12.

Donnerstein, Edward. (1985). Unpublished transcript of testimony to the Attorney General's Commission on Pornography Hearings, Houston, pp. 5–33.

Donnerstein, Edward, & Linz, Daniel. (1985). Presentation paper to the Attorney General's Commission on Pornography, Houston.

Einsiedel, Edna. (1986). Social science report. Prepared for the Attorney General's Commission on Pornography, U.S. Department of Justice, Washington, D.C.

Finkelhor, David. (1984). *Child sexual abuse: New theory and research.* New York: Free Press.

Hite, Shere. (1981). *The Hite report on male sexuality.* New York: Alfred Knopf.

Malamuth, Neil. (1981). Rape fantasies as a function of exposure to violent sexual stimuli. *Archives of Sexual Behavior, 10*, 33–47.

Malamuth, Neil. (1985). Unpublished transcript of testimony to the Attorney General's Commission on Pornography Hearings, Houston, pp. 68–110.

Malamuth, Neil. (1986). Do sexually violent media indirectly contribute to anti-social behavior? Paper prepared for the Surgeon General's Workshop on Pornography and Public Health, Arlington, Vir.

Malamuth, Neil, & Check, James. (1981). The effects of mass media exposure on acceptance of violence against women: A field experiment. *Journal of Research in Personality, 15*, 436–46.

Maxwell, Kristin, & Check, James. (June 1992). Adolescents' rape myth attitudes and acceptance of forced sexual intercourse. Paper presented at the Canadian Psychological Association Meetings, Quebec. (Abstract)

McKenzie-Mohr, Doug, & Zanna, Mark. (1990). Treating women as sexual objects: Look to the (gender schematic) male who has viewed pornography. *Personality and Social Psychology Bulletin, 16* (2), 296–308.

Medea, Andra, & Thompson, Kathleen. (1974). *Against rape.* New York: Farrar, Straus and Giroux.

Page, Stewart. (1989). Misrepresentation of pornography research: Psychology's role. *American Psychologist, 42* (10), 578–580.

Page, Stewart. (1990a). The turnaround on pornography research: Some implications for psychology and women. *Canadian Psychology, 31* (4), 359–367.

Page, Stewart. (1990b). On Linz and Donnerstein's view of pornography research. *Canadian Psychology, 31* (4), 371–373.

Rachman, S., & Hodgson, R. J. (1968). Experimentally-induced "sexual fetishism": Replication and development. *Psychological Record, 18*, 25–27.

Russell, Diana. (1975). *The politics of rape.* New York: Stein and Day.

Russell, Diana. (1984). *Sexual exploitation: Rape, child sexual abuse, and workplace harassment.* Beverly Hills: Sage.

Russell, Diana (Ed.). (1993a). *Making violence sexy: Feminist views on pornography.* New York: Teachers College Press.

Russell, Diana. (1993b). The experts cop out. In Diana Russell (Ed.), *Making violence sexy: Feminist views on pornography* (pp. 151–166). New York: Teachers College Press.

Scully, Diana. (1985). The role of violent pornography in justifying rape. Paper prepared for the Attorney General's Commission on Pornography Hearings, Houston.

Theodorson, George, and Theodorson, Achilles. (1979). *A modern dictionary of sociology.* New York: Barnes and Noble.

Zillmann, Dolf, & Bryant, Jennings. (1984). Effects of massive exposure to pornography. In Neil Malamuth and Edward Donnerstein (Eds.), *Pornography and sexual aggression* (pp. 115–138). New York: Academic Press.

Why Censoring Pornography Would Not Reduce Discrimination or Violence against Women

NADINE STROSSEN

The only thing pornography is known to cause directly is the solitary act of masturbation. As for corruption, the only immediate victim is English prose.

Gore Vidal

Catharine MacKinnon and Andrea Dworkin advocate the adoption of laws that would allow women to take civil action against anyone involved in the production, sale, or distribution of pornography on the grounds that they had been hurt by such material. Contrary to MacKinnon and Dworkin's assertions, these laws would undermine rather than advance important women's rights and human rights causes. For the sake of argument let's make the purely hypothetical assumption that we could fix social problems: let's pretend we could wave a magic wand that would miraculously make the laws do what they are supposed to without trampling on rights that are vital to everyone, and without stifling speech that serves women.

Even in this "Never-Never Land," where we could neutralize its negative side effects, would censorship "cure"—or at least reduce—the discrimina-

tion and violence against women allegedly caused by pornography? That is the assumption that underlies the feminist procensorship position, fueling the argument that we should trade in our free speech rights to promote women's safety and equality rights. In fact, though, the hoped-for benefits of censorship are as hypothetical as our exercise in wishing away the evils of censorship. I will show this by examining the largely unexamined assumption that censorship would reduce sexism and violence against women. This assumption rests, in turn, on three others: that exposure to sexist, violent imagery leads to sexist, violent behavior; that the effective suppression of pornography would significantly reduce exposure to sexist, violent imagery; and that censorship would effectively suppress pornography.

To justify censoring pornography on the rationale that it would reduce violence or discrimination against women, one would have to provide actual support for all three of these assumptions. Each presupposes the others. Yet the only one of them that has received substantial attention is the first—that exposure to sexist, violent imagery leads to sexist, violent behavior—and, as I show later in this chapter, there is no credible evidence to bear it out. Even feminist advocates of censoring pornography have acknowledged that this asserted causal connection cannot be proven, and therefore fall back on the argument that it should be accepted "on faith." Catharine MacKinnon has captured this fallback position well through her defensive double negative: "There is no evidence that pornography does no harm."

Of course, given the impossibility of proving that there is *no* evidence of *no* harm, we would have no free speech, and indeed no freedom of any kind, were such a burden of proof actually to be imposed on those seeking to enjoy their liberties. To appreciate this, just substitute for the word "pornography" in MacKinnon's pronouncement any other type of expression or any other human right. We would have to acknowledge that "there is no evidence" that television does no harm, or that editorials criticizing government officials do no

Epigraph quoted in David Futrelle, "The Politics of Porn, Shameful Pleasures," *In These Times*, 7 March 1994, pp. 14–17.

harm, or that religious sermons do no harm, and so forth. There certainly is no evidence that feminist writing in general, or MacKinnon's in particular, does no harm.

In its *Butler* decision (1992), accepting the antipornography feminist position, the Canadian Supreme Court also accepted this dangerous intuitive approach to limiting sexual expression, stating, "It might be suggested that proof of actual harm should be required. . . [I]t is sufficient . . . for Parliament to have a reasonable basis for concluding that harm will result and this requirement does not demand actual proof of harm."[1]

Even if we were willing to follow the Canadian Supreme Court and procensorship feminists in believing, without evidence, that exposure to sexist, violent imagery does lead to sexist, violent behavior, we still should not accept their calls for censorship. Even if we assumed that *seeing* pornography leads to committing sexist and violent actions, it still would not follow that *censoring* pornography would reduce sexism or violence, due to flaws in the remaining two assumptions: we still would have to prove that pornography has a corner on the sexism and violence market, and that pornography is in fact entirely suppressible.

Even if pornography could be completely suppressed, the sexist, violent imagery that pervades the mainstream media would remain untouched. Therefore, if exposure to such materials caused violence and sexism, these problems would still remain with us. But no censorship regime could completely suppress pornography. It would continue to exist underground. In this respect, censorship would bring us the worst of both worlds. On one hand, as we have just seen from examining the Canadian situation, suppressive laws make it difficult to obtain a wide range of sexually oriented materials, so that most people would not have access to those materials. On the other hand, though, some such materials would continue to be produced and consumed no matter what. Every governmental effort to prohibit any allegedly harmful material has always caused this kind of "double

trouble." Witness the infamous "Prohibition" of alcohol earlier in this century, for example.

Let's now examine in more detail the fallacies in each of the three assumptions underlying the feminist procensorship stance. And let's start with the single assumption that has been the focus of discussion—the alleged causal relationship between exposure to sexist, violent imagery and sexist, violent behavior.

MONKEY SEE, MONKEY DO?

Aside from the mere fear that sexual expression might cause discrimination or violence against women, advocates of censorship attempt to rely on four types of evidence concerning this alleged causal link: laboratory research data concerning the attitudinal effects of showing various types of sexually explicit materials to volunteer subjects, who are usually male college students; correlational data concerning availability of sexually oriented materials and antifemale discrimination or violence; anecdotal data consisting of accounts by sex offenders and their victims concerning any role that pornography may have played in the offenses; and studies of sex offenders, assessing factors that may have led to their crimes.

As even some leading procensorship feminists have acknowledged, along with the Canadian Supreme Court in *Butler*, none of these types of "evidence" proves that pornography harms women. Rather than retracing the previous works that have reviewed this evidence and reaffirmed its failure to substantiate the alleged causal connection, I will simply summarize their conclusions.

LABORATORY EXPERIMENTS

The most comprehensive recent review of the social science data is contained in Marcia Pally's book *Sex and Sensibility: Reflections on Forbidden Mirrors and the Will to Censor* (1994).[2] It exhaus-

---

1. *Butler v. the Queen* 1 SCR 452 (1992), p. 505.

2. Marcia Pally, *Sex and Sensibility: Reflections on Forbidden Mirrors and the Will to Censor* (Hopewell, N.J.: Ecco Press, 1994).

tively canvasses laboratory studies that have evaluated the impact of exposing experimental subjects to sexually explicit expression of many varieties and concludes that no credible evidence substantiates a clear causal connection between any type of sexually explicit material and any sexist or violent behavior. The book draws the same conclusion from its thorough review of field and correlational studies, as well as sociological surveys, in the U.S., Canada, Europe, and Asia.

Numerous academic and governmental surveys of the social science studies have similarly rejected the purported link between sexual expression and aggression. The National Research Council's Panel on Understanding and Preventing Violence concluded, in 1993: "Demonstrated empirical links between pornography and sex crimes in general are weak or absent."[3]

Given the overwhelming consensus that laboratory studies do not demonstrate a causal tie between exposure to sexually explicit imagery and violent behavior, the Meese Pornography Commission Report's contrary conclusion, not surprisingly, has been the subject of heated criticism, including criticism by dissenting commissioners and by the very social scientists on whose research the report purportedly relied.

The many grounds on which the commission's report was widely repudiated include the following: six of the commission's eleven members already were committed antipornography crusaders when they were appointed to it; the commission was poorly funded and undertook no research; its hearings were slanted toward preconceived antipornography conclusions in terms of the witnesses invited to testify and the questions they were asked; and, in assessing the alleged harmful effects of pornography, the commission's report relied essentially upon morality, expressly noting at several points that its conclusions were based on "common sense," "personal insight," and "intuition."

Two of the Meese commission's harshest critics were, interestingly, two female members of that very commission, Judith Becker and Ellen Levine. Becker is a psychiatrist and psychologist whose entire extensive career has been devoted to studying sexual violence and abuse, from both research and clinical perspectives. Levine is a journalist who has focused on women's issues, and who edits a popular women's magazine. In their formal dissent from the commission's report, they concluded: "[T]he social science research has not been designed to evaluate the relationship between exposure to pornography and the commission of sexual crimes; therefore efforts to tease the current data into proof of a casual [sic] link between these acts simply cannot be accepted."[4]

Three of the foremost researchers concerned with the alleged causal relationship between sexually explicit materials and sexual violence, Edward Donnerstein, Daniel Linz, and Steven Penrod, also have sharply disputed the Meese commission's findings about a purported causal relationship.[5]

Because the feminist censorship proposals aim at sexually explicit material that allegedly is "degrading" to women, it is especially noteworthy that research data show no link between exposure to "degrading" sexually explicit material and sexual aggression.

Even two research literature surveys that were conducted for the Meese commission, one by the University of Calgary professor Edna Einsiedel and the other by then-Surgeon General C. Everett Koop, also failed to find any link between "degrading" pornography and sex crimes or aggression. Surgeon General Koop's survey concluded that only two reliable generalizations could be made about the impact of exposure to "degrading" sexual material on its viewers: it caused them to think that a variety of sexual practices were more common

3. Albert J. Reiss, Jr., and Jeffrey A. Roth, eds., *Understanding and Preventing Violence* (Washington, D.C.: National Academy Press, 1993), p. 111. (A project for the National Research Council.)

4. Judith Becker and Ellen Levine, paper presented to a meeting of the National Coalition against Censorship, New York, 17 June 1986.

5. Daniel Linz, Steven D. Penrod, and Edward Donnerstein, "The Attorney General's Commission on Pornography: The Gaps between 'Findings' and Facts," *American Bar Foundation Research Journal* 4 (Fall 1987): 713–736, at 723.

than they had previously believed, and it caused them to more accurately estimate the prevalence of varied sexual practices.[6]

Experiments also fail to establish any link between women's exposure to such materials and their development of negative self-images. Carol Krafka found that, in comparison with other women, women who were exposed to sexually "degrading" materials did not engage in more sex-role stereotyping; neither did they experience lower self-esteem, have less satisfaction with their body image, accept more antiwoman myths about rape, or show greater acceptance of violence against women.[7] Similar conclusions have been reached by Donnerstein, Linz, and Penrod.[8]

CORRELATIONAL DATA

Both the Meese commission and procensorship feminists have attempted to rely on studies that allegedly show a correlation between the availability of sexually explicit materials and sexual offense rates. Of course, though, a positive correlation between two phenomena does not prove that one causes the other. Accordingly, even if the studies did consistently show a positive correlation between the prevalence of sexual materials and sexual offenses—which they do not—they still would not establish that exposure to the materials *caused* the rise in offenses. The same correlation could also reflect the opposite causal chain—if, for example, rapists relieved their violent acts by purchasing sexually violent magazines or videotapes.

Any correlation between the availability of sexual materials and the rate of sex offenses could also

reflect an independent factor that causes increases in both. Cynthia Gentry's correlational studies have identified just such an independent variable in geographical areas that have high rates of both the circulation of sexually explicit magazines and sexual violence: namely, a high population of men between the ages of eighteen and thirty-four.[9] Similarly, Larry Baron and Murray Straus have noted that areas where both sexual materials and sexual aggression are prevalent are characterized by a "hypermasculated or macho culture pattern," which may well be the underlying causal agent.[10] Accordingly, Joseph Scott and Loretta Schwalm found that communities with higher rape rates experienced stronger sales not only of porn magazines, but also of *all* male-oriented magazines, including *Field and Stream*.[11]

Even more damning to the attempt to rest the "porn-causes-rape-or-discrimination" theory on alleged correlations is that there simply are no consistent correlations. While the asserted correlation would not be *sufficient* to prove the claimed causal connection, it is *necessary* to prove that connection. Therefore, the existence of the alleged causal relationship is conclusively refuted by the fact that levels of violence and discrimination against women are often *inversely* related to the availability of sexually explicit materials, including violent sexually explicit materials. This inverse relationship appears in various kinds of comparisons: between different states within the United States, between different countries, and between different periods within the same country.

Within the United States, the Baron and Straus research has shown no consistent pattern between the availability of sexual materials and the number

6. Edward Mulvey and Jeffrey Haugaard, *Surgeon General's Workshop on Pornography and Public Health* (Arlington, Va.: U.S. Department of Health and Human Services, 1986).

7. Carol Krafka, "Sexually Explicit, Sexually Violent, and Violent Media: Effects of Multiple Naturalistic Exposures and Debriefing on Female Viewers" (Ph.D.diss., University of Wisconsin, 1985), p. 29.

8. Daniel Linz, Edward Donnerstein, and Steven Penrod, "The Effects of Long-Term Exposure to Violent and Sexually Degrading Depictions of Women," *Journal of Personality and Social Psychology 55* (1988): 758–768.

9. Cynthia Gentry, "Pornography and Rape: An Empirical Analysis," *Deviant Behavior: An Interdisciplinary Journal 12* (1991): 277–288, at 284.

10. Larry Baron and Murray Straus, "Four Theories of Rape: A Macrosociological Analysis," *Social Problems 34*, no. 5 (1987): 467–489.

11. Joseph Scott and Loretta Schwalm, "Pornography and Rape: An Examination of Adult Theater Rates and Rapes by State," in J. E. Scott and T. Hirchi (eds.), *Controversial Issues in Crime and Justice* (Beverly Hills, Calif. Sage, 1988).

of rapes from state to state. Utah is the lowest-rank-ing state in the availability of sexual materials but twenty-fifth in the number of rapes, whereas New Hampshire ranks ninth highest in the availability of sexual materials but only forty-fourth in the number of rapes.

The lack of a consistent correlation between por-nography consumption and violence against women is underscored by one claim of the procen-sorship feminists themselves: they maintain that the availability and consumption of pornography, including violent pornography, have been increas-ing throughout the United States. At the same time, though, the rates of sex crimes have been de-creasing or remaining steady. The Bureau of Justice Statistics reports that between 1973 and 1987, the national rape rate remained steady and the at-tempted rape rate decreased. Because these data were gathered from household surveys rather than from police records, they are considered to be the most accurate measures of the incidence of crimes. These data also cover the period during which feminists helped to create a social, political, and le-gal climate that should have encouraged higher per-centages of rape victims to report their assaults. Thus, the fact that rapes reported to the Bureau of Justice Statistics have not increased provokes seri-ous questions about the procensorship feminists' theories of pornography-induced harm.[12] Similar questions are raised by data showing a decrease in wife battery between 1975 and 1985, again despite changes that should have encouraged the increased reporting of this chronically underreported crime.[13]

Noting that "[t]he mass-market pornography . . . industr[y] took off after World War II," Marcia Pally has commented, "In the decades since the 1950s, with the marketing of sexual material . . ., the country has seen the greatest advances in sensi-tivity to violence against women and children. Be-fore the . . . mass publication of sexual images, no rape or incest hot lines and battered women's shel-ters existed; date and marital rape were not yet phrases in the language. Should one conclude that the presence of pornography . . . has inspired pub-lic outrage at sexual crimes?"[14] Pally's rhetorical question underscores the illogicality of presuming that just because two phenomena happen to coex-ist, they therefore are causally linked. I have already shown that any correlation that might exist be-tween the increased availability of pornography and *increased* misogynistic discrimination or vio-lence could well be explained by other factors. The same is true for any correlation that might exist be-tween the increased availability of pornography and *decreased* misogynistic discrimination or vio-lence.

In a comparative state-by-state analysis, Larry Baron and Murray Straus have found a positive correlation between the circulation of porno-graphic magazines and the state's "index of gender equality," a composite of twenty-four indicators of economic, political, and legal equality.[15] As the re-searchers have observed, these findings may sug-gest that both sexually explicit material and gender equality flourish in tolerant climates with fewer re-strictions on speech.

The absence of any consistent correlation be-tween the availability of sexual materials and sexual violence is also clear in international comparisons. On the one hand, violence and discrimination against women are common in countries where sexually oriented material is almost completely un-available, including Saudi Arabia, Iran, and China (where the sale and distribution of erotica is now a capital offense). On the other hand, violence against women is uncommon in countries where such material is readily available, including Den-mark, Germany, and Japan.

Furthermore, patterns in other countries over time show no correlation between the increased availability of sexually explicit materials and in-creased violence against women. The 1991 analysis by University of Copenhagen professor Berl

12. Bureau of Justice Statistics, *Criminal Victimization in the United States* (Washington, D.C.: Government Printing Office, 1990); Pally, *Sex and Sensibility*, p. 22.

13. Richard J. Gelles and Murray Straus, *Intimate Vio-lence: The Causes and Consequences of Abuse in the American Family* (New York: Touchstone, 1989), p. 112.

14. Pally, *Sex and Sensibility*, pp. 21, 23.
15. Baron and Straus, "Four Theories of Rape."

Kutchinsky revealed that, while nonsexual violent crime had increased up to 300 percent in Denmark, Sweden, and West Germany from 1964 to 1984, all three countries' rape rates either declined or remained constant during this same period, despite their lifting of restrictions on sexual materials. Kutchinsky's studies further show that sex crimes against girls dropped from 30 per 100,000 to 5 per 100,000 between 1965, when Denmark liberalized its obscenity laws, and 1982.

In the decade 1964–1974, there was a much greater increase in rape rates in Singapore, which tightly restricts sexually oriented expression, than in Sweden, which had liberalized its obscenity laws during that period. In Japan, where sexually explicit materials are easily accessible and stress themes of bondage, rape, and violence, rape rates decreased 45 percent during the same decade. Moreover, Japan reports a rape rate of 2.4 per 100,000 people, compared with 34.5 in the United States, although violent erotica is more prevalent in Japan.[16]

ANECDOTES AND SUSPICIONS

As Seventh Circuit Court of Appeals Judge Richard Posner observed about MacKinnon's book *Only Words*, "MacKinnon's treatment of the central issue of pornography as she herself poses it—the harm that pornography does to women—is shockingly casual. Much of her evidence is anecdotal, and in a nation of 260 million people, anecdotes are a weak form of evidence."[17] Many procensorship advocates attempt to rest their case on self-serving "porn-made-me-do-it" claims by sexual offenders, as well as on statements by victims or police officers that sexual offenders had sexually explicit materials in their possession at the time they committed their crimes.

The logical fallacy of relying on anecdotes to establish a general causal connection between exposure to sexual materials and violence against women was aptly noted by the journalist Ellen Willis: "Anti-porn activists cite cases of sexual killers who were also users of pornography, but this is no more logical than arguing that marriage causes rape because some rapists are married."[18]

Even assuming that sexual materials really were the triggering factors behind some specific crimes, that could not justify restrictions on such materials. As the former Supreme Court justice William O. Douglas wrote, "The First Amendment demands more than a horrible example or two of the perpetrator of a crime of sexual violence, in whose pocket is found a pornographic book, before it allows the Nation to be saddled with a regime of censorship."[19] If we attempted to ban all words or images that had ever been blamed for inspiring or instigating particular crimes by some aberrant or antisocial individual, we would end up with little left to read or view. Throughout history and around the world, criminals have regularly blamed their conduct on a sweeping array of words and images in books, movies, and television.

As noted by the report of the British Committee on Obscenity and Film Censorship (1979), "For those who are susceptible to them, the stimuli to aggressive behavior are all around us."[20] To illustrate the innumerable crimes that have been incited by words or images, the committee cited a young man who attempted to kill his parents with a meat cleaver after watching a dramatized version of Dostoyevsky's *The Brothers Karamazov*, and a Jamaican man of African descent in London who raped a White woman, saying that the televised showing of Alex Haley's *Roots* had "inspired" him to treat her as White men had treated Black women. Additional examples cited by the Ohio State University law professor Earl Finbar Murphy

---

16. Pally, *Sex and Sensibility*, pp. 57–61.

17. Richard Posner, "Obsession," review of *Only Words* by Catharine MacKinnon, *New Republic*, 18 October 1993, pp. 31–36, at 34.

18. Ellen Willis, "An Unholy Alliance," *New York Newsday*, 25 February 1992, p. 78.

19. *Memoirs v. Massachusetts*, 383 U.S. 413, 432 (1966) (concurring).

20. Williams Committee, *The British Inquiry into Obscenity and Film Censorship* (London: Home Office Research and Planning Unit, 1979).

underscore that word blaming and image blaming extend to many religious works, too:

> Heinrich Pommerenke, who was a rapist, abuser, and mass slayer of women in Germany, was prompted to his series of ghastly deeds by Cecil B. DeMille's *The Ten Commandments.*
>
> During the scene of the Jewish women dancing about the Golden Calf, all the doubts of his life became clear: Women were the source of the world's troubles and it was his mission to both punish them for this and to execute them. Leaving the theater, he slew the first victim in a park nearby. John George Haigh, the British vampire who sucked his victims' blood through soda straws and dissolved their drained bodies in acid baths, first had his murder-inciting dreams and vampire longings from watching the "voluptuous" procedure of—an Anglican High Church Service.[21]

Were we to ban words or images on the grounds that they had incited some susceptible individuals to commit crimes, the Bible would be in great jeopardy. No other work has more often been blamed for more heinous crimes by the perpetrators of such crimes. The Bible has been named as the instigating or justifying factor for many individual and mass crimes, ranging from the religious wars, inquisitions, witch burnings, and pogroms of earlier eras to systematic child abuse and ritual murders today.

Marcia Pally's *Sex and Sensibility* contains a lengthy litany of some of the multitudinous, horrific bad acts that have been blamed on the "Good Book." She also cites some of the many passages depicting the "graphic, sexually explicit subordination of women" that would allow the entire Bible to be banned under the procensorship feminists' antipornography law. Pally writes,

> [T]he Bible has unbeatable worldwide sales and includes detailed justification of child abuse, wife battery, rape, and the daily humiliation of women. Short stories running through the text serve as models for sexual assault and the mauling of children. The entire set of books is available to children, who are encouraged or required to read it. It is printed and distributed by some of the world's most powerful organizations. . . .
>
> With refreshing frankness, the Bible tells men it is their rightful place to rule women. . . . [It] specifies exactly how many shekels less than men women are worth. Genesis 19:1–8 tells one of many tales about fathers setting up their daughters to be gang raped. Even more prevalent are . . . glamorized war stories in which the fruits of victory are the local girls. . . . [P]erhaps most gruesome is the snuff story about the guy who set his maid up to be gang raped and, after her death from the assault, cut her body up into little pieces. . . . Unlike movies and television programs, these tales are generally taken to be true, not simulated, accounts.[22]

In 1992, Gene Kasmar petitioned the Brooklyn Center, Minnesota, school board to ban the Bible from school classrooms and libraries on the ground that it is lewd, indecent, obscene, offensive, violent, and dangerous to women and children. He specifically complained about biblical references to concubines, explicit sex, child abuse, incest, nakedness, and mistreatment of women—all subjects, significantly, that would trigger the feminist-style antipornography laws.

In response, the chief counsel of Pat Robertson's American Center for Law and Justice in Virginia, Jay Sekulow, flew to Minnesota and argued that the Bible "is worthy of study for its literary and historic qualities."[23] While the Brooklyn Center school board apparently agreed with this assessment, voting unanimously to reject Kasmar's petition, it must be recalled that Sekulow's argument would be unavailing under Dworkin-MacKinnon-type antipornography laws. Under the

---

21. Earl Finbar Murphy, "The Value of Pornography," *Wayne Law Review 10* (1964): 655–680, at 668.

22. Pally, *Sex and Sensibility*, pp. 99–100.

23. Associated Press, "Atheist Loses Fight to Ban Bible at School," *Chicago Tribune*, 11 November 1992.

MacDworkin model law, any work could be banned on the basis of even one isolated passage that meets the definition of pornography, and the work could not be saved by any serious literary, historic, or other value it might offer. Consequently, the feminist antipornography law could be used by Kasmar and others to ban the Bible not only from public schools, but also from public libraries, bookstores, and all other venues.

The countless expressive works that have been blamed for crimes include many that convey profeminist messages. Therefore, an anecdotal, image-blaming rationale for censorship would condemn many feminist works. For example, the television movie *The Burning Bed*, which told the true story of a battered wife who set fire to her sleeping husband, was blamed for some "copycat" crimes, as well as for some acts of violence by men against women. The argument that such incidents would justify suppression would mark the end of any films or other works depicting—and deploring—the real violence that plagues the lives of too many actual women.

Under a censorship regime that permits anecdotal, book-blaming "evidence," all other feminist materials would be equally endangered, not "just" works that depict the violence that has been inflicted on women. That is because, as feminist writings themselves have observed, some sexual assaults are committed by men who feel threatened by the women's movement. Should feminist works therefore be banned on the theory that they might well motivate a man to act out his misogynistic aggression?

STUDIES OF SEX OFFENDERS

The scientists who have investigated the impact of exposure to sexual materials in real life have not found that either sexual materials or attitudes toward women play any significant role in prompting actual violence. In general, these studies show that sex offenders had less exposure to sexually explicit materials than most men, that they first saw such materials at a later age than nonoffenders, that they were overwhelmingly more likely to have been pun-

ished for looking at them as teenagers, and that they often find sexual images more distressing than arousing.[24]

While no evidence substantiates that viewing pornography leads to violence and discrimination against women, some evidence indicates that, if anything, there may well be an inverse causal relationship between exposure to sexually explicit materials and misogynistic violence or discrimination. One of the leading researchers in this area, Edward Donnerstein of the University of California at Santa Barbara, has written, "A good amount of research strongly supports the position that exposure to erotica can reduce aggressive responses in people who are predisposed to aggress."[25] Similarly, John Money, of Johns Hopkins Medical School, a leading expert on sexual violence, has noted that most people with criminal sexualities were raised with strict, antisexual, repressive attitudes. He predicts that the "current repressive attitudes toward sex will breed an ever-widening epidemic of aberrant sexual behavior."[26]

In one 1989 experiment, males who had been exposed to pornography were more willing to come to the aid of a female subject who appeared to be hurt than were men who had been exposed to other stimuli.[27] Laboratory studies further indicate that there may well be an inverse causal relationship between exposure to violent sexually explicit material and sexual arousal. For example, in 1991, Howard Barbaree and William Marshall, of Queen's College in Ontario, found: "For most men, hearing a description of an encounter where the man is forcing the woman to have sex, and the woman is in distress or pain, dampens the arousal by about 50 percent compared to arousal levels using a scene of consenting lovemaking. . . . Ordinarily violence inhibits

24. Pally, *Sex and Sensibility*, pp. 25–61.
25. Edward Donnerstein, "Erotica and Human Aggression," in *Aggression: Theoretical and Empirical Reviews*, ed. Richard Green and Edward Donnerstein (New York: Academic Press, 1983), pp. 127–128.
26. Quoted in Jane Brody, "Scientists Trace Aberrant Sexuality," *New York Times*, 23 January 1990.
27. Pally, *Sex and Sensibility*, p. 50.

sexual arousal in men. A blood flow loss of 50 percent means a man would not be able to penetrate a woman."[28]

The foregoing research findings are certainly more consistent with what feminist scholars have been writing about rape than is the procensorship feminists' pornocentric analysis: namely, rape is not a crime about sex, but rather, about violence.[29]

SEE NO PORNOGRAPHY, SEE NO SEXIST AND VIOLENT IMAGERY?

Pornography constitutes only a small subset of the sexist or violent imagery that pervades our culture and media. The New York Law School professor Carlin Meyer recently conducted a comprehensive survey of the views of women's sexuality, status, and gender roles that are purveyed in nonpornographic media:

Today, mainstream television, film, advertising, music, art, and popular (including religious) literature are the primary propagators of Western views of sexuality and sex roles. Not only do we read, see and experience their language and imagery more often and at earlier ages than we do most explicit sexual representation, but precisely because mainstream imagery is ordinary and everyday, it more powerfully convinces us that it depicts the world as it is or ought to be.[30]

Other cultural and media analysts have likewise concluded that more-damaging sexist imagery is more broadly purveyed through mainstream, nonsexual representations. Thelma McCormack, direc-

tor of York University's Feminist Studies Centre, has concluded that "the enemy of women's equality is our mainstream culture with its images of women as family-centered," rather than imagery of women as sexual. According to McCormack,

Surveys and public opinion studies confirm the connection between gender-role traditionalism and an acceptance or belief in the normality of a stratified social system. The more traditional a person's views are about women, the more likely he or she is to accept inequality as inevitable, functional, natural, desirable and immutable. In short, if any image of woman can be said to influence our thinking about gender equality, it is the domestic woman not the Dionysian one.[31]

Social science researchers have found that acceptance of the rape myth and other misogynistic attitudes concerning women and violence are just as likely to result from exposure to many types of mass media—from soap operas to popular commercial films—as from even intense exposure to violent, misogynistic sexually explicit materials.[32] Accordingly, if we really wanted to purge all sexist, violent representations from our culture, we would have to cast the net far beyond pornography, notwithstanding how comprehensive and elastic that category is. Would even procensorship feminists want to deal such a death-blow to First Amendment freedoms?

CENSOR PORNOGRAPHY, SEE NO PORNOGRAPHY?

Procensorship feminists themselves have acknowledged that censorship would probably just drive pornography underground. Indeed, as recently as 1987, Catharine MacKinnon recognized that "por-

---

28. Howard Barbaree and William Marshall, "The Role of Male Sexual Arousal in Rape: Six Models," *Journal of Consulting and Clinical Psychology 59*, no. 5 (1991): 621–630; Pally, *Sex and Sensibility*, pp. 44–45.

29. Susan Brownmiller, *Against Our Will: Men, Women, and Rape* (New York: Simon & Schuster, 1975); Susan Estrich, *Real Rape* (Cambridge, Mass.: Harvard University Press, 1987).

30. Carlin Meyer, "Sex, Censorship, and Women's Liberation" (unpublished), pp. 42–43. A revised version of this manuscript was published in *Texas Law Review 72* (1994): 1097–1201.

31. Thelma McCormack, "If Pornography Is the Theory, Is Inequality the Practice?" (presented at public forum, *Refusing Censorship: Feminists and Activists Fight Back*, York, Canada, 12 November 1992), p. 12.

32. Edward Donnerstein, Daniel Linz, and Steven Penrod, *The Question of Pornography: Research Findings and Policy Implications* (New York: Free Press, 1987), p. 107.

nography cannot be reformed or suppressed or banned."[33]

The assumption that censorship would substantially reduce the availability or impact of pornography also overlooks evidence that censorship makes some viewers more desirous of pornography and more receptive to its imagery. This "forbidden fruits" effect has been corroborated by historical experience and social science research. All recent studies of the suppression of sexual expression, including Walter Kendrick's book *The Secret Museum: Pornography in Modern Culture* (1987) and Edward de Grazia's book *Girls Lean Back Everywhere: The Law of Obscenity and the Assault on Genius* (1992), demonstrate that any censorship effort simply increases the attention that a targeted work receives. Social scientific studies that were included in the report of the President's Commission on Obscenity and Pornography (1970) suggested that censorship of sexually explicit materials may increase their desirability and impact, and also that a viewer's awareness that sexually oriented parts of a film have been censored may lead to frustration and subsequent aggressive behavior.[34]

The foregoing data about the impact of censoring pornography are consistent with broader research findings: the evidence suggests that censorship of *any* material increases an audience's desire to obtain the material and disposes the audience to be more receptive to it.[35] Critical viewing skills, and the ability to regard media images skeptically and analytically, atrophy under a censorial regime. A public that learns to question everything it sees or hears is better equipped to reject culturally propagated values than is one that assumes the media have been purged of all "incorrect" perspectives.

Even assuming for the sake of argument that there were a causal link between pornography and antifemale discrimination and violence, the insignificant contribution that censorship might make to reducing them would not outweigh the substantial damage that censorship would do to feminist goals. From the lack of actual evidence to substantiate the alleged causal link, the conclusion follows even more inescapably: *Censoring pornography would do women more harm than good.*

---

33. Catharine MacKinnon, "Not a Moral Issue," *Yale Law and Policy Review 2* (1984): 321–345, at 325.

34. Percy H. Tannenbaum, "Emotional Arousal as a Mediator of Communication Effects," *Technical Report of the U.S. Commission on Obscenity and Pornography 8* (1971), p. 353.

35. Timothy C. Brock, "Erotic Materials: A Commodity Theory Analysis of Availability and Desirability," *Technical Report of the U.S. Commission on Obscenity and Pornography 6* (1971), pp. 131–137.

Sexual Orientation:

Is It Determined by Biology?

One of the most dramatic changes in psychology and psychiatry in the past thirty years has been the movement away from viewing lesbianism and homosexuality as deviant. Until mid-century, the traditional approach was to treat homosexuals and lesbians as deeply disturbed deviants in need of treatment. Bonnie Strickland, one of the pioneers in fashioning a new view of homosexuality, says she feels privileged to be part of a new wave of psychologists who are documenting that "gay and lesbian people are not diseased and perverted" (1995, p. 139).

The shift in the attitude toward homosexuality may have begun with the publication of the research of Kinsey and his associates (Kinsey et al., 1953). Homosexuality, along with other behaviors thought to be abnormal, was shown by Kinsey to be fairly widespread. In addition to the finding that 8 percent of men and 4 percent of women had been exclusively homosexual for a period of at least three years during adulthood, the Kinsey group found that 37 percent of men and 20 percent of women reported at least one homosexual experience that resulted in orgasm. Breaking with past patterns of research, which focused on lesbians who were patients in psychotherapy, investigators began to study lesbians who were not in therapy. Reviews of this literature (Mannion, 1981) indicated that the psychological adjustment of these lesbians did not differ significantly from that of heterosexual women, and, in some cases, the lesbians were less neurotic than their heterosexual counterparts. The changing view of homosexuality is underscored by the reversal of the American Psychiatric Association's position. The 1968 edition of the *Diagnostic and Statistical Manual* (DSM-II), the association's bible for making psychiatric diagnoses, classified homosexuality along with disorders such as child molestation as a "sexual deviance." Five years later, the board of trustees of the association voted to remove "homosexuality per se" from its list of psychiatric disorders, replacing it with a new category, Ego-Dystonic Homosexuality, which covered gays and lesbians who experienced distress over their sexual orientation (see Kupers article in this book).

The origin of homosexuality has also been the subject of extensive debate over the years. Much of that discussion has revolved around the question: do homosexual men and women develop a permanent sexual orientation prenatally or early in life, as the essentialists maintain, or do they choose their sexual orientation within a social context? The essentialist idea that homosexuality is a core way of being has gained a good deal of support in recent years. Simon LeVay (1991) found that in gay men, part of the anterior hypothalamus—the brain region that controls sexual behavior—has the anatomical form normally found in women instead of the one typically found in heterosexual men. LeVay's article was widely heralded as proof that homosexuality was linked to brain differences. Those who favored a biological explanation of homosexuality also found support in a report by Money, Schwartz, and Lewis (1984) that girls who were subjected to extra-high levels of testosterone in the womb were likely to be tomboys and had an increased chance of being lesbians when they grow up. A more recent study also showed that women who had been exposed to diethylstilbestrol, a synthetic estrogen, had a greater chance of becoming bisexual or homosexual than females who had not been exposed (Meyer-Bahlburg et al., 1995).

Several studies of children's behavior have strengthened the essentialist view of homosexuality. Bailey and Zucker's (1995) meta-analysis of sixteen retrospective studies of women found that homosexual women were more tomboyish when they were growing up than their heterosexual counterparts. Long-term studies by Zuger (1984) and Green (1987) found that a large percentage of "feminine" boys become adults with homosexual/bisexual orientations. Research by Bailey and Pillard (1991) reinforced the notion that homosexuality is inherited. They studied 161 homosexual men who were either identical twins (who possess the same genes), fraternal twins (who share about half their genes), or adoptive brothers with no genes in common. The result—53 percent of the sets of identical twins were homosexual, compared with 22 percent of the fraternal twins and 11 percent of the adoptive twins—suggested that genetics plays a large role in determining sexual orientation. A separate study of lesbian twins yielded similar results (Bailey et al., 1993).

These biological and genetic studies have been widely criticized. For example, Byne and Parsons (1993) point out that almost half the brothers of the homosexual identical twins in Bailey and Pillard's 1991 study were heterosexual despite sharing not only their genes but also prenatal and familial environments with their twins. Moreover, Patricia Hersch (1993) argues that since most people fall somewhere along a sexual continuum, it is simplistic to categorize them as either homosexual or heterosexual.

In the following article, J. Michael Bailey and Richard C. Pillard argue that one's sexual orientation is determined by biology. Celia Kitzinger and Sue Wilkinson reject this essentialist position, contending that women's sexuality is fluid and dynamic rather than static and fixed.

REFERENCES

American Psychiatric Association. (1968). *Diagnostic and statistical manual of mental disorders* (2nd ed.). Washington, D.C.: American Psychiatric Association.

Bailey, J. M., and Pillard, R. C. (1991). A genetic study of male sexual orientation. *Archives of General Psychology*, 48, 1089–1096.

Bailey, J. M., Pillard, R. C., Neale, M. C., & Agyei, Y.

(1993). Heritable factors influence sexual orientation in women. *Archives of General Psychology, 50*, 217–223.

Bailey, J. M., and K. J. Zucker, 1995. Childhood sex-typed behavior and sexual orientation: A conceptual analysis and quantitative review. *Developmental Psychology, 31*, 43–55.

Byne, W., and B. Parsons, 1993. Human sexual orientation: The biologic theories reappraised. *Archives of General Psychology, 50*, 228–239.

Green, R. 1987. *The "sissy boy syndrome" and the development of homosexuality.* New Haven: Yale University Press.

Hersch, P. 1993. What is gay? What is straight? In W. Dudley (Ed.), *Homosexuality: Opposing Viewpoints.* San Diego: Greenhaven Press.

Kinsey, A. C., Pomeroy, W. B., Martin, C. E., & Gebhard, P. H. (1953). *Sexual behavior in the human female.* Philadelphia: Saunders.

LeVay, S. (1991). A difference in hypothalamic structure between heterosexual and homosexual men. *Science, 253*, 1034–1037.

Mannion, K. 1981. Psychology and the lesbian: A critical view of the research. In S. Cox (ed.), *Female psychology: The emerging self* (2nd ed.), 256–274. New York: St. Martin's Press.

Meyer-Bahlburg, H. F. L., A. A. Erhardt, L. R. Rosen, R. S. Gruen, N. P. Veridiano, F. H. Vann, and H. F. Neuwalder, 1995. Prenatal estrogens and the development of homosexual orientation. *Developmental Psychology, 31*, 12–21.

Money, J., M. Schwartz, and V. G. Lewis, 1984. Adult heterosexual status and fetal hormonal masculinization and demasculinization: 46, XX congenital virilizing adrenal hyperplasia, and 46, XY androgen-insensitivity syndrome compared. *Psychoneuroendocrinology, 9*, 405–414.

Strickland, B. R. 1995. Research on sexual orientation and human development: A commentary. *Developmental Psychology, 31*, 137–140.

Zuger, B. (1984). Early effeminate behavior in boys: Outcome and significance for homosexuality. *Journal of Nervous and Mental Disease, 172*, 90–97.

ADDITIONAL READING

Garnets, L. D., and Kimmel, D. C. eds. 1993. *Psychological perspectives on lesbian and gay male experiences.* New York: Columbia University Press.

Golombok, S., and F. Tasker, 1996. Do parents influence the sexual orientation of their children? Findings from a longitudinal study of lesbian families. *Developmental Psychology, 32*, 3–11.

Greene, B. 1994. Lesbian women of color: Triple Jeopardy. In L. Comas-Diaz and B. Greene, eds., *Women of color: Integrating ethnic and gender identities in psychotherapy*, 389–427. New York: Guilford Press.

Hamer, D. H., and P. Copeland, 1994. *The science of desire: The search for the gay gene and the biology of behavior.* New York: Simon and Schuster.

Pool, R. E. 1994. *Eve's rib: The biological roots of sex differences.* New York: Crown.

Rothblum, E. D. (1994). Transforming lesbian sexuality. *Psychology of Women Quarterly, 18*, 627–641.

The Innateness of Homosexuality

J. MICHAEL BAILEY AND

RICHARD C. PILLARD

Scientists and the public have become increasingly interested in the question of why some people are homosexual and others heterosexual, partly because several scientific studies of different types have supported the theory that sexual orientation is largely innate. The political and social implications of this research have been hotly debated.

The most consistent evidence for the innateness of sexual orientation comes from genetic studies. Both male and female sexual orientation run in families; gay men have more gay brothers (Pillard & Weinrich 1986; Bailey et al., 1991) and lesbians more lesbian sisters than average (Pillard 1990; Bailey & Benishay 1993). It is not clear whether gay men have more lesbian sisters or lesbians have more gay brothers. A trait may run in families for either environmental or genetic reasons. The best available way to distinguish is to compare genetically identical or monozygotic (MZ) twins with dizygotic (DZ) twins, who are no more genetically alike than any other brothers or sisters. Such studies are valid if the environments of MZ twins are not in general significantly more similar than the environments of DZ twins. This assumption is often criticized on the grounds that MZ twins are treated more alike and therefore have more closely similar experiences (see, e.g., Byne and Parsons 1993). But studies have never shown that the experiences usually cited (such as looking more alike or being dressed alike) have significant influence on personality.

In our two genetic studies (Bailey and Pillard 1991; Bailey et al. 1993), one with male and one with female subjects, we included not only MZ and DZ twins, but also a third group, homosexual men and women with brothers or sisters who were genetically unrelated by virtue of adoption. In both studies, similarity of sexual orientation was correlated with genetic similarity. Among MZ twins of gay men, 53 percent were gay, compared with 22 percent of their DZ twins and 11 percent of adoptive brothers. Among MZ twins of lesbian women, 48 percent were lesbian, compared with 16 percent of DZ twins and 6 percent of adoptive sisters. Statistical analysis showed that for both sexes the heritability of sexual orientation (the proportion of individual variation associated with genetic difference) was about 50 percent. Investigators in two later twin studies came to similar conclusions (King & McDonald, 1992; Whitam et al., 1992). One group found higher and the other lower overall twin concordance (matching) for homosexuality than we did, but both found that MZ twins were more highly concordant than DZ twins.

One other study (Eckert et al., 1986) is worth mentioning because it concerns what many believe to be ideal subjects: MZ twins who were reared apart and therefore cannot have had nearly identical childhood environments. The subjects of the study were two homosexual men; the identical twin brother of each was also homosexual. Although this sample is much too small to justify definite conclusions, the result is suggestive. Incidentally, the study did not find a hereditary influence on female sexual orientation: none of four female identical twin pairs was concordant for homosexuality.

Existing studies have one potentially serious limitation: their subjects were all recruited through advertisements in gay- and lesbian-oriented publications. Such advertisements may be more appealing to gay people with gay twins than to gay people with heterosexual twins. But that bias would account for the findings only if it were stronger for MZ twins than for DZ twins (Bailey and Pillard 1991), and there is no reason to believe that it is.

Another source of evidence for innateness is a body of neuroendocrine and neuroanatomical research suggesting that sexual orientation is largely determined by prenatal effects of androgens (male hormones) on certain regions of the brain (Byne & Parsons, 1993; Ellis & Ames, 1987; Meyer-Bahlburg, 1984). The theory states that in either sex, when these regions are affected by high levels of androgens at a critical time, they are masculinized, and the person in question is sexually attracted to women as an adult. If the body is not producing enough androgens or the relevant tissue is insensitive to them, these brain regions are not masculinized, and the outcome in adulthood is attraction to men. Obviously, the hormonal activity or brain sensitivity to hormones could have a genetic source.

Several lines of research support the neuroendocrine hypothesis (Adkins-Regan, 1988; Byne and Parsons 1993; Meyer-Bahlburg 1984). Female rats and mice who receive a dose of androgens sufficiently early in their development will often display male mating behavior, such as mounting. Males deprived of androgens at an early stage often show female patterns, such as lordosis (arched back). Admittedly, mounting and lordosis are not directly analogous to human sexual orientation, since the physical movements performed during copulation do not indicate the sex to which one is attracted. Nevertheless, these studies are significant, because they indicate that sex-typical behavior is altered by a change in early androgen exposure. Researchers have consistently found that gay men and women tend to recall that as children they behaved in ways atypical of their sex (Bailey and Zucker 1995; Bell et al. 1981; Grellert et al. 1982; Harry 1983; Whitam 1977). Although there are many exceptions, gay men often report that they were considered sissies, and lesbians that they were regarded as tomboys. This suggests that homosexual men and women have been subjected to some influence usually confined to the opposite sex. Furthermore, childhood behavior also changes

in monkeys when the fetus is exposed to unusual levels of androgens. Female rhesus monkeys treated in this way are more likely to engage in the rough-and-tumble play typical of males.

Similar conclusions can be drawn from studies of girls and women with congenital adrenal hyperplasia (CAH), a genetic disorder that causes the adrenal glands of the fetus to secrete large amounts of androgens (Ehrhardt et al., 1968; Money et al., 1984; Dittmann et al., 1992; Zucker et al., 1992). Newborn girls with this condition may have genitalia that look almost masculine (although this is surgically correctable). According to several studies, they are often tomboys who prefer masculine toys and rough play, and as adults they have a higher than average rate of homosexuality (Berenbaum and Hines 1992; Ehrhardt et al. 1968; Ehrhardt and Baker 1974). Women prenatally exposed to diethylstilbesterol (DES), which masculinizes sexual behavior in some animals, also have a higher than average level of homosexual feelings. (Admittedly, only a minority of women with CAH or a history of exposure to DES acknowledge homosexual tendencies.)

The most important and widely discussed neuroanatomical finding on homosexuality was reported by Simon LeVay (1991) in an autopsy study of the brains of nineteen gay men, sixteen heterosexual men, and six women. He examined cell groups (nuclei) in a region of the hypothalamus that was known to be important in differentiating typical male from typical female sexual behavior in certain animals. Two of the nuclei had previously been shown to be larger in men than in women; LeVay found the same sex difference in one of them, the third interstitial nucleus of the anterior hypothalamus (INAH-3). He also found that the INAH-3 was no larger in gay men than in heterosexual women. The differences were statistical averages; in some gay men and heterosexual women, the INAH-3 was as large as in most heterosexual men. Thus the size of this brain region cannot be the sole cause of sexual orientation, and may not be the cause at all. Nevertheless, LeVay's findings suggest that gay men and heterosexual women often share a feature of brain anatomy that is related to sexual behavior.

LeVay's research has been intensely and critically scrutinized. Since all the gay men in the study died of AIDS, it has been suggested that the differences in brain structure might be due to that disease. But some of LeVay's heterosexual men had also died of AIDS, and the INAH-3 in these men was no smaller than in other heterosexual men. Another criticism is that the presumably heterosexual group could have included some homosexuals, since the available medical records did not indicate sexual history. But given recent surveys suggesting that the rate of homosexuality is rather low, it seems unlikely that a heterosexual control group would include a significant proportion of hidden homosexuals. Even if some of the men thought to be heterosexual were actually homosexual, they might have been the ones with smaller INAH-3s. In that case, the real difference between heterosexual and homosexual men would be even larger than the difference found by LeVay. Finally, some have suggested that the difference in brain structure might be an effect of homosexual activity. But research on other mammals indicates that sex differences in the hypothalamus develop early as a response to innate hormonal influences; they are not modified by later experience.

In at least one other study differences in male sexual orientation have been associated with differences in brain structure. Laura Allen and Roger Gorski (1992) found that the anterior commissure of the corpus callosum (which joins the brain's two hemispheres) is relatively larger in heterosexual women and homosexual men than in heterosexual men. Since this part of the brain is not directly involved in sexual behavior, this finding suggests that early homosexual activity has more general effects.

Critics insist that the accumulated biological evidence has little significance, since no single study is strong enough to establish the case definitely. We disagree. It is impossible to achieve perfection in research with human subjects, but here several different kinds of studies with different research strategies and different limitations have reached similar conclusions. A critic who rejects them all begins to sound strained. For example, it has been suggested that girls with CAH are treated more like boys because of their masculine appearing genitalia, or simply because their parents know about the condition (Byne and Parsons 1993; Bleier, 1984). But how likely is it that the behavioral masculinization of CAH females is totally unrelated to the behavioral masculinization of female rhesus monkeys who are given androgens at a critical period? In any case, investigators have failed to find any evidence that girls with CAH are treated like boys.

Scientific theories must be judged by comparison with the alternatives. The two main competitors in this field are psychoanalysis and socialization theory. Psychoanalytic theories of homosexuality, which emphasize the influence of family conflicts in early childhood, suffer from the same well-known deficiency as the rest of psychoanalysis—inadequate impressionistic data collected under uncontrolled conditions. Although there is some evidence that (as psychoanalysis would predict) fathers are rather distant from their gay sons, this effect is small and may be explained by the fathers' uneasiness about their sons' unusual behavior.

Today sex differences in behavior are more often thought to be the result of socialization by parents, peers, and the culture as a whole. But such processes cannot readily explain why a minority develops homosexually. All the available evidence suggests that parents of homosexuals and parents of heterosexuals treat their children similarly. According to a socialization theory, sexual orientation would depend largely on modeling (imitation) and positive reinforcement (rewards) for appropriate gender behavior. But in our society, homosexuals are obviously *not* rewarded for their behavior, and the vast majority of their potential models are heterosexual. These socialization mechanisms have been arranged as if to ensure a heterosexual outcome.

Some critics amalgamate psychoanalytic and socialization theories. They suggest that a boy or girl with certain genetically influenced personality traits who is raised in a certain kind of family has unusual childhood experiences that contribute to adult homosexual orientation. This theory is both vague and implausible. It is vague because the personality traits, family influences, and childhood experiences involved are not specified, and implausible because no personality trait has been shown to distinguish homosexual men and women from heterosexuals.

Because MZ twins are not perfectly matched for sexual orientation, environment must play a role in the genesis of homosexuality and heterosexuality, but the environmental influences could be purely biological rather than psychological or social. We simply do not know. Although the issue is not settled and the studies must be replicated, biological theories of sexual orientation are far more promising than any current alternatives. They deserve the attention of scientists and funding agencies so that this debate can be resolved in the laboratory.

REFERENCES

Adkins-Regan, E. (1988). Sex hormones and sexual orientation in animals. *Psychobiology*, 16, 335–347.

Allen, L. S., & Gorski, R. A. (1992). Sexual orientation and the size of the anterior commissure of the human brain. *Proceedings of the National Academy of Sciences*, 89, 7199–7202.

Bailey, J. M., & Benishay, D. (1993). Familial aggregation of female sexual orientation. *American Journal of Psychiatry*, 150, 272–277.

Bailey, J. M., and Pillard, R. C. (1991). A genetic study of male sexual orientation. *Archives of General Psychiatry*, 48, 1089–1096.

Bailey, J. M., R. C. Pillard, M. C. Neale, and Y. Agyei, 1993. Heritable factors influence female sexual orientation. *Archives of General Psychiatry*, 50, 217–223.

Bailey, J. M., L. Willerman, and C. Parks, 1991. A test of maternal stress hypothesis of human male sexuality. *Archives of Sexual Behavior*, 20, 277–293.

Bailey. J. M., and K. J. Zucker, 1995. Childhood sex-typed behavior and sexual orientation: A conceptual analysis and quantitative review. *Developmental Psychology*, 31, 43–55.

Bell, A. P., M. S. Weinberg, and S. K. Hammersmith, 1981. *Sexual preference: Its development in men and women.* Bloomington: Indiana University Press.

Berenbaum, S. A., and M. Hines, 1992. Early androgens are related to childhood sex-typed toy preferences. *Psychological Science*, 3, 203–206.

Bleier, R. 1984. *Science and gender: A critique of biology and its theories on women.* New York: Pergamon.

Byne, W., & Parsons, B. (1993). Human sexual orientation: The biologic theories reappraised. *Archives of General Psychiatry*, 50, 228–239.

Dittmann, R. W., Kappes, M. E., & Kappes, M. H. (1992).

Sexual behavior in adolescent and adult females with congenital adrenal hyperplasia. *Psychoneuroendocrinology*, 17, 153–170.

Eckert, E. D., Bouchard, T. J., Bohlen, J., & Heston, L. L. (1986). Homosexuality in monozygotic twins reared apart. *British Journal of Psychiatry*, 148, 421–425.

Ehrhardt, A. A., and S. W. Baker, 1974. Fetal androgens, human central nervous system differentiation and behavior sex differences. In R. C. Friedman, R. M. Richart, and R. L. Vande Wiele (eds.), *Sex differences in behavior*, 33–51. New York: Wiley.

Ehrhardt, A. A., Evers, K., & Money, J. 1968. Influence of androgen and some aspects of sexually dimorphic behavior in women with late-treated adrenogenital syndrome. *Johns Hopkins Medical Journal*, 123, 115–122.

Ellis, L., & M. A. Ames, 1987. Neurohormonal functioning and sexual orientation: A theory of homosexuality-heterosexuality. *Psychological Bulletin*, 101, 233–258.

Grellert, E. A., M. D. Newcomb, and P. M. Bentler, 1982. Childhood play activities of male and female homosexuals and heterosexuals. *Archives of Sexual Behavior*, 11, 451–478.

Harry, J. 1983. Defeminization and adult psychological well-being among male homosexuals. *Archives of Sexual Behavior*, 12, 1–19.

King, M., and E. McDonald, 1992. Homosexuals who are twins: A study of 46 probands. *British Journal of Psychiatry*, 160, 407–409.

LeVay, S. (1991). A difference in hypothalamic structure between heterosexual and homosexual men. *Science*, 253, 1034–1037.

Meyer-Bahlburg, H. (1984). Psychoendocrine research on sexual orientation: Current status and future options. In G. J. De Vries, J. P. C. De Bruin, H. M. B. Uylings, and M. A. Corner (eds.), *Progress in brain research*, vol. 61, 375–398. Amsterdam: Elsevier.

Money, J., Schwartz, M., & Lewis, V. G. (1984). Adult heterosexual status and fetal hormonal masculinization and demasculinization. *Psychoneuroendocrinology*, 9, 405–414.

Pillard, R. C. (1990). The Kinsey Scale: Is it familial? In D. P. McWhirter, S. A. Sanders, & J. M. Reinisch (eds.), *Homosexuality/heterosexuality: Concepts of sexual orientation*, 88–100. New York: Oxford University Press.

Pillard, R. C., and J. D. Weinrich, 1986. Evidence of familial nature of male homosexuality. *Archives of General Psychiatry*, 43, 808–812.

Whitam, F. L. (1977). Childhood indicators of male homosexuality. *Archives of Sexual Behavior*, 6, 89–96.

Whitam, F. L., M. Diamond, and Martin, J. 1992. Homosexual orientation in twins: A report on 61 pairs and three triplet sets. Paper presented at Annual Meeting, International Academy of Sex Research, Prague, Czechoslovakia.

Zucker, K. J., Bradley, S. J., Oliver, G., Hood, J. E., Blake, J., & Fleming, S. (1992). Psychosexual assessment of women with congenital adrenal hyperplasia: Preliminary analyses. Paper presented at Annual Meeting, International Academy of Sex Research, Prague, Czechoslovakia.

NO

Transitions from Heterosexuality to Lesbianism: The Discursive Production of Lesbian Identities

CELIA KITZINGER AND

SUE WILKINSON

After more than two decades of social construction-ist approaches to sexual identity (e.g., Gagnon & Si-mon, 1973; C. Kitzinger, 1987; McIntosh, 1968/1992; Plummer, 1981, 1992; Weeks, 1977), biological models of lesbianism and male homo-sexuality are becoming increasingly popular, both in the scientific literature (e.g., Ellis & Ames, 1987; Le-Vay, 1991) and in the media. Although biological and early socialization models may present homo-sexuality as either a natural variation or an unnatu-ral deviation from the "norm" of heterosexuality, "caused" variously by brain structure or function, genetic or hormonal influences, or early childhood experiences, they invariably assume heterosexuality as a natural, unproblematic category (see, e.g., Money, 1988, p. 11). Such an analysis fails to recog-nize that the category *homosexual* can only exist in relation to the category *heterosexual* (part of the so-cial constructionist argument) and is in direct con-tradiction to those radical feminist analyses of heterosexuality that present it as neither natural nor normal, but rather as a coercive patriarchal institu-tion (e.g., Adams, Lenskyj, Masters, & Randall, 1990; Rich, 1987; Wilkinson & Kitzinger, 1993).

There is now a large body of work predicated on the assumption that lesbianism and male homo-sexuality are *essences*—core, fundamental ways of being that are determined prenatally or in early childhood. Key researchers in the field concur on this point: According to Bell, Weinberg, and Ham-mersmith (1981), adult homosexuality stems from homosexual feelings experienced during childhood and adolescence; according to Money (1988, p. 124), "the most important formative years for ho-mosexuality, bisexuality, and heterosexuality are those of late infancy and prepubertal childhood." Within this framework, identifying oneself as ho-mosexual (which is referred to by the lesbian and gay community as *coming out*) is merely a process of learning to recognize and accept what one was all along: Indeed, the very expression *coming out* suggests that the lesbian has always been inside, awaiting debut (Hollander & Haber, 1992).

This idea, that homosexuality and heterosexual-ity are fixed early on and persist relatively immuta-ble to change, is reflected in the literature documenting the failure of conversion therapies (e.g., Halderman, 1991). It is frequently suggested that the essentialism of such theories is a "straw man" erected by the social constructionists as a foil for their own perspective (cf. Stein, 1990, p. 326), but as has been argued elsewhere (C. Kitzinger, in press), such essentialist models of lesbianism and gay male identity development are, in fact, the norm, reflecting and perpetuating popular theories about homosexuality.

Essentialist arguments of this type fail to address the experience of many women. Recent research on heterosexuals who become lesbian (Golden, 1987) and on lesbians who become heterosexual (Bart, 1993) emphasizes the "fluctuating," "fluid," and "dynamic" nature of sexuality for "protean" women (pp. 246–247). Women's sexual fluidity has long been apparent in the psychological and sexological literature, but it is often submerged in the data rather than explicitly theorized. Drawing on data from Kinsey, Pomeroy, Martin, and Gebhard (1953), McIntosh (1968/1992) pointed out that

It is interesting to notice that although at the age of 20 far more men than women have homosexual and bisexual patterns (27% as against 11%), by the age of 35 the figures are both the same (13%). Women seem to broaden their sexual experience as they get older, whereas more men become narrower and more specialised. (p. 154)

Most women who self-identify as lesbian do so only after an earlier period in their lives during which they identified as heterosexual. Researchers typically find that at least a quarter of their lesbian samples have been married (25 percent: Saghir & Robins, 1973; 35 percent: Bell & Weinberg, 1978), and estimates of the number of lesbians with heterosexual sexual experience range from 58 percent (Kenyon, 1968) to 84 percent (Bell & Weinberg, 1978).

Indeed, past heterosexual experience is taken for granted so much in lesbian circles that lesbians who have never been involved with men have complained of the oppressiveness of this assumption (Jo, Strega, & Ruston, 1990). Many self-identified lesbians report that they occasionally engage in heterosexual sex—46 percent in one survey (Bright, 1992, p. 136), a third of these with gay or bisexual men (suggesting that, even for men, essentialist models of sexual identity are seriously problematic)—while Kinsey et al. (1953) reported that 28 percent of all women in their U.S. sample have had sexual experience with another woman. The accounts such women (and men) present of their experience constitute inconvenient data from an essentialist perspective, which assumes an innate or fixed sexual identity and is, perhaps, why such data are undertheorized in the literature.

Our research aims to explore the psychological processes involved for women in making transitions from heterosexuality to lesbianism without resorting to essentialist models of sexuality, according to which such women would finally be discovering their "real" selves after a long period of repression or denial, or, conversely, adopting an inauthentic lifestyle in opposition to their real orientation. Very little research to date has addressed the processes by which such women negotiate transi-

tions to lesbianism (but see Cassingham & O'Neil, 1993; Charbonneau & Lander, 1991; French, 1992).

In seeking a theoretical model within which to conceptualize transitions to lesbianism after a substantial period of heterosexuality, we start from the assumption that adult women who make such transitions are no more driven by biology or subconscious urges than they are when, for instance, they change jobs; such choices could be viewed as influenced by a mixture of personal reevaluation, practical necessity, political values, chance, and opportunity. This might suggest that the transition process could then be conceptualized within the framework of the literatures on transitions as (a) stressful disjunctions in an individual's life or (b) markers of developmental stage or role change. However, the sexist and heterosexist assumptions underpinning the tradition of work on stressful life events (e.g., Fisher & Reason, 1988) would seem to render it largely unusable as a framework for examining transitions in sexual identity. Similarly, classic studies based on stage theories of life span development have been heavily criticized for their male bias and for cohort effects (e.g., Barnett & Baruch, 1978; Rossi, 1980). Moreover, in neither the life stress tradition nor the stage-role change tradition has the transition to lesbianism been addressed.[1]

Models of homosexual identity development have also been based on stage theories (e.g., Coleman, 1981/1982; Troiden, 1979). Criticisms of these models have been directed against their male bias (with the notable exception of Cass [1979, 1984]), despite much evidence of fundamental differences between lesbian and male homosexual experience (e.g., DeMonteflores & Schultz, 1978; Hart & Richardson, 1981). Critics have also noted these models' reification of stages (Weinberg, 1984), their lack of acknowledgment of the situational determinants of identity (Omark, 1981, quoted in Troiden, 1984), and their insistence on a single linear developmental path in the face of the

---

1. A single exception is Penelope (1993), who offered a tongue-in-cheek analysis of how the transition to lesbianism might occur at each stage of the female life span.

"dazzling idiosyncrasy" of sexual identity (Suppe, 1984, p. 17).

Such models are reviewed by Minton and McDonald (1984), whose own three-stage version is typical of the genre: The first (*egocentric*) stage typically occurs in childhood or adolescence and entails genital contact, emotional attachment, and fantasies about a member of one's own sex; in the second (*sociocentric*) stage, conventional assumptions about homosexuality as deviant, sick, or sinful are internalized, leading to secrecy, guilt, and isolation; and in the final (*universalistic*) stage, the individual realizes that societal norms can be critically evaluated, is able to accept and develop a positive homosexual identity, and is able to integrate this identity with all other aspects of self. Faderman (1985) pointed out that women who come to lesbianism through radical feminism appear to go through Minton and McDonald's stages in reverse order. This not only contributes to the critique of stage theories as rigidly sequential, but it is also a salient critique for the present study, given that such women constitute a subgroup of those who make transitions from heterosexuality to lesbianism.

The key criticism of such models, however, is their essentialism. They assume the existence of homosexuality as an innate, or early acquired, sexual orientation. The development of a homosexual identity, in this view, simply entails a gradually developing awareness and acceptance of one's real self. Sexual identity development is conceptualized either as a process of natural unfolding, albeit dependent on environmental interactions, much like any other process of development, or as a voyage of discovery. For example, Coleman (1981/1982) explicitly supports a biological basis for sexual preference, whereas Minton and McDonald (1984) state that "the initial phase of homosexual identity formation appears to emerge in childhood or adolescence," although they leave open the question of whether homosexuality "can be traced to early social learning or biological predisposition" (p. 97). Not surprisingly, then, the literature on homosexual identity development focuses almost exclusively on adolescence (e.g., Gonsiorek & Rudolph, 1991).

This focus on adolescence is a consequence of an essentialism that assumes a dormant, true lesbian self waiting to be discovered or revealed at puberty or shortly thereafter. This kind of model has important implications for women who change their sexual identity from heterosexual to homosexual after a substantial period of heterosexuality. Such women tend to be conceptualized in one of two ways: Either (a) they were "really" lesbians all along but were repressing or denying it—this argument includes the concept of the latent homosexual (e.g., Socarides, 1965)—or (b) they are "not really" lesbians now—Bergler (1954), for example, identified twelve varieties of spurious homosexuality. The label pseudohomosexual is also used to discredit women who present their lesbianism in political terms and who are seen as distorting their natural sexual inclinations in the service of ideology (Defries, 1976).

The process of coming out in adulthood has been almost entirely neglected, and, as Gonsiorek and Weinrich (1991) note: "There is essentially no research on the longitudinal stability of sexual orientation over the adult life span" (p. 8; see also C. Kitzinger & Wilkinson, 1993a). The present study was designed to redress this dearth of information by focusing on disjunctures in sexual identity in adult life, specifically transitions to lesbianism after a substantial period of heterosexuality, and by seeking to explore the psychological processes entailed in such transitions.

The approach adopted here was a metalevel perspective regarding both biological and early socialization models as particular rhetorical constructions, used for specific purposes. In so doing, we drew on the sociology of knowledge (e.g., Knorr-Cetina & Mulkay, 1983; Simons, 1989) and on a social constructionist perspective (e.g., Gergen, 1985; Stein, 1990), especially work on the construction of self and identity (e.g., Shotter & Gergen, 1989). For a detailed discussion of this approach to research on homosexuality, see C. Kitzinger (1987, chapters 1 and 2).

It must be emphasized that in social constructionist, discourse analytic research, the focus is on participants' accounts as primary data rather than on the compilation of accurate and reliable facts about lesbian transitions. The aim is not to reveal the real histories, motives, and life events of the participants but to understand how they construct, negotiate, and interpret their experience. A more extended rationale for eliciting and assessing lesbian accounts is given by C. Kitzinger (1987, chapter 3). An introduction to the principles and practice of discourse analysis is provided by Potter and Wetherell (1987).

METHOD

PARTICIPANTS

Criteria for inclusion in this study were that participants should report having a minimum of ten years' active heterosexual behavior, including coitus; no sense of uncertainty or doubt about being heterosexual during this period; and a current identity as unequivocally lesbian (with or without sexual experience with women).

Participants were recruited by using friendship pyramiding (Vetere, 1972). Twenty women were interviewed specifically about the psychological processes of transition from heterosexuality to lesbianism; sixty others who satisfied the criteria for inclusion were drawn from a larger project on lesbian identities, of which transition processes were only one aspect (C. Kitzinger, 1987).

Because the focus of this study is on the development of lesbian identity, only women who, at the time of interview, identified as lesbian were included. The question as to why some women, with otherwise similar sexual and emotional profiles, instead identify as bisexual, heterosexual, or refuse any label is beyond the scope of the present project (but see Hutchins & Kaahumanu, 1991). Similarly, because the focus was on the development of lesbian identities, we decided not to exclude those without same-sex sexual experience, although in fact only one such woman volunteered for this study.

This study, then, is based on interviews with eighty lesbians, 68 percent of whom had been married. The average participant began to have heterosexual sexual relations at age eighteen, identified

herself as lesbian at age thirty-four, and took part in the interviews at age thirty-six. All of the participants were White; the majority (87 percent) were in professional or skilled occupations, with only 20 percent identifying themselves as working class.[2] Because the aim of this study was to explore commonalities in accounts of transitions, it was not considered appropriate to subdivide and analyze our sample by demographic variables. In recognition of the fact that this study was limited mainly to a sample of White, middle-class lesbians, we also drew on published accounts by lesbians about their coming out experiences that reflect a broad range of ethnic and class backgrounds. We used all such accounts available to us at the time of conducting the research.

MATERIALS AND PROCEDURE

All of the participants were interviewed by C.K. in their own homes. With the exception of three women, who were available only for telephone interviews, all of the participants were interviewed face-to-face. Interviews lasted an average of one and one-half hours.

The interview schedule for the larger project on lesbian identities (sixty interviews) was developed to elicit discourses of lesbian identity in an open-ended and flexible way. All twenty-three questions are quoted in full in C. Kitzinger (1987, pp. 74–75). For the purposes of the present research, the key questions were as follows (with follow-ups in parentheses):

Question 5: How did you first find out about lesbianism? (Feelings about it?)

Question 6: When did you first begin to think that maybe that was what you were? (Was there something particular that happened that made you think you might be lesbian?)

Question 7: What did you do about it? (Seek out other gay people? Seek out counseling? Information in books? Feelings about it?)

---

2. This does not add up to 100 percent because several women in professional or skilled occupations identified themselves as working class.

Question 8: Had you had sex with men before you decided you were a lesbian? (Why or why not? Did you like it? Sex with men now, or in the future? Sexual feelings for men?)

Question 9: Have you had sex with a woman? (Why not? Tell me about your first lover: How did you meet her? How did you become sexually involved? How did you feel about it? What happened to that relationship?)

All of the women included as participants in the specific project on the transition from heterosexuality to lesbianism (twenty interviews) satisfied the criteria specified earlier (determined in a preinterview telephone screening check). The key question in this project was, Tell me about the time when you first began to think of yourself as a lesbian. Subsidiary questions were, How old were you then? How did you feel about it? What did you do about it? Was sex an important part of your decision making? What things helped you during this time? What things made it harder for you during this time? Do you remember a specific point at which you said "Yes, I am a lesbian"? How do you think your life is different because you have become a lesbian?

Additional material was collected from each participant concerning date of birth, place of birth, marital status, ethnicity, social class, and employment. All interviews were tape-recorded with the consent of participants and were transcribed and coded by C.K. The coded data were then subjected to a number of phases of discourse analysis, including the determination of patterns in the data (variability and consistency of discourse use) and examination of the functions and effects of specific discourses or types of discourse use. These procedures follow the ten stages in the analysis of discourse outlined by Potter and Wetherell (1987, pp. 160–176).

RESULTS AND DISCUSSION

Our presentation of women's accounts of transitions from heterosexuality to lesbianism is organized under three broad headings. First, the section *Getting There* examines accounts of the preparatory

"work" that has to be done to create a context in which a transition in sexual identity is possible and looks at strategies used to avoid confronting the possibility of a lesbian identity. Second, the section *Making and Describing the Transition to Lesbian Identity* includes accounts of the transitions themselves: how they are defined and marked; how such experiences are described; and their consequences, costs, and benefits. Finally, the section *Going On* considers the accounts of the new lesbian after transition: the continuing development of her identity and her reflections on the past and future. In reporting the results, we follow the discourse analytic convention of illustrating our analytic categories with substantial extracts from the interview transcripts. Where appropriate, we give some indication of the frequency with which particular discursive strategies and accounts are used.[3]

GETTING THERE: BARRIERS AND RESISTANCES
TO IDENTIFYING AS LESBIAN

Compulsory heterosexuality. In becoming lesbians, women are assuming an identity they were taught to avoid. Most women, as girls, are encouraged to conform to norms of femininity and heterosexuality (S. Kitzinger & Kitzinger, 1991, pp. 264–279). Lesbianism was described by the vast majority of participants as shrouded in silence and invisibility, or was rendered perverse and abnormal:

> My concept of Lesbian—although I didn't really know the word until late adolescence—was formed by my unconsciously responding to the gaps, the silences and hesitations. . . . Women related to men or ???—*blank*—there was nothingness. Nothingness was loaded with dread, the fear of the unknown. (Anne, 1990, p. 38)

> Acknowledging my lesbianism was a very slow process—partly because of not knowing other

3. The frequencies given are based on the spontaneous emergence of themes in our participants' discourse: These are likely to be gross underestimates when compared with the percentages of women reporting such experiences in response to a survey questionnaire.

lesbians, partly because of the fear I felt. . . . People beat up lesbians. People exclude lesbians. People say we're not normal. My whole life was heterosexual and it felt like my whole life was under threat.[4]

Despite feminist analyses of heterosexuality as an institution that has to be "managed, organised, propagandised, and maintained by force" (Rich, 1987, p. 50), the assumption often remains that most women are either innately heterosexual or have "freely chosen" a heterosexual identity (C. Kitzinger & Wilkinson, 1993b). It is little wonder that women who violate this assumption by asserting a lesbian identity are subject to rejection, hostility, and violence (e.g., Herek & Berill, 1992) and that most women express their awareness of this state of affairs.

Multiple oppressions. For women already oppressed for their ethnicity, age, social class, or disability, claiming a lesbian identity is at once exhilarating and threatening to self and society. Beck (1982) described the disbelief and veiled hostility she encountered on telling people she was working on a book about Jewish lesbians:

> My answer was met with startled laughter and unmasked surprise bordering on disbelief, "Are there *many*?"—as if the juxtaposition Jewish/lesbian were just too much. . . . If you tried to claim both identities—publicly and politically—you were exceeding the limits of what was permitted to the marginal. You were in danger of being perceived as ridiculous—and threatening. (p. xiii)

Lesbians with disabilities, Black lesbians, and women who became lesbians in their sixties or seventies have all written of the obstacles put in their paths not just by antilesbianism but also by "ableism," racism, anti-Semitism, and ageism (Browne, Connors, & Stern, 1985; Macdonald & Rich, 1983; Smith, 1983). A substantial minority ($n = 17$) of lesbians in our sample reported other

4. All otherwise unattributed quotations are taken from the interviews in this study.

oppressions being used to negate their attempts to claim a lesbian identity:

> Discovering I had MS [multiple sclerosis] at the same time that I fell in love with Sarah made everything much more complicated—partly because of what it meant for us, of course, but also because Mike [husband] and Jim [marriage counselor] both came up with the idea I wasn't really a lesbian—I wanted to *be* Sarah, as someone younger and healthy.

Other—ageist—examples follow in the subsection "*It's just a phase.*"

Blocking it out. About a quarter ($n = 19$) of the participants who became lesbians after a substantial period of heterosexuality described how they had earlier in their lives refused to allow themselves even to address the question, Am I a lesbian? Asking oneself the question admits the possibility of the answer "yes," and that answer often felt too dangerous. The following two women finally identified as lesbian in their forties:

> The first time I fell in love with a woman I was twenty-five and pregnant with my second child. I thought, "What's this? Are you bisexual or what?" And then I pushed it to the back of my mind. There was no way I could deal with it because I had these children, and a husband, and no way of supporting myself. So I just didn't think about it.

> I had a growing feeling that I wanted . . . well, I didn't know what I did want. . . . I blocked it out; I never finished that sentence even in my own mind. Looking back, it's obvious that I wanted to know women closely and, clearly, sexually, but I couldn't and didn't believe it. It seemed too extraordinary, too way out, too unlike my life, which was a secure middle-class life with a husband and two children. There wasn't any room for my fantasies—I tucked them away and hid them even from myself.

In refusing to address the question, in pushing it to the back of their minds or blocking it out, these women seemed to be buying time. On a smaller scale, some women on the verge of coming out as lesbian succeeded in postponing their moment of self-labeling until after some event in their lives that would be disrupted by their lesbianism: a much wanted exotic holiday with a husband ("I couldn't face the decision until after the holiday—I needed it so badly, I was so exhausted and run down") or parents' golden wedding anniversary ("There was going to be this really big family party. How could I ruin it?"). Others bargained with themselves, promising to think about whether or not they might be lesbian "if I don't get pregnant in the next six months," "when the children start school," "when my husband gets a promotion," or "when the children are all married."

When women in this sample did finally address the question Am I a lesbian? they recalled having used various strategies used to avoid the answer "yes":

"We're just good friends." One woman described how she was "in love with a woman and even though I did everything that is classic in the situation of being in love, I didn't think of it as being in love because you could only be in love with a man." Another told how she met another woman when they were students in 1954: Unable even to "notice" let alone express their love for each other, both married and lived hundreds of miles apart until, after twenty years of friendship expressed through frequent phone calls and letters, and infrequent visits, both became involved in feminism:

> All that Corky and I never said began to unravel. . . . We talked about our lives and the women we had become, and began to talk about the nature of a woman's love for other women. Corky reached for my hand and took it. We continued walking, holding on to one another. Later I wondered how it could have happened that we waited twenty years to clasp hands. (Poor, 1982)

Many lesbians' coming out stories (almost half of our sample: $n = 38$) reiterated this story of passionate feeling, never named as passion. Several ($n = 9$) acknowledged the role of the women's liberation movement as providing a catalyst for reexamination of such feelings and a context in which they could be named (Charbonneau & Lander, 1991).

"It's just sex—I was only experimenting, and anyway I'm sexually attracted to men too." The notion that no real lesbian ever feels any sexual attraction for men also prevented some women's self-identification. Some lesbians in our sample did report feeling sexually attracted to men. One woman told us: "I always enjoyed heterosexual sex—it was fine, an enjoyable sport, a means to an end, a way of achieving an orgasm." Another felt differently: "Sex with men was always a nightmare." Whether a woman has had or enjoyed sex with men was not a reliable guide to whether she became a lesbian. Some women did, however, report clinging to their sexual attraction for men as a way of avoiding the lesbian label: "After Judy and I made love for the first time I got very scared that this meant I was a lesbian. I withdrew right away. I said, 'This doesn't mean I'm a lesbian. I just wanted to try it, and it was nice, but I don't want to do it again.' And then I went out and got myself screwed by four or five men in order to *prove* I wasn't a lesbian." In 61 percent of first same-sex sexual experiences, neither woman identifies herself as a lesbian (Vetere, 1972); furthermore, a heterosexual woman who has a sexual experience with a woman has only about a 50 percent chance of developing a lesbian identity (DeMonteflores & Schultz, 1978).

"It's just a phase." In retrospect, this argument was often used by women in midlife as a justification for not coming out when they were younger: "After I came out as lesbian at the age of forty-two, I remembered the passionate affair I'd had for two years with another girl at school. We told ourselves that it didn't mean anything; we were just practicing for the real thing"; or "I kept telling myself it was just a delayed adolescent phase. I was waiting to grow out of it." Looking at their current lives, they described their feelings as being caused by postnatal depression, empty-nest syndrome, or menopause. Others in their lives also used such developmental causes to dismiss their experience: "My husband said it was the menopause. He actually got textbooks out of the library with cases of women who thought they were lesbian during the

menopause and who subsequently turned out not to be, after they'd totally wrecked their lives."

"I'm in love with a person who happens to be a woman." This form of resistance to naming oneself as lesbian is well-documented in lesbian coming out stories and psychological research alike (Cass 1979; C. Kitzinger, 1987). Women have said, for example:

> We loved each other as "people who just happen to be female." . . . I was not a Lesbian. I just happened to be head over heels in love with another woman who was not a Lesbian either. (Dobkin, 1990, p. 3)

> I got involved in a sexual relationship with another woman and it was her first sexual relationship too, so that meant the transition to becoming lesbian was quite slow. I spent four or five months saying "I am in love with this woman," but not thinking that made me a lesbian.

An account of lesbianism in terms of romantic love enables the woman to present her supposedly deviant experience as conforming to the dominant heterosexual culture, and hence as morally unimpeachable. In one study of lesbian identity development, 45 percent of respondents did not see themselves as lesbian as a result of their first relationship (DeMonteflores & Schultz, 1978); this was also the case for more than half (*n* = 49) of the women in our sample.

"I can't be a lesbian because I . . . have children/enjoy cooking/have long hair/can't fix my own car." Direct recourse to lesbian stereotypes was another very common strategy, reported by nearly three-quarters (*n* = 57) of our sample:

> I read *The Well of Loneliness* [Hall, 1928/1981] and some psychology textbooks. They told me that lesbians were aggressive, jealous, doomed, masculine, perverted, and sick. I was tremendously reassured. I knew that I couldn't possibly be one of those!

> It seems hard to believe, but in the early part of our relationship we didn't use the word "lesbian" for the powerful feelings we were experiencing. . . . After the first giddiness had passed,

I began to try on the word lesbian: me? No! I would look funny in a crew cut. Certainly I could never learn to smoke cigars! My own stereotypes interfered with the unfolding of my new identity. Lesbians aren't mothers, I thought to myself; they probably don't like to cook or weave or do any of the things I like. (Spencer, 1989, p. 106)

"She's the lesbian, not me." Yet another way of avoiding claiming the lesbian label is to attribute it to the other. One researcher described how "two of the women in my sample were heterosexually married, but were involved in an intense affair with each other. Both maintained that they were heterosexuals. However, both attributed lesbianism to the *other*" (Ponse, 1978, p. 192). A lesbian in our sample remembered her first coming out in the following way:

> It was about five months into my relationship with Elaine and we were sitting talking and I actually sort of said, "*you* lesbians . . ." and Elaine said, "What!?" You know, it was just too difficult to say "*us* lesbians." It was so hard to say, "Yes, I am a lesbian, a *lesbian*!" And Elaine said, "What are you then?" and I said, "I . . . am . . . a . . . lesbian." It was an extraordinary moment.

When someone challenges a woman's heterosexual identity, as Elaine challenged her lover in the extract above, she may still not accept the label *lesbian*. A quarter (*n* = 21) of the lesbians in our sample told painful stories about women lovers who fled from a lesbian identity: "She told me she was sexually attracted to me, and the next day she showed up with an engagement ring": "She got married two months after we first slept together": "We were involved for nearly two years. She kept saying she was going to leave her husband and she said she wasn't sleeping with him. As time went by it was obvious that she wasn't going to leave, and then she told me she was pregnant."

The fear and horror invested in the single word *lesbian* are such that women who are passionately involved with other women sometimes continue to construct accounts that maintain their heterosexual identity. Psychologists and psychiatrists collude with this process when they attempt to reassure women that they are probably "not lesbians really" or when they construct rigid definitions of lesbianism such that the majority of lesbians are excluded (e.g., Defries, 1976; Shively, Jones, & DeCecco, 1984).

MAKING AND DESCRIBING THE TRANSITION TO LESBIAN IDENTITY

The woman who makes a transition to lesbianism, then, has already come a long way to reach the point in which claiming a lesbian identity is possible. How then does she make—and describe—the transition itself?

Over three-quarters ($n = 71$) of the women in our sample described having sex or falling in love with a woman as the marker of their transition to lesbianism:

> Within two days of meeting Barbara it became clear to me that I was a lesbian. I remember I was standing on a train platform and I came to the conclusion that I *must* be a lesbian, because I fancied her something rotten, and I couldn't *possibly* deny that, so I must be a lesbian, and please *please* God, could she feel the same way.

> Loving and making love with Ruth was the most amazing thing in my whole life ever. How could I *not* be a lesbian after that!

Insofar as sex with, or love for, other women is part of the commonsense definition of lesbianism, citing these important events in their own lives as moments of revelation is, for the women in our sample, to make sense of their personal histories in these terms. However, what is obscured in the telling of these stories is the ordinariness of the experiences described: Many women love other women or have sex with them, but this alone does not make them lesbians. To make a transition to lesbianism, it is necessary for a woman to acknowledge a passion for another woman, to claim a lesbian identity as one's own. This may entail piecing together fragmented experience and remembering

and naming such fragments to form a coherent whole:

> I only started thinking that I was a lesbian last year. I did have a relationship with a woman about four years ago, after my marriage broke up, but I was convinced that I wasn't a lesbian at the time. I just *knew* I wasn't a lesbian. I was always so sure that I was a normal heterosexual woman, and the fact that I was in a sexual relationship with a woman didn't do anything to change my identity. . . . And then last year I joined a CR [consciousness raising] group and there were three lesbians in it, and I was quite fascinated by them. What did they *do?* I wondered what the difference between me and them was, these women who were so sure they were lesbians. And then, more recently, I was affected by the political lesbianism paper, the Leeds Revolutionary Feminist Paper, and now I know I'm a lesbian and will never have a relationship with a man again.[5] Nothing really happened except my consciousness getting raised.

It is certainly not the case that a woman has to experience sex with other women to identify as lesbian; she may even specifically decide not to do so:

> I decided I was a lesbian without sleeping with a woman. I didn't feel that my sense of identity was dependent on immediate sexual activity. I certainly don't think heterosexual women should have sex with lesbians as a way of deciding whether they're lesbians—because then some other poor woman has an experiment conducted on her.

For those who have already decided they are lesbians, sex may be no more than a confirmation, or simply a consequence, of that decision: "It wasn't particularly significant the first time I slept with a woman. When it happened, I suddenly realized I'd done all the important stuff before that. Sex with a woman marked the end of the transition, not the beginning."

5. This paper is reprinted in Onlywomen Press (1981).

How do women describe the experience of transition to lesbianism? Poet Adrienne Rich first identified as lesbian at the age of 47, after marriage and three children:

I have an indestructible memory of walking along a particular block in New York City, the hour after I had acknowledged to myself that I loved a woman, feeling invincible. For the first time in my life I experienced sexuality as clarifying my mind instead of hazing it over; that passion, once named, flung a long, imperative beam of light into my future. I knew my life was decisively and forever different. (Rich, 1979, p. 12)

This account has several typical features. There is often what one woman described as an "essential awakening," a moment of recognition, of first naming her lesbianism to herself:

It was a really special moment. I was going out with this man and I was bored out of my head but I was lying to myself, trying to talk myself into liking him, into believing he was potentially quite a nice bloke. And my friend Karen said, "but Pauline, you don't even sound as if you *like* him." And we'd talked before about how maybe I could be a lesbian, and she just looked at me and said, "You *are!*" and I said "I *am!*" and we celebrated it, and I knew there was no going back.

A specific moment of naming oneself as lesbian was identified by a third ($n = 26$) of our sample.

A sense of self-discovery came through vividly in some women's accounts: They talked exuberantly of being reborn, of becoming alive or awake for the first time, of seeing the world anew. That moment of first naming was described as "an explosion of aliveness," "like waking up having been half asleep all my life," "like a conversion experience," and "like emerging from a chrysalis." One woman who became lesbian at the age of fifty-two said: "It was as if, all those years before, I'd been starving for something and didn't even know it. And now I grabbed for it, rolled in it, sucked it in ravenously, devouring an essence of life I never

even knew existed before." (Sally, in Lewis, 1979, p. 66).

Far from the liberal notion that becoming lesbian is an insignificant shift, such a transition was experienced by the majority of women in our sample as a very dramatic change: "a quantum leap," "it completely changed my life," "my world was suddenly fundamentally and radically different." One woman (a psychologist) told us: "The moment I said I was lesbian, everything was both the same and utterly different: It was like the alternating cube, or the crone and the young girl drawing— something switches inside your head and the world never looks the same again." Seeking to articulate the enormity of the change they are experiencing, a substantial number of women described it in terms of altered perceptions: "It was like seeing everything in color after only having seen black and white all my life," "life suddenly became three-dimensional," "the world swung into focus instead of being a confusing blur."

Few women, however, were able to face the first acknowledgement of their lesbianism without conflicting reactions. The split was generally described as being one between their relief, happiness, and sense of wholeness or rightness about their lesbianism on the one hand and their fear, on the other, of its implications in a society in which the predominant view of lesbianism is still very negative.

I was looking at myself in the mirror, and I thought, "that woman is a lesbian," and then I allowed myself to notice that it was me I was talking about. And when that happened, I felt whole for the first time, and also absolutely terrified.

I had a dream one night, and I woke up after the dream and I remembered it immediately, and in the dream I was making love with Jillian, and it was lovely. It was a lovely, beautiful dream—one of the nicest I've had for years! And when I woke up, I had two thoughts simultaneously which were "Wow! How lovely!" and "Oh no, I'm *not* that."

Becoming a lesbian involves taking a leap into the unknown, claiming an outlaw identity. Material costs, particularly of leaving a marital relationship, can include the loss of insurance and pension benefits, possibly home and possessions, and perhaps even children or a job (Kirkpatrick, 1989/1993): "He made over the pension lump sum to his father, and asked [his company] to take my name off the health insurance scheme. It even turned out that what I thought was 'my' car—I'd paid for it!— was registered in his name."

The move into a new world is accompanied by a move out of the old one. Social circles in which these women once moved freely and unquestioningly—to which heterosexuality provides an easy passport—were now seen as closed to them, and the women in our sample often described a painful sense of being outsiders to the world in which they once may have felt perfectly at home (see, e.g., Wilton, 1993). A substantial number of women in our sample talked about their sense of loss, of grieving for the old familiar world left behind—grief for the loss of relationships with a husband or boyfriend, grief for the pain caused to parents, and often the loss of those relationships, too (Thompson, 1992). Despite this, only two or three of the women in our sample expressed major regrets about having made the transition to lesbianism. In a similar vein, Cassingham and O'Neil (1993) also reported that none of their sample of thirty-six previously married women regretted the decision to change her sexual identity.

Some women also described a sense of loss for the person they once knew themselves to be. One woman described how, two weeks after first saying to herself (and her husband of fifteen years), "I am a lesbian," she sat for hours staring at the family photograph albums "trying to work out which one was me." Shortly after moving out of the matrimonial home, another woman described how she stood in the aisle of a supermarket with an empty trolley, staring at the shelves in total bafflement "because I was a lesbian now, and I didn't know what kind of groceries lesbians bought." These are vivid examples of common themes: dislocation from the past, the experience of autobiographical

rupture, and an apparent need for total self-reconstruction.

GOING ON: POSTTRANSITION

Completing a transition from a heterosexual to a lesbian identity does not mean the achievement of a static identity—a sort of terminal lesbianism. Once a woman has said to herself "I am a lesbian," she continues to discover what being a lesbian will mean for her, how she wants to live her life as a lesbian, and what kind of lesbian she wants to be. In an important sense, she becomes lesbian, and then yet more lesbian. (Although none of our interviewees saw heterosexuality or bisexuality as possible future identities, these are, of course, posttransition possibilities; cf. Bart [1993]. Here, however, we focus on the continuing posttransition construction of a lesbian identity.) Key aspects of developing and maintaining a lesbian self appear to be retrospective accounting ("How did I get to be here?") and future planning ("Where am I going now?").

The reconstruction of a past that offers a sense of continuity with the present meant that early experiences with women, probably shared by heterosexual and lesbian alike, often assumed an enormous importance for most ($n = 66$) women in our sample. Previously unrecognized feelings or forgotten experiences were brought to light. A fifty-two-year-old woman, married for twenty-two years, described how she began to remember her lesbianism when she first became involved in feminist consciousness-raising groups:

> When that happened, I got in touch with my own background. And remembered that I had had these kinds of thoughts as a high-school kid, that I had had crushes on women, that not only that, that I had had two small sexual experiences with women, and both were cases where I had touched their breasts. And that there was a period in my all-girls high school where I had worn men's shirts. (quoted in Ponse, 1978, p. 162)

One woman in our sample who came out as lesbian at the age of twenty-seven said: "In fact I did have a brief holiday relationship with a girl when I was fourteen, but I'd completely forgotten about it. I'd pushed it to the back of my mind as not being significant. In fact, it was very significant, but until recently that experience seemed very separate from my adult life."

It can seem, from stories like these, as though a woman's whole life was an unconscious acting-out of her lesbian destiny, only now apprehended as such. But same-sex erotic relationships are part of many women's experience (Bell & Weinberg, 1978). Many women who later identify themselves as heterosexual have learned to forget these feelings, to dismiss them as unimportant compared with their feelings for men, or to think of them as mere adolescent preparations for adult heterosexuality—and they are supported in this by the rigid definitions and misleading stereotypes of lesbianism identified earlier. For women in our sample, becoming a lesbian often meant reinterpreting these experiences within a different framework.

Almost all of the women in our sample ($n = 72$) reported that one of the first things they became aware of as new lesbians was the oppression to which they are likely to be subjected. Even though they may have had an intellectual understanding of antilesbianism, most said that they were unprepared for how it feels to be unable to touch lovers in public for fear of assault, or to be unable to talk freely about weekend activities with colleagues at work for fear of reprisals. One woman said: "Now that I was excluded from them, I became acutely conscious of all the goodies you get by being heterosexual."

Creating a lesbian future involved, for many women in our sample, discovering and becoming involved in lesbian communities. New lesbians described becoming part of a world in which taken-for-granted truths are questioned and in which there is the possibility, in community with other lesbians, of developing a different culture and different values. However, some new lesbians ($n = 11$) described disillusionment when their idealistic expectations of warm acceptance into a utopian sisterhood came up against reality: "Anyone

who identified as a dyke I put up on a pedestal. I didn't know anything about what being a lesbian meant, and I allowed them to define it all for me. I used to think that all lesbians were wonderful. Now I think we all have the potential to be wonderful, but lots of us aren't."

The initial processes of coming out as lesbian were described by most women in our sample as a mixed experience: of pain (and perhaps fear) as the old world offers rejection and oppression, but also of joy and excitement as a new world opens up and its possibilities are glimpsed:

> I had no idea how difficult it was going to be. Not just the mess surrounding leaving my husband, losing one of my children, financial insecurity, loss of privilege, safety, and status, but what it means and continues to mean to be a lesbian in this world—the weight and force of being "wrong," "bad," "wicked," "perverted," outside and ultimately apart from the codes and concepts of everyone else—vulnerable in the extreme. I had no idea how good it was going to be. Not only the warmth, the feeling of being on the same side, the sensuality, friendship, renewed energy, but the freedom to begin to think and act in new ways. (Mohin, 1981, pp. 59–60)

CONCLUSION

This study documents the existence of women who have made a transition to lesbianism after a substantial period of commitment to heterosexuality, and we have illustrated the discursive strategies and accounting mechanisms through which such an identity change is accomplished and sustained. This evidence of the discursive production of lesbian identities does not fit easily into an essentialist framework within which lesbianism is conceptualized as an innate or intrinsic characteristic of the individual, to be acknowledged or discovered, or to be denied or repressed. The emphasis on the constitutive nature of discourse in enabling the construction of identity accounts is characteristic of the social constructionist perspective; as such, our work contributes to the elucidation of processes involved in the construction of self and identity (cf. Shotter & Gergen, 1989).

When a woman makes a transition to lesbianism, the appropriate question (from a social constructionist perspective) is not: Am I a lesbian? —with concomitant attempts to match actual experience against some assumed template of "real" prototypical lesbian experience. The question is, rather, Do I want to be a lesbian?—meaning Do I want to construct my experience in that way? From our perspective, there is no essential lesbian self, no set of uniquely lesbian experiences that can be discovered through introspection. What may feel like self-discovery—and that, not surprisingly (given the prominence of discovery accounting) was a frequently used discourse in our data and that of Charbonneau and Lander (1991)—is better considered as self-reconstruction:

> "True insight" is the application of socially derived intelligibility systems, conditions of "genuine self-knowledge" are a formalisation of our common rules for interpreting or describing social action. . . . Breakthroughs in self understanding are primarily breakthroughs in one's capacity to master an intelligibility system as it applies to one's own behaviour. Self-knowledge is not thereby increased; it is only reconstructed anew. (Gergen, 1977, p. 32)

Within such a social constructionist framework, we have offered an account of the ways in which women in transition construct and interpret their changing identities in relation to their constructions of the category lesbian. This has included the rootedness of such accounts in popular and scientific views of lesbianism, and the functions apparently served by particular types of accounting. Our account, of course, is also a construction based on the availability of a particular range of discourses and on our own assessments of these discourses.

Just as proponents of essentialism produce, as evidence for their theories, the stories of lesbians and gay men who "remember feeling different" or who were sexually attracted to the same sex from an early age, so we, as social constructionists, have produced the stories of women who reported constructing their lesbian identities.

It is not our intent, however, to use our participants' reported experience of transition from heterosexuality to lesbianism to support a social constructionist explanation of sexual identity in a manner paralleling the essentialists' use of the personal testimonies of those who "always knew they were gay." In part, this is because, just as social constructionists discount "born that way" (and similar) participant accounts as rooted in popular and scientific ways of explaining the world (rather than as transparent accounts revealing truths about experience), so essentialists, as mentioned earlier, can (and do) dismiss accounts using the language of choice as self-serving justifications and post hoc rationalizations for a predetermined sexual orientation only now revealed to conscious awareness.

At issue here is far more than a technical problem of interview methodology. Rather, in laying claim to the right to accept some participants' versions as true while discrediting others, social scientists are engaged in "a politics of experience" (C. Kitzinger & Perkins, 1993; Pollner, 1975, p. 427).

For one to take a radical social constructionist stance implies not only to regard personal accounts as constitutive, rather than reflective, of social "facts," but also to recognize that within this framework it is not possible to adjudicate between essentialism and social constructionism, because this debate itself is socially constructed. We have argued elsewhere (C. Kitzinger, in press) that the essentialist-social constructionist debate is not resolvable with reference to empirical fact, and it is not our intention (nor do we believe it possible) to prove essentialism wrong with our data here. Data cannot settle questions of epistemology. Rather, the contribution made by this article is to "up the stakes" for social scientists who want to maintain essentialist accounts of lesbian identity. It is not impossible to explain our findings with reference to essentialist theories, but they are inconvenient findings from an essentialist point of view—and far more difficult to incorporate into essentialist theories that assume a fixed sexual identity than are those accounts of lesbians and gay men who speak of having been "born that way." By documenting these accounts of women's transitions from heterosexuality to lesbianism, we hope to force other researchers to defend themselves against our inconvenient data (and our interpretations of them) by refining and elaborating their own essentialisms, in response to our development of social constructionism. Only through such critical engagements, and through developments within both theoretical frameworks, can a vital and comprehensive psychology of lesbianism be developed.

REFERENCES

Adams, M. L., Lenskyj, H., Masters, P., & Randall, M. (eds.). (1990). Confronting heterosexuality [Special issue]. *Resources for Feminist Research/Documentation sur la Recherché Feministe*, 19 (3/4).

Anne, S. (1990). Opening the door. In J. Penelope & S. Valentine (eds.), *Finding the lesbians: Personal accounts from around the world* (pp. 36–41). Freedom, Calif.: Crossing.

Barnett, R. C., & Baruch, G. K. (1978). Women in the middle years: A critique of research and theory. *Psychology of Women Quarterly*, 3, 187–197.

Bart, P. B. (1993). Protean woman: The liquidity of female sexuality and the tenaciousness of lesbian identity. In S. Wilkinson & C. Kitzinger (eds.), *Heterosexuality: A Feminism & Psychology reader* (pp. 246–252). London: Sage.

Beck, E. T. (ed.). (1982). *Nice Jewish girls: A lesbian anthology*. Watertown, Mass.: Persephone.

Bell, A. P., & Weinberg, M. S. (1978). *Homosexualities: A study of diversity among men and women*. London: Mitchell Beazley.

Bell, A. P., Weinberg, M. S., & Hammersmith, S. K. (1981). *Sexual preference: Its development in men and women*. Bloomington: Indiana University Press.

Bergler, E. (1954). Spurious homosexuality. *Psychiatric Quarterly Supplement*, 28, 68–77.

Bright, S. (1992). *Susie Bright's sexual reality: A virtual sex world reader*. Pittsburgh: Cleis.

Browne, S. E., Connors, D., & Stern, N. (eds.). (1985). *With the power of each breath: A disabled women's anthology*. Pittsburgh: Cleis.

Cass, V. (1979). Homosexual identity formation: A theoretical model. *Journal of Homosexuality*, 4, 219–241.

Cass, V. (1984). Homosexual identity: A concept in need of definition. *Journal of Homosexuality*, 9, 105–126.

Cassingham, B. J., & O'Neil, S. M. (1993). *And then I met this woman: Previously married women's journeys into lesbian relationships*. Racine, Wisc. Mother Courage.

Charbonneau, C., & Lander, P. S. (1991). Redefining sexuality: Women becoming lesbian in midlife. In B. Sang, J. War-

show, & A. J. Smith (eds.), *Lesbians at midlife: The creative transition* (pp. 35–43). San Francisco: Spinsters.

Coleman, E. (1981/1982). Developmental stages of the coming out process. *Journal of Homosexuality*, 7, 31–43.

Defries, Z. (1976). Pseudohomosexuality in feminist students. *American Journal of Psychiatry*, 133, 400–404.

DeMonteflores, C., & Schultz, S. J. (1978). Coming out: Similarities and differences for lesbians and gay men. *Journal of Social Issues*, 34, 59–72.

Dobkin, A. (1990). Foreword: Finding the lesbians is good for us and good for women. In J. Penelope & S. Valentine (eds.), *Finding the lesbians: Personal accounts from around the world* (pp. 3–17). Freedom, Calif.: Crossing.

Ellis, L., & Ames, M. A. (1987). Neurohormonal functioning and sexual orientation: A theory of homosexuality-heterosexuality. *Psychological Bulletin*, 101, 233–258.

Faderman, L. (1985). The "new gay" lesbians. *Journal of Homosexuality*, 10, 65–75.

Fisher, S., & Reason, J. (eds.). (1988). *Handbook of life stress, cognition and health*. Chichester, England: Wiley.

French, M. (1992). Loves, sexualities and marriages: Strategies and adjustments. In K. Plummer (ed.), *Modern homosexualities: Fragments of lesbian and gay experience* (pp. 87–97). London: Routledge.

Gagnon, J. H., & Simon, W. S. (1973). *Sexual conduct: The social sources of human sexuality*. Chicago: Aldine.

Gergen, K. J. (1977). The social construction of self-knowledge. In T. Mischel (ed.), *The self: Psychological and philosophical issues* (pp. 28–56). Oxford, England: Blackwell.

Gergen, K. J. (1985). The social constructionist movement in modern psychology. *American Psychologist*, 40, 266–275.

Golden, C. (1987). Diversity and variability in women's sexual identities. In Boston Lesbian Psychologies Collective (eds.), *Lesbian psychologies: Explorations and challenges* (pp. 19–34). Urbana-Champaign: University of Illinois Press.

Gonsiorek, J. C., & Rudolph, J. R. (1991). Homosexual identity: Coming out and other developmental events. In J. C. Gonsiorek & J. D. Weinrich (eds.), *Homosexuality: Research implications for public policy* (pp. 161–176). Newbury Park, Calif.: Sage.

Gonsiorek, J. C., & Weinrich, J. D. (eds.). (1991). *Homosexuality: Research implications for public policy*. Newbury Park, Calif.: Sage.

Halderman, D. C. (1991). Sexual orientation conversion therapy for gay men and lesbians: A scientific examination. In J. C. Gonsiorek & J. D. Weinrich (eds.), *Homosexuality: Research implications for public policy* (pp. 149–160). Newbury Park, Calif.: Sage.

Hall, R. (1981). *The well of loneliness*. New York: Bard Avon. (Original work published 1928.)

Hart, J., & Richardson, D. (eds.). (1981). *The theory and practice of homosexuality*. London: Routledge.

Herek, G., & Berrill, K. (eds.). (1992). *Hate crimes: Confronting violence against lesbians and gay men*. Newbury Park, Calif.: Sage.

Hollander, J., & Haber, L. (1992). Ecological transition: Using Bronfenbrenner's model to study sexual identity change. *Health Care for Women International*, 13, 121–129.

Hutchins, L., & Kaahumanu, L. (eds.). (1991). *Bi any other name: Bisexual people speak out*. Boston: Alyson.

Jo, B., Strega, L., & Ruston. (1990). *Dykes-loving-dykes: Dyke separatist politics for lesbians only*. Oakland, Calif.: Jo, Strega & Ruston.

Kenyon, F. E. (1968). Studies in female homosexuality: Psychological test results. *Journal of Consulting and Clinical Psychology*, 32, 510–513.

Kinsey, A. C., Pomeroy, W. B., Martin, C. E., & Gebhard, P. H. (1953). *Sexual behavior in the human female*. Philadelphia: Saunders.

Kirkpatrick, M. (1993). Middle age and the lesbian experience. In M. L. Andersen & P. H. Collins (eds.), *Race, class and gender: An anthology* (pp. 287–296). Belmont, Calif.: Wadsworth. (Original work published 1989 in *Women's Studies Quarterly*, 17, 87–96.)

Kitzinger, C. (1987). *The social construction of lesbianism*. London: Sage.

Kitzinger, C. (in press). Social constructionism: Implications for lesbian and gay psychology. In A. D'Augelli & C. Patterson (eds.). *Lesbian, gay and bisexual identities across the lifespan: Psychological perspectives on personal, relational and community processes*. New York: Oxford University Press.

Kitzinger, C., & Perkins, R. (1993). *Changing our minds: Lesbian feminism and psychology*. New York: New York University Press.

Kitzinger, C., & Wilkinson, S. (1993a). The precariousness of heterosexual feminist identities. In M. Kennedy, C. Lubelska, & V. Walsh (eds.). *Making connections: Women's studies, women's movements, women's lives* (pp. 24–36). London: Taylor & Francis.

Kitzinger, C., & Wilkinson, S. (1993b). Theorizing heterosexuality. In S. Wilkinson & C. Kitzinger (eds.). *Heterosexuality: A Feminism & Psychology reader* (pp. 1–32). London: Sage.

Kitzinger, S., & Kitzinger, C. (1991). *Tough questions: Talking straight with your kids about the real world*. Boston: Harvard Common Press.

Knorr-Cetina, K., & Mulkay, M. (eds.). (1983). *Science observed*. London: Sage.

LeVay, S. (1991, August 30). A difference in hypothalamic structure between heterosexual and homosexual men. *Science*, 253, 1034–1037.

Lewis, S. G. (1979). *Sunday's women: A report on lesbian life today*. Boston: Beacon.

Macdonald, B., & Rich, C. (1983). *Look me in the eye: Old women, aging and ageism*. San Francisco: Spinsters, Ink.

McIntosh, M. (1992). The homosexual role. In E. Stein (ed.). *Forms of desire: Sexual orientation and the social constructionist controversy* (pp. 152–164). New York: Routledge. (Original work published 1968 in *Social Problems*, 16, 182–192.)

Minton, H. L., & McDonald, G. J. (1984). Homosexual identity formation as a developmental process. *Journal of Homosexuality*, 9, 91–104.

Mohin, L. (1981). Statement from [an] individual member of the collective. In *Love your enemy? The debate between heterosexual feminism and political lesbianism* (pp. 59–60). London: Onlywomen.

Money, J. (1988). *Gay, straight, and in-between: The sexology of erotic orientation*. Oxford: Oxford University Press.

Onlywomen Press. (1981). *Love your enemy? The debate between heterosexual feminism and political lesbianism*. London: Author.

Penelope, J. (1993). Heterosexual identity: Out of the closets. In S. Wilkinson & C. Kitzinger (eds.), *Heterosexuality: A Feminism & Psychology reader* (pp. 261–265). London: Sage.

Plummer, K. (Ed.). (1981). *The making of the modern homosexual*. London: Hutchinson.

Plummer, K. (ed.). (1992). *Modern homosexualities: Fragments of lesbian and gay experience*. London: Routledge.

Pollner, M. (1975). The very coinage of your brain: The anatomy of reality disjunctures. *Philosophy of the Social Sciences*, 5, 411–430.

Ponse, B. (1978). *Identities in the lesbian world: The social construction of self*. Westport, Conn.: Greenwood.

Poor, M. (1982). Older lesbians. In M. Cruikshank (ed.), *Lesbian studies: Present and future* (pp. 57–69). New York: Feminist.

Potter, J., & Wetherell, M. (1987). *Discourse and social psychology: Beyond attitudes and behaviour*. London: Sage.

Rich, A. (1979). Foreword. In A. Rich, *On lies, secrets, silence: Selected prose 1966–1978* (pp. 9–18). London: Virago.

Rich, A. (1987). Compulsory heterosexuality and lesbian existence. In A. Rich, *Blood, bread, and poetry: Selected prose 1979–1985* (pp. 23–75). London: Virago.

Rossi, A. S. (1980). Life-span theories and women's lives. *Signs*, 6, 4–32.

Saghir, M. T., & Robins, E. (1973). *Male and female homosexuality: A comprehensive investigation*. Baltimore: Wilkins & Wilkins.

Shively, M. G., Jones, C., & DeCecco, J. P. (1984). Research on sexual orientations: Definitions and methods. *Journal of Homosexuality*, 9, 127–136.

Shotter, J., & Gergen, K. J. (eds.). (1989). *Texts of identity*. London: Sage.

Simons, H. W. (ed.). (1989). *Rhetoric in the human sciences*. London: Sage.

Smith, B. (ed.). (1983). *Home girls: A Black feminist anthology*. New York: Kitchen Table, Women of Color.

Socarides, C. W. (1965). Female homosexuality. In R. Slovenko (ed.), *Sexual behavior and the law* (pp. 172–190). Springfield, Ill.: Charles C. Thomas.

Spencer. (1989). Coming out. In J. Penelope & S. J. Wolfe (eds.), *The original coming out stories* (pp. 105–119). Freedom, Calif.: Crossing.

Stein, E. (ed.). (1990). *Forms of desire: Sexual orientation and the social constructionist controversy*. New York: Routledge.

Suppe, F. (1984). In defense of a multidimensional approach to sexual identity. *Journal of Homosexuality*, 10, 7–14.

Thompson, C. A. (1992). Lesbian grief and loss issues in the coming out process. *Women and Therapy*, 12, 175–185.

Troiden, R. R. (1979). Becoming homosexual: A model for gay identity acquisition. *Psychiatry*, 42, 362–373.

Troiden, R. R. (1984). Self, self-concept, identity, and homosexual identity: Constructs in need of definition and differentiation. *Journal of Homosexuality*, 10, 97–109.

Vetere, V. A. (1972). The role of friendship in the development and maintenance of lesbian love relationships. *Journal of Homosexuality*, 8, 51–67.

Weeks, J. (1977). *Coming out: Homosexual politics in Britain from the nineteenth century to the present*. London: Quartet.

Weinberg, T. S. (1984). Biology, ideology and the reification of developmental stages in the study of homosexual identities. *Journal of Homosexuality*, 10, 77–84.

Wilkinson, S., & Kitzinger, C. (eds.). (1993). *Heterosexuality: A Feminism & Psychology reader*. London: Sage.

Wilton, T. (1993). Sisterhood in the service of patriarchy: Heterosexual women's friendships and male power. In S. Wilkinson & C. Kitzinger (eds.), *Heterosexuality: A Feminism & Psychology reader* (pp. 273–276). London: Sage.

PART IV

Violence

Domestic Violence: Are Women as Likely

as Men to Initiate Physical Assaults

in Partner Relationships?

Domestic violence, an all but ignored topic twenty-five years ago, is now recognized as a major problem in American life. David Buss and Neil Malamuth write: "At no other time in history have issues of conflict between the sexes become so salient in social science and public discourse" (1996, p. 3). The first shelter for battered women and their children was established in Pasadena, California, in 1964, the result of an effort by the local Alanon chapter to provide for the families of abusive alcoholics (Barnett & LaViolette, 1993). A feminist analysis of the problem began with books like Erin Pizzey's *Scream Quietly or the Neighbors Will Hear* (1974) and the formation of the National Organization for Women's Task Force on Battered Women/Household Violence in 1975.

If nothing else, the growing attention to battering has increased awareness of the scope of the problem. Women, for example, are more likely to be injured or killed by current or former male partners than by anyone else (Koss et al., 1994). C. Everett Koop, the former surgeon general, has labeled domestic violence "the number one health problem for women in the United States, causing more injuries to women than automobile accidents, muggings, and rapes combined" (quoted in Brooks & Silverstein, 1995, pp. 282–283). And according to the American Medical Association, battering is "a silent, violent epidemic" in which more than 700,000 women are sexually assaulted each year, or one woman every 45 seconds (Doctor Group . . ., 1995, p. 21).

Research indicates that when these findings are corrected for socioeconomic class, it appears that White, Hispanic, and Black women experience similar levels of violence. However, ethnicity does play a role in determining how women respond to battering. White women are more likely to seek help from social service agencies, while Black women are inclined to turn to a minister or the police (Matlin, 1996). Asian-American women, on the other hand, are less likely than other ethnic groups to report battering. This is especially true of older Asian women because of their language difficulties and a lack of familiarity with the social service system (Ho, 1990).

When the problem first gained attention, a good deal of the discussion revolved around the notion that battered women somehow contributed to their own victimization or were masochists who enjoyed pain (Shainess, 1977; Goldstein, 1983). "They must like it," Lenore Walker was told, "or else they would leave" (1993, p. vii). There are many reasons why battered women stay in abusive relationships. Although battering cuts across all socioeconomic classes, Rhona Mahony (1995) notes that a woman who is poor or economically dependent on her partner is much more likely to be beaten by him.

Women with some degree of economic independence can leave the battering situation, but unfortunately, most women lack the resources to pick up and move to a new home. Other women may fear family disapproval or retaliation if they leave, or they might hope that the marriage can be saved. As Walker (1979) has pointed out, battering often follows a cycle: a period of rising tensions leading to violence, followed by a honeymoon period in which the batterer begs forgiveness. It is this third phase, if it is something more than a mere cessation of abuse, that can give the women ground for optimism. After all, studies have shown that 73–85 percent of battered women are not assaulted until after they have made a major commitment to their abuser or married him. Positive feelings generated before the battering began can reinforce a woman's hopes that the batterer can reform. The fact that battering takes place in a relationship built on love and trust makes this type of victimization all the more damaging (McHugh et al., 1993).

Spousal abuse usually includes one or more of the following: physical violence, forced sexual acts such as marital rape, destruction of the victim's property, and psychological harm such as verbal assault or threats of injury (McHugh et al., 1993). Although the term *battered woman syndrome* is still widely used to describe these responses, many psychologists now prefer to view them, like reactions to rape or child sexual abuse, as examples of posttraumatic stress disorder. Battered women may experience a sense of learned helplessness, confused thinking, sleeping problems, a reduced interest in significant activities, frightening flashbacks, or partial psychogenic amnesia. Many victims do not need any more help than guaranteed safety from further abuse and strong support from family, friends, or battered-women-shelter staffs. Some, however, may need specific aid, like Survivor Therapy (Walker, 1994).

Although most of the studies on domestic violence have focused on battered women, some researchers insist that men are abused as often as women. Suzanne Steinmetz, for example, estimated that 250,000 husbands are battered each year by their wives (Battered . . ., 1978). A number of critics have dismissed out of hand what they characterize as "the myth of the battered husband syndrome," pointing out that since men are not reluctant to speak out, it is peculiar that these victims have failed to identify themselves (Straton, 1994).

Nevertheless, in the following article, Murray A. Straus, codirector of the Family Research Laboratory at the University of New Hampshire, maintains that abuse of male partners has largely been ignored. Demie Kurz challenges Straus's use of data and argues that his focus on female violence has reduced public sympathy for women.

REFERENCES

Barnett, O. W., & LaViolette, A. D. (1993). *It could happen to anyone: Why battered women stay.* Newbury Park, Calif.: Sage.

The battered husbands. (1978, March 20). *Time,* p. 69.

Brooks, G. R., & Silverstein, L. B. (1995). Understanding the dark side of masculinity: An interactive systems model. In R. F. Levant & W. S. Pollack (Eds.), *A new psychology of men* (pp. 280–333). New York: Basic Books.

Buss, D. M., & Malamuth, N. M. (1996). Introduction. In D. M. Buss & N. M. Malamuth (Eds.), *Sex, power, conflict: Evolutionary and feminist perspectives* (pp. 3–5). New York: Oxford University Press.

Doctor group says violence imperils nation. (1995). *New York Times*, Nov. 7.

Goldstein, D. (1983). Spousal abuse. In A. Goldstein (ed.), *Prevention and control of aggression* (pp. 37–65). New York: Pergamon Press.

Ho, C. K. (1990). An analysis of domestic violence in Asian American communities: A multicultural approach to counseling. In L. S. Brown & M. P. P. Root (Eds.), *Diversity and complexity in family therapy* (pp. 129–150). New York: Haworth Press.

Koss, M. P., Goodman, L. A., Browne, A., Fitzgerald, L. F., Keita, G. P., & Russo, N. F. (1994). *No safe haven: Male violence against women at home, at work, and in the community*. Washington, D.C.: American Psychological Association.

Mahony, R. (1995). *Kidding ourselves: Breadwinning, babies, and bargaining power*. New York: Basic Books.

Matlin, M. W. (1996). *The psychology of women* (3rd ed.). Fort Worth, Tex. Harcourt Brace.

McHugh, M. C., Frieze, I. H., & Browne, A. (1993). Research on battered women and their assailants. In F. L. Denmark & M. A. Paludi (Eds.), *Psychology of women: A handbook of issues and theories* (pp. 513–552). Westport, Conn.: Greenwood Press.

Pizzey, E. (1974). *Scream quietly or the neighbors will hear*. Harmondsworth, England: Penguin.

Shainess, N. (1977). Psychological aspects of wife-battering. In M. Roy (Ed.), *Battered women* (pp. 111–119). New York: Van Nostrand Reinhold.

Straton, J. C. (1994). Thy myth of the "battered husband syndrome." *masculinities*, 2 (4), 79–82.

Walker, L. E. (1979). *The battered woman*. New York: Harper & Row.

Walker, L. E. (1993). Foreword. In O. W. Barnett & A. D. LaViolette (Eds.), *It could happen to anyone: Why battered women stay* (pp. vii-ix). Newbury Park, Calif.: Sage.

Walker, L. E. (1994). *Abused women and survivor therapy*. Washington, D.C.: American Psychological Association.

ADDITIONAL READING

Bender, D., Leone, B., Szumski, B., de Koster, K., Swisher, K. L., Wekesser, C., & Barbour, W. (Eds.) (1994). *Violence against women*. San Diego: Greenhaven Press.

Dutton, D. G., with Susan K. Golant. (1995). *The batterer: A psychological profile*. New York: Basic Books.

Dutton, M. A. (1993). *Empowering and healing the battered woman*. New York: Springer.

Geller, J. A. (1992). *Breaking destructive patterns: Multiple strategies for treating partner abuse*. New York: Free Press.

Island, D. (1991). *Men who beat the men who love them: Battered gay men and domestic violence*. New York: Harrington Park Press.

Kanuha, V. (1994). Women of color in battering relationships. In L. Comas-Diaz & B. Greene (eds.), *Women of color: Integrating ethnic and gender identities in psychotherapy* (pp. 428–454). New York: Guilford Press.

Lamb, S. (1991). Acts without agents: An analysis of linguistic avoidance in journal articles on men who batter women. *American Journal of Orthopsychiatry*, 61 (2), 250–257.

Renzetti, C. (1992). *Violent betrayal: Partner abuse in lesbian relationships*. Newbury Park, Calif.: Sage.

Tifft, L. L. (1993). *Battering of women: The failure of intervention and the case for prevention*. Boulder, Colo.: Westview Press.

Physical Assaults by Women Partners: A Major Social Problem

MURRAY A. STRAUS

The first purpose of this chapter is to review research that shows that women initiate and carry out physical assaults on their partners as often as men do. A second purpose is to show that, despite the much lower probability of physical injury resulting from attacks by women, assaults by women are a serious social problem, just as it would be if men "only" slapped their wives or "only" slapped female fellow employees and produced no injury. One of the main reasons "minor" assaults by women are such an important problem is that they put women in danger of much more severe retaliation by men. They also help perpetuate the implicit cultural norms that make the marriage license a hitting license. It will be argued that, to end woman beating, it is essential for women also to end the seemingly harmless pattern of slapping, kicking, or throwing things at male partners who persist in some outrageous behavior and "won't listen to reason."

The chapter focuses exclusively on physical assaults, even though they are not necessarily the most damaging type of abuse. One can hurt a partner deeply—even drive the person to suicide—without ever lifting a finger. Verbal aggression may be even more damaging than physical attacks (Vissing, Straus, Gelles, & Harrop, 1991). This chapter is concerned only with physical assaults be-

cause, with rare exception, the controversy has been about "violence"—that is physical assaults—by women partners.

DEFINITION AND MEASUREMENT OF ASSAULT

The National Crime Panel Report defines *assault* as "an unlawful physical attack by one person upon another" (U.S. Department of Justice, 1976). It is important to note that neither this definition nor the one used for reporting assaults to the Federal Bureau of Investigation (1989) requires injury or bodily contact. Thus if one person chases another, attempting to hit or stab the victim with a stick or a knife, and the victim escapes, the attack is still a felony-level crime—an "aggravated assault"—even though the victim was not touched. Nevertheless, in the real world, the occurrence of an injury makes a difference in what the police, prosecutors, and juries do. Consequently, injury will also be considered in this chapter.

GENDER DIFFERENCES IN PARTNER ASSAULT AND HOMICIDE RATES
NATIONAL FAMILY VIOLENCE SURVEYS

The National Family Violence Surveys obtained data from nationally representative samples of 2,143 married and cohabiting couples in 1975 and 6,002 couples in 1985 (information on the sample and methodology is given in Gelles & Straus, 1988; Straus & Gelles, 1986, 1990). Previously published findings have shown that, in both surveys, the rate of woman-to-man assault was about the same (actually slightly higher) than the man-to-woman assault rate (Straus & Gelles, 1986, 1990). However, the seeming equality may occur because of a tendency by men to underreport their own assaults (Dutton, 1988; Edleson & Brygger, 1986; Jouriles & O'Leary, 1985; Stets & Straus, 1990; Szinovacz, 1983). To avoid the problem of male underreporting, the assault rates were recomputed for this chapter on the basis of information provided by the 2,994 women in the 1985 National Family Violence Survey. The resulting overall rate for assaults by women is 124 per 1,000 couples, compared with 122 per 1,000 for assaults by men *as reported by women*. This difference is not great enough to be statistically significant. Separate rates were also computed for minor and severe assaults. The rate of minor assaults by women was 78 per 1,000 couples, and the rate of minor assaults by men was 72 per 1,000. The severe assault rate was 46 per 1,000 couples for assaults by women and 50 per 1,000 for assaults by men. Neither difference is statistically significant. As these rates are based exclusively on information provided by women respondents, the near equality in assault rates cannot be attributed to a gender bias in reporting.

Female assault rates based on the Conflict Tactics Scales (CTS) can be misleading because the CTS does not measure the purpose of the violence, such as whether it is in self-defense, nor does it measure injuries resulting from assaults (Straus, 1977, 1980; Straus, Gelles, & Steinmetz, 1980). That information must be obtained by additional questions, and the 1985 National Family Violence Survey included questions on who initiated violence and questions on injuries.

Injury adjusted rates. Stets and Straus (1990) and Brush (1990) provide data that can be used to adjust the rates to take into account whether the assault resulted in an injury. Stets and Straus found a rate of 3 percent for injury-producing assaults by men and 0.4 percent for injury-producing assaults by women. Somewhat lower injury rates were found by Brush for another large national sample—1.2 percent of injury-producing assaults by men and 0.2 percent for injury-producing assaults by women. An "injury adjusted" rate was computed using the higher of the two injury estimates. The resulting rate of injury-producing assaults by men is 3.7 per 1,000 (122 × .03 = 3.66), and the rate of injury-producing assaults by women is much lower—0.5 per 1,000 (124 × .004 = 0.49). Thus the injury adjusted rate for assaults by men is six times greater than the rate of domestic assaults by women.

Although the injury adjusted rates correspond more closely to police and National Crime Victimization Survey statistics (see below), there are several disadvantages to rates based on injury (Straus, 1990b, pp. 79–83), two of which will be mentioned. One of the disadvantages is that the criterion of injury contradicts the new domestic assault legislation and new police policies. These statutes and policies premise restraining orders and encourage arrest on the basis of attacks. They do not require observable injury.

Another disadvantage of using injury as a criterion for domestic assault is that injury-based rates omit the 97 percent of assaults by men that do not result in injury but that are nonetheless a serious social problem. Without an adjustment for injury, the National Family Violence Survey produces an estimate of more than 6 million women assaulted by a male partner each year, of which 1.8 million are "severe" assaults (Straus & Gelles, 1990). If the injury-adjusted rate is used, the estimate is reduced to 188,000 assaulted women per year. The figure of 1.8 million seriously assaulted women every year has been used in many legislative hearings and countless feminist publications to indicate the prevalence of the problem. If that estimate had to be replaced by 188,000, it would understate the extent of the problem and could handicap efforts to educate the public and secure funding for shelters and other services. Fortunately, that is not necessary. Both estimates can be used, because they highlight different aspects of the problem.

OTHER SURVEYS

Married and cohabiting couples. Although there may be exceptions that I missed, every study among the more than thirty describing some type of sample that is not self-selective (such as community random samples and samples of college student dating couples) has found a rate of assault by women on male partners that is about the same as the rate of assault by men on female partners. These studies include research by such respected scholars as Scanzoni (1978) and Tyree and Malone (1991) and large-scale studies such as the Los Angeles Epidemiology Catchment Area study (Sorenson & Telles, 1991), the National Survey of Families and Households (Brush, 1990), and the survey conducted for the Kentucky Commission on Women (Schulman, 1979).

The Kentucky study also brings out a troublesome question of scientific ethics, because it is one of several in which the data on assaults by women were intentionally suppressed. The existence of those data became known only because Hornung, McCullough, and Sugimoto (1981) obtained the computer tape and found that, among the violent couples, 38 percent of the attacks were by women on men who, as reported by the women themselves, had not attacked them. Some of the other studies that found approximately equal rates are cited in Straus and Gelles (1990, pp. 95–105).

Dating couples. Sugarman and Hotaling (1989) summarize the results of twenty-one studies that reported gender differences in assault. They found that the average assault rate was 329 per 1,000 for men and 393 per 1,000 for women. Sugarman and Hotaling comment that a "surprising finding . . . is the higher proportion of females than males who self-report having expressed violence in a dating relationship" (p. 8). Moreover, other studies published since their review further confirm the high rate of assault by women in dating relationships (see, e.g., Pirog-Good & Stets, 1989; Stets & Straus, 1990).

Samples of "battered women." Studies of residents in shelters for battered women are sometimes cited to show that it is only their male partners who are violent. However, these studies rarely obtain or report information on assaults by women, and when they do, they ask only about self-defense. Pagelow's (1981) questionnaire, for example, presents respondents with a list of "factors responsible for causing the battering," but the list does not include an attack by the woman, therefore precluding finding information on female-initiated assaults. One of the few exceptions is in the work of Walker (1984), who found that one out of four women in battering relationships had answered affirmatively that they had "used physical force to get something [they] wanted" (p. 174). Another is the study by Giles-Sims (1983) that found that in the year prior to coming to a shelter, 50 percent of the women reported assaulting their partners, and

in the six months after leaving the shelter, 41.7 percent reported an assault against a partner. These assaults could all have been in self-defense, but Giles-Sims's case study data suggest that this is not likely.

GOVERNMENT CRIME STATISTICS

National Crime Victimization Survey. The National Crime Victimization Survey (NCVS) is an annual study of approximately 60,000 households, conducted for the Department of Justice by the Bureau of the Census. Analysis of the NCVS for the period 1973–1975 by Gaquin (1977–1978) found an extremely low rate of partner violence—2.2 per 1,000 couples. By comparison, the 1985 National Family Violence Survey found a rate of 161 per 1,000, which is 73 times higher. The NCVS rate for assaults by men is 3.9 per 1,000; the rate is 0.3 for assaults by women. Thus, according to the NCVS, the rate of domestic assaults by men is 13 times greater than the rate of assaults by women.

The extremely low rates of assaults found by the NCVS may be accounted for by the fact that NCVS interviews were conducted with both partners present, and victims may have been reluctant to respond out of fear of further violence. Perhaps even more important, the NCVS is presented to respondents as a study of crime. The difficulty with a crime survey as the context for estimating rates of domestic assault is that most people think of being kicked by their partners as wrong, but not a crime in the legal sense. It takes relatively rare circumstances, such as an injury or an attack by a former partner who "has no right to do that," for the attack to be perceived as a crime (Langan & Innes, 1986). This is probably why the NCVS produces such totally implausible statistics as a 75 percent injury rate (compared with an injury rate of less than 3 percent in the two surveys cited earlier) and more assaults by former partners than by current partners. This is because, in the context of a crime survey, people tend to report attacks only when they have been experienced as "real crimes"—because they resulted in injury or were perpetrated by former partners.

Police calls. Data on calls for domestic assaults

to the police are biased in ways that are similar to the bias of the National Crime Victimization Survey. As in the NCVS, at least 93 percent of the cases are missed (Kaufman Kantor & Straus, 1990), probably because there was no injury or threat of serious injury great enough to warrant calling the police. Because the cases for which police are called tend to involve injury or chronic severe assault, and because that tends to be a male pattern, assaults by women are rarely recorded by police. Another reason assaults by women are rare in police statistics is that many men are reluctant to admit that they cannot "handle" their wives. These artifacts produce a rate of assaults by men that is far greater than the rate of assaults by women. Dobash and Dobash (1979), for example, found that only 1 percent of intrafamily assault cases in two Scottish cities were assaults by wives.

PARTNER HOMICIDE RATES

Homicide rates published by the FBI show that only 14 percent of homicide offenders are women (calculated from Federal Bureau of Investigation, 1989, unnumbered table at bottom of p. 9). However, the percentages of female offenders vary tremendously according to the relationships between offenders and victims. Female-perpetrated homicides of strangers occur at a rate that is less than a twentieth the male rate. The female share goes up somewhat for murders of acquaintances. As for murders of family members, women committed them at a rate that was almost half the rate of men in the period 1976–1979 and more than a third of the male rate during the period 1980–1984.

However, family includes all relatives, whereas the main focus of this chapter is couples. Two recent gender-specific estimates of the rates for partner homicide indicate that women murder male partners at a rate that is 56 percent (Straus, 1986) and 62 percent (Browne & Williams, 1989) as great as the rate of partner homicides by men. This is far from equality, but it also indicates that, in partner relationships, even when the assaults are so extreme as to result in death, the rate for women is extremely

high, whereas, as noted above, for murders of strangers the female rate is only a twentieth of the male rate.

SELF-DEFENSE AND ASSAULTS BY WOMEN PARTNERS

In previous work I have explained the high rate of attacks on partners by women as largely a response to or a defense against assault by the partner (Straus, 1977, 1980; Straus et al., 1980). However, new evidence raises questions about that interpretation.

HOMICIDE

For lethal assaults by women, a number of studies suggest that a substantial proportion are self-defense, retaliation, or acts of desperation following years of brutal victimization (Browne, 1987; Browne & Williams, 1989; Jurik, 1989; Jurik & Gregware, 1989). However, Jurik (1989) and Jurik and Gregware's (1989) investigation of twenty-four cases in which women killed partners found that the victim initiated use of physical force in ten (42 percent) of the cases. Jurik and Gregware's table 2 shows that only five out of the twenty-four homicides (21 percent) were in response to "prior abuse" or "threat of abuse/death." Mann's (1990) study of the circumstances surrounding partner homicides by women shows that many women who murder their partners are impulsive and violent and have criminal records. Jurik (1989) and Jurik and Gregware (1989) also report that 60 percent of the women they studied had previous arrests. The widely cited study by Wolfgang (1958) refers to "victim-precipitated" homicides, but the case examples indicate that these homicides include cases of retaliation as well as self-defense.

NATIONAL FAMILY VIOLENCE SURVEY

Woman-only violence. Of the 495 couples in the 1985 National Family Violence Survey for whom one or more assaultive incidents were reported by a woman respondent, the man was the only violent partner in 25.9 percent of the cases, the woman was the only one to be violent in 25.5 percent of the cases, and both were violent in 48.6 percent of the cases. Thus a minimum estimate of violence by women that is not self-defense because the woman is the only one to have used violence in the past twelve months is 25 percent. Brush (1990) reports similar results for the couples in the National Survey of Families and Households.

Perhaps the real gender difference occurs in assaults that carry a greater risk of causing physical injury, such as punching, kicking, and attacks with weapons. This hypothesis was investigated using the 211 women who reported one or more instances of a "severe" assault. The resulting proportions were still close: 35.2 percent; man only, 35.2 percent; and woman only, 29.6 percent.

These findings show that regardless of whether the analysis is based on all assaults or is focused on dangerous assaults, about as many women as men attacked spouses who had not hit them during the one-year referent period. This is inconsistent with the self-defense explanation for the high rate of domestic assault by women. However, it is possible that, among the couples where both assaulted, all the women were acting in self-defense. Even if that unlikely assumption were correct, it would still be true that 25–30 percent of violent relationships are violent solely because of attacks by the woman.

Initiation of attacks. The 1985 National Family Violence Survey asked respondents, "Let's talk about the last time you and your partner got into a physical fight and [the most severe act previously mentioned] happened. In that particular instance, who started the physical conflict, you or your partner?" According to the 446 women involved in violent relationships, their partners struck the first blows in 42.3 percent of the cases, the women hit first in 53.1 percent of the cases, and the women could not remember or could not disentangle who hit first in the remaining 3.1 percent of the cases.

Similar results were obtained by five other studies. Bland and Orne's (1986) study of marital violence and psychiatric disorder in Canada found that women initiated violence somewhat more often than did men. Gryl and Bird (1989) found that "respondents in violent dating relationships in-

dicated that their partners initiated the violence 51% of the time; they initiated it 41% of the time; and both were equally responsible 8% of the time." Saunders (1989) analyzed data on the sequence of events in the 1975 National Family Violence Survey and found that women respondents indicated that they struck the first blow in 40 percent of the cases. Henton, Cate, Koval, Lloyd, and Christopher (1983) found that "in 48.7% . . . of the relationships, the respondent perceived that both partners were responsible for 'starting' the violence" (p. 472). A large-scale Canadian study found that women struck the first blow about as often as men. However, as in the case of the Kentucky survey mentioned earlier, the authors have not published the findings.

IS THE HIGH RATE OF ASSAULT BY WOMEN EXPLAINABLE AS SELF-DEFENSE?

It is remarkable that all six of the studies which investigated who initiates violence found that women initiate violence in a large proportion of cases. However, caution is needed in interpreting these findings, for several reasons.

First, some respondents may have answered the question in terms of who began the argument, not who began hitting. Interviewers were instructed to rephrase the question in such cases. However, there may have been instances in which the misunderstanding of the question went unnoticed.

Second, if the woman hit first, she could still have been defending herself in a situation that she defined as posing a threat of grave harm from which she could not otherwise escape (Browne, 1987; Jurik, 1989; Jurik & Gregware, 1989).

A third reason for caution is the limited data available in the National Family Violence Survey on the context of the assaults. Who initiates an assault and who is injured are important aspects of the contextual information needed for a full understanding of the gendered aspects of intrafamily assault, but they are not sufficient. For example, there may have been an escalation of assaults throughout the relationship, with the original attacks by the man. The fact that the most recent incident happened to be initiated by the female partner ignores the history and the context producing that act, which may be one of utter terror. This scenario is common in cases of women who kill abusive male partners. A battered woman may kill her partner when he is not attacking her, and thus may appear not to be acting in self-defense. As Browne (1987), Jurik (1989), and Jurik and Gregware (1989) show, the traditional criteria for self-defense use assumptions based on male characteristics that ignore physical size and strength differences between men and women and ignore the economic dependency that locks some women into relationships in which they have legitimate grounds for fearing for their lives.

The scenario described above is often recounted by clients of shelters for battered women. However, it is hazardous to extrapolate from the situation of women in those extreme situations to the pattern of assaults that characterizes couples in the general population as represented in the National Family Violence Survey. This issue is discussed more fully later in this chapter. For the moment, let us assume that many of the assaults initiated by women are in response to fear derived from a long prior history of victimization. Even if that is the case, it is a response that tends to elicit further assaults by the male partner (Bowker, 1983; Feld & Straus, 1989; Gelles & Straus, 1988, chap. 7; Straus, 1974).

In the light of these qualifications and cautions, the self-defense explanation of the near equality between men and women in domestic assaults cannot be rejected. However, one can conclude that the research on who hit first does not support the hypothesis that assaults by women are primarily acts of self-defense or retaliation.

GENDER AND CHRONICITY OF ASSAULT

Although the prevalence rate of assaults by women is about the same as that for male partners, men may engage in more repeated attacks. This hypothesis was investigated by computing the mean number of assaults among couples for which at least one assault was reported by a female respondent. According to these 495 women, their partners averaged 7.2 assaults during the year, and they themselves averaged six assaults. Although the frequency of assault by men is greater than the frequency of assault by women, the difference is just short of being statistically significant. If the analysis is restricted to the 165 cases of severe assault, the men averaged 6.1 and the women 4.28 assaults, which is a 42 percent greater frequency of assault by men and is also just short of being statistically significant. If one disregards the tests of statistical significance, these comparisons support the hypothesized greater chronicity of violence by men. At the same time, the fact that the average number of assaults by male partners is higher should not obscure the fact that the violent women carried out an average of six minor and five severe assaults per year, indicating a repetitive pattern by women as well as by men.

THE CLINICAL FALLACY AND THE REPRESENTATIVE SAMPLE FALLACY

The discrepancy between the findings from surveys of family problems and findings based on criminal justice system data or the experiences of women in shelters for battered women does not indicate that one set of statistics is correct and the other not. Both are correct. However, they apply to different groups of people and reflect different aspects of domestic assault. Most of the violence that is revealed by surveys of family problems is relatively minor and relatively infrequent, whereas most of the violence in official statistics is chronic and severe and involves injuries that need medical attention. These two types of violence probably have different etiologies and probably require different types of intervention. It is important not to use findings based on cases known to the police or shelters for battered women as the basis for deciding how to deal with the relatively minor and infrequent violence found in the population in general. That type of unwarranted generalization is often made; it is known as the *clinical fallacy*.

Representative community sample studies have the opposite problem, which can be called the *representative sample fallacy* (Straus, 1990b; see also

Gelles, 1991). Community samples contain very few cases involving injury and severe assaults every week or more often. Men tend to be the predominant aggressors in this type of case, but representative sample studies cannot reveal that, because they include few if any such cases. Ironically, the types of cases that are not covered by community surveys are the most horrible cases and the ones that everyone wants to do something about. However, community surveys can tell us little about what to do about these extreme cases because the samples contain too few to analyze separately.

The controversy over assaults by women largely stems from survey researchers' assumptions that their findings on rates of partner assault by men and women apply to cases known to the police and to shelters, and the similar unwarranted assumption by clinical researchers that the predominance of assaults by men applies to the population at large.

Both community sample data and clinical sample data are needed. Community sample data are essential for informing programs directed at the larger community, especially programs intended to prevent such cases in the first place or to prevent them from developing into clinical cases. Conversely, it is essential to have research on clinical samples, such as those involved with the police or shelters for battered women, in order to have data that do apply to such cases and that therefore provide a realistic basis for programs designed to aid the victims and to end the most serious type of domestic violence.

CONTEXT AND MEANING

The number of assaults by itself, however, ignores the contexts, meanings, and consequences of these assaults. The fact that assaults by women produce far less injury is a critical difference. There are probably other important differences between men and women in assaults on partners. For example, a man may typically hit or threaten to hit to force some specific behavior on pain of injury, whereas a woman may typically slap a partner or pound on his chest as an expression of outrage or in frustra-

tion because of his having turned a deaf ear to repeated attempts to discuss some critical issue (Greenblat, 1983). Despite this presumed difference, both are uses of physical violence for coercion.

A meta-analysis of research on gender differences in aggression by Eagly and Steffen (1986) brings out a related difference in context and meaning. These researchers found no overall difference in aggression by men and women, but less aggression by women if the act would produce harm to the target. These and other differences in context, meaning, and motivation are important for understanding violence by women against partners, but they do not indicate the absence of assault by women. Nor do differences between men and women in the histories, meanings, objectives, and consequences of assaults refute the hypothesis discussed below: that assaults by women help legitimate male violence. Only empirical research can resolve that issue.

VIOLENCE BY WOMEN INCREASES THE PROBABILITY OF WOMAN BEATING

There seems to be an implicit cultural norm permitting or encouraging minor assaults by women in certain circumstances. Stark and McEvoy (1970) found about equal support for a woman hitting a man as for a man hitting a woman. Greenblat (1983) found that both men and women are more accepting of women hitting men than of men hitting women. Data from the National Family Violence Survey also show more public acceptance of a woman slapping a man than of a man slapping a woman. Greenblat suggests that this is because "female aggressors are far less likely to do physical harm" (p. 247). These norms tolerating low-level violence by women are transmitted and learned in many ways. For example, even casual observation of the mass media suggests that just about every day, there are scenes depicting a man who makes an insulting or outrageous statement and an indignant woman who responds by "slapping the cad," thus presenting an implicit model of assault as a morally correct behavior to millions of women.

Let us assume that most of the assaults by women fall into the "slap the cad" genre and are not intended to—and only rarely do—cause physical injury. The danger to women is shown by studies that find that minor violence by women increases the probability of severe assaults by men (Bowker, 1983; Feld & Straus, 1989; Gelles & Straus, 1988, pp. 146–156). Sometimes this is immediate and severe retaliation. Regardless of whether that occurs, however, a more indirect and probably more important effect may be that such morally correct slapping acts out and reinforces the traditional tolerance of assault in relationships. The moral justification of assault implicit when a woman slaps or throws something at a partner for doing something outrageous reinforces his moral justification for slapping her when *she* is doing something outrageous—or when she is obstinate, nasty, or "not listening to reason" as he sees it. To the extent that this is correct, one of the many steps needed in primary prevention of assaults on women is for them to forsake even "harmless" physical attacks on male partners and children. Women must insist on nonviolence from their sisters, just as they rightfully insist on it from men.

It is painful to have to recognize the high rate of domestic assaults by women. Moreover, the statistics are likely to be used by misogynists and apologists for male violence. The problem is similar to that noted by Barbara Hart (1986) in the introduction to a book on lesbian battering: "[It] is painful. It challenges our dream of a lesbian utopia. It contradicts our belief in the inherent nonviolence of women. And the disclosure of violence by lesbians . . . may enhance the arsenal of homophobes. . . . Yet, if we arc to free ourselves, we must free our sisters" (p. 10). My view of recognizing violence by women is parallel to Hart's view on lesbian battering. It is painful, but to do otherwise obstructs a potentially important means of reducing assaults by men—raising the consciousness of women about the implicit norms that are reinforced by a ritualized slap for outrageous behavior on the part of their partners.

It follows from the above that efforts to prevent assaults by men must include attention to assaults by women. Although this may seem like "victim blaming," there is an important difference. Recognizing that assaults by women are one of the many causes of woman beating does not justify such assaults. It is the responsibility of men as well as women to refrain from physical attacks (including retaliation), at home as elsewhere, no matter what the provocation.

DENYING THE EVIDENCE

The findings showing approximately equal rates of partner assault by men and women have been greeted with disbelief and anger by some feminist scholars. There is a large literature which attempts to repudiate the findings. Most of these efforts fall into three categories: (1) criticism of the Conflict Tactics Scales, (2) criticism of the authors of such studies for ignoring the sexist structure of society, and (3) implicitly excusing violence by women by arguing that it must be understood in the context of male oppression.

VALIDITY OF THE CONFLICT TACTICS SCALES

The fact that so many studies have found equal rates of assault has been blamed on deficiencies in the Conflict Tactics Scales (CTS), the instrument used in most of the studies. These critiques contain so many factual errors that the authors could not have examined the CTS firsthand. Because of space limitations I can give only three of the many alleged deficiencies. One example is the assertion that the CTS measures only violence used to settle a conflict and that it ignores purely malicious violence. On the contrary, the instructions ask respondents to describe what happens "when they disagree, get annoyed with the other person, or just have spats or fights because they're in a bad mood or tired or for some other reason." A second erroneous criticism is that the findings are questionable because men underreport their own violence. Although men do underreport, this could not have produced the statistics in this chapter because they are based on data provided by women. Another example is the claim that the CTS gives a biased and limited picture of abuse of partners because it ignores verbal abuse. This is perhaps the most preposterous criticism because a measure of Verbal Aggression is one of the CTS scales.

In addition to factual errors, there are conceptual errors. For example, it is claimed that the CTS is invalid because the continuum of violence in the scales is so broad that it fails to discriminate among the different kinds of violence. Rather, it is the broad continuum that enables one to differentiate cases of minor and severe violence. Perhaps the most important conceptual error is the belief that the CTS is deficient because it does not measure the consequences of physical assault (such as physical and emotional injury) or the causes (such as desire to dominate). This is akin to thinking that a spelling test is inadequate because it does not measure why a child spells badly, or does not measure possible consequences of poor spelling, such as low self-esteem or low evaluations by employers. The concentration of the CTS on acts of physical assault is deliberate and is one of its strengths. Only by having separate measures of assaults, injuries, and context can one, for example, show that acts of violence by men result in more injury than when the same acts are committed by women (Stets & Straus, 1990; Straus, 1990a, 1990b).

Like all tests and scales, the CTS is not perfect. Nevertheless, numerous reviews by scholars who do not have a vested interest in blaming the messenger for the bad news agree that the CTS is the best available instrument (see, e.g., reviews by Grotevant & Carlson, 1989; Hertzberger, 1991.) Its use in many studies since 1973 has established its validity and reliability. New evidence on validity and reliability is published almost monthly by research scholars who are using the CTS in many countries. No other scale meets this standard. Finally, no matter what one thinks of the CTS, at least four studies that did not use the CTS also found roughly equal rates of violence by women.

FAULTY RESEARCH DESIGN DUE TO IGNORING INSTITUTIONALIZED SEXISM

An indirect approach to discounting the findings on equal rates of assault is the claim that the theoretical approach of the studies is invalid because they ignore the sexist structure of society. Since my research has borne the brunt of this criticism, an examination of that research is appropriate. It shows that a paper I presented at a conference in 1973 was the sociological work that introduced most of the feminist explanations of couple violence (Straus, 1976). These feminist approaches include institutionalized male power, cultural norms legitimating male violence against women, and economic inequality between men and women that locks women into violent marriages. These contributions were widely cited until I published "politically incorrect" data on violence by women and was therefore excommunicated from feminist ranks. However, I remain one of the faithful, and have never accepted the excommunication. On the contrary, I have continued to research and write on these issues (see for example Coleman & Straus, 1986, Kolb & Straus, 1974; Straus, 1973, 1976, 1994, Straus et al., 1980; Yllö & Straus, 1990).

EXCUSING ASSAULTS BY WOMEN

The third most popular mode of denying the bad news about assaults by female partners is to explain it away as the result of frustration and anger at being dominated by men. This is parallel to the excuses men give to justify hitting their partners, such as a woman's being unfaithful. In my opinion, parts of some critiques are justifications of violence by women in the guise of feminism. This is a betrayal of the feminist ideal of a nonviolent world. In addition, excusing violence by women and denying overwhelming research evidence may have serious side effects. It may contribute to undermining the credibility of feminist scholarship and contribute to a backlash that can also thwart progress toward the goal of equality between men and women.

CONCLUSIONS

Ending assaults by women needs to be added to efforts to prevent assaults on women for a number of reasons. Perhaps the most fundamental reason is the intrinsic moral wrong of assaulting a partner, as expressed in the fact that such assaults are criminal acts, even when no injury occurs. A second reason is the unintended validation of the traditional cultural norms tolerating a certain level of violence between partners. A third reason is the danger of escalation when women engage in "harmless" minor violence. Feld and Straus (1989) found that if the woman partner also engaged in an assault, it increased the probability that assaults would persist or escalate in severity over the one-year period of their study, whereas if only one partner engaged in physical attacks, the probability of cessation increased. Finally, assault of a partner "models" violence for children. This effect is as strong for assaults by women as it is for assaults by men (Jaffe, Wolfe, & Wilson, 1990; Straus, 1983, 1992a; Straus et al., 1980).

It should be emphasized that the preventive effect of reducing minor assaults by women has not been proven by the evidence in this chapter. It is a plausible inference and a hypothesis for further research. Especially needed are studies to test the hypothesis that "harmless" assaults by women strengthen the implicit moral justification for assaults by men. If the research confirms that hypothesis, it would indicate the need to add reduction of assaults by women to efforts to end woman beating, including public service announcements, police arrest policy, and treatment programs for batterers. Such changes must be made with extreme care for a number of reasons, not the least of which is to avoid implying that violence by women justifies or excuses violence by their partners. Moreover, although women may assault their partners at approximately the same rate as men assault theirs, because of the greater physical, financial, and emotional injury suffered, women are the predominant victims (Stets & Straus, 1990; Straus et al., 1980). Consequently, first priority in services for victims and in prevention and control must continue to be directed toward assaults by men.

This chapter is based on a paper presented at the 1989 meeting of the American Society of Criminology. It is a pleasure to acknowledge the comments and criticisms of the members of the 1989–1990 Family Research Laboratory Seminar, and also those of Angela Browne, Glenda Kaufman Kantor, Coramae Mann, Daniel Saunders, Kirk R. Williams, and Kersti A. Ylló. However, this does not imply their agreement with the arguments presented in this chapter. Part of the data presented here are from the National Family Violence Resurvey, funded by National Institute of Mental Health grant R01MH40027 (Richard J. Gelles and Murray A. Straus, coinvestigators) and by a grant for "family violence research training" from the National Institute of Mental Health (grant T32 MH 15161).

REFERENCES

Bland, R., & Orne, H. (1986). Family violence and psychiatric disorder. *Canadian Journal of Psychiatry*, 31, 129–137.

Bowker, L. H. (1983). *Beating wife-beating.* Lexington, Mass.: Lexington.

Browne, A. (1987). *When battered women kill.* New York: Free Press.

Browne, A., & Williams, K. R. (1989). Exploring the effect of resource availability and the likelihood of female-perpetrated homicides. *Law and Society Review*, 23 (1), 75–94.

Brush, L. D. (1990). Violent acts and injurious outcomes in married couples: Methodological issues in the National Survey of Families and Households. *Gender & Society*, 4, 56–67.

Coleman, D. H., & Straus, M. A. (1986). Marital power, conflict and violence. *Violence and Victims*, 1, 141–157.

Dobash, R. E., & Dobash, R. P. (1979). *Violence against wives: A case against the patriarchy.* New York: Free Press.

Dutton, D. G. (1988). *The domestic assault of women: Psychological and criminal justice perspectives.* Boston: Allyn & Bacon.

Eagly, A. H., & Steffen, V. J. (1986). Gender and aggressive behavior: A meta-analytic review of the social psychological literature. *Psychological Bulletin*, 100, 309–330.

Edleson, J. L., & Brygger, M. P. (1986). Gender differences in reporting of battering incidents. *Family Relations*, 35, 377–382.

Federal Bureau of Investigation. (1989). *Crime in the United States.* Washington, D.C.: U.S. Department of Justice.

Feld, S. L., & Straus, M. A. (1989). Escalation and desistance of wife assault in marriage. *Criminology*, 27, 141–161.

Gaquin, D. A. (1977–1978). Spouse abuse: Data from the National Crime Survey, *Victimology* 2, 632–642.

Gelles, R. J. (1991). Physical violence, child abuse, and child homicide: A continuum of violence or distinct behaviors? *Human Nature*, 2, 59–72.

Gelles, R. J., & Straus, M. A. (1988). *Intimate violence: The causes and consequences of abuse in the American family.* New York: Simon & Schuster.

Giles-Sims, J. (1983). *Wife battering: A systems theory approach.* New York: Guilford.

Greenblat, C. S. (1983). A hit is a hit is a hit . . . or is it? Approval and tolerance of the use of physical force by spouses. In D. Finkelhor, R. J. Gelles, G. T. Hotaling, & M. A. Straus (eds.), *The dark side of families: Current family violence research* (pp. 235–260). Beverly Hills, Calif.: Sage.

Grotevant, H. D., & Carlson, C. I. (1989). *Family assessment: A guide to methods and measures.* New York: Guilford.

Gryl, F. E., & Bird, G. W. (1989). *Close dating relationships among college students: Differences by gender and by use of violence.* Paper presented at the annual meeting of the National Council on Family Relations, New Orleans.

Hart, B. (1986). Preface. In K. Lobel (ed.), *Naming the violence: Speaking out about lesbian battering* (pp. 9–16). Seattle: Seal.

Henton, J., Cate, R., Koval, J., Lloyd, S., & Christopher, S. (1983). Romance and violence in dating relationships. *Journal of Family Issues, 4,* 467–482.

Hertzberger, S. D. (1991). The Conflict Tactics Scales. In D. J. Keyser & R. C. Sweetland (eds.), *Test critiques,* 8. Kansas City: Test Corporation of America.

Hornung, C. A., McCullough, B. C., & Sugimoto, T. (1981). Status relationships in marriage: Risk factors in spouse abuse. *Journal of Marriage and the Family, 43,* 675–692.

Jaffe, P. G., Wolfe, D. A., & Wilson, S. K. (1990). *Children of battered women: Issues in child development and intervention planning.* Newbury Park, Calif.: Sage.

Jouriles, E. N., & O'Leary, K. D. (1985). Interspousal reliability of reports of marital violence. *Journal of Consulting and Clinical Psychology, 53,* 419–421.

Jurik, N. C. (1989). *Women who kill and the reasonable man: The legal issues surrounding female-perpetrated homicide.* Paper presented at the 41st Annual Meeting of the American Society of Criminology, Reno, Nev.

Jurik, N. C., & Gregware, P. (1989). *A method for murder: An interactionist analysis of homicides by women.* Tempe: Arizona State University, School of Justice Studies.

Kaufman Kantor, G., & Straus, M. A. (1990). Response of victims and the police to assaults on wives. In M. A. Straus & R. J. Gelles (eds.), *Physical violence in American families: Risk factors and adaptations to violence in 8,145 families* (pp. 473–486). New Brunswick, N.J.: Transaction.

Kolb, T. M., & Straus, M. A. (1974). Marital power and marital happiness in relation to problem solving ability. *Journal of Marriage and the Family, 36,* 756–766.

Langan, P. A., & Innes, C. A. (1986). Preventing Domestic Violence Against Women. Discussion Paper. Washington, D.C.: U.S. Department of Justice, Bureau of Justice Statistics. Special Report NCJ 102037.

Mann, C. R. (1990). Black female homicide in the United States. *Journal of Interpersonal Violence, 5,* 176–201.

Pagelow, M. D. (1981). *Woman-battering: Victims and their experiences.* Beverly Hills, Calif., Sage.

Pirog-Good, M. A., & Stets, J. E. (eds.). (1989). *Violence in dating relationships: Emerging social issues.* New York: Praeger.

Saunders, D. G. (1989). *Who hits first and who hurts most? Evidence for the greater victimization of women in intimate relationships.* Paper presented at the 41st Annual Meeting of the American Society of Criminology, Reno, Nev.

Scanzoni, J. (1978). *Sex roles, women's work, and marital conflict.* Lexington, Mass.: Lexington.

Schulman, M. (1979). *A survey of spousal violence against women in Kentucky* (Study No. 792701, conducted for Kentucky Commission on Women, sponsored by the U.S. Department of Justice, Law Enforcement Assistance Administration). Washington, D.C.: Government Printing Office.

Sorenson, S. B., & Telles, C. A. (1991). Self-reports of spousal violence in a Mexican-American and non-Hispanic white population. *Violence and Victims, 6,* 3–15.

Stark, R., & McEvoy, J., III. (1970). Middle class violence. *Psychology Today, 4,* 52–65.

Stets, J. E., & Straus, M. A. (1990). Gender differences in reporting marital violence and its medical and psychological consequences. In M. A. Straus & R. J. Gelles (eds.), *Physical violence in American families: Risk factors and adaptations to violence in 8,145 families* (pp. 151–166). New Brunswick, N.J.: Transaction.

Straus, M. A. (1973). A general systems theory approach to a theory of violence between family members. *Social Science Information, 12,* 105–125.

Straus, M. A. (1974). Leveling, civility, and violence in the family. *Journal of Marriage and the Family, 36,* 13–29.

Straus, M. A. (1976). Sexual inequality, cultural norms, and wife-beating. *Victimology, 1,* 54–76.

Straus, M. A. (1977). Normative and behavioral aspects of violence between spouses: Preliminary data on a nationally representative USA sample. In *Violence in Canadian Society.* Symposium sponsored by Simon Fraser University, Department of Criminology, at the University of New Hampshire Family Research Laboratory, Durham.

Straus, M. A. (1980). Victims and aggressors in marital violence. *American Behavioral Scientist, 23,* 681–704.

Straus, M. A. (1983). Ordinary violence, child abuse, and wife-beating: What do they have in common? In D. Finkelhor, R. J. Gelles, G. T. Hotaling, & M. A. Straus (eds.), *The dark side of families: Current family violence research* (pp. 213–234). Beverly Hills, Calif.: Sage.

Straus, M. A. (1986). Domestic violence and homicide antecedents. *Domestic Violence, 62,* 446–465.

Straus, M. A. (1990a). The Conflict Tactics Scales and its critics: An evaluation and new data on validity and reliability. In M. A. Straus & R. J. Gelles (eds.), *Physical violence in American families: Risk factors and adaptations to violence in 8,145 families* (pp. 49–73). New Brunswick, N.J.: Transaction.

Straus, M. A. (1990b). Injury and frequency of assault and the "representative sample fallacy" in measuring wife beating and child abuse. In M. A. Straus & R. J. Gelles (Eds.), *Physical violence in American families: Risk factors and adaptations to violence in 8,145 families* (pp. 75–91). New Brunswick, N.J.: Transaction.

Straus, M. A. (1992a). Children as witnesses to marital violence: A risk factor for lifelong problems among a nationally representative sample of American men and women. In D.

F. Schwarz (ed.), *Children and violence: Report of the Twenty-Third Ross Round-table on Critical Approaches to Common Pediatric Problems in collaboration with the Ambulatory Pediatric Association.* Columbus, Ohio: Ross Laboratories.

Straus, M. A. (1994). State-to-state differences in social inequality and social bonds in relation to assaults on wives in the United States. *Journal of Comparative Family Studies,* 25, 7–24.

Straus, M. A. (1995). Trends in cultural norms and rates of partner violence: An update to 1992. In Sandra M. Stith & M. A. Straus, *Understanding partner violence: Prevalence, causes, consequences and solutions.* Minneapolis: National Council of Family Relations.

Straus, M. A., & Gelles, R. J. (1986). Societal change and change in family violence from 1975 to 1985 as revealed by two national surveys. *Journal of Marriage and the Family,* 48, 465–479.

Straus, M. A., & Gelles, R. J. (eds.). (1990). *Physical violence in American families: Risk factors and adaptations to violence in 8,145 families.* New Brunswick, N.J.: Transaction.

Straus, M. A., Gelles, R. J., & Steinmetz, S. K. (1980). *Behind closed doors: Violence in the American family.* Garden City, N.Y.: Anchor/Doubleday.

Sugarman, D. B., & Hotaling, G. T. (1989). Dating violence: Prevalence, context, and risk markers. In M. A. Pirog-Good & J. E. Stets (eds.), *Violence in dating relationships: Emerging social issues.* New York: Praeger.

Szinovacz, M. E. (1983). Using couple data as a methodological tool: The case of marital violence. *Journal of Marriage and the Family,* 45, 633–644.

Tyree, A., & Malone, J. (1991). *How can it be that wives hit husbands as much as husbands hit wives and none of us knew it?* Paper presented at the annual meeting of the American Sociological Association.

U.S. Department of Justice. (1976). *Dictionary of criminal justice data terminology.* Washington, D.C.: National Criminal Justice Information Service.

Vissing, Y. M., Straus, M. A., Gelles, R. J., & Harrop, J. W. (1991). Verbal aggression by parents and psychosocial problems of children. *Child Abuse and Neglect,* 15, 223–238.

Walker, L. E. A. (1984). *The battered woman syndrome.* New York: Springer.

Wolfgang, M. E. (1958). *Patterns of criminal homicide.* Philadelphia: University of Pennsylvania Press.

Yllö, K. A., & Straus, M. A. (1990). Patriarchy and violence against wives: The impact of structural and normative factors. In M. A. Straus & R. J. Gelles (eds.), *Physical violence in American families: Risk factors and adaptations to violence in 8,145 families.* New Brunswick, N.J.: Transaction.

Physical Assaults
by Male Partners:
A Major Social Problem

DEMIE KURZ

Are women violent toward men? This question has been asked repeatedly, particularly in recent years, as the issue of domestic violence has gained national recognition. The women's movement, which brought the issue of battered women to public attention in the late 1970s, claims that it is men who are violent (Dobash & Dobash, 1992; Jones, 1994). Currently advocates for battered women in many professions and organizations accept this analysis and use it to promote change in the legal, medical, and social service responses to battered women (American Medical Association, 1992; Buzawa & Buzawa, 1996; Dobash and Dobash, 1992; Jones, 1994; Koss, 1990; Novello et al., 1992).

Among social scientists, however, there has been controversy about the nature of violence in intimate relationships, particularly the question of whether women are violent toward men. One group of social scientists adopts a perspective that has been called the violence-against-women perspective (Dobash and Dobash, 1992) and argue that women are the victims of violence in relationships with men (Daly and Wilson, 1988; Dobash and Dobash, 1992; Ellis and DeKeseredy, 1996; Kurz, 1995; Loseke, 1992; Saunders, 1988; Stanko, 1987; Yllö, 1993; Yllö and Bograd, 1988). These researchers include those who identify with the feminist tradition. They claim that, historically, the law

has promoted women's subordination and condoned husbands' use of force in marriage. The other social scientists are the "family violence" researchers (Brinkerhoff and Lupri, 1988; Gelles, 1993; Gelles and Cornell, 1985; Gelles and Straus, 1988; McNeely and Mann, 1990; McNeely and Robinson-Simpson, 1987; Shupe, Stacey, and Hazelwood, 1987; Stets, 1990; Straus, this volume; Straus and Gelles, 1990), who argue that the real problem is "spouse abuse" and "family violence." These researchers believe that women as well as men are violent, and some claim that women "initiate and carry out physical assaults on their partners as often as men do" (Straus, this volume).

This debate over men's and women's use of violence has significant consequences for popular and academic conceptions of battered women, and for social policy. How a problem is framed determines the amount of concern that is generated for that problem as well as the solutions that are proposed. Research findings influence whether the media and the public take battered women seriously or whether they view them as equally blameworthy partners in family violence. Violence-against-women researchers fear that a focus framing the problem as spouse abuse will lead to decreased funding for shelters, a diversion of resources to "battered men," and/or increased arrests of women in "domestic disputes" under mandatory-arrest policies. More generally, violence-against-women researchers fear that the discourse of "spouse abuse" obscures the cause of violence against women—inequality and male dominance.

In this chapter I argue that the violence-against-women point of view best explains the nature and the extent of violence between men and women in intimate relationships. Violence-against-women researchers argue that violence between intimates takes place within a context of inequality between men and women in marriage, while family-violence proponents promote a gender-neutral view of power in intimate relationships. I will compare the evidence and theories presented by the proponents of each perspective, and I will argue that the family-violence view is based on false assumptions about the nature of marriage and of equality between men and women.

A VIOLENCE-AGAINST-WOMEN PERSPECTIVE

Researchers who take a violence-against-women perspective argue that overwhelmingly it is women, not men, who are the victims of violence. They support their point of view with official crime statistics, data from the criminal justice system and hospitals, interviews with victims of battering and with batterers, and historical evidence. As Dobash and Dobash (1992:265) note, data from victimization surveys, from court statistics, and from police files in the United States and Canada indicate that in 90–95 percent of cases of assaults within a family context, women are the victims of male violence. A number of researchers have examined National Crime Survey data and found that wives were the victims of violence at the hands of their husbands in the overwhelming majority of cases. In his analysis of National Crime Survey data, Schwartz (1987) found that only 4 percent of men claimed to be victims of violence at the hands of their wives. In the remaining 96 percent, wives claimed to be the victims of violence at the hands of their husbands. Other researchers who have analyzed National Crime Survey data have reported similar findings (McLeod, 1984; Gaquin, 1977/78). In their study of police records in Scotland, Dobash and Dobash (1979) found that when gender was recorded, women were targets in 94 percent and offenders in 3 percent of cases. Other studies based on data from the criminal justice system show similar results (Kincaid, 1982; Quarm and Schwartz, 1985).

Data on injury patterns confirm that it is women, not men, who sustain injuries in conflicts between males and females in intimate relationships. Brush (1990), in an analysis of NSFH (National Survey of Families and Households) data, found that women were significantly more likely than men to be injured in disputes involving violent tactics. Berk and his colleagues (1983), based on their examination of police records, concluded

that in 95 percent of cases it is the woman who is injured and that even when both partners are injured, the woman's injuries are nearly three times as severe as the man's. Data from hospitals (JAMA, 1990; Kurz, 1990; McLeer and Anwar 1989; Stark and Flitcraft, 1996) show women to be overwhelmingly the injured party. These data lead violence-against-women researchers to reject the concept of spouse abuse, the idea that women are equally as violent as men.

Data from divorcing couples also provide evidence that women are more frequently the targets of violence than men. In their study of 362 separating husbands and wives, Ellis and Stuckless (1993) report that more than 40 percent of separating wives and 17 percent of separating husbands state that they were injured by their partners at some time during the relationship. In a random sample of divorced women with children from Philadelphia County, Kurz (1995) found that 70 percent of women reported experiencing violence at least once during their marriage, 54 percent two to three times, and 37% more than two to three times, findings similar to those in other studies (Fields, 1978; Parker and Schumacher, 1977).

Researchers have also reported high rates of abuse after separation. Indeed, most surveys of postseparation abuse report more abuse after separation than during relationships (Wilson & Daly, 1993). Further, during separation women are not only at greater risk of injury, they are also at greater risk of death. Data gathered in Canada; New South Wales, Australia; and Chicago demonstrate that women are much more likely to be killed by their husbands after separating from them than when they are still living with them (Wilson & Daly, 1993). These wives are at significantly high risk within the first two months of leaving a relationship (Schwartz, 1987, Wilson & Daly, 1993). Data indicate that separated and divorced women are also at increased risk of rape (Bowker, 1981; Solicitor General of Canada, 1985; U.S. Dept. of Justice, 1987).

Researchers who take a violence-against-women perspective claim that the use of violence by men to control female intimates has long been condoned by major social institutions. The first law in the United States to recognize a husband's right to control his wife with physical force was an 1824 ruling by the Supreme Court of Mississippi that permitted the husband "to exercise the right of moderate chastisement in cases of great emergency" (quoted in Browne 1987, p. 166). This, and similar rulings in Maryland and Massachusetts, were based on English common law, which gave a husband the right of "correction" of his wife, although he was supposed to use it in moderation. As Angela Browne (1987) observes, "In 1871 wife beating was made illegal in Alabama. The court stated: 'The privilege, ancient though it be, to beat her with a stick, to pull her hair, choke her, spit in her face or kick her about the floor, or to inflict upon her like indignities, is not now acknowledged by our law. . . . The wife is entitled to the same protection of the law that the husband can invoke for himself' " (p. 167). A North Carolina court made a similar decision in 1874, but limited the kinds of cases in which the court should intervene: "If no permanent injury has been inflicted, nor malice, cruelty nor dangerous violence shown by the husband, it is better to draw the curtain, shut out the public gaze, and leave the parties to forget and forgive" (quoted in Browne, 1987, p. 167). Until recent legal reforms were enacted, the "curtain rule" was widely used by the legal system to justify its nonintervention in wife-abuse cases.

The law and the nature of marriage have changed dramatically since the early twentieth century; however, violence-against-women researchers claim that these institutions continue to condone violence against women. While new laws have criminalized battering, we do not know whether these laws will be enforced (Buzawa & Buzawa, 1996; Kurz, 1992). A recent study suggests that even police who receive training in how to make a criminal response to battering cases may continue to view battered women as unfortunate victims of personal and social problems such as poverty and, in the absence of strong police department support, view arrests as low priority and not part of their "real" work (Ferraro, 1989). To the extent that these laws are not viewed seriously, the legal

system will continue to treat battering as an individual problem rather than as criminal behavior.

Violence-against-women researchers, particularly those who are feminists, argue that marriage still institutionalizes the control of wives by husbands through the structure of husband-wife roles. As long as women are responsible for domestic work, child care, and emotional and psychological support, and men's primary identity is that of provider and revolves around employment, the husband has the more important status and also controls the majority of decisions in the family (Kurz, 1995). It is through such a system, coupled with the acceptance of physical force as a means of control, that, in the words of the Dobashes (1979), the wife becomes an "appropriate victim" of physical and psychological abuse. Feminists argue further that the use of violence for control in marriage is perpetuated not only through norms about a man's rights in marriage but through women's continued economic dependence on their husbands, which makes it difficult to leave a violent relationship. This dependence is increased by the lack of adequate child care and job training, which would enable women to get jobs with which they could support themselves.

Citing interview data from men and women that demonstrate that battering incidents occur when husbands try to make their wives comply with their wishes, violence-against-women researchers believe that men still use violence as a way to control female partners. Based on data from interviews with 109 battered women, Dobash and Dobash (1979) demonstrate how over the course of their marriages, batterers increasingly control wives through intimidation and isolation, findings confirmed by other interview studies (Kurz, 1995; Pagelow, 1981; Walker, 1984). Violence is therefore just one of a variety of controls that men may try to exercise over female partners; others are anger and psychological abuse (Dobash and Dobash, 1992; Mederos, 1987; Yllö, 1993). Interviews with batterers (Adams, 1988; Dobash and Dobash, 1979; Ptacek, 1988) show that men believe they are justified in their use of violence, particularly when their wives do not conform to the ideal of the "good wife."

Some researchers have also found that male dominance is a factor in other types of violence in the family. For example, Bowker, Arbitell, and McFerron (1988) found that 70 percent of wife beaters also physically abused their children and argue that the most important cause and context of child abuse is current abuse of a woman by a male intimate. These researchers also found that the severity of wife beating predicted the severity of child abuse and that the greater the degree of husband dominance, the greater the likelihood of child abuse. Similarly, Stark and Flitcraft (1985), in their review of medical records, found that children whose mothers are battered are more than twice as likely to be physically abused as children whose mothers are not battered. They also believe that purposive violence by male intimates against women is the most important context for child abuse (Margolin, 1992).

Finally, violence-against-women researchers demonstrate that a variety of institutions, in addition to the law and the family, condone male dominance and reinforce battering on an ongoing, everyday basis. Some have demonstrated how this occurs through the labeling and processing of abused women by frontline health care workers who have the most contact with these women. Stark and Flitcraft (1996) have argued that due to patriarchal medical ideologies and practices, health care practitioners have failed to recognize battering and instead label battered women as having psychological or psychosomatic problems. These researchers claim that the actions of health care workers serve to perpetuate battering relationships and argue that the medical system duplicates and reinforces the patriarchal structure of the family. Kurz (1990) has documented how individual staff in emergency rooms come to define battered women as not "true medical cases," but "social" ones, and feel that they make extra work and trouble for medical practitioners. Battered women who do not look like "typical victims" are frequently not recognized as battered and are sent back home,

without any recognition of or attention to their battering.

Other studies address the issue of how violence against women is taught and reinforced in such institutions as the military (Russell, 1989) and sports (Messner, 1989). Sanday (1991) and others (Martin and Hanmer, 1989) have studied the ways in which fraternity practices and rituals, in promoting loyalty to a brotherhood of men, legitimate gang rape and other types of violence against women. Kanin (1984) suggests that the college date rapists he studied came from a more highly sexualized subculture than non-date rapists.

THE FAMILY-VIOLENCE PERSPECTIVE AND ITS CRITICS

In stark contrast to violence-against-women researchers, family-violence researchers focus on what they see as the problem of "spouse abuse," on the use of violence by women as well as men. They claim that women as well as men are perpetrators of physical violence (McNeely and Mann, 1990; McNeely and Robinson-Simpson, 1987; Steinmetz and Lucca, 1988), and some claim that women are as violent within the family as are men (Shupe, Stacey, and Hazelwood, 1987; Stets and Straus, 1990; Straus, this volume; Straus and Gelles, 1986). In this section I argue that when researchers claim that women are as violent as men, they do so on the basis of faulty data and assumptions about gender and the family.

Family-violence researchers typically base their claims about women's use of violence on data collected using the Conflict Tactics Scales (CTS) (Straus, 1979), instruments that require respondents to identify conflict tactics they have used in the previous year. These range from nonviolent tactics (calm discussion), to the most violent tactics (use of a knife or gun). Using this scale, family-violence researchers (Straus, this volume; Straus and Gelles, 1986; Straus et al., 1980) find similar percentages of husbands and wives using violent tactics. On the basis of these data, some family-violence researchers conclude that "husband battering" is a serious problem and even that there is a "battered husband syndrome" (Steinmetz 1977/1978, 1987; Steinmetz and Lucca, 1988). Findings based on the CTS have been replicated by a number of researchers here and abroad (Brinkerhoff and Lupri, 1988; Nisonoff and Bitman, 1979; Stets, 1990), including for dating relationships (Arias et al., 1987; DeMaris, 1987; Lane and Gwartney-Gibbs, 1985).

Findings from the 1985 National Family Violence Survey, based on women's responses to the Conflict Tactics Scales, show that both wife and husband were violent in 48.6 percent of cases, the husband only was violent in 25.9 percent of cases, and the wife only was violent in 25.5 percent of cases (Straus, this volume). Straus concludes from these data that "regardless of whether the analysis is based on all assaults, or is focused on dangerous assaults, about as many women as men attacked a spouse who had not hit them during the one-year referent period." Citing other studies that show the same results, he concludes that these figures are "inconsistent with the 'self-defense' explanation for the high rate of domestic assault by women."

Violence-against-women researchers (Berk et al., 1983; Dobash et al., 1992; Saunders, 1989; Stark & Flitcraft, 1996; Yllö, 1993) argue that the data showing that women are as violent as men, particularly data based on the Conflict Tactics Scales, are misleading and flawed. These researchers believe that the validity of the scales is undermined because the continuum of violence in the scales is so broad that it fails to discriminate among different kinds of violence (Dobash & Dobash 1979, 1992; Stark and Flitcraft 1985). For example, the CTS contains the item "bit, kicked, or hit with a fist." Thus, a woman who bites is equated with a man who kicks or hits with a fist. Another item, "hit or tried to hit with an object," which is counted as severe violence, is similarly ambiguous. Further, critics argue, the scale does not take into account self-defense.

In support of their position, violence-against-women researchers also point to the findings of studies in which women were asked about their use of violence. For example, Saunders (1988) found that in the vast majority of cases, women attributed

their use of violent tactics to self-defense and fighting back. Emery et al. (1989), in an interview study based on a small sample of women who were victims of dating violence, found that most women spoke of self-defense. Some women also spoke of using violence in frustration and anger at being dominated by their partners and in retaliation for their partners' violent behavior.

Further, violence-against-women researchers point out that the CTS focuses narrowly on counting acts of violence. Such a focus draws attention away from related patterns of control and abuse in relationships, including psychological abuse and sexual abuse, and does not address other means of intimidation and domination, including verbal abuse, the use of suicide threats, or the use of violence against property, pets, children, or other relatives. Similarly, the conception of violence as a "conflict tactic" fails to convey the connection between the use of violence and the exercise of power. Yllö (1993) argues that violence is better conceptualized as a "tactic of coercive control to maintain the husband's power."

In addition to their view that women commit as many violent acts as men, family-violence researchers claim that women initiate violence as frequently as men. They draw this conclusion on the basis of responses to a question in the National Family Violence Survey about who initiated conflicts in the relationship. The NFVS, based on the CTS, found that in 53 percent of cases wives reported that they hit first, while their partners initiated the violence in 42 percent of cases (Straus, this volume). These findings have led family-violence researchers to a new focus on women's use of violence (Straus, this volume). Even though husbands use much more serious types of violence, these researchers now claim that violence by women against their husbands must be considered a serious problem.

Let us briefly examine the logic of the family-violence position that women initiate violence as often as men. Straus (this volume) turns our attention to occasions when a woman slaps a man. He refers to a "typical case" in which a woman uses acts of violence because a man who is acting like a "cad" has done something offensive to her: "Let us assume that most of the assaults by women fall into the 'slap the cad' genre and are not intended to—and only rarely do—cause physical injury." He then focuses on the woman's "assaults" and goes on to argue that a woman who "slaps the cad" is in effect provoking her partner by providing him with a justification for hitting: "Such morally correct slapping acts out and reinforces the traditional tolerance of assault in relationships. The moral justification of assault implicit when a woman slaps or throws something at a partner for doing something outrageous reinforces his moral justification for slapping her when *she* is doing something outrageous—or when she is obstinate, nasty, or 'not listening to reason' as he sees it." After claiming that assaults by wives are one of the "causes" of assaults by husbands, he concludes with a stern warning that all women must forsake violence: "One of the many steps needed in primary prevention of assaults on wives is for women to forsake even 'harmless' physical attacks on male partners and children. Women must insist on nonviolence from their sisters, just as they rightfully insist on it from men."

In a few sentences, Straus proceeds from women's defensive behavior to a focus on women as provoking the violence. What is wrong with this logic? While eliminating violence should be a high-priority goal for all men, women, and children, this reframing of the issue puts the blame and responsibility for the violence on the woman. Targeting women's behavior removes the focus from what men might be doing to women. What does it mean that he is acting like a "cad"? Does this refer to unwanted sexual advances, the belittling of the woman, verbal intimidation, drunken frenzy? Who is responsible here? Focusing on the woman's behavior provides support for typical excuses and justifications by batterers, such as "She provoked me to do this" (Ptacek, 1988).

Another problem with asking a single question about who initiated the violence is that it does not focus on the meaning and context of female violence against male partners. For example, there were no questions asked about women's motives

for striking first. We know that male physical and sexual violence against women is often preceded by name-calling and other types of psychological abuse (Browne, 1987), and that women may view these behaviors as early warning signs of violence and hit first in hopes of preventing their partners from using violence (Saunders, 1989). Hanmer and Saunders (1984) have noted that many women hit first because of a "well-founded fear" of being beaten or raped by their husbands or male intimates. Thus, even when women do initiate violence, it may very well be an act of self-defense.

In my view there are many reasons it would be better if we all could be nonviolent—it may well be true that violence provokes more violence. However, we must understand the power dynamics behind the use of violence in particular types of relationships—we must examine who feels entitled to use violence and why. The violence-against-women perspective addresses these critical questions about the context of violence.

A brief examination of the theoretical perspective of family-violence researchers shows the faulty assumptions that guide their interpretation of the data. As one would expect from their findings, as well as their use of the terms *family violence* and *spouse abuse*, family-violence researchers take a family-systems approach to analyzing husbands' and wives' use of violence. They believe that the origins of the problem of violence lie in the nature of the family, not in the relationship between husband and wife (Gelles and Straus, 1988; Straus, this volume), and that violence affects all family relationships. According to Straus, Gelles, and Steinmetz (1980): "A fundamental solution to the problem of wife-beating has to go beyond a concern with how to control assaulting husbands. It seems as if violence is built into the very structure of the society and family system itself. . . . It [wife-beating] is only one aspect of the general pattern of family violence, which includes parent-child violence, child-to-child violence, and wife-to-husband violence" (p. 44).

Family-violence researchers (Gelles, 1993; Gelles and Straus, 1988) believe that violence in the contemporary American family is caused by a variety of social-structural factors, including stresses from difficult working conditions, unemployment, financial insecurity, and health problems. They also believe that husbands and wives are affected by wider social norms condoning violence as a means of solving conflict, and they see evidence of the cultural acceptance of violence in television programming, folklore, and fairy tales (Straus, 1980), and in surveys showing widespread public acceptance of violence. Straus also cites sexism as a factor in family violence; while he believes men and women are equally violent, he claims women are more victimized by family violence because of "the greater physical, financial, and emotional injury suffered by women" (Straus, this volume).

Proponents of the family-violence perspective make some important points about the prevalence of violence in American society; however, from a violence-against-women perspective, the family-violence view is seriously flawed. While cultural norms of violence and stressful living conditions may influence individuals' use of violence, these wider cultural norms and social conditions are mediated by the norms of particular institutions. In the case of the institution of marriage, norms promoting male dominance in heterosexual relationships and males' right to use force have a direct influence on behavior in marriage.

Family-violence researchers do acknowledge male dominance when they argue that sexism is an important factor in domestic violence and that women are the ones who are most seriously hurt in battering relationships. However, from the perspective of a violence against women researcher, sexism is not just *a* factor in domestic violence. Rather, gender is one of the fundamental organizing principles of society. It is a social relation that enters into and partially constitutes all other social relations and activities and pervades the entire social context in which a person lives. Thus, violence-against-women researchers criticize family-violence researchers for equating spouse abuse, elder abuse, and child abuse, because women become just one of a number of victims. Violence-against-women researchers believe that wife abuse should be compared to related types of violence against women,

such as rape, marital rape, sexual harassment, and incest (Wardell et al., 1983), all of which are also products of male dominance.

Violence-against-women researchers believe that family-violence researchers disregard the influence of gender on marriage and heterosexual relationships and see power in the family as a gender-neutral phenomenon. Family-violence researchers claim that "violence is used by the most powerful family member as a means of legitimizing his or her dominant position" (Straus et al., 1980, p. 193) and believe that power can as equally be held by a wife as by a husband. According to violence-against-women researchers, this view of the exercise of power as gender-neutral misrepresents the nature of marriage as a partnership of equals. Marriage has been and still is structured so that husbands have more power than wives. Men are the primary wage earners, and women, as those responsible for child rearing and household work, do not typically have the same bargaining power as their husbands. Thus power is not gender-neutral; it is structured into the institution of marriage in such a way that women are disadvantaged.

To conclude, the basic assumptions of the family-violence and violence-against-women approaches to domestic violence are irreconcilable. Further, each group has voiced strong disagreements with the other. Family-violence researchers argue that the legitimate sociological approach to the issue of violence in the family should be a "multicausal" one and believe that violence-against-women perspectives, particularly those identified as feminist, are biased by a single-minded focus on gender (Straus, 1991). Further, family-violence researchers criticize feminist work as "political" (Gelles, 1983; Straus, 1991) and charge that they have been harassed for studying violent women (Gelles & Straus, 1988, p. 106; Straus, 1991). They believe that findings about women's violence have been "suppressed" because they are not "politically correct" (Straus, this volume). Such statements posit a conspiracy of feminists to keep the truth from being known, rather than an understanding that different theories and methods lead to different conclusions.

Violence-against-women researchers fear that the family-violence approach will reinforce existing popular conceptions that women cause their own victimization by provoking their male partners. They fear that such views will lead to policy outcomes that are harmful to women. Family-violence researchers acknowledge that their research has been used to provide testimony against battered women in court cases and to minimize the need for shelters (Straus & Gelles, 1986:471; Gelles and Straus, 1988:90); however, they argue that this is less "costly" than the "denial and suppression" of violence by women (Straus and Gelles, 1986, p. 471). The question is, "costly for whom?"

Another concern of violence-against-women researchers is that if funders come to believe that family violence is a mutual occurrence between spouses, or that there is a "battered husband syndrome," there will be decreased support for shelters for battered women. Violence-against-women researchers also fear a diversion of resources to shelters for "battered men." Straus's work has been cited to provide evidence that women assault men (Lewin, 1992, p. 12). Men's rights groups cite the "battered husband syndrome" when lobbying for custody and child support issues from a men's rights perspective (Ansberry, 1988; Fathers for Equal Rights Organization, 1988; McNeely and Robinson-Simpson, 1987).

Violence-against-women researchers also fear that the family-violence perspective will reinforce the individualist bias in the field of counseling—that counselors will focus on clients' individual and personal problems without identifying the inequality between men and women that is the context for battering (Adams, 1988). They disagree with those family-violence proponents who argue that violence is caused primarily by frustration, poor social skills, or inability to control anger (Hotaling, Straus, and Lincoln, 1990; Shupe et al., 1987; Steinmetz 1986). Finally, violence-against-women researchers worry that a belief in "spouse abuse" or a "battered husband syndrome" will encourage police who operate under mandatory-arrest statutes to arrest women in domestic disputes.

While some researchers claim that women are as violent as men in intimate relationships, in this chapter I have argued that women are typically victims, not perpetrators of violence in intimate relationships. I have shown how norms and practices of male dominance promote the use of violence by men toward female intimates. The proponents of the family-violence perspective, in arguing that women are violent toward men, disregard gender and its determining role in structuring marital and other heterosexual relationships.

Data on the use of conflict tactics and acts of violence must be interpreted in the context of power differences in male-female relationships. Abstracted from their context, data on who initiates and uses violence promote faulty conclusions. To interpret violence in the family, we must understand how gender shapes the exercise of power in heterosexual relationships.

REFERENCES

Adams, D. (1988). Treatment models of men who batter. In K. Yllö & M. Bograd (eds.), *Feminist perspectives on wife abuse* (pp. 176–199). Newbury Park, Calif.: Sage.

American Medical Association Council on Ethical and Judicial Affairs (1992). Physicians and domestic violence: Ethical considerations. *Journal of the American Medical Association*, 267, 3190–3193.

Ansberry, C. (1988). Calling sexes equal in domestic violence, article stirs clash among rights groups. *Wall Street Journal*, 5 May.

Arias, I., Samios, M., & O'Leary, K. D. (1987). Prevalence and correlates of physical aggression during courtship. *Journal of Interpersonal Violence*, 2, 82–90.

Berk, R., Berk, S. F., Loseke, D., & Rauma, D. (1983). Mutual combat and other family violence myths. In D. Finkelhor, R. J. Gelles, G. T. Hotaling, & M. A. Straus (eds.), *The dark side of families: Current family violence research* (pp. 197–212). Beverly Hills, Calif.: Sage.

Bowker, L. (1981). Women as victims: An examination of the results of L.E.A.A.'s National Crime Survey Program. *Women and Crime in America* 158, 164–165.

Bowker, L., Arbitell, M., and McFerron, J. R. (1988). On the relationship between wife beating and child abuse. In K. Yllö & M. Bograd (eds.), *Feminist perspectives on wife abuse* (pp. 158–174). Newbury Park, Calif.: Sage.

Brinkerhoff, M., & Lupri, E. (1988). Interspousal violence. *Canadian Journal of Sociology* 13, 407–434.

Browne, A. (1987). *Battered women who kill.* New York: Free Press.

Brush, Lisa D. (1990). Violent acts and injurious outcomes

in married couples: Methodological issues in the National Survey of Families and Households. *Gender & Society*, 4, 56–67.

Buzawa, E. S., & Buzawa, C. G. (1996). *Domestic violence: The criminal justice response*. Newbury Park, Calif.: Sage.

Daly, M., and Wilson, M. (1988). *Homicide*. New York: Aldine DeGruyter.

DeMaris, A. (1987). The efficacy of a spouse abuse model in accounting for courtship violence. *Journal of Family Issues*, 8, 291–305.

Dobash, R.E., & Dobash, R. (1979). *Violence against wives*. New York: Free Press.

———. (1992). *Women, violence and social change*. London: Routledge, 1992.

Dobash, R., Dobash, R. E., Wilson, M., & Daly, M. (1992). The myth of sexual symmetry in marital violence. *Social Problems*, 39, 71–91.

Ellis, D., & DeKeseredy, W. S. (1996). *The wrong stuff: An introduction to the sociological study of deviance*. (2d ed.). Toronto: Allyn & Bacon.

Ellis, D., & Stuckless, N. (1993). *Hitting and splitting: Predatory pre-separation abuse among separating spouses*. Mediation Pilot Project Report 7. Submitted to the attorney general of Ontario.

Emery, B., Lloyd, S., & Castleton, A. (1989). Why women hit: A feminist perspective. Paper presented at the Annual Conference of the National Conference on Family Relations, New Orleans.

Fathers for Equal Rights Organization (1988). *Father's Review*, February, 1.

Ferraro, K. (1989). Policing woman battering. *Social Problems* 36, 61–74.

Fields, M. D. (1977/1978). Wife-beating: Facts and figures. *Victimology*, 2, 643–647.

Gaquin, D. A. (1977/1978) Spouse abuse: Data from the National Crime Survey. *Victimology*, 2, 632–643.

Gelles, R. (1983). An exchange/social control theory. In D. Finkelhor, R. J. Gelles, G. T. Hotaling, & M. A. Straus (eds.), *The dark side of families: Current family violence research* (pp. 151–165). Beverly Hills, Calif.: Sage.

Gelles, R. (1993). Through a sociological lens: Social structure and family violence. In R. J. Gelles and D. Loseke (eds.), Current controversies on family violence (pp. 31–46). Newbury Park, Calif.: Sage.

Gelles, R., & Cornell, C. (1985). *Intimate violence in families*. Beverly Hills, Calif.: Sage.

Gelles, R., & Straus, M. (1988). *Intimate violence*. New York: Simon & Schuster.

Hanmer, J., & Saunders, S. (1984). *Well-founded fear: A community study of violence to women*. London: Hutchinson.

Hotaling, G., Straus, M., & Lincoln, A. (1990). Intrafamily violence and crime outside the family. In M. Straus & R. Gelles (eds.), *Physical violence in American families* (pp. 431–470). New Brunswick, N.J.: Transaction.

JAMA, Journal of the American Medical Association. (1990).

Domestic violence intervention calls for more than treating injuries, 264, 939.

Jones, A. 1994. *Next time, she'll be dead: Battering & how to stop it*. Boston: Beacon Press.

Kanin, E. (1984). Date rape: Unofficial criminals and victims. *Victimology* 9, 95–108.

Kincaid, P. J. (1982). *The omitted reality: Husband-wife violence in Ontario and policy implications for education*. Maple, Ontario: Learners.

Koss, M. (1990). The women's mental health research agenda: Violence against women. *American Psychologist*, 45, 374–380.

Kurz, D. (1990). Interventions with battered women in health care settings. *Victims and Violence*, 5, 243–256.

———. (1992). Battering and the criminal justice system: A feminist view. In E. Buzawa and C. Buzawa (eds.), *Domestic violence: The criminal justice response* (pp. 21–38). Westport, Conn.: Auburn House.

———. (1995). *For richer, for poorer: Mothers confront divorce*. New York: Routledge.

Lane, K. E., and Gwartney-Gibbs, P. A. (1985). Violence in the context of dating and sex. *Journal of Family Issues*, 6, 45–59.

Lewin, T. (1992). Battered men sounding equal-rights battle cry. *New York Times*, April 20.

Loseke, D. (1992). *The battered woman and shelters: The social construction of wife abuse*. New York: SUNY Press.

Margolin, L. (1992). Beyond maternal blame: Physical child abuse as a phenomenon of gender. *Journal of Family Issues* 13, 410–423.

Martin, P. Y., and Hanmer, R. (1989). Fraternities and rape on campus. *Gender & Society*, 3, 457–473.

McLeer, S., & Anwar, R. (1989). A study of battered women presenting in an emergency department. *American Journal of Public Health*, 79, 65–66.

McLeod, M. (1984). Women against men: An examination of domestic violence based on an analysis of official data and national victimization data. *Justice Quarterly*, 1, 171–193.

McNeely, R., & Mann, C. 1990. Domestic violence is a human issue. *Journal of Interpersonal Violence* 5, 129–132.

McNeely, R., & G. Robinson-Simpson. (1987). The truth about domestic violence: A falsely framed issue. *Social Work* 32, 485–490.

Mederos, F. (1987). Theorizing continuities and discontinuities between "normal" men and abusive men: Work in progress. Paper presented at the Third National Family Violence Research Conference, University of New Hampshire, Durham.

Messner, M. (1989). When bodies are weapons: Masculinity and violence in sport. *International Review of Sociology of Sport*, 25, 203–220.

Nisonoff, L., & Bitman, I. 1979. Spouse abuse: Incidence and relationship to selected demographic variables. *Victimology* 4, 131–140.

Novello, A., Rosenberg, M., Saltzman, L., & Shosky, J. 1992.

From the surgeon general, U.S. Public Health Service. *JAMA, Journal of the American Medical Association, 267*, 3132.

Pagelow, M. (1981). *Woman-battering: Victims and their experiences.* Beverly Hills, Calif.: Sage.

Parker, B., & Schumacher, D. (1977). The battered wife syndrome and violence in the nuclear family of origin: A controlled pilot study. *American Journal of Public Health 67*, 760–761.

Ptacek, J. (1988). Why do men batter their wives? In K. Yllö & M. Bograd (eds.), *Feminist perspectives on wife abuse* (pp. 133–57). Newbury Park, Calif.: Sage.

Quarm, D., & Schwartz, M. (1985). Domestic violence in criminal court. In C. Schweber and C. Feinman (eds.), *Criminal justice politics and women: The aftermath of legally mandated change* (pp. 29–46). New York: Haworth.

Russell, D. (1989). Sexism, violence, and the nuclear mentality. In D. Russell (ed.), *Exposing nuclear phallocies* (pp. 63–74). New York: Plenum.

Sanday, P. R. (1991). *Fraternity gang rape: Sex, brotherhood and privilege on campus.* New York: New York University Press.

Saunders, D. (1988). Wife abuse, husband abuse, or mutual combat? In K. Yllö & M. Bograd (eds.), *Feminist perspectives on wife abuse* (pp. 90–113). Newbury Park, Calif.: Sage.

———. (1989). Who hits first and who hurts most? Evidence for the greater victimization of women in intimate relationships. Paper presented at the American Society of Criminology, Reno, Nev.

Schwartz, M. D. (1987). Gender and injury in spousal assault. *Sociological Focus, 20*, 61–75.

Shupe, A., Stacey, W., & Hazelwood, R. (1987). *Violent men, violent couples: The dynamics of domestic violence.* Lexington, Mass.: Lexington.

Solicitor General of Canada. (1985). Canadian urban victimization survey: Female victims of crime, 4.

Stanko, E. (1987). Typical violence, normal precaution: Men, women, and interpersonal violence in the U.S., England, Wales and Scotland. In J. Hanmer and M. Maynard (eds.), *Women, violence, and social control* (pp. 122–134). London: Macmillan, 1987.

Stark, E., & Flitcraft, A. (1985). Woman battering, child abuse and social heredity: What is the relationship? In N. Johnson (ed.), *Marital violence* (pp. 147–171). London: Routledge.

———. (1996). *Women at risk: Domestic violence and women's health.* Newbury Park, Calif.: Sage.

Steinmetz, S. (1977/1978). The battered husband syndrome. *Victimology, 2*, 499–509.

———. (1987). Family violence: Past, present, and future. In M. Sussman & S. Steinmetz (eds.), *Handbook of marriage and the family* (pp. 725–765). New York: Plenum.

Steinmetz, S., & Lucca, J. (1988). Husband battering. In V. Van Hasselt, R. Morrison, A. Bellack, & M. Hersen (eds.), *Handbook of family violence* (pp. 233–246). New York: Plenum.

Stets, J. 1990. Verbal and physical aggression in marriage. *Journal of Marriage and the Family 52*, 501–514.

Stets, J., & Straus, M. (1990). Gender differences in reporting marital violence and its medical and psychological consequences. In M. Straus & R. Gelles (eds.), *Physical violence in American families* (pp. 151–166). New Brunswick, N.J.: Transaction.

Straus, M. (1979). Measuring intrafamily conflict and violence: The conflict tactics (CT) scales. *Journal of Marriage and the Family, 41*, 75–88.

Straus, M. (1980). Victims and aggressors in marital violence. *American Behavioral Scientist, 23*, 681–704.

———. (1991). New theory and old canards about family violence research. *Social Problems, 38*, 180–197.

Straus, M., & Gelles, R. (1986). Societal change and change in family violence from 1975 to 1985 as revealed by two national surveys. *Journal of Marriage and the Family, 48*, 465–479.

———. (1990). How violent are American families? Estimates for the national family violence resurvey and other studies. In M. Straus & R. Gelles (eds.), *Physical violence in American families* (pp. 95–112). New Brunswick, N.J.: Transaction.

Straus, M., Gelles, R., & Steinmetz, S. (1980). *Behind closed doors: Violence in the American family.* Garden City, N.Y.: Doubleday.

United States Dept. of Justice. (1987). Violent crime by strangers and non-strangers. Special Report, January.

Walker, L. (1984). *The battered woman syndrome.* New York: Springer.

Wardell, L., Gillespie, C., & Leffler, A. (1983). Science and violence against women. In D. Finkelhor, R. J. Gelles, G. T. Hotaling, & M. A. Straus (eds.), *The dark side of families: Current family violence research* (pp. 69–84). Beverly Hills, Calif.: Sage.

Wilson, M., & Daly, M. (1993). Spousal homicide risk and estrangement. *Violence and Victims 8*, 3–15.

Yllö, K. (1993). Through a feminist lens: Gender, power, and violence. In R. Gelles & D. Loseke (eds.), *Current controversies on family violence* (pp. 47–62). Newbury Park, Calif.: Sage.

Yllö, K., & Bograd, M. (eds.). (1988). *Feminist perspectives on wife abuse.* Newbury Park, Calif.: Sage.

Rape: Are Rape Statistics Exaggerated?

In 1991, date rape, which had been widely discussed on college campuses during the previous decade, attracted national attention when a woman claimed that she had been raped by William Kennedy Smith, a nephew of Senator Ted Kennedy. The couple met in a Florida bar and went for a walk on the beach at the Kennedy estate. She claimed she had been raped; he claimed it was consensual sex. Millions saw the trial on television, and the case became a media event. The six-person jury, four of whom were women, eventually found Smith not guilty (Friedman, 1993). The fact that boxer Mike Tyson, in another high-profile case, was convicted of date rape suggests that the race and class of the defendant may play an important role in court decisions. On the other hand, the race of the victim is also important in terms of the attention the crime receives. Although Black women run a greater risk of being assaulted, media attention is disproportionately focused on White women (Lott, 1994).

As the Smith and Tyson cases demonstrate, the definition of rape can be quite controversial. When a group of male subjects was asked whether they would force a woman to have sex against her will if they could get away with it, about half said they would. On the other hand, when asked whether they would rape a woman if they knew they could get away with it, only about 15 percent said they would. Those who responded differently to the second question apparently didn't realize that there is no difference between rape and forcing a woman to have sex against her will (Malamuth, 1989a, 1989b).

The FBI defines rape as attempted or completed forcible vaginal intercourse against a woman's will. State laws have expanded the definition to include men as well as women, anal and oral penetration as well as vaginal intercourse. The laws also define rape as intercourse with someone unable to consent because of youth, mental illness, mental retardation, or intoxication (Koss & Cook, 1993). Some feminists have gone beyond the legal definitions. Robin Morgan would extend the definition of rape to include "any time sexual intercourse occurs when it has not been instigated by the woman, out of her own genuine affection and desire." Consequently, she would define as rape a situation in which a woman engages in sex out of "fear of losing the guy, fear of being thought a prude, fear of hurting his fragile feelings, *fear*" (Morgan, 1974, p. 84).

In their survey of 3,187 female students at thirty-two colleges across the country, Koss and her colleagues (1987) found that many women share the confusion about what constitutes rape. Only 27 percent of the women who had experienced acts by men that met the standard definition of rape (unwanted sexual penetration) labeled the experience as rape. That is, they responded that they had unwillingly experienced sexual intercourse, but answered "no" to the question: "Have you ever been raped?" The data also indicated that eight out of ten rapes or attempted rapes involved someone the victim knew, and more than half (57 percent) of these assaults occurred on a date.

At first glance, the large percentage of women who did not acknowledge that they had been raped is perplexing. Parrot (1991) suggests four scenarios that might explain their behavior: concern for the rapist; blaming themselves for the incident; repression; and/or the nature of the victim's definition of rape. Kahn, Mathie, and Torgler (1994) found that women who do not label their experience as rape have a narrow picture in their mind of what constitutes rape. They envision rape as an event involving a stranger who employs considerable violence, including the use or threatened use of a weapon. In other words, unwanted sex performed in a less forceful manner by an acquaintance or a date does not match their notion of rape.

Koss's figures differ dramatically from the rape statistics in the traditional data sources: the FBI's Uniform Crime Reports, which are based on crimes reported to the police, and higher numbers, drawn from the National Crime Victimization Survey, which asks a sample of people if they have been victims of a crime. Interestingly, the Department of Justice revised its survey in 1992. Instead of asking respondents whether they had been attacked, they specifically asked whether they had been victims of rape. The result was a dramatic increase in the reported incidence of rape. The 1995 Department of Justice report concluded that there were 310,000 rapes or attempted rapes in 1992-1993, double the number recorded in the previous survey (Schafran, 1995). Ronet Bachman, coauthor of the report, declared that the Justice Department always knew that women were more likely to be raped by someone they were acquainted with, but she was shocked to find that four out of five women who are raped or sexually assaulted knew their attackers, a figure that Koss and her colleagues had come up with a decade earlier (Vobejda, 1995).

Despite the fact that the findings of Koss and her colleagues have been widely cited in the psychological literature, they have come under fire from critics. Katie Roiphe, a self-styled feminist, claims that the increase in the number of reported rapes is due to an expanded definition of rape. According to Roiphe, "there is a gray area in which someone's rape may be another person's bad night" (1993, p. 54). The danger, she says, is that if *rape* is used to mean so many things, the word loses its meaning.

If nothing else, the controversy surrounding rape statistics demonstrates that the results depend on who is asking the questions and what questions are being asked. Neil Gilbert, in the following article, argues that Koss and her fellow researchers have engaged in what he identifies as "advocacy research," an attempt to "persuade the public and policymakers that a problem is vastly larger than commonly recognized." Charlene Muehlenhard and her colleagues disagree, contending that Gilbert and Roiphe have misinterpreted the findings of Koss and her associates.

REFERENCES

Friedman, L. (1993). *Crime and punishment in American history.* New York: Basic.

Kahn, A. S., Mathie, V. A., & Torgler, C. (1994). Rape scripts and rape acknowledgment. *Psychology of Women Quarterly, 18,* 53-66.

Koss, M. P., & Cook, S. L. (1993). Facing the facts: Date and acquaintance rape are significant problems for women. In R. J. Gelles & D. R. Loseke (Eds.), *Current controversies in family violence* (pp. 104-119). Newbury Park, Calif.: Sage.

Koss, M. P., Gidycz, C. A., & Wisniewski, N. (1987). The scope of rape: Incidence and prevalence of sexual aggression and victimization in a national sample of higher education students. *Journal of Consulting and Clinical Psychology, 55,* 162-170.

Lott, B. (1994). *Women's lives: Themes and variations in gender learning* (2nd ed.). Pacific Grove, Calif.: Brooks/Cole.

Malamuth, N. M. (1989a). The attraction to sexual aggression scale: I. *Journal of Sex Research, 26,* 26-49.

Malamuth, N. M. (1989b). The attraction to sexual aggression scale: II. *Journal of Sex Research, 26,* 324-354.

Morgan, R. (1974). Theory and practice: Pornography and rape. In R. Morgan (ed.), *The word of a woman: Feminist dispatches, 1968-1992.* New York: Norton.

Parrot, A. (1991). Institutionalized response: How can acquaintance rape be prevented? In A. Parrot & L. Bechhofer (Eds.), *Acquaintance rape: The hidden crime* (pp. 355-367). New York: John Wiley & Sons.

Roiphe, K. (1993). *The morning after: Sex, fear and feminism on campus.* Boston: Little, Brown.

Schafran, L. H. (1995). Rape is still underreported. *New York Times,* August 26 p. 19.

Vobejda, B. (1995). The known factor in rape. *Washington Post National Weekly Edition,* August 21–27 p. 37.

ADDITIONAL READING

Abbey, A., Ross, L. T., McDuffie, D., & McAuslan, P. Alcohol, misperception, and sexual assault: How and why are they linked? In D. M. Buss & N. M. Malamuth (eds.), *Sex, power, conflict: Evolutionary and feminist perspectives* (pp. 138–161). New York: Oxford University Press.

Bohner, G. (1996). The threat of rape: Its psychological impact on nonvictimized women. In D. M. Buss & N. M. Malamuth (eds.), *Sex, power, conflict: Evolutionary and feminist perspectives* (pp. 162–178). New York: Oxford University Press.

Cook, S. L. (1995). Acceptance and expectation of sexual aggression in college students. *Psychology of Women Quarterly, 19,* 181–194.

Lonsway, K. A., & Fitzgerald, L. F. (1994). Rape myths: In review. *Psychology of Women Quarterly, 18,* 133–164.

Muehlenhard, C. L., Danoff-Burg, S., & Powch, I. G. (1996). Is rape sex or violence? Conceptual issues and implications. In D. M. Buss & N. M. Malamuth (eds.), *Sex, power, conflict: Evolutionary and feminist perspectives* (pp. 119–137). New York: Oxford University Press.

Quina, K., & Carlson, N. L. (1989). *Rape, incest, and sexual harassment: A guide for helping survivors.* New York: Praeger.

Sanday, P. R. (1996). *A woman scorned: Acquaintance rape on trial.* New York: Doubleday.

Wyatt, G. E. (1992). The sociocultural context of African American and white American women's rape. *Journal of Social Issues, 48,* 77–91.

Advocacy Research

Exaggerates Rape Statistics

NEIL GILBERT

Over the past decade, problems like stranger abduction, child abuse, elder abuse, and homelessness have been magnified by advocacy research. But these efforts are modest in comparison with the remarkably powerful campaign of advocacy research inspired by the rape crisis movement of the early 1990s.[1] According to the alarming accounts routinely voiced by radical feminist groups, about one in every two women will be a victim of rape or attempted rape an average of two times in her life, and many more will suffer other forms of sexual molestation. These claims are based on figures from several studies, among which the *Ms.* magazine Campus Project on Sexual Assault, directed by Mary Koss, and Diana Russell's survey of sexual exploitation are the largest, most widely disseminated, and frequently cited. Both studies were funded by the National Institute of Mental Health, which gave them the imprimatur of a respected federal agency. Often quoted in newspapers and journals, on television, and in the 1991 and 1993 Senate reports on the Violence Against Women

1. Some advocates deny the existence of the rape crisis movement, but as Barbara Collins and Mary Whalen (1989:61) explain it, "The rape crisis movement was a radical feminist social issue that emerged in the early 1970s—feminist because the movement was conceived by women whose primary concerns focused on women's experiences, radical because it sought to dismantle the existing social order." By 1979 there were about 1,000 rape crisis centers forming the organizational core of the movement (Amir and Amir, 1979).

Bill, the findings from these studies have gained authority through repetition. Most of the time, however, those who cite the findings take them at face value, understanding neither where the numbers come from nor what they actually represent. A critical analysis of the studies will demonstrate how social scientists practice the craft of advocacy research and why the media and the public are often deceived by their studies.

RAPE RESEARCH: EXAMINING THE FACTS

The *Ms.* study directed by Koss involved a survey of 6,159 students at thirty-two colleges. As Koss defines the problem, 27 percent of the female college students in her study had been victims of rape (15 percent) or attempted rape (12 percent) an average of two times between the ages of fourteen and twenty-one. Using the same survey questions, which she claims represent a strict legal description of the crime of rape, Koss calculates that during a twelve-month period 17 percent of college women were victims of rape or attempted rape and that more than half of the victims were assaulted twice (Koss, 1988; Koss, Gidycz, and Wisniewski, 1987; Warshaw, 1988). If victimization continued at this annual rate, we would expect well over half of all college women to suffer an incident of rape or attempted rape over the course of four years and more than one-quarter of them to be victimized twice.

There are several reasons for serious researchers to question the magnitude of sexual assault conveyed by the *Ms.* findings. To begin with, there is a notable discrepancy between Koss's definition of rape and the way most of the women whom she labeled as victims interpreted their experiences. When asked directly, 73 percent of the students whom Koss categorized as victims of rape did not think that they had been raped. This discrepancy is underscored by the subsequent behavior of a high proportion of those identified as victims: 42 percent had sex again with the man who supposedly raped them. Of those categorized as victims of attempted rape, 35 percent later had sex with the purported offender (Koss, 1988; Koss, Gidycz, and Wisniewski, 1987).

Although the exact legal definition of rape varies by state, most definitions involve sexual penetration accomplished against a person's will by means of physical force or threat of bodily harm or when the victim is incapable of giving consent; the latter condition usually involves cases in which the victim is mentally ill, developmentally disabled, or intentionally incapacitated through the administration of intoxicating or anesthetic substances.

Rape and attempted rape were operationally defined in the *Ms.* study by five questions, three of which referred to the threat or use of "some degree of physical force." The other two questions asked: "Have you had a man attempt sexual intercourse (get on top of you, attempt to insert his penis) when you didn't want to by giving you alcohol or drugs, but intercourse did not occur? Have you had sexual intercourse when you didn't want to because a man gave you alcohol or drugs?" (Koss, 1988; Koss, Gidycz, and Wisniewski, 1987). Forty-four percent of all the women identified as victims of rape and attempted rape in the previous year were so labeled because they responded positively to these awkward and vaguely worded questions. What does it mean to have sex "because" a man gives you drugs or alcohol? A positive response does not indicate whether duress, intoxication, force, or the threat of force was present; whether the woman's judgment or control was substantially impaired; or whether the man purposefully got the woman drunk to prevent her from resisting his sexual advances. Perhaps the woman was trading sex for drugs; or perhaps a few drinks lowered her inhibitions so that she consented to an act that she later regretted.[2] Koss assumes that a positive an-

swer signifies that the respondent engaged in sexual intercourse against her will because she was intoxicated to the point of being unable to deny consent (and that the man had administered the alcohol for this purpose). Although the question could have been clearly worded to denote "intentional incapacitation of the victim," only a mind reader could detect whether an affirmative response to the question as it stands corresponds to the legal definition of rape.

In an attempt to resolve this problem, Koss and Cook (1993a:3) first take the question as originally reported, "Have you had sexual intercourse with a man when you didn't want to because he gave you drugs or alcohol?" and claim that it included the words "to make you cooperate." Rather than helping the case, this revised version suggests that instead of being too drunk to deny consent, the woman actually cooperated in the act of intercourse after taking drugs and alcohol. After noting this criticism of their attempt to clarify the case by altering the original definition, Koss and Cook (1993b:106) concede that "for the sake of discussion it is helpful to examine what happens to the prevalence figures when these instances are removed."[3] According to Koss and Cook's revised estimates, when the item dealing with drugs and alcohol is removed, the prevalence rate of rape and attempted rape declines by one-third.[4]

During Koss's (1990) testimony in the Senate Judiciary Committee Hearings on the Violence Against Women Act, it emerged that three-quarters of the respondents classified as victims in the *Ms.* study did not think they had been raped. The committee chair, Joseph Biden, said: "My daughter is not going to have any doubt." But no one asked

---

2. In Prince Georges County, Maryland, where more than one in four allegations of rape in 1990–91 were unfounded (that is, the women admitted that their charges were false, or the police found no evidence that a rape had occurred), the former head of criminal investigations concluded that the high rate of false reports was due in part "to frequent cases of sex-for-drug transactions gone sour" (Buckley, 1992:81).

3. Later, in an interview with Nara Schoenberg and Sam Roe (1993), Koss acknowledged that the drug and alcohol questions, two of the five items used to define victims of rape and attempted rape, were ambiguous.

4. From the form in which the data are reported in Koss's earlier studies it is not possible to verify the new estimate. But, as noted earlier, calculations that can be made from the original data show that the one-year incidence rate declines by 44 percent when the item dealing with intercourse under the influence of drugs or alcohol is removed.

why all these other young college women did not know that they had experienced the brutal and terrifying crime of rape. On how they interpreted the event, Koss (1990:40) reported to the committee: "Among college women who had an experience that met legal requirements for rape, only a quarter labeled their experience as rape. Another quarter thought their experience was some kind of crime, but not rape. The remaining half did not think their experience qualified as any type of crime."

A different account of how the students interpreted their experience had been published several years earlier by Koss and her colleagues (Koss et al., 1988). According to that report, 11 percent of the students said they "don't feel victimized," 49 percent labeled the experience "miscommunication," 14 percent labeled it "crime, but not rape," and 27 percent said it was rape. Although there was no indication that other data might have been available on this question, three years later a surprisingly different distribution of responses was put forth. In answer to questions raised about the fact that most of the victims did not think they had been raped (Gilbert, 1991a, b), Koss offered four new versions of the students' responses; in none did she mention that 49 percent thought it a matter of miscommunication. First, in a breathtaking disregard for the data that she had originally published, Koss (1991b:6) wrote that the students labeled as victims viewed the incident as follows: "One quarter thought it was rape, one quarter thought it was some kind of crime but did not believe it qualified as rape, one quarter thought it was sexual abuse but did not think it qualified as a crime, and one quarter did not feel victimized." In a later paper, Koss (1991a:9) revised the gist of these new findings: "One quarter thought it was some kind of crime, but did not realize it qualified as rape; one quarter thought it was serious sexual abuse, but did not know it qualified as a crime." Two years later, yet another revision of these findings was published. Koss (1993) continued to deny that virtually half of the students labeled their experience a case of miscommunication; she claimed instead that "only one in ten victims said she felt unvictimized by the experience. The remaining nine who felt vic-

timized were split between those who thought their experience was rape (the 27% fraction Mr. Gilbert quotes), those who thought their experience was a crime but might not be called rape, and those who thought their incident was extremely traumatic but was not a crime." Finally, in a fourth effort, Koss and Cook (1993b:107) explain: "In fact, half the rape victims identified in the national survey considered their experience as rape or some crime similar to rape."

These inconsistencies aside, the additional data are difficult to interpret. If one-quarter thought the incidents involved a crime but not rape, what kind of crime did they have in mind? Were they referring to an illegal activity like drinking under age or taking drugs?[5] Despite Koss's elaboration of the data originally reported, in the first version of the findings 60 percent of the students either did not feel victimized or thought the incident was a case of miscommunication. Although in the second, third, and fourth versions Koss claims that many more of the students assessed the sexual encounter in negative terms, the fact remains that 73 percent did not think they had been raped.

Moving beyond the experience of college students, Diana Russell's study is another source often quoted as evidence that rape has reached, as she describes it, "epidemic proportions throughout society" (1984, 1991). In addition to reporting a

---

5. In reviewing the research methodology for the *Ms.* study, Koss (1988; Koss, Gidycz, and Wisniewski, 1987) explains that previous reliability and validity studies conducted on the ten-item Sexual Experience Survey (SES) instrument showed that few of the female respondents misinterpreted the questions of rape. Examining the earlier studies, however, we find that the original SES instrument (Koss and Oros, 1982) differed from the version used in the *Ms.* study in at least one important respect; the original instrument contained neither of the questions dealing with rape or attempted rape that happened "because a man gave you alcohol or drugs." In a brief report on the assessment of validity, Koss and Gidycz (1985:423) note: "To explore the veracity of the self-reported sexual experiences, the Sexual Experience Survey (original wording) was administered to approximately 4,000 students." This suggests that the findings on validity would not include the vague items on "intentional incapacitation" absent from the original version of the SES instrument.

prevalence rate of 38 percent to 54 percent for child sexual abuse, she (1984) found that 44 percent of the women in her sample were victims of rape (26 percent) or attempted rape (18 percent) an average of twice in their life and that many other women suffered experiences in marriage that, if not rape, were very close to it. If mutually desired intercourse and rape are placed at the ends of a continuum, Russell (1982:356) explains, "our study suggests that a considerable amount of marital sex is probably closer to the rape end of the continuum." Indeed, beyond marital sex, Russell (1984:121, 1975:261) suggests that, according to this view, "much of what passes for normal heterosexual intercourse would be seen as close to rape." Although this analysis of sex relations is not as censorious as that of Andrea Dworkin (1988), for whom all heterosexual sex is rape, it leans in that direction.

Using her San Francisco findings, Russell offers a detailed analysis to extrapolate not only the lifetime probability but also the national incidence of rape and attempted rape in 1978. She explains: "The incidence figure for rape in the Russell survey . . . was 35 per 1000 females. (This includes cases of rape and attempted rape that occurred to residents of San Francisco, both inside and outside the city.) This is *24 times higher* than the 1.71 per 1000 females [in San Francisco] reported by the Uniform Crime Reports" (1984:46, emphasis in original). On the basis of this calculation, Russell takes the 1978 *Uniform Crime Report's* figure of 67,131 for all the cases of rape and attempted rape in the United States and multiplies it by 24, which yields her estimate of 1.6 million incidents that year nationwide.

Faulty logic and poor arithmetic invalidate this analysis. First, the initial calculation is incorrect. The San Francisco rate of 35 per 1,000 is 20.5 times (not 24 times) higher than the 1.71 per 1,000 in the *Uniform Crime Report.* Ignoring for a moment this arithmetic error, let us look at the logic of the second calculation, where Russell assumes a correspondence between the Uniform Crime Report rates for San Francisco and the nation. If Russell's sample had an incidence rate twenty-four times

higher than the report's rate for San Francisco, we need only multiply by twenty-four the national rate given in the report to project the local difference on a national scale. However, those who study this subject know very well that the reported rates of rape are considerably higher for metropolitan areas than for the national population (Johnson, 1980). Indeed, the *Uniform Crime Report's* total of 67,131 cases of rape and attempted rape in 1978 amounted to a national rate of 0.6 per 1,000 females, which was about one-third the rate of 1.7 per 1,000 females that the report showed for San Francisco (U.S. Bureau of the Census, 1986). Thus, if we include the initial arithmetic error, Russell's national estimate of the incidence of sexual assault exaggerates by about 350 percent the figure that would result from simply an accurate reading of her own data.

A common tactic of advocacy researchers is to declare that their estimates are not only accurate but well replicated in many other studies. In support of the *Ms.* survey findings, for example, Koss often adduces additional studies as sources of independent verification. But if we take a close look at the studies that she usually cites, we find very little replication. Some of the studies (Ageton, 1983) use different definitions of forced sexual behavior (including verbal persuasion and psychological coercion) and involve small or nonrepresentative samples that are inadmissible as a basis for serious estimates of the size of the problem. Other studies are referred to without explanation or critical examination. Thus, for example, Koss and Cook (1993b) cite two studies using representative samples that show the prevalence rate of rape for college students in the 12 percent range, a figure not far from the 15 percent reported in the *Ms.* findings. One of these studies, conducted by Koss and Oros (1982), used the original version of the Sexual Experience Survey instrument to measure rape, which excluded items dealing with unwanted intercourse when "a man gives you drugs or alcohol." The second study defined rape as forced oral sex or intercourse, where force included verbal persuasion: "This study showed that most of the sexual encounters were forced through verbal persuasion-protestations by the male to 'go further' because of sexual need, arousal, or love." According to this definition, the conventional script of nagging and pleading—"Everyone does it," "If you really loved me, you'd do it," "I need it," "You will like it"—is transformed into a version of rape. After verbal persuasion, the form of force experienced most frequently by students was "use of alcohol or drugs," though the researcher neither elaborates on this category nor claims that it reflects intentional incapacitation of the victim (Yegidis, 1986:53).

As further evidence that the study results are verified by other research, Koss and Cook (1993b:110) refer to the National Victim Center (1992) study: "In a just released telephone survey of more than 4,000 women in a nationally representative sample, the rate of rape was reported to be 14%, although this rate excluded rapes of women unable to consent." This figure is close to the 15 percent rate reported in the *Ms.* study. What Koss and Cook fail to tell the reader is that approximately 40 percent of the rapes reported in the National Victim Center study occurred to women between the ages of fourteen and twenty-four, resulting in an estimated rate of 5 percent for that age-group.[6] According to Koss's findings in the *Ms.* study, 15 percent of college women are victims of rape between the ages of fourteen and twenty-one. Thus, for almost the same age cohort, Koss found a rate of rape three times higher than that detected in the National Victim Center survey.

6. In fact, the rate of rape found in the National Victim Center study was 13 percent. Data on the age of the victims at the time of the rape are grouped; data on those younger than eleven are lumped together, as are data on those eleven to seventeen, eighteen to twenty-four, and twenty-five and older. To calculate the percentage of victims in the fourteen to twenty-four cohort, I took a proportional rate of the eleven-to seventeen-year-olds (18 percent) and added that to the 22 percent in the eighteen-to twenty-four-year-old group. Because these data on the age of rape victims include cases in which some women were raped more than once, the estimate is based on the assumption that the cases of multiple rapes were distributed proportionately among the age-groups.

DISTORTED MEASURES AND INEQUITABLE POLICY

In the deliberations on federal policy regarding violence against women, advocacy research on rape was accepted almost at face value. In the opening statement during the Senate Judiciary Committee hearings on the Violence Against Women Act in 1990, Biden explained: "One out of every four college women will have been attacked by a rapist before they graduate, and one in seven will have been raped. Less than 5 percent of these women will report these rapes to the police. Rape remains the least reported of all major crimes. . . . Dr. Koss will tell us today the actual number of college women raped is more than 14 times the number reported by official governmental statistics. Indeed, while studies suggest that about 1,275 women were raped at America's three largest universities last year, only three rapes—only three—were reported to the police" (U.S. Senate, 1991:3). Without a blink, the panel was informed that unreported rapes of college women are more than twenty times, more than fourteen times, and—simultaneously—more than four hundred times the number of incidents reported to the police. In fact, as we noted earlier, the unreported rate, according to Koss's figures, would be one thousand times higher than the rate of rape and attempted rape reported on college campuses.

Expert opinions solicited for the hearings reinforced the figures presented by Chairman Biden as authoritative measures of rape; his data came directly from the *Ms.* study, whose severe shortcomings we have already examined. The first professionals testifying before the committee were introduced as "two nationally prominent experts in this field. . . . Ms. Warshaw is the author of the foremost book published on acquaintance rape and the attitudes that lead to it, entitled *I Never Called It Rape.*" And Dr. Koss "has studied the incidence and prevalence of rape more extensively than any other social scientist in this country" (U.S. Senate, 1991:27). Robin Warshaw (1988) is a journalist, and the full title of her book is *I Never Called It Rape: The Ms. Report on Recognizing, Fighting, and Surviving Date and Acquaintance Rape.* Its afterword is by none other than Mary Koss, who directed the *Ms.* study.

Owing in large part to the credibility attributed to advocacy research, the Violence Against Women Act of 1993, under Title IV (Safe Campuses for Women), proposes the appropriation of $20 million for rape education and prevention programs to make college campuses safe for women. Extrapolating from the 408 reported cases of rape and attempted rape on 500 campuses with five million college students in 1992 yields approximately 1,000 reported incidents at all colleges in the United States. The appropriation proposed under Title IV thus amounts to $20,000 per reported case (U.S. Senate, 1993).

Whatever the value of these programs, the cost is remarkably high compared with the amount allocated per reported case of rape victim off college campuses; among those cases, poor and minority women are vastly overrepresented (U.S. Bureau of Justice Statistics, 1992). According to FBI (1993) data, there were altogether 109,062 reported cases of rape and attempted rape nationwide in 1992. Given these rates, to make the rest of society as safe as college campuses would require an expenditure of over $2 billion on education and prevention programs (or more than twice the appropriations proposed under all five titles of the act combined). Compared with the $20 million designated for college campuses ($20,000 per reported case), the Violence Against Women Act proposes an appropriation of $65 million (approximately $650 per reported case) for prevention and education programs to serve the broader community (U.S. Senate, 1993).[7] Under this arrangement, the sum distributed for education and prevention programs on college campuses is disproportionate; worse, most college victims, according to the *Ms.* study, do not know they have been raped. And relatively meager resources will be invested in similar programs for low-income and minority communities, where authentic victims need all the help that society can offer.

Some might argue that the need is really greater on college campuses because the rate of underreporting is much higher there than in other places. But we have little reason to assume that middle-class college students are less likely to report being raped than women from other backgrounds. Indeed, organized efforts have been made to facilitate reporting by college students. During the past decade, rape crisis counseling and supportive services have been established on most major campuses. Staffed by professionals highly sensitive to the social and psychological violations of rape, these services provide a sympathetic environment in which victims may come forward for assistance without having to make official reports to the police. Reliable data on how many rape victims are served by these programs are difficult to obtain, but individual accounts suggest that the demand is not excessive.[8] The director of counseling services at Lafayette College, for example, reports that over the course of five years services were provided to about a dozen students who confided that they were sexually assaulted (Forbes and Kirts, 1993). Offering an account of a typical Saturday night at the Rape Crisis Center at Columbia University, Peter Hellman (1993) reports: "Nobody called; nobody came."

It is difficult to criticize advocacy research without giving the impression that one cares less about the problems of victims than do those engaged in magnifying the size of the problems. But a citizen or social scientist may be deeply concerned about problems like rape, child abuse, and homelessness yet still wish to see a rigorous and objective analysis of their dimensions. Advocacy researchers who

7. Although prevention and education funds are disproportionately targeted to college campuses, an appropriation of $100 million is earmarked for "high-density crime areas" for the purposes of expanding police protection, prosecuting offenders, and improving data collection.

8. In 1990, for example, the staff of the rape counseling program on the University of California, Berkeley, campus were unable to cite the exact number of women seen that year. They estimated having served forty to eighty cases, including some clients who were not students and some who were seen for problems other than rape. It was unclear whether the cases were counted according to number of contacts or number of individuals served.

uncover a problem, measure it with reasonable accuracy, and bring it to light perform a valuable service by raising public consciousness. Social equity is advanced when emerging problems are scrupulously assessed and brought to the attention of policymakers. The current trend in advocacy research, however, is to inflate problems and redefine them in line with the advocates' ideological preferences. The few impose their definitions of social ills on the many. Though creating sensational headlines, this type of advocacy research invites the formulation of social policies that are likely to be neither effective nor fair.

REFERENCES

Ageton, S. 1983. *Sexual assault among adolescents: A national study*. Final report to the National Institute of Mental Health.

Amir, D., and M. Amir. 1979. Rape crisis centers: An arena for ideological conflicts. *Victimology* 4(2), pp. 247–57.

Buckley, Stephen. 1992. Unfounded reports of rape confound area police investigations. *Washington Post*, June 27.

Collins, B., & Whalen, B. (1989). The rape crisis movement: Radical or reformist? *Social Work* 34, 61–65.

Dworkin, Andrea. 1988. *Letters from a war zone*. London: Secker and Warburg.

Federal Bureau of Investigation. 1993. *Crime in the United States: Uniform Crime Reports, 1992*. Washington, D.C.: Government Printing Office.

Forbes, Karen, and Donald Kirts. 1993. Letters to the editor. *The Lafayette*, October 29, p. 5.

Gilbert, Neil. 1991a. The campus rape scare. *Wall Street Journal*, June 27, p. 10.

———. 1991b. The phantom epidemic of sexual assault. *Public Interest* 103 (Spring), pp. 54–65.

Hellman, Peter. 1993. Crying rape: The politics of date rape on campus. *New York*, March 8, pp. 32–37.

Johnson, Allan. 1980. On the prevalence of rape in the United States. *Signs* 6(1), pp. 137–45.

Koss, Mary. 1988. Hidden rape: Sexual aggression and victimization in a national sample of students in higher education. In A. W. Burgess, ed., *Rape and Sexual Assault II*. New York: Garland.

———. 1990. Testimony in Senate hearings on women and violence. In *Women and violence: Hearings before the Committee on the Judiciary*, 101st Cong., 2nd sess. Part 2. Washington, D.C.: Government Printing Office.

———. 1991a. Rape on campus: Facing the facts. University of Arizona, Tucson. Mimeo.

———. 1991b. Statistics show sexual assaults are more prevalent than many realize. *Los Angeles Daily Journal*, July 17.

———. 1993. Letters to the editor. *Wall Street Journal*, August 3.

Koss, Mary, and Sarah Cook. 1993a. Facing the facts: Date and acquaintance rape. Final draft of chapter prepared for *Current controversies on family violence*.

———. 1993b. Facing the facts: Date and acquaintance rape are significant problems for women. In Richard Gelles and Donileen Loseke, eds., *Current controversies on family violence*. Beverly Hills, Calif.: Sage.

Koss, Mary, Thomas Dinero, Cynthia Seibel, and Susan Cox. 1988. Stranger and acquaintance rape: Are there differences in the victim's experience? *Psychology of Women Quarterly* 12, pp. 1–24.

Koss, Mary, and Christine Gidycz. 1985. Sexual experiences survey: Reliability and validity. *Journal of Consulting and Clinical Psychology* 53(3), pp. 422–23.

Koss, Mary, Christine Gidycz, and Nadine Wisniewski. 1987. The scope of rape: Incidence and prevalence of sexual aggression and victimization in a national sample of higher education students. *Journal of Consulting and Clinical Psychology* 55(2), pp. 162–70.

Koss, Mary, and Cheryl Oros. 1982. The Sexual Experiences Survey: A research instrument investigating sexual aggression and victimization. *Journal of Consulting and Clinical Psychology* 50(3), pp. 455–57.

National Victim Center. 1992. *Rape in America: A report to the nation*. Arlington, Va.: National Victims Center.

Russell, Diana. 1975. *The politics of rape*. New York: Stein and Day.

———. 1982. *Rape in marriage*. New York: Macmillan.

———. 1984. *Sexual exploitation: Rape, child sexual abuse, and workplace harrassment*. Beverly Hills, Calif.: Sage.

———. 1991. The epidemic of sexual violence against women: A national crisis. Seabury Lecture, University of California, Berkeley, November 25.

Schoenberg, Nara, and Sam Roe. 1993. Rape: The making of an epidemic. *Toledo Blade*. October 10, 11, 12.

U.S. Bureau of the Census. 1986. *Statistical abstract of the United States, 1987*. Washington, D.C.: Government Printing Office.

U.S. Bureau of Justice Statistics. 1994. *Criminal victimization in the United States, 1992*. Washington, D.C.: Government Printing Office.

U.S. Senate. 1991. *Women and violence: Hearings before the Committee on the Judiciary*. 101st Cong., 2nd sess. Part 2. Washington, D.C.: Government Printing Office.

———. 1993. *S.11 Violence Against Women Act 1993*, 103rd Cong., 1st sess. Washington, D.C.: Government Printing Office.

Warshaw, Robin. 1988. *I never called it rape: The Ms. report on recognizing, fighting, and surviving date and acquaintance rape*. New York: Harper and Row.

Yegidis, Bonnie. 1986. Date rape and other forced sexual encounters among college students. *Journal of Sex Education and Therapy* 12, pp. 51–54.

NO

Rape Statistics

Are Not Exaggerated

Charlene L. Muehlenhard,

Barrie J. Highby, Joi L. Phelps,

and Susie C. Sympson

Since the early 1970s, feminists concerned about women's welfare have worked hard to make our social and legal systems more sensitive to victims of rape and other forms of sexual coercion. In the past twenty-five years, rape crisis centers have been established, rape laws have been reformed, and research on rape has proliferated and moved away from the victim-blaming theories that were prominent even into the 1970s (Estrich, 1987; Muehlenhard, Harney, & Jones, 1992). Recently, however, feminist research and political action have been disparaged by critics who have charged, among other things, that rape statistics have been exaggerated. In this article, we focus on two of the most outspoken proponents of that thesis: Neil Gilbert, professor of social welfare at the University of California at Berkeley, and Katie Roiphe, author of *The Morning After: Sex, Fear, and Feminism on Campus*. Although they raised numerous issues, because of space constraints, we address only one of their arguments: that rape statistics have been exaggerated.

Gilbert (1991) wrote about "the phantom epidemic of sexual assault" (p. 54). Roiphe (1993) also questioned frequently cited rape statistics: "If 25 percent of my female friends were really being raped, wouldn't I know it?" (p. 52). Are feminist re-searchers' rape statistics merely, to use Gilbert's phrase, "advocacy numbers" (p. 63)?

BACKGROUND

To provide readers with a background for understanding these allegations, we briefly discuss some studies that Gilbert and Roiphe have criticized. They have frequently referred to a study by Mary Koss and her colleagues (Koss, Dinero, Seibel, & Cox, 1988; Koss, Gidycz, & Wisniewski, 1987). This study is sometimes called the *Ms.* study of campus rape because the staff of *Ms.* magazine assisted with it; however, the study was peer reviewed and funded by the National Institute of Mental Health. Koss studied 3,187 women and 2,972 men at thirty-two randomly selected institutions of higher education across the United States. She asked women about their experiences as victims—and men about their experiences as perpetrators—of various forms of sexual coercion. Perhaps most widely quoted is her finding that one in four college women had experienced either rape or attempted rape since age fourteen. More specifically, 15.4 percent had been raped, and an additional 12.1 percent had experienced attempted rape.

Gilbert (1995) has also referred to Diana Russell's (1984) study of a community sample of 930 randomly selected women, ages eighteen to eighty-five and older, in San Francisco. Russell defined rape as "forced intercourse (i.e., penile-vaginal penetration), or intercourse obtained by threat of force, or intercourse completed when the woman was drugged, unconscious, asleep, or otherwise totally helpless and hence unable to consent" (p. 35). Russell found that 24 percent of these women had been raped; this figure increases to 44 percent when attempted rape is included.

Roiphe quoted a chapter written by Muehlenhard and Schrag (1991) entitled "Nonviolent Sexual Coercion." In that chapter, we examined several "types of sexual coercion that would not be legally classified as 'rape' but nevertheless have a powerful, insidious effect on women in our society" (p. 115). These types of sexual coercion included, for example, discrimination against lesbians, which pressures them to choose between sex they do not want (i.e., heterosexual sex) and no sex at all; assumptions about the nature of marriage, which make it difficult for wives to refuse unwanted sex with their husbands; and—the focus of Roiphe's criticism—verbal sexual coercion, "unwanted sexual activity because of a man's verbal arguments, not including verbal threats of physical force" (p. 122).

Both Gilbert and Roiphe have criticized these studies as exaggerating the prevalence of rape. We will now examine some of their criticisms.

GILBERT'S AND ROIPHE'S MISREPRESENTATION OF THE DATA

Both Gilbert and Roiphe have misinterpreted Koss's and Russell's findings and then criticized their distorted interpretations as exaggerated. For example, Koss found that one in four *women* had experienced either rape or attempted rape; Roiphe (1993) distorted this finding to say that "sex is, in one in four *cases*, against your will" (p. 21, emphasis added). Clearly, saying that one in four women has ever experienced rape or attempted rape, as Koss did, is different from saying that one in four cases of sex is involuntary—Roiphe's version of Koss's findings.

Both Gilbert and Roiphe compared Koss's or Russell's *lifetime prevalence rates* with *annual incidence rates* obtained from unreliable sources. For example, Gilbert (1991) cited National Crime Surveys that uncovered only about one case or rape per thousand women per year (an annual rate of 0.1 percent). National Crime Surveys have been notoriously unreliable sources of data on rape for many reasons, including that none of the screening questions even asked about rape (see Koss, 1992; Russell, 1984). When Gilbert stated that "the difference between a sexual-assault rate of 25 or 50 percent and one of 0.1 percent is more than a matter of degree" (p. 64), he was comparing lifetime rates found in Koss's and Russell's carefully done studies with the annual rate found in a study that did not ask about rape. Roiphe made a similar erroneous comparison (p. 54).

WHO SHOULD DECIDE WHETHER RAPE HAS OCCURRED?

Gilbert and Roiphe have made much of the fact that 73 percent of the women who fit Koss's definition of rape victims did not regard themselves as having been raped. Gilbert (quoted by Kahn, 1991) stated, "This implies that women don't know when they're being raped until a researcher tells them. . . . This is insulting" (p. 7C). Rather than asking women, "Have you ever been raped?" Koss developed a three-part operational definition of rape based on Ohio law. It is standard scientific practice for researchers to establish their own operational definitions. For example, a scientist doing research on gifted children would establish her or his own definition of the term "gifted" rather than letting individuals decide for themselves whether they were gifted.

Asking women whether they have ever been raped is likely to evoke images of strangers leaping from dark alleys; incidents of forced sex that do not fit this image would be missed. All too often in this culture, forced sex involving an unarmed assailant known to the victim is not considered "real rape" (Estrich, 1987). It is not surprising that women learn to use the word *rape* the way it is commonly used in this culture, but researchers should not be constrained by such narrow usage of the word.

How one labels unwanted sex does not indicate the severity of its consequences. Although victims of acquaintance rape (as defined by Koss) were less likely than victims of stranger rape to label their experiences as rape (23.1 percent vs. 55.0 percent, respectively), the two groups did not differ significantly in their levels of depression, anxiety, problems with relationships, problems with sex, or thoughts of suicide (Koss et al., 1988).

HOW SHOULD RAPE BE DEFINED?

Gilbert and Roiphe have criticized feminist researchers' definitions of rape as overly broad and thus leading to inflated statistics. Their two main criticisms are about items related to alcohol and items related to verbal sexual coercion. (For further discussion of definitions of rape, see Muehlenhard, Powch, Phelps, & Giusti, 1992.)

Alcohol. Both Gilbert (1995) and Roiphe (1993) have criticized Koss's item that asks, "Have you ever had sexual intercourse when you didn't want to because a man gave you alcohol or drugs?" (Koss et al., 1987, p. 167). Koss based her definition on Ohio law, which criminalizes "sexual conduct with another person . . . [when] for the purpose of preventing resistance the offender substantially impairs the other person's judgment or control by administering any drug or intoxicant to the other person" (Koss et al., 1987, p. 166). We agree that, in some ways, Koss's definition may be too broad; for example, it might be interpreted to include the exchange of sex for drugs or regrets about behavior that was consensual at the time, both of which we see as problematic but not as rape. In other ways, however, Koss's definition—and Ohio's law—might be too narrow. For example, Kansas's legal definition of rape includes nonconsensual intercourse "when the victim is incapable of giving consent . . . because of the effect of any alcoholic liquor, narcotic, drug or other substance, which condition was known by the offender or was reasonably apparent to the offender" (Rape, 1993, p. 323), *regardless of the source* of the alcohol or drugs.

Even without the alcohol-and-drug question, 9 percent of the women in the study by Koss et al. reported unwanted sexual intercourse—and 6 percent reported unwanted "anal or oral intercourse or penetration by objects other than the penis"— "because a man threatened or used some degree of physical force (twisting your arm, holding you down, etc.) to make you" (1987, p. 167). These are not trivial percentages.

Verbal sexual coercion. Both Gilbert (1995) and Roiphe (1993) have criticized feminist researchers for including verbal sexual coercion in their definitions of rape. We have two responses to this: (1) Gilbert and Roiphe are wrong; most feminist rape researchers have not defined verbal sexual coercion as rape. (2) Nevertheless, this does not mean that verbal coercion is unimportant.

Koss asked women about verbal sexual coercion but did not include it in her definition of rape or her rape statistics (see Koss et al., 1987, pp.

166–167). Russell also omitted verbal sexual coercion from her definition of rape: "Some respondents reported *feeling* forced rather than *being* forced, or having intercourse because of a threat that was not a threat of physical force or bodily harm. These cases were not counted as instances of rape or attempted rape" (p. 37). Thus, Gilbert's and Roiphe's claims that these studies yielded exaggerated numbers because of the inclusion of verbal sexual coercion are false.

Roiphe criticized Muehlenhard and Schrag's chapter on nonviolent sexual coercion, writing that "psychologists Charlene Muelenhard [sic] and Jennifer Schrag include the remarks 'He said he'd break up with me if I didn't,' 'He said I was frigid,' and 'He said everyone's doing it' in the category of verbal coercion. . . . The suggestion lurking beneath this definition of rape is that men are not just physically but intellectually and emotionally more powerful than women" (pp. 67–68).

Roiphe's comments are misleading; Muehlenhard and Schrag (1991) specifically stated that this form of sexual coercion "would not be legally classified as 'rape' " (p. 115). We called it "verbal sexual coercion"; we never called it rape.

That verbal sexual coercion is not rape as defined by law or by Muehlenhard and Schrag, however, does not mean that it is inconsequential or unimportant to address. In a prospective study in which women were assessed twice, three months apart, those who had been verbally sexually coerced during the three-month interim showed greater increases in depression from Time 1 to Time 2 than did other women. Furthermore, compared with women who had not been coerced, women who had been verbally coerced reported feeling more anxious, depressed, self-blaming, and demoralized and less self-confident after the incident (Jones & Muehlenhard, 1993).

Roiphe argued that addressing verbal sexual coercion portrays women as weak and passive: "By protecting women against verbal coercion, these feminists [Muehlenhard & Schrag] are promoting the view of women as weak-willed, alabaster bodies, whose virtue must be protected" (p. 67). Advocating consensual sex does not construct women as weak or passive. Men as well as women engage in unwanted sexual activity for a variety of reasons, including physical or verbal coercion by the other person, peer pressure, and internalized gender-role expectations to perform sexually (Muehlenhard & Cook, 1988). A thorough analysis of sexual coercion must go beyond obvious physical force and take into account stereotyped gender roles and other aspects of the social context. Our goal is not to portray women as weak-willed or alabaster-bodied. Our goal is for people—women and men—to engage in sex only when they freely consent, not because sex is the least undesirable of several undesirable options. We have no problem with sex that is sedate or wild or crazy, done in pairs, groups, or alone—as long as it's consensual!

REFERENCES

Estrich, S. (1987). *Real rape: How the legal system victimizes women who say no*. Cambridge: Harvard University Press.

Gilbert, N. (1991). The phantom epidemic of sexual assault. *The Public Interest, 103*, 54–65.

Gilbert, N. (1995). *Welfare justice: Restoring social equality*. New Haven: Yale University Press.

Jones, J. M., & Muehlenhard, C. L. (1993). *The impact of verbal and physical sexual coercion on women's psychological health*. Poster presented at the 1993 Kansas Series in Clinical Psychology, Lawrence, Kans., April.

Kahn, A. (1991). Professor challenges studies on date rape as exaggerated. *Lawrence Journal World*, May 31, 7C.

Koss, M. P. (1992). The underdetection of rape: Methodological choices influence incidence estimates. *Journal of Social Issues, 48* (1), 61–75.

Koss, M. P., Dinero, T. E., Seibel, C. A., & Cox, S. L. (1988). Stranger and acquaintance rape: Are there differences in the victim's experience? *Psychology of Women Quarterly, 12*, 1–23.

Koss, M. P., Gidycz, C. A., & Wisniewski, N. (1987). The scope of rape: Incidence and prevalence of sexual aggression and victimization in a national sample of higher education students. *Journal of Consulting and Clinical Psychology, 55*, 162–170.

Muehlenhard, C. L., & Cook, S. W. (1988). Men's self-reports of unwanted sexual activity. *The Journal of Sex Research, 24*, 58–72.

Muehlenhard, C. L., Harney, P. A., & Jones, J. M. (1992). From "victim-precipitated rape" to "date rape": How far have we come? *Annual Review of Sex Research, 3*, 219–253.

Muehlenhard, C. L., Powch, I. G., Phelps, J. L., & Giusti, L. M. (1992). Definitions of rape: Scientific and political implications. *Journal of Social Issues, 48* (1), 23–44.

Muehlenhard, C. L., & Schrag, J. (1991). Nonviolent sexual coercion. In A. Parrot & L. Bechhofer (eds.), *Acquaintance rape: The hidden crime* (pp. 115–128). New York: John Wiley and Sons.

Rape. *1993 cumulative supplement to the Kansas statutes annotated*, 21–3502, pp. 323–324.

Roiphe, K. (1993). *The morning after: Sex, fear, and feminism on campus*. Boston: Little, Brown.

Russell, D. E. H. (1984). *Sexual exploitation: Rape, child sexual abuse, and workplace harassment*. Beverly Hills, Calif.: Sage.

PART V

Knowing
and
Learning

Ways of Knowing:

Do Women and Men Have

Different Ways of Knowing?

Women's Ways of Knowing (*WWK*) (1986), one of the most widely cited books on women's intellectual development, won the Distinguished Publication Award of the Association for Women in Psychology in 1987. Mary Belenky, Blythe Clinchy, Nancy Goldberger, and Jill Tarule built on the theories of Carol Gilligan, outlined in her groundbreaking book *In a Different Voice* (1982). Working within a feminist framework, Gilligan challenged Lawrence Kohlberg's model of moral reasoning, which tended to locate women at level 3, characterized by a "regard for pleasing others," while placing men at a higher level of development, distinguished by a concern with law and justice. Gilligan pointed out a paradox: the traits traditionally associated with the "goodness" of women—caring and sensitivity to others—are the very same characteristics that render them inferior on moral-judgment scales. Arguing that women are oriented toward attachment and "connectedness" to others while men are inclined toward individuation and "separateness" from others, Gilligan suggested that there could be two parallel developments in moral reasoning: women's "ethic of care" could be viewed as the equivalent of men's "ethic of justice."

Like Gilligan, the *WWK* authors restricted their subject pool to women. And just as Gilligan provided a feminist critique of Kohlberg's work, the *WWK* authors undertook a woman-centered reformulation of the research of William Perry (1970) and his nine-stage model of intellectual and ethical development, based on interviews with Harvard undergraduates in the 1950s and 1960s. *Women's Ways of Knowing* identifies five stages in women's intellectual development. Concluding that women's thinking does not fit into Perry's categories, Belenky, Clinchy, Goldberger, and Tarule contrast "separate" (male-oriented) and "connected" (female-oriented) ways of knowing. Men, they claim, pursue knowledge through an individual, objective, impersonal, adversarial approach while women feel more comfortable learning in a collective and supportive context where they can empathize with another person's viewpoint and form an intimate attachment to what they are studying.

Separateness, with its emphasis on scientific objectivity, is clearly the accepted mode of learning in academe. The *WWK* authors suggest that this may be at the root of many women's discomfort with traditional educational methods. "We observed," they write, "that women often feel alienated in academic settings and experience formal education as either peripheral or irrelevant to their central interests and development" (1986, p. 4). *Women's Ways of Knowing* sold more than 250,000 copies in its first edition. Although it was hailed by a number of reviewers, including Sara Neustadtl, who likened the authors to "Joans of Arc guided by the sound of women's voices" (1986, p. 26), the book is not without its critics. Mary Crawford (1989) has called attention to the methodological problem of trying to demonstrate the unique attributes of women without comparable data on the male experience. Many feminists are also troubled by a thesis that seems to reinforce the notion that men think rationally while women rely on intuition. An argument that women *do not* think like men can easily be translated into the claim that women *cannot* think like men and therefore should have no place in the public sphere (Crawford & Marecek, 1989).

An issue that constantly crops up in this type of research is whether the identified differences represent essential, universal characteristics or stem from other factors, such as women's socioeconomic position, education, or ethnicity (Pollitt, 1994; Harding, 1986). Based on interviews with women and men of Color from a variety of cultural backgrounds, including African Americans, Native Americans, and Asian Americans, Nancy Goldberger (1996) argues that women's ways of knowing are not an artifact of educated White women.

The concept of a unique women's approach to knowledge remains a controversial issue. Is there a "woman's way of knowing," as Nancy Goldberger argues in the following essay, or are Mary Brabeck and Ann Larned correct in claiming that there is insufficient evidence to support this contention?

REFERENCES

Belenky, M. F., Clinchy, B. M., Goldberger, N. R., & Tarule, J. M. (1986). *Women's ways of knowing: The development of self, voice and mind.* New York: Basic Books.

Crawford, M. (1989). Agreeing to differ: Feminist epistemologies and women's ways of knowing. In M. Crawford & M. Gentry (Eds.), *Gender and thought: Psychological perspectives* (pp. 128–145). New York: Springer-Verlag.

Crawford, M., & Marecek, J. (1989). Psychology reconstructs the female: 1968–1989. *Psychology of Women Quarterly, 13,* 147–165.

Gilligan, C. (1982). *In a different voice: Psychological theory and women's development.* Cambridge, Mass.: Harvard University Press.

Goldberger, N. (1996). Cultural Imperatives and diversity in ways of knowing. In N. Goldberger, J. Tarule, B. Clinchy, & M. Belenky, (Eds.), *Knowledge, difference, and power: Essays inspired by Women's Ways of Knowing.* New York: Basic Books.

Harding, S. (1986). Women's ways of knowing: The development of self, voice and mind. *Women's Review of Books, 4,* p. 6.

Neustadtl, S. (1986, October 5). They hear different voices. *New York Times Book Review,* p. 26.

Perry, W. G. (1970). *Forms of Intellectual and ethical development in the college years.* New York: Holt, Rinehart, & Winston.

Pollitt, K. (1994). *Reasonable creatures: Feminism and society in American culture at the end of the twentieth century.* New York: Alfred A. Knopf.

ADDITIONAL READING

Berger, M. M. (Ed.) (1983). *Women beyond Freud: New concepts of feminine psychology.* New York: Brunner/Mazel.

Bohan, J. S. (1993). Regarding gender: Essentialism, constructionism, and feminist psychology. *Psychology of Women Quarterly, 17* (1), 5–21.

Garber, L. (Ed.) (1994). *Tilting the tower: Lesbians teaching queer subjects.* New York: Routledge.

Gaskell, J., & Willinsky, J. (Eds.) (1995). *Gender informs curriculum: From enrichment to transformation.* New York: Teachers College Press.

Goldberger, N. R., & Veroff, J. B. (Eds.) (1995). *The culture and psychology reader.* New York: New York University Press.

Griffin, G. (Ed.). (1994). *Changing our lives: Doing women's studies.* Boulder, Colo.: Pluto Press.

Gunew, S. (Ed.). (1990). *Feminist knowledge: Critique and construct.* New York: Routledge.

Tong, R. (1989). *Feminist thought: A comprehensive introduction.* Boulder, Colo.: Westview Press.

Ways of Knowing: Does Gender Matter?

NANCY GOLDBERGER

In a large interview-based study on ways of knowing (Belenky, Clinchy, Goldberger, and Tarule, 1986) my colleagues and I asked women the following questions: How do you know what you know? Where does your knowledge come from? To whom or to what do you turn when you want answers? Is there such a thing as "truth" or "right answers"? What makes an expert? We wanted to understand and describe the variety of ways women go about making meaning for themselves in a world that devalues women's authority and voices. Although William Perry in an important earlier study (1970) had explored the way young men think about the nature and acquisition of knowledge and how their thoughts change during their college years, no one had asked, How do women know?

Our initial study was based on a broad sample of 135 rural and urban women of different ages, classes, ethnic backgrounds, and educational histories. It provided an unusual look into the lives of women who, though different from one another in many ways, were subject to common sex stereotypes and sex role socialization processes and presumably shared common experiences by virtue of their gender.

Based on these original interviews, we described in our book *Women's Ways of Knowing* (Belenky, Clinchy, Goldberger, and Tarule, 1986) five knowledge perspectives, or frameworks from which women view themselves and the world, and make meaning of their lives. Since the original study, my colleagues and I have interviewed an even broader demographic sample of women and men so that we could extend our thinking about the roles of gender, class, race, and ethnicity in the development of epistemological perspectives and approaches to learning. Our new work (described in Goldberger, Tarule, Clinchy, and Belenky, 1996), like the original, uncovers themes concerning human psychology and development that have been ignored or are missing in major developmental theories but that are prominent in the stories of women (and men) from several classes and cultures. These stories reveal a great deal about the varieties of ways people think about power, self-other dilemmas, personal authority and voice, and relationships and groups.

SETTING THE CONTEXT: A BRIEF HISTORY

Our research was and continues to be guided by the belief that individuals, not just philosophers, have implicit theories about knowledge and truth that shape the way they see the world, the way they think about themselves, and the way they relate to authority. We believe that personal theories of knowledge and experiences of gender and self, as they shift throughout the life cycle, are culturally embedded. One shapes and is shaped by one's cultural context; meaning-making is both an intrapsychic and extrapsychic phenomenon. We all grow up in families, communities, and cultures that affect the definitional boundaries for "male" and "female," but each of us also constructs narratives of self, gender, family, authority, and truth that evolve as we encounter new ideas and an ever-widening variety of people and outlooks on life. As we point out (Belenky, Clinchy, Goldberger, and Tarule, 1986, 1996; Goldberger, 1996), even family histories are rewritten (that is, they are reinterpreted) as people shift from one knowledge perspective to another.

The process of constantly revising and reinterpreting our own histories—as de Laurentis (1986) and Alcoff (1988) have noted—leads to a shifting "positionality" with respect to our identities as "woman" or "knower." One's definition of *woman* or *knower* changes as one's social position changes in an ever-shifting cultural context. As the feminist Allison Jaggar has put it (1983), we each know the world and speak from a particular standpoint, or "position in society from which certain features of reality come into prominence and from which others are obscured" (p. 382). As we grow and change, and perhaps shift class and social roles, we see the world differently. Thus, as many feminists argue, all knowledge is situated. I agree.

This emphasis on the central role of social context in meaning-making has recently become a major concern for professional training in psychology. Clinical psychologists are now mandated to become culture-sensitive and competent to work with culturally diverse patient populations. This implies that psychology has become more attuned to how psyche and culture construct each other as well as to diversity in ways of knowing (Shweder, 1991; Goldberger and Veroff, 1995). Many American citizens, especially biracial or bicultural individuals, are shaped in part by what may be divergent or even conflicting world views and ways of knowing that arise out of their minority status in the dominant culture.

Most of the women my colleagues and I interviewed were able to tell us about their history as makers of meaning and how they had changed over time. In some cases an individual's primary and current approach to knowing was clearly a manifestation of the approach to knowing valued by her immediate community or cultural reference group. In other cases, individuals were more conscious of the culture-embeddedness of ways of knowing and more interested in exploring alternative epistemologies espoused by cultures and subcultures other than their own. Most women reported transitional periods and changes in positional perspective that led to major shifts in the way they thought about knowledge and truth. Catalysts for such epistemological revolutions, we found, differed from person to person, although some common ones were education, childbearing, family trauma, difficult or challenging relationships, exposure to other cultures, a new kind of work or work environment, and psychotherapy.

Other psychological theorists have pointed out the relevance of one's personal epistemology (ways of knowing) to everyday experience and decision-making. Greeno (1989) has argued that children's beliefs about the origin and nature of knowledge have been understudied until recently but are central to our understanding of the vast and disparate research on cognitive development and approaches to learning. Magolda (1992) has related epistemology to learning styles and cognitive complexity. Others (Perry, 1970; Loevinger, 1976; Kitchener and King, 1981; Kitchener, 1983; Chenin, 1984; Unger, Draper, and Pendergrass, 1986) have demonstrated how shifts in ways of knowing, beginning in adolescence and continuing throughout adulthood, are directly related to self-concept, social perceptions and attributions, orientation to the future, and moral judgments. Culture theorists (Gardner, 1995; Ogbu, 1981; Shweder, 1991) have argued that multiple intelligences and ways of knowing evolve as individuals respond to cultural imperatives and learn the lessons necessary to grow, survive, and become functioning members of the larger culture as well as their subcultures and communities.

WAYS OF KNOWING

In our original work (Belenky, Clinchy, Goldberger, and Tarule, 1986), we described five different epistemological perspectives apparent in the data we gathered from our interviews with women. These five ways of knowing should be considered as frameworks for meaning-making that can evolve over time rather than as enduring traits or personality types. They are not fixed categories but rough schemata that will undoubtedly be elaborated on and even changed as ways of knowing are studied across culture groups, classes, and other sources of human difference. Whether gender matters in the study of ways of knowing and how gender matters, if it does, are questions for future study as we analyze the intersection of culture, power, situation, and historical moment. For now, I shall summarize the five knowledge perspectives as we originally described them.

I. *Silence* is a perspective in which women experience themselves as mindless and subject to powerful external authorities. In a sense, this is not a way of knowing but a way of not knowing. Such women do not dare to know or think of themselves as knowers. Women who have emerged from this kind of silence tell us that their silence has been a way of surviving in what they experienced as a dangerous environment. Although silence is also an issue for women at other epistemological positions, we decided to call this particular subgroup of our interviewees the silent women because the absence of voice was as striking as the fragile and hidden sense of self.

For these women, to know, or to use words to protest the actions of others—that is, to speak out—is to court danger and retaliation. What distinguishes silent women is their isolation, fearfulness, and acceptance of the status quo. Silent women are women living out the most pernicious form of structural genderized oppression and sexual abuse. Their families and communities and schools have usually planted and reinforced their belief that they are not smart and know nothing. Such women tend to drop out of school during or immediately after high school.

II. *Received knowing* is a perspective in which a woman conceives of herself as capable of receiving, even reproducing, knowledge from external authorities but not capable of creating knowledge on her own. Knowledge, she believes, originates outside the self. The received knower tends to discount the importance of her own experience in the process of knowing.

The received knower listens carefully to the voices of authority. She achieves a sense of personal power by identifying with and conforming to the social norms of her primary group. Her self-concept is organized around social roles and expectations. She models herself after the cultural ideals of what a woman should be, ideals transmitted by her church, her family, or her teachers.

The received knower is a vehicle for the transmission of social stereotypes. When she speaks, her voice is one of imitation. What she has learned from her good authorities (however "good" is constructed in her community) she can then transmit and teach to others. She derives both pleasure and security from trusting, listening to, and learning from external authorities. Discussion of changes in beliefs or alternative ways to live can be unwanted or even threatening to the received knower who is secure in her community.

III. *Subjective knowing* is a perspective in which truth is found internally. Knowledge is conceived of as personal, private, and subjective. Thought is not seen as central to the process of knowing. As one woman put it, "I try not to think. If you trust yourself, you just know." Subjective knowers value gut knowledge over what they believe to be illegitimate theorizing by self-appointed authorities; thus, they display little respect for official, certified authority. Other people's opinions do not often change the mind of the subjective knower because she tends to be locked inside her own subjectivity; however, like-minded people may be sought out and used to affirm her opinions.

In our study, many of the women who viewed the world from a subjectivist perspective had come to this way of knowing following a rejection of what they experienced as failed male authority. Their interviews were replete with observations about gender relations, power and disempowerment, anger and distrust. The theme of birth and rebirth was common as these women described how they were revolutionizing their lives, discarding abusive relationships, and disengaging themselves from responsibilities to others. They were busy redefining for themselves what it means to be a woman.

IV. From the *procedural knowing* perspective, the emphasis is on learning and applying objective procedures for obtaining and communicating knowledge—the criteria for which are held by and agreed on by the members of a discipline, guild, or culture group. Authority is external (as it is for received knowers), but it resides with the intellectual elite (not with all authority, as the received knower assumes). In our original sample, procedural knowers—whether adolescents or adults—were primarily students whom we interviewed in either high schools or colleges. Higher education, particularly the kind of education one obtains in the liberal arts colleges and universities that promote critical analytical thinking, can push the received knower into procedural knowing. Thus, authority is external and resides with the academic experts until the student has mastered the "right" way to know, is initiated into the community of scholars, and becomes a knower, presumably with power and influence in the public sector.

With the advent and use of reason come a sense of mastery and personal competence. Many women are delighted to be initiated into the public world of the academy or the workplace, in which they assume they can attain the same degree of recognition, achievement, and power as men. And many do succeed. We have found, however, that a number of highly competent women suffer from a feeling of alienation from their own successes and products. They express a feeling of nonownership of their work. They feel they are still learning by rote and thinking by someone else's recipe. They have lost touch with a sense of "I." A number of the stories we gathered from women suggest that this sense of alienation from the self can eventuate in a crisis of identity and meaning that brings some such women into therapy. Others, who may not seek therapy, precipitously drop out of school or leave the disciplines in which they have been studying, claiming that the academy or the professions are not real life. They set out on a journey in search of the "unknown woman" (Koller, 1983), that is, themselves.

This kind of disaffection and frustration seems to be common among female law students. Although they are admitted to law schools in numbers equal to men, women report feeling silenced and experience a high degree of alienation in law school (Weiss and Melling, 1988). A report of legal education at one law school detailed the female students' distress at the hostile competition and adversarial pedagogy that evidently affect their academic performance (Guinier, Fine, and Balin, 1994). The adversarial pedagogy (grounded in the Socratic method) that these women object to is quite simi-

lar to what we have called separate knowing—a kind of procedural approach to knowing that uses dispassionate detachment, doubt and skepticism, and challenge to others in order to defend one's own position.

In *Women's Ways of Knowing*, we contrast separate knowing with what we call connected knowing, which is based on the premise that in order to understand another person's point of view or ideas, one must enter into the place of the other and adopt the person's terms. Connected knowers are not dispassionate, unbiased observers. They are biased in favor of that which they are trying to understand. They assume a stance of believing rather than doubting. The heart of connected knowing is active imagination, that is, figuratively climbing into the head of another. In connected knowing, objectivity is achieved by entering the perspective of the other and by reasoning along with the other. In our new book (Goldberger, Tarule, Clinchy, and Belenky, 1996) both Blythe Clinchy and Sara Ruddick expand on how connected knowing is an objective strategy for knowing.

Whether women embrace separate or connected procedural knowing, our interviews suggest that many women are conflicted about the suggestion that they need to learn to "think like a man" and learn the "right" way or socially normative way to know.

V. *Constructed knowing* is a position at which women view all knowledge as contextual and relative. Truth, right answers, and even facts must always be evaluated within the contextual frame within which they arise. Women with this perspective recognize that to claim "I know" is to acknowledge the historical, cultural, and subjective position from which the "I" speaks. Constructed knowers experience themselves as creators of knowledge, and they come to value and draw on multiple ways of knowing—objective and subjective, connected and separate—to enlarge their reality and understanding of the world. They believe that different routes to knowing have their place, logic, and usefulness.

Even though constructed knowers acknowledge the tentativeness of knowledge, they struggle toward a "commitment within relativism" (Perry, 1970). It is at this position that a person achieves a critical consciousness (Freire, 1971) and a capacity for reflective judgment that takes into account personal history, social and historical context, and structural inequality. It is from this position that a person makes informed choices and commitments, and conceives of her life and her acts as political.

THE "RIGHT" WAY TO KNOW

The account that my colleagues and I give of women's ways of knowing is our story of how different women struggle to come to terms with covert and overt social pressures to learn the "right" way to know. Some women yield to cultural norms; others do not. The families, schools, and communities in which women grow up affect the educational routes they take and the perspectives on knowing that they develop. Although our work is, in part, about women's experiences of feeling silenced and intellectually devalued, it is also about women's efforts to gain a voice and claim the powers of their own minds. We look at the phenomenon of women's self-doubt and ask how our American culture gives women mixed messages about who has the right to speak, who has authority, and how one best goes about learning and developing.

Social acceptability, manifested as a preoccupation with the correct or right way to know, was an issue in many of our interviews with women. Not all women felt that their approach to knowing was socially acceptable or valid; they experienced themselves as somehow out of the mainstream; many doubted themselves and their minds. Today, both men and women in the Western world are taught to value what is assumed to be the objective, "male" mind and to devalue knowing that is identified as female and is assumed to be, among other things, overly emotional and personalized. Our androcentric culture sends out the message to women that in order to succeed they need to "learn to think like a man."

Assumptions about the best, or most advanced, or most scientific and objective ways of knowing

are not just a modern concern. Questions about the origins and nature of knowledge—and the best way to know—have preoccupied philosophers for centuries. In various historical eras there have emerged different answers, different means for seeking truth, even different ways of asking what are considered to be the important questions about human nature and human knowing (Kuhn, 1970; Sampson, 1978; Gergen, 1985; Watzlawick, 1984; Antony and Witt, 1992; Alcoff and Potter, 1992). In any society there are privileged epistemologies—the socially valued ways of knowing for establishing and evaluating truth claims—that assume normative standing. Such social norms affect and delimit individual ways of knowing. When a person or group subscribes to ways of knowing that fall outside the margins of the normative epistemology of their culture, any analysis of their divergent ways of knowing must necessarily also be an analysis of the power relationships within their community, workplace, or culture (Miller, 1976/1987; Howard, 1987; Collins, 1990). Certain perspectives, ways of knowing, and value frameworks are more apparent in and more emphasized by women than men at this point in the history of Western culture. In a sense, one can say that, in any culture, knowledge is genderized in that women "carry" certain kinds of knowledge (for example, knowledge concerning nutrition or conflict resolution or maintenance of social ties); men carry other sorts of knowledge. Some of the ways of knowing identified in the United States as female or feminine have been highly valued in other historical eras and in other cultures.

Increasing attention has been paid lately to how the value attached to different ways of knowing varies as a function of racial, class, and cultural background. Collins (1990) has explored the politics and history of Afro-American knowledge and thought in her development of what she calls a Black feminist epistemology. She emphasizes the importance of concrete experience, dialogue and narrative, and the ethic of caring and connection in assessing knowledge claims. Wisdom, not knowledge, is given high credence among Afro-Americans because "mother wit" is needed to deal with "educated fools" (p. 208). These same values are echoed in the stories of the women we identified as connected knowers. Luttrell (1989) has analyzed how Black and White working-class women define and claim knowledge. The women she interviewed relied on personal experience and common sense but also included intuition as central to knowing (as did our subjectivists). Belenky, Bond, and Weinstock (in press) are studying ways of knowing and the development of voice in a group of disadvantaged rural mothers for whom silence and received knowledge are prominent. In my own work (Goldberger, 1996) I am focusing on the effects of acculturation on individuals from different ethnic communities, races, and immigrant groups as they are channeled into the American educational system, with its normative standards concerning the right way to know. What is becoming apparent to me, as I listen to stories about the undermining and loss of the indigenous culture's approaches to knowing, is the pain and compromise that accompany such social change. People whom my students and I have interviewed have told anguished stories about familiar ways of meaning-making, endorsed by their community and culture, that they lost when they were exposed to mainstream privileged American thought and interpretive frameworks.

THE METAPHORS OF VOICE AND SILENCE

People who work with, live with, and listen to women know that the metaphors of silence and voice are potent ones. Gaining a voice has come to be equated with personal empowerment. Whether a woman develops a sense of the power of her mind is closely allied to the development of a sense of personal voice and authority. In my recent interviews, I have been paying close attention to how women, people of color, and other members of the so-called subordinate social groups speak about being silent and feeling silenced as they describe their lives and developmental histories. I have found that silence is an issue not just for a subset of women, as we implied in our book, but is a common experience, albeit with a host of both positive

and negative connotations, for almost all people. There is a big difference, however, between self-imposed and externally imposed silences. Feeling silenced and feeling unheard are painful and frustrating experiences, so women tell us, when imposed from without. To be ignored when you speak is the equivalent of being told "You know nothing. You have nothing to say worth hearing."

But it is also clear from the women's interviews that self-silencing sometimes takes place. Silence can be a source of retreat, of safety, or it can be a source of self-renewal. Sometimes, according to her wisdom about the situation and the moment, a woman may choose not to speak. Some women tell about learning how to temper their voices so that when they do speak, they have a better chance of being heard.

In *Women's Ways of Knowing*, we described in some detail the distinctive family patterns and "politics of family talk" common to each epistemological perspective. From early ages on, children learn rules of speaking and listening. These rules (and the associated assumptions about where truth lies) are carried into adulthood and greatly affect the way an individual constructs authority and expertise. One-way talk, inequality in parental communications, and disallowed questioning all contribute to the silencing of children's sense of mind and voice. Mutuality in communication, listening and dialogue, and respect even for half-formed ideas all contribute to a growing sense of personal authority and voice. It is these lessons, learned first in families and then in schools and later in the workplace, that greatly affect developing self-confidence and feelings of intellectual worth. Too often, in American families, girls and women are socialized to be seen, not heard.

FEMINIST CONTROVERSY ON THE PSYCHOLOGY OF DIFFERENCE

Since *Women's Ways of Knowing* was published in 1986, considerable academic debate has taken place among feminist theorists concerning our work and the political implications of an emphasis on gender sameness versus difference. Our work is now considered part of a larger body of theory—which I shall call different voice theory—that identifies, typically through interviews with women, some of the issues, themes, and perspectives in human development and thought that have been submerged or ignored (and often devalued) by the normative masculinist culture. Among the work classified as part of different voice theory, in addition to our work on ways of knowing, is the work of Jean Baker Miller and the Stone Center on self-in-relation (Miller, 1976/1987; Jordan, Kaplan, Miller, Stiver, and Surrey, 1991), the work of Carol Gilligan and her colleagues on the ethic of care (Gilligan, 1982; Gilligan, Ward, and Taylor, 1988; Gilligan, Lyons, and Hanmer, 1990; Brown and Gilligan, 1992), and the analysis by philosopher Sara Ruddick of what she calls "maternal thinking" (1980, 1989), which grows out of maternal practice.

It is through the efforts of different voice theorists that attention has turned to what is positive about the characteristics of knowing and thinking that have long been associated with the feminine. Within the spectrum of various feminist positions, different voice theory has been categorized by Offen (1988) and Noddings (1990) as "relational feminism" because it highlights the role of care and connection in women's lives. It has also been categorized by Hare-Mustin and Marecek (1990) and others as theory with an "alpha bias," that is, the inclination to emphasize male-female differences, as opposed to "beta-bias" theory, which minimizes difference. Considerable controversy has emerged over whether relational feminism and different voice theory are essentialist (that is, implicitly arguing for natural or enduring differences between the sexes). By focusing on women as a group, some critics argue, relational feminists and different voice theorists only fuel old stereotypes of women. They warn that any focus on gender differences or women's distinctive attributes or perspectives, even those that grow out of differences in cultural experience, can be appropriated by political adversaries (who hold to the "difference is deficit" position), turned against women, and used to endorse male privilege. But as the feminist historian Karen Offen has pointed out (1988), if we reject relational feminism because it can be misappropriated, then we must reject individualist and beta-bias feminism on the same grounds. Ignoring differences and the sociopolitical context as well as the relational aspects of most women's lives can lead to the alienation of ordinary women from mainstream feminism. Many women have gained a sense of power (even if illusory), a voice, control, and an enhancement of self-esteem through the valuing of "women's ways." Even more important, in these days of backlash against feminism and multiculturalism (two movements that have emphasized the importance of listening to different voices and analyzing the social construction of "otherness"), it seems politically unstrategic to minimize difference and implicitly ally oneself with the forces from the right who would have us return to a White-only, middle-class, masculinist culture. As young female law students have passionately argued (Weiss and Melling, 1988), to minimize differences and to "focus on sameness limits criticism and change; it means accepting the world as constructed by men, challenging only women's exclusion from it, and acceding to our forced integration into the dominant culture" (p. 1301). Furthermore, by casting the feminist theoretical dilemma as a matter of choice between two poles (sameness versus difference), such feminists as Spelman (1988), Mednick (1989), Hare-Mustin and Marecek (1990), and Bohan (1993), who bring essentialism charges against other feminist theorists, risk fueling the polarization and controversy already apparent in feminist circles (Hirsch and Keller, 1990; Martin, 1992).

DOES GENDER MATTER?

It is true that some of the women my colleagues and I interviewed hold essentialist positions and believe in the natural separation of the sexes. As theorists, however, we do not argue that essential, universal, highly dichotomized, and enduring differences exist between men and women. We maintain that gender is both culturally and psychologically constructed. In an ideal world, gender would not matter, but in this world, gender does matter—and it will continue to matter as long as social power and influence are inequitably distributed, and as long as certain attitudes and values and ways of knowing are considered to be feminine and therefore lesser.

At this point in my own intellectual development, I value a critical analysis of differences that arise out of such social categories as gender, race, class, or ethnicity because of the historical power of such categories, even though I recognize that an overemphasis on the explanatory power of these social categories can mask important situational and individual differences within social categories. I argue that we must focus on difference and listen carefully to the stories of marginalized people so that we can better understand the logic of individual courses of action in different social contexts. Life stories can teach us how some people's lives simply do not conform to theoretical prescriptions and normative standards. By listening to different voices—voices from the margin—and exploring difference, we can challenge authority and old assumptions and paradigms. It is by understanding the epistemological biases behind different strategies of empowerment that we can evaluate and choose the most effective ways to act in and on the world—an evaluation that is as important to educational and clinical intervention as it is to political and social action. In learning to live with diversity in a pluralistic world, all of us must learn how to make a connection with difference.

Our task, if we are to live successfully as citizens in a world where differences matter, is to find and strengthen our voices, to learn to hear the voices of others, and to develop the art of really talking with other people who are separated from us by gender or race or class or culture or partisan politics.

REFERENCES

Alcoff, L. (1988). Cultural feminism versus post-structuralism: The identity crisis in feminist theory. *Signs: Journal of Women in Culture and Society*, 13 (3), 405–436.

Alcoff, L., and Potter, E. (Eds.) (1992). *Feminist epistemologies*. New York: Routledge.

Antony, L., and Witt, C. (Eds.) (1992). *A mind of one's own*. Boulder: Westview Press.

Belenky, M., Bond, L., and Weinstock, J. (in press). *A tradition with no name: Public homeplaces and the development of women, families, and communities*. New York: Basic Books.

Belenky, M., Clinchy, B., Goldberger, N., and Tarule, J. (1986). *Women's ways of knowing: The development of self, voice, and mind*. New York: Basic Books.

Belenky, M., Clinchy, B., Goldberger, N., and Tarule, J. (1996). *Women's ways of knowing: The development of self, voice, and mind*. (2nd ed.) New York: Basic Books.

Bohan, J. S. (1993). Regarding gender: Essentialism, constructionism, and feminist psychology. *Psychology of Women Quarterly*, 17 (1), 5–22.

Brown, L. M., and Gilligan, C. (1992). *Meeting at the crossroads: Women's psychology and girl's development*. Cambridge, Mass.: Harvard University Press.

Chinen, A. B. (1984). Modal logic: A new paradigm of development and late-life potential. *Human Development*, 27, 42–56.

Clinchy, B. (1989). The development of thoughtfulness in college women: Integrating reason and care. *American Behavioral Scientist*, 32, 647–657.

Collins, P. H. (1989). The social construction of black feminist thought. *Signs: Journal of Women in Culture and Society*, 14 (4), 745–773.

Collins, P. H. (1990). *Black feminist thought: Knowledge, consciousness, and the politics of empowerment*. Boston: Unwin Hyman.

de Laurentis, T. (1986). Feminist studies/critical studies: Issues, terms and context. In T. de Laurentis (Ed.), *Feminist studies/critical studies*. Bloomington: Indiana University Press (1–19).

Freire, P. (1971). *The pedagogy of the oppressed*. New York: Seaview.

Gardner, H. (1995). The development of competence in culturally defined domains. In N. Goldberger and J. Veroff (Eds.), *The culture and psychology reader*. New York: New York University Press.

Gergen, K. J. (1985). The social constructionist movement in modern psychology. *American Psychologist*, 40, 255–265.

Gilligan, C. (1982). *In a different voice: Psychological theory and women's development*. Cambridge, Mass.: Harvard University Press.

Gilligan, C., Lyons, N., and Hanmer, T. (Eds.) (1990). *Making connections: The relational worlds of adolescent girls at Emma Willard School*. Cambridge, Mass.: Harvard University Press.

Gilligan, C., Ward, J. W., and Taylor, J. McL. (Eds.) (1988). *Mapping the moral domain: A contribution of women's thinking to psychological theory and education*. Center for the Study of Gender, Education, and Human Development. Distributed by Harvard University Press.

Goldberger, N. (1996). Cultural imperatives and diversity in Ways of Knowing. In N. Goldberger, J. Tarule, B. Clinchy, and M. Belenky (Eds.), *Knowledge, difference, and power: Essays inspired by Women's Ways of Knowing*. New York: Basic Books.

Goldberger, N., Tarule, J., Clinchy, B., and Belenky, M.

(Eds.) (1996). *Knowledge, difference, and power: Essays inspired by Women's Ways of Knowing*. New York: Basic Books.

Goldberger, N., and Veroff, J. (Eds.) (1995). *The culture and psychology reader*. New York: New York University Press.

Greeno, J. G. (1989). A perspective on thinking. Special Issue: Children and their development. *American Psychologist*, 44 (2), 134–141.

Guinier, L., Fine, M., and Balin, J. (1994). Becoming gentlemen: Women's experiences at one Ivy-League law school. *University of Pennsylvania Law Review*, 143 (1) 1–110.

Harding, S. (1986). *The science question in feminism*. Ithaca: Cornell University Press.

Hare-Mustin, R. T., and Marecek, J. (Eds.) (1990). *Making a difference: Psychology and the construction of gender*. New Haven: Yale University Press.

Hirsch, M., and Keller, E. F. (Eds.) (1990). *Conflicts in feminism*. New York: Routledge.

Howard, J. A. (1987). Dilemmas in feminist theorizing: Politics and the academy. *Current Perspectives in Social Theory*, 8, 279–312.

Jaggar, A. (1983). *Feminist politics and human nature*. Totowa, N.J.: Rowan and Allanheld.

Jordan, J. V., Kaplan, A. G., Miller, J. B., Stiver, I. P., and Surrey, J. L. (1991). *Women's growth in connection: Writings from the Stone Center*. New York: Guilford Press.

Kitchener, K. (1983). Cognition, metacognition, and epistemic cognition. *Human Development*, 26, 222–232.

Kitchener, K., and King, P. M. (1981). Reflective judgment: concepts of justification and their relationship to age and education. *Journal of Applied Developmental Psychology*, 2, 89–116.

Koller, A. (1983). *An unknown woman*. New York: Bantam.

Kuhn, T. S. (1970). *The structure of scientific revolutions*. 2nd ed. Chicago: University of Chicago Press.

Loevinger, J. (1976). *Ego development*. San Francisco: Jossey-Bass.

Luttrell, W. (1989). Working-class women's ways of knowing: Effects of gender, race, and class. *Sociology of Education*, 62 (January), 33–46.

Magolda, M. B. (1992). *Knowing and reasoning in college: Gender related patterns in students' intellectual development*. San Francisco: Jossey Bass.

Martin, J. R. (1992). Methodological essentialism, false difference, and other dangerous traps. *Signs: Journal of Women and Society*, 19 (3), 630–657.

Mednick, M. T. (1989). On the politics of psychological constructs: Stop the bandwagon, I want to get off. *American Psychologist*, 44, 1118–1123.

Miller, J. B. (1976/1987). *Toward a new psychology of women*. Boston: Beacon Press.

Noddings, N. (1990). Feminist critiques in the professions. *AERA Annual Review of Research*, 16, 393–424.

Offen, K. (1988). Defining feminism: A comparative historical approach. *Signs: Journal of Women in Culture and Society*, 14 (1), 119–157.

Ogbu, J. U. (1995). Origins of human competence: A cultural-ecological perspective. In Goldberger, N., and J. Veroff (Eds.), *The culture and psychology reader*. New York: New York University Press.

Perry, W. G. (1970). *Forms of intellectual and ethical development in the college years*. New York: Holt, Rinehart, and Winston.

Ruddick, S. (1980). Maternal thinking. *Feminist Studies*, 6, 70–96.

Ruddick, S. (1989). *Maternal thinking: Toward a politics of peace*. Boston: Beacon Press.

Sampson, E. E. (1978). Scientific paradigm and social value: Wanted—a scientific revolution. *Journal of Personality and Social Psychology*, 36, 1332–1343.

Shweder, R. (1991). *Thinking through cultures: Expeditions in cultural psychology*. Cambridge, Mass.: Harvard University Press.

Spelman, E. (1988). *Inessential woman*. Boston: Beacon Press.

Unger, R., Draper, R. D., and Pendergrass, M. L. (1986). Personal epistemology and personal experience. *Journal of Social Issues*, 42, 67–79.

Watzlawick, P. (Ed.) (1984). *The invented reality: How do we know what we believe we know*. New York: Norton.

Weiss, C., and Melling, L. (1988). The legal education of twenty women. *Stanford Law Review*, 40 (5), 1299–1369.

NO

What We Do Not Know about Women's Ways of Knowing

MARY M. BRABECK AND

ANN G. LARNED

There is much in Nancy Goldberger's essay with which we agree. We agree that epistemologies—ways of knowing and making meaning—result from experience as well as maturation. We agree that epistemologies change over time and with socialization, and are related to other developmental constructs such as identity, conceptions of self, and morality. We also agree that for many women socialization into cultural norms is problematic; frequently because of socialization women do not develop to their full potential. We agree that knowledge and ways of knowing are valued differently in different historical times and cultures, and we agree that across times and cultures that which is identified as female is devalued.

We disagree, however, that there is a "women's way of knowing." More specifically, we disagree that sufficient evidence exists to support the contention that there is a form of epistemological development that is distinctly associated with women to a greater degree than with men. Furthermore, we disagree that it is "politically unstrategic to minimize difference," at least insofar as claims of difference are made about epistemic and cognitive development. Gender differences ought to be minimized, we argue, if the difference between men's and women's ways of knowing is not empirically demonstrated. Empirically unsupported assertions of gender differences reinforce gender stereotypes

because they erroneously emphasize gender over ethnicity, race, socioeconomic state, educational experience, or other equally compelling explanations for the sources of diversity in the ways people think and make meaning.

DEFINITIONS OF THE CONSTRUCT OF WOMEN'S WAYS OF KNOWING

Part of the problem in examining the empirical evidence for claims regarding women's ways of knowing is that this construct is difficult to define. In her essay, Goldberger defines the construct as "the variety of ways women go about making meaning for themselves" and women's "implicit theories about knowledge and truth." Goldberger says that she and her colleagues assessed women's ways of telling "about their history as makers of meaning and how they had changed over time," indicating that metacognition, or the ability to think about one's thinking, is involved. These issues belong in the domain of epistemological development and are similar to the questions asked by Perry (1970) and Kitchener and King (1981) from whom the Belenky team (1986) drew many of their interview questions. Meaning making is appropriately assessed through questions about what one knows, the nature of truth, and the roles of authority, evidence, and experts in knowledge and knowledge claims.

Goldberger, however, also defines women's ways of knowing as "frameworks from which women view themselves and the world" and as the "ways people think about power, self-other dilemmas, personal authority and voice, and relationships and groups." This definition suggests that the construct involves issues of identity and the ability to analyze the association of gender with power and equity. Goldberger describes women's ways of knowing as strength of conviction, self-assurance, or commitment to what one knows: "Whether a woman develops a sense of the power of her mind is closely allied to the development of a sense of personal voice and authority." Goldberger further defines women's ways of knowing as "the process of constantly revising and reinterpreting our own histories . . . a shifting 'positionality' with respect to our identities as 'woman' or 'knower.' " This suggests that the construct involves gender identity, gender role socialization, and self-awareness of these roles. Finally, women's ways of knowing are described as the content of knowledge resulting from gender socialization: "Women 'carry' certain kinds of knowledge (for example, knowledge concerning nutrition or conflict resolution or maintenance of social ties); men carry other sorts of knowledge."

It is beyond the scope of this essay to assess the various domains that are encompassed in the diverse definitions of the construct. A thorough examination of the empirical validity of the claim that women and men differ in ways of knowing would entail examination of gender differences in identity, self-concept, self-awareness, gender role identity, gender role socialization, reflection on gender and power, and knowledge content. Other issues that Goldberger's essay raises will not be addressed here: Is the model developmental? What is developing? What is the mechanism for development (change or growth)? What is the philosophical foundation for the claims regarding connected knowing? These questions are important to a full discussion of the theory. We shall restrict our discussion here, however, to the issue of gender differences in ways of knowing or in epistemological development.

We use the phrase *epistemological development* to refer to the development of knowledge, beliefs, and ways of knowing. We include in this definition both the Enlightenment notion of rationalism and the postmodern and feminist critiques of dualisms and absolutes (Alcoff & Potter, 1993). That is, like Goldberger, we reject the masculinist bias toward rationality as the *only* source of knowledge. But we take the position that while there are many sources of knowledge, no way of knowing is privileged along gender lines. Research examining how we come to know what we know and how experience and maturation affect our ways of knowing extends back to Piaget (1972). The Women's Ways of Knowing (WWK) theory joins at least 11 recently articulated theoretical models of adolescent and adult cognitive development (Brabeck, 1984). We shall discuss the WWK model within that larger body of literature. Belenky et al.'s (1986) insights from the original interviews were arrived at through qualitative methods. Our discussion addresses the existing empirical evidence, mostly resulting from quantitative studies, regarding the claim that women's ways of knowing are uniquely associated with women.

EMPIRICAL STUDIES OF WOMEN'S WAYS OF KNOWING AS "DIFFERENT VOICE" THEORY

The original study on which the WWK model was based included interviews with 135 women but no men (Belenky et al., 1986). Content analysis of the interviews revealed five ways of knowing, described in Goldberger's essay. In the absence of comparison groups, it is difficult to know whether the observations regarding ways of knowing can be attributed to gender (as the authors claim) or to some other factor. Goldberger, for example, notes for "silent women" that "their silence has been a way of surviving in what they experienced as a dangerous environment." Perhaps the response of silence that researchers found is a defensive reaction to the effects of abuse. To examine this question would require that one assess men and women who have experienced different levels or types of abuse.

Goldberger links her theory to relational theories, or "different voice" theories, such as those of Gilligan (Gilligan, 1982; Gilligan & Belenky, 1980; Gilligan, Ward, & Taylor, 1988) and the Stone Center (Jordan et al., 1991). She cites their work as supporting the WWK theory. These standpoint theories claim that men and women differ in conceptions of self, relationships, and moral orientation. The evidential argument is circular; relational theorists point to each other to substantiate their contention that women and men have different voices, ways of knowing, and ways of connecting or being in relationship. Goldberger's evidence is Gilligan, Gilligan's evidence is Miller, and Miller and colleagues (Jordan et al., 1991) say that they are developing theory and have clinical observations, not empirical data. Ironically, different voice theorists speak in one voice.

The most extensively researched different voice theory is Carol Gilligan's. But the evidence to support her assertions of gender differences is either lacking or refutes the claim. Walker's (1986) meta-analysis to test the hypothesis that males were more advanced in moral reasoning than females, as measured by the Kohlbergian interview, was not significant. The effect size (Cohen's d) was $+.046$, indicating that gender accounts for only one-twentieth of one percent of the variance in moral reasoning scores ($r^2=0.0005$). These results corroborated Walker's (1984) earlier meta-analysis that showed no consistent differences in males' and females' moral reasoning scores. Of the 152 samples, 85.5% (130 samples) reported nonsignificant gender differences. Females had higher scores in 5.9% (9 samples), and males were higher in 8.6% (13 samples). The few differences favoring females tended to occur in homogeneous samples of school and university students; those favoring males were in more heterogeneous samples in which the sexes differed in education and occupation. Thus, education rather than gender appears to be important in accounting for individual differences in moral reasoning.

In a similar investigation into gender differences in moral reasoning, Thoma (1986) conducted a meta-analysis on 56 samples of more than six thousand participants who responded to the Defining Issues Test, Rest's (1979) objective test of comprehension and preference of moral issues. Thoma reported that at every age and educational level, females scored significantly higher than males, but less than one-half of one percent of the variance could be attributed to gender. Further, he found that education was 250 times more powerful in predicting moral judgment level than gender. A meta-analysis (Bebeau & Brabeck, 1989) of the Defining Issues Test scores of seven groups of dental students (593 men and 184 women) indicated a mean of 47.20 for males and a mean of 47.60 for females, with an effect size of $d=.03$, indicating a high degree of similarity between male and female

dental students. Results of these meta-analytic studies are supported by the longitudinal work of Colby and colleagues (1983), who have shown that females are as likely as males to advance in the sequential order of development predicted by Kohlberg's theory. Furthermore, research examining gender differences in Gilligan's (1982) care orientation indicates that the type of dilemma that is discussed (that is, a moral dilemma involving a personal issue or relationship, versus a dilemma over conflicting claims about individual rights) is a better predictor of moral orientation than gender (Walker, 1985). Thus, the different voice theory domain has not withstood the test of empirical scrutiny in the domain of moral development. Nevertheless, the myth of gender differences in moral voice continues (Hurd & Brabeck, in press).

Like Gilligan's popular different moral voice theory, the WWK model is one of the most referenced developmental models in the literature. A review of the *Social Science Citation Index* from 1987 to 1994 revealed more than 450 citations across at least ten academic fields. A random sampling of the articles that cited the Belenky et al. (1986) work referred to WWK as an empirically demonstrated difference between men and women. Nevertheless, a thorough search of the literature revealed only seven empirical articles that examined gender differences in ways of knowing. Of these, three employed only samples of women and four included both men and women. This paucity of independent empirical work is surprising given the attention the decade-old theory has received, including calls for empirical inquiry into the theoretical claims (Brabeck, 1993; Crawford & Marecek, 1989). Goldberger refers to neither the studies that examine the theory nor the articles that have suggested that the assertions are overdrawn given the available evidence (Brabeck, 1994). The empirical tests of the claim that there is a gender difference in the five women's ways of knowing perspectives will be reviewed next.

Of the three empirical studies that examined samples of women only, each used a different measure of ways of knowing. Buczynski (1993) developed a paper-and-pencil measure by testing 348 predominantly white young women between the ages of 18 and 25. Her 48-item questionnaire, the WOKI (Ways of Knowing Instrument), was patterned after Belenky et al.'s (1986) five perspectives of knowing. But several of the items listed in Buczynski's questionnaire do not seem directly related to a way of acquiring knowledge or epistemology. For example, an item coded as "silent knower" was, "When we have a discussion in class on a certain topic I usually do not participate in the discussion." This may represent either fear of isolation or an individual's response style. Another item was, "Sometimes I feel like I am on a speeding freight train [in] that I have no control over the events in my life." This and the two other items that made up the "subjective knowledge" scale seem to represent personality identity rather than epistemology. We found no other studies that used this questionnaire, and without a sample of men, or any instrument validation information, we cannot know whether the WOKI assesses perspectives that represent a distinct women's way of knowing.

In her class of undergraduate women, Ortman (1993) explored the WWK claim that education for women should be different from that for men. She organized the class around theoretical ideas about education for women and used a self-report essay at the end of the term, which asked women to assess their own Belenky et al. (1986) knowing perspective. Eighty-two percent of her students reported that they were procedural knowers, and most reported they were connected rather than separate knowers. In this study most students identified a progression from one way of knowing to the next, with seniors reporting themselves at a more developed (constructed) way of knowing. We cannot determine from this study whether students accurately classified their way of knowing. This is particularly problematic because Belenky et al. (1986) and Goldberger present the connected perspective in a more favorable light for women than the separate perspective. Perhaps Ortman's instruction reflected that bias.

Finally, Bredemeier and colleagues (1991) interviewed 47 women college athletes using procedures outlined in the Belenky et al. (1986) book. This qualitative study reported no silent knowers, few

who evidenced received ways of knowing, and few constructive knowers. Most women scored at either separate procedural or connected procedural levels. Although this study suggests that there is diversity in ways of knowing among women, it does not shed light on claims of gender differences because a male comparison group was not measured.

We identified four studies that compared males and females. In each of these studies, the "way of knowing" construct was defined and measured differently. Two of the studies measured women's ways of knowing using concepts of separate and connected knowing (Clinchy, 1989; Lang-Takac & Osterweil, 1992). A related study examined gender differences in connected and separate moral reasoning (Wingfield & Haste, 1987). A fourth study assessed the five WWK perspectives of knowing and examined how these perspectives were related to relativistic thought among men and women (Orr & Luszcz, 1994).

Lang-Takac and Osterweil (1992) used four self-report scales to assess the degree of separate or connected knowing in 30 Israeli males and 30 Israeli females with similar ethnic backgrounds, education, and stages of life. They defined separateness as "emotional self-other differentiation and independence" (p. 279) and "in terms of empathy and intimacy" (p. 280). Their results did reveal differences between men and women in separate and connected knowing, although they found only weak correlations between the constructs. Because separate and connected knowing are different orientations of procedural knowledge, one would expect a relation between these perspectives. But no evidence shows how well these items measure separateness and connectedness, as Belenky et al. (1986) define them.

Clinchy (1989), one of the original architects of the WWK theory, asked male and female students to respond to comments that reflect either "argumentative" or "connected" conversation. Here separate knowing was called "the doubting, argumentative, adversarial mode of discourse" (p. 649). Connected knowers play the "believing game" by "deliberately bias[ing] themselves in favor of the thing they are examining" (p. 651). Clinchy found that men's and women's conversation modes differed, with men preferring argument as a style of conversation and women preferring connected conversation. But the definitions of separate and connected knowing in Clinchy's study vary markedly from the constructs of separateness and connectedness used in the Goldberger article.

A third study did not directly test the WWK theory but examined a related construct. Wingfield and Haste (1987) asked nine adolescent boys and nine adolescent girls about friendship, loyalty, and understanding of the political and social order. These interviews were scored for connected and separate *moral* reasoning. Although males and females evidenced both separate and connected knowing, a chi-square analysis indicated that males were significantly more likely to be scored as using a separate orientation and females were more likely to be scored as using a connected orientation. Wingfield and Haste suggested that connected and separate knowing affected moral reasoning and claimed that their results support Gilligan's theory. Their study, however, was not designed to assess whether there was a woman's way of knowing.

Finally, Orr and Luszcz (1994) examined whether the constructed way of knowing (Belenky et al.'s fifth perspective) could be predicted by the use of relativistic operations (Sinnott, 1981). They assessed 30 female and 30 male university students at an Australian university by presenting the students with two everyday problems (a modified form of the WWK interview). They reported that "the ways of knowing described by Belenky et al. (1986) are not unique to women" (p. 230). Neither age nor education was related to ways of knowing, suggesting that the perspectives do not follow a developmental sequence. Gender differences were found for subjective (more frequent among women) and procedural (more frequent among men) knowing. But there were no gender differences in either connected-procedural or separate-procedural knowing, nor were there differences in received or constructed knowing. The authors conclude that gender explanations for the different knowing perspectives should be rejected in favor of more plausible explanations such as educational

level, occupational background, age, or experience (Orr & Luszcz, 1994).

Our literature review indicates that the studies that have tested the WWK claims are sparse and that explanations for variability in responses to the WWK interview questions are better attributable to factors other than gender. In the few cases in which gender differences as predicted by the WWK theory were found, differences in men's and women's education, occupation, social status, or age offer equally plausible explanations for the results. Are there gender differences in women's ways of knowing as defined by other theories of intellectual development? We turn to that question next.

OTHER THEORIES OF ADULT INTELLECTUAL DEVELOPMENT AND TESTS OF GENDER DIFFERENCES

Since the 1970s at least 11 theories of adolescent and adult cognitive development beyond Piaget's stage of formal operations have been developed (see Brabeck, 1984; Brabeck & Wood, 1990; King & Kitchener, 1994). These theories all claim that the passage from adolescence to adulthood is marked by changes in ways of thinking about thinking; the capacity to engage in more abstract reasoning; a more complex understanding of the role of authorities and evidence in knowledge; a shift from absolute, dualistic thinking to contextualized knowledge; and increased ability to reflect on knowledge claims. Although most researchers have used both males and females in their studies, none of these theories have hypothesized or reported consistent gender differences in adult cognitive development.

Nancy Goldberger maintains that until the Belenky et al. (1986) book, "no one had asked, How do women know?" She makes this assertion in part because William Perry's (1970) model of college students' intellectual and ethical development was originally developed through interviews with Harvard students at a time when Harvard did not admit women. Gilligan (1982) based her charge of sexism in Kohlberg's research on a similar observation. Since the 1970s, however, researchers and theorists have developed models of adult intellectual development based on interviews with both men and women. Arlin's (1975) model of problem finding, Sinnott's (1981) relativistic operations, Moshman and Timmons' (1982) stages in construction of logical necessity, Labouvie-Vief's (1982) modes of mature autonomy, Fischer's (1980) cognitive skills theory, Riegel's (1979) dialectical operations, Basseches' (1980) dialectical schemata, Broughton's (1978) levels of self, mind, reality, and knowledge, and Kitchener and King's (1981) reflective judgment theory were not developed with only male students in mind.

Two theories of adult intellectual development warrant special attention: William Perry's theory of intellectual and ethical development (1970) and Patricia King and Karen Kitchener's theory of reflective judgment (1994). Both these theories are closely tied to the WWK theory in that these theories were based on interview questions later used by Belenky et al. (1986), and researchers have empirically tested the question of gender differences in both theories.

Although early work on Perry's theory (for example, Widick & Simpson, 1978) did not examine gender differences, a few later studies have examined gender and epistemological development as measured by the Perry model. A study conducted by Durham, Hays, and Martinez (1994) found no significant gender differences in students' sociocognitive development in a sample of 20 females and 6 males of predominantly Chicano origin, matched with a stratified random sample of Anglo-American students.

A longitudinal study (Baxter Magolda, 1990, 1992, 1995) examined gender differences in Perry's levels of intellectual development, and the extent to which co-curricular activities (that is, out-of-class experiences) contributed to students' intellectual development. Baxter Magolda used the Measure of Epistemological Reflection (MER) interview (Baxter Magolda & Porterfield, 1985) and a one-hour interview to assess Perry's first five positions and Belenky et al.'s five perspectives. She tested 50 men and 51 women in their first year of college and followed 80 through each of the four years of school-

ing. Her participants in postcollege testing remained relatively gender balanced, and 27 women and 21 men were tested in the seventh year of the study (Baxter Magolda, 1995). During their first year males and females came to view knowledge as more uncertain, and no gender differences were detected in reasoning or preferences in either peer interactive or independent activities (Baxter Magolda, 1990). Overall, regardless of gender, co-curricular activities greatly contributed to a student's intellectual development. During the sophomore and junior years, differences between males' and females' cognitive development were negligible. Although both males and females used "relational" knowing (similar to Belenky et al.'s connected knowing) and "impersonal" knowing (similar to Perry's levels), the college women used the relational pattern of knowing slightly more often than the college men. In their postcollege years, these gender-related patterns disappeared, and the young adults Baxter Magolda interviewed (1995) showed an integration of relational and impersonal knowing. The results of Baxter Magolda's studies illustrate that educational level and social experience contribute to an individual's intellectual development, that both relational and impersonal patterns of knowing are identifiable in qualitative studies involving (primarily White) college students, and that males and females are equally capable of using both patterns of knowing.

Noting that Perry had confounded two domains, epistemology and identity, Kitchener and King (1981) developed a model to assess epistemic development or reflective judgment. Reflective judgment involves reasoning about "the kinds of problematic situations that are truly controversial" (p. 7). Reflective judgment research assesses the rational ability to state and defend one's beliefs, "based on the evaluation and integration of existing data and theory into a solution about the problem at hand, a solution that can be rationally defended as most plausible or reasonable, taking into account the sets of conditions under which the problem is being solved" (p. 8). King and Kitchener (1994) provided a summary of 32 studies (with more than 1700 participants) that tested the claims of the theory. Of 17 studies that included males and females, 3 did not examine gender differences, 7 found no differences between males and females, 6 found males higher in reflective judgment scores, and 1 reported a class-by-gender interaction, with traditional-age women third-year students and nontraditional-age first-year students (but not traditional-age first-year students) scoring higher than their male counterparts. In addition they reported Wood's (1985) analysis of the Kitchener and King longitudinal data, which found gender differences in physical growth spurts suggesting differences in timing of developmental changes. Given the confounding factors of differential opportunities, maturation rates, and timing of development, King and Kitchener (1994) reasoned that a conclusion about gender differences in reflective judgment "remains to be seen" (p. 177). We agree. The evidence from the theories of intellectual development under investigation for more than two and a half decades does not support the hypothesis that women engage in a different way of knowing than do men.

Should One Study Gender Differences?

Ultimately it is the assertion of difference between males and females, regardless of the specific construct under investigation, that Goldberger defends. Claims of difference, she argues, in and of themselves are valuable: by "exploring difference, we can challenge authority and old assumptions and paradigms." It is, we think, because Goldberger values diversity that she champions the cause of listening to the marginalized. Because she values questioning the established paradigms (such as Perry's claims about intellectual development), she raises questions about their universal applicability. We agree that understanding individuals within specific sociopolitical realities is better than acting on stereotypes, and that prevailing truth ought to be subjected to scrutiny in light of new evidence and insight. We agree that an analysis of power and politics is essential to an adequate understanding of individuals in context. We also agree

that women have less access to power and privilege than men in the United States, although the differences are far less than in other countries. But, what does knowing about gender add to the information about an individual if one is looking at epistemological development? Do men and women use different thought strategies or rational methods? Are there gender differences in ways of knowing? Goldberger says "yes" but provides no strong evidence to support that answer. We say "no." Our stand does not reflect a belief that the study of gender differences is useless or politically dangerous to women. Rather, we believe that to focus on gender dualisms without relying on empirical evidence ignores diversity and often reinforces gender stereotypes. We therefore raise concerns about *how* one studies gender differences.

The study of gender differences raises three related but different questions. The first question is empirical: Is there a difference between men and women's ways of knowing? Only if the first question is affirmative, must one address the second: What is the basis, the source, or the factors responsible for the observed difference? Finally when one understands the origin of the observed difference, one can and must address the "so what?" question: What are the educational, occupational, and social implications of an observed difference? This essay focuses on the first question.

Nancy Goldberger skips over the first question and addresses the second and third. Without demonstrating a difference in men's and women's ways of knowing, she argues from a theory of origins: *because* women are more devalued, more likely to experience abuse, more oppressed, and more likely to be ignored than are men, women *must* think, know, and understand the world differently. On the basis of this reasoning, a number of educators (such as Ortman, 1993) have begun to describe different learning environments for girls and women. We suggest that before we rush to create separate learning experiences to promote "women's ways," we first clarify the construct (epistemic development? relational focus? identity issue? emotional responsiveness? empathy? defensive response to abuse?). We must then ask the three questions relevant to claims of gender differences. First, do gender differences exist? While qualitative methods can generate new insights and new theory, quantitative methods are more appropriate for testing generalizability from a sample to a population. Such an inquiry must consider girls and women, boys and men, in our diverse ethnicities; educational, social, economic backgrounds; physical, mental, and emotional challenges; sexual orientations; and ages. Second, *if* we find gender differences, we must investigate the origin of these differences (abuse? prejudice? devaluing? inappropriate learning environments?), and third, we must work to develop appropriate social and educational experiences (challenges and supports) to enhance the development of girls and boys, women and men. Ignoring any of these steps may lead to undesirable results.

Lisa Delpit (1995) described the educational practices popularized by well-meaning teachers who based their teaching on studies conducted on middle-class White children by well-meaning academics. These practices developed for White middle-class children, Delpit argues, were educational disasters for many children of Color. Generalization from small homogeneous samples is risky business. When uncritically applied in the classroom, these generalizations can be devastating for many students. WWK theory has not been researched enough to be a foundation for educational interventions. No one would approve a medical intervention based on the evidence available regarding women's ways of knowing. Yet given that WWK was cited in 188 of the 454 educational articles we surveyed—that is, 41%—we fear that such prescriptions are being made. Belenky et al. (1986) and Goldberger in this volume present women's ways of knowing in a light that affirms and celebrates women. But that is not sufficient reason for adopting their model for educational practice. It has not yet been demonstrated that there are women's ways of knowing.

The authors thank Karen Arnold, Tom Bidell, Tracey Hurd, and Ilda King for reading and commenting on an earlier draft of this paper.

REFERENCES

Alcoff, L., & Potter, E. (Eds.). (1993) *Feminist Epistemologies.* New York: Routledge.

Arlin, P. K. (1975). Cognitive development in adulthood: A fifth stage? *Developmental Psychology, 11,* 602–606.

Basseches, M. (1980). Dialectical schemata: A framework for the empirical study of the development of dialectical thinking. *Human Development, 23,* 400–421.

Baxter Magolda, M. B. (1990). Gender differences in epistemological development. *Journal of College Student Development, 31,* 555–561.

Baxter Magolda, M. B. (1992). Cocurricular influences on college students' intellectual development. *Journal of College Student Development, 33,* 203–213.

Baxter Magolda, M. B. (1995). The integration of relational and impersonal knowing in young adults' epistemological development. *Journal of College Student Development, 36* (3), 205–216.

Baxter Magolda, M. B., & Porterfield, W. D. (1985). A new approach to assess intellectual development on the Perry scheme. *Journal of College Student Personnel, 26,* 343–351.

Bebeau, M., & Brabeck, M. M. (1989). Ethical sensitivity and moral reasoning among men and women in the professions. In M. Brabeck (Ed.), *Who Cares? Theory, Research and Educational Implications of the Ethic of Care* (pp. 144–163). New York: Praeger.

Belenky, M. F., Clinchy, B. M., Goldberger, N., & Tarule, J. M. (1986). *Women's Ways of Knowing: The Development of Self, Voice and Mind.* New York: Basic Books.

Brabeck, M. (1984). Longitudinal studies of intellectual development during adulthood: Theoretical and research models. *Journal of Research and Development in Education, 17* (3), 12–27.

Brabeck, M. M. (Ed.). (1989). *Who Cares? Theory, Research and Educational Implications of the Ethic of Care.* New York: Praeger.

Brabeck, M. M. (1993). Recommendations for re-examining women's ways of knowing. *New Ideas in Psychology, 11* (2), 253–258.

Brabeck, M. (1994). Review of the book *Developing Reflective Judgment: Understanding and Promoting Intellectual Growth and Critical Thinking in Adolescents and Adults. Journal of Adult Development, 1* (4), 261–263.

Brabeck, M., & Wood, P. K. (1990). Cross-sectional and longitudinal evidence for differences between well-structured problem solving abilities. In M. L. Commons, C. Armon, L. Kohlberg, F. A. Richards, T. A. Grotzer, & J. D. Sinnott (Eds.), *Adult Development, Vol. 2: Models and Methods in the Study of Adolescent and Adult Thought* (pp. 133–146). New York: Praeger.

Bredemeier, B. J. L., Desertrain, G. S., Fisher, L. A., Getty, D., Slocum, N. E., Stephens, D. E., & Warren, J. M. (1991). Epistemological perspectives among women who participate in physical activity. *Journal of Applied Sport Psychology 3,* 87–107.

Broughton, J. (1978). Development of concepts of self, mind, reality and knowledge. *New Directions for Child Development, 1,* 75–100.

Buczynski, P. (1993). The development of a paper-and-pencil measure of Belenky, Clinchy, Goldberger and Tarule's (1986) conceptual model of women's ways-of-knowing instrument. *Journal of College Student Development, 34,* 197–200.

Clinchy, B. M. (1989). The development of thoughtfulness in college women. *American Behavioral Scientist, 32* (6), 647–657.

Colby, A., Kohlberg, L., Gibbs, J., & Lieberman, M. (1983). A longitudinal study of moral judgment. *Monographs of the Society for Research in Child Development, 48* (1–2). Serial No. 200.

Crawford, M., & Marecek, J. (1989). Psychology reconstructs the female: 1968–1988. *Psychology of Women Quarterly, 13,* 147–165.

Delpit, L. (1995). *Other People's Children: Cultural Conflict in the Classroom.* New York: New Press.

Durham, R. L., Hays, J., & Martinez, R. (1994). Socio-cognitive development among Chicano and Anglo American college students. *Journal of College Student Development, 35,* 178–182.

Fischer, K. W. (1980). A theory of cognitive development: The control and construction of hierarchies of skills. *Psychological Review, 87,* 477–531.

Gilligan, C. (1982). *In a Different Voice: Psychological Theory and Women's Development.* Cambridge, Mass.: Harvard University Press.

Gilligan, C., & Belenky, M. F. (1980). A naturalistic study of abortion decisions. In R. L. Selman & R. Yando (Eds.), *New Directions for Child Development: Clinical-Developmental Psychology* (no. 7, pp. 69–90). San Francisco: Jossey-Bass.

Gilligan, C., Ward, J. V., & Taylor, J. M. (1988). *Making Connections: The Relational Worlds of Adolescent Girls at Emma Willard School.* Cambridge, Mass.: Harvard University Graduate School of Education.

Hurd, T., & Brabeck, M. (in press). The ethic of care as revealed in college textbooks, 1970–1990: An empirical examination of alpha and beta bias. *Teaching of Psychology.*

Jordan, J. V., Kaplan, A. G., Miller, J. B., Stiver, I. P., and Surrey, J. L. (Eds.) (1991). *Women's Growth in Connection.* New York: Guilford Press.

King, P. M., & Kitchener, K. S. (1994). *Developing reflective judgment.* San Francisco: Jossey-Bass.

Kitchener, K. S., & King, P. M. (1981). Reflective judgment: Concepts of justification and their relationship to age and education. *Journal of Applied Development Psychology, 2,* 89–116.

Labouvie-Vief, G. (1982). Dynamic development and mature autonomy. A theoretical prologue. *Human Development, 25,* 161–191.

Lang-Takac, E., & Osterweil, Z. (1992). Separateness and connectedness: Differences between the genders. *Sex Roles, 27* (5–6), 277–289.

Moshman, D., & Timmons, M. (1982). The construction of logical necessity. *Human Development, 25,* 309–323.

Orr, R., & Luszcz, M. (1994). Rethinking women's ways of knowing: Gender commonalties and intersections with post-formal thought. *Journal of Adult Development, 1* (4), 225–233.

Ortman, P.E. (1993). A feminist approach to teaching learning theory with educational applications. *Teaching of Psychology, 20* (1), 38–40.

Perry, W. (1970). *Forms of Intellectual and Ethical Development in the College Years.* New York: Holt, Rinehart and Winston.

Piaget, J. (1972). Intellectual evolution from adolescence to adulthood. *Human Development, 15,* 1–12.

Reigel, K. F. (1979). *Foundations of Dialectical Psychology.* New York: Academic Press.

Rest, J. R. (1979). *Development in Judging Moral Issues.* Minneapolis: University of Minnesota Press.

Sinnott, J. (1981). The theory of relativity: A metatheory for development? *Human Development, 25,* 293–311.

Thoma, S. (1986). Estimating gender differences in the comprehension and preference of moral issues. *Developmental Review, 6* (2), 165–180.

Walker, L.J. (1984). Sex differences in the development of moral reasoning: A critical review. *Child Development, 55,* 677–691.

Walker, L.J. (1985). Sexism in Kohlberg's Moral Psychology? In W.M. Kurtines and J. L. Gewirtz (Eds.), *Moral Development: An Introduction* (pp. 83–107). Boston: Allyn and Bacon.

Walker, L. J. (1986). Sex differences in the development of moral reasoning: A rejoinder to Baumrind. *Child Development, 57,* 522–526.

Widick, C., & Simpson, D. (1978). Developmental concepts in college instruction. In C. A. Parker (Ed.), *Encouraging Development in College Students* (pp. 27–59). Minneapolis: University of Minnesota Press.

Wingfield, L., & Haste, H. (1987). Connectedness and separateness: Cognitive style or moral orientation? *Journal of Moral Education, 15,* 214–225.

Wood, P.K. (1985). A statistical examination of necessary but not sufficient antecedents of problem solving behavior. Ph.D. diss. University of Minnesota. *Dissertations Abstracts International, 46,* 2055.

Mathematics: Is Biology the Cause of Gender Differences in Performance?

A great deal of research has been devoted to the debate over gender similarities and differences in mathematics achievement. One of the major reasons for the continuing interest in this topic is the significant role that mathematics plays in academic and career success. A study done by Lucy Sells at the University of California at Berkeley in the early 1970s showed that whereas 57 percent of the incoming male students had four years of high school math, this was true of only 8 percent of the female students. Thus 92 percent of the first-year female students could not enroll in fifteen of the twenty majors at the university (such as engineering, computer science, physics) because they required a strong mathematics background. In effect, mathematics became, in Sells's (1978) words, a "critical filter" that served to close off a number of occupations to women. The vital importance of mathematics for women's careers is clear. In a study that tracked more than twelve thousand women from high school graduation in 1972 until they were thirty-two, Adelman (1991) found that those who took more than two college-level mathematics courses had a much better chance of achieving salary equity with men than did those women who opted for other courses.

Impressed by Sells's findings, which at that point had not yet been published, Sheila Tobias brought the issue to the attention of the public in a 1976 article in *Ms.* magazine in which she traced the problem of the underenrollment of women in math courses to "math anxiety." In her book, appropriately entitled *Overcoming Math Anxiety* (1978, 1993), Tobias argued that girls are encouraged to drop mathematics at an early age while social forces encourage boys to pursue such courses.

In 1980, Camilla P. Benbow and Julian C. Stanley shifted the focus of the discussion when they reported large sex differences in the mean scores of talented seventh- and eighth-graders on the mathematical part of the College Board's Scholastic Aptitude Test (SAT). Noting that both sexes had similar formal educational training, they suggested that the sex differences resulted from an innate male talent for mathematics. Not surprisingly in light of the long-held popular belief that men were better than women at math, a media blitz heralded the Benbow and Stanley study. In the same week, a *Newsweek* (Williams, 1980) headline asked "Do Males Have a Math Gene?" while *Time* (Gender factor, 1980) declared, "A new study says that males may be naturally abler than females." Scholars quickly joined the controversy: forty-two researchers responded to a later article by Benbow (1988), expressing a variety of opinions on the subject (Unger & Crawford, 1996).

Benbow and her colleagues' research triggered much criticism. Carol Jacklin (1989) challenged their speculation about the biological causes for their results, noting that they provided no biological data to back it up. Jacquelynne Eccles and her colleagues have identified a number of factors that may explain why women avoid math, including parental influence (Jacobs & Eccles, 1992) and teachers' expectations (Yee & Eccles, 1988). Eccles (1989) has also developed a model of academic choice that draws on decision making, achievement, and attribution theory. She notes that girls begin to have less confidence in their math ability in the seventh grade; consequently, they choose to take fewer math courses because they believe they will not do well and because they attach less importance to activities and careers in mathematics and science than do their male counterparts. In fact, Chipman and Wilson (1985) believe that self-confidence is a better predictor of who will take additional math courses than actual math achievement.

Questions have also been raised as to the validity of the SAT scores. As Shea (1994) has demonstrated, women receive lower SAT scores than men, yet receive higher grade-point averages in college. Findings like these have led such colleges as MIT to include factors other than SAT scores in their admissions decisions (Matlin, 1996). Evidence also shows that women's math avoidance has dropped substantially since Sells's original study. In 1985, 45 percent of students taking the SAT who reported having had four or more years of high school math courses were women. Two years later, 46 percent of the bachelor's degrees in mathematics went to women (Mednick & Thomas, 1993).

Much work also needs to be done on the interaction of gender with race, ethnicity, class, and cultural diversity in mathematics achievement (Secada, 1992). International comparisons of students show few or no gender differences within countries but large differences between countries. In one study, the lowest average score in grade five in Japan was higher than the highest score in the United States (Kimball, 1995). Studies like this suggest that it is simplistic to draw conclusions about gender from comparison studies within a particular country.

Nevertheless, Benbow and David Lubinski continue their argument that there are biological explanations for the excess number of mathematically talented males. In contrast, Janet Hyde argues that it makes no sense to search for a biological cause for male math superiority because there is little evidence of gender difference in mathematical performance in the general population.

REFERENCES

Adelman, C. (1991). *Women at thirtysomething: Paradoxes of attainment.* Washington, D.C.: U.S. Department of Education.

Benbow, C. P. (1988). Sex differences in mathematical reasoning ability in intellectually talented preadolescents: Their nature, effects, and possible causes. *Behavioral and Brain Sciences, 11,* 169–232.

Benbow, C. P., & Stanley, J. (1980). Sex differences in mathematical ability: Fact or artifact? *Science, 210,* 1262–1264.

Chipman, S. F., & Wilson, D. M. (1985). Understanding mathematics course enrollment and math achievement: A synthesis of the research. In S. F. Chipman, L. R. Brush, & D. M. Wilson (Eds.), *Women and mathematics: Balancing the equation* (pp. 275–328). Hillsdale, N.J.: Erlbaum.

Eccles, J. S. (1989). Bringing young women to math and science. In M. Crawford & M. Gentry (Eds.), *Gender and thought: Psychological perspectives* (pp. 36–58). New York: Springer-Verlag.

Gender factor in math. (1980, December 15). *Time*, p. 57.

Jacklin, C. N. (1989). Female and male: Issues of gender. *American Psychologist, 44*, 127–133.

Jacobs, J. E., & Eccles, J. S. (1992). The impact of mothers' gender-role stereotypic beliefs on mothers' and children's ability perceptions. *Journal of Personality and Social Psychology, 63*, 932–944.

Kimball, M. (1995). *Feminist visions of gender similarities and differences.* New York: Harrington Park Press.

Matlin, M. W. (1996). *The psychology of women* (3rd ed.). Fort Worth, Tex.: Harcourt Brace Jovanovich.

Mednick, M. T., & Thomas, V. G. (1993). Women and the psychology of achievement: A view from the eighties. In F. L. Denmark & M. A. Paludi (Eds.), *Psychology of women: A handbook of issues and theories* (pp. 585–626). Westport, Conn.: Greenwood Press.

Secada, W. G. (1992). Race, ethnicity, social class, language, and achievement mathematics. In D. A. Grouws (Ed.), *Handbook of research on mathematics teaching and learning* (pp. 623–660). New York: Macmillan.

Sells, L. W. (1978). Mathematics—a critical filter. *Science Teacher, 45*, 28–29.

Shea, C. (1994, September 7). "Gender gap" on examinations shrank again this year. *Chronicle of Higher Education*, p. A54.

Tobias, S. (1976, September). Math anxiety: Why is a smart girl like you counting on your fingers? *Ms., 5*, 56–59, 92.

Tobias, S. (1978, 1993). *Overcoming math anxiety.* New York: Norton.

Unger, R., & Crawford, M. (1996). *Women and gender: A feminist psychology.* New York: McGraw-Hill.

Williams, D. A., with King, P. (1980, December 15). Do males have a math gene? *Newsweek*, p. 73.

Yee, D. K., & Eccles, J. S. (1988). Parent perceptions and attributions for children's math achievement. *Sex Roles, 19*, 317–333.

ADDITIONAL READING

Burton, L. (Ed.) (1993). *Gender and mathematics: An international perspective.* London: Cassell.

Eccles, J. S. (1994). Understanding women's educational and occupational choices: Applying the Eccles et al. model of achievement-related choices. *Psychology of Women Quarterly, 18* (4), 585–609.

Geary, D. C. (1994). *Children's mathematical development: research and practical applications.* Washington, D.C.: American Psychological Association.

Geary, D. C. (in press). Sexual selection and sex differences in mathematical abilities. *Behavioral and Brain Sciences.*

Leder, G. C. (1992). Mathematics and gender: Changing perspectives. In D. A. Grouws (Ed.), *Handbook of research on mathematics teaching and learning* (pp. 597–622). New York: Macmillan.

McGuinness, D. (1993). Gender differences in cognitive style: Implications for mathematics performance and achievement. In L. A. Penner, G. M. Batsche, H. M. Knoff, & D. L. Nelson (Eds.), *The challenge in mathematics and science education: Psychology's response* (pp. 251–274). Washington, D.C.: American Psychological Association.

Rogers, P., & Kaiser, G. (Eds.) (1995). *Equity in mathematics education: Influences of feminism & culture.* Bristol, Penn.: Taylor & Francis.

Sadker, M., & Sadker, D. (1994). *Failing at fairness: How America's schools cheat girls.* New York: Scribner.

Wertheim, M. (1995). *Pythagoras' trousers: God, physics, and the gender wars.* New York: Times Books.

YES

Psychological Profiles of the Mathematically Talented: Some Sex Differences and Evidence Supporting Their Biological Basis

CAMILLA PERSSON BENBOW AND

DAVID LUBINSKI

Ever since its founding by Julian C. Stanley at Johns Hopkins University in 1971, the Study of Mathematically Precocious Youth's (SMPY's) research and educational programming has focused on exceptional achievements in mathematics, engineering, and the physical sciences, and on the young individuals with the potential to produce them. These were fortuitous choices, given that our increasingly technological society requires many well-trained scientists in just these areas. Furthermore, the importance of mathematical ability for scientific achievement and creativity has become more evident with time. Krutetskii (1976, p. 6), for example, noted that "the development of the sciences has been characterized recently by a tendency for them to become more mathematical. . . . Mathematical methods and mathematical style are penetrating everywhere." Kuhn (1962) was most probably correct in ascribing an overwhelming majority of "scientific revolutions" to the work of mathematically brilliant individuals, criticisms of the selectivity of his examples notwithstanding.

Thus, individuals seen as having the most potential for high academic achievement and subsequent creative production in the physical sciences are those whose mathematical reasoning abilities are exceptionally high (Benbow & Arjmand 1990, Green 1989, Walberg et al. 1984), the very individuals on whom SMPY chose to focus its research program. Here, we present a psychological profile of the mathematically talented, especially as it relates to the constellation of personal attributes critical for the manifestation of exceptional scientific contributions, the sex differences found therein, and some biological foundations for these phenotypic manifestations. We begin with a discussion of mathematical talent and the importance of considering a label such as "gifted" as a continuous rather than a categorical concept. A common arbitrary point for the label of giftedness is an ability level in the top 1%. Such a cutoff procedure can be misleading, because many people fail to appreciate the extent of individual differences within the top 1%. The top 1% of almost all ability ranges (for general intelligence, those with IQs from about 135 to over 200) cover a range just as broad as that from the bottom 2% to the top 2% (an IQ range of about 66 to 134).

INDIVIDUAL DIFFERENCES IN THE TOP 1%: THEIR PSYCHOLOGICAL IMPLICATIONS

Many firmly hold that being within the top 1% in mathematical ability is sufficient for the production of exceptional scientific achievements (e.g., MacKinnon 1962, Renzulli 1986, Wallach 1976); that is, above a certain ability threshold (here, the top 1%, but many maintain that lower levels apply), other factors become increasingly important for the emergence of advanced scientific achievements and creativity. What many educators and social scientists do not realize is that the range of giftedness includes about one-third of the *entire* ability range, and this range is seldom investigated systematically with the necessary methodological requirements (see Lubinski & Dawis 1992).

We (Benbow 1992) undertook the task of empirically determining if indeed there is such a point of diminishing returns in the distribution of mathematical ability, a point beyond which even greater mathematical talent has little usefulness. About 2000 students were identified by SMPY as being in the top 1% in mathematical reasoning ability in the 7th or 8th grade (13-year-olds), through use of out-of-level testing with the College Board Scholastic Aptitude Test-Mathematics (SAT-M) (i.e., 7–8th-graders took a test designed for above-average 11th and 12th-graders [16–18-year-olds]). These students had been included in SMPY's planned 50-year longitudinal study, which includes a total of 5000 students identified over 20 years, and, as part of the longitudinal study, had been surveyed 5 and 10 years after their identification at age 13 (Lubinski & Benbow 1994). We (Benbow 1992) elected to compare the mathematics-science achievement profiles of those students whose SAT-M scores placed them in the top quartile of the top 1% with those whose scores placed them in the bottom quartile of the top 1%. Sample sizes averaged 100 females and 367 males for the top 25%, and 282 females and 248 males for the bottom 25%. Data on a variety of criteria—earning a college degree in the sciences, intellectual level of college attended, academic honors, grade-point average, and intensity of involvement in mathematics and science—all favoured the top quartile, irrespective of sex. Of the 37 variables studied, 34 showed significant differences favoring the high SAT-M group, but, more important, most were substantively meaningful.

We (Benbow 1992) also conducted predictive validation assessments using the full range of talent in this sample, correlating the students' 8th-grade SAT-M scores with their College Board Achievement Test scores in mathematics or science attained at the end of high school (i.e., 4–5 years later). The correlations ranged from 0.16 to 0.57, with a mean of 0.40 for females and 0.45 for the males (approximate sample sizes are $n = 95$ females and $n = 223$ males, because different numbers of students elected to take specific tests). The predictive validities for Advanced Placement (AP) calculus examination scores averaged 0.43 for fe-

males and 0.38 for males. (It should be stressed that the above were raw correlations, not corrected for attenuation.)

These data clearly reveal that individual differences in the top 1% in ability do have important psychological implications, yet such individual differences are seldom observed for the following reasons: (1) out-of-level testing is required to detect and separate the top 1%; (2) sample sizes of individuals within the top 1% tend to be small; and (3) the criteria themselves tend to lack sufficient ceilings (Lubinski & Dawis 1992). Nonetheless, irrespective of the individual differences within the top 1%, it must be acknowledged that the most important attribute for successful performance in any highly select domain often has the least variation among the factors that contribute to achievement in that domain, a finding that transcends all types of talents or skills (Lubinski & Dawis 1992, Lubinski & Humphreys 1990a). This is because the variance in the critical attributes tends to be suppressed within elite educational and occupational populations through self-selection and institutionalized selection procedures. Thus, for individuals within the most prestigious scientific occupations, mathematical ability might have minuscule variation relative to the normal variation, but remain at center stage. What then are some of the other factors that contribute to success? We turn to that issue next and to the theoretical model guiding our work for some clues.

THE THEORETICAL MODEL FOR SMPY'S RESEARCH

The conceptual framework guiding our research on mathematical talent draws on three already existing theoretical perspectives (Dawis & Lofquist 1984, Tannenbaum 1983, Zuckerman 1977) and incorporates some of what is already known about the development of talent and personal preferences for contrasting educational and vocational paths. Primarily, our work is based on a well-known model of vocational adjustment, the Theory of Work Adjustment, a model first introduced in the 1960s by Rene V. Dawis and Lloyd H. Lofquist at the University of Minnesota (Dawis & Lofquist 1984, Lofquist & Dawis 1969, 1991). Although it is formulated to explain work adjustment, an especially attractive feature of this model is that it can be readily extended to critical *antecedents* to vocational adjustment, such as choice of college major and preferred density of course work in contrasting disciplines.

According to the Theory of Work Adjustment, to ascertain an individual's optimal learning and work environments one must first parse the individual's "work personality" and the environment into two broad but complementary subdomains. An individual's work personality primarily comprises his or her (i) repertoire of specific skills or abilities and (ii) personal preferences for the content found in contrasting educational and vocational environments. In contrast, different environmental contexts (educational curricula and occupations) are classified in terms of (i) their ability requirements and (ii) their tendency to reinforce personal preferences. Optimal educational and work environments for an individual are those for which two levels of correspondence can be established, *satisfactoriness* and *satisfaction*. Satisfactoriness is the correspondence between an individual's abilities and the ability requirements of a particular educational or occupational environment, whereas satisfaction is the correspondence between an individual's preferences and the types of reinforcers provided by a particular occupation or educational track. The extent to which satisfactoriness and satisfaction are achieved determines educational and career choice, degree of commitment, and occupational tenure.

An important implication of this model is that both abilities and preferences must be assessed, concurrently, to ascertain the suitability of a given individual for a particular educational or career track (see Lubinski & Thompson 1986). Similarly, both components of the educational and vocational environment (response requirements *and* reward systems) need to be evaluated to estimate whether both dimensions of correspondence are likely to be achieved.

Which abilities and preferences should be assessed when the educational or work environment is engineering or physical science? For these disciplines, as noted above, especially high mathematical reasoning ability is a requirement. High spatial-mechanical reasoning ability (probably the second most significant personal attribute and one that is frequently underappreciated; Humphreys et al. 1993) is also important. Verbal ability is somewhat less critical but still important. Investigative interests (scientific) and theoretical values (intellectual and philosophical) are among the most salient personal preferences of people who gravitate toward scientific environments, find their content reinforcing (for developing intellectual talent), and maintain a commitment toward these kinds of disciplines (Dawis 1991, Dawis & Lofquist 1984, Holland 1985, Lubinski & Benbow 1992, 1994, MacKinnon 1962, Roe 1953, Southern & Plant 1968). The physical sciences also require intense abilities and preferences for manipulating and working with sophisticated objects and gadgets. Individuals with pronounced or relatively high social values (or a stronger need for contact with people) gain less reinforcement in such environments.

If the abilities and preferences that are important for adjustment in scientific environments are not all in place, high achievement in the sciences is most unlikely. We propose that high achievement and creativity in science emanate from the following configural pattern of personal attributes: high mathematical reasoning ability, high spatial-mechanical reasoning ability, high theoretical values and investigative interests, and a relatively low need for contact with people in learning environments and vocational settings. These characteristics, coupled with an intense commitment to mastery of one's chosen discipline and energy for work (see below), are the sine qua non for high scientific achievement. For all of these attributes to be salient in any one individual is rare, but not as rare as noteworthy scientific achievements.

Possession of these personal attributes by themselves is insufficient. Those who have the personal potential to manifest exceptional achievement also require an environment appropriate to facilitate the emergence of world-class scientific accomplishment. Bloom (1985), for example, noted from his interviews of talented performers in a variety of disciplines that special experiences, sometimes interventions, were important in their development. (This is what we attempt to provide in our summer programs for the gifted, described in detail elsewhere; Benbow 1986a, Stanley 1973, Stanley et al. 1974.)

Moreover, Zuckerman (1977), in her analysis of Nobel Laureates' careers, saw that their development or emergence fit well with the model of "the accumulation of advantage." That is, individuals with exceptional scientific achievements almost always show promise extremely early in their careers, and this precocity appears not only to respond to but also to create greater opportunities for intellectual development. For example, most Laureates were advantaged in their graduate work by attending a distinguished university (10 universities produced 55% of the Laureates) and by studying with the best minds of the day—thereby begetting a pattern of eminence creating eminence.

Tannenbaum (1983) postulated that great performance or productivity results from a rare blend of superior general intellect, distinctive special aptitudes, the right combination of non-intellectual traits, a challenging environment, and the smile of good fortune at crucial periods of life. (The first three components seem to parallel the abilities and preferences discussed in the Theory of Work Adjustment, and the latter two the work of Zuckerman.) According to Tannenbaum, success depends on a combination of facilitators, whereas failure results from even a single deficit. By virtue of its veto power, then, every one of the five qualifiers is a requisite for high achievement, and none of them has sufficient strength to overcome appreciable inadequacies in the others.

The above serves as the scaffolding for our work on the dispositional determinants of scientific educational and career paths of the gifted. It is also the starting point for our attempts to facilitate the optimal development of their intellectual talents. However, a consistent finding from SMPY (and other research programs studying the highly able or normal samples) is that these abilities and preferences, and commitment to work in general, differ between the sexes. An investigation of these sex differences led to the first evaluation of the Theory of Work Adjustment, with the results described below.

SEX DIFFERENCES ORGANIZED AROUND THE THEORY OF WORK ADJUSTMENT: A PRELIMINARY APPRAISAL

SEX DIFFERENCES IN ABILITIES

Among SMPY's mathematically gifted 13-year-olds, differences favor males in mathematical reasoning ability but not in verbal reasoning, where there are no differences (Benbow 1988, Lubinski & Benbow 1992). Our gifted males score approximately one-half of a standard deviation higher than the females on the SAT-M, our measure of mathematical reasoning. Males' SAT-M scores are also more dispersed. The resulting proportion of males and females at age 13 at various cut-off scores on SAT-M is approximately as follows: ≥ 500 (average score of college-bound 12th-grade [18-year-old] males), 2:1; ≥ 600, 4:1; and ≥ 700 (top 1 in 10,000 for 7th-graders [13-year-olds], 13:1 (Benbow & Stanley 1983). These ratios have remained relatively stable over the past 20 years and have now been observed among mathematically gifted students in the 3rd grade (8-year-olds), (Mills et al. 1993) and cross-culturally (though they are smaller in Asian populations; Lubinski & Benbow 1992). They have profound implications for the mathematics-science pipeline, because far fewer females than males qualify for advanced training in disciplines that place a premium on mathematical reasoning.

The picture intensifies when the other cognitive abilities important for achieving advanced educational credentials in the physical sciences are examined. Although mathematically talented students, whether male or female, tend to have highly developed spatial and mechanical reasoning abilities, those of the males do appear higher (Benbow et al. 1983, Benbow & Minor 1990, Humphreys et al. 1993, Lubinski & Benbow 1992, Lubinski & Humphreys 1990b). Sex differences in mathematical reasoning ability are consistently found, paralleling findings described above for the entire nation. Although there are no meaningful differences in SAT-Verbal or Advanced Raven (a non-verbal test of general intelligence) scores, there are substantial differences between boys and girls in spatial and mechanical reasoning abilities, not unlike those observed 20 years ago by SMPY.

Thus, at age 13, sex differences in mathematical reasoning ability are compounded by differences in spatial and mechanical reasoning abilities. At the end of high school and college, these differences remain and are accompanied by differences favoring males in mathematics and science achievement test scores (Benbow & Minor 1986, Benbow & Stanley 1982, Stanley et al. 1992).

SEX DIFFERENCES IN PREFERENCES

Abilities are but one class of variables that affect educational and career decisions. Preferences for certain environments and occupational reinforcers are another. Accompanying sex differences in abilities are prominent differences in critical preferences for maintaining a commitment to careers in the mathematics-science area. Mathematically talented males as young as 13 are more theoretically oriented than females on the Allport-Vernon-Lindzey (1970) study of values (SOV) (Lubinski & Benbow 1992); furthermore, their primary interests lie in the investigative and (secondarily) the realistic (working with mechanical gadgets) sectors of Holland's hexagon of vocational interests (C. P. Benbow & D. Lubinski, unpublished work 1992, Fox et al. 1976). In contrast, mathematically talented females are more socially and aesthetically oriented and have interests that are more evenly divided among investigative, social, and artistic pursuits (C. P. Benbow & D. Lubinski, unpublished work 1992, Fox et al. 1976, Lubinski & Benbow 1992). It appears that females are more balanced and less narrowly focused in terms of their interests and values. Females have more competing interests and abilities, which draw them to a broader spectrum of educational and vocational pursuits.

An alternative way to capture the essence of the sex differences in preferences is worth further elaboration. It takes us back to Thorndike (1911) and one of the most celebrated dimensions of individual differences, "people versus things." In normative samples, as well as among the gifted, females tend to gravitate towards the former, while males gravitate towards the latter (Lubinski & Benbow 1992, Lubinski & Humphreys 1990a); this dimension is found to be one of the best predictors of career choice among the highly able 10 years after its assessment (Lubinski, Benbow, & Sanders, 1993). Given the female preference within the sciences for biology and medicine over the physical sciences (Lubinski & Benbow 1992), we have suggested that sex differences in vocational preferences are perhaps more precisely labeled as organic versus inorganic content (Benbow & Lubinski 1993, Lubinski et al. 1993).

In conclusion, males are more likely than females to have a profile of abilities and preferences congruent with studying science, even among the mathematically precocious (see Lubinski & Benbow 1992). That is, in scientific disciplines, males are more likely than females to achieve correspondence for both satisfaction and satisfactoriness. The effect of this difference, however, is magnified by the huge difference between the sexes in commitment to full-time work, a difference that has remained fairly consistent over the past 20 years in SMPY investigations: 95% of gifted males versus 55% of gifted females plan to work full time until retirement (C. P. Benbow & D. Lubinski, unpublished work 1992). This latter difference is particularly important for scientific achievement because scientists of any note almost always devote extremely long hours to work. Thus, we propose that the differing ability and preference profiles and commitment to full-time work of males and females will lead them to find personal fulfillment in different careers. Moreover, given the nature of these differences (larger means and standard deviations for males in relevant abilities [Stanley et al. 1992], plus larger mean differences favoring males on relevant interests and values), sex differences in science achievement should be especially pronounced at the exceptional levels.

CONSEQUENCES OF SEX DIFFERENCES IN ABILITIES
AND PREFERENCES

Although students are not formally selected for advanced training on the basis of their theoretical values, their investigative interests, or their spatial and mechanical reasoning abilities (but they are on mathematical and verbal reasoning ability), students appear to self-select areas of concentration on the basis of these attributes, whether or not they are explicitly aware of their abilities and preferences (Humphreys et al. 1993). Disparate male-to-female proportions in mathematics-science achievement thereby ensue. Indeed, that seems to be precisely the case for SMPY's mathematically talented individuals. SMPY's 10-year follow-up of its first cohort of mathematically talented students at age 23 revealed that more males than females were entering mathematics or science career tracks (51% versus 32%), especially in the inorganic sciences, and males had higher educational aspirations (Lubinski & Benbow 1992). Together, these trends lead to a somewhat startling result—less than 1% of females in the top 1% of mathematical ability from SMPY's first cohort are pursuing doctorates in mathematics, engineering, or physical science. About 8% of such males were doing so. Similar discrepancies were found (C. P. Benbow & D. Lubinski, unpublished work 1992) for two other cohorts of mathematically talented students being surveyed by SMPY: among students with mathematical abilities in at least the top 0.5%, 12% of females compared with 27% of males were pursuing doctorates in mathematics, engineering, and physical science, while among 18-year-old students in the top 1 in 10,000 in mathematical ability (SAT-M $\geq$ 700 before age 13) 77% of males and 47% of females were pursuing bachelor's degrees in those areas. What are the prospects for the future? Will these large differences in career choice remain with us? As long as sex differences in critical ability and preference profiles remain stable, as they have done the past 20 years for the gifted, corresponding disparities along the mathematics-science pipeline will also remain.

SMPY's work in the area of sex differences suggests that the Theory of Work Adjustment provides an adequate explanation of career choice among the gifted. Sex differences in achievement in the physical sciences seem to be a natural result of sex differences in personal attributes related to contrasting paths for fulfillment in the world of work—at least, that is what our data would suggest. Also, because differences in abilities and value dimensions between boys and girls are in place long before high school (Lubinski & Benbow 1992), we have suggested the hypothesis, and found evidence for it, that abilities and preferences may partly channel sex differences in specific coursework attitudes and course selection in high school and college and, in turn, directly contribute to male-female disparities in advanced educational credentials in mathematics and science (Lubinski, Benbow, & Sanders, 1993).

SOME POSSIBLE BIOLOGICAL LINKAGES WITH MATHEMATICAL TALENT

When one is confronted with sex differences such as those described above, especially those in the area of abilities, the natural question to ask is, Why? Why do females, as a group, have poorer mathematical reasoning ability than males? This is a complex question, which cannot be given full justice here. Our work with the mathematically talented leads us to ask not why females have poorer mathematical reasoning ability but, rather, why there is an excess of mathematically talented males. Although most causal analyses of differences between the sexes in abilities (as well as preferences) stress socialization mechanisms (Halpern 1992, Lytton & Romney 1991), relevant variables may exist at more basic biological levels (Bouchard et al. 1990).

Our investigations into the biological bases of mathematical talent have been guided by the work of the late Norman Geschwind (Geschwind & Behan 1982). Geschwind had proposed that prenatal exposure to high levels of testosterone would: (1) affect the thymus gland and, thereby, the immune system; and (2) affect the development of the left and right hemispheres of the brain in such a way as to enhance right hemisphere functioning, which, in turn, increases the likelihood of left-handedness. Geschwind put forward this theory to explain the relationship between left-handedness and various immune and auto immune disorders as well as learning disabilities. We, however, used his theory to frame our biologically oriented work on mathematical talent, because mathematical reasoning has been suggested to be specialized within the right hemisphere of the brain. Our approach has been fruitful, leading us to identify several physiological correlates of extreme mathematical talent. These include left-handedness, immune disorders, myopia, and enhanced right-hemispheric functioning (Benbow 1986b, O'Boyle et al. 1991, O'Boyle & Benbow 1990, Lubinski & Humphreys 1992)—all consistent with Geschwind's hormonal hypothesis. This has now led to some electroencephalogram (EEG) studies, described below.

In two studies, patterns of brain activation or inhibition in relation to sex and precocity were investigated. EEG activity was monitored over the left and right hemispheres while gifted and average-ability subjects of both sexes viewed two types of stimuli, one type requiring verbal processing and the other requiring spatial processing. During verbal processing, gifted boys and girls exhibited greater activity than controls, with activation localized in the frontal lobes rather than in the temporal lobes, as in the subjects of average ability. During spatial processing, gifted and average-ability females did not differ from each other, but did differ from the two groups of males. However, gifted and average-ability males did differ, with gifted males demonstrating the capacity to selectively inhibit regions of the left hemisphere and thereby allow the right hemisphere to predominate in the processing. These findings suggest that different patterns of brain activation and inhibition underlie precocity and its expression in at least a subset of males, a finding that might eventually be tied to the sex differences described above. We hope that psychophysiologists and neuropsychologists will examine this possibility further in subsequent empirical research.

Exceptional achievements and creative contributions in mathematics, engineering, and the physical sciences are within the exclusive purview of individuals with mathematical talent, a talent that can be reliably identified as early as age 13. Although many believe that being within the top 1% is sufficient for scientific excellence, there are vast individual differences within the top 1% of ability that are found to co-vary with a host of meaningful academic and vocational criteria when methods appropriate to reveal these relationships are used. Mathematical talent is not all that is necessary for the emergence of scientific eminence. Those who have the potential to manifest exceptional scientific achievements are those who also possess exceptional spatial and mechanical reasoning abilities, as well as a high theoretical orientation in combination with a relatively low social value orientation, coupled with high investigative interests. On the preference dimension for "people versus things," exceptional physical scientists tend to be located on the "things" end of this well-known spectrum of individual differences. Such individuals require special encounters with the appropriate environment to facilitate the emergence of world-class scientific achievement. Finally, mathematical talent seems to have biological co-variates, with the patterns of brain activation and inhibition underlying precocity and its expression differing between at least a subset of males and females.

This work was supported by a grant from the National Science Foundation (MDR 8855625).

REFERENCES

Allport, G.W., Vernon, P.E., Lindzey, G. 1970. Manual for the study of values. Houghton Mifflin, Boston.

Benbow, C.P. 1986a. SMPY's model for teaching mathematically precocious students. In: Renzulli, J.S. (ed.) Systems and models in programs for the gifted and talented. Creative Learning Press, Mansfield Center, CT, pp. 1–25.

Benbow, C.P. 1986b. Physiological correlates of extreme intellectual precocity. Neuropsychologia 24:719–725.

Benbow, C.P. 1988. Sex differences in mathematical reasoning ability among the intellectually talented: Their characterization, consequences, and possible explanations. Behav. Brain Sci. 11:169–232.

Benbow, C.P. 1992. Academic achievement in mathematics and science between ages 13 and 23: Are there differences among students in the top one percent of mathematical ability? J. Educ. Psychol. 84:51–61.

Benbow, C.P., Arjmand O. 1990. Predictors of high academic achievement in mathematics and science by mathematically talented students: A longitudinal study. J. Educ. Psychol. 82:430–441.

Benbow, C.P., Lubinski, D. 1993. Consequences of gender differences in mathematical reasoning ability: Some biological linkages. In: Haug, M., Whalen, R.E., Aron, C., Olsen, K.L. (eds.) The development of sex differences and similarities in behaviour. Kluwer, The Hague (NATO Ser) pp. 87–109.

Benbow, C.P., Minor, L.L. 1986. Mathematically talented males and females and achievement in high school sciences. Am. Educ. Res. J. 23:425–436.

Benbow, C.P., Minor, L.L. 1990. Cognitive profiles of verbally and mathematically precocious students: Implications for the identification of the gifted. Gift. Child Q. 34:21–26.

Benbow, C.P., Stanley, J.C. 1982. Consequences in high school and college of sex differences in mathematical reasoning ability: A longitudinal perspective. Am. Educ. Res. J. 19:598–622.

Benbow, C.P., Stanley, J.C. 1983. Sex differences in mathematical reasoning ability: More facts. Science 222:1029–1031.

Benbow, C.P., Stanley, J.C., Zonderman, A.B., Kirk, M.K. 1983. Structure of intelligence in intellectually precocious individuals and their parents. Intelligence 7:129–152.

Bloom, B.S. (ed.) 1985. Developing talent in young people. Ballantine Books, New York.

Bouchard, T.J., Lykken, D.T., McGue, M., Tellegen, A., Segal, N. 1990. Sources of human psychological differences: The Minnesota study of twins reared apart. Science 250:223–228.

Cohen, J. 1988. Statistical power analysis for the behavioral sciences, 2nd ed. Lawrence Erlbaum, Hillsdale, NJ.

Dawis, R.V. 1991. Vocational interests, values, and preferences. In: Dunnette, M., Hough, L. (eds.) Handbook of industrial and organizational psychology, 2nd ed. Consulting Psychologists Press, Palo Alto, CA, vol 2:833–871.

Dawis, R.V., Lofquist, L.H. 1984. A psychological theory of work adjustment: An individual differences model and its applications. University of Minnesota Press, Minneapolis.

Fox, L.H., Pasternak, S.R., Peiser, N.L. 1976. Career-related interests of adolescent boys and girls. In: Keating DP (ed.) Intellectual talent: Research and development. Johns Hopkins University Press, Baltimore, p. 242–261.

Geschwind, N., Behan, P. 1982. Left-handedness: Associations with immune disease, migraine, and developmental learning disorders. Proc. Natl. Acad. Sci. USA 79:5097–5100.

Green, K.C. 1989. A profile of undergraduates in the sciences. Am. Sci. 77:475–480.

Halpern, D.F. 1992. Sex differences in cognitive abilities, 2nd ed. Lawrence Erlbaum, Hillsdale, NJ.

Holland, J.L. 1985. Making vocational choices: A theory of vocational personalities and work environments, 2nd ed. Prentice-Hall, Englewood Cliffs, NJ.

Humphreys, L.G., Lubinski, D., Yao, G. 1993. Utility of predicting group membership: Exemplified by the role of spatial visualization in becoming an engineer, physical scientist, or artist. J. Appl. Psychol. 78:250–261.

Krutetskii, V.A. 1976. The psychology of mathematical abilities in school children. Kilpatrick J., Wirszup I. (eds.) Teller J. (transl.). University of Chicago Press, Chicago.

Kuhn, T.S. 1962. The structure of scientific revolutions. University of Chicago Press, Chicago.

Lofquist, L.H., Dawis, R.V. 1969. Adjustment to work. Appleton-Century-Crofts, New York.

Lofquist, L.H., Dawis, R.V. 1991. Essentials of person environment correspondence counseling. University of Minnesota Press, Minneapolis.

Lubinski, D., Benbow, C.P. 1992. Gender differences in abilities and preferences among the gifted: Implications for the math/science pipeline. Curr. Dir. Psychol. Sci. 1:61–66.

Lubinski, D., Benbow, C.P. 1994. The Study of Mathematically Precocious Youth: Its planned 50-year study of intellectual talent. In: Subotnik, R., Arnold, K. (eds) Beyond Terman: Longitudinal studies in contemporary gifted education. Norwood, NJ. Ablex.

Lubinski, D., Benbow, C.P., Sanders, C.E. 1993. Reconceptualizing gender differences in achievement among the gifted: An outcome of contrasting attributes for personal fulfillment in the world of work. In: Heller, K.A., Mönks, E.J., Passow, A.H. (eds.) International handbook for research on giftedness and talent. Pergamon Press, Oxford, pp. 575–602.

Lubinski, D., Dawis, R.V. 1992. Aptitudes, skills, and proficiency. In: Dunnette, M.D., Hough, L.M. (eds.) The handbook of industrial and organizational psychology, 2nd ed. Consulting Psychologists Press, Palo Alto, CA, vol 3:3–59.

Lubinski, D., Humphreys, L.G. 1990a. Assessing spurious "moderator effects": Illustrated substantively with the hypothesized ("synergistic") relation between spatial visualization and mathematical ability. Psychol. Bull. 107:327–355.

Lubinski, D., Humphreys, L.G. 1990b. A broadly based analysis of mathematical giftedness. Intelligence 14:327–355.

Lubinski, D., Humphreys, L.G. 1992. Some medical and bodily correlates of mathematical giftedness and commensurate levels of socioeconomic status. Intelligence 16:99–115.

Lubinski, D., Thompson, T. 1986. Functional units of human behavior and their integration: A dispositional analysis. In: Thompson, T., Zeiler, M. (eds.), Analysis and integration of behavioral units. Lawrence Erlbaum, Hillsdale, NJ, pp. 275–314.

Lytton, H., Romney, D.M. 1991. Parents' differential socialization of boys and girls: A meta-analysis. Psychol. Bull. 109: 267–296.

MacKinnon, D.W. 1962. The nature and nurture of creative talent. Am. Psychol. 17:484–495.

Mills, C.J., Ablard, K., & Heinrich, S. 1993. Gender differences in academically talented young students' mathematical reasoning: Patterns across age and subskills. J. Educ. Psychol. 85: 1–7.

O'Boyle, M.W., Benbow, C.P. 1990. Enhanced right hemisphere involvement during cognitive processing may relate to intellectual precocity. Neuropsychologia 28:211–216.

O'Boyle, M.W., Alexander, J., Benbow, C.P. 1991. Enhanced right hemisphere activation in the mathematically precocious: A preliminary EEG investigation. Brain Cognit. 17:138–153.

Renzulli, J.S. 1986. The three-ring conception of giftedness: A developmental model for creative productivity. In: Sternberg, R.J., Davidson, J.E. (eds.) Conceptions of giftedness. Cambridge University Press, New York, pp. 53–92.

Roe, A. 1953. The making of a scientist. Dodd, Mead, New York.

Southern, M.L., Plant, W.T. 1968. Personality characteristics of very bright adults. J. Soc. Psychol. 75:119–126.

Stanley, J.C. 1973. Accelerating the educational progress of intellectually gifted youths. Educ. Psychol. 10:133–146.

Stanley, J.C., Keating, D.P., Fox, L.H. (eds.) 1974. Mathematical talent: Discovery, description, and development. Johns Hopkins University Press, Baltimore.

Stanley, J.C., Benbow, C.P., Brody, L.E., Dauber, S., Lupkowski, A.E. 1992. Gender differences on eighty-six nationally standardized aptitude and achievement tests. In: Colangelo, N., Assouline, S.G., Ambroson, D.L. (eds.) Talent development. Trillium Press, Unionville, NY, pp. 42–65.

Tannenbaum, A. 1983. Gifted children: Psychological and educational perspectives. Macmillan, New York.

Thorndike, E.L. 1911. Individuality. Riverside Press, Cambridge, MA.

Walberg, H.J., Strykowski, B.F., Rovai, E., Hung, S.S. 1984. Exceptional performance. Rev. Educ. Res. 54:84–112.

Wallach, M.A. 1976. Tests tell us little about talent. Am. Sci. 64:57–63.

Zuckerman, H. 1977. Scientific élite: Nobel Laureates in the United States. Free Press, New York.

Gender Differences in Math Performance: Not Big, Not Biological

JANET SHIBLEY HYDE

More than two decades ago, Julian Stanley initiated a program of research at Johns Hopkins University, focusing on seventh and eighth graders whose test scores showed that they had exceptional mathematical talent (see, for example, Stanley et al., 1974). The project is called the Study of Mathematically Precocious Youth (SMPY). Camilla Benbow, now at Iowa State University, and David Lubinski have continued this research (Benbow & Lubinski, this volume). What are the claims of these researchers? Do these claims hold up under scrutiny?

The SMPY researchers make two assertions that are relevant to our consideration of gender and mathematics (Benbow & Lubinski, this volume): (1) In samples of exceptionally mathematically talented adolescents, considerably more males are found than females. Moreover, even in this highly selected group, the males outscore the females. In short, boys are better at math than girls are. (2) This gender difference in mathematical ability is due to biological factors. In the sections that follow, I shall examine the evidence for each of the assertions, as well as other implications of the research.

ARE THERE GENDER DIFFERENCES IN MATHEMATICS PERFORMANCE?

The SMPY sample is not a random sample of the population of children of that age, nor was it intended to be. Because it is not a random sample, we cannot generalize SMPY results to the rest of the population. That is, Benbow and Lubinski's results apply only to the mathematical top 1%, not to the other 99% of the population. For the most part, Benbow and Lubinski are careful to speak only about gender differences among the mathematically talented. Other publications by researchers on this project, however, have strayed to talking about gender differences in math ability, with the implication that the general population is the focus (for example, Benbow & Stanley, 1980). This unwarranted generalization has two problems. First, it is poor science. Second, because this research has been highly publicized, it may lead members of the public to believe that *substantial gender differences in mathematical ability exist in the general population*. Let's consider the second point in more detail.

When Benbow and Stanley's article on gender differences in math ability was published in 1980, it received widespread coverage in newspapers and news magazines, and even on radio and television. At the same time, another team of researchers, Jacobs and Eccles (1985), were in the middle of a project on gender and math. They were following adolescents from the general population and their parents in a longitudinal study. Before the publicity about Benbow and Stanley's results appeared, Jacobs and Eccles had already asked parents for their estimates of their child's math abilities and for their gender-role stereotypes regarding math abilities. They were then able to ask these same questions to these parents again, following the publicity about Benbow and Stanley's research; they also asked the parents whether they had read or seen anything about the research. Media exposure had a particularly strong effect on mothers of daughters. Following exposure to the media messages, these women rated their daughters' math competence significantly lower than they had before being exposed, and significantly lower than women who had not been exposed.

There is a danger, then, that people reading this research may think that the results say "boys are better at math than girls are," when in fact the results at most show that "among the highly mathematically talented, boys are better at math than girls are." This misunderstanding is more than just an intellectual problem. It has been demonstrated to have an effect on whether mothers think their daughters are good at math, and mothers' beliefs, in turn, have been shown to influence their daughters' thinking about their own math competence (Eccles, 1987).

This overgeneralization of the results might not be too much of a problem, though, if other researchers, studying the general population, found the same patterns of gender differences that Benbow and Lubinski found. What do studies based on general samples say?

To answer this question my colleagues and I used a technique called meta-analysis (Hyde et al., 1990). Meta-analysis is essentially a statistical technique for combining the results of many studies. It allowed us to see whether, averaged over the many studies of gender and math that have been collected, there is a significant gender difference, what the direction of the difference is, and how large the difference is. The statistic we computed in the meta-analysis is called d.[1] Positive values of d indicate that males scored better, and negative values indicate that females scored better. Generally, a d value of 0.20 is considered to be a small difference, $d = 0.50$ is considered a moderate difference, and $d = 0.80$ is considered large (Cohen, 1969).

We were able to locate a hundred studies of gender and math, representing the testing of more than 3 million people, for our meta-analysis (Hyde et al., 1990). Some of the studies were not based on samples of the general population (for example, studies of mathematically precocious youth). When we looked just at studies based on samples of the general population, we found $d = -0.05$. That is, girls scored higher (the value is negative). But this difference is so small that it indicates that

1. The formula for d is as follows: $d = (M_M - M_F) / s$, where M_M is the mean score for males, M_F is the mean score for females, and s is the average within-gender standard deviation.

no gender difference exists. This is quite a different result than one might expect after reading Benbow and Lubinski's essay.

More recently, these results were confirmed in a meta-analysis by Hedges and Nowell (1995). They examined data from five large, well-sampled nationwide studies of high school students' performance on standardized tests. Across the samples, the effect size for gender differences in mathematics performance ranged from $d = +0.03$ to $+0.24$, with an average $d = +.16$. This difference indicates better performance by males (the value is positive), but the difference is small and, given that the test takers were high school students (a point to be discussed further below), the findings are quite consistent with our earlier meta-analysis. In the general population, the gender difference in mathematics performance is not large.

We also conducted some additional analyses to determine the following: (1) Are there age trends in the gender difference—for example, might there be no gender difference in elementary school but a large difference in adolescence? and (2) Do the gender differences depend on the cognitive level of the math test —that is, are gender differences larger for problem solving (as measured in story problems) than for simpler problems that involve only computation (Hyde et al., 1990)? Benbow and Lubinski concern themselves only with mathematical problem solving, because this is the ability that is crucial for advanced careers in engineering and the physical sciences. Our additional analyses indicated that there were no gender differences in computation at any age—if anything, females have a small advantage in elementary school and middle school. For problem solving, the pattern was more complex. There were no gender differences in elementary school or middle school. A small-to-moderate gender difference emerged favoring males, though, in high school ($d = 0.29$) and the college years ($d = 0.32$).

It is crucial to notice that the gender difference in mathematical problem solving does not emerge until high school, precisely the time at which mathematics courses become optional. Girls are less likely than boys to choose to take optional math courses. To compound the problem, high school girls are also less likely to enroll in courses in the physical sciences. Some experts in math education believe that problem solving is taught very little in most math classrooms, which emphasize computation. Math problem solving may be taught more in science courses. High school girls taking a standardized math test, then, are at a triple disadvantage compared with high school boys. They have taken fewer math courses, it has been longer since they took a math course, and they have taken fewer science courses. We should not be surprised that high school girls score somewhat lower on tests of mathematical problem solving. What is surprising is that researchers would search for biological explanations when the environmental ones are so clear.

In conclusion, studies of the general population find no gender differences in mathematics performance, with the exception of a difference favoring males in problem solving, emerging in high school. This difference most likely is explained by the lesser enrollment of girls in optional math and science courses.

THE BIOLOGICAL EVIDENCE

Benbow and Lubinski (this volume) base their argument that gender differences in mathematics performance are biological—and here it is not clear whether they are talking just about the gifted or about the general population—on a theory by Geschwind. He argued that being exposed to high levels of testosterone prenatally enhances the functioning of the right hemisphere of the brain, which is generally responsible for processing spatial problems (and the left hemisphere is primarily responsible for processing verbal problems). Benbow and Lubinski reason, by implication, that because males are exposed to more testosterone prenatally, they will perform better on math problems.

Benbow and Lubinski present two categories of evidence. First, they refer to several studies that find an association between mathematical talent, left-handedness, and right-hemispheric functioning. Readers are provided with so little detail about

these studies, however, that they cannot evaluate them. Second, they describe two electroencephalogram studies in which electrical activity in the brains of mathematically gifted and control boys and girls was recorded while they were working on either verbal problems or spatial problems. The results lead them to conclude that different patterns of brain activity underlie mathematical precocity in males. The important thing to notice about these studies, though, is that the boys and girls were not solving mathematical problems—rather, they were engaged in verbal or spatial problem solving. How can one conclude that gender differences in mathematical precocity have a biological basis when the students were not even doing math problems?

The evidence for biological causes of possible gender differences in math problem-solving ability, then, is more in the realm of speculation than in the realm of solid evidence.

THE GREATER MALE VARIABILITY HYPOTHESIS

The Greater Male Variability Hypothesis was proposed more than one hundred years ago (Ellis, 1894; Shields, 1975). It states that, regardless of whether gender differences exist in mean (average) scores, males are more variable than females. In statistical terms, the hypothesis says that the variance (or standard deviation) for males is larger than the variance for females. The result would be—even in the absence of an average gender difference—a greater number of males at the high end of the distribution and also at the low end. The hypothesis originated from the observation in the 1800s that there were more eminent men than women, and more men than women in homes for the mentally deficient (Ellis, 1894).

Two meta-analyses of the 1990s have addressed the issue of greater male variability in mathematics performance. Feingold (1992) examined the performance of eighth through twelfth graders on standardized tests. He computed a statistic called the variance ratio, which is the ratio of the variance for males to the variance for females. If the variance ratio is 1.0, males and females are equally variable. If the ratio is greater than 1.0, males have more variability (variance) than females, and if the ratio is less than 1.0, females have greater variability. Feingold found that the variance ratio for performance on math tests was approximately 1.11. That is, males were slightly more variable.

Hedges and Nowell (1995), in a meta-analysis discussed earlier, also looked at the variance ratio. For mathematics, they found variance ratios ranging between 1.05 and 1.25, with an average of 1.15, a figure very close to Feingold's. Again, the results indicate that males are slightly more variable.

It may be, then, that the excess of males in samples of the highly mathematically talented is due not to average gender differences in math ability but to greater variability in the distribution of males' scores. This explanation, unfortunately, raises at least as many questions as it answers. Chief among these questions is, What causes greater variability among males? Scientists have not tackled this one yet.

WHY ARE THERE FEW WOMEN IN HIGH-MATH-ABILITY CAREERS? A FEMINIST ANALYSIS

Benbow and Lubinski express a concern—one that many others share—about why so few women choose careers, such as engineering and the physical sciences, that require high math ability. I call this the Dearth of Women Phenomenon. Based on the Theory of Work Adjustment, Benbow and Lubinski conclude that the Dearth of Women Phenomenon is due to (1) gender differences in the number of people having the critical level of math *ability* for these careers; and (2) gender differences in *preferences* for studying and working in the content areas of engineering and the physical sciences. That is, Benbow and Lubinski argue that a combination of ability and preference is at work.

Feminist analysis makes a distinction between internal attributions for phenomena and external attributions (Hyde, 1996). Internal attributions refer to causes internal to the individual, such as ability. External attributions refer to causes external to the individual, such as discrimination, parents' atti-

tudes, and so on. Feminist theorists are generally critical of internal attributions, such as blaming rape on a woman's seductiveness. Such internal attributions often amount to blaming the victim. Feminist theorists instead emphasize external attributions; rape, for example, is viewed as the result of socializing males to be aggressive and to associate sex with aggression.

The crucial point is that Benbow and Lubinski construct two internal attributions for the Dearth of Women Phenomenon: ability and personal preferences. In so doing, they ignore dozens of other explanations that rely on external attributions. Examples include the following:

1. The fields of science and engineering lack role models for women. Women are dramatically underrepresented on university science and mathematics faculties, for example (Holloway, 1993; Koshland, 1988).

2. Sexual harassment of women is associated with highly gender-segregated, male-dominated fields (Fitzgerald, 1993; Gutek, 1985).

3. Math and science courses are not taught in a manner that is interesting and compelling to women (Holloway, 1993).

4. Males have substantially more informal experience with physical science than females. By the eleventh grade, for example, 49% of males compared with 17% of females report that they have used an electricity meter (that is, the equivalent of $d = +0.95$; Linn & Hyde, 1989).

Cross-cultural evidence supports the view that the dearth of women in science is due to culture, not biology. In the United States, 15% of B.S. degrees in physics go to women and 11% of Ph.D.s in physics go to women. Among tenure track faculty in physics, women are only about 3%. In contrast, in France 21% of Ph.D.s in physics go to women and 23% of university faculty in physics are women. In Italy, the figures are identical to those for France: 21% and 23%. Even in Turkey, 23% of physics faculty members are women. Cross-culturally, the percentage does not approach an equitable 50% except in Hungary, where 47% of physics faculty in universities are women (Dresselhaus et al.

1994). If women constitute only 3% of physics faculty in the United States because of biological factors, it is difficult to explain how women have achieved so much more in physics in other countries. Culture, not biology, shapes women's success in science.

Four conclusions are warranted regarding gender, math, and the mathematically precocious:

1. Although there may be gender differences in math performance in samples of mathematically gifted youth, these findings should not be generalized to the rest of the population.

2. Meta-analysis shows that, in the general population, gender differences in mathematics performance are close to zero, with the exception of math problem solving, where a difference favoring males emerges in the high school years.

3. The evidence of biological causes of gender differences in math performance is at present mostly speculative. Moreover, because there is little evidence of a gender difference in math performance in the general population, it makes no sense to search for a biological cause of difference.

4. A likely explanation for gender differences in math problem solving in high school involves girls' lesser enrollment in math and science courses in high school.

Whether we are concerned with scientific research or with social action, the best strategy is to discover why girls are less likely to take high school math and science courses (see, for example, Eccles, 1987) and then to make efforts to change these factors. These efforts may involve developing girl-friendly math classrooms, or special programs that help girls learn the relevance of math for careers they may want to pursue in adulthood. These strategies will be most effective if we really want to do something about women and math.

REFERENCES

Benbow, C. P., & Stanley, J. C. (1980). Sex differences in mathematical ability: Fact or artifact? *Science, 210,* 1262–1264.

Cohen, J. (1969). *Statistical power analysis for the behavioral sciences.* New York: Academic Press.

Dresselhaus, M. D., Franz, J. R., & Clark, B. C. (1994). Interventions to increase the participation of women in physics. *Science, 263,* 1392–1393.

Eccles, J. (1987). Gender roles and women's achievement-related decisions. *Psychology of Women Quarterly, 11,* 135–172.

Ellis, H. (1894). *Man and woman: A study of human secondary sexual characters.* New York: Scribner's.

Feingold, A. (1992). Sex differences in variability in intellectual abilities: A new look at an old controversy. *Review of Educational Research, 62,* 61–84.

Fitzgerald, L. F. (1993). Sexual harassment. *American Psychologist, 48,* 1070–1076.

Gutek, B. A. (1985). *Sex and the workplace.* San Francisco: Jossey-Bass.

Hedges, L. V., & Nowell, A. (1995). Sex differences in mental test scores, variability, and numbers of high-scoring individuals. *Science, 269,* 41–45.

Holloway, M. (1993, November). A lab of her own. *Scientific American,* 94–103.

Hyde, J. S. (1996). *Half the human experience: The psychology of women.* 5th ed., Lexington, Mass.: D. C. Heath.

Hyde, J. S., Fennema, E., & Lamon, S. J. (1990). Gender differences in mathematics performance: A meta-analysis. *Psychological Bulletin, 107,* 139–155.

Jacobs, J., & Eccles, J. S. (1985). Science and the media: Benbow and Stanley revisited. *Educational Researcher, 14,* 20–25.

Koshland, D. E. (1988). Women in science. *Science, 239,* 1473.

Linn, M. C., & Hyde, J. S. (1989, November). Gender, mathematics, and science. *Educational Researcher, 18,* 17–27.

Shields, S. A. (1975). Functionalism, Darwinism, and the psychology of women: A study in social myth. *American Psychologist, 30,* 739–754.

Stanley, J. C., Keating, D. P., Fox, L. H. (Eds.) (1974). *Mathematical talent: Discovery, description, and development.* Baltimore: Johns Hopkins University Press.

PART VI

The Workplace

Leadership: Do Women and Men Have Different Ways of Leading?

Most of the research on women's leadership in the 1970s and 1980s focused on the question of why women were less likely than men to be leaders. Any number of reasons, in addition to job discrimination, have been used to explain the relatively small number of female leaders: fear of success (M. Horner, 1972), fear of failure (A. Horner, 1989), low self-confidence (Hancock, 1989), career-family conflict (Schwartz, 1989), and low-status aspirations (Hannah & Kahn, 1989). Recently, Powell and Butterfield (1994) added the speculation that women are less likely to apply for leadership positions because they anticipate being blocked by a "glass ceiling," the invisible barrier that blocks them from top jobs.

As more and more women secured managerial positions in the 1990s, researchers began examining the similarities and differences in female and male leadership styles. In a meta-analysis of studies on the subject, Eagly and Johnson (1990) found that women and men generally exhibited similar leadership styles, with women demonstrating a slightly greater tendency to adopt a democratic or participatory approach. Those women who do adopt a more autocratic male style of leadership, however, are more likely to receive negative treatment (Eagly, Makhijani & Klonsky, 1992). In a follow-up synthesis of research on the relative effectiveness of women and men managers, Eagly and her colleagues (1995) discovered that women are judged more capable in roles that are defined in relatively feminine terms, whereas men are viewed as more capable in roles defined in relatively masculine terms.

In an article in the *Harvard Business Review* (1990), Judy Rosener, a professor in the Graduate School of Management at the University of California, Irvine, broke with the growing consensus in the psychology literature when she argued that women and men had different leadership styles. Just as Belenky et al. (1986) found a woman's way of knowing and Tannen (1990) identified a woman's way of talking, Rosener detected a woman's way of leading. Women, she contended, are comfortable with ambiguity, and favor a collaborative style that tends to empower workers. But, because women do not fit the male hierarchical model, they have not been viewed as potential leaders. The result is that in 1995, nine years after Hymowitz and Schellhardt (1986) coined the term *glass ceiling*, the U.S. Glass Ceiling Commission revealed that only 3–5 percent of top U.S. executives were female ("Glass Ceiling?" 1995). In *America's Competitive Secret* (1995), Rosener argues that the need to place women in top management is a matter of not only equity but also economics. She believes that this untapped pool of well-educated professional women will give America a competitive edge in today's fast-changing, service-oriented world of business.

Some critics are wary of Rosener's focus on sex differences in leadership styles. Myra Strober, a Stanford labor economist, fears that an emphasis on differences can reinforce gender stereotypes and wonders further if a belief in female superiority would undermine the argument for affirmative action. Rosener finds it ironic that when the characteristics associated with women were negative, gender was seen as relevant, but now that they are positive, no one wants to talk about them (Noble, 1993).

Do women make better managers? In the following chapters, Judy Rosener argues that they do. Gary N. Powell, who believes that neither sex has a special advantage, disagrees and warns us that Rosener's ideas could lead to a ghettoization of women managers.

REFERENCES

Belenky, M. F., Clinchy, B. M., Goldberger, N. R., & Tarule, J. M. (1986). *Women's ways of knowing: The development of self, voice, and mind.* New York: Basic Books.

Eagly, A. H., & Johnson, B. T. (1990). Gender and leadership style: A meta-analysis. *Psychological Bulletin, 108*, 233–256.

Eagly, A. H., Karau, S. J., & Makhijani, M. (1995). Gender and the effectiveness of leaders: A meta-analysis. *Psychological Bulletin, 117*, 125–145.

Eagly, A. H., Makhijani, M. G., & Klonsky, B. G. (1992). Gender and the evaluation of leaders: A meta-analysis. *Psychological Bulletin, 111*, 3–22.

Glass ceiling? It's more like a steel cage. (1995, March 20). *Los Angeles Times*, p. 4.

Hancock, E. (1989). *The girl within.* New York: Fawcett Columbine.

Hannah, J. S., & Kahn, S. E. (1989). The relationship of socioeconomic status and gender to the occupational choices of Grade 12 students. *Journal of Vocational Behavior, 34* (2), 161–178.

Horner, A. J. (1989). *The wish for power and the fear of having it.* New York: Jason Aronson.

Horner, M. (1972). Toward an understanding of achievement-related conflicts in women. *Journal of Social Issues, 28*, 157–175.

Hymowitz, C., & Schellhardt, T. (1986, March 24). The glass ceiling: Why women can't seem to break the invisible barrier that blocks them from top jobs. *Wall Street Journal*, A special report: The corporate woman, pp. 1, 4–5.

Noble, B. P. The debate over *la différence*. (1993, August 15). *New York Times*, p. 6.

Powell, G. N., & Butterfield, D. A. (1994). Investigating the "glass ceiling" phenomenon: An empirical study of actual promotions to top management. *Academy of Management Journal, 37*, 68–86.

Rosener, J. B. (1990). Ways women lead. *Harvard Business Review, 68*, 119–125.

Rosener, J. B. (1995). *America's competitive secret: Utilizing women as a management strategy.* New York: Oxford University Press.

Schwartz, F. N. (1989). Management women and the new facts of life. *Harvard Business Review, 67*, 65–76.

Tannen, D. (1990). *You just don't understand: Women and men in conversation.* New York: William Morrow.

ADDITIONAL READING

Cantor, D. W., & Bernay, T. (1992). *Women in power: The secrets of leadership.* New York: Houghton Mifflin.

Driscoll, D. M., & Goldberg, C. (1993). *Members of the club: The coming age of executive women.* New York: Free Press.

Haslett, B. J., Geis, F. L., & Carter, M. R. (1992). *The organizational woman: Power and paradox.* Norwood, N.J.: Ablex.

Heifetz, R. A. (1994). *Leadership without easy answers.* Cambridge, Mass.: Harvard University Press.

Heim, P., with Golant, S. K. (1992). *Hardball for women: Winning at the game of business.* Los Angeles: Lowell House.

Jamieson, K. H. (1995). *Beyond the double bind: Women and leadership.* New York: Oxford University Press.

Morrison, A. M. (1992). *The new leaders: Guidelines on leadership diversity in America.* San Francisco: Jossey-Bass.

Van Nostrand, C. H. (1993). *Gender-responsible leadership: Detecting bias, implementing interventions.* Newbury Park, Calif.: Sage.

Leadership and the Paradox of Gender

JUDY B. ROSENER

In the context of American management, the one best model has traditionally been the command-and-control model. Organizations using this model are hierarchical and have clear lines of authority. Decisions are made from the top down, and it is assumed that those at the top know best. Performance is judged on individual rather than group contribution, and criteria for advancement have as much to do with fitting in as with competence. As its name suggests, the command-and-control model strongly resembles the military. It is no surprise that books about military leaders like Norman Schwarzkopf and Colin Powell, and corporate CEOs like Ross Perot and Lee Iacocca, are popular with businessmen. Their stories and philosophies reinforce the belief that success comes from being a commanding male manager.

American institutions tend to look alike. They have similar structures and practices and similar kinds of leaders.[1] Typically, American executives are White, male, heterosexual, and married with children. They are individualists, linear thinkers, sports fans, and usually military veterans. They also tend to be workaholics and graduates of prestigious colleges. They value their families but spend little

time with them.[2] Although there are many women who aspire to and are qualified for positions of power in major organizations, female leaders remain the exception rather than the rule. As Julie Newcomb Hill, CEO of Costain Homes, has said, "There's only so much shelf space for women at the top of organizations."[3]

Given the success of American institutions in the past, it can't be denied that the command-and-control model worked. And because White males created and led most organizations, it isn't surprising that they occupy the most powerful positions. But as Yogi Berra said years ago, "The future ain't what it used to be." The economic climate has changed, and organizations and theories of management must change, too. It has become apparent that the command-and-control model does not always produce optimal results.

However, to say that command-and-control leadership is no longer the one best model is not to say that it has lost its value. It has not. Rather, there *is* no one best model, and command-and-control leadership is only *one of many models* that can help an organization compete in today's work environment.

Increasingly, what I have described as the interactive leadership model is seen as desirable and complementary to the command-and-control model. The interactive style involves managing in a collaborative rather than top-down fashion. It is characterized by the use of a reward system that values group as well as individual contributions, the empowerment of workers at all levels, multidirectional feedback and performance evaluation, and a strong emphasis on interpersonal as well as technical skills. This style is well suited to fast-changing organizations that require flexibility, individual and group self-direction, and comfort with the sharing of power and information. It is the style many profes-

---

1. Korn/Ferry International with the UCLA Anderson Graduate School of Management, *The Executive Profile: A Decade of Change in Corporate Leadership* (1990).

2. Marilyn Loden and Judy Rosener, *Workforce America! Managing Employee Diversity as a Vital Resource* (Homewood, Ill.: Business One Irwin, 1991), 42–44.

3. Julie Newcomb Hill, conversation with author, August 1994.

sional women tend to prefer. Yet because it differs from the male command-and-control style, women have not been viewed as potential leaders. Instead they have been the target of books advising them that if they want to succeed, they have to think and act like men.[4] Implicit in this idea is the assumption that the "right" or "best" way to run an organization is the White male way.

Over time, women develop a particular set of skills and values shaped by their life experiences. For example, they are comfortable with ambiguity because their lives are full of uncertainty. They are good at juggling and completing many tasks simultaneously because that is the story of their daily existence. It isn't strange to see a woman feeding a baby, watching the news on TV, listening to her husband, and thinking about how to solve a problem at work, all at the same time. Not so with men, who more often than not have the luxury of focusing on one or two things at a time. It is not strange for women to change plans and moods as often as sheets, because household chores and family responsibilities are not easily scheduled and women rarely have others to take care of their schedules for them. Women simultaneously have to satisfy the different needs and conflicting demands of husbands, parents, in-laws, children, friends, and fellow workers. Consequently, they develop negotiating skills that are often different from those of men.

I am not suggesting that men do not also experience ambiguity and conflicting demands. Henry Mintzberg, in *The Nature of Managerial Work*, points out that the daily experience of men is punctuated with interruptions.[5] However, most male executives resent interruptions and often use their secretaries to shield them from distractions. Women executives tend to see unscheduled tasks and encounters not as unwelcome interruptions but rather as opportunities to connect.[6] And men generally do not have to juggle household chores with managerial work responsibilities, whereas most professional women work a "second shift" that never goes away.[7]

This second-shift responsibility, along with women's tendency to speak "in a different voice" and "women's ways of knowing," differentiates them from their male colleagues at work.[8] These differences, in my opinion, help explain why women never fully measure up to the standards of what American business leaders consider to be the executive model.

I don't think there's much doubt that the attributes and behaviors associated with women are those of the interactive leadership style. It would be simplistic and reductive to say that the interactive style is the exclusive province of women and the command-and-control style the exclusive province of men. All men do not behave in the same way, nor do all women. Clearly, gender differences exist along a continuum. But there is by now a large body of academic and popular literature suggesting that women and men do indeed tend to differ in the ways they think and act.[9] My own research has convinced me that these differences are real and that they carry over into leadership styles.

4. See, for example, Margaret Hennig and Ann Jardim, *The Managerial Woman* (New York: Pocket Books, 1976); Betty Lehan Harragan, *Games Mother Never Taught You* (New York: Warner Books, 1977); Bette Ann Stead, *Women in Management* (Englewood Cliffs, N.J.: Prentice-Hall, 1978); Alice G. Sargent, *Beyond Sex Roles* (St. Paul, Minn.: West Publishing, 1977, 1985); Ann Harriman, *Women/Men/Management* (New York: Praeger, 1985); Lynda L. Moore, *Not As Far As You Think* (Lexington, Mass.: Lexington Books / D. C. Heath, 1986).

5. Henry Mintzberg, *The Nature of Managerial Work* (New York: Harper and Row, 1973), vii-x.

6. Sally Helgeson, *The Female Advantage: Women's Ways of Leadership* (New York: Doubleday/Currency, 1990), 10, 20.

7. Arlie Hochschild with Anne Machung, *The Second Shift: Working Women and the Revolution at Home* (New York: Viking, 1989).

8. See Carol Gilligan, *In a Different Voice* (Cambridge, Mass.: Harvard University Press, 1982); Mary Field Belenky et al., *Women's Ways of Knowing* (New York: Basic Books, 1986).

9. See, for example, Gilligan, *In a Different Voice;* Belenky et al., *Women's Ways of Knowing;* Deborah Tannen, *You Just Don't Understand* (New York: William Morrow, 1990); John Gray, *Men Are from Mars, Women Are from Venus* (New York: HarperCollins, 1992).

As early as 1978, in his famous book *Leadership*, James MacGregor Burns mentioned a male bias in the concept of leadership. He argued that leadership should be seen as a process in which leaders engaged and mobilized the human needs and aspirations of followers. When that happened, he said, women would be recognized as leaders and men would change their leadership style.[10] Tom Peters, author of the best-selling *In Search of Excellence*, makes reference in many of his syndicated newspaper columns to the effectiveness of female attributes in organizations that call for flexibility.

Burns and Peters are exceptions in the leadership literature, however. A great deal has been written about the subject,[11] but most studies suggest that men and women display similar leadership traits, such as vision, intelligence, charisma, commitment, and drive. Male and female leaders look alike in this context because most leadership studies focus on the traits themselves rather than how they are operationalized. Having observed female leaders, I was interested in testing the hypothesis that while men and women share general leadership traits, their leadership styles are quite different. I was convinced that those who had conducted leadership studies asked the wrong questions and looked in the wrong places for answers. They looked at large companies, large universities, and large government agencies. It might be expected that women leaders in these kinds of organizations would lead like men. In order to be promoted, they probably had to adopt the command-and-control leadership style. I wondered what happened to women (and men) who chose to lead in a different way. Where did they go? Did they succeed using a different leadership style?

In 1989, to answer these questions, I conducted a nationwide study of men and women leaders in diverse professions. In particular, I focused on a group of successful women leaders to ascertain how they exercised power, what kind of leadership style they preferred, and what kinds of organizations they worked in. As a basis for comparison, I looked at a similar group of male leaders at the same time. That study formed the basis of my article "Ways Women Lead," which was published in the *Harvard Business Review* in late 1990 and became a lightning rod for debate about gender differences in a management context.[12] I found that women, on average, exhibited and preferred the interactive leadership style, and men the command-and-control leadership style, and that the interactive style is particularly effective in flexible, nonhierarchical organizations of the kind that perform best in a climate of rapid change. My findings did not suggest that one style is better or worse than the other, only that men and women tend to lead differently and that interactive leaders tend to be most successful in nontraditional organizations.

As I have said, the inattention to human resource utilization in management thinking, along with the related assumption that "cream rises to the top," in part explains why organizations have not looked to women as leaders and why women are still so scarce in top management. However, I believe there is another factor at work, what I call the paradox of gender.

Paradox of Gender

- When attributes or behaviors associated with women are considered negative or of little value, gender is seen as relevant.
- When attributes or behaviors associated with women are considered positive or valuable, gender is seen as irrelevant.

As long as the command-and-control management style dominated organizations, female-linked behaviors such as consensus building, power sharing, and comfort with ambiguity were considered signs of weakness, and gender was the explanation. These behaviors, judged wanting in comparison to command-and-control behaviors, were supposedly what made women unfit for leadership roles. But as doubts about the effectiveness of the command-and-control model made their way into the execu-

10. James MacGregor Burns, *Leadership* (New York: Harper Torchbooks, 1978).

11. See Barnard Bass, *Handbook of Leadership* (New York: Free Press, 1974), 59–88.

12. Judy B. Rosener, "Ways Women Lead," *Harvard Business Review*, November-December 1990, 119–25.

tive suite, these same behaviors began to appear in a positive light and were no longer considered female. They were now simply good leadership traits. It is revealing, for example, that in defending the role of intuition and emotion in management decisions, Herbert Simon[13] made no mention of the prevailing view of these qualities as "female" and therefore irrational and unreliable. Similarly, when the attributes associated with the interactive leadership style are considered organizationally effective, they are often presented as gender neutral. Ironically, in some organizations men are now being trained to be interactive leaders while women are still hitting the glass ceiling because they *are* interactive leaders.

13. Herbert A. Simon, "Making Management Decisions: The Role of Intuition and Emotion," *Academy of Management Executive*, February 1987, 57–63.

NO

Leadership and Gender:

Vive la Différence?

GARY N. POWELL

There has been a dramatic change in the face of management over the past two decades. That face is now female more than one-third of the time. What are the implications for the practice of management? Most of us are aware of traditional stereotypes about male-female differences, but how well do these stereotypes apply to the managerial ranks? Do female and male managers differ in their basic responses to work situations and in their overall effectiveness (and if so, in what ways?), or are they really quite similar?

If you believe recent books and articles in business magazines, female and male managers bring different personal qualities to their jobs. For example, Jan Grant, in an *Organizational Dynamics* article entitled "Women as Managers: What They Can Offer to Organizations,"[1] argues that women have unique qualities that make them particularly well suited to be managers. She says that instead of forcing women to fit the male model of managerial success, which stresses such qualities as independence, competitiveness, forcefulness, and analytical thinking, organizations should place greater emphasis on such female qualities as affiliation and attachment, cooperativeness, nurturance, and emotionality.

Felice Schwartz's *Harvard Business Review* article, "Management Women and the New Facts of

Life,"[2] triggered a national debate over the merits of "mommy tracks" (although she did not use the term herself). She proposed that corporations (1) distinguish between "career-primary women," who put their careers first, and "career-and-family" women, who seek a balance between career and family; (2) nurture the careers of the former group as potential top executives; and (3) offer flexible work arrangements and family supports to the latter group in exchange for lower opportunities for career advancement. Women were assumed to be more interested in such arrangements than men and were therefore less likely to be suitable top executives; there has been less discussion over the merits of "daddy tracks."

Judy Rosener, in her book *America's Competitive Secret: Utilizing Women as a Management Strategy*, distinguishes between male and female leadership styles. In contrast to the "command-and-control" model more associated with males, she finds that women prefer an "interactive" style, which is shaped by their life experiences and involves "managing in a collaborative rather than top-down fashion."[3] Marilyn Loden, in a book entitled *Feminine Leadership, or How to Succeed in Business Without Being One of the Boys*, similarly concludes that female managers are more capable than male managers of exhibiting "feminine leadership," which she sees organizations as needing more than ever. She summarizes her view about male-female differences in the managerial ranks in three words: "Vive la différence!"[4]

Women and men certainly differ in their success within the ranks of management. Although women have made great strides in entering management since 1970, with the overall proportion of

1. J. Grant, "Women as Managers: What They Can Offer to Organizations," *Organizational Dynamics*, 16 (No. 3, Winter 1988): 56–63.

2. F. N. Schwartz, "Management Women and the New Facts of Life," *Harvard Business Review*, 67 (No. 1, January-February 1989): 65–76.

3. J. B. Rosener, *America's Competitive Secret: Utilizing Women as a Management Strategy* (New York: Oxford University Press, 1995).

4. M. Loden, *Feminine Leadership, or How to Succeed in Business Without Being One of the Boys* (New York: Times Books, 1985), p. 79.

women managers rising from 16 percent to 42 percent, the proportion of women who hold *top* management positions is less than 5 percent.[5] This may simply be because the average male manager is older and more experienced than the average female manager. After all, managerial careers invariably start at the bottom. If there were no basic differences between male and female managers, it would be just a matter of time until the proportion of women was about the same at all managerial levels.

But *are* there basic differences between male and female managers? According to traditional gender stereotypes, males are more masculine (e.g., self-reliant, aggressive, competitive, decisive) and females more feminine (e.g., sympathetic, gentle, shy, sensitive to the needs of others).[6] Grant's, Rosener's, and Loden's views of male-female differences mirror these stereotypes. But the applicability of these stereotypes to managers is debated. Four distinct points of view have emerged:

1. *No differences.* Women who pursue the nontraditional career of manager reject the feminine stereotype and have goals, motives, personalities, and behaviors that are similar to those of men who pursue managerial careers.

2. *Stereotypical differences favoring men.* Female and male managers differ in ways predicted by gender stereotypes as a result of early socialization experiences that leave men better suited to be managers.

3. *Stereotypical differences favoring women.* Female and male managers differ in accordance with gender stereotypes owing to early socialization experiences, but managers in today's work world need feminine traits in particular.

4. *Nonstereotypical differences.* Female and male managers differ in ways opposite to gender stereotypes because women managers have had to be exceptional to compensate for early socialization experiences that are different from those of men.

In this chapter, I briefly review the evidence on gender differences in management that has been gathered since women managers were first noticed by researchers in the mid-1970s to determine the level of support for each of these points of view.[7] Possible differences in personal traits, behavior, effectiveness, values, commitment, and subordinates' responses are considered, then implications of the review are discussed.

Do Female and Male Managers Differ?

One of the most extensive research studies ever conducted of managers and their personal characteristics took place in the Bell System through its parent, the American Telephone and Telegraph Company (AT&T). Prior to the court-ordered 1984 divestiture of its regional operating companies, the Bell System was the nation's largest business enterprise. In the late 1970s and early 1980s AT&T initiated a study of 344 lower-level managers who were considered to be representative of those managers from whom Bell's future middle- and upper-level managers would come. Nearly half of those studied were women.[8]

These managers went through three days of assessment exercises. Extensive comparisons were made in terms of background, work interests, personality, motivation, abilities, and overall managerial potential. Women had advantages in administrative ability, interpersonal skills and sensitivity, written communication skills, energy, and inner work standards. Men had advantages in

5. U.S. Department of Labor, Bureau of Labor Statistics, *Employment and Earnings*, 39 (No. 5, May 1992), computed from table A-22, p. 29; A. B. Fisher, "When Will Women Get to the Top?" *Fortune*, 126 (No. 6, 21 September 1992): 44–56.

6. For a review of research on gender stereotypes, see R. D. Ashmore, F. K. Del Boca, and A. J. Wohlers, "Gender Stereotypes," in *The Social Psychology of Female-Male Relations: A Critical Analysis of Central Concepts*, ed. R. D. Ashmore and F. K. Del Boca (Orlando, Fla.: Academic Press, 1986).

7. For a more extensive report of this review with complete references, see G. N. Powell, "Managing People," in *Women and Men in Management*, 2nd ed. (Newbury Park, Calif.: Sage, 1993).

8. A. Howard and D. W. Bray, *Managerial Lives in Transition: Advancing Age and Changing Times* (New York: Guilford Press, 1988).

company loyalty, motivation to advance within the company, and attentiveness to power structures. The greatest gender difference was masculinity/femininity: men were more likely to have traditionally masculine interests, whereas women were more likely to have traditionally feminine interests. There were no gender differences in intellectual ability, leadership ability, oral communication skills, or stability of performance. When the assessors took these tradeoffs into account, they judged women and men to have similar managerial potential. Forty-five percent of the women and 39 percent of the men were judged to have the potential to attain middle management in the Bell System within ten years. Douglas Bray, who directed the AT&T studies until he was succeeded by Ann Howard, concluded: "Vive la no différence!"

Other research on the personality and motivation of managers generally has found few gender differences. Both male and female managers are high in their motivation to manage. Many researchers have found that women and men managers score essentially the same on psychological tests of needs and motives that are supposed to predict managerial success. When differences have been found in the relative strength of motives possessed by female and male managers, they have generally favored women and been contrary to gender stereotypes. In a study of nearly 2,000 managers that was similar to the AT&T study in scope but examined managers from different organizations, Susan Donnell and Jay Hall found that women managers reported lower basic needs and higher needs for self-actualization. Women were seen as exhibiting a "more mature and higher-achieving motivational profile" than their male counterparts, being more concerned with opportunities for growth, autonomy, and challenge and less concerned with work environment and pay.[9]

Most studies of gender differences in managerial or leader behavior have examined two aspects of leadership style. The first, called *task style*, refers to the extent to which the manager initiates work activity, organizes it, and defines the way work is to be done. The second, called *interpersonal style*, refers to the extent to which the manager engages in activities that tend to the morale and welfare of people in the work setting. Task and interpersonal styles of leadership are typically regarded as independent dimensions. That is, a manager may be high in both task and interpersonal styles, low in both, or high in one but not the other. A third aspect of leadership style that has been frequently studied is the extent to which the leader exhibits *democratic leadership*, which allows subordinates to participate in decision making, versus *autocratic leadership*, which discourages such participation; these are considered to be opposites.

Although a "meta-analysis" of research studies found gender differences in each of these three dimensions of leadership style, the size of the difference varied, as did the circumstances under which it appeared. Small gender differences were found in task style and interpersonal style; however, these differences appeared only for subjects in laboratory experiments and for nonleaders who were assessed on how they would behave if they were actually leaders. There were no gender differences in the task and interpersonal styles of actual managers. In contrast, a more pronounced gender difference was found in democratic versus autocratic leadership. Women tended to be more democratic, less autocratic leaders than men, a difference that appeared for individuals in all settings—actual managers, nonmanagers, and subjects in laboratory experiments. These results offer support for both the no-differences and the stereotypical-differences views.[10]

A separate meta-analysis found no sex difference in overall leader effectiveness. Still, men fared better in such male-dominated work environments as the military, whereas women fared better in

9. S. M. Donnell and J. Hall, "Men and Women as Managers: A Significant Case of No Significant Difference," *Organizational Dynamics*, 8 (No. 4, Spring 1980), p. 71.

10. A. H. Eagly and B. T. Johnson, "Gender and Leadership Style: A Meta-Analysis," *Psychological Bulletin*, 108 (1990): 233–256; A. H. Eagly, "Sex Differences in Human Social Behavior: Meta-Analytic Studies of Social Psychological Research," in *The Development of Sex Differences and Similarities in Behavior*, ed. M. Haug, R. E. Whalen, C. Aron, and K. L. Olsen (Dordrecht, Netherlands: Kluwer Academic, 1993).

such female-dominated work settings as schools. These results support a no-differences view overall, but a stereotypical-differences view within work environments dominated by either sex.[11]

The values of managers, especially top executives, usually receive attention only when a corporate scandal takes place. Personal values have considerable influence on how managers handle the responsibilities of their jobs. Values may influence perceptions of others, solutions to problems, and the sense of what constitutes individual and organizational success. Values also influence what managers believe to be ethical and unethical behavior and whether they accept or resist organizational pressures and goals. Most evidence suggests that similarities outweigh differences in the value systems of male and female managers. With few exceptions, gender differences have not been found in the work values and personal business ethics of managers.[12]

The sense of commitment that managers bring to their work is also important, at least as far as their organizations are concerned. More committed managers might be expected to work longer hours when the need arises, to relocate when the organization wishes, and to place a greater importance on the interests of the organization than on personal interests when the two are in conflict. Managers who are less committed are more likely to believe that "a job is a job" and to balk when they are asked to do anything that is outside their normal routines. Gender stereotypes suggest that women lack the high level of commitment essential for a successful managerial career, but a meta-analysis found no gender difference in commitment to either professional or nonprofessional

jobs. Instead, commitment is better explained by other factors. Age and education are positively linked to commitment, for example. Greater job satisfaction, more meaningful work, and greater utilization of skills are also associated with stronger commitment.[13]

Even if male and female managers did not differ in any respect, subordinates could still have different preferences for working with them or respond to them differently. A tendency to prefer male managers to female managers is present in many workers. A survey of employed adult Americans found that almost half preferred a boss of a specific sex. Among those workers who expressed a preference, 85 percent of men and 65 percent of women said they would rather work for a male boss. In contrast, studies of actual managers and their subordinates have typically found that subordinates express similar satisfaction with male and female managers. Overall, subordinates do not appear to respond differently to male and female leaders for whom they have actually worked. Once subordinates have experienced both female and male managers, the effects of gender stereotypes tend to disappear, and managers are treated more as individuals than as representatives of their sex.[14]

In summary, the title of this section of the chapter posed the question "Do female and male managers differ?" The research evidence suggests the answer: "They differ in some ways and at some times, but, for the most part, they do not differ."

11. A. H. Eagly, S. J. Karau, and J. B. Johnson, "Gender and the Effectiveness of Leaders: A Meta-Analysis," *Psychological Bulletin*, 117 (1995): 125–145.

12. C. Mottaz, "Gender Differences in Work Satisfaction, Work-Related Rewards and Values, and the Determinants of Work Satisfaction," *Human Relations*, 39 (1986): 359–378; G. E. Stevens, "The Personal Business Ethics of Male and Female Managers: A Comparative Study" (Paper delivered at the Annual Meeting of the Academy of Management, Dallas, 1983).

13. F. F. Aven, Jr., B. Parker, and G. M. McEvoy, "Gender and Attitudinal Commitment to Organizations: A Meta-Analysis," *Journal of Business Research*, 26 (1993): 63–73; L. H. Chusmir, "Job Commitment and the Organizational Woman," *Academy of Management Review*, 7 (1982): 595–602.

14. M. B. Rubner, "More Workers Prefer a Man in Charge," *American Demographics*, 13 (No. 6, June 1991): 11; J. Adams, R. W. Rice, and D. Instone, "Follower Attitudes Toward Women and Judgments Concerning Performance by Female and Male Leaders," *Academy of Management Journal*, 27 (1984): 636–643; H. F. Ezell, C. A. Odewahn, and J. D. Sherman, "The Effects of Having Been Supervised by a Woman on Perceptions of Female Managerial Competence," *Personnel Psychology*, 34 (1981): 291–299.

Although the AT&T study found several gender differences in managerial traits, these differences offset each other in the determination of overall management potential. In motivational profiles found in other studies, female managers tend to have the preferred managerial traits. Women and men do not differ in their effectiveness as leaders, although some situations favor women and others favor men. A stereotypical difference is present in the tendency to exhibit democratic versus autocratic leadership. In contrast, gender differences in task and interpersonal styles are confined to laboratory studies and are not present in the leadership styles of actual managers. Results outside the laboratory suggest an absence of gender differences in values and commitment. Actual male and female managers provoke similar responses in subordinates. Thus, few gender differences favoring either men or women have been found.

Overall, this review supports the no-differences view of gender differences in management. This does not necessarily mean that female and male managers are completely interchangeable, however. The leadership roles that women and men hold in organizations typically provide clear guidelines for acceptable behavior. Managers become socialized into their roles early in their careers. In addition, they are selected by their organizations to fill leadership roles because they are seen as meeting a specific set of attitudinal and behavioral criteria. These factors decrease the likelihood that female and male managers will differ substantially in the personal qualities they exhibit on their jobs, even if they are initially inclined to act differently. Because women remain in the minority in the managerial ranks, especially in the upper levels, they experience strong pressures to conform to standards based on a stereotypically masculine view of managerial effectiveness.

IMPLICATIONS FOR ORGANIZATIONS

The implications of this review are clear: *If there are no differences between male and female managers, organizations should not act as if there are.* Instead, they should follow two principles in their actions:

1. To be gender blind in how they fill managerial positions, except when consciously trying to offset the effects of past discrimination.

2. To minimize differences in the job experiences of equally qualified male and female managers, so that artificial gender differences in career patterns and success do not arise.

Organizations should do whatever they can to equalize the job experiences of equally qualified female and male managers. This means abandoning the model of a successful career as an uninterrupted sequence of promotions to positions of greater responsibility heading toward the top ranks. All too often, any request to take time out from a career for family reasons, by either a woman or a man, is seen as evidence of lack of career commitment.

Grant, Rosener, and Loden based their recommendations on a stereotypical-differences-favoring-women view. Although this view receives some support in my review, especially in women's greater tendency to exhibit democratic versus autocratic leadership, it is not supported by the bulk of the research evidence. Nevertheless, it has been used as the basis for sweeping assertions. Grant argues, for example, that organizations will benefit from placing greater value on women's special qualities.

These "human resources" skills are critical in helping to stop the tide of alienation, apathy, cynicism, and low morale in organizations. . . . If organizations are to become more humane, less alienating, and more responsive to the individuals who work for them, they will probably need to learn to value process as well as product. Women have an extensive involvement in the processes of our society—an involvement that derives from their greater participation in the reproductive process and their early experience of family life. . . . Thus women may indeed be the most radical force available in bringing about organizational change.[15]

15. Grant, p. 62.

Human resources skills are certainly essential to today's organizations. Corporations that are concerned only with getting a product out and pay little attention to their employees' needs are unlikely to have a committed workforce or to be effective in the long run. But women are at risk when corporations assume that women have a monopoly on human resources skills. The risk is that they will be placed exclusively in managerial jobs that call for social sensitivity and interpersonal skills—for example, jobs in public relations, human resources management, consumer affairs, and corporate social responsibility. These jobs are typically staff functions, peripheral to the more powerful line functions of finance, sales, and production, and are seldom regarded in exalted terms by line personnel. Women managers are found disproportionately in such jobs, outside the career paths that most frequently lead to top management jobs. Corporations that rely on Grant's assertions about women's special abilities could very well perpetuate this trend.

Thus it is very important that the facts about gender differences in management be disseminated to key decision makers. When individuals hold onto stereotypical views about gender differences that are not supported by the research evidence, either of two approaches may be tried.

1. Send them to programs like cultural diversity workshops to make them aware of the ways in which biases related to gender (as well as race, age, etc.) can affect their decisions, and to learn how to keep these biases from occurring. For example, Levi Strauss put all of its executives, including the president, through an intense three-day program designed to make them examine their attitudes toward women and minorities on the job. In Ortho Pharmaceuticals, Avon, and Citizens Insurance, every *employee* receives diversity awareness training.[16]

2. Recognize that beliefs and attitudes are difficult to change, and focus on changing behavior instead. If people are motivated by an effective performance appraisal and reward system backed by the CEO to be gender blind in their decision making, they often come to believe in what they are doing.

Schwartz based her recommendations on a real gender difference: more women than men leave work for family reasons owing to the demands of maternity and the differing traditions and expectations of the sexes. But her solution substitutes a different type of gender difference: that such women remain at work with permanently reduced career opportunities. It does not recognize that women's career orientation may change during their careers. Women could temporarily leave the fast track for the mommy track but be ready and able to resume the fast track later. Once classified as career-and-family, however, they would find it difficult to be reclassified as career-primary, even if their career commitment returned to its original level.

More women and men are adopting a holistic approach to their careers and lives. By providing the opportunity for alternative work schedules and family supports for all employees, not just career-and-family women, as Schwartz recommended, organizations can help women and men achieve their full potential for success. Firms that offer flexible work arrangements not only are more likely to retain their employees. They may also attract more qualified employees (even for less pay) who view the opportunity to take advantage of a flexible work arrangement as a worthwhile substitute for higher pay at another firm.[17]

Corporations could offer "parent tracks" rather than mommy tracks and accurately believe that they were treating their female and male employees alike. However, if women opted for such programs

16. T. Cox, Jr., *Cultural Diversity in Organizations: Theory, Research and Practice* (San Francisco: Berrett-Koehler, 1993), pp. 236–237; B. Zeitz and L. Dusky, "Levi Strauss," in *The Best Companies for Women* (New York: Simon & Schuster, 1988).

17. M. A. Ferber and B. O'Farrell with L. R. Allen, eds., *Work and Family: Policies for a Changing Work Force* (Washington, D.C.: National Academy Press, 1991); D. E. Friedman and E. Galinsky, "Work and Family Issues: A Legitimate Business Concern," in *Work, Families, and Organizations*, ed. S. Zedeck (San Francisco: Jossey-Bass, 1992).

more than men did (as is often the case) and if any-one who opted for one was held back in pursuing a future managerial career, the programs would con-tribute to a gender difference in access to top man-agement positions. Automatic restrictions should not be placed on the later career prospects of indi-viduals who choose alternative work arrangements. Those who wish to return to the fast track should be allowed to do so once they demonstrate the nec-essary skills and commitment.

Organizations need to create both standard and flexible career paths so *all* the needs of *all* their em-ployees may be fully met. A firm that develops a flexible as well as a core workforce may find consid-erable advantages during downturns in the busi-ness cycle, for layoffs may be avoided in favor of sabbaticals for those who prefer a flexible career pattern. Organizations need to reorganize their workforces in this manner to better meet the needs of employees and the pressures of business cycles.

There are other ways by which organizations can minimize gender differences in managers' job experiences. The majority of top male and female executives have had one or more mentors, and mentorship has been critical to their advancement and success. But lower-level female managers have greater difficulty in finding mentors than male managers at equivalent levels, because of the smaller number of female top executives and the preference people have for mentoring people like themselves. This gives lower-level male managers an advantage in achieving career success.[18]

Some companies try to overcome barriers of gender by assigning highly placed mentors to promising lower-level managers. At the Bank of America, senior executives are asked to serve as mentors for three or four junior managers for a year at a time. Formal mentoring programs have also been implemented at Jewel Companies, Aetna, Bell Labs, Merrill Lynch, Federal Express, and the U.S. General Accounting Office. Good mentoring

relationships cannot be engineered, however. They must emerge from the spontaneous and mutual in-volvement of two people who see value in relating to each other. If people feel coerced into or mis-matched in mentoring relationships, the relation-ships are likely to flounder. Instead, a better approach for organizations is to offer educational programs about mentoring and its role in career development, then to identify who is doing good mentoring and reward them for it.[19]

Companies also influence job experiences through the training and development programs that they encourage or require their managers to take. These programs contribute to a gender differ-ence in job experiences if (1) men and women are systematically diagnosed to have different develop-mental needs and thereby go through different pro-grams, or (2) men and women are deliberately segregated in such programs. Female managers do not need to be sent off by themselves for assertive-ness training, as they were in the past. They need access to advanced training and development activi-ties, such as executive MBAs or executive leader-ship workshops, just the way male managers do.

The Executive Women Workshop offered by the Center for Creative Leadership (CCL) and simi-lar programs are open only to women. In addition, some firms, such as Northwestern Bell, have their own executive leadership programs for women only. These programs are intended "to give female managers the unique opportunity to understand their individual developmental needs and establish personal and career objectives," as the CCL catalog puts it. In general, however, women and men should be recommended for training and develop-ment programs according to their individual needs, not their sex. Almost half of the companies regarded as "the best companies for women" rely on training and workshops to develop their high-potential managerial talent. Many of these compa-

18. G. R. Roche, "Much Ado About Mentors," *Harvard Business Review*, 79 (No. 1, January-February 1979): 14–28; B. R. Ragins, "Barriers to Mentoring: The Female Manager's Dilemma," *Human Relations*, 42 (1989): 1–22.

19. K. E. Kram, "Mentoring in the Workplace," in *Career Development in Organizations*, ed. D. T. Hall and Associates (San Francisco: Jossey-Bass, 1986); M. Murray with M. A. Owen, *Beyond the Myths and Magic of Mentoring: How to Fa-cilitate an Effective Mentoring Program* (San Francisco: Jossey-Bass, 1991).

nies, including Bidermann Industries, General Mills, Hewitt Associates, Neiman-Marcus, and PepsiCo, have no special programs for women; they simply enroll the best and brightest people, regardless of sex.[20]

Organizations should not assume that male and female managers differ in personal qualities. They should also make sure that their policies, practices, and programs minimize the creation of gender differences in managers' experiences on the job. There is little reason to believe that either women or men make superior managers. Instead, there are likely to be excellent, average, and poor managers within each sex. Success in today's highly competitive marketplace requires organizations to make the best use of the talent available to them. They need to identify, develop, encourage, and promote the most effective managers, whether men or women. If they do so, what expression will best capture the difference between them and their less successful competitors? *Vive la différence!*

20. Center for Creative Leadership, "Executive Women Workshop," in *1992 Programs Catalog* (Greensboro, N.C.: Center for Creative Leadership, 1992), p. 8; Zeitz and Dusky.

Discrimination: Is Sex Stereotyping the Cause of Workplace Discrimination?

Early in 1988 Brenda Taylor, an assistant state attorney in Broward County, Florida, was criticized by her supervisor because of the way she dressed. He told Taylor, who favors designer blouses, ornate jewelry, tight-fitting skirts, and spike heels, that she looked like a "bimbo" (Lacayo, 1988). When Taylor complained to the federal Equal Employment Opportunity Commission (EEOC), she was fired. Taylor charged discrimination; the state attorney's office claimed that she had been dismissed for poor performance. Ironically, the Taylor episode occurred at a time when another discrimination case, *Price Waterhouse v. Hopkins*, was on its way to the U.S. Supreme Court. Unlike Taylor, who ran into trouble because she was too feminine, Ann Hopkins, the mother of three young children, was denied a promotion because she was not feminine enough.

Some of the facts in the Hopkins case were not in dispute. Price Waterhouse, one of the "big eight" accounting firms, held out the prospect of a partnership as a reward for meritorious work. Of the 662 partners in 1982, only seven were women. That year, after four years' work as a manager in the company's Washington office, Hopkins was nominated for partnership because "her strong character, independence and integrity are well recognized by her clients and peers" (Glaberson, 1988, p. 38). Hopkins had also helped bring some $40 million in business to the firm, far more than the other eighty-seven nominees, all of whom were male. She seemed a sure winner, but when the votes were counted, Hopkins was not one of the forty-seven applicants invited to become partners, and her candidacy was put on hold.

What went wrong? As Hopkins subsequently learned, the voting partners turned her down because this "lady partner candidate" was "macho, harsh and aggressive," "overcompensated for being a woman," and needed a "course at charm school." Even one of her supporters suggested that she might improve her chances if she would "walk more femininely, talk more femininely, dress more femininely, wear makeup, have her hair styled, and wear jewelry" (Fiske et al., 1991). With her chances for partnership rapidly diminishing, Hopkins filed a sex-discrimination claim with the EEOC, contending that the promotion process had violated Title VII of the 1964 Civil Rights Act, which prohibits job discrimination. Shortly afterward, she submitted her resignation, stating that she found conditions at Price Waterhouse intolerable. After Hopkins won in a lower court and the U.S. Court of Appeals, Price Waterhouse's appeal was heard before the U.S. Supreme Court, where the judges again found in her favor.

Taylor's and Hopkins's cases dramatize the double bind faced by many professional women who must walk a narrow line between appearing too feminine or too businesslike. If they behave according to the female stereotype, which calls for them to be passive, docile, and noncompetitive, they run the risk of being passed over for promotion because they lack characteristics associated with leadership positions, such as assertiveness and dominance. On the other hand, if they depart from the female image, they run into the problem experienced by Hopkins.

Her case is also unique because it was the first time the Supreme Court heard psychological evidence about sex stereotyping (Fiske et al., 1991). Dr. Susan Fiske, a social psychologist who testified as an expert witness, identified for the court the antecedent conditions that encourage stereotyping, such as being an "isolated one- or few-of-a-kind individual in an otherwise homogenous environment" (Fiske et al., 1991, p. 1050)—exactly the situation in which Hopkins found herself. Evidence for the salience of gender in the decision-making process could be found in the comment of one partner, who declared that he did not see why women were being proposed for partnerships when they were not even suited to be senior managers (Fiske et al., 1991). That Hopkins was attempting to move into a position deemed nontraditional for women only increased the chances for negative stereotyping. The result, as Fiske pointed out, was that Hopkins was evaluated on such narrow gender-related criteria as her social skills instead of her success in generating business for the company.

In the appeal to the Supreme Court, Price Waterhouse dismissed Fiske's testimony as "intuitively divined" and "gossamer evidence" (Fiske, 1992). The thrust of its argument was to challenge the validity of research on stereotyping in a case dealing with discrimination. At that point, the American Psychological Association (APA) filed an amicus curiae brief prepared by a panel of social and industrial/organizational psychologists who supported the scientific validity of gender-stereotyping research. Fiske and her colleagues' efforts were rewarded when the Court found in Hopkins's favor and ordered the company to grant her a partnership and pay her $371,000 in back wages. The Court noted: "An employer who objects to aggressiveness in women but whose positions require this trait places women in an intolerable Catch 22: out of a job if they behave aggressively and out of a job if they don't. Title VII [of the Civil Rights Act] lifts women out of this bind" (Fiske et al., 1991, p. 1055).

The difficulties experienced by Ann Hopkins, a White woman, are often exacerbated for women of Color. Although the number of professional women of Color has increased in recent years, they continue to experience the dual burden of racism and sexism. Hortensia Amaro and her colleagues (1987) found that the psychological distress of Hispanic women was closely associated with the discrimination experienced by 82 percent of their subjects. The problems that women of Color encounter in the workplace are heightened by their status as the token Black, Asian, or Latin woman. Tokenism carries with it a number of stressors, including being viewed as the representative of one's race. A White male's mistake is an individual error; a Black woman's mistake, however, is a sign of racial inferiority (Unger and Crawford, 1996). Women of Color may also fall into the category of "now you see them; now you don't." They are often showcased by a company to prove that it is complying with affirmative action requirements. On the other hand, women of Color, along with White women, often find themselves ignored by White male managers at business meetings (Comas-Diaz & Greene, 1994).

In the next chapter Gerald V. Barrett and Scott B. Morris challenge the APA's brief, arguing that it was based on selective evidence and that the APA erred in accepting Hopkins's position on disputed facts. Fiske and her colleagues follow with a categorical denial of these charges.

REFERENCES

Amaro, H., Russo, N. F., & Johnson, J. (1987). Family and work predictors of psychological well-being among Hispanic women professionals. *Psychology of Women Quarterly, 11*, 505–521.

Comas-Diaz, L., & Greene, B. (1994). Women of Color with professional status. In L. Comas-Diaz & B. Greene (Eds.), *Women of Color: Integrating ethnic and gender identities in psychotherapy* (pp. 347–388). New York: Guilford Press.

Fiske, S. T. (1992). Sex stereotyping as evidence of discrimination in the workplace. *Radcliffe Quarterly, 78*, 24–27.

Fiske, S. T., Bersoff, D. N., Borgida, E., Deaux, K., & Heilman, M. E. (1991). Social science research on trial: Use of sex stereotyping research in *Price Waterhouse v. Hopkins. American Psychologist, 46* (10), 1049–1060.

Glaberson, W. (1988, October 30). Determined to be heard: Four Americans and their journeys to the Supreme Court. *New York Times Magazine*, pp. 32–36, 38, 40.

Lacayo, R. (1988, November 14). A hard nose and a short skirt. *Time*, p. 98.

Unger, R., & Crawford, M. (1996). *Women and gender: A feminist psychology.* New York: McGraw-Hill.

ADDITIONAL READING

Clayton, S. D., & Crosby, F. J. (1992). *Justice, gender, and affirmative action.* Ann Arbor: University of Michigan Press.

Fried, N. E. (1994). *Sex, laws and stereotypes: Authentic workplace anecdotes and practical tips for dealing with ADA, sexual harassment, workplace violence and beyond.* Dublin, Ohio: Intermediaries Press.

Goodman, J. (1993). Evaluating psychological expertise on questions of social fact: The case of *Price Waterhouse v. Hopkins. Law and Human Behavior, 17*, 249–255.

Hopkins, A. (1996). *So ordered: Making partner the hard way.* Amherst: University of Massachusetts Press.

Lott, B., & Maluso, D. (Eds.) (1995). *The social psychology of interpersonal discrimination.* New York: Guilford Press.

National Council for Research on Women. (1996). Affirmative action: Beyond the glass ceiling and the sticky floor. *Issues Quarterly, 1*, 1–28.

NO

The American Psychological Association's Amicus Curiae Brief in *Price Waterhouse v. Hopkins*

GERALD V. BARRETT AND

SCOTT B. MORRIS

On several occasions, the American Psychological Association (APA) has submitted amicus curiae briefs to the Supreme Court. Through these briefs, the APA can inform the courts of the scientific evidence pertaining to a particular issue. These briefs represent an important service that the APA can provide to the courts and thereby to society.

A problem arises from a difference in the style of writing a legal brief versus a scientific review. Legal briefs are designed to present convincing arguments and evidence to support these arguments. Presenting alternative evidence is the responsibility of the opposing party. A scientific review, on the other hand, is expected to present an unbiased account of the literature and to report contradictory evidence when it exists. These two distinct and often conflicting philosophies must be combined when drafting a brief, and often the values of the legal system predominate over the values of science.

Grisso and Saks (1991) make a strong argument for the scientific perspective. They argue that the value of APA amicus briefs is not their ability to persuade the courts concerning particular legal is-

sues. Instead, the APA should help the courts avoid faulty assumptions about human behavior.

If the APA forfeits its impartiality and produces briefs that are slanted in favor of one side, it may lose its credibility as a source of scientific knowledge. If the courts do not accept APA briefs as scientific authority, their value to society will be lost. Thus, it is of critical importance that the APA ensure the thoroughness and validity of these amicus curiae briefs.

The scientific merit of three of APA's amicus curiae briefs has previously been questioned (Elliott, 1991; Gardner, Sherer & Tester, 1989). It was argued that many of the assertions in these briefs were not supported by the empirical evidence. As Judge Bazelon (1982) warned, psychologists must resist the temptation to exaggerate their psychological knowledge, because in the long run doing so will only reduce their effectiveness to society and the courts.

To demonstrate the effects of adopting legal rather than scientific values, this chapter will examine a brief (APA, 1991) submitted by the APA in *Price Waterhouse v. Hopkins* (1989) concerning the effects of stereotyping on discrimination against women. In a recent *American Psychologist* article, this brief was offered as a positive example of the APA's involvement in the legal arena (Fiske et al., 1991). However, we believe that the brief differed from the usual scientific review in three ways. First, the brief argued in the alternative (i.e., theories were used when they supported an argument but were ignored when their predictions did not support the brief's position). Second, the brief accepted the contention of Ms. Hopkins on several points that were disputed by Price Waterhouse, and failed to indicate that these were disputed facts. Third, the literature review presented in the brief selectively cited the literature, giving the illusion of a consistent body of research when, in fact, the research on stereotyping and discrimination is inconclusive. These methods, though not uncommon in legal arguments, are not accepted practice in the scientific community.

As Scarr (1988) has recently emphasized, when dealing with controversial areas such as gender, it is important for authors to clarify their views. We wish to clarify the purpose of this chapter. First, we are not attempting to convince the reader that sex discrimination never occurs in some organizations or that Hopkins was not a victim of discrimination. Research exists that demonstrates discrimination and stereotyping. Conversely, there are a number of studies showing no discrimination against women. Second, we support the concept of the APA submitting amicus curiae briefs. We believe these briefs can make an important contribution to the legal process, with the proviso that the brief accurately reflect the supporting research.

BACKGROUND

The case concerned Ann Hopkins, who failed to obtain a partnership at Price Waterhouse, a major accounting firm. She sued for sex discrimination, and the district court ruled that stereotypes had an impermissible effect on the decision (*Hopkins v. Price Waterhouse*, 1985). When the case was appealed to the Supreme Court, the APA (1991) submitted an amicus curiae brief in support of Ms. Hopkins. The Supreme Court discussed the issue of stereotypes as a basis for sex discrimination, and though not fully supporting Ms. Hopkins, it did remand the case to the lower courts (*Price Waterhouse v. Hopkins*, 1989). After reevaluating the evidence, the district court concluded that "Price Waterhouse intentionally maintained an evaluation system that permitted negative, sexually-stereotyped comments to influence partnership selection" (*Hopkins v. Price Waterhouse*, 1990, p. 1205). Although the courts recognized that there was some uncertainty about the extent to which the comments were tainted by stereotypes, they accepted the testimony of the plaintiff's expert witness (which was supported by the APA brief) that stereotypes played a major determining role in the decision. Ms. Hopkins was granted a full partnership in the accounting firm and awarded $371,000 in back pay.

THEORETICAL FRAMEWORK OF THE APA'S AMICUS BRIEF

This chapter will not attempt an in-depth examination of the theoretical work on stereotyping. It is important to note, however, that several different theories explain how stereotypes might lead to discrimination. The brief draws upon several of these theoretical frameworks. A variety of processes (e.g., descriptive stereotypes, normative stereotypes, attributions) were assumed to contribute to discrimination, even though in some situations the theories make completely opposite predictions.

For example, the lack-of-fit model (Heilman, 1983) states that women will be devalued when the stereotype of the applicant does not match the stereotype of the job. In this model, discrimination is most likely when an extremely feminine woman is applying for a traditionally masculine job. There would be less bias against masculine females because they would have a better fit with the masculine job. The normative stereotype model (Costrich et al., 1975) proposes that discrimination will occur when the applicant displays out-of-role behavior. This theory would predict *more* bias against a masculine female.

Unfortunately, the brief fails to provide a consistent framework to explain these apparently inconsistent predictions. Instead, it argues in the alternative, using a theory when it supports the claim of discrimination but ignoring the same theory when it predicts no discrimination.

DISPUTED FACTS

The brief makes several statements about the conditions surrounding the decision not to promote Ms. Hopkins. This is a matter of direct evidence, not scientific evidence, and should not have been presented in an APA amicus brief. In addition, these statements refer to points of dispute in the trial. We do not believe it is appropriate for the drafters of a brief to make decisions about the truth or falsity of direct evidence. During the trial, relevant evidence came from witnesses, records, documents, and exhibits. The trial process includes determining the credibility of witnesses from observation of their behavior. This evidence was not examined by the drafters of the brief. Instead, they fully accepted the assertions of the plaintiff.

Several statements in the APA's brief clearly indicate that the plaintiff's contention was accepted as fact. The brief states that Ms. Hopkins's detractors referred to her behavior as "abrasive" (p. 1065). In fact, according to Price Waterhouse's brief, the trial transcript indicates that Ms. Hopkins and her supporters also described her as "abrasive" (*Price Waterhouse v. Hopkins*, 1988a, p. 74). At another point, the APA's brief asserts that Hopkins brought in $40 million worth of new business (p. 1066). Price Waterhouse argued that this money came from massive proposals prepared by teams of managers and partners and could not be credited to specific individuals (*Price Waterhouse v. Hopkins*, 1988b, p. 183).

We do not propose that the information in the brief is incorrect, only that the brief presents one side of several disputed facts. Judgments about these facts are best made through legal proceedings. The APA should restrict itself to providing scientific evidence.

SLANTED PORTRAYAL OF THE RESEARCH LITERATURE

The avowed purpose of the APA brief was to "inform this Court of the scientific thought regarding stereotyping, particularly as it affects judgments of women in work settings" (p. 1061). However, the brief failed to present the scientific literature accurately. The brief gives the impression of a consistent body of research indicating that sex stereotypes affect business decisions. In fact, the research on stereotyping and sex bias is inconclusive. Although research supporting the APA position is provided in the brief, a large body of contradictory research was ignored. In addition, many of the conclusions in the brief are drawn primarily from laboratory research, with questionable generalizability to actual work situations.

STEREOTYPING OF WORKING WOMEN

The brief claims that categorization on the basis of sex is common and that these sex stereotypes influence how people interpret the behavior of others. There is substantial evidence that when people make abstract descriptions of the typical man and woman, the sexes are perceived differently (Broverman et al., 1972; Rosen & Jerdee, 1978; Schein, 1973, 1975). This does not necessarily mean, however, that women will be seen or treated differently in a work situation. For example, the characteristics of the typical woman are not used to describe female managers (Heilman et al., 1989).

The Iron Maiden. The brief alleges that people who did not value Ms. Hopkins's performance at Price Waterhouse fitted her into the stereotype of "the 'Iron Maiden'—a frequent subcategory for career women who are perceived to be unfeminine" (p. 1065). Taylor (1981) describes the Iron Maiden as cold and aloof. Such women are perceived as tough or dangerous by their coworkers (Kanter, 1977a, p. 236).

The only support for the concept is the classic book by Kanter, *Men and Women of the Corporation* (1977a). Several other citations were given to support this argument, but none provides evidence that working women are perceived as so-called Iron Maidens. Kanter hypothesizes that working women are cast into stereotyped roles, such as the mother, seductress, pet, and Iron Maiden. These stereotyped roles are not based on any empirical data. They are a result of Kanter's speculations from a case study of one organization. The speculations come from informal interviews of sixteen women who had recently begun working in the organization as sales personnel, as well as their male peers and managers (Kanter, 1977b). No female managers were actually interviewed. The Iron Maiden concept came from the fact that Kanter heard about a female in the organization who was cast into that role. We find no other supporting evidence for the concept of the Iron Maiden.

Token Status. The brief claims further that stereotyping is especially likely when there are few women in the workforce. Increased attention to these token or rare individuals "causes observers to form more 'packaged' stereotypic impressions than they otherwise would" (p. 1067). Three papers are cited for this statement. The first is Kanter (1977a), which we have already discussed. The second citation was a review chapter by Taylor (1981), which discussed other research, none of which was in a work setting.

The third study (Taylor et al., 1978) looked at the traits and roles ascribed to token men and women. There was no indication that people are more likely to attribute stereotypical traits to token women. Although the authors concluded that token individuals were more likely to be seen as playing a stereotypical role, this effect was not statistically significant ($p < .09$). Thus, there is little evidence to support the proposed negative consequences of token status.

BIAS AGAINST WORKING WOMEN

The brief emphasizes the point that females are devalued when compared to equivalent males. The majority of the research cited to support this claim follows the "paper-people" research design. The typical research study presents some information concerning an applicant for a position with either a male or a female name attached to it. The paper-people design is a useful technique for investigating the decision process, especially when actual managers are used as subjects. However, it is important to also examine decisions in real organizations before generalizing research from the laboratory.

Initial Selection. A common theme is exemplified by the following quotation from the APA amicus curiae brief: "A multitude of studies have shown that providing precisely the same information about job qualifications or job performance and merely varying the identity associated with the information as either male or female leads to differential and negative evaluations of the woman or her work. This is true when women apply for jobs or seek promotions once on the job " (pp. 1065–1066). Most of the research cited to support this statement looked at decisions made by college students. Although there is some support for the existence of a pro-male bias (Dipboye, Arvey & Terpstra, 1977), other references indicate that sex has no effect on hiring decisions (Terborg & Ilgen, 1975) or that sex bias occurs only when little relevant information is given

(Heilman, 1984). A number of studies not cited in the brief have found no indication of sex bias when college students make simulated hiring decisions (Fusilier & Hitt, 1983; Gordon & Owens, 1988; McDonald & Hakel, 1985; Renwick & Tosi, 1978).

A consistent finding from these studies is the small amount of variance accounted for by sex in the hiring decisions. The APA brief references a meta-analysis which found that, on average, sex accounted for 4 percent of the variance in the hiring recommendations, although there was substantial variability in the effects (Olian, Schwab & Haberfeld, 1988).

In another cited study of sex bias (Zikmund, Hitt & Pickens, 1978), resumes were mailed to 100 personnel directors. Only 9 positive responses were received, and of these, more were received when gender was not specified than when the applicant was female. The APA brief did not mention a subsequent study by the same authors. In the expanded study, resumes were sent to 200 personnel directors (Hitt, Zikmund & Pickens, 1982). There was no significant sex effect, but there was a tendency for females to be preferred over males. Similar results have been obtained from research in which personnel professionals, managers, or recruiters screen hypothetical resumes or actual applicants; the most consistent finding is that sex is not a significant factor (Graves & Powell, 1988; Hitt & Zikmund, 1985; Kryger & Shikiar, 1978; Oliphant & Alexander, 1982; Rosen & Mericle, 1979).

The brief fails to cite a single study of actual selection decisions in real-world organizations. Studies of interviewers selecting actual applicants for organizations have consistently shown that there is no discrimination in the initial selection process, and, in fact, females are often rated higher than male applicants (Amsden & Moser, 1975; Arvey et al., 1987; Elliott, 1981; Parsons & Liden, 1984; Raza & Carpenter, 1987).

Performance Appraisal. The brief cites two reviews (Heilman, 1983; Nieva & Gutek, 1980) as support for the statement that "performance of women in traditionally male jobs is very often devalued simply because they are women" (p. 1066).

These reviews point out that although many studies support the claim of sex bias in evaluation, a number of studies have produced conflicting results. The statements in the brief do not reflect the mixed nature of the research literature.

The APA brief claims that "even when behavior is held constant in carefully controlled laboratory conditions, males are seen as more influential, more confident, and somewhat more deserving of respect than women, perceptions consonant with sex stereotypes" (p. 1064). The support for this statement is based in part upon the research of Taylor et al. (1978). In this study, college students observed and evaluated the participants in a conversation. Males were seen to be significantly more influential, confident, and analytical, but they were not seen as more competent or deserving of respect than females.

Other more direct, relevant research, which used the familiar paper-person methodology, involved college and graduate students rating the performance of males and females in a variety of occupations. The results were consistent in showing no sex differences—or, at times, differences favoring the females—in the evaluation of managers (Hall & Hall, 1976; Moore, 1984) and other occupations (Bigoness, 1976; Schmitt & Lappin, 1980).

Perhaps the most surprising aspect of the brief's evaluation of performance appraisal research is the complete failure to cite any studies of male and female employees in actual work organizations to support their allegations of discrimination. There are a number of studies on performance appraisal of nonmanagerial employees that show either no sex discrimination (Pulakos et al., 1989; Thompson & Thompson, 1985) or a slight bias favoring females (Mobley, 1982). The research has also found no evidence of sex discrimination in performance evaluations of male and female managers (Deaux, 1979; Peters et al., 1984; Tsui & Gutek, 1984; Wexley & Pulakos, 1982).

Promotions. The court case (*Price Waterhouse v. Hopkins*, 1989) revolved around a promotion decision. One would suppose that the APA brief concentrated on studies that showed that there was discrimination against females in the promotion process. This was not the case. The cited research provides only partial support for the statement that "the choice by men to hire or promote comparable men over women is the most pertinent example" of biased decision making (p. 1064). Heilman and Stopeck (1985a) are cited to support the assertion of sex discrimination in promotion. They found that attractiveness was detrimental for women and beneficial for men. Sex alone was not significant. In a companion study (1985b), they found that the unattractive female was actually rated the highest for promotion to a managerial position. These two studies hardly support the proposition that men are promoted over comparable women.

The brief also cites Heilman and Guzzo (1978) to support the following statement: "That these evaluations are not based on competence results in judgments detrimentally affecting the degree to which organizational rewards are accorded women and impedes career progress" (APA, 1991, p. 1066). This study involved twenty-nine MBA students who rated the appropriateness of different personnel actions for "paper" male or female employees. The analysis showed a main effect for cause of performance and no differences due to the employee's sex. Once again research is cited for a proposition when, in fact, the actual research results do not support the claim of sex discrimination. Other studies have shown that sex was not an important variable in simulated promotion decisions made by students (Frank & Drucker, 1977) or actual managers (London & Stumpf, 1983; Mai-Dalton, Feldman-Summers & Mitchell, 1979; Stumpf & London, 1981).

Research having the most potential external validity would be that which deals with actual ongoing organizations that are involved in making promotion decisions. The brief does not cite any studies that involve managers or assessors making actual promotion decisions in any type of organization. We located two studies in the literature that involved the evaluation of over 5,000 women and 9,000 men. Both of the studies were consistent in showing that when females were evaluated in an assessment center for promotion within the organization, equivalent evaluations were given to males and females and there was no evidence of any sex bias (Moses & Boehm, 1975; Walsh, Weinberg & Fairfield, 1987).

PENALTIES FOR OUT-OF-ROLE BEHAVIOR

The brief emphasizes the point that when women perform masculine tasks or jobs, they will be devalued. If a female does well on the job, the assumption will be made that her success was not based on her ability or effort but on luck or some other extraneous variable. In addition, a woman cannot show masculine traits. For a female leader to be judged in a favorable fashion, she must adhere to the "feminine" stereotype.

Females Are Devalued When Performing Masculine Jobs. The APA amicus brief states that the performance of women can be devalued simply because they are performing a traditionally male job. Taynor and Deaux (1975) were cited in the brief to support this proposition. In their study, undergraduate students evaluated males and females performing what were considered "traditional" male and female tasks (confronting a gunman and talking to a child). There were no differences in the performance ratings of the males and females. However, women who performed well on a masculine task were seen as more deserving of a reward than men who performed in an equal fashion. If we were to follow the equity theory proposed by Taynor and Deaux and believe that Ms. Hopkins was performing a masculine job, then we would predict that Ms. Hopkins would be seen as more deserving of a reward than a comparable male.

Other research, using the paper-people research design, has found that females are rated equally or as even more suitable for a masculine job than comparable males. This has been found to be true for the jobs of management trainee (Muchinsky & Harris, 1977), football photographer (Heilman, Martell & Simon, 1988), and sports reporter (Sharp & Post, 1980).

Attributions Given for Women's Success. The brief contends that the success of highly accomplished women is attributed to luck rather than ability. One citation to support this concept is Deaux and Emswiller (1974). This research design involved evaluating a person who was attempting to identify a tire jack that was flashed on the TV screen for one second. Subjects tended to attribute a female's success with this "masculine task" to luck. Conversely, for males who did well on this "masculine task," there were more attributions made to ability. Obviously, the task used in this study has little to do with "highly accomplished performance."

Garland and Price (1977) were also cited for the proposition that attributions made concerning women resulted in their being devalued. This study involved responses by undergraduates to paper female managers. There was no comparison between the attributions made about female managers versus male managers. In fact, for successful women hard work was seen as the most important factor for success, and ability was seen as the second most important attribute. Both were seen as more important than luck. Other research has found that the sex of the manager was not related to the reasons given for success or failure (Butterfield & Powell, 1981; Rose, 1978).

Devaluation of Masculine Women. The brief argues that women will be judged negatively if they do not conform to the feminine stereotype. Research by Bartol and Butterfield (1976) is cited as support for this proposition. The now familiar design had undergraduates rate paper male and female managers with identical qualifications. The implications of this study for the evaluation of masculine women are ambiguous. While female managers using one masculine leadership style (initiating structure) were devalued relative to male managers, female managers using another masculine style (production emphasis) were not devalued. Other research has shown that ratings of leadership style are not affected by the sex of the manager (Butterfield & Bartol, 1977; Izraeli, 1987; Izraeli & Izraeli, 1985; Lee & Alvares, 1977).

The research of Rosen and Jerdee (1973) included samples of bank supervisors and undergraduates as subjects. The subjects rated the performance of paper male and female supervisors. The authors concluded that "stereotypes of an aggressive, threatening role being appropriate for male supervisors and a compassionate, helping role being appropriate for female supervisors were not upheld by the data" (p. 47).

Other studies cited in the brief support the claim of bias against women who display "out-of-role" behavior (Costrich et al., 1975; Hagen & Kahn, 1975; Jago & Vroom, 1982; Wiley & Eskilson, 1982). However, other research indicates that women who display masculine behavior are actually valued more highly than a comparison male (Dipboye & Wiley, 1977, 1978; Jackson, 1983a, 1983b; Spence & Helmreich, 1972; Spence, Helmreich & Stapp, 1975).

METHODS TO REDUCE THE EFFECTS OF STEREOTYPING

The APA amicus brief acknowledges that stereotyping is a normal part of the thinking process and, therefore, cannot be completely eliminated. However, the brief provides several suggestions on how organizations can minimize the impact of sex stereotypes.

The brief suggests that "interdependence undercuts stereotyping and encourages more accurate, particularized impressions," and concludes from this that "an organization that makes team work explicit, makes promotions depend on group products, and emphasizes supervisors' responsibilities for their subordinates' success can reduce stereotyping" (p. 1069). The research cited to support this advice has questionable generalizability to the work setting. The subject population of the first study consisted of boys who were attending a summer camp forty years ago (Sherif & Sherif, 1953). The second study was based on the responses of college students, over forty years ago, who were solving puzzles in groups (Deutsch, 1949). The third study involved college students evaluating the likeability of a purported schizophrenic (Neuberg & Fiske, 1987).

None of the studies involved subjects who (1) were older than typical undergraduate college students, (2) were working in an organization, (3) had supervisory responsibility, or (4) were involved in

seeking promotion. One must question the extent to which the research can be generalized to actual organizations.

CONCLUSION

Two value systems, legal and scientific, must be balanced when drafting an amicus curiae brief. But the legal values can easily predominate over the values of science (Elliott, 1991; Gardner et al., 1989). As noted by Fiske et al. (1991), the APA's brief can be considered a success if one considers the persuasiveness of its arguments and, in particular, its probable influence on the Supreme Court's decision in *Price Waterhouse v. Hopkins* (1989). However, Grisso and Saks (1991) argue that the goal of a science translation brief should be to inform, rather than persuade, the courts. If the purpose of the *Price Waterhouse* brief was to inform the Court of the scientific thought regarding stereotyping, its accomplishment falls far short of that goal.

The brief differs from accepted scientific practice in three ways. First, the presentation of the theoretical basis of discrimination is inconsistent and fails to successfully resolve discrepancies among the theoretical models. Second, the brief's portrayal of the conditions at Price Waterhouse is biased in favor of Ms. Hopkins's case. The brief fails to acknowledge that several of the points were disputed during the trial. Third, the brief does not present an accurate picture of the research literature on stereotyping.

If the APA purports to discuss scientific thought, then it has an obligation to present an accurate summary of the relevant literature, not just the literature that supports preconceived conclusions. A careful examination of the literature reveals that the arguments in the brief are often not supported by the cited literature and that a large body of contradictory research is not discussed in the brief. The brief cites thirty-three studies to support the arguments discussed in this chapter. Between 40 percent and 100 percent of these studies did not support the arguments for which they were cited. We located a total of seventy-eight studies that contradict the brief's conclusions, only twenty-nine of which were conducted in actual work set-tings. Our review of the APA brief leads us to the conclusion that the pattern of citations and infer-ences drawn from them goes beyond customary scientific practice. As a particularly vivid example, there are several instances where the brief cites re-search in support of an argument (e.g., Bartol & Butterfield, 1976; Deaux & Emswiller, 1974; Dip-boye, Arvey & Terpstra, 1977; Dipboye, Fromkin & Wilback, 1975; Heilman, 1984; Heilman & Stopek, 1985a; Rosen & Jerdee, 1974; Zikmund, Hitt & Pickens, 1978), yet ignores other research by the same authors when that research contradicts the brief's argument (Butterfield & Bartol, 1977; Butterfield & Powell, 1981; Deaux, 1979; Dipboye & Wiley, 1977, 1978; Heilman, Martell & Simon, 1988; Heilman & Stopek, 1985b; Hitt & Zikmund, 1985; Hitt, Zikmund & Pickens, 1982; Rosen & Mericle, 1979).

A substantial body of literature questions whether studies using college students can be used to infer the behavior of managers making actual personnel decisions (Barr & Hitt, 1986; Bernardin & Villanova, 1986; Gordon, Slade & Schmitt, 1986, 1987; Gorman, Clover & Doherty, 1978; Ilgen & Favero, 1985; Rozelle & Baxter, 1981). Despite the persistent claim that stereotyping affects women in real work settings, most of the literature cited in the brief involves college students evaluating paper people. In fact, of the 105 references in the brief, only one examined the evaluation of managers in a real organization. This study examined ratings by subordinates rather than superiors and found no differences in the rated performance of male and fe-male supervisors (Day & Stogdill, 1972).

The problems outlined here illuminate a need to change amicus curiae briefs. We suggest that two possible corrective actions be taken to improve them. First, we believe an amicus brief should pre-sent only conclusions from the scientific literature and should not make judgments about disputed facts. Second, we suggest that all APA amicus cu-riae briefs be given priority publication in a rele-vant journal (e.g., *American Psychologist, Journal of Applied Psychology, Personnel Psychology, Profes-sional Psychology, Law and Human Behavior*) ac-cording to the subject matter of the brief. This will allow the brief's arguments to receive the critical scrutiny of the entire psychology community. We are not suggesting that publication occur before an amicus curiae brief can be submitted to the Su-preme Court. Time constraints make that impracti-cal. However, the knowledge that the briefs will be published in a timely manner may encourage thor-ough consideration of the literature.

The authors would like to thank Ralph Alexander, Terri Baumgardner, Dennis Doverspike, Rick DeShon, Jan Dorsett, Lynn Kahney, Paul Levy, Robert Lord, Karen Ma-her, Marty Murphy, Jackie Szmania, and Linda Subich for their comments.

REFERENCES

American Psychological Association.(1991). In the Supreme Court of the United States: *Price Waterhouse v. Ann B. Hop-kins*. Amicus curiae brief for The American Psychological Association. *American Psychologist, 46*, 1061–1070.

Amsden, A. H., & Moser, C. (1975). Supply and mobility of women economists: Job search and affirmative action. *American Economic Review, 65*, 83–91.

Arvey, R. D., Miller, H. E., Gould; R., & Burch, P. (1987). In-terview validity for selecting sales clerks. *Personnel Psychol-ogy, 40*, 1–12.

Barr, S. H., & Hitt, M. A. (1986). A comparison of selection decision models in manager versus student samples. *Person-nel Psychology, 39*, 599–617.

Bartol, K. M., & Butterfield, D. A. (1976). Sex effects in evalu-ating leaders. *Journal of Applied Psychology, 61*, 446–454.

Bazelon, D. L. (1982). Veils, values, and social responsibility. *American Psychologist, 37*, 115–121.

Bernardin, H. J., & Villanova, P. (1986). Performance ap-praisal. In E. A. Locke (Ed.), *Generalizing from laboratory to field settings* (pp. 43–62). Lexington, Mass.: Lexington Books.

Bigoness, W. J. (1976). Effect of applicants' sex, race, and per-formance on employers' performance ratings: Some addi-tional findings. *Journal of Applied Psychology, 61*, 80–84.

Broverman, I. K., Vogel, S. R., Broverman, D. M., Clarkson, F. E., & Rosenkrantz, P. S. (1972). *Journal of Social Issues, 2*, 59–78.

Butterfield, D. A., & Bartol, K. M. (1977). Evaluators of leader behavior: A missing element in leadership theory. In J. G. Hunt & L. L. Larson (Eds.), *Leadership: The Cutting Edge* (pp. 167–188). Carbondale: Southern Illinois Univer-sity Press.

Butterfield, D. A., & Powell, G. N. (1981). Effect of group performance, leader sex, and rater sex on ratings of leader behavior. *Organizational Behavior and Human Performance, 28*, 129–141.

Costrich, N., Feinstein, J., Kidder, L., Marecek, J., & Pascale, L. (1975). When stereotypes hurt: Three studies of penalties for sex-role reversals. *Journal of Experimental Social Psychology, 11*, 520–530.

Day, D. R., & Stogdill, R. M. (1972). Leader behavior of male and female supervisors: A comparative study. *Personnel Psychology, 25*, 353–360.

Deaux, K. (1979). Self-evaluations of male and female managers. *Sex Roles, 5*, 571–580.

Deaux, K., & Emswiller, T. (1974). Explanations of successful performance on sex-linked tasks: What is skill for the male is luck for the female. *Journal of Personality and Social Psychology, 29*, 80–85.

Deutsch, M. (1949). An experimental study of the effects of cooperation and competition upon group process. *Human Relations, 2*, 199–231.

Dipboye, R. L., Arvey, R. D., & Terpstra, D. E. (1977). Sex and physical attractiveness of raters and applicants as determinants of resume evaluations. *Journal of Applied Psychology, 3*, 288–294

Dipboye, R. L., Fromkin, H. L., & Wilback, H. (1975). Relative importance of applicant sex, attractiveness, and scholastic standing in evaluation of job applicant resumes. *Journal of Applied Psychology, 60*, 39–43.

Dipboye, R. L., & Wiley, J. W. (1977). Reactions of college recruiters to interviewee sex and self-presentation style. *Journal of Vocational Behavior, 10*, 1–12.

Dipboye, R. L., & Wiley, J. W. (1978). Reactions of male raters to interviewee self-presentation style and sex: Extensions of previous research. *Journal of Vocational Behavior, 13*, 192–203.

Elliott, A. G. P. (1981). Sex and decision making in the selection interview: A real-life study. *Journal of Occupational Psychology, 54*, 265–273.

Elliott, R. (1991). Social science data and the APA: The Lockhart brief as a case in point. *Law and Human Behavior, 15*, 65–82.

Fiske, S. T., Bersoff, D. N., Borgida, E., Deaux, K., & Heilman, M. E. (1991). Social science research on trial: Use of sex stereotyping research in *Price Waterhouse v. Hopkins*. *American Psychologist, 46*, 1049–1060.

Frank, F. D., & Drucker, J. (1977). The influence of evaluatees' sex on evaluations of a response on a managerial selection instrument. *Sex Roles, 3*, 59–64.

Fusilier, M. R., & Hitt, M. A. (1983). Effects of age, race, sex, and employment experience on students' perceptions of job applications. *Perceptual and Motor Skills, 57*, 1127–1134.

Gardner, W., Scherer, D., & Tester, M. (1989). Asserting scientific authority: Cognitive development and adolescent legal rights. *American Psychologist, 44*, 895–902.

Garland, H., & Price, K. H. (1977). Attitudes toward women in management and attributions for their success and failure in a managerial position. *Journal of Applied Psychology, 62*, 29–33.

Gordon, M. E., Slade, L. A., & Schmitt, N. (1986). The "sci-

ence of the sophomore" revisited: From conjecture to empiricism. *Academy of Management Review, 11*, 191–207.

Gordon, M. E., Slade, L. A., & Schmitt, N. (1987). Student guinea pigs: Porcine predictors and particularistic phenomena. *Academy of Management Review, 12*, 160–163.

Gordon, R. A., & Owens, S. D. (1988). The effect of job level and amount of information on the evaluation of male and female job applicants. *Journal of Employment Counseling, 25*, 160–171.

Gorman, C. D., Clover, W. H., & Doherty, M. E. (1978). Can we learn anything about interviewing real people from "interviews" of paper people? Two studies of the external validity of a paradigm. *Organizational Behavior and Human Performance, 22*, 165–192.

Graves, L. M., & Powell, G. N. (1988). An investigation of sex discrimination in recruiters' evaluations of actual applicants. *Journal of Applied Psychology, 73*(1), 20–29.

Grisso, T., & Saks, M. J. (1991). Psychology's influence on constitutional interpretation: A comment on how to succeed. *Law and Human Behavior, 15*, 205–211.

Hagen, R. L., & Kahn, A. (1975). Discrimination against competent women. *Journal of Applied Social Psychology, 5*, 362–376.

Hall, F. S., & Hall, D. T. (1976). Effects of job incumbents' race and sex on evaluations of managerial performance. *Academy of Management Journal, 19*, 476–481.

Heilman, M. E. (1983). Sex bias in work settings: The lack of fit model. *Research in Organizational Behavior, 5*, 269–298.

Heilman, M. E. (1984). Information as a deterrent against sex discrimination: The effects of applicant sex and information type on preliminary employment decisions. *Organizational Behavior and Human Performance, 33*, 174–186.

Heilman, M. E., Block, C. J., Martell, R. F., & Simon, M. C. (1989). Has anything changed? Current characterizations of men, women, and managers. *Journal of Applied Psychology, 74*, 935–942.

Heilman, M. E., & Guzzo, R. A. (1978). The perceived cause of work success as a mediator of sex discrimination in organizations. *Organizational Behavior and Human Performance, 21*, 346–357.

Heilman, M. E., Martell, R. F., & Simon, M. C. (1988). The vagaries of sex bias: Conditions regulating the undervaluation, equivaluation, and overvaluation of female job applicants. *Organizational Behavior and Human Decision Processes, 41*, 98–110.

Heilman, M. E., & Stopeck, M. H. (1985a). Attractiveness and corporate success: Different causal attributions for males and females. *Journal of Applied Psychology, 70*, 379–388.

Heilman, M. E., & Stopeck, M. H. (1985b). Being attractive, advantage or disadvantage? Performance-based evaluations and recommended personnel actions as a function of appearance, sex, and job type. *Organizational Behavior and Human Decision Processes, 35*, 202–215.

Hitt, M. A., & Zikmund, W. G. (1985). Forewarned is forearmed: Potential between and within sex discrimination. *Sex Roles, 12,* 807–812.

Hitt, M. A., Zikmund, W. G., & Pickens, B. A. (1982). Discrimination in industrial employment: An investigation of race and sex bias among professionals. *Work and Occupations, 9,* 217–231.

Hopkins v. Price Waterhouse, 618 F.Supp. 1109 (D.C.D.C. 1985).

Hopkins v. Price Waterhouse, 737 F.Supp. 1202 (D.C. Cir. 1990).

Ilgen, D. R., & Favero, J. L. (1985). Limits in generalization from psychological research to performance appraisal processes. *Academy of Management Review, 10,* 311–321.

Izraeli, D. N. (1987). Sex effects in the evaluation of influence tactics. *Journal of Occupational Behavior, 8,* 79–86.

Izraeli, D. N., & Izraeli, D. (1985). Sex effects in evaluating leaders: A replication study. *Journal of Applied Psychology, 70,* 540–546.

Jackson, L. A. (1983a). Gender, physical attractiveness, and sex role in occupational treatment discrimination: The influence of trait and role assumptions. *Journal of Applied Social Psychology, 13,* 443–458.

Jackson, L. A. (1983b). The influence of sex, physical attractiveness, sex role, and occupational sex-linkage on perceptions of occupational suitability. *Journal of Applied Social Psychology, 13,* 31–44.

Jago, A. G., & Vroom, V. H. (1982). Sex differences in the incidence and evaluation of participative leader behavior. *Journal of Applied Psychology, 67,* 776–783.

Kanter, R. M. (1977a). *Men and women of the corporation.* New York: Basic Books.

Kanter, R. M. (1977b). Some effects of proportions on group life: Skewed sex ratios and responses to token women. *American Journal of Sociology, 82,* 965–990.

Kryger, B. R., & Shikiar, R. (1978). Sexual discrimination in the use of letters of recommendation: A case of reverse discrimination. *Journal of Applied Psychology, 63,* 309–314.

Lee, D. M., & Alvares, K. M. (1977). Effects of sex on descriptions and evaluations of supervisory behavior in a simulated industrial setting. *Journal of Applied Psychology, 62,* 405–410.

London, M., & Stumpf, S. A. (1983). Effects of candidate characteristics on management promotion decisions: An experimental study. *Personnel Psychology, 36,* 241–259.

Mai-Dalton, R. R., Feldman-Summers, S., & Mitchell, T. R. (1979). Effect of employee gender and behavioral style on the evaluations of male and female banking executives. *Journal of Applied Psychology, 64,* 221–226.

McDonald, T., & Hakel, M. D. (1985). Effects of applicant race, sex, suitability, and answers on interviewers' questioning strategy and ratings. *Personnel Psychology, 38,* 321–334.

Mobley, W. H. (1982). Supervisor and employee race and sex effects on performance appraisals: A field study of adverse impact and generalizability. *Academy of Management Journal, 25,* 598–606.

Moore, D. P. (1984). Evaluating in-role and out-of-role performers. *Academy of Management Journal, 27,* 603–618.

Moses, J. L., & Boehm, V. R. (1975). Relationship of assessment-center performance to management progress of women. *Journal of Applied Psychology, 60,* 527–529.

Muchinsky, P. M., & Harris, S. L. (1977). The effect of applicant sex and scholastic standing on the evaluation of job applicant resumes in sex-typed occupations. *Journal of Vocational Behavior, 11,* 95–108.

Neuberg, S. L., & Fiske, S. T. (1987). Motivational influences on impression formation: Outcome dependency, accuracy-driven attention, and individuating processes. *Journal of Personality and Social Psychology, 53,* 431–444.

Nieva, V. F., & Gutek, B. A. (1980). Sex effects on evaluation. *Academy of Management Review, 5,* 267–276.

Olian, J. D., Schwab, D. P., & Haberfeld, Y. (1988). The impact of applicant gender compared to qualifications on hiring recommendations: A meta-analysis of experimental studies. *Organizational Behavior and Human Decision Processes, 41,* 180–195.

Oliphant, V. N., & Alexander, E. R., III. (1982). Reactions to resumes as a function of resume determinateness, applicant characteristics, and sex of raters. *Personnel Psychology, 35,* 829–842.

Parsons, C. K., & Liden, R. C. (1984). Interviewer perceptions of applicant qualifications: A multivariate field study of demographic characteristics and nonverbal cues. *Journal of Applied Psychology, 69,* 557–568.

Peters, L. H., O'Connor, E. J., Weekley, J., Pooyan, A., Frank, B., & Erenkrantz, B. (1984). Sex bias and managerial evaluations: A replication and extension. *Journal of Applied Psychology, 69,* 349–352.

Price Waterhouse v. Hopkins (1988a). Brief for the petitioner. *Labor Law Series,* 1988/89 Term of Court, *22,* 61–117.

Price Waterhouse v. Hopkins (1988b, October Term). Reply brief for petitioner. *Labor Law Series,* 1988/89 Term of Court, *22,* 177–198.

Price Waterhouse v. Hopkins, 490 U.S. 228 (1989).

Pulakos, E. D., White, L. A., Oppler, S. H., & Borman, W. C. (1989). Examination of race and sex effects on performance ratings. *Journal of Applied Psychology, 74,* 770–780.

Raza, S. M., & Carpenter, V. N. (1987). A model of hiring decisions in real employment interviews. *Journal of Applied Psychology, 72,* 596–603.

Renwick, P. A., & Tosi, H. (1978). The effects of sex, marital status, and educational background on selection decisions. *Academy of Management Journal, 21,* 93–103.

Rose, G. L. (1978). Sex effects of effort attributions in managerial performance evaluation. *Organizational Behavior and Human Performance, 21,* 367–378.

Rosen, B., & Jerdee, T. H. (1973). The influence of sex-role stereotypes on evaluations of male and female supervisory behavior. *Journal of Applied Psychology, 57,* 47–48.

Rosen, B., & Jerdee, T. H. (1974). Effects of applicant's sex and difficulty of job on evaluations of candidates for managerial positions. *Journal of Applied Psychology, 59,* 511–512.

Rosen, B., & Jerdee, T. H. (1978). Perceived sex differences in managerially relevant characteristics. *Sex Roles, 4,* 837–843.

Rosen, B., & Mericle, M. F. (1979). Influence of strong versus weak fair employment policies and applicant's sex on selection decisions and salary recommendations in a management simulation. *Journal of Applied Psychology, 64,* 435–439.

Rozelle, R. M., & Baxter, J. C. (1981). Influence of role pressures on the perceiver: Judgments of videotaped interviews varying judge accountability and responsibility. *Journal of Applied Psychology, 66,* 437–441.

Scarr, S. (1988). Race and gender as psychological variables. *American Psychologist, 43,* 56–59.

Schein, V. E. (1973). The relationship between sex role stereotypes and requisite management characteristics. *Journal of Applied Psychology, 57,* 95–100.

Schein, V. E. (1975). Relationships between sex role stereotypes and requisite management characteristics among female managers. *Journal of Applied Psychology, 60,* 340–344.

Schmitt, N., & Lappin, M. (1980). Race and sex as determinants of the mean and variance of performance ratings. *Journal of Applied Psychology, 65,* 428–435.

Sharp, C., & Post, R. (1980). Evaluation of male and female applicants for sex-congruent and sex-incongruent jobs. *Sex Roles, 6,* 391–401.

Sherif, M., & Sherif, C. W. (1953). *Groups in harmony and tension: An integration of studies on intergroup relations.* New York: Harper.

Spence, J. T., & Helmreich, R. (1972). Who likes competent women? Competence, sex-role congruence of interests, and subjects' attitudes toward women as determinants of interpersonal attraction. *Journal of Applied Social Psychology, 2,* 197–213.

Spence, J. T., Helmreich, R., & Stapp, J. (1975). Likability, sex-role congruence of interest, and competence: It all depends on how you ask. *Journal of Applied Social Psychology, 5,* 93–109.

Stumpf, S. A., & London, M. (1981). Capturing rater policies in evaluating candidates for promotion. *Academy of Management Journal, 24,* 752–766.

Taylor, S. E. (1981). A categorization approach to stereotyping. In D. L. Hamilton (Ed.), *Cognitive processes in stereotyping and intergroup behavior* (pp. 83–114). Hillsdale, NJ: Erlbaum.

Taylor, S. E., Fiske, S. T., Etcoff, N. L., & Ruderman, A. J. (1978). Categorical and contextual bases of person memory and stereotyping. *Journal of Personality and Social Psychology, 36,* 778–793.

Taynor, J., & Deaux, K. (1975). Equity and perceived sex differences: Role behavior as defined by the task, the mode, and the actor. *Journal of Personality and Social Psychology, 32,* 381–390.

Terborg, J. R., & Ilgen, D. R. (1975). A theoretical approach to sex discrimination in traditionally masculine occupations. *Organizational Behavior and Human Performance, 13,* 352–376.

Thompson, D. E., & Thompson, T. A. (1985). Task-based performance appraisal for blue-collar jobs: Evaluation of race and sex effects. *Journal of Applied Psychology, 70,* 747–753.

Tsui, A. S., & Gutek, B. A. (1984). A role of set analysis of gender differences in performance, affective relationships, and career success of industrial middle managers. *Academy of Management Journal, 27,* 619–635.

Walsh, J. P., Weinberg, R. M., & Fairfield, M. L. (1987). The effects of gender on assessment center evaluations. *Journal of Occupational Psychology, 60,* 305–309.

Wexley, K. N., & Pulakos, E. D. (1982). Sex effects on performance ratings in manager-subordinate dyads: A field study. *Journal of Applied Psychology, 67,* 433–439.

Wiley, M. G., & Eskilson, A. (1982). Coping in the corporation: Sex role constraints. *Journal of Applied Social Psychology, 12,* 1–11.

Zikmund, W. G., Hitt, M. A., & Pickens, B. A. (1978). Influence of sex and scholastic performance on reactions to job applicant resumes. *Journal of Applied Psychology, 63,* 252–254.

What Constitutes a Scientific Review? A Majority Retort to Barrett and Morris

Susan T. Fiske,

Donald N. Bersoff,

Eugene Borgida, Kay Deaux,

and Madeline E. Heilman

Barrett and Morris (in this volume) attack the American Psychological Association *amicus* brief in *Price Waterhouse v. Hopkins* as failing to adhere to the values of science in three respects. First, they claim that the amicus used theories in convenient but logically inconsistent ways. A straightforward reading of the theories indicates that Barrett and Morris simply confuse the descriptive (e.g., "women typically are incompetent") and prescriptive (e.g., "women should be nice") aspects of gender stereotypes. Second, Barrett and Morris claim that the APA used facts disputed by the employer, thereby biasing the brief. However, these facts were accepted at all levels of the court system, thereby establishing them as "fact" for the record, to which the Supreme Court and the APA were then bound. Third, Barrett and Morris claim the amicus literature review was biased. Yet, rather than support that claim with a full review, they present highly selected results that are biased, incomplete, misleading, and inaccurate. Independent quantitative reviews undertaken since the brief support its central arguments and dispute the Barrett-Morris interpretations. In short, none of their arguments is supported.

> I. Empirical research on sex stereotyping has been conducted over many decades and is generally accepted in the scientific community.
> II. Stereotyping under certain conditions can create discriminatory consequences for stereotyped groups, including women.
> > A. Stereotypes about women shape perceptions about women's typical and acceptable roles in society.
> > B. Sex stereotypes have demonstrably negative effects on women in work settings.
> III. The conditions that promote stereotyping were present in the petitioner's work setting.
> IV. Although petitioner was found to have taken no effective steps to prevent its discriminatory stereotyping of respondent, methods are available to monitor and reduce the effects of stereotyping. (American Psychological Association, 1991)

So stated the major arguments in the American Psychological Association (APA) amicus brief in *Price Waterhouse v. Hopkins* (1989). These simple and straightforward points have evoked a lengthy attack by Barrett and Morris.

It seems odd that Barrett and Morris should criticize the amicus for lacking scientific integrity. Their analysis distorts and fundamentally misunderstands both the amicus and the literature it reviews. The critique does not stand up to the scrutiny of basic research nor the values it upholds. Barrett and Morris build their complaint on the backs of a troika of straw figures. They argue that the brief submitted by APA (1) ignored theories and evidence when they did not support the brief's arguments; (2) accepted as fact issues that were disputed by the employer, Price Waterhouse (PW); and (3) selectively cited research in such a way as to falsely portray the data as consistent. As we shall show, however, it does not take much firepower to topple these three straw figures.

WHO ABUSED THEORIES?

Barrett and Morris claim that contradictory theories are used to support mutually inconsistent explanations of how stereotypes can lead to discrimination, each theory being used when it supports an argument and ignored when it contradicts one. This point is totally without foundation. The authors' ill-informed comments highlight a dramatic failure to understand the named theories in particular and the field of gender stereotyping in general. The brief itself makes quite clear the respective explanatory domains of the presented theories. On the one hand, lack-of-fit theories explain how *descriptive* sex stereotypes (e.g., viewing the typical woman as less analytically competent than the typical man) can diminish a woman's expected competence when a job is male sex typed (i.e., requires analytic competence). Negative evaluations of women's work and potential can result. On the other hand, when evidence of good performance is undeniable and unambiguous, a woman's success may be dismissed by attributions to hard work or luck, which are less praiseworthy than competence. These ideas do not conflict at all, but instead derive from the same conceptual base, namely, descriptive stereotypes implying incompetence at male-sex-typed tasks.

The brief also discusses the consequences of *prescriptive* or normative sex stereotypes (e.g., women should be nice and passive; men should be strong and aggressive). Here, the issue no longer is acknowledgment of competence. Rather, this aspect of the stereotyping process explains the penalties that result from perceived violation of acceptable sex-role-appropriate behaviors. These penalties tend to take the form not of unfavorable competence evaluations but of unfavorable interpersonal and mental health evaluations. Because many behaviors considered inappropriate for women are the very ones deemed necessary to be "competent" in a traditionally male job, sex stereotypes create a double bind for women. Their competence is undervalued if they behave in traditionally feminine ways, while their interpersonal skills are derogated and their mental health is questioned if they be-

have in traditionally masculine ways. These ideas, which are spelled out clearly in the brief and articulated in the Supreme Court decision, are not mutually inconsistent, nor are they used selectively; quite simply, they concern different aspects of stereotypes, a point somehow lost on Barrett and Morris.

WHAT DISPUTED FACTS?

Whatever the (lack of) merit of the authors' other arguments, their complaint regarding "disputed facts" is undermined by their lack of knowledge of the law and the legal system. Barrett and Morris assert that matters of direct evidence should not be contained in a scientifically oriented amicus brief. They accuse the brief's authors of making unilateral decisions about the veracity of disputed direct evidence, a task that Barrett and Morris argued is "best made through legal proceedings." Although they do not accuse the APA of dissembling about the facts, they do allege that "the brief presents one side of several disputed facts" and that its portrayal of the facts was "biased in favor of Ms. Hopkins's case."

There are at least four responses to these arguments. First, there is no rule, policy, custom, or rational basis for barring the use of what Barrett and Morris call "direct evidence" in an amicus brief. To the contrary, a legal or scientific argument often depends on such factual evidence.

Second, even though Barrett and Morris make "disputed facts" one of the cornerstones of their critique, the facts that they cite as in dispute are not significant. They were not germane to the decision of the APA to submit a brief in the case, to the arguments the APA made in it, and, most important, to the Supreme Court's ultimate opinion in *Price Waterhouse*.

Third, Barrett and Morris are simply wrong that the "facts" they complain about are in dispute, at least as far as the legal system is concerned. As they suggest, the rare bits of factual evidence used by the APA were determined in legal proceedings. Price Waterhouse may continue to dispute the existence of certain facts, but an assertion in a civil case such as this one becomes a fact in law when a trial court decides, after hearing all admissible evidence, that more likely than not, the assertion is true. A party who continues to dispute the facts found by the trial court may appeal, which PW did. The appeals court may overturn factual findings if the appellant (PW here) can show that the trial judge's determinations were clearly erroneous. In the few cases that are subsequently reviewed by the U.S. Supreme Court, the Court in almost all instances is bound by the facts found below. Although PW may still believe in its perception of the facts, none of the facts that Judge Gesell found and accepted were ever changed, even though the case not only came before Judge Gesell twice but was reviewed on two occasions by an intermediate court of appeals and, ultimately, by the Supreme Court. The APA did not make any independent determination of the facts; like the Supreme Court, it was bound by the findings in the record and relied on that record in writing the brief. By the time a case goes to the Supreme Court, in other words, the facts have been decided; the Supreme Court does not engage in fact finding.

Finally, and most important, there is the existence of one crucial and incontrovertible fact central to the APA's brief: the agreement in this case by courts at all levels of the judicial process that PW engaged in sexual stereotyping of Ann Hopkins and thus violated Title VII of the 1964 Civil Rights Act. Affirming Judge Gesell's conclusion of law, the court of appeals agreed that "the partnership selection process at Price Waterhouse was impermissibly infected by stereotypical attitudes toward female candidates" (*Price Waterhouse v. Hopkins*, 1987, p. 468). And a majority on the Supreme Court, not known recently for upholding the civil rights of individuals against organizations or governmental entities, specifically rejected PW's assertion that stereotyping was not present in the way it chose partners. In sum, then, Barrett and Morris's criticism of the APA with regard to the issue of disputed facts is about as off the mark as PW's promotion policies.

WHO IS SELECTIVELY CITING RESEARCH?

The Barrett-Morris arguments do not perform any better when they turn to the substance of the research, which forms the main body of their article. To advance their claim that the amicus distorted the existing literature, they isolate what they call its four main arguments (note: *not* arguments I-IV given at the outset of this chapter), and cite literature that they claim takes exception to each one. Their main point seems to be that the literature review undertaken in the amicus brief was fundamentally flawed and perhaps even intentionally biased. As the scientists who drafted the APA amicus brief, we would have been interested to see alternative reviews of the relevant literatures that could further advance our knowledge in this area. Unfortunately, this review does not. Their review has several fatal flaws, so it does not live up to its mission as an unbiased consideration of the amicus. It does not add even a constructive iota to the amicus nor does it provide a useful set of criticisms, for the several reasons detailed below.

SEVEN OUT OF THIRTY-ONE: 22 PERCENT

An initial and fundamental flaw in the structure of the Barrett-Morris complaint is that it ignores the majority (77 percent) of the arguments in the brief. It focuses on seven out of thirty-one arguments in the brief—fewer than a quarter. Such tactics might impress someone who never read the brief, but to someone who has read it carefully, they do not undermine its validity except by oblique innuendo. The number of ignored arguments can be documented: Under Point I of the brief, all three arguments were ignored; under IIA, six out of seven arguments were ignored; under IIB, two out of six were ignored; under III, nine out of ten were ignored; and under IV, four out of five were ignored. One can only conclude that the authors found the remaining twenty-four arguments fully convincing, or at least could not find even the few isolated examples that served as exceptions to the general conclusions drawn in the few arguments they did choose to attempt to refute. What were the isolated arguments that Barrett and Morris chose to tackle, and how do their criticisms stand up? Poorly, when one has the space to examine each of their objections in more detail.

Stereotyping of Working Women. The first argument criticized is the existence of a subtype of the overall female stereotype sometimes called an Iron Maiden (after Kanter, 1977); she is perceived to be an unfeminine, unyielding woman who is independent of men. The Iron Maiden argument identifies not so much a stereotyping process as a description of the contents of one possible subtype. As such, it only requires documented examples of its usage. The authors mistakenly claim that the only existing support for this concept is Kanter's case study, and they criticize this study as not being empirically based; yet one would think it the very sort of externally valid examination of an operating organization that would meet the authors' complaints elsewhere in their critique about "paper" people.[1]

Quite clearly, the Iron Maiden subtype describes people's dislike of women perceived to be less nice, passive, and dependent than required by the prescriptive aspect of sex stereotypes. For example, when compared with successful managers (sex unspecified), highly successful women managers are portrayed as more bitter, quarrelsome, selfish, and power hungry than successful men managers are (Heilman et al., 1989). This general point is well documented (Fiske et al., 1991, p. 1050). The authors implicitly acknowledge this by failing to argue with the more general point that women who behave in masculine (tough, aggressive) ways are

disliked; men who behave in masculine ways are, of course, not penalized—quite the contrary. The authors fail to acknowledge the overall weight of the literature on this point.

Moreover, they misunderstand the scattered studies they do cite. For example, the authors misrepresent the results of the Heilman et al. (1989) study. It compared discrepancies between characterizations of successful managers both with "women in general" and with "women managers"; it did not compare women in general with women managers. Even so, the authors have distorted these data; the characterizations of women in general overlap a good deal with those of women managers, and the overlap tends to be in attributes that are particularly damning in terms of organizational functioning. This point is made quite clearly in the original article but is ignored by Barrett and Morris.

The authors' discussion of token status is simply inaccurate. The three citations given illustrate converging evidence for a phenomenon. Kanter's (1977) research is strong precisely because it is a case study of a real organization, relying on the accounts of the employees. Taylor's (1981) research is useful because it finds evidence for the same phenomenon in a more controlled laboratory setting. The robustness of the solo phenomenon is indicated in a meta-analysis since conducted by Mullen (personal communication, May 20, 1992). Across several studies, he tested the prediction that people would be more likely to process information about solo targets in gender-stereotypic terms as a direct function of the proportionate rarity of the targeted sex in the group. He found that the effect was nontrivial ($r = .20$); this effect size is larger than the effect size of the recent well-known medical research showing that aspirin reduces stroke episodes. And it is significant ($p < .0001$). Forty studies showing *no effect whatsoever* would be needed to reduce the combined probability of this effect to $p = .05$. So the effect seems well established in the laboratory.

An additional study using MBA students evaluating standard employment applications shows the same thing (Heilman, 1980). And a recent study of 486 work groups across a variety of jobs and organizations also shows that women receive more

---

1. The review returns again and again to the complaint that the studies cited in the brief used only paper persons. Yet the authors persist in citing some of the same types of studies when they view them as compatible with their own points. Moreover, not all the studies cited in the brief or in the underlying literature review use paper stimuli. The authors cannot have it both ways. As any introductory psychology class is taught, laboratory studies are useful for internal validity, and case studies, such as the book by Kanter, are useful for external validity. Each can be criticized for what it does not do, but together they reinforce each other. The authors do not address this fundamental point either in their own sampling of the literature or in their criticism of the amicus.

negative evaluations as their proportions decrease in the group, even controlling for gender differences in abilities, education, and experience (Sackett, DuBois & Noe, 1991). The point here is that the brief reports a sample of converging laboratory and field evidence of the solo phenomenon. Other research, existing at the time, supported its analysis, and subsequent research more than bears it out, both in the lab and in the field. Barrett and Morris simply failed to carry out a scientifically responsible review of the relevant literature on this topic (see A Lesson in Literature Review, below).

Bias Against Working Women. The second point that Barrett and Morris criticize is that women are often evaluated less positively than men, given comparable credentials and performance. The brief notes that such stereotyping depends, among other things, on the information available and on the setting. This conclusion was based not only on the citations given in the brief but also on the Ruble and Ruble (1982) review of 250 sex-stereotyping studies, Nieva and Gutek's (1980) review of 58 performance evaluation studies, Deaux's (1985) *Annual Review* chapter citing over 250 articles on sex and gender, Fiske and Taylor's (1984) *Social Cognition* book citing 1,300 references, and more. Our description of this literature was based on the weight of all the evidence as read by other experts and ourselves. That was our charge from the APA, and we carried it out.

By contrast, Barrett and Morris take a shotgun approach, making ad hoc complaints about isolated studies failing to find discrimination on particular subsidiary measures. In a now-familiar pattern, they miscite studies. We will describe the misrepresentation of some studies closest to home. First, Barrett and Morris misread one study as saying that "sex bias occurs only when little relevant information is given (Heilman, 1984)." In this study, there was an overall main effect for gender (favoring men) in personnel decisions. The authors simply chose to ignore this. Indeed, the study's goal was to understand the conditions that would mitigate against this baseline effect, and one of its most interesting findings was that discrimination failed to occur *only* when explicitly relevant information was provided. Hence, the only condition that Barrett and Morris cite was, oddly enough, the very exception to the general trend, rather than the general conclusion of the study, as they misleadingly imply.

As a second example, Barrett and Morris cite a 1979 study by Deaux as saying, "The research has also found no evidence of sex discrimination in performance evaluations of male and female managers." The focus of that study was on *self*-evaluations of male and female managers, although data on evaluations by supervisors were collected and reported (these data were less controlled, because some supervisors were evaluating several managers while others were evaluating a single manager). Two points are crucial here: (1) Because male and female managers were selected from the available samples in the organizations, we have no evidence as to what their true performance level was. In fact, given access discrimination, we might assume that women managers in the 1970s were more highly selected and more qualified than the men who occupied the same positions within the companies. If this were the case, then equivalent ratings of male and female performance by supervisors could in fact be discriminatory rather than unbiased. (2) Supervisors' ratings in that study did show no difference in evaluations of performance, ability, motivation, initiative, and ability to accept praise or criticism. However, significant differences *were* found in the ratings of manager friendliness, relations with the supervisor, and difficulty of assignments, all in favor of the male manager. Marginally significant (.09) were differences in rated moodiness, with women regarded as moodier than men. Thus Barrett and Morris were somewhat selective in their reporting of the findings.

As a third example, the Heilman and Stopeck (1985a) study is cited as showing that, in promotion decisions, "attractiveness was detrimental for women and beneficial for men. Sex alone was not significant." This study actually concerns causal attributions for corporate success, not decisions about promotion; it is not correctly depicted in the text. The following comment, "the unattractive female was actually rated the highest for promotion," in reference to the Heilman and Stopeck (1985b) study is simply wrong. No statistical comparison of the sort was reported; the authors are inferring this difference from a table, but the comparison was not conducted because it was not relevant to the hypotheses of the study. Also, Barrett and Morris simply ignore other data about organizational rewards and work-related evaluations that do not support their point. More broadly, the researchers' interest was in comparing the degree to which men and women were evaluated and treated differently as a function of their appearance. It was expected, and found, that attractiveness was a liability for women at the managerial level; Heilman and Stopeck explained this on the basis of the perceived femininity of the attractive woman and the greater perceived lack of fit between her attributes and those required for the job. This is perfectly consistent with the ideas in the brief.

Central to the problem seems to be the Barrett-Morris confusion about the consequences of the descriptive and prescriptive aspects of stereotyping. Penalties for out-of-role behavior tend to be in interpersonal judgments, not in competence judgments. So, even if the authors' analysis of these two studies were correct (e.g., unattractive appearance is equivalent to out-of-role behavior), the findings would not be inconsistent with other research reported, for the focal outcomes in these studies were, in both cases, competence judgments. It is the woman who is behaving in a way that "fits" the masculine job who is seen as the more competent, but that behavior may also earn her a good measure of unpopularity. This is what the brief means by a double bind. Barrett and Morris blur the distinction between these two possible negative outcomes and therefore see inconsistencies where, according to the brief's formulation, there are none.

As yet another example, Barrett and Morris allege that Heilman and Guzzo (1978) do "not support the claim of sex discrimination." This comment shows a total misunderstanding of the ideas underlying the research and of the research process itself. The point, of course, is that, typically women's performance is not attributed to ability; the research was designed to show the conse-

quences of such attributions. Not looking at the total pattern of findings in a factorial design and not attending to the purpose of the research is inexcusable. Picking out bits and pieces of data and presenting them out of context for the sake of debate is questionable ethically and, at the very least, is bad scholarship.

Moving away from our own previously published work, let us take up two sets of research findings (Moses & Boehm, 1975; Walsh, Weinberg & Fairfield, 1987) that, according to Barrett and Morris, demonstrate a lack of sex bias in actual promotion decisions. These can, in fact, be viewed as consistent with our arguments. In both of these studies, women were evaluated for promotion in an assessment center; the procedure entails intensive evaluation of performance-relevant characteristics in a simulated work environment by a group of highly trained assessors. Therefore, information was made available about the women, the information itself was highly relevant to the job and unambiguous in its implications for performance, and the determinations had to be justified to peers. It is precisely under these conditions, the brief and the existing literature would contend, that stereotypic thinking does not translate into discriminatory behavior.

One could go through a similar exercise regarding the rest of this section of the review, but we will not belabor the point. Several of the other "contradictory" results presented throughout the chapter can also be accounted for by these ideas. It is only in the context of a theory that all these results can be pulled together into a meaningful whole. Our published work has variously provided such theories, whereas Barrett and Morris's "theory" seems to be limited to the simple claim that women are simply not discriminated against. Barrett's published work on statistical regressions in wage discrimination suits comes to a similar conclusion (e.g., Barrett et al., 1986; Barrett & Sansonetti, 1988). Consistent with Barrett's having been an expert witness in over eighty cases (Barrett & Associates, 1992), the agenda of these effects takes a particular perspective. This would not be a problem if the literature review were comprehensive and accurate, but it is not. In the absence of apparent objectivity, other agendas may be relevant.[2]

The gender stereotyping literature shows clear and consistent patterns of converging evidence to indicate the specific conditions under which discrimination is most and least likely to occur. The point is that one's interpretation of any given study depends on its fit to the larger literature, something Barrett and Morris fail to consider. This is not a mixed literature, according to the consensus of experts in the field (see A Lesson in Literature Review, below). Without a truly comprehensive, quantitative literature review, one cannot characterize the literature as mixed and inconclusive.

Barrett and Morris do cite one meta-analysis also cited in the brief, which they note reported a small *average* effect size, although it was significant and there was substantial variability in the results. The argument (small amount of variance explained) is a common one in psychology because of the assumption that it limits the practical significance of a finding. However, some of our most eminent scholars and sophisticated statisticians have argued that even very small effect sizes can have profound practical effects (Abelson, 1985; Cohen, 1990; Rosenthal, 1990; Rosnow & Rosenthal, 1989; for discussions of Rosenthal, 1990, see Crow, 1991; McGraw, 1991; Rosenthal, 1991; Strahan, 1991). They make two essential points: First, a small r can refer to nontrivial percentage differences. Effect sizes in medical research, for example, are not necessarily bigger. If one is in the 10 percent who will be saved by the new treatment, that small effect matters a lot. Conversely, if one is in the 10 percent who lose jobs because of discrimination, that small effect can destroy one's life. The legal system deals in individual rights, not in odds.

Second, small effects aggregate over time (Abelson, 1985). If small odds of being victimized by discrimination in any one performance evaluation are

aggregated over a lifelong career, they can amount to a substantial record of discrimination, and the cumulative effect can be devastating.

Finally, as noted below (see A Lesson in Basic Research), it is precisely the variability across studies and across conditions within studies that is designed to specify the conditions under which stereotyping does and does not occur. These studies are not designed to be surveys of discrimination's frequency in the population; instead, they are basic research on what moderates the effects—another point lost on Barrett and Morris.

Penalties for Out-of-Role Behavior. The third point addressed in the review is penalties for out-of-role behavior: women are often devalued in traditionally masculine jobs, and they must conform to female stereotypes. Again, the Barrett and Morris strategy is to identify a few contrary results, some miscited, but not to acknowledge the thorough literature reviews that come to contrary conclusions. Describing a few exceptions does not address the relative weight of literature on each side of the issue.

As an example of a miscited study on this point, research by Taynor and Deaux (1975) is referenced in footnote 31 of the amicus and referred to by Barrett and Morris. A study by Taynor and Deaux published in 1973 used a similar paradigm and obtained similar findings. Barrett and Morris ignore some critical features of those studies. First, the performance outcome in those studies was unambiguous, and it was recognized and commended by authority figures. Thus, unlike in most job situations, there was no question as to whether the person had done well. Second, in both studies the successful woman was considered to have exerted more effort, but not to have more ability than the man. Further, in the 1975 study, which varied mode of action, the man was rated as behaving more logically than the equivalently performing female, *and* a logical mode was regarded more favorably than an intuitive/sensitive mode.

Another miscited study (Heilman, Martell & Simon, 1988) is taken totally out of context. The one condition cited is the one the original article used to illustrate just how extraordinary a situation

2. In contrast, none of the amicus authors obtains income on a regular basis from consulting in gender discrimination cases. Fiske has turned down at least forty opportunities, pursuing only those very few that were of particular scientific interest, including both management and plaintiff clients. The other authors have consulted rarely or never.

must be to get the reversal seized upon by Barrett and Morris. The general pattern of data and the rationale for this predicted effect are completely ignored, as is the main effect for applicant sex, indicating that *women generally were judged less favorably* than men in terms of competence ratings and assessments of likely career success.

Barrett and Morris also claim that "the brief contends that the success of highly accomplished women is attributed to luck rather than ability." This crucially misrepresents the brief itself. The brief contends that luck *or hard work* is used to explain women's success rather than ability or competence. This "error" makes the entire section of their review superfluous.[3]

Methods to Reduce the Effects of Stereotyping. This section misrepresents the brief again. The brief outlines three conditions that act to reduce stereotypic thought and sex discrimination. These are entirely ignored in the review, as is most of the literature presented in the corresponding section of the brief. Again, there is selectivity at work, this time in the representation of the brief itself.

Of the several remedies for stereotyping, just one argument is selected for criticism, namely, that interdependence undercuts stereotyping. Barrett and Morris criticize the three cited interdependence papers as lacking generalizability. They ignore a larger literature clearly supporting the effectiveness of teamwork in undermining stereotyping and discrimination. Though not limited to gender, much of the intergroup relations literature focuses on interdependence as a remedy in real-world settings (e.g., Miller & Brewer, 1984), and the interdependence principle is applicable.

Moreover, Barrett and Morris fail to appreciate that laboratory research is designed to demonstrate fundamental processes (i.e., people pay more care-

ful attention to those on whom their outcomes depend). These processes generalize over forty years of research and a wide variety of subject populations. It is easy to claim that laboratory results will not generalize, but there is an elementary lesson in methodology that Barrett and Morris fail to grasp in three respects. To be convincing, the generalizability critique must do three things: First, one would have to show that there are compelling, well-established *principles* predicting that real-world settings bring particular, identifiable factors that would eliminate the obtained effects. Second, one should pick a literature that does not already contain real-world examples. In fact, the laboratory research was based on real-world experiences with the success of teamwork in destroying discrimination. Third, one would have to find general flaws in the literature common to all the studies. Piecemeal ad hoc criticism that differs study by study fails to deal with converging evidence. The inevitable weaknesses in any one study are compensated by similar results from another study that may have other weaknesses. Perhaps if Barrett and Morris were more oriented toward basic research and less toward the techniques of the witness stand, they would appreciate this scientific principle.

Conclusion. An outsider reading only the Barrett and Morris chapter might walk away with the mistaken impression that the gender stereotyping literature is a quagmire and that experts cannot agree. In our view, that would be an error. There is remarkable consensus on the effects of stereotypes and discrimination, and a robust literature indicating the conditions under which they do and do not apply. The consensus of experts and even elementary textbooks runs totally contrary to the decidedly idiosyncratic Barrett-Morris reading. At the time of the original failure to promote Hopkins in 1982, the time of the original testimony in 1984, and the time the brief was written in 1988, basic textbooks in social and industrial/organizational psychology described gender stereotyping as a barrier to women in organizations (e.g., Baron & Byrne, 1981; Muchinsky, 1987). We cite undergraduate textbooks not so much to make them the authority here as to describe the consensus of the

---

3. Moreover, the description of the Deaux and Emswiller (1974) task is slightly distorted. The objects that the performer was judging included not only a tire jack but also a variety of objects that either men or women were believed to have a high degree of experience and presumably expertise with. In addition, the information about the person's performance level, as provided to the subjects, made it clear that the performance was of high quality.

field about the state of the world when Hopkins was reviewed for partner.

A LESSON IN BASIC RESEARCH

On what basis do Barrett and Morris assert that the research on stereotyping and sex bias is inconclusive? Where is this large body of contradictory research that "was ignored"? Is there a comprehensive body of literature that has demonstrated that stereotyping does *not* lead to sex bias? The authors seem to be alluding to individual research studies or even conditions within studies that do not indicate sex discrimination. But the brief was not asserting that sex discrimination always occurs. In fact, much of the cited research attempts to identify the conditions that inhibit its occurrence, so of course they contain conditions in which discrimination fails to occur; they were designed precisely to do so. The brief was explicitly written to educate the Court about the stereotyping process, and the literature reviewed was literature informative about that process, not a survey of the incidence of sex discrimination.

This also helps explain the brief's emphasis on experimental research. This type of research uniquely enables one to study a phenomenon causally, to test out various mediating processes that can account for it, and to identify the moderating conditions that regulate when it does or does not occur. Given the objectives of the brief, to educate the Court about the nature of the stereotyping process and the way it operates to foster discrimination, a heavy reliance on experimental research was wholly appropriate and optimally informative.

In sum, the Barrett-Morris treatment of basic research demonstrates an utter failure to understand why one does research, much less how one interprets the findings. The idea of having a theoretical framework that can guide research and help to integrate results across many studies seems totally alien to the authors. Clearly they do not understand that if a phenomenon is to be understood, it is critical not only to document it but also to explore the process giving rise to it and to determine the conditions that regulate its occurrence. This process of

identifying moderators of an effect is important theoretically, and it also has crucial implications for intervention. Therefore, what most crucially informs basic theory-driven research is the interaction (i.e., moderating) effect, not the main effect. The authors deal in logically irrelevant main effects that average over control conditions showing discrimination and experimental conditions designed to eliminate discrimination. The main point of such studies is to identify those very eliminating conditions. The meaning of the research lies in the comparison of findings within a given study, not in isolated bits and pieces of data taken totally out of context.

Barrett and Morris repeatedly pick one or two cells from an experimental design, usually the ones that are predicted to be the exception that demonstrates the rule, and use them to make their case. No heed is paid to the rationale for the research, the hypotheses, or the pattern of results in all conditions of the design. They also pick and choose which results to report—sometimes chastising the authors of the brief for using examples that lack general sex effects and sometimes ignoring these very same effects when they do occur.

Finally, on several occasions, the authors have reported data incorrectly, making unwarranted inferences about unreported and nonsignificant statistical differences and making blanket statements about results that are far from true to the data. In all these ways, the review falls short of adding to the scientific debate and can only misinform legal scholars who follow it.

A LESSON IN LITERATURE REVIEW

The Barrett-Morris literature review is biased, incomplete, and adversarial. It simply locates a few studies or conditions here and there that disagree with the amicus arguments. As such, it adds nothing to our knowledge of this area or to our evaluation of the brief. The only way to critically test the objectivity of the APA brief would be to undertake several careful, complete meta-analytic reviews of the relevant literatures, testing each of the arguments made in the brief. In fact, such meta-analytic reviews have been conducted since the brief, and they support its arguments. The meta-analysis of solo status and stereotyping was mentioned previously. Another meta-analytic review, based on fifty-six documents reporting sixty-one studies, addresses gender and leadership, concluding that the *average* discriminatory effect size was small (this does not eliminate its practical importance, as noted earlier). But more important, the review identifies the conditions under which negative evaluations (collapsed over competence, evaluation, and style) are most likely to occur: "Women in leadership positions were devalued relative to their male counterparts when leadership was carried out in stereotypically masculine styles, particularly when this style was autocratic or directive. In addition, the devaluation of women was greater when leaders occupied male-dominated roles and when the evaluators were men" (Eagly, Makhijani & Klonsky, 1992). One could hardly ask for a more concise confirmation of the APA's conclusions regarding Ann Hopkins's situation. Such a review most certainly would have been included in the amicus had it been available at the time the amicus was developed.

Another *Psychological Bulletin* meta-analysis by Swim et al. (1989) argues that the gender discrimination effect in evaluation of task performance is small; nevertheless, "one obvious but erroneous implication might be that people do not hold gender stereotypes or use such stereotypes when thinking about others. . . . People's evaluations of men and women are a complex function of a set of factors that influence the process of gender stereotyping" (p. 423). As in the Eagly et al. article and as in our earlier Lesson in Basic Research, the meta-analysis identifies conditions under which sex stereotypes do and do not surface. In this case, Swim et al. note the informational conditions that encourage and discourage stereotyping, a point also made in the brief. Moreover, Swim et al. suggest five other factors, not examined therein, that might moderate gender stereotyping. Of course, the Goldberg paradigm reviewed by Swim et al. is only one paradigm out of many for studying sex stereotyping, but this is the level of analysis necessary for responsible lit-

erature review in that it is publicly accountable for its inclusion criteria.

The amicus brief was drafted by four psychologists expert in sex stereotyping research—three social psychologists (Borgida, Deaux, Fiske) and one industrial/organizational psychologist (Heilman). It was prepared for submission by an attorney who is also a psychologist (Bersoff). The brief represented their best judgment of the state of the field, and the studies cited were illustrative of the points being made. Such a narrative approach was appropriate to the task, given the time and technical constraints of brief writing. The brief itself was not an exhaustive or meta-analytic literature review, nor could it be, given the constraints of space, time, and audience imposed by the case.

On the other hand, the Barrett-Morris article has no such excuse. It admits to not being a comprehensive literature review, but in fact, it ends up being arbitrary and unconvincing. Of course, there are a few empirical findings contrary to the conclusions of the brief. As any psychologist knows, some isolated results always contradict the major conclusions of the literature. Meta-analytic reviews are the methodologically responsible way to evaluate their import. Although such a meta-analysis is not within the scope of an amicus brief, it is now de rigueur in the *Psychological Bulletin* and any other APA journal publishing responsible literature reviews.

The main virtue of a meta-analysis is that its inclusion criteria are publicly specified. A meta-analytic review includes every study published in specifiable outlets in a specifiable time period that meets specifiable criteria. If one disagrees with the meta-analysis, one can disagree with the selection criteria or the analysis methods, but at least the paradigm is explicit in such a meta-analysis.

But the Barrett-Morris chapter does not even attempt an objectively conducted meta-analytic review. The basis for selecting results to cite in the Barrett and Morris chapter is only that they contradict the amicus. In a literature with thousands of relevant studies, that is not a sufficient criterion. Barrett and Morris impressively intone that they have identified 78 studies that directly contradict the brief. This number is less than impressive if one considers that (1) many of those studies are selectively or wrongly cited, as illustrated above, and (2) the literature itself contained 1,765 articles on sex-role attitudes from 1967 to 1982 alone, and over 300 on gender stereotypes from 1974 to 1987 (APA, 1991, footnote 8). Taking 78 out of a couple of thousand studies hardly makes the point. One has to make an argument that the cited studies are in the majority, so one must review the entire literature to draw any reasonable conclusions. Otherwise, their argument amounts to a logical flaw: If there were ninety-six findings supporting one view and four supporting the opposite, one cannot review the four exceptions and claim that their conclusions are the important ones.

In short, their review ignores the bulk of the literature. There is simply no basis for the sweeping statement "The arguments in the brief are often not supported by the cited literature and . . . a large body of contradictory research is not discussed in the brief." As the first author knows, for he wrote to Fiske for the references, the amicus brief was based on a bibliography of numerous citations, which included several previous literature reviews. The amicus brief does not (and should not) cite hundreds of studies; instead it uses "e.g." citations as illustrative. Such a brief is appropriately based on the expert opinions of the professionals drafting it. Not coincidentally, Judge Gesell, in his own independent sampling of the research literature (references were not supplied by the plaintiff or her expert), reached the same conclusions.

Barrett and Morris would have to back up their opinions by establishing a substantial weight of literature and professional background in the area. This their chapter simply fails to do. Neither author is an expert in the substantive literature of sex stereotyping, the chapter was not reviewed by experts in gender stereotyping, and the Barrett-Morris sampling of the literature does nothing to establish that expertise. Being an expert in regression analysis applied to salary discrimination does not require or imply a *substantive* expertise in the area of stereotyping and discrimination per se. Nor does the Barrett-Morris article present a compre-

hensive literature review of research as evidence to establish substantive expertise. Their conclusion that "the pattern of citations and inferences drawn from them goes beyond customary scientific practice" might seem a quotable quote for some future expert witness, but it is not scientifically supported. Sweeping and groundless statements are not exactly science.

SOME WORDS ABOUT TIMING OF PUBLICATION

Finally, the authors imply that the drafters of the amicus were engaged in a subversive attempt to hide the brief because they somehow knew it would not stand up to public scrutiny. This misrepresents the process in several respects, many of which the authors must have known.

First, in the bibliography sent to Barrett at his request long before he submitted the critique for publication, opposing results are indeed cited. However, the drafters made a professional judgment about the quality and weight of those studies as compared to the rest of the literature. But it is not as if the amicus drafters hid that information from anyone who requested it. Moreover, the innuendo that the brief drafters knew of the alternative literature but were suppressing it is simply based on groundless suspicion. As noted, the drafters were aware of a variety of literature, made it available to those professionals who asked, and made an informed judgment about the relative weight of the empirical evidence on each side.

Second, the amicus drafting team included one person (Borgida) known as a gadfly who critically reevaluates some taken-for-granted assumptions of sex-stereotyping research. If the drafters had intended to present a biased review, such a person would not have been included. The brief passed muster with Borgida. Similarly, the drafters included an expert in sex stereotyping within organizations (Heilman); the external validity of the cited studies and the conclusions of the review were approved by this person as well. The amicus team also included another industrial/organizational psychologist, Ralph Alexander, appointed by the APA to monitor the sections on subjective criteria (see footnote 45 of the brief). In short, the APA constructed the team to include a range of expertise and opinion; the amicus reflected the resulting consensus.

Third, the brief was always intended for submission to the *American Psychologist*, but the authors waited for the outcome of the continuing litigation in order to present the complete story to APA readers. The brief was submitted in June 1988, and the Supreme Court heard the case in October, handing down its decision in May 1989, which included a remand to Gesell. Ideas for an article accompanying the brief were solicited immediately, in June 1989. Material was received from all the authors over the following academic year while we waited for Gesell's decision on remand. This decision was made May 14, 1990. Fiske circulated a draft of the article ten days later (May 24, 1990), and we submitted it to *American Psychologist* on August 24, 1990. We received reviews from the journal over six months later (March 5, 1991), conferred and submitted a revision two months later (June 4, 1991), and received a final acceptance on July 18, for publication in October 1991. The authors can hardly be faulted for delay. On the contrary, perhaps we should have waited longer, for meanwhile Price Waterhouse appealed Judge Gesell's remanded decision, and the appellate decision was in December 1990; Price Waterhouse petitioned to have the case reviewed again by the Supreme Court, but its request was eventually denied. In short, the amicus team planned from the outset to accompany the brief with an explanation of the process and the details of the case. To imply, as they do, that coercion is needed to guarantee objectivity is simply inaccurate and insulting.

Fourth, it is an insult to imply, as they also do, that the brief authors purposefully misrepresented their own work. None of our own published studies that are cited are in fact inconsistent with the ideas presented, and many more of our studies that *are* consistent with the ideas presented are not cited in the brief because of space considerations.

In conclusion, it has unfortunately required many pages to address the Barrett-Morris critique, which takes an unintegrated, scattershot approach that defies a brief response. In our opinion, their review is not of sufficient quality to merit so much consideration, for it is riddled with logical inconsistencies, and it does not meet its own standards of objectivity. In fact, its flaws exemplify its own criticisms. Indeed, one wonders to what values their own chapter subscribes and to what ends.

REFERENCES

Abelson, R. P. (1985). A variance explanation paradox: When a little is a lot. *Psychological Bulletin, 97,* 129–133.

American Psychological Association (1991). In the Supreme Court of the United States: *Price Waterhouse v. Ann B. Hopkins:* Amicus curiae brief for The American Psychological Association. *American Psychologist, 46,* 1061–1070.

Baron, R. A., & Byrne, D. (1981). *Social psychology: Understanding human interaction.* Boston: Allyn and Bacon.

Barrett & Associates, Inc. (1992). *Capability statement.* Akron, Ohio.

Barrett, G. V., Alexander, R. A., Anesgart, M. N., & Doverspike, D. (1986). Frequently encountered problems in the application of regression analysis to the investigation of sex discrimination in salaries. *Public Personnel Management, 15,* 143–156.

Barrett, G. V., & Sansonetti, D. M. (1988). Issues concerning the use of regression analysis in salary discrimination cases. *Personnel Psychology, 41,* 503–516.

Cohen, J. (1990). Things I have learned (so far). *American Psychologist, 45,* 1304–1312.

Crow, E. L. (1991). Response to Rosenthal's comment "How are we doing in soft psychology?" *American Psychologist, 46,* 1083.

Deaux, K. (1979). Self evaluations of male and female managers. *Sex Roles, 5,* 571–580.

Deaux, K. (1985). Sex and gender. *Annual Review of Psychology, 36,* 49–81.

Deaux, K., & Emswiller, T. (1974). Explanations of successful performance in sex-linked tasks: What is skill for the male is luck for the female. *Journal of Personality and Social Psychology, 29,* 80–85.

Eagly, A. H., Makhijani, M. G., & Klonsky, B. G. (1992). Gender and evaluation of leaders: A meta-analysis. *Psychological Bulletin, 111,* 3–22.

Fiske, S. T., Bersoff, D. N., Borgida, E., Deaux, K., & Heilman, M. E. (1991). Social science research on trial: The use of sex stereotyping research in *Price Waterhouse vs. Hopkins. American Psychologist, 46,* 1049–1060.

Fiske, S. T., & Taylor, S. E. (1984). *Social cognition.* New York: Random House.

Heilman, M. E. (1980). The impact of situational factors on personnel decisions concerning women: Varying the sex composition of the applicant pool. *Organizational Behavior and Human Performance, 26,* 386–395.

Heilman, M. E. (1984). Information as a deterrent against sex discrimination: The effects of applicant sex and information type on preliminary employment decisions. *Organizational Behavior and Human Performance, 33*, 174–186.

Heilman, M. E., Block, C. J., Martell, R. F., & Simon, M. C. (1989). Has anything changed? Current characterizations of men, women, and managers. *Journal of Applied Psychology, 74*, 935–942.

Heilman, M. E., & Guzzo, R. A. (1978). The perceived cause of work success as a mediator of sex discrimination in organizations. *Organizational Behavior and Human Performance, 21*, 346–357.

Heilman, M. E., Martell, R., & Simon, M. (1988). The vagaries of bias: Conditions regulating the undervaluation, equivaluation, and overvaluation of female job applicants. *Organizational Behavior and Human Performance, 41*, 98–110.

Heilman, M. E., & Stopeck, M. H. (1985a). Attractiveness and corporate success: Different causal attributions for males and females. *Journal of Applied Psychology, 70*, 379–388.

Heilman, M. E., & Stopeck, M. H. (1985b). Being attractive, advantage or disadvantage? Performance-based evaluations and recommended personnel actions as a function of appearance, sex, and job type. *Organizational Behavior and Human Decision Processes, 35*, 202–215.

Kanter, R. (1977). *Men and women of the corporation.* New York: Basic Books.

McGraw, K. O. (1991). Problems with the BESD: A comment on Rosenthal's "How are we doing in soft psychology?" *American Psychologist, 46*, 1084–1086.

Miller, N., & Brewer, M. B. (Eds.) (1984). *Groups in contact: The psychology of desegregation.* New York: Academic Press.

Moses, J. L., & Boehm, V. R. (1975). Relationship of assessment-center performance to management progress of women. *Journal of Applied Psychology, 60*, 527–529.

Muchinsky, P. M. (1987). *Psychology applied to work: An introduction to industrial/organizational psychology* (2nd ed.). Pacific Grove, Calif.: Brooks-Cole.

Mullen, B., personal communication, May 20, 1992.

Nieva, V. F., & Gutek, B. A. (1980). Sex effects on evaluation. *Academy of Management Review, 5*, 267–276.

Price Waterhouse v. Hopkins, 825 F.2d 458 (D.C. Cir. 1987).

Price Waterhouse v. Hopkins, 109 S. Ct. 1775 (1989).

Rosenthal, R. (1990). How are we doing in soft psychology? *American Psychologist, 45*, 775–776.

Rosenthal, R. (1991). Effect sizes: Pearson's correlation, its display via the BESD, and alternative indices. *American Psychologist, 46*, 1086–1087.

Rosnow, R. L., & Rosenthal, R. (1989). Statistical procedures and the justification of knowledge in psychological science. *American Psychologist, 44*, 1276–1284.

Ruble, D. N., & Ruble, T. L. (1982). Sex stereotypes. In A. G. Miller (Ed.), *In the eye of the beholder: Contemporary issues in stereotyping* (pp. 188–252). New York: Praeger.

Sackett, P. R., DuBois, C. L. Z., & Noe, A. W. (1991). Tokenism in performance evaluations: The effects of work group representation on male-female and White-Black differences in performance ratings. *Journal of Applied Psychology, 76*, 263–267.

Strahan, R. F. (1991). Remarks on the binominal effect size display. *American Psychologist, 46*, 1083–1084.

Swim, J., Borgida, E., Maruyama, G., & Myers, D. G. (1989). Joan McKay versus John McKay: Do gender stereotypes bias evaluations? *Psychological Bulletin, 105*, 409–429.

Taylor, S. E. (1981). A categorization approach to stereotyping. In D. L. Hamilton (Ed.), *Cognitive processes in stereotyping and intergroup behavior* (pp. 83–114). Hillsdale, N.J.: Erlbaum.

Taynor, J., & Deaux, K. (1973). When women are more deserving than men: Equity, attribution, and perceived sex differences. *Journal of Personality and Social Psychology, 28*, 360–367.

Taynor, J., & Deaux, K. (1975). Equity and perceived sex differences: Role behavior as defined by the task, the mode, and the action. *Journal of Personality and Social Psychology, 32*, 381–390.

Walsh, J. P., Weinberg, R. M., & Fairfield, M. L. (1987). The effects of gender on assessment center evaluations. *Journal of Occupational Psychology, 60*, 305–309.

Diagnosis: Is There Gender Bias in the 1994 *Diagnostic and Statistical Manual* (DSM-IV)?

The question of whether there is gender bias in psychotherapy is a highly charged issue dating back to the beginning of the current women's movement. The classic study by Inge Broverman and her colleagues (1970), which suggested that therapists have different standards of mental health for men and women, provided ammunition to those critics who charged psychotherapy with sexism. The Broverman study has been faulted for flawed methodology (Widiger & Settle, 1987), and subsequent replications have not found the same sex bias (Phillips & Gilroy, 1985). This may indicate that sexism has declined among mental health professionals. However, there is also the possibility that Broverman et al.'s research design is no longer sensitive enough to detect the subtle sex biases of today's more sophisticated therapists working in a more gender-conscious climate.

Many recent complaints of gender bias in psychotherapy focus on the American Psychiatric Association's *Diagnostic and Statistical Manual of Mental Disorders* (DSM). The first DSM, published in 1952, in an attempt to standardize psychiatric nomenclature, identified fifty-nine mental disorders. Since that time the manual has undergone several revisions: DSM-II in 1968, DSM-III in 1980, and DSM-III-R in 1987. The current 886-page edition, DSM-IV (1994), lists more than 300 disorders. Whether or not a disorder is included in the manual can determine if insurers will pay for a patient's treatment. The manual's influence is illustrated by the fact that a minor revision of the DSM-III's criteria for schizoid personality disorder in 1987 led to an 800-percent increase in the number of patients meeting the criteria in the following year (Morey, 1988).

Unlike DSM-III-R, which paid little attention to the role of culture, the 1994 edition contains information on the effects of culture and ethnicity on both diagnosis and treatment. Culture-bound syndromes are now identified. For example, "nervios," defined as feelings of stress and mood changes, is typically seen in Latinos in the southwestern United States and Central America (Ginorio et al., 1995; Hughes & Wintrob, 1995). The manual also includes "Acculturation Problems" as a new category without necessarily identifying them as symptoms of mental disorder (Lu et al., 1995).

Critics, however, continue to attack the manual's treatment of women. At various times, five areas of the DSM have been targeted as potentially harmful to women: Borderline Personality Disorder, Histrionic Personality Disorder, Dependent Personality Disorder, Self-defeating Personality Disorder, and Premenstrual Dysphoria Disorder. Kroll (1988) believes that personality disorders have been criticized for sex bias because they seem to represent social conventions more than medical diseases. For example, Becker and Lamb note that the essential characteristics of Borderline Personality Disorder, "a pervasive pattern of instability of interpersonal relationships, self-image, and affects," is applied to women more often than men at a rate of anywhere from 2 to 1 to 9 to 1 (1994, p. 55).

Not surprisingly, two of the disorders that represent exaggerated versions of feminine traits are also much more likely to be applied to women than to men. A patient suffering from Histrionic Personality Disorder "tends to be attention seeking, self-dramatizing, excessively gregarious, seductive . . . vain, and demanding." Dependent Personality Disorder, on the other hand, "describes a pattern of excessive reliance on others that is reflected in the person's tendency to permit others to make important decisions, . . . to tolerate mistreatment, and fail to be appropriately assertive" (Frances et al., 1995, pp. 373, 377).

Feminist psychologists have complained that many of what the DSM classifies as personality disorders represent responses to situational problems rather than enduring personality traits. For example, they identify tolerating mistreatment as possibly an appropriate coping strategy for a woman in a battering situation who fears that any sign of assertiveness will lead to greater physical harm. Moreover, many traits associated with personality disorders subside or disappear when the patient moves out of the abusive situation (Committee on Women in Psychology, 1985).

A similar criticism was raised against the inclusion of Self-defeating Personality Disorder in DSM-III-R (1987), which was listed in the Appendix as a diagnostic category needing further study. Criteria for the disorder included helping others at the price of failing to accomplish one's own goals and engaging in excessive self-sacrifice. Originally entitled Masochistic Personality Disorder, the designation was changed in an attempt to distance it from Freud's concept of moral masochism, which implied that someone so labeled derived unconscious pleasure from suffering. As Carol Tavris (1992) pointed out, putting other people first is virtually a role requirement for women in our culture. A firestorm of criticism, charging that a diagnosis of Self-defeating Personality Disorder was tantamount to blaming the victim, forced the American Psychiatric Association to withdraw it from the 1994 manual (Caplan, 1995).

A similar effort to dislodge Premenstrual Dysphoria Disorder from the DSM-IV, however, failed. The dispute over this disorder, which remains in the Appendix, pending further study, mirrors many of the objections to the manual's treatment of women. Critics contend that not only is there little or no supporting scientific evidence for it, but a diagnosis of Premenstrual Dysphoria Disorder pathologizes a large number of women with premenstrual problems (Caplan, 1995). Its defenders argue, however, that the criteria for the disorder establish a high symptom threshold that would likely apply to only some 3–5 percent of women (Frances et al., 1995).

In the following articles, Terry Kupers argues that DSM-IV has failed to eliminate gender bias and that it continues to pathologize nonmainstream behaviors and attitudes. Ruth Ross and her colleagues disagree. They contend that by addressing the issue of gender bias, the DSM-IV Task Force has increased the applicability and usefulness of the manual for the treatment of both men and women.

REFERENCES

American Psychiatric Association. (1987). *Diagnostic and statistical manual of mental disorders* (3rd ed. rev.). Washington, D.C.: American Psychiatric Association.

American Psychiatric Association. (1994). *Diagnostic and statistical manual of mental disorders* (4th ed.). Washington, D.C.: American Psychiatric Association.

Becker, D., & Lamb, S. (1994). Sex bias in the diagnosis of borderline personality disorder and posttraumatic stress disorder. *Professional Psychology: Research and Practice, 25,* 55–61.

Broverman, I., Broverman, D. M., Clarkson, F. E., Rosenkrantz, P. S., & Vogel, S. R. (1970). Sex role stereotypes and clinical judgments of mental health. *Journal of Consulting and Clinical Psychology, 34,* 1–7.

Caplan, P. J. (1995). *They say you're crazy: How the world's most powerful psychiatrists decide who's normal.* Reading, Mass.: Addison-Wesley.

Committee on Women in Psychology. (October 1985). Statement on proposed diagnostic categories for DSM-III-R. Washington, D.C.: American Psychological Association.

Frances, A., First, M. B., & Pincus, H. A. (1995). *DSM-IV guidebook.* Washington, D.C.: American Psychiatric Press.

Ginorio, A. B., Gutierrez, L., Cauce, A. M., & Acosta, M. (1995). Psychological issues for Latinas. In H. Lan-

drine (Ed.), *Bringing cultural diversity to feminist psychology: Theory, research, and practice* (pp. 241- 263). Washington, D.C.: American Psychological Association.

Hughes, C. C., & Wintrob, R. M. (1995). Culture-bound syndromes and the cultural context of clinical psychiatry. *Review of Psychiatry, 14,* 565–597.

Kroll, J. K. (1988). *The challenge of the borderline patient: Competency in diagnosis and treatment.* New York: Norton.

Lu, F. G., Russell, F. L., & Mezzich, J. E. (1995). Issues in the assessment and diagnosis of culturally diverse individuals. *Review of Psychiatry, 14,* 477–510.

Morey, L. C. (1988). Personality disorders in DSM-III and DSM-III-R: Convergence, coverage and internal consistency. *American Journal of Psychiatry, 145,* 573–577.

Phillips, R. D., & Gilroy, F. D. (1985). Sex role stereotypes and clinical judgments of mental health: The Broverman findings re-examined. *Sex Roles, 12,* 179–193.

Tavris, C. (1992). *The mismeasure of women.* New York: Simon & Schuster.

Widiger, T. A., & Settle, S. A. (1987). Broverman et al. revisited: An artifactual sex bias. *Journal of Personality and Social Psychology, 53,* 463–469.

ADDITIONAL READING

Frances, A., First, M. B., & Pincus, H. A. (1995). DSM-IV: Its value and limitations. *Harvard Mental Health Letter, 11,* 4–6.

Garb, H. N. (1995). Sex bias and the diagnosis of borderline personality disorder. *Professional Psychology: Research and Practice, 26,* 526.

Kirk, S. A., & Kutchins, H. (1992). *The selling of DSM:*

The rhetoric of science in psychiatry. New York: Aldine de Gruyter.

Ussher, J. M. (1991). *Women's madness: Misogyny or mental illness?* Amherst: University of Massachusetts Press.

Willie, C. V., Rieker, P. P., Kramer, B. M., & Brown, B. S. (Eds). (1995). *Mental health, racism and sexism.* Pittsburgh: University of Pittsburgh Press.

The Politics of Psychiatry:

Gender and Sexual Preference

in DSM-IV

TERRY A. KUPERS

The fourth edition of the *Diagnostic and Statistical Manual of Mental Disorders* (DSM-IV), published by the American Psychiatric Association (APA) in 1994, contains the official list of diagnostic categories. It is touted as an improvement over previous editions, more precise in its descriptions of mental disorders, more rigorous in its criteria for establishing diagnoses. There is some effort to take gender and sexual orientation into consideration, as well as race and ethnicity. And there are claims of greater objectivity on account of the improvements, the detail, and the attention to cultural contexts. But is the new edition really an improvement, or merely a more rigorous rationalization for pathologizing nonmainstream behaviors and attitudes? And how successful have the authors been in transcending past gender biases? A meaningful discussion of these questions requires reading between the lines as well as attending to the social and historical context.

A LONGER, MORE DETAILED LIST OF DIAGNOSTIC CATEGORIES

The first thing to note about the DSM-IV is its size, 886 pages. DSM-I (APA, 1952) contained 130 pages; DSM-II (APA, 1968) contained 134 pages; DSM-III (APA, 1980) contained 481 pages. (A revised DSM-III, DSM-III-R, was published in 1987,

but I will leave it out of this summary for simplicity's sake.) In each edition there are new disorders, new groupings of disorders, some deletions, and various revisions in the way well-established disorders are viewed.

For instance, with the publication of the third edition in 1980, Panic Disorder, Post-traumatic Stress Disorder, Social Phobia, and Agoraphobia were added. The last two diagnoses had been lumped under the category Phobias in DSM-II; in DSM-III they, along with Panic Disorder and PTSD, became subtypes of the group of Anxiety Disorders. And with the publication of DSM-III some names were changed, for instance Manic-Depressive Disorder (DSM-II) became Bipolar Disorder (DSM-III); and some categories were dropped, notably homosexuality.

Again, in DSM-IV, there are new categories (Substance-Induced Anxiety Disorder, Sibling Relational Problem, Physical and Sexual Abuse of Adult); there are name changes (Multiple Personality Disorder becomes Dissociative Identity Disorder); there are new groupings (Gender Identity Disorders subsumes what used to be three groupings: Gender Identity Disorder of Childhood, of Adolescence, and of Adulthood); and there are deletions (Passive-aggressive Personality Disorder, Transsexualism). Relatively few new categories were added to DSM-IV, the emphasis being on more detail in the descriptions, presumably to increase inter-rater reliability. And the fourth edition makes the diagnostic categories relatively less exclusive so that one does not need to be as careful to rule out one category in order to pin down the diagnosis of another. Consequently a given individual is more likely to be assigned two or more "comorbid" diagnoses, for instance Obsessive Compulsive Disorder with Depression or with Alcohol Dependence.

TWO EXPLANATIONS FOR A LONGER, MORE DETAILED DSM

Why has the DSM grown thicker, the list of disorders longer? There are two basic explanations, one built upon a positivist notion of scientific progress, the other on the notion that our concepts of mental health and mental disorder are socially and historically constructed.

According to the positivist model, which underlies the stance of orthodox psychiatry and rationalizes its current turn toward biologism (for a critique see Cohen, 1993), advancing technology, and newer research findings permit us to discover mental disorders which always existed, but went undetected until now because our understanding of the brain and mental functioning was not as sophisticated as it is today. Joel Kovel (1980) says it well: "Psychiatry's self-image (is) of a medical profession whose growth is a matter of increasing mastery over a phenomenon, mental illness, which is supposed to be always present, a part of nature passively awaiting the controlling hand of science" (p. 72). The emphasis in DSM-IV on extensive reviews of clinical and research literatures and the conduct of field trials with revised diagnostic categories reflect this assumption. The goal is to see how much consistency can be achieved among diagnosticians.

Then there is the rush to develop "Treatment Guidelines," keyed to DSM-IV categories. For instance, the APA recently released its "Practice Guidelines for the Treatment of Patients with Bipolar Disorder" (APA, 1994b). Treatment guidelines provide medical centers and third-party payers with a rationale for allowing some benefits and disallowing others. Thus scientific truth is defined in terms of consensus among certain clinicians, mainly psychiatrists who have clout in the APA, about the proper diagnosis and treatment of each disorder.

Confident that their opinions about the existence of mental disorders constitute a science that is advancing rapidly and unfalteringly, psychiatrists and their collaborators are not very likely to uncover the biases and social interests that determine the path of their scientific endeavors, for instance the fact that a significant part of their research is funded by pharmaceutical companies that would like very much to see them identify mental disorders for which the treatment of choice is a pharmaceutical agent.

The social/historical model holds that "the disorder and the remedy are both parts of the same social process, and that they form a unity subject to the total history of the society in which they take place" (Kovel, 1980, p. 72). Our concept of mental health as well as our categories of mental disorder are socially constructed, and people in power determine what constitutes mental disorder among those they have power over (Conrad, 1980; Foucault, 1965). Jean Baker Miller (1976), building on Hegel's Master/Slave dialectic, points out that in the interest of continuing domination, the dominant group is the model for "normal human relationships" while the subordinate group is viewed as inferior in one way or another (Blacks are intellectually inferior, women are "ruled by emotion"). Thomas and Sillen (1974) point out that slaves who ran away from their owners' plantations in the antebellum South received the diagnosis "drapetomania," literally, "flight-from-home madness" (p. 2).

Elizabeth Packard's husband declared in 1860 that her disagreement with his religious views was evidence of insanity; and because the laws of Illinois as well as the male asylum psychiatrist were on his side, he was able to have her locked in an asylum (Chesler, 1972). Hughes (1990) uncovers some of the gender biases in the testimony of families who had a member admitted to an asylum in late nineteenth-century Alabama. To skip to the present, is it merely coincidental that just when middle-class women are entering the workplace in record numbers, premenstrual syndrome is declared a form of mental disorder?

Social theory provides two related answers to the question of why the DSM grows longer and more detailed in successive editions. First, the growth of the mental health industry depends on the expansion of the list of diagnostic categories. The number of psychiatrists, psychologists, and psychotherapists has grown considerably in recent years, as has the variety of psychotropic medications. As clinicians examine and treat a larger proportion of the citizenry, more diagnoses are needed to justify the whole endeavor. I will return to this point in the section on childhood disorders.

Second, our consciousness and everyday lives have become increasingly regimented and administered over the past century, and as a result the average citizen is permitted fewer eccentricities before deviance is declared. The Industrial Revolution required a disciplined workforce capable of sufficient delayed gratification to endure long hours at hard labor for less than fair wages. Those who could not work had to be marginalized as criminals, beggars, or lunatics. This was the period when great leaps were made in the description of such psychotic conditions as dementia praecox, later to be renamed schizophrenia. Since the explosive growth of consumerism in the 1920s, newer, milder diagnoses are needed for those who are capable of working, who buy into the promise of ad campaigns that the purchase of one commodity after another will lead to happiness, and yet are unable to attain the kind of happiness portrayed in advertisements and films. The successful but still unhappy people must be neurotic; perhaps they need psychoanalysis, psychotherapy, a tranquilizer, or an antidepressant.

While the positivist model directs our attention toward the gathering of ever more empirical data and the evolution of more sophisticated statistical analyses, the social/historical model permits us to understand the way social interests determine our views on psychopathology as well as our views on what constitutes scientific progress.

ABOUT HOMOSEXUALITY

The debate about homosexuality in the late 1960s and early 1970s included mass demonstrations at annual meetings of the APA. The straight male leadership was forced to back down, voting in 1973 to delete the category of homosexuality from the official list of mental disorders. The change was reflected in the next edition, DSM-III, in 1980.

But the stigmatization did not end there. The official list of mental disorders is merely the tip of the iceberg when it comes to pathologizing. Psychoanalysts and psychotherapists pathologize constantly, deciding, for instance, when to intervene in the patient's story and make an interpretation. There is the decision to interpret something and not

to interpret something else, and the clinician's views about normalcy and pathology determine her or his choices. In the 1920s, analysts repeatedly interpreted penis envy in women (for a summary of psychoanalytic views on gender, see Connell, 1994). Why did they not choose instead to interpret the pathology in men's defensive need to exclude women from the halls of power? In the 1960s, analysts interpreted the radical activism of young adults as a sign of psychopathology. Why did they not interpret the inactivism of others (including themselves) in the face of great social upheavals (Kupers, 1993b)?

I do not believe there is anything inherently wrong with pathologizing certain human characteristics. Sedgwick (1982) argues convincingly that the attempt by libertarians and radical therapists in the sixties to get rid of the entire concept of mental illness was misguided at best. The question is which human traits shall be pathologized. Throughout the history of the mental health professions, why has homosexuality consistently been the target for pathologizing while homophobia has never appeared among the list of mental disorders? The unstated biases reflected in these choices do not disappear just because one category of mental disorder is deleted.

Still, in the struggle to transcend homophobia, it is a positive development when homosexuality is removed from the list of mental disorders. In its place, in DSM-III (1980), a new category was added, Ego-Dystonic Homosexuality, designed for gays and lesbians who would prefer to be straight but were having trouble converting their desires. Since this category became, in practice, a substitute for the category of homosexuality, its deletion in DSM-IV is another positive step—likely motivated by the presence of more women and gays on the task force and work groups that developed DSM-IV. The APA even calls for all professional organizations and individuals "to do all that is possible to decrease the stigma related to homosexuality" (APA, 1993, p. 686).

But the pathologization of homosexuality remains. Consider this statement, made two years after the APA decided to stop diagnosing homosexuality, by Otto Kernberg (1975), a prominent psychoanalyst:

We may classify male homosexuality along a continuum that differentiates the degree of severity of pathology of internalized object relations. First, there are cases of homosexuality with a predominance of genital, oedipal factors, in which the homosexual relation reflects a sexual submission to the parent of the same sex as a defense against oedipal rivalry. . . . In a second and more severe type, the male homosexual has a conflictual identification with an image of his mother and treats his homosexual objects as a representation of his own infantile self. . . . In a third type of homosexual relation, the homosexual partner is "loved" as an extension of the patient's own pathological grandiose self. . . . This, the most severe type of homosexual involvement, is characteristic of homosexuality in the context of narcissistic personality structure proper, and constitutes the prognostically most severe type of homosexuality. (pp. 328–29)

I am not aware of any disclaimer of this formulation by Kernberg, who is listed as an adviser to the authors of DSM-IV. Even though the diagnosis of homosexuality is no longer officially sanctioned, a clinician, following Kernberg and other prominent experts, might assign a gay man the DSM-IV diagnoses Gender Identity Disorder, Sexually Attracted to Males (APA, 1994a, p. 534) with Narcissistic Personality; or Transvestic Fetishism (p. 530) with Narcissistic Personality Disorder; and other clinicians would get the point. There is also continuing debate about whether the goal in treating homosexuals should be conversion to heterosexuality (Socarides, Kaufman, Gottlieb, & Isay, 1994). In other words, long after the category is removed from the official list and the APA advocates destigmatization, prominent clinicians continue to pathologize homosexuality while showing no interest in creating a category for homophobia.

WOMEN'S DISORDERS

Women have evolved a strong voice within establishment psychiatry. The list of contributors to DSM-II (1968) contains the names of thirty-seven men and three women, whereas the equivalent list for DSM-IV (1994a) contains the names of twenty-six men and eleven women. (It is not as easy to determine how many gays and lesbians were involved.) As a result, there were rancorous debates about the pathologization of women's experiences and characteristics prior to the publication of DSM-IV. Two proposed diagnostic categories were at issue: "Self-defeating Personality" (for women who find themselves repeatedly victimized by abusive men) and "Late Luteal Phase Dysphoric Disorder" (the luteal phase of the menstrual cycle begins at ovulation and ends at menses, and this diagnosis is synonymous with PMS). Feminist psychiatrists and psychologists argued that the former diagnosis stigmatized and blamed the victims of domestic abuse (Caplan, 1987). They prevailed: Self-defeating Personality was not included in DSM-IV. Meanwhile the categories Sexual Abuse of Adult (APA, 1994a, p. 682) and Physical Abuse of Adult (p. 682) were added to the official list, permitting the clinician to diagnose pathology in the perpetrator.

In regard to Late Luteal Phase Dysphoric Disorder, the question was why pathologize the woman's natural cycles? Why not pathologize instead men's need to avoid all signs of emotion and dependency while maintaining an obsessively steady pace (Spitzer et al., 1989)? I coined the term "pathological arrhythmicity" for this disorder in men (Kupers, 1993a). The debate about PMS was not as intense as the one about Self-defeating Personality. Some women clinicians claimed that a category for PMS might serve to increase sensitivity among male colleagues to the experiences of women. The debate ended in compromise: Premenstrual Dysphoric Disorder is included in an appendix of DSM-IV designated ". . . For Further Study."

But remember, the official manual is merely the tip of the iceberg when it comes to pathologizing. Penis envy was never an official diagnostic category, yet it was frequently diagnosed. Phyllis Chesler (1972) explains how the diagnosis of Hysteria in women has served to maintain their subordination: "Both psychotherapy and marriage enable women to express and defuse their anger by experiencing it as a form of emotional illness, by translating it into hysterical symptoms: frigidity, chronic depression, phobias, and the like" (p. 122). Hysteria is a rare diagnosis today, and women are more likely diagnosed Borderline Character Disorder, Multiple Personality Disorder (there is intense debate about the existence of this disorder, connected with the debate about "recovered memories" of childhood molestation), or Somatization Disorder. Judith Herman (1992) points out that among women assigned these modern diagnostic substitutes for hysteria are a significant number who were molested as girls, but these diagnoses divert attention away from the early traumas and focus the clinician's attention instead on the woman's personal flaws. She proposes that instead of diagnosing Borderline Character Disorder and Somatization Disorder in so many women today, we consider the diagnosis "Complex Post-traumatic Stress Disorder," the residual condition resulting from repeated childhood sexual and physical abuse. Thus far Complex PTSD has not made its way into the DSM.

Another relevant critique of the way women's characteristics are selectively pathologized comes from the staff of the Stone Center at Wellesley College (Jordan, Kaplan, Miller, Stiver, & Surrey, 1991). They believe that this culture's overvaluation of autonomy and independence leaves something to be desired in terms of community and the capacity to be intimate, and that a very male notion of independence and autonomy is at the core of traditional clinical descriptions of psychopathology. Women are pathologized because of their emphasis on connection and interdependence. They call for a redrawing of the line between psychopathology and mental health so that women's need for connection and community will be viewed as an admirable trait rather than a symptom.

The APA has not heeded this group's call. The category Dependent Personality Disorder remains in DSM-IV and is assigned disproportionately to women, while no equivalent category has been devised to describe the male dread of intimacy and dependency. The description of Dependent Personality Disorder contains the very bias that clinicians from the Stone Center are concerned about. Consider this sentence: "Individuals with this disorder have difficulty initiating projects or doing things independently" (APA, 1994a, p. 666). Often there is a choice between two contrasting ways to handle problems at work: one way being for the individual to come up with a totally independent solution and get credit for doing so at promotion time; another being for several coworkers to brainstorm, work together to figure out a solution collectively, and share the credit. It is as if official psychiatry has decided that individual action is preferred and the search for collaborative solutions (more usual for women workers in today's corporate culture) is pathological. Thus, in spite of improvements in DSM-IV regarding gender bias, many problems remain.

What About the Men?

I have already mentioned several diagnoses that might be included in a DSM but are not: homophobia, "pathological arrhythmicity," and the dread of dependency. There are other male behaviors we might wish to pathologize: dependence on pornography, workaholism, friendlessness, the need for sexual conquests, the tendency to react to aging by deserting one's same-age female partner and taking up with someone the age of one's children, and so forth.

There is a brief and very telling statement about the gender distribution of each mental disorder in DSM-IV. Disorders diagnosed more frequently in males include Conduct Disorder in boys and adolescents, Obsessive-Compulsive Personality Disorder (distinct from Obsessive-Compulsive Disorder, or OCD, which is distributed equally between the sexes), Narcissistic Personality Disorder, Paraphilias, Antisocial Personality Disorder, Intermittent Explosive Disorder, and Pathological Gambling. A comparable list of conditions diagnosed more often in women includes Histrionic Personality Disorder, some forms of Depression, Eating Disorders, Dissociative Identity Disorder, Kleptomania, Panic Disorder, Somatization Disorder, Agoraphobia, and Borderline Personality Disorder.

Could there be a clearer reflection of gender stereotypes? But why are the same qualities that compose the stereotypes—the unfeeling, action-oriented, sexually aggressive, misbehaving male; and the emotional, dependent, weight-conscious, frightened, and sickly woman—so much the basis for pathologizing each gender? Perhaps the diagnostic categories serve to create an upper limit for the very characteristics that are socially encouraged in each gender. Boys are encouraged to be active, rough, aggressive, sexually adventurous, steady, and rational. But when boys become too aggressive they are assigned the diagnosis Conduct Disorder or Intermittent Explosive Disorder, when men become too steady and rational they are diagnosed Obsessive-Compulsive Personality Disorder, when men break the rules too badly in the sexual realm they are considered Paraphiliacs, and so forth. It is a little like the college and pro football teams that encourage players to be hyperaggressive and then have to discipline some of them when they draw negative publicity by raping women after a game. The mental disorders typically assigned to men, like the fines assigned for the overly aggressive football players, serve to keep the lid on the very behaviors that are being encouraged. Similarly, women are encouraged from early childhood to be emotional and connected with others, but if they are too emotional they are diagnosed Histrionic Personality Disorder, and if they are too connected they are diagnosed Dependent Personality Disorder. There is little if any support for creating new, improved forms of masculinity and femininity in DSM-IV.

CHILDHOOD DISORDERS AND THE SHAPING OF GENDER

The main thing to notice about the section of DSM-IV on childhood and adolescent disorders is that the list of disorders is growing. In DSM-II (1968) there were two subsections containing a total of seven disorders, whereas in DSM-IV (1994a) there are ten subsections and thirty-two disorders. Most of the enlargement occurred between DSM-II and DSM-III, the authors of DSM-IV being more

interested in providing detailed descriptions for established disorders than in adding new ones to the official list. Still, the number of children who see mental health professionals and undergo psychotherapy or receive psychotropic medications is growing, and children are being taken to see professionals at younger ages.

Consider three childhood disorders from the list in DSM-IV: Attention Deficit/Hyperactivity Disorder (ADHD), Oppositional Defiant Disorder, and Gender Identity Disorder. What if Oscar Wilde had been given one or more of these diagnoses when he was six or eight years old? What if Ritalin had been prescribed to limit his energy level or he had been given Prozac to control his nonconformist notions about gender and sexuality? What if there had been a way at that time to predict which children might become gay or antisocial (research of this kind is proliferating today), and preventive treatment had been instituted? Would Wilde's vision have been the same, would he have created great literature? This is not to say that Wilde was mentally disordered, or that mental disorder is a prerequisite for works of genius. Rather I am selecting Wilde to illustrate the point that earlier diagnosis and treatment of mental disorders in children runs the risk of stigmatizing unusual men and women, creating less tolerance for experimentation in the realm of gender roles, and thereby limiting the historical possibilities for transforming gender relations.

Of course, in some children, for instance those who compulsively pull out their hair or those who cannot sit still long enough to finish a classroom assignment, professional intervention can have positive effects. I am not arguing that any particular child should be denied examination and treatment. But when children in unprecedented numbers are taken to see professionals, there are social ramifications. One is that approaches to social problems are reduced to the search for psychopathology in individual children. For instance, consider the difficulty teachers have maintaining order in classrooms containing ever-larger numbers of students as budgets for public instruction decline. The teacher cannot reduce the size of the class, but he or she can tell the parents of problematic children that their kids suffer from ADHD and need to be taking Ritalin. In general, it is when we despair about the prospects for social transformation—e.g., making public education a higher social priority—that we tend to reduce social problems to the pathology of individuals. Breggin and Breggin (1994) outline the dangers of this development, though they tend to polarize the discussion by minimizing the positive contributions of child psychiatry and psychotherapy.

Of course, there is money to be made from the quest for earlier detection of mental disorders in children. An even more alarming implication is that society has embarked on the early correction of all deviations from the "straight" path of development. As our lives as workers and consumers become more routinized, and as the gap between the rich and the poor grows wider, concerned parents begin to wonder if their children are going to be among the winners or the losers. This motivates them to watch for early signs of mental disorder and hurry their children off to a mental health professional at the first sign of hyperactivity, school failure, impulsive behavior, or gender impropriety.

There are class and race differences. Diagnosing children in the inner city with Conduct Disorder and Oppositional Defiant Disorder does not usually lead to quality treatment (the public mental health service system is shrinking rapidly); but the diagnoses do serve to rationalize the fact that low-income, inner city children are less likely than their middle-class cohorts to find fulfilling work and are more likely to wind up behind bars. People actually begin to believe it is the psychopathology of poor people, not social inequity, that causes unemployment and criminality. As we pathologize more "off-beat" qualities, we are inadvertently tightening the bounds around what is considered "normal" behavior for boys and girls. Nothing is said about this social inequity in DSM-IV, and this silence is quite worrisome.

CONCLUSION

The DSM-IV is definitely an improvement over previous editions. There is more participation by women in the work groups; Homosexuality has been deleted from the list of disorders, as has DSM-III's Ego-Dystonic Homosexuality; the proposal to add Self-defeating Personality has been defeated; and there are sections on racial and ethnic differences (that do not go far enough toward correcting racial bias in the diagnostic process—but I will leave that issue for a future discussion). Meanwhile, the DSM grows longer, the descriptions of mental disorders become more codified, and psychiatry has little or nothing to say about the social ramifications of its pathologizing.

Traditional psychiatry looks backward, diagnosing mental illness in those who do not fit yesterday's prescribed social roles. Emotionality as well as assertiveness in women, rebellion on the part of minority members, and homosexuality have all been pathologized. As previously stigmatized groups gain power within the mental health professions, diagnoses are modified. DSM-IV reflects admirable progress in terms of the inclusion of diverse groups and the concerted effort to minimize gender bias and homophobia wherever it can be identified. Still, the fourth edition of DSM continues to pathologize deviation from yesterday's gender roles.

Instead of a longer, more detailed list of mental disorders, we need a system of psychopathology that is informed by a vision of a better society. We could begin by envisioning that society, one in which gender equality reigns and there is no homophobia or any other form of domination. Then, by extrapolating backward from that vision, we could pathologize the qualities that would make a person dysfunctional in that more equitable and just social order. Racism, misogyny, and homophobia would head the list of psychopathologies. This kind of pathologizing might even serve to bring about the vision. Unfortunately, far from solving the problems of gender bias and homophobia, the improvements in DSM-IV will serve largely to appease potential dissenters as the mental health professions evolve an ever more conformist manual of psychopathology.

↳ good for conclusion of psych lecture

REFERENCES

American Psychiatric Association. (1952). *Diagnostic and statistical manual of mental disorders.* Washington, D.C.: Author.

American Psychiatric Association. (1968). *Diagnostic and statistical manual of mental disorders* (2nd ed.). Washington, D.C.: Author.

American Psychiatric Association. (1980). *Diagnostic and statistical manual of mental disorders* (3rd ed.). Washington, D.C.: Author.

American Psychiatric Association. (1993). Position statement on homosexuality. *American Journal of Psychiatry, 150,* 686.

American Psychiatric Association. (1994a). *Diagnostic and statistical manual of mental disorders* (4th ed.). Washington, D.C.: Author.

American Psychiatric Association. (1994b). Practice guideline for the treatment of patients with bipolar disorder. *American Journal of Psychiatry, 151,* Supplement, 1–36.

Breggin, P. R., & Breggin, G. R. (1994). *The war against children.* New York: St. Martin's Press.

Caplan, P. J. (1987). The psychiatric association's failure to meet its own standards: The dangers of self-defeating personality disorder as a category. *Journal of Personality Disorders, 1,* 178–182.

Chesler, P. (1972). *Women and madness.* New York: Avon.

Cohen, C. (1993). The biomedicalization of psychiatry: A critical overview. *Community Mental Health Journal, 29,* 509–522.

Connell, R. W. (1994). Psychoanalysis on masculinity. In H. Brod & M. Kaufman (Eds.), *Theorizing masculinities* (pp. 11–38). Thousand Oaks, Calif.: Sage.

Conrad, P. (1980). On the medicalization of deviance and social control. In D. Ingleby (Ed.), *Critical psychiatry* (pp. 102–119). New York: Pantheon.

Foucault, M. (1965). *Madness and civilization.* New York: Pantheon.

Herman, J. (1992). *Trauma and recovery: The aftermath of violence—From domestic abuse to political terror.* New York: Basic Books.

Hughes, J. S. (1990). The madness of separate spheres: Insanity and masculinity in Victorian Alabama. In M. C. Carnes & C. Griffen (Eds.), *Meanings for manhood: Constructions of masculinity in Victorian America* (pp. 67–78). Chicago: University of Chicago Press.

Jordan, J., Kaplan, A., Miller, J. B., Stiver, I.P., and Surrey, J. L. (1991). *Women's growth in connection: Writings from the Stone Center.* New York: Guilford Press.

Kernberg, O. F. (1975). *Borderline conditions and pathological narcissism.* New York: Jason Aronson.

Kovel, J. (1980). The American mental health industry. In D. Ingleby (Ed.), *Critical psychiatry* (pp. 72–101). New York: Pantheon.

Kupers, T. A. (1993a). *Revisioning men's lives: Gender, intimacy and power.* New York: Guilford.

Kupers, T. A. (1993b). Psychotherapy, neutrality and the role of activism. *Community Mental Health Journal, 29,* 523–534.

Miller, J. B. (1976). *Toward a new psychology of women.* Boston: Beacon Press.

Sedgwick, P. (1982). *Psychopolitics: Laing, Foucault, Goffman, Szasz and the future of mass psychiatry.* New York: Harper & Row.

Socarides, C. W., Kaufman, B., Gottlieb, F., & Isay, R. (1994). Letters about reparative therapy. *American Journal of Psychiatry, 151,* 157–59.

Spitzer, R. L., Severino, S. K., Williams, J. B., & Parry, B. L. (1989). Late luteal phase dysphoric disorder and DSM-III-R. *American Journal of Psychiatry, 146,* 892–897.

Thomas, A., & Sillen, S. (1974). *Racism and psychiatry.* Secaucus, N.J.: Citadel.

NO

Gender Issues in DSM-IV

RUTH ROSS, ALLEN FRANCES, AND

THOMAS A. WIDIGER

HOW TO UNDERSTAND DIFFERENCES IN GENDER PREVALENCES

A number of psychiatric disorders have markedly different rates of occurrence in women and men. It is not clear whether these differences are inherent to actual differences in psychopathology between women and men or are the artifactual result of biases in ascertainment, definition, or assessment (Brown 1986; Davidson and Abramovitz 1980; Deaux 1985; Earls 1987; Hamilton et al. 1986; Kaplan 1983; Lewine et al. 1984; Loring and Powell 1988; Russell 1985; Sherman 1980; Smith 1980; Snyder et al. 1985; Widiger and Nietzel 1984; Widiger and Settle 1987; Widiger and Spitzer 1991; Widom 1984; Zeldow 1984). Gender differences in treatment seeking or referral patterns may explain the different gender ratios that occur in community samples as opposed to more selected clinical samples. For example, there is a higher ratio of women with major depressive disorder in clinical than in epidemiological samples, perhaps because women are more likely to recognize and admit to depression. In contrast, there is a higher ratio of men with schizophrenia in clinical than in epidemiological samples, perhaps because men with schizophrenia are more disruptive and likely to require treatment intervention. However, there also appear to be data supporting the view that a higher rate of major depression in women is a real and not artifactual finding. Biases in definition may also play a role in gender differences in preva-

lence. There may also be gender differences in prevalence because of biases in the evaluator that may lead to misinterpretation of the diagnostic criteria. It is likely that there are also real differences in prevalence, at least for certain disorders (e.g., conduct disorder, antisocial personality disorder) that reflect real differences between women and men.

GENDER AND THE PERSONALITY DISORDER CRITERIA

Another extremely controversial issue has been the question of a possible gender bias within the DSM-III-R criteria sets, particularly for the diagnoses of histrionic personality disorder and dependent personality disorder (Hirschfeld et al. 1991, 1996; Pfohl 1996). Both of these personality disorders are diagnosed much more frequently in women than in men. Histrionic personality disorder and dependent personality disorder appear to involve, at least in part, stereotypic feminine traits (Kaplan 1983; Sprock et al. 1990; Walker 1994) that could be mislabeled as personality disorder in a gender-biased system. In contrast, others have argued that histrionic personality disorder and dependent personality disorder are diagnosed more frequently in women than in men not because of definition or assessment bias but precisely because these personality disorders involve maladaptive variants of stereotypic feminine traits, just as antisocial personality disorder and obsessive-compulsive personality disorder involve maladaptive variants of stereotypic masculine traits and are diagnosed more frequently in men (Widiger and Spitzer 1991; Widiger et al. 1994b; Williams and Spitzer 1983). There is no reason to assume that each personality disorder will occur with an equal frequency across genders. To the extent that some personality traits are more prevalent or predominant within one gender (e.g., Eagly and Crowley 1986; Eagly and Steffen 1986), one might expect personality disorders that represent maladaptive or excessive variants of these traits to be more prevalent within that gender. However, concerns about a possible gender bias are also understandable. The DSM-III/DSM-III-R personality disorder criteria were constructed, for the most part, by males with little input from systematic empirical research. It would not be surprising to find that male clinicians would have a lower threshold for the attribution of maladaptive feminine traits than for the attribution of maladaptive masculine traits.

It is also important to ensure that empirically derived criteria sets do not impel or exaggerate gender differences through research that is confined largely to one gender. This risk is perhaps easiest to demonstrate in the case of antisocial personality disorder. As a matter of convenience, studies on antisocial personality disorder have often been confined to males; as a result, the diagnostic criteria that performed best within these studies are criteria that work best for males with this disorder. For example, it is possible that the DSM-III-R criteria for antisocial personality disorder, with such behaviors as forcing someone into a sexual activity before age fifteen or beating one's spouse after the age of fifteen, were biased toward the manner in which males expressed antisocial personality traits. More males than females may indeed have antisocial personality disorder, but to the extent that the diagnostic criteria were based on research confined to male subjects, the criteria set may result in the underdiagnosis of females with this disorder. Moreover, there is evidence that antisocial personality traits in females may be misdiagnosed as histrionic (Ford and Widiger 1989; Hamilton et al. 1986).

The DSM-IV Personality Disorders Work Group addressed this problem in a variety of ways. The DSM-IV field trials on antisocial personality disorder were analyzed separately for males and for females to assess whether any proposed revisions would be detrimental to the diagnosis of antisocial personality disorder in females. In addition, individual criteria were revised to be more gender neutral. For example, the DSM-III-R histrionic personality disorder item "is inappropriately sexually seductive in appearance or behavior" (American Psychiatric Association 1987, p. 349) was revised to "interaction with others is often characterized by inappropriate sexually seductive or pro-

vocative behavior" (American Psychiatric Association 1994, p. 657). This item was revised to emphasize seductive or provocative behavior rather than just appearance, because normal sexual attractiveness can be readily confused with sexual seductiveness and because females may be more likely to be perceived as sexually seductive in appearance given the social pressure concerning physical attractiveness in females. Provocative or seductive behavior is perhaps less prone to gender-biased attributions than seductive appearance. Likewise, the criteria set for conduct disorder was revised in part to include antisocial behaviors that tend to occur in females (e.g., staying out at night despite parental prohibitions before age thirteen).

Gender variations in the expression of personality disorders are also discussed in the "Specific Culture, Age, and Gender Features" sections of the texts for these disorders. For example, in the discussion of histrionic personality disorder, it is noted that

the behavioral expression of histrionic personality disorder may be influenced by sex role stereotypes. For example, a man with this disorder may dress and behave in a manner often identified as "macho" and may seek to be the center of attention by bragging about athletic skills, whereas a woman, for example, may choose very feminine clothes and talk about how much she impressed her dance instructor. (American Psychiatric Association 1994, p. 656)

The text discussions also caution against the imposition of gender-biased assumptions when making personality disorder diagnoses—for example, noting that "there has been some concern that antisocial personality disorder may be underdiagnosed in females, particularly because of the emphasis on aggressive items in the definition of conduct disorder" (American Psychiatric Association 1994, p. 647) or cautioning in the text for dependent personality disorder that "societies may differentially foster and discourage dependent behavior in males and females" (American Psychiatric Association 1994, p. 667).

To the extent that there are clearly established gender variations in the expression of a personality disorder (or any disorder), the authors of the future DSM-V may eventually consider developing separate criteria sets for each gender. This is already done for gender identity disorder, in which such differences are inherent in the disorder itself. However, there is currently insufficient research to support such an approach in DSM-IV.

SELF-DEFEATING PERSONALITY DISORDER

The inclusion of the self-defeating personality disorder (originally called masochistic personality disorder) in the appendix to DSM-III-R generated substantial controversy (Caplan 1987, 1991; Rosewater 1987; Walker 1987, 1994). In considering whether to continue to include self-defeating personality disorder in the DSM-IV appendix, the conceptual and empirical foundation for this proposed disorder was thoroughly studied by the DSM-IV Personality Disorders Work Group and by the Task Force on DSM-IV. As a culmination of its review process, the Personality Disorders Work Group recommended that self-defeating personality disorder not be included in the main body or the appendix of DSM-IV (Widiger, in press).

The literature review for self-defeating personality disorder (Fiester, 1996) indicated that this newly proposed diagnosis has received very little research attention and that there have been only a few investigations of real patients (the few available studies have focused more on surveys or the diagnosis of illustrative written case examples). The work group was also concerned about the inherent difficulty of accurately diagnosing self-defeating personality disorder in the presence of a harsh environmental context or when other psychiatric disorders are present. The clinical studies suggested that self-defeating personality disorder would overlap a great deal with the eleven other personality disorders that are included in DSM-III-R. This is a serious problem because most clinicians and researchers believe that we are already burdened by the inclusion of too many personality disorders in DSM-III-R, creating a system that is cumbersome to use in clinical and research practice and usually results in multiple diagnoses.

However useful the concept of masochism remains in the practice of psychotherapy, the work group discussions revealed that there are structural problems that prevent the simple translation of the psychodynamic construct of masochism to the psychiatric diagnosis of personality disorder. The criteria set of self-defeating personality disorder was an attempt to provide a descriptive operationalization of the psychodynamic construct that unconscious forces may lead to a masochistic pattern of interpersonal relationships and behaviors. The analytic literature has attributed this masochistic pattern to a variety of unconscious motivations, including self-punishment consequent to superego pathology; an external reenactment of introjected early sadomasochistic relationships; self-directed aggression as a defense against sadism; and pathological narcissism. In the psychotherapy situation, the evaluation of these unconscious motivations usually requires a careful and prolonged assessment of the patient's transferential attitudes and behaviors in the treatment relationship. This judgment depends on a good deal of psychodynamic expertise and inference and usually can be confirmed only by the patient's masochistic treatment behavior, not just by the evaluation of problems presented in the diagnostic interview. The self-defeating personality disorder criteria represented an attempt to draft a set of behavioral and interpersonal criteria that would capture the surface manifestations of the presumed unconscious motivation for masochistic behavior. This turned out to be an inherently impossible task. One cannot convert this particular psychodynamic construct inferring unconscious masochistic motivation into a behavioral (and less inferential) criteria set that is not confounded by the individual's interactions with the environment. This effort failed because it cannot be done, not just because of any deficiencies in the specific self-defeating personality disorder criteria that were selected. It was not simply a matter of studying and improving the existing criteria set. The basic issue is that much "self-defeating" behavior occurs for reasons other than the specific "masochistic" unconscious motivations that are meant to be at the heart of the self-defeating personality disorder concept. It is usually impossible within the context of a general psychiatric evaluation to determine whether the individual's pattern of self-defeating behavior is an expression of unconscious motivation that would play out over and over again regardless of the environment in which the individual exists or whether the "self-defeating" pattern of behavior is an understandable and perhaps adaptive result of the need to survive in a harsh and punishing environment.

In addition many mental disorders are characterized by behaviors and symptoms that are "self-defeating" in their effect but not "masochistic" in their unconscious motivations. This is particularly true for chronic depression but is also true for many other psychiatric disorders. The concept of self-defeating personality disorder is inherently confounded with self-defeating aspects that are secondary consequences of other mental disorders. There were also no studies to document that the diagnosis described a behavior pattern that was not already adequately represented by an existing Axis I or Axis II diagnosis. Although self-defeating behaviors are encountered commonly enough in clinical practice, it is not clear that the self-defeating personality disorder diagnosis is specific in capturing the central or predominant pathology in most of these cases.

Another major concern that was factored into the consideration of the proposed self-defeating personality disorder diagnosis was that the diagnosis might be used to blame victims of (spouse) abuse for their own victimization (Fiester 1991; Widiger, 1995; Widiger and Frances 1989). The proposed criteria set did provide an exclusion criterion such that the items would not be considered present if they occurred exclusively in response to or in anticipation of being physically, sexually, or psychologically abused. However, many of the instruments that were developed to assess self-defeating personality disorder failed to consider this exclusion criterion, and many victims are reluctant to acknowledge the presence of actual abuse. The research on self-defeating personality disorder often failed to consider the occurrence and influence of victimization on the diagnosis (e.g.,

Spitzer et al. 1989), and the research on victimization has failed to assess adequately for the role and influence of self-defeating personality traits (e.g., Walker 1984).

Although there undoubtedly are individuals with self-defeating personality patterns, the utility and validity of the construct as a psychiatric diagnosis has not yet been established, and the Personality Disorders Work Group concluded that its provision within an appendix to DSM-IV would provide the diagnosis with a credibility or recognition that it did not yet warrant. A diagnosis that has the potential for misuse should be held to an especially high standard of validation before it is given any official credibility. Nevertheless, the concept of self-defeating unconscious motivations is sometimes useful in understanding or treating individuals encountered in clinical practice.

SADISTIC PERSONALITY DISORDER

Sadistic personality disorder was included in the appendix to DSM-III-R based almost completely on anecdotal case reports. In considering whether to continue to include this proposed diagnosis in the DSM-IV appendix, the Personality Disorders Work Group undertook a literature review on sadistic personality disorder (Fiester and Gay 1991). The group found that little research on sadistic personality disorder had been done and that the only published studies were by the original proponents of the disorder (i.e., Fiester and Gay 1991; Gay, in press; Spitzer et al. 1991). Based on the lack of systematic research supporting this diagnosis and the potential for misuse, the Personality Disorders Work Group recommended that it not be included in the appendix to DSM-IV (Widiger 1995).

PREMENSTRUAL DYSPHORIC DISORDER

As mentioned earlier, the inclusion of late luteal phase dysphoric disorder, as it was then called, in the appendix to DSM-III-R produced one of the more heated controversies surrounding the publication of DSM-III-R (Chait 1986; Eckholm 1985; Hamilton and Gallant 1988; Holtzman 1988; Reid

1987). Proponents maintained that late luteal phase dysphoric disorder is a clinically significant condition that is supported by research and clinical literature and that its omission might lead to underdiagnosis, misdiagnosis, failure to give appropriate treatment, and stigmatization by blaming individual women with the problem for their symptoms. Opponents referred to the paucity of clinical and research literature and warned that inclusion might encourage inappropriate diagnosis and treatment and also had the potential to stigmatize women in general. There were concerns about whether there were sufficient data to generate a valid and reliable criteria set for this proposed disorder. Questions were also raised as to whether it was best conceptualized as a mental disorder (rather than an endocrinological or gynecological one) and whether a disorder related to male hormones should be included.

A Late Luteal Phase Work Group was formed and given responsibility for making a recommendation, based on empirical data, as to whether late luteal phase dysphoric disorder should continue to appear in the appendix of DSM-IV, should be included in the main body of the manual, should be included in the section for "Other Clinically Significant Conditions That May Be a Focus of Clinical Attention," or should be left out altogether (American Psychiatric Association 1991). To make a recommendation on this issue, the work group conducted an exhaustive literature review that included clinical and research studies on both premenstrual syndrome and late luteal phase dysphoric disorder. Because late luteal phase dysphoric disorder first appeared in the nomenclature in 1987, published studies using the proposed late luteal phase dysphoric disorder criteria from DSM-III-R were limited, but these increased in number during the period of the review from 1988 to 1992 (Gold et al., in press). The purpose of this literature review was to try to determine "if there is a clinically significant mental disorder associated with the menstrual cycle that can be separated from other mental disorders" (Gold, in press). More than five hundred articles on premenstrual syndrome and late luteal phase dysphoric disorder

were reviewed, and information on prevalence, association with preexisting mental disorders, course of illness and prognosis, familial factors, biological and treatment studies, and social, forensic, and occupational issues were examined. The group identified a number of methodological problems in the literature: variable or unclearly specified definitions of premenstrual syndrome, small sample sizes, lack of control groups, prospective daily ratings not used, possibly biased sample selection, failure to delineate timing and duration of symptoms, and failure to collect adequate hormonal samples. Despite these problems, the work group determined that, based on the literature review, a relatively circumscribed group of women (perhaps 3%-5%) suffer from severe and clinically significant dysphoria related to the premenstrual period.

The work group also carried out a reanalysis of previously collected data from more than six hundred subjects from five sites (Hurt et al. 1992; Severino et al., in press). The results of this reanalysis supported the clinical usefulness of the criteria set for late luteal phase dysphoric disorder but suggested some changes in emphasis to reflect that the disturbance is most closely related to mood disorder and to emphasize the dysphoric nature of the symptoms. The revised proposed criteria require severe impairment and minimize physical symptoms.

The literature review and data reanalysis were widely circulated for comments and critique among thirty-six advisers who were selected to represent a range of different perspectives, including individuals who had done research on the disorder and others who were very concerned about its possible misuse. The group attempted to formulate criteria that would be optimal for research purposes and could also be easily and consistently applied by clinicians. They focused on where the disorder should be placed in the classification and what it should be called (Gold, in press). They concluded that the name *late luteal phase dysphoric disorder* was cumbersome and somewhat misleading (because the symptoms may not be related to the endocrinological changes of the late luteal phase) and proposed the name *premenstrual dysphoric disorder* (Gold, in press).

A detailed summary of the work group process and the rationale for the final task force decision will be provided in the fourth volume of the *DSM-IV Sourcebook* (Gold, in press). The final decision of the Task Force on DSM-IV was to continue to include the disorder, renamed *premenstrual dysphoric disorder*, in the appendix to the manual, and not to make it part of the official nomenclature. It was decided to refer to premenstrual dysphoric disorder as an example of a depressive disorder not otherwise specified for purposes of differential diagnosis, rather than as an example of a mental disorder not otherwise specified, based on the fact that the data seem to support a strong mood component in the disorder. The appendix in which the criteria set for premenstrual dysphoric disorder is included is titled "Criteria Sets and Axes Provided for Further Study." The introduction to the appendix states that "the task force determined that there was insufficient information to warrant inclusion of these proposals as official categories or axes in DSM-IV" (American Psychiatric Association 1994, p. 703). It is noted that "the items, thresholds, and durations contained in the research criteria sets are intended to provide a common language for researchers and clinicians who are interested in studying these disorders. It is hoped that such research will help to determine the possible utility of these proposed categories and will result in refinement of the criteria sets" (American Psychiatric Association 1994, p. 703).

The decision to include premenstrual dysphoric disorder in the appendix to DSM-IV received widespread media attention (e.g., Alvardo 1993; Seligman and Gelman 1993; Spam 1993). In some cases, these accounts were fair and balanced accounts of the issues involved (Spam 1993). Unfortunately, many articles reported inaccurate information and contributed to the controversy by fostering the impression that the developers of DSM-IV were attempting to pathologize a large part of the female population. They often stated that premenstrual dysphoric disorder would be included in the main body of the manual as an

official diagnosis or claimed that the much more common premenstrual syndrome would be considered a mental disorder in the DSM-IV diagnostic system.

However, the "Differential Diagnosis" section of the text that accompanies the proposed research criteria for premenstrual dysphoric disorder in the DSM-IV appendix states that

> the transient mood changes that many females experience around the time of their period should not be considered a mental disorder. Premenstrual dysphoric disorder should be considered only when the symptoms markedly interfere with work or school or with usual social activities and relationships with others (e.g., avoidance of social activities, decreased productivity and efficiency at work or school). Premenstrual dysphoric disorder can be distinguished from the far more common "premenstrual syndrome" by using prospective daily ratings and the strict criteria listed below. It differs from the "premenstrual syndrome" in its characteristic pattern of symptoms, their severity, and the resulting impairment. (American Psychiatric Association 1994, p. 716)

Although there is a lack of a consistent definition of premenstrual syndrome, the proposed research criteria set for premenstrual dysphoric disorder is an attempt to define a severe dysphoric disorder that causes clinically significant impairment and is not to be confused with the milder premenstrual syndrome. The text for premenstrual dysphoric disorder notes,

> it is estimated that at least 75% of women report minor or isolated premenstrual changes. Limited studies suggest an occurrence of "premenstrual syndrome" (variably defined) of 20%-50%, and that 3%-5% of women experience symptoms that may meet the criteria for this proposed disorder (American Psychiatric Association 1994, p. 716).

It was, in part, because of the tentative nature of the criteria that it was decided to continue to place premenstrual dysphoric disorder in the appendix so that further studies in larger populations could investigate the validity and reliability of the items selected and the ability of the criteria to discriminate these symptoms from milder premenstrual syndrome.

The proposed DSM-IV criteria set for premenstrual dysphoric disorder requires that five or more of the following symptoms (with at least one being one of the first four) be present most of the time during the last week of the luteal phase in most menstrual cycles during the past year (American Psychiatric Association 1994, p. 717):

1) feeling sad, hopeless, or self-deprecating; 2) feeling tense, anxious or "on edge"; 3) marked lability of mood interspersed with frequent tearfulness; 4) persistent irritability, anger, and increased interpersonal conflicts; 5) decreased interest in usual activities, which may be associated with withdrawal from social relationships; 6) difficulty concentrating; 7) feeling fatigued, lethargic, or lacking in energy; 8) marked changes in appetite, which may be associated with binge eating or craving certain foods; 9) hypersomnia or insomnia; 10) a subjective feeling of being overwhelmed or out of control; and 11) physical symptoms such as breast tenderness or swelling, headaches, or sensations of "bloating" or weight gain, with tightness of fit of clothing, shoes, or rings. There may also be joint or muscle pain. The symptoms may be accompanied by suicidal thoughts. (American Psychiatric Association 1994, p. 715)

The symptoms must begin to remit within a few days after the onset of the follicular phase and be absent in the week postmenses. The disturbance must markedly interfere with work or school or usual social activities and relationships with others and must not be merely an exacerbation of the symptoms of another mental disorder. The symptoms described in the criteria set must be confirmed by prospective daily ratings during at least two consecutive symptomatic cycles. The criteria set describes a pattern of symptoms that is far more severe and impairing than what is usually called premenstrual syndrome, despite the vari-

ations in definitions of premenstrual syndrome. DSM-IV states that the symptoms of premenstrual dysphoric disorder are "typically . . . of comparable severity (but not duration) to those of a major depressive episode" (American Psychiatric Association 1994, p. 715).

DISSOCIATIVE DISORDERS

The increased attention given to dissociative amnesia and dissociative identity disorder (formerly called multiple personality disorder) has occasioned a heated controversy concerning whether these were previously underrecognized or whether they are now being overdiagnosed. This question is pertinent for this chapter because both of these categories are diagnosed more frequently in women and may be associated with early childhood sexual abuse. In preparing the texts for these disorders, an effort was made to inform clinicians about the issues involved without taking sides. For example, the text for dissociative amnesia includes the following statement in the "Prevalence" section:

In recent years in the United States, there has been an increase in reported cases of dissociative amnesia that involves previously forgotten early childhood traumas. This increase has been subject to very different interpretations. Some believe that the greater awareness of the diagnosis among mental health professionals has resulted in the identification of cases that were previously undiagnosed. In contrast, others believe that the syndrome has been overdiagnosed in individuals who are highly suggestible. (American Psychiatric Association 1994, p. 479)

The "Differential Diagnosis" section of the text for dissociative amnesia includes the following caution:

Care must be exercised in evaluating the accuracy of retrieved memories, because the informants are often highly suggestible. There has been considerable controversy concerning amnesia related to reported physical or sexual abuse, particularly when abuse is alleged to have occurred during early childhood. Some clinicians believe that there has been an underreporting of such events, especially because the victims are often children and perpetrators are inclined to deny or distort their actions. However, other clinicians are concerned that there may be overreporting, particularly given the unreliability of childhood memories. There is currently no method for establishing with certainty the accuracy of such retrieved memories in the absence of corroborative evidence. (American Psychiatric Association 1994, pp. 480–481)

The "Prevalence" section for dissociative identity disorder includes a statement very similar to the one given for dissociative amnesia, and the "Differential Diagnosis" section includes the following:

> Controversy exists concerning the differential diagnosis between dissociative identity disorder and a variety of other mental disorders, including schizophrenia and other psychotic disorders, bipolar disorder, with rapid cycling, anxiety disorders, somatization disorders, and personality disorders. Some clinicians believe that dissociative identity disorder has been underdiagnosed (e.g., the presence of more than one dissociated personality state may be mistaken for a delusion or the communication from one identity to another may be mistaken for an auditory hallucination, leading to confusion with the psychotic disorders; shifts between identity states may be confused with cyclical mood fluctuations leading to confusion with bipolar disorder). In contrast, others are concerned that dissociative identity disorder may be overdiagnosed relative to other mental disorders based on the media interest in the disorder and the suggestible nature of the individuals. Factors that may support a diagnosis of dissociative identity disorder are the presence of clearcut dissociative symptomatology with sudden shifts in identity states, reversible amnesia, and high scores on measures of dissociation and hypnotizability in individuals who do not have the characteristic presentations of another men-

tal disorder. (American Psychiatric Association 1994, p. 487)

CONCLUSION

For most of the diagnoses in DSM-IV, the emphasis on documentation and empirical data as the foundation for change resulted in remarkably little controversy. However, the gender issues related to diagnosis that have historically been subject to controversy continued to be the subject of disagreement during the development of DSM-IV. In part, this may have resulted from the fact that systematic research efforts on gender differences have begun only recently. However, the larger social questions these issues touch on made it more difficult to settle them on empirical grounds alone or even to reach a shared interpretation of the data that are available. Ultimately it is for others to judge, but we believe that the DSM-IV development process was characterized by serious attempts to base decisions on a fair and balanced interpretation of the available data on gender-related issues in diagnosis. It is hoped that the new section "Culture, Age, and Gender Features" that is included in the texts for many disorders will be helpful in alerting clinicians to gender-related differences in presentation and to possible gender-related pitfalls in making diagnoses. However, perhaps the most important gender-related accomplishment of DSM-IV has been to stimulate and encourage debate on issues related to gender and diagnosis. It is hoped that when possible problems related to gender are noted in the text for specific disorders, this will stimulate studies on those disorders that will inform the next revision of DSM and lead to more accurate diagnostic information.

The major questions concerning the relationship between gender and psychiatric diagnosis remain largely unanswered. It is not at all clear whether and to what extent marked differences in gender prevalence of certain diagnoses reflect true gender differences or are artifacts of ascertainment, definition, or assessment. For those gender differences that do stand up to improved methodological rigor in diagnosis, the next step will be to identify the mechanisms involved in these differences in psychopathology.

REFERENCES

Alvardo, D. Furor over new diagnosis for PMS. San Jose Mercury News, May 22, 1993, p. 1A.

American Psychiatric Association. DSM-IV Options Book: Work in Progress (9/1/91). Washington, D. C., American Psychiatric Association, 1991.

American Psychiatric Association. Diagnostic and Statistical Manual of Mental Disorders, 3rd Edition, Revised. Washington, D. C., American Psychiatric Association, 1987.

American Psychiatric Association. Diagnostic and Statistical Manual of Mental Disorders, 4th Edition. Washington, D.C., American Psychiatric Association, 1994.

Brown, L. S. Gender-role analysis: A neglected component of psychological assessment. Psychotherapy 23:243–248, 1986.

Caplan, P. The psychiatric association's failure to meet its own standards: The dangers of self-defeating personality disorder as a category. Journal of Personality Disorders 1:178–182, 1987.

Caplan, P. J. How do they decide who is normal? The bizarre, but true, tale of the DSM process. Canadian Psychology 32:162–170, 1991.

Chait, L. R. Premenstrual syndrome and our sisters in crime: A feminist dilemma. Women's Rights Law Reporter 9:267–293, 1986.

Davidson, C. V., Abramovitz, S. I. Sex bias in clinical judgment: Later empirical returns. Psychology of Women Quarterly 4:377–395, 1980.

Deaux, K. Sex and gender. Ann. Rev. Psychol. 36:49–81, 1985.

Eagly, A. H., Crowley, M. Gender and helping behavior: A meta-analytic review of the social psychology literature. Psychol. Bull. 100:283–308, 1986.

Eagly, A. H., Steffen, V. J. Gender and aggressive behavior: A meta-analytic review of the social psychological literature. Psychol. Bull. 100:309–330, 1986.

Earls, F. Sex differences in psychiatric disorders: Origins and developmental influences. Psychiatric Developments 1:1–23, 1987.

Eckholm, E. Premenstrual problems seem to beset baboons. The New York Times, June 4, 1985, p. C2.

Fiester, S. J. Self-defeating personality disorder: A review of data and recommendations for DSM-IV. Journal of Personality Disorders 5:194–209, 1991.

Fiester, S. J. Self-defeating personality disorder, in DSM-IV Sourcebook, Vol 2. Edited by Widiger, T. A., Frances, A. J, Pincus, H. A., et al. Washington, D. C., American Psychiatric Association, 1996.

Fiester, S. J., Gay, M. Sadistic personality disorder: A review of data and recommendations for DSM-IV. Journal of Personality Disorders 5:376–385, 1991.

Fiester, S. J., Gay, M. Sadistic personality disorder, in DSM-

IV Sourcebook, Vol 2. Edited by Widiger, T. A., Frances, A. J, Pincus, H. A., et al. Washington, D. C., American Psychiatric Association, 1996.

Ford, M., Widiger, T. Sex bias in the diagnosis of histrionic and antisocial personality disorders. J. Consult. Clin. Psychol. 57:301–305, 1989.

Gallant, S. J. A., Hamilton, J. A. On a premenstrual psychiatric diagnosis: What's in a name? Professional Psychology: Research and Practice 19:271–278, 1988.

Gay, M. Sadistic personality disorder in a child abusing population. Child Abuse Negl. (in press).

Gold, J. H. Late luteal phase dysphoric disorder and the DSM-IV, in DSM-IV Sourcebook, Vol 4. Edited by Widiger, T. A., Frances, A. J., Pincus, H. A., et al. Washington, D. C., American Psychiatric Association (1996).

Gold, J. H., Endicott, J., Parry, B. L., et al. Late luteal phase dysphoric disorder, in DSM-IV Sourcebook, Vol 2. Edited by Widiger, T. A., Frances, A. J., Pincus, H. A., et al. Washington, D. C., American Psychiatric Association (in press).

Hamilton, S., Rothbart, M., Dawes, R. M. Sex bias, diagnosis, and DSM-III. Sex Roles 15:269–274, 1986.

Hirschfeld, R. M. A., Shea, M. T., Weise, R. Dependent personality disorder: Perspectives for DSM-IV. Journal of Personality Disorders 5:135–149, 1991.

Hirschfeld, R. M. A., Shea, M. T., Talbot, K. M. Dependent personality disorder, in DSM-IV Sourcebook, Vol 2. Edited by Widiger, T. A., Frances, A. J., Pincus, H. A., et al. Washington, D. C., American Psychiatric Association, 1996.

Holtzman, E. Premenstrual syndrome as a legal defense, in The Premenstrual Syndromes. Edited by Gise, L. H., Kose, N. G., Berkowitz, R. L. New York, Churchill Livingstone, 1988, pp. 137–143.

Hurt, S. W., Schnurr, P. P., Severino, S. K., et al. Late luteal phase dysphoric disorder in 670 women evaluated for premenstrual complaints. Am. J. Psychiatry 149:525–530, 1992.

Kaplan, M. A woman's view of DSM-III. Am. Psychol. 38:786–792, 1983.

Lewine, R., Burbach, D., Meltzer, H. Y. Effect of diagnostic criteria on the ratio of male to female schizophrenic patients. Am. J. Psychiatry 141:84–87, 1984.

Loring, M., Powell, B. Gender, race, and DSM-III: A study of the objectivity of psychiatric diagnostic behavior. J. Health Soc. Behav. 29:1–22, 1988.

Pfohl, B. Histrionic personality disorder, in DSM-IV Sourcebook, Vol 2. Edited by Widiger, T. A., Frances, A. J., Pincus, H. A., et al. Washington, D.C., American Psychiatric Association, 1996.

Reid, R. L. Premenstrual syndrome. AACC ENDO 5:1–12, 1987.

Rosewater, L. B. A critical analysis of the proposed self-defeating personality disorder. Journal of Personality Disorders 1:190–195, 1987.

Russell, D. Psychiatric diagnosis and the oppression of women. Int. J. Soc. Psychiatry 31:298–305, 1985.

Seligman, J., Gelman, D. Is it sadness or madness? Psychiatrists clash over how to classify PMS. Newsweek, March 15, 1993, p. 66.

Severino, S. K. et al. Database reanalysis, in DSM-IV Sourcebook, Vol 4. Edited by Widiger, T. A., Frances, A. J., Pincus, H. A., et al. Washington, D. C., American Psychiatric Association (in press).

Sherman, J. A. Therapist attitudes and sex-role stereotyping, in Women and Psychotherapy. Edited by Brodsky, A. M., Hare-Mustin, R. T. New York, Guilford Press, 1980, pp. 34–66.

Smith, M. L. Sex bias in counseling and psychotherapy. Psychol. Bull. 187:392–407, 1980.

Snyder, S., Goodpaster, W. A., Pitts, W. M., et al. Demography of psychiatric patients with borderline personality traits. Psychopathology 18:38–49, 1985.

Spam, P. Vicious cycle: The politics of periods. Washington Post, July 8, 1993, pp. C1-C2.

Spitzer, R. L., Williams, J. B. W., Kass, F., et al. National field trial of the DSM-III-R diagnostic criteria for self-defeating personality disorder. Am. J. Psychiatry 146:1561–1567, 1989.

Spitzer, R. L., Fiester, S. J., Gay, M., et al. Results of a survey of forensic psychiatrists on the validity of the sadistic personality disorder diagnosis. Am. J. Psychiatry 148:875–879, 1991.

Sprock, J., Blashfield, R. K., Smith, B. Gender weighting of DSM-III-R personality disorder criteria. Am. J. Psychiatry 147:586–590, 1990.

Walker, L. E. A. The Battered Woman Syndrome. New York, Springer, 1984.

Walker, L. E. A. Inadequacies of the masochistic personality disorder diagnosis for women. Journal of Personality Disorders 1:183–189, 1987.

Walker, L. E. A. Are personality disorders gender biased? in Controversial Issues in Mental Health. Edited by Kirk, S. A., Einbinder, S. D. Boston, Allyn & Bacon, 1994, pp. 22–30.

Widiger, T. A. Deletion of self-defeating and sadistic personality disorders, in DSM-IV Personality Disorders. Edited by Livesley, W. J. New York, Guilford, 1995.

Widiger, T. A., Frances, A. J. Controversies concerning the self-defeating personality disorder, in Self-Defeating Behaviors: Experimental Research, Clinical Impressions, and Practical Implications. Edited by Curtis, R. C. New York, Plenum, 1989, pp. 289–309.

Widiger, T., Nietzel, M. Kaplan's view of DSM-III: The data revisited. Am. Psychol. 39:1319–1320, 1984.

Widiger, T., Settle, S. Broverman et al. revisited: An artifactual sex bias. J. Pers. Soc. Psychol. 53:463–469, 1987.

Widiger, T. A., Spitzer, R. L. Sex bias in the diagnosis of personality disorders: Conceptual and methodological issues. Clinical Psychology Review 11:1–22, 1991.

Widiger, T. A., Corbitt, E., Funtowicz, M. Rejoinder to Dr. Walker, in Controversial Issues in Mental Health. Edited by Kirk, S. A., Einbinder, S. D. Boston, Allyn & Bacon, 1994b, pp. 30–38.

Widom, C. W. Sex roles and psychopathology, in Sex Roles and Psychopathology. Edited by Widom, C. S. New York, Plenum, 1984, pp. 3–17.

Williams, J. B. W., Spitzer, R. L. The issue of sex bias in DSM-III: A critique of "A woman's view of DSM-III" by Marcie Kaplan. Am. Psychol. 38:793–798, 1983.

Zeldow, P. B. Sex roles, psychological assessment, and patient management, in Sex Roles and Psychopathology. Edited by Widom, C. S. New York, Plenum, 1984, pp. 355–374.

Relational Therapy: Is the Stone Center's Relational Theory a Source of Empowerment for Women?

In the 1970s, feminists challenged psychology's perception of women's role. Germaine Greer, after describing how psychologists tried to persuade women that they were mentally ill, concluded, "Psychologists cannot fix the world, so they fix women" (1970, p. 83). Phyllis Chesler, in *Women and Madness* (1972), saw it all as a power play: women were being driven mad by men who were trying to keep them in their place.

Old ideas gave way as a new psychology of women was born. This explosion of knowledge followed several paths. While some researchers believed that their work would degenderize behavior, others, like Jean Baker Miller (1976), turned the old theories on their head. Women's "dependency," once viewed as a source of their problems, was now rein-terpreted as relationship skills such as sensitivity, empathy, and care for others, skills that were beneficial not only to women's development but to the larger society. These abilities, according to Chodorow (1978), emerged during child rearing when little girls are brought up to be like their mother, with a capacity for caretaking, empathy, and relationship built into their self-definition. Little boys, on the other hand, are taught to be as different from their mother as possible. Encouraged to be more autonomous and self-sufficient, men are discouraged from relating to others and become threatened by closeness.

Jean Baker Miller, Judith V. Jordan, Janet Surrey, Alexandra Kaplan, and Irene Stiver, members of Wellesley College's Stone Center and the Jean Baker Miller Training Institute, have pioneered in developing a therapy model to help women recognize their relational needs. Women, according to Miller, do not want to be "dependent or independent." What they desire is "to be in relationship with others . . . to understand the other's feelings . . . to contribute to the other . . . wanting the nature of the relationship to be one in which the other person(s) is engaged in this way" (1991, p. 22).

The Stone Center group is not talking about the traditional concept of altruism, which suggests sacrifice. To engage in the type of relationship they are describing is to feel better and more gratified while at the same time developing a sense of self-worth and effectiveness (Miller, 1991). Utilizing the relational theory of women's development described in their book, *Women's Growth in Connection* (1991), the five authors have shown how empathy, mutual empowerment, and dependency can be applied to the clinical treatment of such problems as depression, posttraumatic stress disorder, anxiety attacks, self-destructive patterns, and problems that interfere with daily functioning. Karen Johnson and Tom Ferguson, authors of a guidebook on the psychology of women, hailed their work as coming "closest to creating a comprehensive pro-female psychological theory that rivals Freud's pro-male perspective" (1990, p. 36).

Some feminists have reservations about a theory that glorifies women's relational skills. One problem, they argue, is that it replaces the old male model with a new model of female chauvinism. "Before, men criticized women for not thinking; now women criticize men for not feeling" (Peay, 1994, pp. 26–27). Others fear that the emphasis on women's nurturing and interpersonal behavior constitutes a retrograde movement that reinforces the notion of separate spheres for women. Naomi Wolf contends that "the social pressure on women to exhibit 'connection' and suppress 'autonomy' can inhibit women's assertiveness" (1993, p. 24). Moreover, as Rachel Hare-Mustin and Jeanne Marecek (1988) suggest, rather than being an essential female quality, women's concern with caring and empathy may stem from their subordinate position in society.

Some have suggested that the Stone Center's model might better be described as a relational theory of White women's development because it may not be applicable to women of Color (Golden, 1996). Others, however, argue that relational theory may represent a way of connecting feminist psychology to multicultural and cross-cultural psychology (J. Y. Kawamoto, 1995). Lillian Comas-Diaz (1994) claims that relational theory is relevant to women of Color, although it has to be modified to fit individual life experiences. The African-American mother-daughter relationship, for example, differs from that of mainstream women in that it involves supplying the daughter with information on what it is like to be an African-American in American society (Greene, 1990). Latina mother-daughter relationships follow their own path, which is a more egalitarian one (Garcia-Preto, 1990). Stephen Bergman even believes that the relational model may be relevant to men. Although the details of men's development differ in several important ways, he notes, "men as well as women are motivated by a primary desire for connection" (1995, p. 68).

In the following articles, Marcia Westkott charges that the relational theory of women's development serves to perpetuate male privilege. Judith V. Jordan challenges this assertion and argues that the relational model developed at the Stone Center validates women's unique experiences and conflicts and can be a source of empowerment for women.

REFERENCES

Bergman, S. J. (1995). Men's psychological development: A relational perspective. In R. F. Levant & W. S. Pollack (Eds.), *A new psychology of men* (pp. 68–90). New York: Basic Books.

Chesler, P. (1972). *Women and madness.* New York: Doubleday.

Chodorow, N. (1978). *The reproduction of mothering.* Berkeley: University of California Press.

Comas-Diaz, L. D. (1994). An integrative approach. In L. Comas-Diaz & B. Greene (Eds.), *Women of Color: Integrating ethnic and gender identities in psychotherapy* (pp. 287–318). New York: Guilford Press.

Garcia-Preto, N. (1990). Hispanic mothers. *Journal of Feminist Therapy, 2,* 15–21.

Golden, C. (1996). Relational theories of White women's development. In J. C. Chrisler, C. Golden, &

P. D. Rozee (Eds.), *Lectures on the psychology of women* (pp. 229–242). New York: McGraw-Hill.

Greene, B. (1990). What has gone before: The legacy of racism and sexism in the lives of Black mothers and daughters. *Women and therapy, 9*, 207–230.

Greer, G. (1970). *The female eunuch.* New York: McGraw-Hill.

Hare-Mustin, R. T., & Marecek, J. (1988). The meaning of difference: Gender, theory, postmodernism and psychology. *American Psychologist, 43*, 455–464.

Johnson, K., & Ferguson, T. (1990). *Trusting ourselves: The sourcebook on the psychology of women.* New York: Atlantic Monthly Press.

Jordan, J. V., Kaplan, A. G., Miller, J. B., Stiver, I. P., & Surrey, J. L. (1991). *Women's growth in connection: Writings from the Stone Center.* New York: Guilford Press.

Kawamoto, J. Y. (1995). A Japanese American therapist discovers feminist therapy. In J. Adleman & G. M. Enguidanos (Eds.), *Racism in the lives of women: Testimony, theory, and guides to antiracist practice* (pp. 65–73). New York: Haworth Press.

Miller, J. B. (1976). Toward a new psychology of women. Boston: Beacon Press.

Miller, J. B. (1991). The development of women's sense of self. In J. V. Jordan, A. G. Kaplan, J. B. Miller, I. P. Stiver, & J. L. Surrey, *Women's growth in connection: Writings from the Stone Center* (pp. 11–26). New York: Guilford Press.

Peay, P. (July-August, 1994). What do women want? *Common Boundary*, pp. 22–34.

Wolf, N. (November 29, 1993). Are opinions male? The barriers that shut women up. *New Republic*, pp. 20–26.

ADDITIONAL READING

Adleman, J., & Enguidanos, G. M. (Eds.). (1995). *Racism in the lives of women: Testimony, theory, and guides to antiracist practice.* New York: Haworth Press.

Brown, L. S. (1994). *Subversive dialogues: Theory in feminist therapy.* New York: Basic Books.

Brown, L. S., & Ballou, M. (1992). *Feminist conceptualizations: The future of personality theory and psychopathology.* New York: Guilford Press.

Gilligan, C. (1991). Women's psychological development: Implications for psychotherapy. In C. Gilligan, A. G. Rogers, & D. L. Tolman (Eds.), *Women, girls and psychotherapy: Reframing resistance.* Special Issue, *Women and Therapy, 11*, 5–31.

Kaschak, E. (1992). *Engendered lives: A new psychology of women's experience.* New York: Basic Books.

Miller, J. B., Stiver, I. P., Jordan, J. V., & Surrey, J. L. (1995). The psychology of women: A relational approach. In J. Fadiman and R. Frager (Eds.), *Personality and personal growth* (pp. 159–179). New York: HarperCollins.

Philipson, I. J. (1993). *On the shoulders of women: The feminization of psychotherapy.* New York: Guilford Press.

Tatum, B. D. (1993). Racial identity development and relational theory: The case of Black women in White communities. Work in Progress No. 63. Wellesley, Mass.: Stone Center Working Paper Series.

NO

On the New Psychology of Women: A Cautionary View

MARCIA C. WESTKOTT

For nearly two decades writers on the psychology of women have questioned the male bias in theories of psychological health and development. In 1970 Broverman et al. charted the terms of what was to become the new feminist critique: their findings showed that clinicians implicitly associated psychological maturity and health with stereotypical male characteristics, but identified normal female traits as the same as those they associated with psychological immaturity or dysfunctioning. The feminist agenda has since been to question and redefine this culturally rooted, professionally accepted equation. The following essay describes the new paradigm that has emerged from this feminist project, analyzes its elaboration in the work of the Stone Center at Wellesley College, and critiques the paradigm from the perspective of Karen Horney.

In 1976 Jean Baker Miller initiated the feminist reevaluation with her thesis that "women have developed the foundations of extremely valuable psychological qualities" (p. 26), but that gender inequality causes these qualities or strengths to go unrecognized or devalued. Among the strengths that Miller identified was "women's great desire for affiliation" (pp. 88–89). Although this female predilection has been a source of women's problems, it can also be, she argued, the basis for important social values. Indeed, Miller concluded her influential book with the hope that it is precisely the affiliative qualities that women have developed—traits that

are "dysfunctional for success in the world as it is" —that may be those which are most needed for transforming the world into a more humane place (p. 124).

In 1978 Nancy Chodorow extended Miller's work by proposing that a female affiliative or relational self emerges from a structure of parenting in which mothers treat their sons and daughters differently. Daughters, who are treated as projections of the mother, never fully separate from her and thus come to define themselves as connected to or continuous with others. Boys, who are treated as more separate by their mothers, come to identify themselves as differentiated from others and possess more rigid ego boundaries than their sisters. Thus, "the basic feminine sense of self is connected to the world, the basic masculine sense of self is separate" (Chodorow 1978, p. 169).

Like Miller, Chodorow was critical of the social systems that reflect the male psyche, in particular the alienated work world of capitalist societies (Chodorow 1978, pp. 218–19). But unlike Miller, Chodorow's solution emphasized gender balance rather than a release of women's strengths upon a resisting world. In calling for men to participate equally in parenting, she advocated a realignment that would have "people of both genders with the positive capacities each has, but without the destructive extremes these currently tend toward" (p. 218). Chodorow's androgynous golden mean of individuated but affiliated mothers and fathers nurturing the next generation of balanced children was nevertheless dependent upon a change in *male* behavior. Assuming the public sphere changes for women initiated by the women's movement, Chodorow suggested that it is up to men to complete the rectification of the gender imbalance by engaging in the affiliative, nurturing activities of the private, domestic sphere (p. 218). Thus, like Miller's, Chodorow's solution was one that called for a universal valuing of those relational qualities traditionally identified with women.

Building on both Miller and Chodorow, Carol Gilligan (1982) expanded the theme to the redefinition of moral development. She grounded her work in a critique of Kohlberg's scale of six stages of moral judgment (Kohlberg 1973), a measurement constructed from interviews with only males but presumed to be universally applicable. Gilligan noted that females generally advanced only to Kohlberg's third level, in which morality is perceived as interpersonal and goodness defined as helping others. She argued that girls and women fall short of the higher levels, where the application of rules and universal principles of justice prevail over concern for specific relationships, not because females are morally deficient but because the scale itself is male-biased and irrelevant to women's own hierarchy of values (Gilligan 1982, pp. 18–19). Gilligan proposed that women and girls engage in moral judgments according to a different set of imperatives—a "different voice"—from that which men and boys follow: "The moral imperative that emerges repeatedly in interviews with women is an injunction to care, a responsibility to discern and alleviate the 'real and recognizable trouble' of this world. For men, the moral imperative appears rather as an injunction to respect the rights of others and thus to protect from interference the rights to life and self-fulfillment" (p. 100).

Paralleling Chodorow, Gilligan (1982) advocated an integration of both male and female moral perspectives to create an androgynous whole that combines a morality of responsibility to others with a morality of rights and principles (p. 100). Like Miller, Gilligan viewed the devaluation of women's concern for relationships and care for others and the elevation of the male emphasis on individual achievement and autonomy to be "more a commentary on the society than a problem in women's development" (p. 171). Like both Miller and Chodorow, Gilligan proposed to correct the male bias in both psychological models and behavioral norms by valuing the traditional female traits of affiliating and caring for others.

These works by Miller, Chodorow, and Gilligan have wielded considerable influence on the scholarship about women during the last decade. For example, they have inspired a spate of new studies, including books on women's cognitive development (Belenky et al. 1986), on educational philoso-phy (Noddings 1984), and on theories of war (Elshtain 1987). Three volumes of the *Psychology of Women Quarterly* from the mid-1980s (1985–87) included nineteen articles with forty-six references to at least one of the works by Miller, Chodorow, or Gilligan. This subsequent work has filled in the new paradigm of women's psychology that challenges universal models of psychological functioning and development, exposes its male bias, and makes the argument not only that female characteristics have been neglected or devalued but that they are positive human traits necessary for all people to cultivate.

The quality that has been singled out as most significant is the female relational disposition, variously defined in terms of women's need to affiliate with others, to take care of others, to nurture or mother them, to empathize, to be connected, to relate. This is often contrasted with an opposing psychological makeup that is associated with traditional models of (male) development: the differentiated, individuated self whose maturational goals are autonomy and personal success (for example, Levinson 1978). The problem of gender inequality is seen to be part of a larger problem in which some privileged groups (notably White, Western males) pursue their own individualistic goals at the expense of other groups (in particular, Third World people, people of Color, women, and children). The solution is a democratization which promotes equal opportunity, equality, and justice—goals which given the conditions of domination require a cultivation of the very devalued traits assigned to women: care, cooperation, empathy, and sense of responsibility for others. The argument is that social and political conditions require that these traditional female traits be universalized as a new ethic of care and cooperation. Men need to learn them, and women need to stop doubting themselves and instead build on the relational strengths to transform the world into their own image (for example, Eisler 1987).

The most systematic attempt to elaborate the new paradigm is occurring at the Stone Center for Developmental Services and Studies at Wellesley College, which was originally under the directorship of Jean Baker Miller. A group of clinicians and researchers there has assumed the positive value of women's relationality and, through a series of working papers, has explored its implications for both clinical practice (Kaplan 1984) and an understanding of women's psychology as it relates to such issues as power (J. B. Miller 1982), work (Stiver 1983), eating patterns (Surrey 1984), and violence (Swift 1987). Mostly, however, the work of the group is united by exploring and developing "the self-in-relation theory" (see especially Surrey 1985) of female and, by implication, human development.[1]

The Stone Center theory is grounded in an ethical vision in which the self is posited as containing two equally demanding but compatible needs: the need for recognition by *and* the need to understand the other (Surrey 1983, p. 8). These needs are socially constructed desires, created out of the physical and social contexts of mother-child interaction. The realization of the compatible needs is a mutually empathetic relationship. According to Jordan (1983), empathy does not entail a permanent blurring or loss of the self in the other but is based upon a separate sense of oneself that is temporarily relaxed to allow for attunement to the other's meaning systems and feelings (Jordan 1986, p. 2). Empathy occurs within the framework of intersubjectivity, the disposition to hold "the other's subjectivity as central to the interaction with that individual" (p. 2). In a relationship characterized by mutuality, self and other both express empathy and inter-subjectivity, giving and taking in a way that affirms not only self and other individually but also "the larger relational unit" that transcends them (p. 2).

Indeed, maintaining the larger relational unit itself becomes the ultimate end, because it is the condition sine qua non that meets the needs of the self.

For this reason the emphasis in the theoretical writings of the Stone Center is upon sustaining connection with the other. The self-in-relation abhors and dreads isolation, disconnection, and loss of the other, for this absence produces a fundamental loss of the self. Therefore, because maintaining the relationship is all-important, the two fundamental needs are not equally weighted: recognizing the other as a means of sustaining the relationship is implicitly given greater value than the desire for recognition. If connection is necessary for self-definition, then creating the conditions that keep the other connected becomes the primary personal agenda.

Although Stone Center psychologists routinely mention the importance of the need for "self-empathy" (Jordan 1984, p. 9), self-growth (J.B. Miller 1984, pp. 13–14), and personal empowerment (J. B. Miller 1982, p. 5), they reject the idea of personal desire being met in the absence of relationship. They regard such an individualist concept of motive to be dangerous. According to Jordan (1987), "Any system that emphasizes the ascendancy of individual desire as the legitimate basis for definition of self and interpersonal relationship is fraught with the possibility of creating violent relationships based on competition of need and the necessity for establishing hierarchies of dominance, entitlement, and power" (p. 9). The idea of the dangerous individual desire is replaced with a basic relational desire that is by definition informed by "empathy, noncomparativeness, and mutuality . . . involving empathetic responsiveness and a sense of compassion in a context of caring for the well-being of others (Jordan 1987, p. 9).

How is this deep motive for connection and compassion created? Following most developmental theories, the Stone Center psychologists attribute personality to the early patterns of parent-child, especially mother-child, interaction. According to Jean Baker Miller (1984), the infant, through the interaction with the caretaker, "begins to develop an internal representation of her/himself as a 'being in relationship.' This is the beginning of a sense of 'self' which reflects what is happening *between* people . . . pick[ing] up the feel-

---

1. The Stone Center Group has more recently moved away from using the term *self-in-relation* in favor of the term *connection*. Nevertheless, the more recent work continues to build on the earlier theoretical writings on the self-in-relation that posited the development of a core female sense of self connected to or related to others. See, for example, J. B. Miller (1988).

ings of the other person. . . . The child experiences a sense of comfort only as the other is also comfortable" (p. 3). The emergent sense of self is one whose core is "attended to by the other(s); and who begins to attend to the emotions of the other(s) . . . a self inseparable from dynamic interaction" (p. 4). Human growth is a process of engaging in "progressively complex relationships" (Kaplan and Klein 1985, p. 3) rather than in separating from caretakers by pursuing goals of autonomy and power. Maturity is defined in terms of "relational competence" (Surrey 1987, p. 8), "empathy" (Jordan 1984, p. 3), "clarity in connection" (Jordan 1987, p. 7), and the ability to create and sustain mutual intersubjectivity (Jordan 1986, p. 2). This, then, is their maturational ideal: the true relational self, who reflects the earliest human interpersonal experience, realizing its "motive for connection" in mutually empathetic relationships. Relationship is, thus, both the context in which the self develops and the goal for which it strives.

Despite their emphasis on the essential importance of mutuality as the social realization of the self-in-relation, the Stone Center psychologists contend that this goal is rarely attained in adult male-female relationships. The obstacle, argues Miller, is the traditional gender system, which promotes the unrealistic goal of autonomy and "power-over" for men and devalues the truly human activity of relational connectedness and caring as female responsibility (J. B. Miller 1982, p. 2). The cultural expectation that women, but not men, must care for others closes men off from their humanity, places a lopsided burden upon women, and makes male-female mutuality impossible (J. B. Miller 1983, pp. 3–5). Men take for granted that women will be caring and empathetic, but they implicitly and explicitly devalue women and refuse to reciprocate. Women, on the other hand, are drawn to relating to the other and caring for him but are neither validated in this role nor given empathetic support and nurturing in response (Stiver 1984, p. 8). If one were to interpret caretaking in our culture from the perspective of the Stone Center's critique, one would conclude that women care and men take.

Like Chodorow, the Stone Center psychologists explain the psychological reproduction of these culturally based gender types as the consequence of the mother's response to sexual differences in her children. Mothers encourage relational dispositions in their daughters and discourage them in their sons. However, unlike Chodorow, who advocates an androgynous balance of these traditional patterns of child rearing, the Stone Center psychologists contend that the mother-daughter pattern of interaction comes closest to promoting the growth of the healthy (i.e., relational) self and should, therefore, be considered the model for all parenting (Surrey 1985, p. 43; 1987, p. 6).

The developmental theory of the self-in-relation is grounded in the assumption that all infants have an attentiveness to the feeling state of the mother or caretaker. According to Surrey (1985), this disposition is encouraged in daughters but not in sons because of the mother's "ease with and interest in emotional sharing" with her daughter (p. 4; see also Surrey 1983, p. 6; J. B. Miller 1984, p. 4), which does not exist with the son. Consequently, the daughter's mother-attentiveness is reinforced, promoting in her "the basic sense of 'learning to listen,' to orient and attune to the other person through feelings" (Surrey 1985, p. 4). The mother's continued response of listening, empathizing, and reinforcing the daughter's responses to her creates what Surrey calls the "open relationship" between mother and daughter. This interactive context helps to form the daughter's "increasing ability for mutual empathy" through which the mother and daughter "become highly responsive to the feeling states of the other." Surrey describes the development of this mutuality more fully:

Through the girl's awareness and identification with her mother as the "mothering one" and through the mother's interest in being understood and cared for, the daughter as well as the mother become mobilized to care for, respond to or attend to the well-being and the development of the other. Moreover, they care for and take care of the relationship between them. This is the motivational dynamic of mutual empowerment, the inherent energizing force of real relationship. It becomes important for the girl to experience validation of her own developing empathetic competence. Thus, mothers empower their daughters by allowing them to feel successful at understanding and giving support at whatever level is appropriate at a particular period of development. In fact, part of learning to be a "good enough" daughter involves learning to be a "good enough" mother or "empathetic relator" to one's mother and later to other important people. This ongoing process begins to allow for experience and practice in "mothering" and "relational caretaking." (p. 5)

Thus, a girl develops a self-in-relation both through her mother's "ease" in responding to infant female attunement, and through her "expecting empathy and caretaking from [her] daughter" (Surrey 1983, p. 9). This sense of self that emerges in the daughter is characterized by an "ongoing capacity to consider one's actions in light of other people's needs, feelings, and perceptions" (Surrey 1987, p. 6). She comes to feel that "maintaining the relationship(s) with the main people in her . . . life is still *the* most important thing" (J. B. Miller 1984, p. 6). And her "self-esteem is based in feeling that she is a part of relationships and is taking care of relationships" (p. 5) through which she can express empathy, care, and "clarity in connection" with others (Jordan 1987).

The popularity of the new paradigm, including the work of the Stone Center, reflects the failure of traditional psychologies to reflect and explain women's lives. First, the new approach places a positive value on women's characteristics by turning traditional psychologies upside down. Instead of arguing that women are just as capable or mature or healthy as men, based upon a yardstick derived from male experience, these authors assume a distinct female psychology that has its own unique merits. Whereas traditional psychology once thought of the female as *l'homme manqué*, the new women's psychology now posits the feminine relational traits as *personne supérieure*.

Moreover, the Stone Center writings suggest a new feminist ideal for adult relationships in which self and other are neither locked into an endless battle for dominance nor resigned to a destructive hierarchy. Rather, their concept of mutuality promises a revisioning of the personal politics of need and desire in which meeting the needs of each becomes mutually fulfilling for both self and other. In their claims that such mutuality is regrettably absent in male-female relationships, but that the capacity for it is present in women, the Stone Center writers imply a transformation of the heterosexual paradigm along the line that others have associated with lesbian relationships and women's friendships (e.g., Raymond 1986). Thus, the mutuality that is possible between women emerges by implication as a new model for heterosexual reform. And, indeed, this reform extends beyond personal dyads to an argument for the feminization of social life and political structures, a transformation of patriarchy itself.

In addition, the writings of the Stone Center have rejected an object relations model of adult development in favor of an approach more consistent with recent work by more empirically oriented theorists like Daniel Stern (1985). In brief, they reject the object relations assumption that the developmental task is the individuation of the self out of a presumed original oneness with "the mother." In contrast, consistent with Stern, the Stone Center writers do not assume the mother-child bond as an ontological given (an ontology that I suspect may reflect wishful thinking). Rather they see it as a human relationship that must be created for the well-being of the child. This shift not only redefines the task of development as the creation of relationships, but also shifts the ethics of parenting from letting go in the context of an assumed bond to creating a bond that promotes individual growth. Jean Miller's more recent work (1988) suggests the possibilities of a feminist developmental psychology from this new perspective.

Finally, by identifying women's psychological traits as strengths, the writers on the new women's psychology offer individual women hope and a basis upon which to develop their self-worth and inner strength. The Stone Center writers emphasize that women can begin a therapeutic process by tapping resources they already have developed rather than engaging in perpetual self-criticism for not living up to (male-derived) maturational goals that are antithetical to their own deeply rooted dispositions.

Despite these breakthroughs, however, I believe that the Stone Center authors inadvertently reproduce the very patriarchal values that they criticize in traditional paradigms. The problem occurs through their abstracting the mother-daughter relationship from the wider patriarchal contexts in which this bond is actually cultivated, and then idealizing the relationship as if it were free of patriarchal influence. The result is a concept of the female psyche that appears to be not only out of sync with patriarchy but also free of it, as if the idealized qualities of care and relationality were not themselves informed by patriarchal meanings and purposes. The consequence is a mystification of the patriarchal interests that are served by women's empathetic and relational traits.

The problem is best identified in the Stone Center's theoretical writings on female development. Recall that the self-in-relation emerges from a dynamic in which a mother expresses both an ease and interest in emotional sharing with her daughter and a need to be understood and cared for by her daughter. The mother's desire to be cared for is of particular significance because it is the source of the daughter's development of empathy as a permanent feature of her character. The daughter is encouraged to respond to her mother's needs and is rewarded for doing so by receiving in return both care and gratitude.

The work of the Stone Center theorists celebrates the process through which a daughter learns to be "a 'good enough' mother or 'empathetic relator' to one's mother and later to other people" (Surrey 1985, p. 5). What is missing from their account is an understanding of the fact that the needs of the infant or child and the needs of the adult are not of the same magnitude, and that the difference in age, capability, and maturation necessarily creates an imbalance in the relationship. Indeed, when one reads the Stone Center formulations of the mother-daughter relationship, one has little indication that this is an interaction between an adult

and a child. Their descriptions of the dyad read more like interactions between peers, as if the mutual empathy that is posited as the ideal *adult* engagement is projected back onto the mother-daughter relationship.

The blurring of differences in age, need, and authority between mother and daughter serves to deflect attention from the unique needs of the child and to legitimate the mother's right to have her needs met by her daughter. The Stone Center writers do not question what they describe as "the mother's interest in being understood and cared for" by her daughter (Surrey 1985, p. 5). Instead, they accept it as a given. This assumption, however, has buried within it a belief that has a profound consequence for explaining the mother-daughter relationship. This belief is that mothers *should* be able to gratify their needs for care and understanding through interacting with their daughters. Instead of questioning this prerogative or placing it in the context of cultural values that foster it, the Stone Center psychologists reproduce it uncritically, implying that it is "natural" or unproblematic. However, by doing so, they close off the possibility for interpreting it as a parent's *use* of her child, a practice which others (e.g., A. Miller 1981, 1983, 1984) have argued has harmful developmental consequences. Thus, by projecting the model of ideal adult mutuality back on the mother-daughter relationship—a projection which presumes the right of the mother to have her needs met by her daughter—the Stone Center theory mystifies both the real power difference between mother and daughter (which permits a mother to impose her needs) and the possible detrimental consequences of this imposition for the daughter's development.

One of the sources of this mystification is the abstraction of the mother-daughter relationship from the wider cultural contexts in which it is actually embedded. The Stone Center writers do describe a cultural context, but they limit discussion of its consequences to adult male-female relationships. According to Jean Baker Miller (1983), traditional gender arrangements are so deeply rooted in male domination and female subordination that mutual empathy between women and men is impossible (pp. 4–5). The Stone Center psychologists provide numerous examples from clinical practice of women struggling with the absence of reciprocal empathy and understanding in their relationships with men (e.g., Jordan 1984, p. 7; 1986, pp. 8–10; J.B. Miller 1986, p. 4). Yet, except for incidental comments that the absence could lead to a mother's overidentification with her children (J. B. Miller 1972; Stiver 1986), these writers provide no systematic analysis of the implications of their critique of the gender system for their theory of the mother-daughter relationship.

If they had placed their model of the mother-daughter relationship in the context of the gender system that they criticize, the Stone Center theorists might have interpreted differently their assumption of a mother's need for care and understanding from her daughter. They might have identified the likelihood that a woman who cannot find mutual empathy or care and understanding in her relationship with an adult man might indeed turn to her daughter to meet those needs, not because it is "natural" or "given," but because the mother, too, has internalized the belief that only females are to care for others. This is the cultural devaluation of both women and the socially necessary need for care that pervades our society, an argument that Miller made eloquently in her 1976 book. A mother's acting on that belief in her relationship with her daughter is not a failure of mothers *per se*, but an understandable expression of this wider system of values.

Reinterpreted from the perspective of the gendered context of the mother's need for care, the Stone Center model of the mother-daughter bond assumes a different meaning. A mother who turns to her daughter in order to meet her own needs does not create the conditions for the blossoming of the self but instead confounds her own needs for care and recognition with her responsibilities as a caretaker. By turning to her daughter to provide adult mutuality, a mother can, in effect, create a nurturing reversal, seeking care from one who is too young to give it.

In my interpretation of Karen Horney's work (Westkott 1986), I argued that this kind of contra-dictory and needy behavior fosters anxiety in a child and results in the child's developing defensive strategies to create a sense of safety (Horney 1937, pp. 85–86). From the standpoint of Horney's work, the caring, empathetic qualities that the mother seeks from her daughter and that the daughter offers in return are not the expressions of an essentially human, relational self, but the protective devices of one who feels that she *must* display these behaviors in order to gain her mother's love and acceptance.[2]

From this perspective, the empathetic qualities of the self-in-relation actually constitute a defensive structure. Hence, I suggest that the self-in-relation is not the authentic self that the Stone Center theorists presume it to be, but the idealized "false" self that Horney associated with self-effacement and living according to others' expectations (Horney 1937, pp. 119–20; 1950, pp. 168). According to this interpretation, the self-in-relation finds acceptance from others through displaying the altruistic qualities of "unselfishness, goodness, generosity, humility, saintliness, nobility, sympathy" that she believes will win her love (Horney 1950, p. 222). These are the "shoulds" of her defensive system: doing for others, caring for them, making their needs the sources of her motives, complying with others' demands for recognition. The defensive, altruistic self emerges from a childhood in which girls are sexualized and otherwise devalued. The sexualization ranges from overt incest to more subtle forms of sexually suggestive, intrusive, and controlling treatment. Through being sexualized, a girl learns that she is an object to be used for the purposes and pleasures of others, especially men. Other forms of devaluation deny a girl's integrity as a self-directed

2. Alice Miller (1981, 1983, 1984) has explored the consequences of parents' narcissistic use of their children, a practice which promotes children making themselves into "gifts" for their parents. Jessica Benjamin (1988) argues that the absence of recognition of the child and her authentic, unique needs creates a compliant and obedient, that is, masochistic, female self who is unable to distinguish what she wants from what her mother, and later others, want. I read Horney's work as a prefiguring of this theme.

person and are conveyed in what Karen Horney called "the thousand little daily experiences of a child" (Horney 1942, p. 49), for example, constraining a girl's freedom, ignoring her accomplishments or valuing only those that serve others, subtly or blatantly discouraging her aspirations, paying little or no attention to her activities or to her interpretations of herself and the world around her. Thus, if a girl learns through being sexualized that she is an object to be used for male pleasure or purposes, she learns that lesson again from the devaluation of her efforts to become a self-directed human being. Sexualization of a girl's body transforms her desire into desirability; devaluation of her agency shifts the fulfillment of her needs into a wish to be valued through meeting the needs of others. These two forms of treating a girl as an object rather than a subject thus mirror one another: every devaluation of her agency confirms her sexual subordination, and every sexualizing encounter deepens her sense that her actions are valuable only if they are pleasing to others.

How does this translation take place? How does a girl internalize this experience of being treated as an object so as to take her self to be only an object for others? Horney's theory offers an explanation that suggests the ways that cultural values become internalized. The psychodynamics of family life, which express female devaluation and sexualization, reproduce our "masculine civilization's" pattern of preference for males, an assumption that meeting the needs of men takes preference over meeting those of women, and that men are, in the final analysis, superior to women (Horney 1939, p. 170). When these values get conveyed in parents' interaction with their daughters in the behaviors of sexualization and devaluation, they form a social reality that threatens a child's safety. The need for safety, along with the desire to satisfy one's desires, is an ontological category in Horney's psychology. But because it establishes the condition for satisfying one's desires, safety is the primary requirement. "People can renounce food, money, attention, affection as long as they are only renouncing satisfaction, but they cannot renounce these things if

without them they would be or feel in danger of destitution or starvation or of being helplessly exposed to hostility, in other words, if they would lose their feeling of safety" (Horney 1939, p. 73). The theoretical primacy that Horney places on safety implies that the infant or child is not simply or primarily a bundle of desires but a being at risk, dependent on the ethical conduct—the care—of others. When a child is treated with warmth and care by the adults in her life, she is treated as an end in herself and not as a means to meeting the needs of others (Westkott 1986, pp. 66–71).

However, the culturally infused familial patterns of sexualization and devaluation create for girls an experience of danger, not safety. In the face of being treated as an object *for* others, a child will respond with fear and anger. Fear is the understandable reaction to feelings of helplessness in the face of the absence of genuine parental affection and love. Anger is also an understandable response; it is a way of fighting back, of protesting the behavior of others and expressing legitimate anger. However, because female anger is unladylike, because it calls into question the authority of sexualizing and devaluating adults, a girl's anger intensifies the danger. Thus, out of fear of reprisal or loss of whatever love and safety are possible, a girl represses her anger. In the process, the feared and resented parent becomes admired, and the child becomes the object of her own hostility. This "shift from true rebellion to untrue admiration" (Horney 1942 p. 51) is a solution to the experience of danger. By admiring the devaluing and/or sexualizing parent, the girl diffuses interpersonal conflict.

The conflict, however, becomes internalized. It manifests as an inner psychological tension between feelings of worthlessness (the anger turned back upon the self) and the feminine behaviors that are pleasing to the devaluing and sexualizing adults (compliance as a strategy of safety). These forms of compliance—seductive and self-abnegating femininity—constitute the defensive false or idealized self that unfortunately gets rewarded for its adherence to appropriate forms of culturally prescribed female behavior. Exhibiting these behaviors and embracing their attendant feelings thus becomes the greatest defense against both self-hatred and social disapproval. It is the way through which compulsory femininity becomes compulsively pursued.

It is possible, I suggest, to interpret the Stone Center's concept of the self-in-relation as a form of the compulsory feminine. By their own accounts, a daughter is expected to nurture her mother, which, I argue, can be a form of devaluating the daughter's own needs for nurturance, care, validation. The relational, altruistic qualities that the daughter then exhibits do not inform the flowering of some true female self but express the acquiescence to a caring and self-abnegating femininity that the mother herself needs. The daughter thus comes to need others to need her as a way of confirming that she is, indeed, empathetic, caring, lovable. Moreover, from the perspective of Horney's theory, the idealized empathetic self is not only a strategic persona that seeks protective gratitude and admiring confirmation from others; it is also an inexorable inner critic that condemns actual behavior for failing to live up to the proud "shoulds" comprising the ideal (Horney 1950, pp. 111–12). Failure to be caring enough or sensitive to others' feelings can incur the wrath of the idealized self-image, fostering a compulsion to live up to the shoulds. One who is dominated by the idealized self cannot escape its wrath. The combination of defensive perfectionism and inevitable shortcomings serves to make anger against the self a permanent feature of character (Horney 1951). But anger is felt not only because one fails to achieve the ideal, but also because one is forced to repress desires for individual self-fulfillment that violate the relational ideal. The idealized relational self, therefore, perpetuates self-criticism and anger as ongoing intrapsychic processes.

Because the self-in-relation theory idealizes the rational, caring qualities, it obscures the ways in which these idealized qualities themselves create oppressive demands and foster inner rage. Ironically, many of the clinical examples presented in the Stone Center works-in-progress series are of angry or depressed women (e.g., J. B. Miller 1983; Jordan 1987, p. 17; Surrey 1985, p. 13). And usually, the clinical advice is to encourage these women to develop greater "self-empathy" or to meet their own needs (e.g., Stiver 1983, pp. 9–10; 1984, p. 10; Surrey 1984, p. 4; 1985, pp. 11–12; Jordan 1984, p. 9). But because empathy for the other is assumed to be a benign need rather than a compulsive demand, the inner anger that can be generated *by* that demand is never adequately addressed.

The self-in-relation theory, like the paradigm it elaborates, attempts to rescue the psychology of women from traditional distortions by inverting the values ascribed to stereotypically male and female traits. But its solution—hoisting the banner of care and relationality above individual achievement and autonomy—creates another danger for women. The expectation that women should be caring and empathetic expresses a deeper cultural belief that men's needs take precedence over women's. The female relational ideal is grounded in, and serves to perpetuate, a context of male privilege. The new paradigm acknowledges this system of male prerogative in adult relationships but fails to understand its deep influence on women's character development. Thus, by celebrating relationality as if its development were free of the effects of female subservience, the new psychology unwittingly advocates an oppressive ideal for women.

Yet in its limitations, as well as in its goals, the new paradigm raises a fundamental ethical question: how do we construct a world in which care for others is humanly possible and universally valued? The answer, I suggest, lies not in an idealization of traditional femininity as a new universal ethic, but in a radical revisioning of the values and practices we associate with both care and gender. Through such critical reformulation we may begin to move beyond present practices that devalue women and the socially necessary need to care.

REFERENCES

Belenky, M. F., Clinchy, B. M., Goldberger, N. R., and Tarule, J. M. 1986. *Women's Ways of Knowing.* New York: Basic Books.

Benjamin, Jessica. 1988. *The Bonds of Love: Psychoanalysis, Feminism, and the Problem of Domination.* New York: Pantheon.

Broverman, I. K., Broverman, D. M., Clarkson, F. D., Rosenkrantz, P. S., and Vogel, S. R. 1970. Sex-Role Stereotypes and Clinical Judgments of Mental Health. *Journal of Consulting and Clinical Psychology* 34, no. 1:1–7.

Chodorow, Nancy. 1978. *The Reproduction of Mothering.* Berkeley: University of California Press.

Eisler, Riane. 1987. *The Chalice and the Blade.* San Francisco: Harper and Row.

Elshtain, Jean B. 1987. *Women and War.* New York: Basic Books.

Gilligan, Carol. 1982. *In a Different Voice: Psychological Theory and Women's Development.* Cambridge: Harvard University Press.

Horney, Karen. 1937. *The Neurotic Personality of Our Time.* New York: Norton.

———. 1939. Can you Take a Stand? *Journal of Adult Education, 11,* 129–132.

———. 1942. *Self Analysis.* New York: Norton.

———. 1945. *Our Inner Conflicts: A Constructive Theory of Neurosis.* New York: Norton.

———. 1950. *Neurosis and Human Growth.* New York: Norton.

———. 1951. On Feeling Abused. *American Journal of Psychoanalysis.* no. 11:5–12.

———. 1967. *Feminine Psychology.* New York: Norton.

Jordan, Judith V. 1983. Women and Empathy: Implications for Psychological Development and Psychotherapy. *Work in Progress* No. 82–02. Wellesley, Mass.: Stone Center Working Paper Series.

———. 1984. Empathy and Self-Boundaries. *Work in Progress* No. 16. Wellesley, Mass.: Stone Center Working Paper Series.

———. 1986. The Meaning of Mutuality. *Work in Progress* No. 23. Wellesley, Mass.: Stone Center Working Paper Series.

———. 1987. Clarity in Connection: Empathic Knowing. Desire and Sexuality. *Work in Progress* No. 29. Wellesley, Mass.: Stone Center Working Paper Series.

Kaplan, Alexandra G. 1984. Female or Male Psychotherapists for Women: New Formulations. *Work in Progress* No. 83–02. Wellesley, Mass.: Stone Center Working Paper Series.

Kaplan, A. G., and Klein, R. 1985. Women's Self Development in Late Adolescence. *Work in Progress* No. 17. Wellesley, Mass.: Stone Center Working Paper Series.

Kohlberg, L. 1973. Continuities and Discontinuities in Childhood and Adult Moral Development Revisited. *Collected Papers on Moral Development and Moral Education.* Cambridge: Harvard University, Moral Education Research Foundation.

Levinson, D. 1978. *The Seasons of a Man's Life.* New York: Knopf.

Miller, Alice. 1981. *The Drama of the Gifted Child.* New York: Basic Books.

———. 1983. *For Your Own Good: Hidden Cruelty in Child-Rearing and the Roots of Violence.* New York: Farrar, Straus, and Giroux.

———. 1984. *Thou Shalt Not Be Aware.* New York: Farrar, Straus, and Giroux.

Miller, Jean Baker. 1972. Sexuality and Inequality: Men's Dilemma (A Note on the Oedipus Complex, Paranoia and Other Psychological Concepts). *American Journal of Psychoanalysis,* no. 32:147–55.

———. 1976. *Toward a New Psychology of Women.* Boston: Beacon Press.

———. 1982. Women and Power. *Work in Progress* No. 82–01. Wellesley, Mass.: Stone Center Working Paper Series.

———. 1983. The Construction of Anger in Women and Men. *Work in Progress* No. 83–01. Wellesley, Mass.: Stone Center Working Paper Series.

———. 1984. The Development of Women's Sense of Self. *Work in Progress* No. 12. Wellesley, Mass.: Stone Center Working Paper Series.

———. 1986. What Do We Mean by Relationships? *Work in Progress* No. 22. Wellesley, Mass.: Stone Center Working Paper Series.

———. 1988. Connections, Disconnections and Violations. *Work in Progress* No. 33. Wellesley, Mass.: Stone Center Working Paper Series.

Noddings, Nel. 1984. *Caring: A Feminine Approach to Ethics and Moral Education.* Berkeley: University of California Press.

Psychology of Women Quarterly, 1986, Volume 10; 1987, Volume 11; 1988, Volume 12.

Raymond, Janice G. 1986. *A Passion for Friends: Toward a Philosophy of Female Affection.* Boston: Beacon Press.

Stern, Daniel N. 1985. *The Interpersonal World of the Infant.* New York: Basic Books.

Stiver, Irene P. 1983. Work Inhibitions in Women. *Work in Progress* No. 82–03. Wellesley, Mass.: Stone Center Working Paper Series.

———. 1984. The Meanings of "Dependency" in Female-Male Relationships. *Work in Progress* No. 83–07. Wellesley, Mass.: Stone Center Working Paper Series.

———. 1986. Beyond the Oedipus Complex: Mothers and Daughters. *Work in Progress* No. 26. Wellesley, Mass.: Stone Center Working Paper Series.

Surrey, Janet L. 1983. The Relational Self in Women: Clinical Implications. *Work in Progress* No. 82–02. Wellesley, Mass.: Stone Center Working Paper Series.

———. 1984. Eating Patterns as a Reflection of Women's Development. *Work in Progress* No. 83–06. Wellesley, Mass.: Stone Center Working Paper Series.

———. 1985. Self-in-Relation, a Theory of Women's Development. *Work in Progress* No. 13. Wellesley, Mass.: Stone Center Working Paper Series.

———. 1987. Relationship and Empowerment. *Work in Progress* No. 30. Wellesley, Mass.: Stone Center Working Paper Series.

Swift, C.F. 1987. Women and Violence: Breaking the Connection. *Work in Progress* No. 27. Wellesley, Mass.: Stone Center Working Paper Series.

Westkott, Marcia. 1986. *The Feminist Legacy of Karen Horney.* New Haven: Yale University Press.

The Relational Model Is a Source of Empowerment for Women

JUDITH V. JORDAN

Marcia Westkott argues that the relational model is "grounded in and perpetuates a context of male privilege, and advocates an oppressive ideal for women" (this volume). My goal in this article is to challenge Westkott's assertion and to demonstrate that the relational model developed at the Stone Center at Wellesley College validates women's unique experiences and conflicts, especially in a cultural milieu that often invalidates or challenges this mode of being in the world; further, this very validation is a source of empowerment for women. This discussion will recast and reformulate notions of women's development, focusing on aspects that reflect hidden or neglected areas of development—specifically, the centrality of human relationships to women's sense of themselves and the importance of the development of the capacity for relatedness.

Although I disagree with many of Westkott's interpretations of the relational model, several of her admonitions are useful. The possibility does exist in a value-oriented model that women will be oppressed by a new set of relational "shoulds." We do not want to burden women with new, impossible standards such as achieving perfectly harmonious, all "good" relationships. Our goal is simply to listen to women's voices and better represent their experiences so they are not judged as deficient by male-centered models of development. It is also im-

portant in response to Westkott's critique that we clarify that we are not encouraging daughters to "take care of" their mothers; such parentification of a child clearly would not serve as a model of healthy functioning. Rather, the kind of mutual empathy that occurs in the mother-daughter relationship is not about caretaking per se but about attunement and co-creation of relationship in which both people are affected by one another. Mutuality also does not signify equality of function or capability. We have attempted to carefully define the concept of mutuality so that people do not confuse it with equality or reciprocity. To counter the charge that we are sending women back into subordination in patriarchal systems by overemphasizing relationship and women as the "keepers of relationship," we want to stress the importance of both competence in women's lives and the courage to move into "good conflict." With regard to diversity, the Stone Center now has several study groups of people from diverse racial, cultural, and sexual orientation backgrounds who are reworking and rethinking this work from different vantage points; those of us working on this model, coming from various backgrounds of privilege, need to be careful not to speak for all women or suggest that there is one truth for all women.

PATRIARCHAL THEORY

Developmental and clinical theory has generally emphasized the growth of the autonomous, individuated self in such a way that early developmental milestones are typically characterized by greater separation from mother and an increasing sense of boundedness, self-control, the self as origin of action and intention, and use of logical, abstract thought. This particular bias, if we may call it that, probably derives from several influences: (1) the modeling of psychology as a science on Newtonian physics, which emphasized notions of discrete entities acting on each other in measurable ways; (2) the emphasis in Western, democratic countries on the sanctity and freedom of the individual; (3) a culture that perceives its task of child rearing as weaning the helpless, dependent infant toward greater self-sufficiency and independence; and (4) a study of the psyche that grew from an understanding of pathology in which the ego was seen as needing to protect itself from assaults both by internal impulses and external demands. Freud commented that "protection against stimuli is an almost more important function for a living organism than reception of stimuli" (Freud, 1920, p. 27). In traditional psychoanalytic theory the individual is seen as growing from an undifferentiated and later embedded and symbiotic phase into an individuated, separate state. These theories arose within a Western patriarchal tradition that emphasizes "mastery over" nature, the importance of instrumentality, growth characterized by increasing capacity for self-sufficiency and separation, and a portrayal of personal security based on "power over" and protection from others. This is what we would call a *separate self* model of personal development.

In the past decade an important impetus for shifting to a different paradigm of the self in developmental-clinical theory has come from feminist psychologists who have been increasingly vocal and articulate about their dissatisfaction with existing models of women's development and the "female self." Although not always explicitly stated, the adequacy of old models for describing men's development is also questioned. "Feminist thought" has been described as "different in every respect: as a practical, particular, contexted, open, and nonsystematic knowledge of the social circumstances in which one has one's being, concerned with achieving a heterarchy of times and places for a plurality of otherwise conflicting voices" (Shotter and Logan, 1988, pp. 75–76). Miller (1976), Chodorow (1978), Gilligan (1982), and the Stone Center theory group (Jordan et al., 1991) are among the new wave of women challenging existing conceptualizations of women's development and personal organization. All note the male (phallocentric) bias in clinical-developmental theory. Miller's work takes a broad psychological-cultural approach to the problem; she explicitly notes, "As we have inherited it, the

notion of 'a self' does not appear to fit women's experience" (Miller, 1984, p. 1). More recently, she has been drawing on clinical work to broaden and deepen her alternative perspective of "being in relation." Gilligan's ideas about the nature of female development derived from her awareness that prevailing theories of moral development (Kohlberg & Gilligan, 1971) were not applicable to women but were being used in such a way that women consistently appeared as defective or deficient moral selves. As Gilligan notes, "The disparity between women's experience and the representation of human development, noted throughout the psychological literature, has generally been seen to signify a problem in women's development. Instead, the failure of women to fit existing models of human growth may point to a problem in the representation, a limitation in the conception of human condition, an omission of certain truths about life" (Gilligan, 1982, pp. 1–2). An important truth being omitted was the power of the ethic of caretaking and relationship in women's lives. Chodorow reexamined object relations theory and found that traditional theory failed to acknowledge the importance of the early and longer lasting bond between the girl and her mother. This bond leads to a different experience of boundaries and identity from what the boy, as objectified other, experiences with mother.

What all these theorists allude to and seek to begin to correct in psychological theory reflects an old tradition, captured in Aristotle's statement that "the female is a female by virtue of a certain lack of qualities; we should regard the female nature as afflicted with a natural defectiveness" (Sanday, 1988, p. 58). When men are studied, when men do the studying, and when male values hold sway in the culture, one cannot expect any other outcome; the other will always be defined in the terms of the subject, and differences will be interpreted as deficiencies, especially in a hierarchical system (Broverman et al., 1970). Very specifically, all of these theorists note the failure of previous theories of "human development" to appreciate the relational nature of women's sense of themselves. Miller and Gilligan also explicitly posit a more contextual, relational paradigm for the study of all self experience.

MUTUALITY

The Stone Center (Jordan et al., 1991) relational perspective on human experience (sometimes referred to as self-in-relation theory) posits that: (1) we grow in, through, and toward relationship; (2) for women, especially, connection with others is central to psychological well-being; and (3) movement toward relational mutuality optimally occurs throughout life, through mutual empathy, responsiveness, and contribution to the growth of each individual and to the relationship. From a relational perspective the movement of relating, of mutual initiative and responsiveness, is the ongoing central dynamic in people's lives.

In mutuality there is both affirmation of one's own experience as well as a paradoxical transcendence of self, a sense that one is part of something larger. Mutuality is disrupted when one person exerts power over another, when a person falls into inauthentic patterns of relating, or when one person closes down or becomes defensive.

Mutuality does not mean equality or sameness; it involves openness to change and growth on both sides where there is interest in the other, in emotional availability, and in responsiveness. With mutuality both people are in and for the relationship which involves attention to other, self, and relationship. It involves a shift from a model of altruism versus egoism, self-sacrifice versus egocentricity into one in which both people contribute to, are sustained by, and are able to grow in the relationship that exists between them.

Early in our work the mother-daughter relationship was studied as an example of the development of mutual empathy (Jordan & Surrey, 1986); it is this work that Westkott most strongly takes issue with. While articulating the structure of the mother-daughter relationship is important to understanding women's unique development, the model presented here is a general model of relationship and is not totally specific to the nuclear mother-daughter relationship of early childhood.

This relationship simply represents the beginning of a structure and process that will be developed through important relationships with other significant people in childhood and throughout life. Such relational development will depend on the availability of many different relationships and of relational networks which can foster and facilitate it.

According to the mother-daughter example, the early attentiveness to feeling states on the part of the daughter and the mother's corresponding ease with and interest in emotional sharing may be the origin of learning to listen to feelings, to orient and attune to the other person—in other words, the origin of a capacity for empathy. Boys, on the other hand, may learn not to listen, to shut out the mother's voice, and in general learn not to be too influenced by others. Following from this early developmental difference, women in adult life experience "being with" psychologically as self-enhancing, whereas men may experience it as invasive, engulfing, or threatening. *Being with* here means both being seen and seeing the other or understanding and being understood, which is the experience of mutual empathy; it includes the interplay of being affected or impacted by another and noticing the impact we have on others. This early open connection is allowed to develop more naturally between mothers and daughters than between mothers and sons. The expectations that the boy separate and move into the male world curtail his early sense of relatedness with mother. For the girl, however, this early mutual empathy may be the origin of "seeing through the eyes of the other."

This, then, is a key aspect of the mother-daughter relationship: The experience of mutual empathy, developed in a matrix of emotional connectedness. The interest, ability, and involvement of the mother in listening and responding, empathizing and mirroring the child has been well described by Winnicott (1971), Kohut (1971), and others, who see this as the beginning of the development of experiences of the self. The mother's emotional openness with the daughter and her attunement to her probably leave the girl feeling emotionally connected, understood, and recognized. In healthy development this sense of connection appears to form the framework for the process of differentiation and gaining a sense of personal clarity. Girls, then, develop the expectation that they can facilitate and enhance their sense of self through psychological connection and grow to expect that the mutual sharing of experience leads to mutual empathy. We at the Stone Center recognize fully that there is clear inequality between mothers and their children in terms of power, cognitive ability, size, and many other factors, and mothers do not expect to be "mothered" by their children (daughters or sons); mothers, however, often report a real deepening of self-awareness and growth in their ongoing experience of relating to a growing child. Westkott views this emphasis on mutuality in the mother-daughter relationship as a pathological form of the mother using the daughter to get taken care of. Mutual empathy and empowerment do not involve creating a parentified child or reversing roles; they simply mean that in this relationship both mother and daughter experience growth, increasing capacity to act, increasing clarity about their own experience and the other person's, and increasing desire for other connections. A large portion of Westkott's disagreement with the relational model seems based on her understanding of the concept of mutuality, a concept which I hope we have clarified in recent writings (Jordan et al., 1991).

In mutuality, one is both affecting the other and being affected by the other; one extends oneself out to the other and is also receptive to the impact of the other. There is openness to influence, emotional availability, and a constantly changing pattern of responding to and affecting the other's state. There is both receptivity and active initiative toward the other. There is a sense of expanding participation, engagement, and openness between the people involved (Jordan, 1986). When empathy and concern flow both ways, there is an intense affirmation of one's own experience and paradoxically a transcendence of the experience of separate self, a sense of self as part of a larger relational unit. Mutual empathy occurs when two people relate to one another in a context of interest in the other,

emotional responsiveness, and cognitive appreciation of the wholeness of the other. Clearly this process occurs in different ways with people at different developmental points; it depends on cognitive and emotional capacities.

Mutual empowerment is another characteristic of growth-enhancing relationships and occurs through mutual sensitivity, mutual empathy, and each caring about the growth of the other. Within the early mother-daughter relationship, and as it develops over the life cycle, we can begin to see the precursors of women's interest, comfort, and sense of purpose and empowerment in relatedness. Mutual empathy and mutual empowerment in the mother-daughter relationship is not a kind of burdensome caregiving that is foisted on the child for the mother's good.

In emphasizing the development of mutuality throughout the lifespan, we are pointing to the possibility of a profound change in the nature of relatedness between people. The expectation of fully developed mutuality in our most important relationships depends heavily on the possibility of changing patriarchal systems of male dominance and female subordination. At a societal level valuing and supporting relational growth are offered as an alternative to the overvaluation of individualism and competitive hierarchies as defining the success of human beings.

AUTHENTICITY AND RELATIONAL SELF

Relational authenticity describes the ongoing effort to represent oneself as fully as possible, to be real, clear, and present in the relationship. It also takes into account the possible impact of one's experience on the other person; in this way it differs from some notion that we should pay attention only to our own needs or our own truths. It often involves the possibility of moving into interpersonal conflict, as the real representation of difference between two people may lead to the need for personal accommodations or shifts in one or both people. Existing images and patterns of relationship may also need to change when authentic voices are heard. The mutually empathic relationship that provides the energy for growth entails both the need to be seen and understood and the need to see and understand the other as fully as possible; this often includes the possibility of interpersonal conflict.

Lacking the capacity to bear conflict, an individual could be in danger of being taken over by another's reality. Learning to be in conflict is learning to work with differences creatively rather than simply getting rid of differences. Traditionally women are taught to accommodate, to make harmony, and to keep things moving smoothly in relationship. This often creates inauthenticity, a sense that one cannot represent one's experience fully in relationship. We need to dispel the myth of the nonangry, totally accommodating woman. And we need to learn that we can stay in connection around interpersonal conflict or anger; clearly, this becomes more complicated when we are threatened with aggression by more powerful others if we choose to move into conflict. Unfortunately, this occurs regularly in systems of dominance and power over.

In the absence of the capacity to move into interpersonal conflict, one is also in danger of losing contact with one's own experience as well as possibly moving into inauthentic relatedness. Gilligan (1982) suggests that this happens normatively for adolescent girls when they begin to believe that they can no longer bring their full experience into relationship and be accepted. Authenticity depends on the capacity to bring one's experiences as fully as possible into connection; mutual relationship encourages mutual authenticity. Power relationships discourage it. Patriarchy discourages authenticity in nondominant groups.

Authenticity is compromised in unequal power relationships; if one is in a position of subordination, one is not allowed authenticity when it is at odds with the dominant's view of reality. Authenticity is further threatened when one person in a relationship is not responsive to the other's real expression of need or feeling; in such situations there is no impact on the other. If a girl or woman cannot find ways to have an impact on available relationships, she will attempt to change the only person possible to change, herself (Miller et al., 1995).

Specifically, she tries to alter her internal image of herself and others. This process leads to what Miller and Stiver have suggested is a major paradox. In order to try to connect in the only relationships available, the child will be keeping more and more of her authentic self out of her relationships. She will be trying to maintain relationships at the price of failing to represent her own experience in them. In this process, she is moving further and further away from connection with her own experience—and she is losing the main source of psychological growth: interactions within relationships. Authenticity, then, is central to a notion of growth in connection. "Relating" out of a place of falseness ("false self," as suggested by Westkott, 1990) does not constitute growth-enhancing connection but rather is a way of disconnecting or moving out of connection.

AUTONOMOUS FUNCTIONING

The prevailing concept of self is modeled on the now-outdated Newtonian physics, a paradigm which posited separate objects possessing clear identifies whose interactions were secondary to their atomistic and bounded structures. The philosophical, sociopolitical context, which supported the development of this notion of self in Western culture, celebrated the sanctity of the individual and the importance of individual rights and entitlements; the individual was seen as needing protection from the presumed aggressive self-interest of others and from the impinging community. In this worldview, a pessimistic expectation of individual selfishness led to an overvaluing of the separate self at the expense of connectedness and community. Self-sufficiency and self-control, then, constituted an important part of the definition of the "ideal man"; self-interest became equated with health, while interest in others' well-being became equated with self-sacrifice or the devalued work of caretakers, that is, women.

Related to this traditional image of self as separate and relationships as impinging was the emphasis on autonomy. *Autonomous* literally means "self-governing." In many models of separation and autonomy, there has been a heavy focus on freedom from restraint by others and from having to attend carefully to the effects of one's actions on others. But is such a state really desirable or possible in any but the most abstracted, nonmutual, nonempathic situations?

In a paradigm that recognizes the relational and interdependent nature of our lives, we might replace autonomy with "the capacity to be clear in our thoughts, feelings, and actions; to act with intention; to be creative and effective, but always with awareness of the source of our energy in relationships and with recognition of the impact of our actions on others." The capacity to integrate individual and relational goals and to deal with conflict within relationships becomes essential. I have referred to this as "clarity in connection" (Jordan, 1987). An appreciation of relational responsibility and context does not impair our effectiveness in the world; rather, it can positively influence and support the direction that our creative and productive energies will take.

The capacity for clarity and for fully representing oneself in relationship, as well as the capacity to engage in conflict, is intrinsic to the relational development of women. Without these capacities, a woman might be in danger of what Westkott suggests would be the development of a false self or resubmersion in systems of patriarchal domination or male privilege. In fully embracing the importance of being able to move into conflict when necessary to represent one's needs and wants, in working toward real mutuality rather than a return to the role as keepers of the relationship, often to their own detriment, women are encouraged to seek real mutuality in all their close relationships, with friends, family, and partners. This means we are seeking profound change in the typical gendered patterns of relationship for both men and women. But we are not suggesting that women attempt this by adopting the predominantly male models of autonomy, self-sufficiency, personal entitlement, or centering on the self. We are suggesting that women follow the more relational paths, developing their competence in a way that does not lead to self-sacrifice or sacrifice of others.

As women have entered traditional male arenas in our society, enormous stresses have been involved. These systems are not attuned to relational issues but are concerned mainly with production and mastery and view the individual as directed primarily toward protection and enhancement of the separate self. These systems create conflicts in women whose very identity is bound up in relationship.

Clearly, what is needed is an integration of relationship, caring, and what has been called autonomous functioning. Women have been called on to act, think, and feel "like a man" when out "in the world" and to maintain traditional female norms "in the home." This assumes, again, a compartmentalization of functioning that is more characteristic of men's functioning than women's. It is a perpetuation of the tendency to make women conform to the male model. Thus, women have to bear the burden of adding the role of money earner or professional to that of nurturer and caregiver. But if, on top of the drain of emotional energy in trying to fill several demanding roles, the woman feels unable to make the transition back and forth between the two modes, she is left feeling inadequate in each. Again, the models do not take into account the special psychology of women. For a real integration to occur, both women and men must be given the opportunity to fully acknowledge, express, and value the relational mode as well as one typified by instrumental competence.

CONCLUSION

The relational model is not one of *self-development*; we suggest instead that all development is about *relational development*, a constant movement of energy and meaning between people, a deeply contextual experience of personhood. In this perspective the enhancement of relatedness may constitute a greater goal than individual gratification and ironically may lead to greater individual fulfillment (Jordan, 1987). Stated more strongly, perhaps the most basic human need is the need to participate in relationship. A relational, dialogic approach suggests that there is an integrative experience of being in and for the relationship. Both people contribute to and both are sustained by, grow in, and depend on the relationship. This does not diminish the significance of other lines of development (such as agency, initiative, or creativity), but these other capacities are developed for women in the context of important relationships and need to be redefined in a relational framework. In a relational model we have attempted to more accurately describe women's unique experience and thus to free women from prevailing models that pathologize and devalue a woman's way of being in the world. We seek to bring women out of the shame created by such denigration by the dominant culture, a shaming process that occurs frequently in regard to the experience of marginalized groups. By implying or directly stating that the other person's experience is deficient or less good, this process of active shaming leads to silence and disempowerment in the marginalized person. In viewing many previously devalued areas of relational attunement and engagement as skills and strengths, not just for women but for the whole culture, we hope to empower women. By thus focusing and building on women's specific strengths, we hope we can help construct clinical, educational, and social strategies for fostering women's (and ultimately all people's) development.

REFERENCES

Broverman, I., Broverman, D., Clarkson, F., Rosenkrantz, P., & Vogel, S. (1970). Sex role stereotype and clinical judgments of mental health. *Journal of Consulting and Counseling Psychology, 43,* 1–7.

Chodorow, N. (1978). *The reproduction of mothering: Psychoanalysis and the sociology of gender.* Berkeley: University of California Press.

Freud, S. (1920). Beyond the pleasure principle. *Standard Edition, 18* (1955). London: Hogarth Press, 3–64.

Gilligan, C. (1982). *In a different voice.* Cambridge: Harvard University Press.

Jordan, J. V. (1986). The meaning of mutuality. *Work in Progress, No. 23.* Wellesley, Mass.: Stone Center Working Paper Series.

———. (1987). Clarity in connection: Empathic knowing, desire and sexuality. *Work in Progress, No. 29.* Wellesley, Mass.: Stone Center Working Paper Series.

Jordan, J. V., Kaplan, A. G., Miller, J. B., Stiver, I. P., & Surrey, J. L. (1991). *Women's growth in connection.* New York: Guilford Press.

Jordan, J. V., & Surrey, J. (1986). The self-in-relation: Empathy and the mother-daughter relationship. In T. Bernay & D. Cantor (Eds.), *The psychology of today's woman: New psychoanalytic visions* (pp. 81–104). New York: Analytic Press.

Kohlberg, L., & Gilligan, C. (1971). The adolescent as a philosopher: The discovery of the self in a postconventional world. *Daedalus, 100,* 1051–1056.

Kohut, H. (1971). *The analysis of the self.* New York: International Universities Press.

Miller, J. B. (1976). *Toward a new psychology of women.* Boston: Beacon Press.

Miller, J. B. (1984). The development of women's sense of self. *Work in Progress, No. 22.* Wellesley, Mass.: Stone Center Working Paper Series.

Miller, J. B., Stiver, I. P., Judith, J. V., Surrey, J. L. (1995). The psychology of women: A relational approach. In J. Fadiman & R. Frager (Eds.), *Personality and personal growth* (pp. 159–179). New York: HarperCollins.

Sanday, P. R. (1988). The reproduction of patriarchy in feminist anthropology. In M. Gergen (Ed.), *Feminist thought and the structure of knowledge* (pp. 49–69). New York: New York University Press.

Shotter, J., & Logan, J. (1988). The pervasiveness of patriarchy: On finding a different voice. In M. Gergen (Ed.), *Feminist thought and the structure of knowledge* (pp. 69–87). New York: New York University Press.

Winnicott, D. W. (1971). *Playing and reality.* New York: Basic Books.

PART VIII

Social Change

Women's Behavior: Do Mothers Harm Their Children When They Work Outside the Home?

Each new report on the increasing number of working mothers touches off another round in the debate over whether this phenomenon has negative effects on children. A double standard is clear; it is rarely, if ever, charged that working fathers cause problems for their children. In a sense, this topic is just one chapter in the voluminous literature on the effects of mothering on infants and children. Even a glance at some of the publications on this subject indicates the narrow line mothers have to tread. On the one hand, they must avoid providing too little mothering, which could cause emotional damage to their children. But they also run the risk of overmothering or smothering their children. Mother-blaming continues to find favor with some writers. Hans Sebald (1976) views "momism" (Wylie, 1942) as America's "silent disease," and Charles Socarides (1995) traces the root cause of homosexuality to "smothering mothers" and "abdicating fathers."

The research of the late 1940s and early 1950s tended to focus on one side of the line: the effects of maternal deprivation. The work of René Spitz (1945) and John Bowlby (1951) called attention to the negative effects of the separation of infants from their mothers. Later psychoanalytic theorists, working from a different premise, similarly focused on the importance of early mothering in the lives of children. Paula Caplan and Ian Hall-McCorquodale (1985) characterized this research as "mother blaming." Essentially this means making mothers scapegoats for everything that can go wrong in parenting: "all psychopathology, from simple behavior problems to juvenile delinquency to schizophrenia itself " (Chess and Thomas, 1982, pp. 213–214). Subsequent studies pointed out that the Spitz and Bowlby data were collected during wartime from understaffed institutions where the lack of sensory and affective stimulation led to the orphans' problems (Hoffman, 1979).

In a sense, concern over the effects of mothers' absence on their children is ironic, because the current effort to reduce the welfare rolls involves encouraging mothers to go to work. In female-headed households with at least one related child under eighteen, 39 percent of White families and 71 percent of Black families fall below the poverty line (Rollins, 1996). For working women who have young children and who earn such low salaries, the real concern is finding adequate help rather than weighing the advantages and disadvantages of childcare. Many women of Color are forced to rely on family and friends, although one study showed that mothers receiving AFDC prefer group care or in-home babysitters to care by a relative outside the home (Sonenstein and Wolf, 1991).

A survey by McCartney and Phillips (1988) found that professional childcare did not harm the mother-child relationship. In fact, recent studies (Clarke-Stewart, 1989; Scarr and Eisenberg, 1993) have shown that children in daycare are more socially skilled than children cared for at home. Mounting evidence that there are few, if any, negative consequences of daycare (Silverstein, 1991) has not quieted what Scarr (1990) characterizes as the "fantasies" surrounding the role of mothers in infant development.

Despite some efforts to shift the research agenda toward documenting the need for high-quality and affordable childcare, the debate continues (Silverstein, 1991). Burton White, who believes that most children will get a better start in life if they are cared for by their parents or other family members, argues that "you need someone close at hand who has a kind of irrational love and commitment to the child, and it is difficult to find such people in substitute care" (quoted in Clark, 1993, p. 1109). Belsky and Eggebeen (1991) agree, declaring that children whose mothers were employed full-time beginning in the first or second year of their child's life were more poorly adjusted than children whose mothers were not employed during their first three years.

The issue of maternal employment is not just an academic question. The expertise of psychologists has been influential in shaping childcare policies. For example, Edward Zigler's testimony before Congress that employers should provide four months of parental leave to meet the developmental needs of infants played an important part in the passage of the Parental Leave Bill (Hyde, 1996). A survey revealed that half of the judges who participated in a 1989 study of the Massachusetts court system believed that women should be at home to greet children after school and that close to half of them were convinced that preschool-age children would probably suffer if their mothers worked outside the home. Such views can have far-reaching implications. In a recent Michigan case, a judge awarded custody to the former boyfriend of a young woman who had enrolled her daughter in daycare while she attended college. Although the young man's only previous involvement in childcare had been a $12-a-week child-support payment, the judge reasoned that he was the better parent because he lived with his mother, who had agreed to take care of the child (Clay, 1995).

Is Penelope Leach correct in asserting that mothers start out with an "irreplaceable bio-emotional advantage in relating to their infants" and that extended time in daycare is likely to damage a newborn's development? Or does the evidence support Diane Eyer's contention that infants and young children benefit from having several caregivers and that few differences exist between infants raised at home and infants receiving quality daycare?

REFERENCES

Belsky, J., & Eggebeen, D. (1991). Early and extensive maternal employment and young children's socioemotional development: Children of the National Longitudinal Survey of Youth. *Journal of Marriage and the Family, 53,* 1083–1110.

Bowlby, J. (1951). The nature of the child's tie to his mother. *International Journal of Psychoanalysis, 39,* 350–373.

Caplan, P. J., & Hall-McCorquodale, I. (1985). Mother blaming in major clinical journals. *American Journal of Orthopsychiatry, 55,* 345–353.

Chess, S., and Thomas, A. (Eds.)(1982). Infant bonding:

Mystique and reality. *American Journal of Orthopsychiatry 52*, 213–222.

Clark, C. S. (1993, December 17). Child care: The issues. *The CQ Researcher*, pp. 1107–1109, 1111–1115.

Clarke-Stewart, A. (1989). Infant day care: Malignant or maligned? *American Psychologist, 44*, 266–273.

Clay, R. (1995, December). Courts reshape the image of the good mother. *APA Monitor*, p 31.

Hoffman, L. W. (1979). Maternal employment, 1979. *American Psychologist, 34*, 859–865.

Hyde, J. (1996). *Half the human experience* (5th ed.). Lexington, Mass.: D. C. Heath.

McCartney, K., and Phillips, D. (1988). Motherhood and child care. In B. Birns and D. Hay, Eds., *Different faces of motherhood*, pp. 157–183. New York: Plenum Press.

Rollins, J. H. (1996). *Women's minds women's bodies: The psychology of women in a biosocial context.* Upper Saddle River, N.J.: Prentice Hall.

Scarr, S. (1990). Mother's proper place: Children's needs and women's rights. *Journal of Social Behavior and Personality, 5*, 507–515.

Scarr, S., & Eisenberg, M. (1993). Child care research: Issues, perspectives, and results. *Annual Review of Psychology, 44*, 613–644.

Sebald, H. (1976). *Momism: The silent disease of America.* Chicago: Nelson-Hall.

Silverstein, L. (1991). Transforming the debate about child care and maternal employment. *American Psychologist, 46*, 1025–1032.

Socarides, C. W. (1995). *Homosexuality: A freedom too far: A psychoanalyst answers 1,000 questions about causes and cures and the impact of the gay rights movement on American society.* Phoenix, Ariz. Adam Margrave Books.

Sonenstein, F. L., & Wolf, D. A. (1991). Satisfaction with childcare: Perspectives on welfare mothers. *Journal of Social Issues, 47*, 15–31.

Spitz, R. A. (1945). Hospitalism: An inquiry into the genesis of psychiatric conditions in early childhood. In R. S. Eissler (Ed.), *The psychoanalytic study of the child*, 1 (pp. 53–75). New York: International Universities Press.

White, Burton. (1993). Quoted in Child care: Should parents be more involved as caregivers? *CQ Researcher.* Washington, D.C.: Congressional Quarterly.

Wylie, P. (1942). *Generation of vipers.* New York: Farrar & Rinehart.

ADDITIONAL READING

Chehrazi, S. S. Ed. (1990). *Psychological issues in day care.* Washington, D.C.: American Psychiatric Press.

Clarke-Stewart, K. A., Gruber, C. P., & Fitzgerald, L. M. (1994). *Children at home and in day care.* Hillsdale, N.J.: Lawrence Erlbaum.

Karen, R. (1994). *Becoming attached: Unfolding the mystery of the infant-mother bond and its impact on later life.* New York: Warner Books.

Hooyman, N. R., & Gonyea, J. (1995). *Feminist perspectives on family care: Policies for gender justice.* Newbury Park, Calif.: Sage.

Hyde, J. S., & McKinley, N. M. (1993). Beliefs about the consequences of maternal employment for children: Psychometric analyses. *Psychology of Women Quarterly, 17*, 177–191.

Lamb, M. E., Sternberg, K. J., Hwang, C. P., & Broberg, A. G. (Eds.). (1992). *Child care in context: Cross-cultural perspectives.* Hillsdale, N.J.: Lawrence Erlbaum.

Silverstein, O., & Rashbaum, B. (1994). *The courage to raise good men.* New York: Viking.

Nurseries and Daycare Centers Do Not Meet Infant Needs

PENELOPE LEACH

Older babies and toddlers do not need their mothers every minute; the necessity for "full-time exclusive mothering" has been exposed as a myth of the postwar West. We know that having their care shared between parents and other adults is not damaging to children and in fact may be enriching; that shared care—albeit of many different kinds—has been the norm in every time and place and remains so in many. And we know that lack of people with whom to share childcare is a major problem in western maternity. Daycare *is* shared care, so why is it not ideal?

The answer comes from many other things we know about children—things that are being conveniently forgotten in the daycare debate. Perhaps the most important is that developmentally infants are *not* children and neither are toddlers—quite. The spiraling strands of development that transform helpless newborns into sociable and socialized small people are plaited into their relationships with known, loved, and loving adults. Those adults do not have to be parents or relations but, unfashionable and unpalatable though the fact may be, it is much easier if they are. Mothers start out with an irreplaceable bio-emotional advantage in relating to their infants, and fathers start out with a lesser one that still puts them ahead of any outsider. That does not make every natural mother or father a "good parent" nor handicap every infant raised otherwise, but it does stack the odds and should inform the debate. Whoever it is who

cares for infants must have permanence, continuity, passion, and a parentlike commitment that is difficult to find or meet outside the vested interests and social expectations of family roles and cannot be adequately replaced by professionalism.

WHY CONTINUOUS INDIVIDUAL CARE MATTERS TO BABIES

If a new baby wants to suck, she will suck your finger or her own, whichever is handiest. She does not know that she is separate from other people; she recognizes no boundaries between self and other.

The long, slow realization of her separate self starts early. The baby not only uses other people as extensions of herself, she uses them as mirrors of her own behavior. In her first days, for instance, she smiles and frowns more or less at random, but within a couple of months she smiles only when she is pleased and sociable and frowns only when she is not. It is the consistently pleased or concerned responses of adults that have taught her which is which.

Responsive and overtly affectionate adults are crucial to all aspects of infants' development. Every time a baby's very existence is celebrated with a spontaneous hug; every time her sounds, expressions, and body language are noticed and answered; every time somebody does something just because she seems to want or enjoy it, a tiny piece is added to the foundation of that baby's future self-image, self-confidence, and social competence. The more of that sensitive, tuned-in experience a baby gets (and the less of its opposite), the better. We cannot measure out "enough," but we know the likely consequences of strict rationing. After the Second World War, thousands of orphaned and refugee babies were kept in institutions where their care was physically excellent but wholly impersonal. Many of those babies failed to thrive; some died for reasons nobody could understand. The researchers of the day eventually concluded that those babies were suffering from "maternal deprivation," but while being with their mothers would certainly have saved them, it was not separation from their particular blood-mothers that removed their will to live but deprivation of individualized, responsive, sociable care. Western countries learned to avoid residential nurseries when they could and to organize differently those they had to have. But the same syndrome became apparent in 1990 when Romania's packed orphanages were revealed to the world. Impersonal residential care is the greatest risky situation but not the only one. Any personal indifference is damaging to infants, even that of a potentially loving mother who becomes so submerged in postnatal depression that it is all she can do to keep her baby fed and warm and clean and more than she can do to offer herself to him, respond to him, glory in him. An outside caregiver has less reason than a mother to celebrate an infant and therefore needs less cause to be indifferent to him. A nursery worker has less reason still to celebrate this infant because she has others to care for who may overload her or whom she may prefer. How well an infant thrives despite any of those situations probably depends on how much time he also spends with someone who cares not just *for* but *about* him. Three hours a day in an understaffed nursery where he is special to nobody is far from ideal for a newborn, but nine hours a day is far more likely to damage his development.

By about three months, infants realize that they are separate from the mothers and others on whom they are totally dependent, and then only sensitive and consistent responses can protect them from the lonely fear of being abandoned and from anxiety about their needs being met. If circumstances allow her to do so, a baby will now learn to recognize and distinguish all the people who regularly come and go within her small space, learn what responses to expect from each person and, gradually, learn how to evoke the responses she wants. A baby who expects particular people to respond to her particular signals in a particular way is confused and distressed when they do not. If a mother who has been smiling and chatting to her three-month-old baby suddenly becomes impassive and silent, the infant will quiet, sober, stare, and probably cry. It is not that the adult's silent, serious

face is frightening in itself (it certainly would not bother the baby if she were studying her mother as she watched television, for instance). What upsets that baby is her unexpected failure to manage and control the interaction and evoke a response. She reacts as we react if somebody cuts us in the street: as if the mother had snubbed her, hurting her feelings.

Many people dislike the notion of babies "managing" adults; it makes them sound manipulative and raises peculiarly western fears that they will become spoiled. But it is only by being allowed, even helped, to find reliable ways of controlling some aspects of adult behavior that a baby can build vital competence and confidence in her own powers of communication. Whether they are six or sixteen months old, most babies try to keep a beloved adult with them all the time, and while they are awake, many are successful. Once they fall asleep, though, they cannot prevent adults from leaving; like it or not, they usually wake up alone. If a baby is to accept that calmly—neither fighting to stay awake so as to prevent it nor panicking when she awakens—she needs to know, from repeated experience, that she can get a parent or accepted substitute (not someone unexpected or strange) back again with a cry or call. All babies are physically helpless, but the babies who *feel* damagingly helpless in the longer term are the ones who cannot trust their special adults to be there and to respond to them.

In the first half-year or so babies are seldom alarmed by strangers (though they may be alarmed by what strangers do). Introduced to an admiring male visitor, for example, a baby will usually try to interact with him as she does with her father. If she does not get the responses she expects she may be puzzled or obviously turned off, but as soon as she is handed back to familiar arms she will switch on again, and after a while she may willingly give the new person another try. That familiar interlude is vital. She can cope with a stranger for a while, but not with an unbroken succession of strangers. Each presents her with subtly different intonations, expressions, and body language, and without reconfirmation from someone she knows well, she gradually loses track of who she is. Handed from one stranger to another, a baby may even panic as an adult can panic in a fairground hall of mirrors, seeing a different distortion of himself wherever he turns. When a baby in his third hour in the temporary childcare facility set up at a conference, or third day in a daycare center, suddenly cries and cannot be comforted, he is usually assumed to be crying for loss of his mother; in truth he is more likely to be crying for loss of his own identity and control, vested in his mother and not yet assured by a sufficiently known worker.

Only adults who know, have known, and will go on knowing an individual baby can provide that vital sense of trust and growing empowerment. Even the best-intentioned and qualified stranger cannot do it because however much she knows about babies in general, she knows nothing about *this* one. The baby eats lunch; the caregiver goes to put her down for a nap but she cries. Training and experience suggest questions but not answers: Is she crying because she is tired and this is her idiosyncratic way through to the relaxation of sleep? Is she crying because she is not tired and therefore does not, today, want to nap? Or is she crying because some minute difference between the stranger and her accustomed caretaker—her smell, her tone, her arrangement of cuddly toys—has broken the usual progression from full belly to slumber? It does not hurt a baby to have to get to know someone new, especially if someone familiar can stay around while she does it. By tomorrow the stranger will seem less strange; if she is still there in a week or two she will be a known friend. But what if someone else is there tomorrow and someone else next week?

Even beloved adults cannot always understand a baby's messages. When they do understand them, they do not always choose to do or give what the baby wants. That's fine. Babies have to learn to communicate more and more clearly (and eventually to speak), and of course they cannot always have what they want. But adults who are tied to infants in reciprocal affection will always *try* to understand, and they will always answer, even if the answer is no. That is what matters; that is what assures infants that

they are real, individual people who can act upon other people, and that is the assurance that will keep them going forward. However carefully she is fed, washed, and protected, and however many mobiles are hung for her, a baby's overall care is not good enough to ensure her optimal development unless she is constantly with people who know her as an individual and who always have the time (and usually the inclination) to listen to and answer her, to cuddle and play, show and share. Those are the people to whom she will attach herself, and that attachment matters.

Every baby needs at least one special person to whom she can attach herself. It is through that first love relationship that she will learn about herself, other people, and the world, experience emotions and learn to cope with them, move through egocentric baby love into trust and eventually toward empathy and the altruism that will one day enable her to give to another person what she now needs for herself. She needs at least one person. More is better, safer. Babies do not have a quota of devotion: if there are several adults around and available to an infant, she will usually select one for her primary, passionate attachment (and, even today, that will probably be her mother), but all of them will be special to her and any one can serve as a life raft when the mother's absence would otherwise leave her drowning in a sea of despair. Every baby will sometimes need such a rescuer. The grieving of a baby who loses her one and only special person—her mother who dies, for example, or the lifelong foster mother from whom she is removed—is agonizing to see because we are looking at genuine tragedy. But the pain of the separations we arrange and connive at every time we change caregivers or leave a baby in the daycare center that has new staff—again—or with an agency babysitter she has never seen, may not be as different as we assume. In her first six, nine, or even twelve months, that baby has no way of knowing that the parent who leaves her will come back, no way of measuring the passage of time, no way of holding the parent's image in her mind so as to anticipate her or his return. Only another known and beloved adult can keep her happily afloat.

WHY NURSERIES AND DAYCARE CENTERS SELDOM MEET THOSE INFANT NEEDS

Vital continuous one-to-one attention can rarely be achieved in group care, however excellent the facility. Babies in their first year each need one primary adult, and while that may be inconvenient, it is not surprising. Human beings do not give birth to litters but almost always to single babies. Women can feed only two at a time (ask any mother of twins) and cannot singlehandedly care for more (ask any mother of triplets). No amount of "training" enables a nursery worker to do better. If one baby is sucking a bottle on her lap when another wakes from a nap and a third drops a toy from his high chair, she cannot respond adequately to them all. If one is unwell and one is tired, she cannot cuddle them both in a way that makes them feel she cares, let alone keep the third busy and safe. And that is three. How many daycare centers really offer a 1:3 adult-child ratio? A recent survey of eighteen British nurseries produced an average ratio of 1:4.6, and data from the comparative licensing study of American states showed that *recommended* ratios for infants ranged from 1:3 in three states to 1:8 in four states. And as all researchers acknowledge, even these figures may overestimate the adult attention available to each baby—as, for example, when two adults have charge of six infants, one will often stay with them while the other cleans up.[1]

In most countries, the majority of daycare centers for infants are not excellent. How could they be? The work is underpaid and undervalued, as well as demanding, so it neither attracts nor keeps high-quality staff. As a recent report to the European Commission put it: "Childcare workers . . . are amongst the lowest paid of women workers. . . .

The conditions of work are also often very poor. . . . Often the pressure of work is such that workers are too exhausted to even think about their work, let alone improve it."[2]

Although both parents and policy-makers assume that center care is professional care, this is seldom true for children under three. In this respect, the United Kingdom fares better than much of the European Community because it has a well-established diploma-level Nursery Nurses' qualification. In those eighteen British nurseries, only 20 percent of the staff lacked any formal training. In most EEC countries, however, it is rare for those who work in daycare centers with this age group to have childcare qualifications of any kind, and in many countries even the basic educational requirements for entry to the work are minimal. In the United States, where federal standards have been abolished and each state makes its own childcare regulations, the current situation is best summed up by the researchers who studied comparative licensing: "The possibility of having a 'qualified' staff is virtually non-existent. . . . In a majority of states, the existing regulations allow these very young children to be cared for by a staff that would have a mean age of 18, has not graduated from high school, and has no previous group day-care experience."

Although higher salaries are desperately needed and might help to attract higher-caliber staff (although they would also raise the costs of care), a real improvement in standards would also require training, better working conditions, and career opportunities. Unfortunately, every such concession to adult needs further reduces fulfillment of the children's. The daycare center's working day, for example, has to be longer than a full office day to allow for parental commuting. A staff's working hours can be reduced by splitting the day into two shifts, but that immediately doubles the number of people with whom infants must interact. As soon as nursery workers are also given proper lunch hours and breaks, sick leave, vacation entitlement,

1. On the British nurseries survey, see P. Moss and E. Melhuish, *Current Issues in Day Care for Young Children* (London: HMSO, 1991). The comparative licensing study of American states, carried out in 1982, is the subject of an interesting study of issues of quality in daycare centers. See K. Young and E. Zigler, "Infant and Toddler Day Care: Regulation and Policy Implications," in E. Zigler & M. Frank (Eds.), *The Parental Leave Crisis* (New Haven: Yale University Press, 1988), pp. 120–140.

2. Report of the European Childcare Network to the European Commission (1989), *Who Cares for Europe's Children?* (Public Document CB-55-89-738-EN-C), p. 25.

in-service training, educational leave, and encouragement to relocate for promotion, there is such constant staff movement that babies are likely to be handled by several different people each day and are unlikely to be handled by those same people all week: some will inevitably be strangers to some of the children, filling in for the known caregivers who are already filling in for parents. And still nursery workers leave. In North America the annual turnover of childcare staff is about 42 percent, and aides come and go even more frequently. It is not uncommon for a group of children to have three "mother figures" in a year. If each baby is not fully attached to each successive caregiver, she will spend many days in limbo; if she is fully attached she will spend many days in grief.

There Is No Evidence That Mothers Harm Their Infants and Toddlers by Working Outside the Home

DIANE E. EYER

Is there scientific evidence that mothers harm their infants and toddlers by working outside the home? In two words: absolutely not. Penelope Leach articulates quite clearly, however, what mothers have been told by expert advisors since the 1830s—mothers are the critical influence on their young children, and the virtuous mother enjoys remaining at home with her charges. The unique influence of the Victorian mother on her children was not an empirical discovery, of course, but rather the product of a social and an economic revolution. Prior to the 1830s, fatherhood in America was accorded all the character-forming importance we now attribute to motherhood. But the emphasis shifted when commerce and industry began to provide more paid work outside the home, where most of the production had formerly taken place. The Industrial Revolution created a conflict about who would mind the home and thereby forgo wages. The solution was to link work to gender identity: The "feminine" woman would now remain at home to become the angel of the hearth, an exemplar of Christian virtue for her children; she would be submissive, nurturing, kind and gentle, and devoted to domesticity. (Poor women, Black women, and Native American women were not in-vited onto the domestic pedestal.) The "masculine" man would be a public figure—independent, aggressive, and individualistic, the breadwinner for his family but no longer the primary mentor of his children.

This facet of our history is essential to understanding attachment theory. Attachment, popularized by John Bowlby in the 1950s, is thought to be based on an instinctual behavior that programs a child to stay close to its caregiver as a means of survival. Therefore, according to Bowlby, mothers must stay home with their children for the first three years of life while this psychobiological relationship is secured. In spite of the warnings of Bowlby and other attachment theorists, however, growing numbers of mothers began to work outside the home, and between 1960 and 1984, married women with children under six nearly tripled their participation in the labor force. Today, 62 percent of mothers are in the labor force (Bianchi, 1995). Psychologists, of course, were increasingly concerned about the psychological damage children would experience because of their mothers' violation of this natural law. In study after study they sought the negative effects of daycare on children who were increasingly leaving their mother's side to join other children in the homes of friends and relatives and in the growing number of professionally run daycare centers. Curiously, while psychologists lamented the damage that middle-class working mothers were doing to their children's attachment and related cognitive functions, they enthusiastically promoted daycare for poor children. Poor children were to be provided with a preschool experience thought to be so positive that it would propel them out of poverty. The Head Start program, launched in 1965, taught cognitive and social skills to children and instructed their mothers on how to tutor their children. The assumption was that these mothers, by virtue of their poverty, were incompetent to teach their own children unaided. Ironically, one cannot help but notice that since the average salary of a Head Start teacher was below the poverty level, the teachers themselves should have been ruled incompetent as well![1]

More than two decades of looking for the "effects of maternal employment" on children have yet to turn up evidence of damage to attachment. In fact, the one consistent, if accidental, finding is that the happiest children tend to be those of mothers who work at jobs they love. The next happiest are likely to be children whose mothers stay home and love doing so (Otto and Atkinson, 1994; Hoffman, 1984; Jackson, 1993). The effect of maternal happiness on women's families, however, is never the subject of research.

The search for damage continues, however. Dozens of studies of "home-reared" versus "childcare-reared" children rest on the assumption that separation from their mothers interrupts young children's attachment process and that childcare-reared children will be less secure. Researchers began these studies in the 1970s, when many children started attending daycare. The mothers and children studied were mostly middle-class, and the children attended quality daycare centers. There are many differences that show up when children who attend daycare are compared with those who do not. Some research finds increased aggression in children who attend daycare, though the aggression seems to be related to aspects of the daycare setting rather than to the interruption of attachment. Some research finds that these children are less cooperative with adults, though many researchers interpret this behavior as independence. Others find accelerated social and intellectual development, though this tends to level off as children enter school. Children of working mothers are found to demonstrate higher cognitive abilities and school achievement, to have more respect for the wide range of women's abilities, and to show more independence. It is impossible to draw sound conclusions about any of these findings because it is not clear to what these differences are attributable.

For example, many of the differences could be due to the fact that certain kinds of families, who already differ from each other in important ways, select certain kinds of care based on those preexisting differences.

As no clear evidence of damage could be found, was maternal employment declared safe? Hardly. The search continued, and the scope of research expanded to include more average-quality daycare than was previously studied and a variety of aspects of the care. Infants and toddlers became the new focus of the damage search, as little injury to the psyches of preschoolers could be unearthed. In 1986, psychologist Jay Belsky declared that infants under twenty-four months who experience more than twenty hours per week of daycare are at risk for insecure attachment to their mothers and greater aggressiveness and noncompliance in early childhood. Although Belsky's findings caused quite a stir, a number of critics cast doubt on his findings. For example, they found the differences between the two groups of daycare and home care infants to be even smaller than Belsky claimed. They also believed that the label of insecure "avoidant" attachment for daycare infants was instead a child's independence.[2]

<hr/>

1. In 1989, the average teacher's salary was $12,074; 47 percent were paid below $10,000. Valery Polokow, *Lives on the edge: Single mothers and their children in the other America.* Chicago: University of Chicago Press, 1993, p. 120. Teacher's aides, of course, were paid even less.

2. Among the problems with Belsky's study is his contention that the infants who experienced daycare showed significantly more insecure-avoidant ("bad") attachment than infants kept at home with their mothers. But in fact there were just about what is considered a normal percentage of attachment types among the infants who attended daycare. However, because Belsky compared them with a group that had a higher than average percentage of "securely" attached children, the discrepancy between the secure and the insecure in the two groups looked bigger. More important, however, was the interpretation of the meaning of insecure-avoidant attachment, which some researchers contended could simply be evidence of independence and familiarity with encountering strangers. Jay Belsky, "Infant day care: A cause for concern?" *Zero to Three* 6: 1–7 (1986). Also see Jay Belsky, "The 'effects' of day care reconsidered," *Early Childhood Research Quarterly* 3:235–72, John Richters and Carolyn Zahn-Waxler, "The infant day care controversy: Current status and future directions," *Early Childhood Research Quarterly* 3 (1988): 319–36, and K. Alison Clarke-Stewart, "Infant day care: Maligned or malignant," *American Psychologist*, February 1989, 266–73.

Parenting advisors ignore the many studies showing that working mothers spend close to the same amount of time with their children as stay-at-home mothers. The differences are only a few hours a week. Moreover, perfectly competent fathers, other relatives, and professional caregivers are engaged in looking after the children in their mother's place. Why the insistence on exclusive maternal care? Can such care really be best for children? How can Penelope Leach counsel fathers of infants to stay in the background while their wives go it alone?

Leach rests her belief on decades of attachment theory and long-established research. The grain of truth around which attachment theory is built is an important one: infants are social creatures who require consistent and loving care. This verity might have passed for common sense in other eras. But in the early part of the twentieth century the increasing use of institutions to care for infants created situations that tested principles of infant care. Unfortunately, the policies invented by professional (male) experts soon proved detrimental to infant health. Infants' emotional needs were therefore eventually rediscovered, if not reinvented, and the discovery contributed to the development of attachment theory.

By the 1940s, researchers in England and America began to notice that their institutional policies were damaging children's health. In the United States, René Spitz and Katherine Wolf (1946) studied infants in nurseries and discovered what they called anaclitic depression. At about six months, infants who did not see their mothers and were cared for by a rotating staff began to develop weepy behavior. After twelve months they simply withdrew their interest in humans and exhibited very sad expressions. They were depressed for lack of a loving consistent caretaker and began to waste away and even to die, according to Spitz, of greater susceptibility to disease. Spitz and Wolf filmed these infants, and their expressions are absolutely haunting. But their own data showed that these infants actually had as many as *fifty* different caretakers in their first eighteen months of life and that they often lay in their cribs all day long with no human attention. There were even covers on the sides of their cribs, presumably so the infants would not disturb one another and make a commotion requiring the attention of the scarce staff. These infants were deprived not only of love but of stimulation. Moreover, most of the infants actually died of a measles epidemic. Yet the cause of their suffering and even death was said to be *maternal* deprivation.

On the other side of the Atlantic, John Bowlby, John Robertson, and other researchers were studying children in hospitals where parental visits were generally discouraged lest the frequent separations make the children unmanageable. The children's negative reactions to being separated from their parents was seen as evidence of their being spoiled. But instead of compensating with nursing care that emphasized consistency, nurses were switched frequently to prevent a child from becoming too attached lest the final separation from them also prove traumatic. But Bowlby and Robertson showed it was the very separation from parents that was causing these children such distress.

The maternal deprivation studies resulted in the reform of these institutions. But they were also used to bolster the rationale for stay-at-home mothering at a time when many middle-class women had tasted the fruits of paid work during World War II. In 1951, Bowlby published *Maternal Care and Mental Health*, a study of war orphans that became a bestseller. Bowlby found the orphans to be generally retarded in their development and to have a variety of emotional problems, all of which he said stemmed from maternal deprivation. Curiously, it does not seem to have occurred to Bowlby that many of the orphans he studied had been through a devastating war and had lost both parents, their homes, and most of the life that had provided them with security. Maternal deprivation was the good doctor's diagnosis, and nobody noticed the rest. In fact, maternal deprivation, Bowlby claimed, going far beyond his data on orphans, could even take place in the seemingly normal home. "Full-time employment of [a] mother," he insisted, "is on a par with the death of a parent, imprisonment of a parent, war, famine," and so forth (p. 73). Moreover, children could suffer maternal

deprivation at home from a variety of maternal failures. For instance, a mother who has "an unconsciously rejecting attitude underlying a loving one"
or who did not "enjoy being at home with her children 365 days a year" would also cause maternal
deprivation (pp. 11,12). Bad mothers were the
cause of children's suffering, and only good mothers could save them, according to Bowlby.

Belief in the almighty power of maternal deprivation was facilitated by the popular theories of Sig-
mund Freud, who said that the proper sex role for
women rested on the desire to be a wife and
mother. Any wavering from this goal was seen as
penis envy—a desire to be masculine rather than
feminine. And penis envy, of course, was a sign of
neurosis, the twentieth-century equivalent of sin.
Neurotic mothers would create neurotic children.
Freud's theory, of course, was a philosophy based
on his clinical practice. It was left to others to attempt to scientifically test the theory.[3]

Bowlby was soon pressed to substantiate his
claims about maternal deprivation—which at first
rested rather loosely on Freudian theory—with empirical evidence. He claimed to have found it in the
laboratory of Harry Harlow (1958) at the University of Wisconsin. Harlow had accidentally discovered that infant monkeys—which he had isolated
for months to keep them free of disease for experi-

ments in learning—had become socially abnormal
as a result of their isolation. Lacking a monkey
caretaker, they emerged frightened and socially bizarre, rocking back and forth, hugging and even
biting themselves, and unable to mate. Those monkeys, which were deprived of *all* animal contact,
were of course said to be suffering from *maternal*
deprivation. Harlow also experimented to see
whether infant monkeys learned to love their mothers, as Freudian theory postulated, because mothers reduced their hunger drive by feeding them. In
a series of experiments examining "motherlove" he
built wire mesh dummies with crude plastic faces
to act as surrogate mothers. In one of these experiments one dummy held a milk-dispensing baby
bottle but provided no tactile comfort; the other
provided no milk but was covered with terry cloth.
When Harlow then frightened the babies, those
"raised by" the wire mesh mother clutched themselves, rocked back and forth, and threw themselves on the floor. When a terry cloth dummy was
available they clung to it. These behaviors were
later said to illustrate the infant's need for an attachment figure and the dire consequences of maternal employment. (Why no mother has thought
to go off to work leaving a terry cloth dummy in
her place is still a mystery!)

Harlow's experiments pointed a new direction
for Bowlby: the analogy of animal behavior,
which eventually became the foundation for attachment theory. In the 1950s, Bowlby began to
develop his theory of attachment, which he
defined as a warm, continuous relationship with a
loving mother or mother substitute. This bond,
formed in infancy, would be the foundation on
which all of the child's other relationships would
be formed. Several researchers, including Mary
Ainsworth (1967; Ainsworth et al., 1978), a former student of Bowlby's, began to identify types
of proximity-promoting signals in infants, such as
crying, cooing, gazing, following, and so forth,
and their mother's responses that take place during the first three years of life and could be said
to constitute this attachment process. Ainsworth
found three types of attachment: secure (about
two-thirds of infants), insecure, and unattached

3. While Freud's assertion about penis envy may sound
preposterous, it rests on his complex theory of child development. He postulates universal age-related developmental
tasks in childhood that, depending on how they are negotiated, determine the adult character. Children whose oral impulses are thwarted in infancy, for instance, are likely to become dependent and addictive personalities in adulthood. As
the sexual impulses of preschool children become predominant, failure to direct and manage these biological urges will
likely cause them to become sexually frigid or impotent or
even homosexual in adulthood. Children's prime love object
at this stage is a parent. A girl must therefore convert her sexual impulse to possess her father (and his penis) by identifying with her mother's essential characteristic—her reproductive capacity. In adulthood, in fact, her sexual fulfillment will
come from childbirth. Women who do not want to have children are unfeminine, unattractive, and neurotic because they
identified with the (owner of) the penis instead of the womb.
Women who find fulfillment in work are male identified,
too, and are therefore candidates for the couch.

(later changed to avoidant), which she saw as related to the level of sensitivity and responsiveness in the mother.

In Scotland, Schaffer and Emerson (1964) found that at about seven months of age infants begin to prefer the company of one person; in 65 percent of cases they prefer their mother, in 5 percent of cases they prefer their father, and in 30 percent, someone else. (Since Ainsworth studied only mothers one cannot help but wonder whether 35 percent of her subjects were primarily attached to someone else and whether that third corresponded to the insecure group or portions of the secure group. Alas, no one thought to ask.)

Of course, simply describing developmentally consistent behaviors was not sufficient to make a case for the primacy of the maternal relationship, so Bowlby turned to ethology and found that imprinting in birds provided, to his mind, an evolutionary imperative for attachment. Konrad Lorenz (1950, 1952) and others had observed that there is a critical period during the first few days of the life of some birds when they attach themselves to their mother, responding to species-specific cues. Once they have responded to this attachment figure, they thereafter follow only it; they are imprinted. Moreover, this early imprinting has implications for later adult behavior. A jackdaw that had attached to Lorenz in infancy later courted him in adulthood, dropping worms on his hat and trying to put them in his mouth and ears in a courting gesture. This behavior was taken as evidence that strong infant attachment provided the emotional bedrock on which adult relationships were founded (Bowlby, 1969). (Why no one interpreted this data to mean that a strong early attachment promotes incest is yet another mystery!)

Psychologists assume that attachment is good because it has helped us to survive, and they have been careful to prescribe good mothering behaviors that they say promote attachment. But baby animals can imprint on inanimate objects (Styrofoam objects, cloth and wire surrogates, bouncing balls, television sets, and so forth). These objects can hardly be assessed for their sensitivity and appropriateness of response to the infant's needs, yet animals attach to them. Moreover, a behavior that was adaptive in one environment might not be so in a contemporary one. Earlier in our evolution it is likely that families remained in close proximity throughout an individual's life, rather than spreading over the planet as they are increasingly doing. Close and long-lasting family bonds were probably essential for survival then, but different conditions prevail today. For these reasons, any suggestion that a particular type of relationship is to be preferred over another because it is "natural" is suspect.

While Bowlby and Ainsworth did not study fathers, a few of their followers did. There was a brief flurry of studies in the late 1970s and early 1980s comparing father attachment to mother attachment. Fathers, apparently, can do it as well as mothers. Moreover, infants often have attachments to both parents, and these can differ in type from one parent to the other. Interestingly, though, fathers' working does not interfere with attachment because fathers' strong emotional investment, according to the research, "suffuses" their interactions and communicates a special caring to the infant. Curiously, no suffusion of care has been identified in mothers whose guilt about working might be eased by such a discovery. More than 90 percent of attachment studies focus on mothers. Although minute variations in maternal attachment are said to account for a variety of aspects of child development, there are virtually no studies connecting father attachment to later child behaviors or personality factors (Silverstein, 1991).

The belief in the importance of exclusive maternal attachment was so strong in the academic and pediatric professions that a virtual army of researchers turned out thousands of attachment studies. The primary yardstick by which attachment was measured was created by Ainsworth. She designed a Strange Situation Test (SST) that determines the quality of attachment by assessing the degree to which an infant uses his mother as a secure base from which to explore and play, and the degree to which an infant seeks comfort in the mother when distressed.[4] This test has been the prime psychological index used in comparisons of children whose mothers work or stay at home. Curiously, Ainsworth's own subjects were not working mothers, and yet only two-thirds had a secure attachment. (So far, no one has suggested that a well-trained child nurse be substituted for the third of mothers who fail to make it into the secure attachment category—in attachment logic a bad mother is better than a good caregiver.)

There is growing agreement even among attachment researchers that the SST is not a valid measure (Eyer, 1996). The test has now been used all over the world, and the proportion of "secure" and "insecure" infants changes with each culture. It could be that the Strange Situation Test is just measuring a child's reaction to stress. Some researchers believe that the behavior Ainsworth calls insecure-avoidant is actually autonomous or independent. Perhaps the child, on reunion with his mother, doesn't need to be held by her. It is also possible that an "avoidant" infant could really be just a placid, friendly baby. Moreover, a "secure" baby could really be dependent and even spoiled. Also, when researchers observe infants in their own homes, they find that sensitive mothering (hardly an objective concept) does not necessarily predict a secure rating in the laboratory test. And when family circumstances change, so does behavior in the SST.

Another fundamental problem with the Strange Situation Test is that it doesn't take into account the infant's own characteristics. Some babies are good-natured and easygoing, others may be sick or cranky, shy or extroverted, stubborn or compliant, and all these factors are going to affect interaction with caretakers, who also have different personalities. A very expressive and active caretaker might overwhelm an infant with a low tolerance for stimulation, and few caretakers can do "well" with a very irritable baby. Moreover, the balance between exploring the world and maintaining safe contact is maintained in a rich and subtle variety of ways by different parent-child pairs. This notion of dividing children into those whose relationships are insecure or secure reflects a clinical concern, a need to identify those who are doing well emotionally and those who are not. Yet the test does not appear to register even severe pathologies. For example, autistic children, who are virtually unable to form or manifest loving relationships, do not differ from normal children in their Strange Situation behavior. What is reflected in the SST is probably just a normal range of human behaviors (Sigman and Ungerer, 1984).

Not surprisingly, the attempt to actually predict later behavior from the quality of the early attachment has largely failed because it is impossible to disentangle attachment from more general factors, such as intelligence, quality of schooling, talent, income, family harmony, and luck. Some studies that followed infants into later childhood have found consistency between early attachment and later child development, but it appears that the consistency is the product of the child's innate characteristics combined with an emotional environment that changes very little from year to year. Early secure attachment does not even predict later attachment, let alone all the global characteristics said to be associated with attachment (Lamb et al. 1985).

When attachment researchers admit into study caretakers other than the mother, it becomes clear that maternal attachment is hardly the only index of children's emotional security. In fact, research continues to show that infants and toddlers prefer their mothers only about 60 percent of the time and often continue to like several people at once. Infants clearly develop attachments with close friends and family as well as paid caregivers. In fact, some research suggests that infants with a dis-

---

4. Babies and mothers are observed in a laboratory in several episodes over twenty minutes: first the mother and baby are together and the baby plays alone; then a stranger joins them; then the mother leaves unobtrusively, returns a few minutes later and settles the baby; she and the stranger leave—this time saying goodbye; then the mother returns. It is assumed that the strange place and person will upset the baby, who will seek security in the mother. If the baby seeks comfort in the mother when she returns, he is securely attached. If he avoids her or is ambivalent about the reunion, then he is insecurely attached. M. Ainsworth, M. Blehar, E. Waters, and S. Wall, *Patterns of attachment: A psychological study of the strange situation* (Hillsdale, N.J. Erlbaum, 1978).

turbed or very unhappy parent thrive with a close attachment to a paid caregiver.

Attachment is not an adequate framework for understanding the developmental significance of parent-child relationships. Security is just one dimension of such relationships. They also differ in mutual warmth and mutual expression of affection; in frequency of conflict; in shared involvement in daily activities; in shared communication about feelings; in shared humor; in the ability to sustain a line of communication; and in the pattern of power and control.

One of the appeals of attachment theory is the simplicity of the idea. It is a concept that everyone can readily grasp: put two people together and you have a relationship. It's a kind of social Velcro. Everyone can visualize attachment. The notion that these processes are instant and automatic adds to their appeal; at least there is one area of life, the relationship of mothers and children, that is secure and predictable.

Unfortunately, the alleged beneficiaries of this attachment paradigm—children—are in fact the victims of it. The countless studies searching for negative effects of nonmaternal care obscure the real childcare needs of the modern family. After all, one of the prime factors promoting good mental health for women and consequently their children is reliable, affordable childcare. With so many mothers of young children in the labor force, you might think that psychologists would finally turn their attention to the real causes of inadequate caregiving, such as poorly paid caregivers, familial poverty, and lack of knowledge about child behavior, but they seem to be fixated on the wonders of biological motherhood.

It's unfortunate that child-raising experts like Penelope Leach, who champion public policy that supports families, are still mired in the hearth angel ideology and its twentieth-century incarnation in attachment theory. Their warnings about nonmaternal care can only increase the confusion and guilt that working mothers experience and lend credence to a research paradigm that deserves none.

REFERENCES

Ainsworth, M. 1967. *Infancy in Uganda: Infant care and the growth of attachment.* Baltimore: Johns Hopkins University Press.

Bianchi, Suzanne. 1995. The changing demographic and socioeconomic characteristics of single-parent families. In *Single-parent families: Diversities, myths, and realities.* S. Hanson et al. (eds.), *Marriage and Family Review* 20: 1–2. New York: Hayworth Press, 1995, pp. 71–97.

Bowlby, John. 1951. *Maternal care and mental health.* 2nd ed. Geneva: World Health Organization, Monograph Series no. 2.

Bowlby, John. 1969. *Attachment.* New York: Basic Books.

Eyer, Diane. 1996. *Motherguilt: How our culture blames mothers for what's wrong with society.* New York: Times Books/Random House, chap. 3.

Hoffman, Lois. 1984. Maternal employment and the child. In M. Perlmutter (ed.), *Parent-child interaction.* Hillsdale, N.J.: Erlbaum.

Jackson, Aurora. 1993. Black, single working mothers in poverty. *Social Work* 38, 1:26–38.

Lamb, Michael, et al. 1985. *Infant-mother attachment: The origins and developmental significance of individual differences in strange-situation behavior.* Hillsdale, N.J.: Erlbaum.

Lorenz, Konrad. 1950. The comparative method in studying innate behavior patterns. In *Physiological mechanisms of animal behavior, symposia of the Society of Experimental Biology in Great Britain,* no. 4. Cambridge: Cambridge University Press.

Lorenz, Konrad. 1952. *King Solomon's ring.* London: Methuen.

Otto, L., and Atkinson, M. 1994. Feedback: Maternal employment . . . A reanalysis and comment. *Journal of Marriage and the Family* 56:501–10.

Schaffer, H., and P. Emerson. 1964. The development of social attachments in infancy. Monographs of the Society for Research in Child Development 29, 3: 1–77.

Sigman, M., and Ungerer, J. 1984. Attachment behaviors in autistic children. *Journal of Autism and Developmental Disorders* 14:231–44.

Silverstein, Louise. 1991. Transforming the debate about child care and maternal employment. *American Psychologist,* October, 1025–32.

Spitz, René, and Wolf, Katherine. 1946. Anaclytic depression. *Psychoanalytic Study of the Child* 2:313–14.

Men's Behavior: Is the Mythopoetic Men's Movement Creating New Obstacles for Women?

Freud once asked, "What do women want?" The question might be asked today of men. The questions are, in fact, interrelated. As stereotypes of women's roles began to crumble in the face of the feminist movement, men were compelled to contemplate the possibility of change in their own attitudes and behavior. It has not been easy. As Terry Kupers notes, men have difficulty discussing what they feel or what they hope to gain from therapy, other than relief of their symptoms. Women, on the other hand, do not have as much trouble "since they share a common oppression" (1995a, p. 2).

This is not the first time in history that men have perceived a threat to their traditional role. Women's success in gaining entrance into previously all-male schools in the nineteenth century, for example, stimulated a new literature on masculinity including W. J. Hunter's *Manhood Wrecked and Rescued* (1900). As the U. S. commissioner of education put it in a 1905 report on coeducation: "The boy in America is not being brought up to punch another boy's head, or to stand having his own punched in a healthy and proper manner. . . . There is a strange and indefinable air coming over the men; a tendency toward a common . . . sexless tone of thought" (Records, 1905, p. 7). One of the best-known efforts to reverse the feared decline in manliness was the creation of the Boy Scout movement in 1910, originally designed to save America's young men from the debilitating influence of mothers, teachers, and female classmates.

Changes in men's situation are, of course, the result of more than modifications of women's conventional roles. Both men and women have been affected by a number of social problems in recent years, including rising job insecurity and declining middle-class wages. Men have reacted to these changes in a number of different, sometimes contradictory ways, ranging from the formation of pro-feminist men's groups to participation in various attempts to restore patriarchal values.

The new psychology of men seeks to improve male-female communication while studying the "gender-role strain" that many men experience (Pollack & Levant, 1995). The concept of gender-role strain stems from the pioneering work of Joseph Pleck (1981, 1995), who argued that males experience anxiety because their gender roles are so contradictory and inconsistent. For example, men are expected to be independent and competitive at work and caring and cooperative at home. Failure to fulfill male role expectations can lead to "low self-esteem and other negative consequences" (Pleck, 1995, p. 12). Just as men in the dominant culture must examine the role expectations that bind them, men of Color must do the same from within their own cultural paradigm (Lazur & Majors, 1995). Meanwhile, other psychologists are exploring the "dark side of masculine role socialization" (Brooks & Silverstein, 1995, p. 281) in order to deal with such problems as violence against women and sexual harassment.

Some men, on the other hand, have labeled any criticism of men's traditional roles as male-bashing. Warren Farrell, for example, argues that feminists have ignored the man who has "seen his marriage become alimony payments, his home become his wife's home, and his children become child-support payments" (1994, p. 26). The solution for men and women, according to the Promise Keepers, a conservative religious organization that has sponsored mass rallies of men across the country, is a return to the days when men were the acknowledged heads of their households (Kupers, 1995a).

More difficult to categorize is the mythopoetic movement, inspired by the best seller *Iron John: A Book About Men* (1990), in which Robert Bly uses a Grimm brothers' tale to argue that men have lost touch with their maleness. Echoing the 1905 commissioner of education's report, Bly discusses men who have gone "soft" and who lack energy. "You often see them," he notes, "with strong women who positively radiate energy" (pp. 2–3). A major problem, he argues, is that changes stemming from the Industrial Revolution have deprived society of the initiation ritual that turns boys into men. Each generation since the mid-nineteenth century has experienced a decrease in the emotional bonding of father and son. Not only are sons unable to learn about masculinity from their mothers, they grow up seeing their fathers through their mother's eyes. As a result, the son often grows up with a "wounded image of his father" (p. 24).

The goal of the mythopoetic men's movement is to heal that wound by helping men get in touch with their true masculine nature through a variety of methods, including therapy sessions, weekend retreats, initiation rites, drumming, and chanting. Even some of the movement's critics see a positive side to it. "Forget the hokey ritualism," says Michael Kimmel. "These are real feelings pouring out" (1995, p. 370). Helping men to get over their anger and disappointment in their fathers can also be a positive step (Kupers, 1995b).

But much of the mythopoetic movement has come in for criticism rather than praise. One group of feminists devoted an entire book to Bly, faulting him for, among other things, mother-blaming and failing to realize that men's inner wounds result from the power system of patriarchy (Hagan, 1992). A number of pro-feminist men agree. Part of the problem, Kupers writes, is that by urging men to get in touch with their male essence, Bly ends up stigmatizing qualities that society desperately needs, some of which are "popularly held to be feminine, such as the capacity to nurture and care about the fate of others [and] to work cooperatively with others instead of always competing" (1995b, p. 226). To Michael Kimmel, a movement whose sole aim seems to be making men feel better about themselves sounds a lot like "sexism with a happy face" (1995, p. 371).

Nevertheless, many men have resonated to Bly's message. Marvin Allen believes that women can also benefit from men meeting separately for the purpose of changing themselves. Michael S. Kimmel and Michael Kaufman disagree, however. They argue that any realistic agenda for changing gender relations must go beyond therapeutic exercises, getting in touch with one's feelings, or going off to the forest to beat drums with the guys.

REFERENCES

Bly, R. (1990). *Iron John: A book about men.* Reading, Mass.: Addison-Wesley.

Brooks, G. R., & Silverstein, L. B. (1995). Understanding the dark side of masculinity: An interactive systems model. In R. F. Levant & W. S. Pollack (Eds.), *A new psychology of men* (pp. 280–333). New York: Basic Books.

Farrell, W. (1994). *The myth of male power.* New York: Simon & Schuster.

Hagan, K. L. (Ed.). (1992). *Women respond to the men's movement.* San Francisco: HarperCollins.

Hunter, W. J. (1900). *Manhood wrecked and rescued: How strength or vigor is lost, and how it may be restored by self-treatment.* New York: Health Culture.

Kimmel, M. S. (1995). Afterword. In M. S. Kimmel (Ed.), *The politics of manhood: Profeminist men respond to the mythopoetic men's movement (and the mythopoetic leaders answer)* (pp. 362–374). Philadelphia: Temple University Press.

Kupers, T. A. (1995a, December). What do men want? *Readings: A Journal of Reviews and Commentary in Mental Health,* pp. 2–5.

Kupers, T. A. (1995b). Soft males and mama's boys: A critique of Bly. In M. S. Kimmel (Ed.), *The politics of manhood: Profeminist men respond to the mythopoetic men's movement (and the mythopoetic leaders answer)* (pp. 222–230). Philadelphia: Temple University Press.

Lazur, R. F., & Majors, R. (1995). Men of color: Ethnocultural variations of male gender role strain. In R. Levant & W. S. Pollack (Eds.), *A new psychology of men* (pp. 337–358). New York: Basic Books.

Pleck, J. H. (1981). *The myth of masculinity.* Cambridge, Mass.: MIT Press.

Pleck, J. H. (1995). The gender role strain paradigm: An update. In R. F. Levant & W. S. Pollack (Eds.), *A new psychology of men* (pp. 11–32). New York: Basic Books.

Pollack, W. S., & Levant, R. F. (1995). Coda: A new psychology of men: Where have we been? Where are we going? In R. F. Levant & W. S. Pollack (Eds.), *A new psychology of men* (pp. 383–387). New York: Basic Books.

Records of the Commissioner of Education. (1905).

ADDITIONAL READING

Betcher, W., & Pollack, W. S. (1993). *In a time of fallen heroes: The re-creation of masculinity.* New York: Atheneum.

Gerson, K. (1993). *No man's land: Men's changing commitments to family and work.* New York: Basic Books.

Kimbrell, A. (1995). *The masculine mystique: The politics of masculinity.* New York: Ballantine.

Kimmel, M. (1996). *Manhood in America: A cultural history.* New York: Free Press.

Kupers, T. A. (1993). *Revisioning men's lives.* New York: Guilford Press.

Levant, R. F., with Kopecky, G. (1995). *Masculinity reconstructed: Changing the rules of manhood—At work, in relationships and in family life.* New York: Dutton.

Rotundo, E. A. (1993). *American manhood: Transformations in masculinity from the revolution to the modern era.* New York: Basic Books.

Wetherell, M., & Griffin, C. (1995). Feminist psychology and the study of men and masculinity: Assumptions and perspectives. In M. Blair, J. Holland, and S. Sheldon (Eds.), *Identity and diversity: Gender and the experience of education* (pp. 81–103). Bristol, Pa.: Open University.

We've Come a Long Way, Too, Baby. And We've Still Got a Ways to Go. So Give Us a Break!

MARVIN ALLEN

I find it distressing that feminism and the media have given such rapt attention to the enigmatic, mythological aspects of the men's movement while ignoring the more grounded and psychologically efficacious elements. A movement rich with diversity, leaders, and goals has been, in the eyes of the media and feminism, reduced to a cult of white-collar drum bangers with visions of kings, warriors, and wild, hairy men dancing in their heads. According to countless newspaper and magazine articles, these seekers of the "deep masculine" were followers of the poet Robert Bly. Whatever Bly said, whether it made sense or not, suddenly became the voice of the men's movement. If Bly came across as a bigot or sexist, then the men's movement was bigoted or sexist. If Bly was a closet patriarch, then *his* movement was a clandestine attempt by threatened men to win back all the power and virility they had lost to the women's movement. Why didn't they pay more attention to such well-balanced and apparently emotionally healthy leaders as Aaron Kipnis (*Knights Without Armor*), Bill Kauth (*A Circle of Men*), or Sam Keen (*Fire in the Belly*)? Other men's leaders like Herb Goldberg (*The Hazards of Being Male*), Warren Farrell (*The Myth of Male Power*), and Asa Baber (*Naked at Gender Gap*) also have some salient, if controversial, ideas to offer the men and women of this country. Without diversity in leadership, a move-

ment gets top-heavy and extremely vulnerable to criticism—much as a thousand acres of corn can be devastated by a single type of bug. By creating an easy target like Bly as *the* leader, and by focusing on only the sensational or unusual elements of men's gatherings, the media was able to discredit and dismantle much of the men's movement in short order.

Most of the 20 percent of American people who have even heard of the men's movement actually believe that the whole thing is about a bunch of White middle-aged middle-class men in the woods dancing around in animal skins, drumming wildly, hugging each other, primal screaming, and whining about their lot in life. Yes, there are drums and dancing and some screaming in many of the outdoor gatherings for men. But that's only a small part of what goes on.

For instance, the Wildman Gatherings I designed and continue to facilitate with my friend and colleague Dick Prosapio are weekend retreats dedicated not only to helping men become more emotionally aware and alive, but also to assisting them in becoming more available, more nurturing husbands, fathers, and friends. Yes, we use certain Native American ceremonies that we believe will help White middle-class Americans become more connected with the beauty and the spirit of Earth. To develop a passion for our planet is one of the goals of the weekend. And, yes, we sing a Native American chant, but we also sing "Amazing Grace." Too bad the media and the feminists couldn't hear the glorious sound of "America the Beautiful" sung by a hundred men, their voices rising up through the pines and into a crisp, starlit night in the mountains of Nevada.

And what of the White middle-class men who are whining about their unfair lot in life? What's that all about? Is it possible that for the first time in their lives many of these men are facing the fact that, as impressionable little boys, they were hurt by an unrealistic masculine code that made a shambles of their natural feelings and pushed them into a robotlike existence? Is it possible that these same men, who seem so cool and collected on the outside, have been hiding the fact that they were deeply hurt by neglectful, emotionally unavailable, or even abusive mothers and dads? And is it whining to finally give vent to all that buried pain, grief, and rage? Is it really so weird to want to be liberated from all those troubling feelings and belief systems that have driven us into aggressive competition, workaholism, alcoholism, perfectionism, passivity, or raging? Is it so strange to want to seek comfort and validation from other men who have endured the same masculine conditioning process and many of the same experiences as we have? Isn't this, after all, what it's all about? Trying to become more emotionally healthy, balanced men? Are we supposed to be able to transform ourselves by just deciding to pull ourselves up by our bootstraps? Or by going to Sunday school? Or in a Saturday afternoon chat with our wife or lover? Is it possible that working in groups of men may be the most effective and efficient way for males to break out of their emotional armor, defensiveness, and isolation?

It seems ironic that some feminists (by the way, I consider myself a feminist who wants to see true equality and fairness between the sexes) complain bitterly about what jerks men are and yet they also complain when men get together to try to change themselves. It seems that men need some time and space to understand what has happened to them; to see the relevance that their personal history has in their present-day lives; to realize that certain ways they have of thinking, feeling, and behaving may be harmful to themselves or their loved ones; to take responsibility for what they've done and are doing; and, finally, to get whatever help is necessary to create positive change in their lives. I know of no better way for the average male to achieve these goals than to be in the company of other like-minded, nonblaming men.

You see, men have come a long way, too, baby. And a significant part of our journey has been through hell in this twentieth century. First there was World War I, then World War II, then the Korean War, the Cold War, the Vietnam War, the Persian Gulf War, and several "skirmishes." Remember, too, that during most of the century

men who didn't volunteer were forced to fight the wars or go to prison, or, at the very least, were considered cowards. To be effective and efficient in these wars and in earning a living, males had to be "toughened up" by parents, schools, churches, media, and the military. As they grew into adulthood, these males were expected to display characteristics of leadership, independence, toughness, courage, responsibility, and quiet stoicism. These traits became synonymous with manliness and played a major role in keeping our country free and our standard of living high. Traditionally, men from other cultures around the world have been conditioned in similar ways.

Unfortunately, however, while millions of American men have had the traditional masculine traits drilled into their heads and hearts, they've been taught very little about the traditional "feminine" ways of being. Without the feminine—I prefer to call them human—qualities of patience, vulnerability, gentleness, compassion, and empathy, these men are destined to become emotionally unbalanced. Millions of American boys continue to be emotionally stunted in this way before they reach their eighteenth birthdays. Many of these boys who didn't get enough good parenting will try to compensate for their low self-esteem and insecurities by following the rules of manhood in an exaggerated fashion.

Thus, under such circumstances, "Be stoic and don't let your feelings get in the way of positive action" becomes "Don't ever cry or show your vulnerable emotions, no matter what." "Be strong enough to get the job done and don't give up too soon" becomes "Don't ever be weak, don't compromise, and never give up." "Be brave" becomes "Don't ever be scared, but if you are, never let anyone know." "Be capable of leading when necessary" becomes "Prove your manliness by controlling and dominating those around you." "Be a responsible provider" becomes "Prove your worth to bosses, coworkers, and wives by pleasing them and achieving at all costs."

After working with thousands of males in the United States, I am convinced that a significant number of men have been so influenced by one or more of these exaggerated masculine rules that their ability to enjoy meaningful relationships or even life itself has been deeply diminished. Although following the manly code may have paved the way for success in business, sports, or war, the toll on their wives, their children, their friends, their planet, and themselves has been unacceptable.

Millions of American men spend a lot more time trying to prove themselves than they do celebrating themselves. They spend more time feeling numb, anxious, or angry than they do feeling joyful. To make matters worse, many of these men just go through the motions in their relationships. Because they can't be vulnerable and haven't developed the necessary communication skills, they are often unable to experience the deep inner satisfaction that should come from intimate relationships with wives, children, and friends. Instead, they may find themselves outside the loop in their own families, spending much of their lives trying to cope with soul-wrenching isolation and loneliness.

Emotionally unbalanced men fall prey to very "unmasculine" feelings of inadequacy, anxiety, depression, and dependency. To avoid or cope with these painful and embarrassing emotions, millions of men have turned to such manly solutions as excess work, alcohol, TV sports, food, sexual compulsions, and even aggression and violence. Unfortunately, these "solutions" not only don't work, they also create more problems. I believe that divorce, addictions, wife battering, child abuse, suicide, and crime could all be reduced by 75 percent or more if men could just become a little more emotionally balanced. Although men who use violence against their wives and children must be stopped and prosecuted to the full extent of the law, we must realize that incarceration alone will not heal these men's problems. They need help in the form of effective and appropriate counseling and treatment. Otherwise, they will just serve the sentence and then repeat the crimes.

There are millions of emotionally unbalanced men who would never rape or physically batter but who are excessively critical, controlling, and emotionally abusive to their wives and children. In mil-lions of other men, emotional imbalance takes the form of sulking, stony silence, and passivity.

These maladies must be addressed if our families and communities are to flourish. As a nation, we must understand that the vast majority of American men are good-hearted, well-intentioned people who, as a group, are reflecting both the positive and the negative effects of traditional masculine conditioning. If we are to replace sexism, racism, and violence with mutual respect, dignity, and equality, surely the first step must include a new masculinity that demands emotional honesty, wholeness, and balance. This new masculinity must also recognize that excellence in relationships is every bit as manly a trait as excellence in business, sports, or war. To do this, men and women must work together in fresh, nonblaming ways to raise awareness and to encourage dialogue that fosters understanding and compassion. To help them develop healthier ways of thinking, feeling, and behaving, men must be encouraged and supported to get the assistance they need from counselors, men's groups, classes, books, and friends. Finally, we must find the wisdom and courage to raise our sons to be the well-balanced, emotionally healthy men that our creator intended them to be.

So for God's sake, let's support the elements of the men's movement that foster true growth and development. Why not take the energy that's being spent fighting Bly and use it to support the practical, psychologically sound aspects of the men's movement? The truth is, that part of the men's movement that smacks of patriarchy or lacks substance and groundedness will go down the drain without much intervention. In fact, if you listen closely you may hear a giant sucking sound right now!

REFERENCES

Baber, Asa. (1992). *Naked at the gender gap: A man's view of the war between the sexes.* New York: Birch Lane Press.
Farrell, Warren. (1993). *The myth of male power: Why men are the disposable sex.* New York: Simon & Schuster.
Goldberg, Herb. (1977). *The hazards of being male: Surviving the myth of masculine privilege.* Bergenfield, N.J.: New American Library.

Kauth, Bill. (1992). *A circle of men: The original manual for men's support groups*. New York: St. Martin's Press.

Keen, Sam. (1991). *Fire in the belly: On being a man*. New York: Bantam.

Kipnis, Aaron. (1991). *Knights without armor: A practical guide for men in the quest of masculine soul*. Los Angeles: Jeremy P. Tarcher.

Weekend Warriors:
The New Men's Movement

MICHAEL S. KIMMEL AND

MICHAEL KAUFMAN

Held up as the end-all of organization leadership, the skills of human relations easily tempt the new administrator into the practice of a tyranny more subtle and more pervasive than that which he means to supplant. No one wants to see the old authoritarian return, but at least it could be said of him that what he wanted primarily from you was your sweat. The new man wants your soul.

—William H. Whyte, *The Organization Man*

Across the United States and Canada, men have been gathering in search of their manhood. Inspired and led by poet Robert Bly, the *éminence grise* of this new men's movement—and whose book, *Iron John*, topped the bestseller lists for more than thirty-five weeks in 1991—dozens of therapists and "mythopoetic" journeymen currently offer workshops, retreats, and seminars to facilitate their "gender journey," to "heal their father wounds" so that they may retrieve the "inner king," the "warrior within," or the "wildman."[1] And hundreds of thousands of men have heeded the call of the wildman, embraced this new masculinity, and become weekend warriors.

1. Robert Bly, *Iron John* (Reading, Mass.: Addison-Wesley, 1990).

The movement has certainly come in for its share of ridicule and derision. Countless magazine articles and newspaper stories and even several TV sitcoms have portrayed the movement as nothing more than a bunch of White upper-middle-class professionals chanting and dancing around bonfires, imitating Native American rituals, and bonding. Recently, feminist women have indicated their suspicions that this men's movement is patriarchy with a New Age face, a critique that is explicitly political. To date, the new men's movement has received virtually no serious analytic scrutiny from men. This essay is an attempt to make sense of that movement, to subject the new men's movement to serious analysis.

Like any other social movement, the new men's movement can best be examined through a set of analytic frames, each designed to illuminate a specific part of the movement. Through an analysis of the major texts of the movement, as well as through participant observation at several men's retreats, we will attempt to make sense of this phenomenon. Specifically, we will want to pose four sets of questions:

1. *Historical and political context.* What specific historical conditions have given rise to this new men's movement? What does the movement have to do with the women's movement? Why now?

2. *Social composition.* To what specific groups of men does this new men's movement appeal? Why these men? What is the class, racial, and ethnic composition of these weekend retreats?

3. *Ideology of masculinity.* What is the vision of social change that the new men's movement embraces? From what sources do participants derive their vision? What is their diagnosis of the causes of malaise among contemporary men?

4. *Organizational dynamics.* What are the organizational vehicles by which the men's movement will accomplish its aims? What does the evocation of ritual, chanting, drumming, and initiation mean in the context of the movement?

By exploring these four aspects of the mythopoetic men's movement, we will be able to assess the consequences of the movement, both for men and women individually and for the larger framework of other movements for social change. In talking about this men's movement, we see it as distinct from the pro-feminist men's movement, even though at least some of the men attracted to Robert Bly also consider themselves pro-feminist. It's also distinct from the self-consciously anti-feminist and misogynist men's rights movement although, again, some other mythopoetic men wander into this camp.

THE MEN'S MOVEMENT AND THE REAL WORLD

CONTEXTS AND COMPOSITION

The first two dimensions of the new men's movement can be fairly briefly summarized. In the past two decades masculinity has been increasingly seen as in "crisis," a widespread confusion over the meaning of manhood. (Much of this discussion applies specifically to the United States and Canada, although there are some points of contact with Australia and western Europe.) From the earliest whines of "men's liberation" in the mid-1970s to the current "Great American Wimp Hunt" and the preoccupation with the diets and fashion tastes of "Real Men," questions of the definitions of masculinity have been contested. That men are confused over the meaning of masculinity has become a media cliché, and hundreds of advice books and magazine columns today advise men on gender issues.

The contemporary crisis of masculinity has structural origins in changing global geopolitical and economic relations, and in the changing dynamics and complexion of the workplace. Our traditional definitions of masculinity had rested on economic autonomy: control over one's labor, control over the product of that labor, and manly self-reliance in the workplace. The public arena, the space in which men habitually had demonstrated and proved their manhood, was racially and sexually homogenous, a homosocial world in which straight White men could be themselves, without fear of the "other." Economic autonomy, coupled with public patriarchy, gave men a secure sense of themselves as men. And if they should fail, they could always head out for the frontier, to the boundaries of civilization, where they could stake a new claim for manhood against the forces of nature.

That world is now gone. The transformation of the workplace—increased factory mechanization, increased bureaucratization of office work—means that fewer and fewer men experience anything resembling autonomy in their work. This century has witnessed a steady erosion of economic autonomy; from 90 percent of U.S. men who owned their own shop or farm at the time of the Civil War to less than 1 out of 10 today. The continental frontier was declared closed at the turn of the century, and since that time we have invented a succession of frontiers to take its place—from the Third World to outer space (the "final frontier") to the corporate "jungle." The current global restructuring finds many former outposts on that frontier demanding inclusion into the economy; decolonization and movements for regional or ethnic autonomy destabilize American hegemony.

Perhaps nothing has had a larger cultural impact in this crisis of masculinity than the recent rise of the women's movement, and also the gay and lesbian movement. By the late 1960s, the civil rights movement had already challenged the dominant view that the public arena and the workplace were virtually preserves for Whites. With the rise of the women's movement, there was a challenge to older and even more fundamental beliefs about men's place in society. Old certainties and gender divisions were challenged, a process augmented by the gay and lesbian movement, which challenged the heterosexual assumptions of those old gender arrangements.

Although these economic, political, and social changes have affected all different groups of men in radically different ways, perhaps the hardest hit *psychologically* were middle-class straight White men from their late twenties through their forties. For these were the men who not only inherited a prescription for manhood that included economic autonomy, public patriarchy, and the frontier safety valve, they were also men who believed themselves *entitled* to the power that attended upon the successful demonstration of masculinity. These men experienced workplace transformation as a threat to their manhood, and the entry of the formerly excluded "others" as a virtual invasion of their privileged space.

As a result, many middle-class White middle-aged heterosexual men — among the most privileged groups in the history of the world — do not experience themselves as powerful. Ironically, although these men are everywhere in power, that aggregate power of that group does not translate into an individual sense of feeling empowered. In fact, this group feels quite powerless. Entitled to partake in the traditional power of masculinity, these men feel besieged by new forces outside of their control, and somewhat at a loss as they observe the women in their lives changing dramatically while they feel increasingly helpless.

It should come as no surprise, then, to observe that the overwhelming majority of the men who are currently involved in the new men's movement are precisely middle-class, middle-aged, White, and heterosexual. The men who feel most besieged, and who have the resources with which to combat that siege, are the most frequent weekend warriors. Attendance of men of Color ranged, over a variety of retreats and conferences in various parts of the United States that we attended, from zero to less than 2 percent, while never greater than 5 percent of the attendees were homosexual men. The majority of the men are between forty and fifty-five, with about 10 percent over sixty and about 5 percent younger than thirty. Professional, white-collar, and managerial levels were present in far greater proportion than blue-collar and working-class men, in part because the expense of the weekend retreats (usually $200 to $500 for a weekend) or the day-long seminars ($50 to $200) makes the retrieval of deep manhood a journey open only to the economically privileged.

The men's movement is the cry of anguish of privileged American men, men who feel lost in a world in which the ideologies of individualism and manly virtue are out of sync with the realities of urban, industrialized, secular society. It retells the tales of overdominant mothers and absent fathers who have betrayed the young boy and deprived him of his inheritance of a sense of personal power. The men's movement taps a longing for the lost innocence of childhood; it is a cry for certainty about the

meaning of manhood in a society where both men's power and rigid gender definitions are being challenged by feminism. These themes, trumpeted by Bly and his followers, link up with the experiences of predominately White heterosexual middle-class and middle-aged readers who have made his book and the movement which surrounds it such a success. Movement leaders speak directly and with compassion to men's uneasiness and discomfort: eloquently to their grief about their relationships with their fathers, to their despair over their relationships with women, to their pain and sense of powerlessness and isolation. What exactly does the men's movement say? What is its diagnosis of the masculine dilemma?

THE SEARCH FOR THE DEEP MASCULINE

The men's movement has many different voices, drawing on many different traditions. Some rely entirely on Greek and Roman mythologies for images of heroic manhood; others use Jungian archetypes or Eastern religions as the foundation for new visions of masculinity. But certain themes are constantly sounded, especially essentialist assumptions about gender distinctions, a contemporary diagnosis of feminization of American manhood, the search for lost fathers (and father figures), and a vision of retrieval of heroic archetypes as models for men. Bly's argument rests on the fusion of (1) a psychological analysis of Jungian archetypes, in which a retelling of fairy tales and myths serve as illustrations; (2) a historical interpretation of the progress of industrialization and modernization on men's lives; (3) an anthropological survey of nonindustrial cultures and their rituals of initiating men into society and providing secure identities for adult men. These are sandwiched between a political critique of contemporary men and a vision for the future of manhood that reclaims lost rituals and grounds men's identities more securely. Since *Iron John*, based on an explication of a Grimm fairy tale, is the touchstone of the men's movement, we can explicate its ideology by deconstructing its seminal text. The fable goes as follows:

> Once upon a time, a hunter volunteers to go into the woods and find out why the King had

lost several of his men. The hunter returned with a Wild Man, who had lived at the bottom of a lake, and had apparently been devouring the others. The King put the Wild Man in a cage in the courtyard. One day, the King's eight year old son was playing near the cage with a ball. The ball rolled into the cage. To get it back, the Wild Man made the boy promise to get the key to his cage and free him. The key was under the boy's mother's pillow. The boy stole the key from under his mother's pillow and opened the cage. The Wild Man walked off into the woods with the boy. (They have set each other free.)

In the woods with Iron John, the boy fails to follow Iron John's instructions, so he is sent off to work, first as a cook's apprentice, later as a gardener. Here, he meets the daughter of the king. He goes off to war, proving himself in battle, although he doesn't take credit for it. At a postbellum festival, he catches three golden apples tossed by the king's daughter in a competition, but the boy rides off in a different suit of armor after catching each one. Eventually, he is brought before the king and asks for the girl's hand in marriage. The big wedding celebration is suddenly interrupted by the entrance of a great King, who walks up to the young man and embraces him. "I am Iron John, who through an enchantment became turned into a Wild Man. You have freed me from that enchantment. All the treasure that I won will from now on belong to you."

Bly uses the Iron John fable to several ends—to suggest manhood as a quest, to heal the split between the dutiful son and the Wild Man, to imply that the son's healing of his own wounds will simultaneously heal the father's wounds, to suggest the possibilities of manly nurture and initiation of men by other men, and, most centrally, to launch his critique of contemporary men.

THE NEW MAN AS WIMP

The mythopoetic men's movement agrees that something is dramatically wrong with American manhood. "The male of the past twenty years has become more thoughtful, more gentle. But by this process he has not become more free. He's a nice boy who pleases not only his mother but also the young woman he is living with," Bly writes (p. 2). The evidence of feminization is abundant; in an earlier essay Bly notes that "the percentage of adult sons still living at home has increased; and we can see much other evidence of the difficulty the male feels in breaking with the mother: the guilt often felt toward the mother; the constant attempt, usually unconscious, to be a nice boy; lack of male friends; absorption in boyish flirtation with women; attempts to carry women's pain, and be their comforters; efforts to change a wife into a mother; abandonment of discipline for 'softness' and 'gentleness'; a general confusion about maleness."[2] The new man is incapable of standing up to women, so eager is he to please. "If his wife or girlfriend, furious, shouts that he is 'chauvinist,' a 'sexist,' a 'man,' he doesn't fight back, but just takes it" (p. 63). In short, the new man turns out to be a wimp; he is the problem, not the solution, and manhood needs to be rescued from such sensitive Mama's boys.

The men's movement assumes a deep, essential manhood, and its retrieval is the solution. Manhood is seen as a deeply seated essence, an ingrained quality awaiting activation in the social world. Intrinsic to every man, manhood is transhistorical and culturally universal. "The structure at the bottom of the male psyche is still as firm as it was twenty thousand years ago," observes Bly, while Moore and Gillette claim that the deep elements of manhood have "remained largely unchanged for millions of years."[3] And it is the exact opposite of the essence of woman: "Male and female make up one pair. . . . One can feel the resonance between opposites in flamenco dancing. Defender and attacker watch each other, attractor and refuser, woman and man, red and red. Each is

2. Robert Bly, "What Men Really Want," in *New Age Journal* (May 1982): 31–51.

3. Robert Moore and Douglas Gillette, *The King Within: Accessing the King in the Male Psyche* (New York: William Morrow, 1992), 49; Bly, *Iron John*, p. 230.

a pole with its separate magnetic charge, each is a nation defending its borders, each is a warrior enjoying the heat of extravagant passion, a distinguished passion which is fierce, eaglelike, mysterious" (Bly, pp. 174–75).

Though masculinity is seen as an inner essence diametrically opposed to femininity, individual men do not inherit manhood through their biological composition. Manhood must be achieved. And it must be validated by other men; women cannot validate manhood. "It takes work to become a man," write Moore and Gillette (1992, p. 234). "Achieving adult male status requires personal courage and the support and nurturing of older men." It is the task of the larger society to facilitate this achievement, because when the actualization of manhood is thwarted, dire consequences result. "If a culture does not deal with the warrior energy . . . it will turn up outside in the form of street gangs, wife beating, drug violence, brutality to children, and aimless murder" (p. 179)—all of which sounds remarkably similar to the words of right-wing ideologue George Gilder.[4] The route to manhood is perilous, but the consequences of failure are far worse.

What then are the appropriate stages of manhood, the stages that each man should follow if he is to activate his deep, essential masculinity? In sum, there are four stages of manhood, each with an accompanying scholarly and mythical apparatus to facilitate its passage: (1) bonding with the mother and breaking away from her (psychological level); (2) bonding with the father and breaking away from him (historical critique of modernity); (3) finding the male mother (anthropological reclamation of initiation ritual); (4) the reentry into adult heterosexual union (reproduction of heterosexuality, gender roles). Each of these is central to the mythopoetic vision.

BAD DEALS FROM MOMS AND DADS

The men's movement embraces a traditional, and rather conservative, rendering of psychoanalytic

4. George Gilder, *Naked Nomads* (New York: Quadrangle, 1974).

theory. The task of becoming men requires a break from our initial identification with the mother. In today's world this isn't simple; men's repudiation of the feminine is thwarted. More than one man "today needs a sword to cut his adult soul away from his mother-bound soul" (Bly, 1990, p. 165). There are two reasons why men have not broken the bond with mother. First, mothers won't let them, remaining locked in somewhat incestuous flirtations with their sons. (This is why the young boy must steal the key from under his mother's pillow—she will not voluntarily give it, and thus him, up.) Second, fathers are not there to facilitate the transfer of identity. Separation from the mother is traditionally facilitated by father, who provides a role model for his son and presents to him an alternative to femininity. But, sadly, men are not doing their job as fathers. It's not entirely men's fault but rather a consequence of modern society. Here, the men's movement adopts a somewhat mythic history of the Industrial Revolution and its consequences for male development.

If we state it as another fairy tale, this myth goes something like this: Once upon a time, the division of labor was fully gendered, but both father and mother remained closely bound to the home and children. Fathers were intimately involved with the development of their sons. As artisans, they brought their sons to their workplace as apprentices; the sons had an intimate appreciation for the work of the father. But the Industrial Revolution changed all that; the separation of spheres imprisoned women in the home, as feminists have long argued, and it exiled men from the home (a fact curiously absent from feminist analysis, Bly seems to think). Now fathers are nowhere to be found in the lives of their sons. The "love unit most damaged by the Industrial Revolution has been the father-son bond," writes Bly (1990, p. 19). This, mythopoets label the "father wound."

The consequences of the father wound are significant, including adolescent male rebellion. "The son does not bond with the father, then, but on the contrary a magnetic repulsion takes place, for by secret processes the father becomes associated in the son's mind with demonic energy, cold

evil, Nazis, concentration camp guards, evil capital-
ists, agents of the CIA, powers of world conspiracy.
Some of the fear felt in the '60s by young leftist
men ('never trust anyone over 30') came from that
well of demons" (Bly, 1982, p. 45). The consequences also include feminism, since father absence "may severely damage the daughter's ability
to participate good-heartedly in later relationships
with men. Much of the rage that some women direct to the patriarchy stems from a vast disappointment over this lack of teaching from their own
fathers" (Bly, 1990, p. 97). Another consequence is
feminist-inspired male bashing. "The emphasis
placed in recent decades on the inadequacy of men,
and the evil of the patriarchal system, encourages
mothers to discount grown men. . . . Between
twenty and thirty percent of American boys now
live in a house with no father present, and the demons have full permission to rage" (pp. 86, 96).
(The reader is left to figure out exactly which demons those might be.)

The absence of the father leaves a void in the
center of every adult man, a psychic wound that
yearns for closure. Without healing the father
wound, men are left only with mother, left literally
with women teaching them how to become men.
But, Bly and his followers argue, only men can really teach men to be authentic men, validate masculinity, and provide a male with a secure sense that
he has arrived at manhood.

MASCULINITY AS PRAXIS

Fortunately, the men's movement has discovered
such a mechanism, developed in nonindustrial cultures over thousands of years, that can substitute
for the absent father and provide the young male
with a secure grounding in gender identity. It is
the male initiation ritual, symbolically reproduced
by thousands of weekend warriors across the nation, men who flock to male-only retreats to tell
stories, beat drums, and re-create initiation rituals
from other cultures. These nonindustrial cultures
are seen as providing a mechanism for young
boys to successfully pass through an arduous rite,
at the end of which they are secure in manhood.

It is never again a question. There is no "man
problem."

In each case, initiation centers around separation
from the world of women and rebirth into the world
of adult men. This is achieved in spatially separate
men's huts or retreats, and during specific tempo-
rally demarcated periods. Like baptism, there is symbolic death of the boy (the profane self, the self born
of woman) and rebirth. Bly recalls one Australian culture in which the adult men construct a twenty- to
thirty-foot-long tunnel of sticks and bushes, and
push the young boys through, only to receive them
with much ceremony at the other end, having now
been reborn "out of the male body" (1982, p. 47). Or
the Kikiyu, who take young boys who are hungry after a day-long fast and sit them down by a fire in the
evening. Each adult male cuts his arm and lets the
blood flow into a gourd which is passed to the young
boys to drink "so that they can see and taste the depth
of the older males' love for them." This represents a
shift from "female milk to male blood" (p. 47).

The purpose of the initiation has a long theoretical legacy. Mircea Eliade argued that initiation "is
equivalent to a revelation of the sacred, of death, of
sexuality, and of the struggle for food. Only after
having acquired these dimensions of human experience does one become truly a man." And sociologist Max Weber commented on the consistency of
these ritual structures in his epic *Economy and Society*. "He who does not pass the heroic trials of the
warrior's training remains a 'woman' just as he
who cannot be awakened to the supernatural remains a 'layman,' " he wrote.[5]

At the conclusion of the initiation ritual, the
young male is socially a man. He has been prepared psychically by separation from mother and
identification with father, and sociologically by
leaving the individual father and becoming one of
the band of brothers. Now he is ready to reconnect
with woman in spiritual and sexual union, seeking
joyous connection, not neurotic demonstration of

---

5. Mircea Eliade, *The Sacred and the Profane* (Chicago:
University of Chicago Press, 1962), 73. Max Weber, *Economy
and Society*, 2 vols. (Berkeley: University of California Press,
1978), 1144.

manhood nor narcissistic self-pleasuring. He is
ready for marriage.

Thus, the spiritual quest for authentic and
deep manhood reproduces traditional norms of
masculinity and femininity, of heterosexuality,
and, in our culture, monogamous marriage; in
short, the men's movement retrieval of mythic
manhood reproduces the entire political package
that Gayle Rubin called the "sex-gender system."[6]
In the present, as in the mythical past, the demonstration of manhood becomes associated with a re-
lentless repudiation of the feminine. Since, in our
era, the father's absence makes this separation
difficult, weekend retreats offer an emotional substitute for real fathers. At these retreats men can
heal their father wound—the grief men feel that
their fathers were not emotionally or physically
present in their lives. They can feel a sense of intimacy and connectedness to other wounded and
searching men. They can discover the depths of
their manhood. This is the movement's promise
for masculine renewal.

FALSE PROMISES

It is a false promise. In this section of this essay, we
will develop a broad-based critique of the mythopoetic men's movement, bringing to bear a variety of
social scientific literatures to understand the limitations of each phase of the men's movement's promise. We will discuss (1) the limitations of
essentialism; (2) the psychoanalytic misdiagnosis;
(3) the anthropological context of male bonding;
(4) and the sociology of regression. We will conclude with an analysis of the value of the feminist
critique of masculinity as a blueprint for men's
transformation.

THE CONSTRUCTION OF ESSENTIALISM

The central assumption in the mythopoetic vision
is an ontological essential difference between

6. Gayle Rubin, "The Traffic in Women," in *Toward an
Anthropology of Women*, ed. Rayna R. Reiter (New York:
Monthly Review Press, 1974).

women and men. For all theorists of the movement, the male-female difference is not socially
constructed and does not vary cross-culturally.
Whether based on Jungian archetypes or bowdler-
ized readings of Eastern religions, or the selection
of myths and fairy tales, the men's movement
claims that men and women are virtually different
species. The mythopoetic search for the "deep masculine" and the psychically "hairy man" is a search
for something that exists as a natural, biological reality. Moore and Gillette claim that the central elements of manhood are the "hard wired
components of our genetically transmitted psychic
machine"—without a hint of awareness of how
gendered and mechanistic is their language (p. 33).

The men's movement, therefore, misses one of
the central insights of social science—that gender is
a product of human action and interaction, that
our definitions of masculinity and femininity are
the products of social discourse and social struggle.
Being a man is distinct from being biologically
male. Essentialism leads the men's movement to
adopt a version of manhood that corresponds
rather neatly with our society's dominant conception of masculinity—man as warrior and con-
queror—and to suggest that this represents the
quintessence of manhood. Thus Moore and Gillette venerate Ronald Reagan's courage during the
hostage crisis and vilify Jimmy Carter as a wimp:
"Emblematic of his weak thinking was his absurd
attempt to dramatize energy conservation by not
lighting the national Christmas tree, an ancient
symbol of eternal life and ongoing vigor. Of more
consequence was his impotent reaction to the Iran
hostage crisis" (p. 167). That this definition of masculinity rests on men's gender power does not have
to enter into the equation—rather, the mythopoetic warrior's quest is to rediscover his masculine
core and experience a bond with his psychic ances-
tors.

HEALING THE MOTHER WOUND

These essentialist assumptions lead Bly and others
to an inversion of feminist psychoanalytic insights
of the past three decades. Following Chodorow,

Dinnerstein, Rubin, Benjamin, and others,[7] we think that the core psychological problem of gender formation for men is, in a sense, not too little separation from mother but too much. In societies where men do little parenting, both young boys and girls have a primary identification with mother. However, the establishment of a boy's identity and his individuality is a psychic process in which the boy struggles to renounce identification with mother and the nurturing she represents, and embrace identification with father. It is a process with enormous costs. "Boys come to define themselves," writes Chodorow, "as more separate and distinct, with a greater sense of rigid ego boundaries and differentiation. The basic feminine sense of self is connected to the world, the basic masculine sense of self is separate" (pp. 174, 169). Such a process has political ramifications: "Dependency on his mother, attachment to her, and identification with her represent that which is not masculine; a boy must reject dependence and deny attachment and identification. Masculine gender role training becomes more rigid than feminine. A boy represses those qualities he takes to be feminine inside himself, and rejects and devalues women and whatever he considers to be feminine in the social world" (Chodorow, p. 181).

Manhood is defined as a flight from femininity and its attendant emotional elements, particularly compassion, nurturance, affection, and dependence. This does not mean that men completely lose these capacities. Rather it means that these things become more or less muted and often experienced as inimical to male power. Though the definition of manhood varies by class and culture, by era and orientation, our hegemonic definitions of masculinity are based on independence, aggression, competition, and the capacity to control and dominate.[8]

This helps to explain men's rage at women, men's rage at their own dependency and weaknesses, and the rage of so many men at gay men (whom they misperceive as failed men).

As a result, most men are afraid of behavior or attitudes that even hint at the feminine. So many men are willing, even eager, to engage in all manner of high-risk behavior, lest they be branded wimps or tainted with the innuendo that they might be homosexual. The whole quest for masculinity is a lifelong set of high-risk behaviors. The costs to men may be on a different level than the costs to women—for example, violence or rape—but men's lived experience involves considerable alienation and pain. Men remain emotionally distant, aggressively risk-taking, preoccupied with power, status, money, accumulating sexual partners, because these are all badges of manhood. We call this obsessive flight from the feminine the "mother wound." Through the mother wound the boy internalizes the categories of gender power of a patriarchal society. The social project of suppressing women and their social power is internalized and unconsciously recreated in the psychic life of the young boy.

The men's movement claims that the root psychological problem for men is that we have not yet cut our psychic umbilical cord. By contrast, we see the problem as the opposite: the relentlessness by which we consciously and unconsciously demonstrate that the cord has been cut. From this difference comes the men's movement's prescription for retrieving manhood: to wrench men away from the home, off to the woods with other men, into a homosocial space where men can validate one another's masculinity. It's a feel-good response, but it does little to address the roots of the problem of either a father wound or a mother wound. Men breaking down their isolation and fears of one another is important, but to get to the core of the problem requires men to play a role in domestic life through equal and shared parenting. Boys would experience men as equally capable of nurture, so that they would not associate nurturing with only one gender, leaving "people of both genders with the positive capacities each has, but without the destruc-

7. Nancy Chodorow, *The Reproduction of Mothering* (Berkeley: University of California Press, 1978); Dorothy Dinnerstein, *The Mermaid and the Minotaur* (New York: Harper and Row, 1976); Rubin, "Traffic"; and Jessica Benjamin, *The Bonds of Love* (New York: Pantheon, 1985); Lillian Rubin, *Intimate Strangers* (New York: Harper and Row, 1982).

8. R. W. Connell, *Gender and Power* (Stanford: Stanford University Press, 1988).

tive extremes these currently tend toward" (Chodorow, p. 218). Men would find their defensive shells pierced by affection and interdependence, thus transforming the definition of masculinity itself, no longer "tied to denial of dependence and devaluation of women." And politically, shared parenting would "reduce men's needs to guard their masculinity and their control of social and cultural spheres which treat and define women as secondary and powerless" (p. 218).

Perhaps more than anything else, it is through the social practices of parenting that men may connect with the emotional qualities that they have rejected in real life—nurturing, compassion, emotional responsiveness, caring. These emotional resources will not be adequately discovered reading a book or stomping through the woods hugging other men who have taken totemic animal names. They are to be found in the simple drudgery of everyday life in the home. Cleaning the toilet, ironing, or washing dishes are not romantic—you don't have to be a "golden eagle" to keep your nest clean. But they are the everyday stuff of nurture and care. They are skills that are learned, not received by divine revelation after howling at the moon in the forest. We need more Ironing Johns, not more Iron Johns.

Although men's entry as equal parents becomes a key part of intergenerational solutions, it isn't only biological fathers who can rediscover their capacity to nurture. Gay men, largely in response to the AIDS crisis, have developed inspiring formal and informal social networks of caregiving, nurturance, and support.

The route to manly nurture is through practicing it in the everyday way that women currently nurture in our society, the ways our mothers—and not usually our fathers—nurtured us. If mothers embody responsibility, care, and nurture, why would Bly suggest that our project is to reject mother and run away from her? Men need to heal the mother wound, to close the gap between the mother who cared for us and the mother we have tried to leave behind as we struggled to get free of her grasp. What we've lost in that process is precisely what we are currently searching for. Healing the mother wound would allow men to feel that their manhood was not inextricably linked to repudiating mother and all she stands for, but rather in reclaiming, as men, a positive connection to the pre-Oedipal mother, the mother who represented to us all those emotions we currently seek: connectedness, interdependence, nurture, and love.

In a distorted way, this is what's at the core of all the pseudo-rituals in the men's movement. Isn't this what getting in touch with the Earth is all about? When workshop leaders encourage men to smear dirt on themselves or take off their shoes and feel the Earth under their feet (even when they happen to be in a carpeted meeting room), they hook into a fierce longing for reconnection with the Earth and with our mothers, who physically embodied our most visceral connection with life and its origins.

ANTHROPOLOGICAL ANDROCENTRISM

The desire to heal men's wounds leads the men's movement to a survey of initiation rituals and rites of passage, the mechanisms by which traditional cultures established manhood as praxis. But here is one of the chief failings of the movement. Even the most cursory glance at the same myths, archetypes, and anthropological borrowings reveals that all the cultures so celebrated by the men's movement as facilitating deep manhood have been precisely those cultures in which women's status was lowest. As male domination is not a category of thought to the movement, it needn't be a category of history. But its absence creates a major analytic and strategic problem.

Bly and the others wander through anthropological literature like postmodern tourists, as if the world's cultures were an enormous shopping mall filled with ritual boutiques. After trying them on, they take several home to make an interesting outfit—part Asian, part African, part Native American. Moore and Gillette snatch theories from Native American cosmology and Jungian archetypes, and images from ancient Egypt, seventh-century Tibet, and the Aztecs, Incas, and Sumerians. All are totally decontextualized. But can these rituals be ripped from their larger cultural contexts, or are they not deeply embedded in the cultures of which they are a part, expressing important unstated psychological and metaphysical assumptions about both the males and females of the culture as well as reflecting the social and economic realities of life, including structures of hierarchy and domination?

Bly argues that these men's rituals helped men achieve stable and secure senses of themselves as men, and that these rituals had nothing to do with the hierarchical relations between women and men. In fact, he hints that where men are secure in their gender identity, life is actually better for women. But what we actually learn from nonindustrial cultures—as opposed to what we might wish we had learned—is that these initiation ceremonies, rituals, and separate spheres have everything to do with women's inequality. One survey of over one hundred nonindustrial cultures found that societies with separate men's huts are those in which women have the least power. Those cultures in which men sleep separately from women are those in which women's status is lowest. "Societies with men's huts are those in which women have the least power," writes geographer Daphne Spain. In short, "institutionalized spatial segregation reinforces prevailing male advantages." Anthropologist Thomas Gregor agrees; men's clubs of all kinds are "associated with strongly patriarchal societies."[9]

Gregor's work on the Mehinaku of central Brazil illustrates the selectivity in the mythic anthropology of the men's movement. The Mehinaku have well institutionalized men's houses where tribal secrets are kept and ritual instruments played and stored. Spatial segregation is strictly enforced. As one man told Gregor, "This house is only for men. Women may not see anything in here. If a woman comes in, then all the men take her into the woods and she is raped. It has always been that way" (p. 27).

The men's movement is quite selective about which societies and which of their customs it should appropriate. The initiation rituals were ones through which men symbolically appropriated women's power of reproduction and childbirth. Such rituals had a central place in early patriarchal cultures. After all, how could men possibly claim to be all-powerful when it was women who had the ultimate power of bringing life into the world? Men thus devalued women's power of reproduction and asserted that only men could give birth to men, symbolized in elaborate rebirthing rituals to bring men into the world.

If our goal was not to reassert male power but to ensure gender equality, then the best approach is not to champion the initiation of men into separate mythic spheres: "When men take care of young children and women control property, boys are apt to grow up with fewer needs to define themselves in opposition to women, and men are less inclined toward antagonistic displays of superiority. When wives are not required to defer to husbands, and men are not encouraged to boast and display fierce hostility, then cultural ideologies are unlikely to portray men as superior and women as inferior."[10]

Interestingly, the interpretations of the myths themselves are asserted to be unambiguous, always leading men away from the home and from women, off into the company of other men. But to take but one example of the dozens of ambiguous readings which might emerge from a confrontation with the original texts, we are reminded that throughout the Odyssey, Odysseus spends his time yearning to be home with his wife and child, looking longingly out at the sea and weeping every night he is away. In Book II, he returns home, following his prophecy to stop wandering. He takes his oar to a place where men do not salt their food (inland) and where they do not recognize the oar (mistaking it for a thresher), and there he plants the oar in the ground and offers a sacrifice. Then his wanderings will be at an end, and he will be at peace. To us, the quest is, like E. T. said, to go home.

What's more, the evocations of some mythic figures as unambiguous heroes is also problematic.

9. Daphne Spain, *Gendered Spaces* (Chapel Hill: University of North Carolina Press, 1992), 76; Thomas Gregor, "No Girls Allowed," *Science* 82 (December 1982): 27.

10. Scott Coltrane, *Family Man* (unpublished ms.), p. 41.

While some mythopoetic leaders advocate the retrieval of Zeus energy, they willfully forget that Zeus was an "incessant rapist, molesting both mortal women and ancient goddesses." His reign ushered in a terrible era for women, according to Robert Graves—the "hitherto intellectually dominant Greek woman degenerated into the unpaid worker and breeder of children wherever Zeus and Apollo were the ruling gods."[11] Loading up on "Zeus juice" may make compelling myth, but it makes for bad gender politics.

These rituals also have consequences for race relations that their purveyors either ignore or disguise as "respect for traditional cultures." To see a group of middle-class White men appropriating "Indian" rituals, wearing "war paint," drumming and chanting, and taking on totemic animal names is more than silly play—more, even, than a "bunch of boys playing games with the cultures of people they don't know how to live next door to."[12] It is politically objectionable, similar to the "Tomahawk Chop" of Atlanta Braves baseball fans. But then again, how wise is the storyteller who asserts, as Bly does, that golden hair is a universal sign of beauty? Perhaps, as Braves fans asserted, participants believe that their behavior honors these Native American traditions. In the postmodern New Age supermarket of the mythopoetic men's movement, though, it feels more like boys playing cowboys and Indians, and letting the Indians win for a change.

There is another, deeper level at which the racism of the new men's movement is even more deeply troubling. Here, we will make a brief historical analogy. During the late nineteenth century, minstrel shows were enormously popular among White working-class men. These shows were particularly popular with young Irish men, and later,

in the first decades of the twentieth century, with young Jewish men. Performers in blackface would imitate Black men, singing and dancing in racial sendups. But what did these blackface performers sing about? They sang of their nostalgia, their longing for home, for the comforts of family, especially Mammy. In a sense, as historians understand it now, these young Irish and Jewish performers and audiences projected their own anxieties and longings—the ones that they could not express for fear of feminization—onto newly freed Black migrants to the cities. Blackface was more about the longings of White immigrants than about the real lives of Black people.

Today, of course, blackface would be immediately transparent as racist. So men's movement leaders encourage what we might call "redface," the appropriation of Native American rituals and symbols—the drum, chants of "ho," warpaint, animal names, etc. And they imagine that these native cultures expressed a deep spirituality, an abiding love and respect for nature, and a palpable sense of brotherhood. What they are really doing, we believe, is projecting onto these cultures their own longings and their own needs. Such a project relies upon racial, and racist, stereotypes.

Some of the faux-religious iconography of the mythopoetic men's movement gets pretty silly. Moore and Gillette suggest a small crystal pyramid be carried around as a "useful portable icon" and that the soundtrack albums for *Spartacus* or *Ben Hur* provide good background music to access the inner King, since they are "particularly evocative of King energy" (pp. 215, 217). As Joseph Conwell wrote in *Manhood's Morning*, a turn-of-the-century advice manual for how to grow up and be a real man, "[r]ot is rot, and it is never more rotten than when it is sandwiched between religious quotations and antiquated poetry."[13]

The weekend warriors join a host of contemporary masculinists who search for the masculine primitive among the shards of advanced industrial

11. Cited in Jane Caputi and Gurdene O. Mackenzie, "Pumping *Iron John*," in *Women Respond to the Men's Movement*, ed. Kay Leigh Hagan (San Francisco: HarperCollins, 1992), 72. See also Harry Brod, "Reply to Bly," *AHP Perspective* (April 1985).

12. Hattie Gossett, "min's movement??? a page drama," in *Women Respond to the Men's Movement*, ed. Kay Leigh Hagan (San Francisco: HarperCollins, 1992), 21.

13. Joseph Alfred Conwell, *Manhood's Morning; or, "Go it while You're Young": A Book for Young Men Between 14 and 28 Years of Age* (Vineland, N.J.: Hominis, 1896), 155.

culture.[14] One Yale senior waxed nostalgic about his years as a member of the secret society Skull and Bones: "I mean, it's a damn shame it's got to end. The fraternity and everything. Someday we should build us all a fraternity house that wouldn't end. And we could initiate all our friends and go off and drink like freshmen and never graduate. Hell! Why build a fraternity house? Let's build one gigantic fraternity system!—Graduating senior, age twenty-one." How different are they from the wealthy members of the Bohemian Club in San Francisco who go off to Bohemian Grove retreats every summer—retreats that are drenched with ritualized male bonding, dancing partially naked in front of campfires, "full of schmaltz and nostalgia"—with corporate CEOs and legislators (and presidents), and other members of the American ruling class,[15] or take part in the occasional Wild Man retreat if he felt the creeping enervation of having to deal with adult women on an equal basis. But in case the impact on women is lost to our dreaming Yalie, let him hear the voice of one of his brothers, another member of Yale's Skull and Bones club. "I would predict an increase in date rape," he prophesied, should the club be forced to admit women.[16]

BOYS' TOWN

The image of the eternal fraternity reveals a partially hidden longing that lies just beneath the surface of Bly's appeal. The search for the deep

masculine is actually a search for lost boyhood, that homosocial innocence of pre-adolescence, at once rough and tumble and sweetly naive. It is an effort to turn back the clock to that time before work and family responsibilities yanked men away from their buddies, from a world of fun. Leslie Fiedler noticed this nostalgic yearning for lost boyhood, a world of homosocial intimacy as the dominant theme in American literature. Unlike European literature, in which the action revolved around adult men and women in domestic entanglements, the American novel allows the young man to escape domesticity by being kidnapped, running away, enlisting in the army, or being shipwrecked. The American romantic couple is Natty Bumppo and Chingachgook, Ishmael and Queequeg, Huck Finn and Jim, the Lone Ranger and Tonto. These couples "proffer a chaste male love as the ultimate emotional experience" revealing an "implacable nostalgia for the infantile, at once wrong headed and somehow admirable," he writes. The authors' "self congratulatory buddy-buddiness" also reveals an "astonishing naivete."[17] "I reckon I gotta light out for the territory," says Huck, "cuz Aunt Sally, she's gonna civilise me, and I can't stand it."

The mythopoetic men's retreats recall the clubhouse with the sign reading "No Girls Allowed" or the movie *Stand By Me*, which captures that last summer before junior high school, before having to posture to impress girls will forever distort the relationships among the boys. What Kenneth Keniston calls the "fallacy of romantic regression" appeals not to men who want to be men, but rather men who want to re-become boys; thus, their antipathy toward women and work is so easily displaced onto mothers who have not been part of their lives for decades. "No one is going to catch me lady and make me a man. I want always to be a little boy and to have fun." So said Peter Pan. So say the men at wildman retreats.

This search for lost boyhood as the search for the authentic masculine helps explain several of the

14. Masculinists, as distinct from either pro-feminist men or self-conscious anti-feminists, are more concerned with what they see as the feminization of men than the feminism of women. In response to this fear of feminization, they attempt to carve out homosocial environments in both the public and private spheres in order to celebrate male bonding and fantasies of escape from women. See Michael Kimmel, "Men's Responses to Feminism at the Turn of the Century," *Gender & Society* 1 (1987). Yale student cited in William F. Buckley, "The Clubhouse" in *About Men*, ed. D. Erickson (New York: Poseidon Press, 1987), 257.

15. See, for example, G. William Domhoff, *The Bohemian Grove and Other Ruling Class Retreats* (New York: Harper and Row, 1974).

16. Cited in *Newsweek*, 23 September 1991.

17. Leslie Fiedler, *Love and Death in the American Novel* (New York: Stein and Day, 1966), 144.

paradoxes that emerge at the men's retreats. The men's movement speaks to men not as fathers but as sons searching for their fathers. But curiously, the attendees at the workshops are middle-aged men, many of whom are fathers themselves. They rarely speak of their own children (and when they do, it's almost exclusively their sons; it's as if daughters do not exist in this world). They speak as sons, of their pain as sons estranged from fathers. That is, they would rather complain about something they can barely change than work toward transforming something that they can: their relationships with their own children and the structured inequalities of power between men and women, adults and children, and one man and another.

However, at the retreats, they are also asked to honor the elders, the older men at the weekend retreats, who are seen to embody a certain deeply male wisdom. Leaders invite us to admire the wisdom of older men, to listen to their stories, learn from the wisdom they have gained through the years. But wait, are these not the same elder men (fathers) who abandoned us? Thus when Bly or his followers speak as fathers, they criticize contemporary men as having followed their mothers, having been dutiful little boys (having been feminized). But when they speak as sons, they are angry and hurt by fathers who behaved exactly as they have.

How do we explain this shift in focus? "I'm not sure why they want to be back in the good old days," observed a woman therapist in 1967. "Do they want to be back there as the father, or do they want to be back there as the child?"[18] When we speak as sons, we are angry and wounded by our fathers. When we speak as fathers, we expect veneration and admiration from sons. We are thus going to have it both ways, particularly whichever way allows us to feel like the innocent victim of other people's disempowering behavior, the victim of what others (fathers or sons) have done to us. This is again the lost (false) innocence of mythic boyhood.

18. Cited in Myron Brenton, *The American Male* (London: George Allen and Unwin, 1967), 107.

But it is also more than that—it is staking a claim for victimhood and entitlement at the same time. This is what explains the emphasis on the role of the little prince in the Iron John story, and explains the way that these men, feeling like boys, want to claim their inner King. The prince is actually not the central figure in Iron John's story; it is Iron John himself, who is liberated by the young boy's quest. As the title indicates, he is the star. But male readers see themselves as the king's son, the prince, and not as Iron John.

But who is the prince? The prince is the rightful heir to power; he will be the king. He is literally *entitled* to power, but he is not yet ready for it. So too, for manhood. Men's movement participants believe themselves entitled to that power, the power that comes from being a man, the power we might call patriarchy, or male privilege. They do not feel that power yet, but they want to, and they feel themselves entitled to it. This is why the men at the mythopoetic retreats find it so much easier to imagine themselves as sons, to call themselves "adult children"—as if the word "adult" was an adjective, modifying the word "child"—rather than as fully adult, responsible to others, and refusing to claim their privileged inheritance.[19]

WHISPERS OF THE HEART

We believe that the mythopoetic quest is misguided, because it reproduces masculinity as a power relation—the power of men over women and the power of some men over other men. But there is no reason to doubt Bly or his followers' sincerity, or their desire to re-create a world of gender certainty. The appeal of this message is in its response to feminism, but not only in the negative sense we have been describing. It is also an indication that millions of men have been forced to grap-

19. It has also been suggested that movement participants are princes because there can only be one king: Bly himself, the symbolic "good" father who facilitates, through traditional analytic transference, the healing of the father wound. But we believe that the mythopoetic men's movement is more than Freudian psychoanalysis on a mass scale; it is also political and ideological.

ple with what it means to be a man. Men are searching, looking for a new sense of meaning. That they've been looking under every possible stone and crystal is no surprise, nor is it a surprise that the most popular solution so far is one that offers a quick and comfortable fix. While the mythopoetic solution may not bring real change, the enthusiasm with which it has been greeted represents, at least in part, a process of change.

A key aspect of that process, a progressive whisper within a reactive structure, is that mythopoetic groups and gatherings can be means for men to break their isolation from other men. Part of patriarchy's interpersonal cement is an isolation that keeps each man fearful of his own masculinity and forces him to go to lengths to prove to the other guys that he's a real man. By breaking the isolation, by setting up opportunities for men to express a range of feelings among themselves and to talk about their fears and loves and challenges, men can take steps toward disassociating manhood and domination and reestablishing it on the basis of connection and harmony with those around us.[20]

This activity of redefinition is seen in the nostalgia for boyhood. We've talked about the regressive side of this nostalgia, but we also must ask why this nostalgia is so powerful. Perhaps it is part of what Barbara Ehrenreich described as men's flight from commitment symbolized by the magazine that extolled a male inhabiting an adult body but acting like a boy at play, literally a Play-boy.[21] But there's more: it is a longing for what men have given up in order to fit into the tight pants of masculinity. Becoming a man required a suppression of a range of human capacities, capabilities, and emotions. But these capacities maintain a nagging presence in our own lives. Few of us completely or effortlessly fit into the dictates of male gender power, particularly in a society where women have demanded equality and have challenged men to examine our own

lives. As we attempt to expand our emotional repertoire, as we learn to reach out to our brothers, sisters, and children, it reawakens a childhood voice that has long been buried. Playing in the woods recalls the days when we were less preoccupied with maintaining our gender barriers, when we felt more at home with the bodies and the tears of other males, and when we felt more at home with ourselves. It isn't that any moment of our lives we were completely free of the rigors of gender acquisition, but rather that gender demands did not yet so completely overwhelm a range of other human characteristics and possibilities. Of course, part of the yearning for the past is a nostalgia for a past that did not completely exist.[22]

The alternative is not to reject personal change and personal growth. It is not for men to start a political movement in the image of other political movements. "Alright, men, let's get out there and get this job done no matter what the cost." It is to hear what women have been telling us for the past two and one-half decades—that personal change is an indispensable element of, and tool for, social change, and that structural social change is an indispensable element for personal change.

It is a personal vision of political change and a political vision of personal change that we propose as an alternative to the men's movement that will allow men's wild and progressive impulses to blossom.

THE FLIGHT FROM FEMINISM

What keeps Bly and his followers from taking this radical course of personal and social change are his protests that his work has nothing to do with women or feminism. Bly writes that his book "does not constitute a challenge to the women's movement," that he "does not seek to turn men against women, nor to return men to their domineering mode that has led to repression of women and their values for centuries" (1990, p. x). But such claims are disingenuous.

---

20. An alternative approach to breaking this isolation but within a profeminist perspective is addressed in Kaufman's *Cracking the Armour: Power, Pain, and the Lives of Men* (Toronto: Viking Canada, 1993).

21. Barbara Ehrenreich, *The Hearts of Men* (New York: Anchor, 1983).

22. Our thanks to Harry Brod for suggesting this final point, the sense of nostalgia for something that did not fully exist.

Though Bly is careful to hedge his comments, the book is full of inferences that reveal how he embraces traditional gender roles: "A mother's job is, after all, to civilize the boy" (p. 11) and "A man who cannot defend his own space cannot defend women and children" (p. 156) and "As more and more mothers work out of the house, and cannot show their daughters what they produce, similar emotions may develop in the daughter's psyche, with a consequent suspicion of grown women" (p. 96).

Alone with other men, Bly gives this anti-feminist tendency fuller play. Journalists Steve Chapple and David Talbot describe an encounter between Bly and his campers at a retreat: "Robert, when we tell women our desires, they tell us we're wrong," shouts out one camper. "So," says Bly, "then you bust them in the mouth because no one has the right to tell another person what their true desires are."[23]

And if Bly sidesteps the issue, his followers do not. One leader of retreats to heal the father wound argues, "A lot of men feel hung out to dry by the women's movement. A lot of men feel that they, personally, are being held responsible for everything that's macho and wrong in the world today: rape, wife-beating, war. They've been feeling very bad about themselves, and so they're overjoyed to recover their maleness and feel proud about themselves as men" (cited in Chapple and Talbot, 195). Ray Raphael celebrates men's ability to do anything women can: "At a time when an enlightened feminism has taken away many of our traditional props, at a time when many of our manly roles have become virtually obsolete, at a time when we have been placed on the defensive in what we perceive as a never-ending competition between the sexes, we have countered by aggressively usurping the roles once played by women."[24] And journalist Trip Gabriel

reports from the gender front that "more than the men's movement cares to admit, it is a reaction to the decades of feminism, a reclaiming of prerogatives that men have long been made to feel defensive about."[25]

Note how each of these men couches the reaction against feminism in terms of men's defensiveness. Men have been made to feel badly about traditional masculinity, about men's violence, rape, pornography, battery, and a litany of other feminist accusations. Their response is not to enlist in the feminist struggle against these excesses of manly behavior but to declare themselves tired of listening.

The retreat to find a revitalized and recharged manhood, embodied in the new men's movement, is most definitely a retreat. It is a retreat from the mother, who embodies, in the practices of mothering, precisely the positive qualities of caring and nurturing that men are running away from her to find. It is a retreat from the historical specificity of the present era, a retreat from political responsibilities to confront male excesses that daily manifest themselves on our streets, in our schools, in our workplaces, in our bedrooms, excesses such as rape, violence, spouse abuse, gay bashing, high-risk sexual behavior, drunk driving. It is a retreat to a highly selective anthropological world of rituals that reproduce men's cultural power over women and that are now used to facilitate a deeper nostalgic retreat to the lost world of innocent boyhood. It is thus a retreat from women, from adult men's responsibilities to embrace women's equality and struggle against those obstacles that continue to lie in the path of gender equality. Male bonding, hailed as the positive outcome of these weekend retreats, is doublesided. Bonding implies connection with others, and it also implies constraints, responsibilities. The deep masculine will never be retrieved by running away from women. Only by fighting for equality, side by side, as equals, can we realize the best of what it means to be a man.

---

23. Cited in Steve Chapple and David Talbot, *Burning Desires* (New York: Simon and Schuster, 1990), 196.

24. Ray Raphael, *The Men from the Boys: Rites of Passage in Male America* (Lincoln: University of Nebraska Press, 1988), 172.

25. Trip Gabriel, "In Touch with the Tool Belt Chromosome," *New York Times*, 22 September 1991, 31.

Index

AAUP. *See* American Association of University Professors
AAUW. *See* American Association of University Women
Abbey, A., 235
Abel, G., 160, 163
Abelson, R. P., 29, 327
Abinanti, A., 84n
Abramovitz, S. I., 348
Acculturation Problems, in DSM-IV, 337
Achievement motivation, 7
Acker, J., 62
ACLU. *See* American Civil Liberties Union
Acquaintance rape, 233, 244, 417. *See also* Rape
ACT. *See* American College Testing Program
Adams, D., 224, 229
Adams, J., 301n
Adams, K. A., 16
Adams, M. L., 188
Adelman, C., 271
Adelman, J., 57
ADHD. *See* Attention Deficit/Hyperactivity Disorder
Adkins-Regan, E., 185
Adleman, J., 361
Adolescence: homosexual identity development during, 190; pornography available during, 162–63
Advocacy research, and rape statistics, 236–46
Aetna, 304
Africa, 44–45
African Americans: Black feminist thought, 59; as category, 65; conversational style of, 79, 94; and discrimination in workplace, 308–09; and domestic violence, 207; increased research on, 5, 55; and knowing, 256–57; learning styles of, 83n; negotiation strategies of, 135; oppression of Black men, 56; poor families, 383; and pornography, 156; psychotherapy with women, 56; racism and sexism against, 66; and rape, 233; and relational theory, 360; and Senate hearings on Clarence Thomas's nomination to Supreme Court, 70; and slavery, 21, 69, 121, 341; and smiling behavior, 102; and Women's Ways of Knowing (WWK) model, 250; working mothers, 383–84
Agency, embedded view of, 139–40
Agentic behavior, 40, 44
Ageton, S., 239
Agoraphobia, 344
Ainsworth, M., 394–97, 396n
Akert, R. M., 112n

Alcoff, L., 252, 256, 262
Alessandri, S. M., 35, 50
Alexander, E. R., III, 313
Alexander, R., 331–32
Allen, L. R., 303n
Allen, L. S., 186
Allen, M., xx, 95, 400–04
Allport, G. W., 278
Almquist, E., 59
Alpha bias, 258
Alvardo, D., 353
Alvares, K. M., 315
AMA. *See* American Medical Association
Amaro, H., 308
American Association of University Professors (AAUP), 9–10
American Association of University Women (AAUW), 50
American Bar Association, 166–67
American Booksellers v. Hudnut, 155
American Center for Law and Justice, 176
American Civil Liberties Union (ACLU), 156
American College Testing Program (ACT), 19, 30
American Indians: increased research on, 5; in law school, 84–85; nonverbal behavior of, 102; rituals of, used in men's movement, 416; and Women's Ways of Knowing (WWK) model, 250
American Medical Association (AMA), 207, 222
American Men's Studies Association, 6
American Psychiatric Association: *Diagnostic and Statistical Manual* (DSM-I), 337, 340; *Diagnostic and Statistical Manual* (DSM-II), 181, 337, 340, 343, 345; *Diagnostic and Statistical Manual* (DSM-III/III-R), 337, 338, 340, 342, 349–52; *Diagnostic and Statistical Manual* (DSM-IV), 337–56; on homosexuality, 181, 342–43, 346; "Practice Guidelines for the Treatment of Patients with Bipolar Disorder," 341
American Psychological Association (APA): amicus curiae brief in *Price Waterhouse v. Hopkins,* 308, 309, 310–17, 321–32; Committee on Women in Psychology, 338; Division of the Psychology of Women, x, 4; Society for the Psychological Study of Men and Masculinity, 6; women's membership in, 3
American Telephone and Telegraph Company (AT&T), 299–300, 302
America's Competitive Secret (Rosener), 292, 298
Ames, M. A., 185, 188

Amir, D., 236n
Amir, M., 236n
Amsden, A. H., 313
Andersen, M. L., 56, 59, 60, 67
Androgyny, 362
Anne, S., 192
Ansberry, C., 229
Anthony, S. B., 109
Antisocial Personality Disorder, 344, 348, 349
Antony, L., 256
Anwar, R., 223
APA. *See* American Psychological Association
Aptheker, B., 61
Arbitell, M., 224
Archer, D., 112n, 114, 120, 123
Archer, J. A., 30, 51
Arias, I., 226
Aries, E., xx, 80, 91–99, 105
Aristotle, 374
Arjmand, O., 274
Arlin, P. K., 266
Arnkoff, D., 96
Arvey, R. D., 313, 317
Asch, S. E., 130n
Ashmore, R. D., 22, 299n
Asian Americans: as category, 65; and discrimination in workplace, 308; and domestic violence, 207; family expectations of, 5; increased research on, 5; and Women's Ways of Knowing (WWK) model, 250
Assaults: definition and measurement of, 210. *See also* Domestic violence
Association for Women in Psychology (AWP), 4
AT&T, 299–300, 302
Atkins, B., 93
Atkinson, J., 7
Atkinson, M., 392
Attachment theory, 49–50, 391–97
Attention Deficit/Hyperactivity Disorder (ADHD), 345–46
Attitude toward Women Scale (AWS), 111
Attorney General's Commission on Pornography, 155
Australia, 102, 407
Authenticity and relational self, 376–77
Autocratic leadership, 300
Autonomous functioning, 377–78
Aven, F. F., Jr., 301n
Avon, 303
AWP. *See* Association for Women in Psychology
AWS. *See* Attitude toward Women Scale
Ayres, I., 135

Baber, A., 402
Bachman, R., 234
Baer, J. L., 79
Bailey, J. M., xx, 182, 184–87
Baken, D., 40
Baker, L., 33
Baker, R. L., 38
Baker, S. W., 185
Bales, R. E., 40

Bales, R. F., 61
Balin, J., 255
Balint, M., 40
Ballou, M., 361
Banaji, M., 106
Bank of America, 304
Barbaree, H., 177–78
Barbour, W., 209
Bardwick, J., 4–5, 4n
Baril, G., 151
Barlow, D., 160
Barnett, M. A., 20, 24
Barnett, O. W., 207
Barnett, R. C., 189
Baron, D., 86n
Baron, L., 173–74
Baron, R. A., 328
Barr, S. H., 317
Barrett, G. V., xx, 309, 310–17, 321–23, 325–31
Barrett & Associates, 326
Bart, P. B., 188, 198
Bartol, K. M., 315, 317
Bartos, O. J., 146
Baruch, G. K., 189
Basow, S. A., 4n
Bass, B., 296n
Basseches, M., 266
Battered husband syndrome, 225, 229. *See also* Domestic violence
Battered woman syndrome, 208. *See also* Domestic violence
Baxter, J. C., 317
Baxter, S., 34
Baxter Magolda, M. B., 266
Bayer, B. M., 56
Bayley, N., 38
Bazelon, D. L., 310
Beal, C. R., 34, 35
Beatty, W. W., 40
Bebeau, M., 263
Beck, E. T., 193
Becker, D., 338
Becker, J., 156, 163, 172
Behan, P., 279
Belenky, M. F., 249–50, 252, 255, 257, 261–66, 268, 291, 295n, 363
Bell, A. P., 185, 188, 189, 199
Bell, R. Q., 40
Bell System, 299–300
Bell Labs, 304
Belsky, J., 384, 392, 392n
Bem, S. L., 8, 17, 35, 165
Benbow, C. P., xx, 271, 272, 274–80, 283–86
Bender, D., 209
Beneke, T., 159, 164
Benishay, D., 184
Benjamin, J., 368n, 413
Benson, J. B., 45, 47
Berenbaum, S. A., 33, 185
Bergen, D. J., 96

Berger, J., 128, 147
Berger, M. M., 250
Bergler, E., 190
Bergman, S., 360
Berill, K., 193
Berk, R., 223, 226
Bernard, J., 16
Bernardin, H. J., 317
Bernay, T., 292
Berra, Y., 294
Bersoff, D. N., xx, 321–32
Bertin, J., 9
Beta-bias theory, 258
Betancourt, H., 19, 57
Betcher, W., 401
Beyond Separate Spheres (Rosenberg), 9
Bezirganian, S., 49
Bianchi, S., 391
Bible, 176
Bickel, O., 70
Biden, J., 237, 240
Bidermann Industries, 305
Bigoness, W. J., 314
Binomial effect size display, 29
Biological causation: of gender differences, 33–52; of gender
    differences in mathematics achievement, 271–87; of non-
    verbal sensitivity, 115; overview of issues concerning gen-
    der differences, 33–35; of sexual orientation, 181–88
Bird, G. W., 214
Birdwhistell, R. L., 104
Bitman, I., 225
Bjorkqvist, K., 21, 36
Blacks: Black feminist thought, 59; as category, 65; conversa-
    tional style of, 79, 94; and discrimination in workplace,
    308–09; and domestic violence, 207; increased research on,
    5, 55; and knowing, 256–57; learning styles of, 83n; nego-
    tiation strategies of, 135; oppression of Black men, 56;
    poor families, 383; and pornography, 156; psychotherapy
    with women, 56; racism and sexism against, 66; and rape,
    233; and relational theory, 360; and Senate hearings on
    Clarence Thomas's nomination to Supreme Court, 70; and
    slavery, 21, 69, 121, 341; and smiling behavior, 102; and
    Women's Ways of Knowing (WWK) model, 250; working
    mothers, 383–84
Blair, J. D., 149
Blanchard, E., 160
Bland, R., 214
Blehar, M., 396n
Bleier, R., 186
Block, J. H., 49
Bloom, B. S., 276–77
Bly, R., 6, 400, 402, 406, 408–12, 414–15, 418–20, 418n
Body language. *See* Nonverbal behavior
Boehm, V. R., 315, 326
Bograd, M., 222
Bohan, J. S., 97, 250, 258
Bohner, G., 235
Bond, L., 257
Bonding, mother-infant, 386–90

Bonoma, T. W., 146
Borderline Character Disorder, 344
Borderline Personality Disorder, 338
Borgida, E., xx, 321–32
Borker, R., 98
Boston Medical and Surgical Journal, 15
Bouchard, T. J., 279
Bowker, L., 215, 216, 223, 224
Bowlby, J., 295, 383, 393–95
Boy Scout movement, 399
*Boys and Girls Are Different: Men, Women, and the Sex Differ-
    ence*, 33
Brabeck, M. M., xxi, 250, 261–68
Bradley, P., 96
Brain research: and mathematics achievement, 280, 285; and
    sexual orientation, 181, 182, 185–86
Brannon, L., 4n
Bray, D. W., 299n, 300
Brazelton, T. B., 38
Brazil, 415
Bredemeier, B. J. L., 264
Breggin, G. R., 346
Breggin, P. R., 346
Brennan-Parks, K., 102
Brenton, M., 418n
Bretherton, I., 48
Brewer, M. B., 328
Briere, J., 165, 166
Bright, S., 189
Brinkerhoff, M., 222, 225
Britain, 175, 389, 393
British Committee on Obscenity and Film Censorship, 175
Broberg, A. G., 385
Brock, T. C., 179n
Brod, H., 419n
Brody, L. R., 102
Brooks, G. R., 207, 401
Broughton, J., 266
Broverman, D. M., 96
Broverman, I. K., 96, 312, 337, 362, 374
Brown, B. R., 135, 146
Brown, B. S., 57, 339
Brown, C. E., 102, 120n, 148
Brown, D., 50
Brown, L. M., 258
Brown, L. S., 56, 348, 361
Brown, R., 109
Browne, A., 213, 214, 224, 227
Browne, S. E., 193
Brownmiller, S., 155, 165, 178n
Brush, L. D., 211, 213, 223
Bryant, J., 161–64, 166, 167
Brygger, M. P., 210
Buck, R., 114, 123
Buckley, S., 237n
Buckley, W. F., 417n
Buczynski, P., 263–64
Bugental, D. E., 101, 128
Bundy, T., 156

Burn, S. M., 4n
Burning Bed, The, 177
Burns, J. M., 296
Burt, M., 165
Burton, L., 273
Busia, A. P. A., 57
Buss, D., 18, 207
Butler v. the Queen, 171
Butterfield, D. A., 291, 315, 317
Buzawa, C. G., 222, 224
Buzawa, E. S., 222, 224
Bylsma, W. H., 136
Byne, W., 182, 184, 185, 186
Byrne, D., 155, 328

Cahill, S. E., 64
California Psychological Inventory, 94
Cameron, D., 80, 98
Campbell, R. R., 157
Campos, J. J., 41
Campus Project on Sexual Assault, 236
Canada, 171, 172, 177–78, 407
Cantor, D. W., 292
Caplan, P. J., 145, 338, 343, 350, 383
Caplow, T., 146
Caputi, J., 416n
CARAT. *See* Communication of Affect Receiving Ability Test
Carli, L. L., xxi, 35, 44–52, 79
Carlisle, J. M., 159
Carlson, C. I., 218
Carlson, N. L., 235
Carpenter, V. N., 313
Carroll, L., 138
Carse, A. L., 157
Carson, G., 86n
Carter, J. D., 120n, 132
Carter, M. R., 292
Cass, V., 189, 195
Cassingham, B. J., 189, 198
Cate, R., 214
Causation, definition of, 158–59
CCL. *See* Center for Creative Leadership
Censorship of pornography, 155–56, 170–79
Center for Creative Leadership (CCL), 304–05
Chait, L. R., 351
Chammah, A. M., 146
Chapple, S., 420
Charbonneau, C., 189, 194, 200
Check, J., 162, 163, 165, 165–66, 166
Chehrazi, S. S., 385
Cherry, L., 48
Chesler, P., 341, 343–44, 359
Chess, S., 383
Child abuse, 225
Childcare. *See* Daycare
Childhood: and attachment theory, 49–50, 391–97; benefits of childcare for, 391–97; J. Benjamin on, 368n; Chodorow on mother-daughter versus mother-son relationships, 362; cross-sex behavior during, 51; daycare as unable to meet

infants' needs, 384, 386–90; developmental milestones during first year of life, 37–42, 44–48; difficult children, 49–50; education of children of Color, 268; Freud on, 374, 394, 394n; gender differences in first year of, 37–42, 44–48; homosexual identity development during, 190; Horney on, 368–70; independence during, 35; and knowing, 253; and maternal deprivation, 393–94; men's movement and parent-child relationship, 410–14; A. Miller on, 368n; parents' influence on gender development during, 34–35, 48–51; play during, 34, 49, 51; psychiatric disorders in, 345–46; relationship theory and mother-child relationship, 362, 364–67, 375–76; working mothers and children's well being, 383–97
China, 174
Chinen, A. B., 253
Chinese-Americans, 5
Chipman, S. F., 272
Chodorow, N., 7, 9, 56, 59, 139, 359, 362, 363, 365, 374, 412–14
Christopher, S., 214
Chusmir, L. H., 301n
Circle of Men, A (Kauth), 402
Citizens Insurance, 303
Civil Rights Act of 1964, 308, 323
Clark, C. S., 384
Clarke, E., 1–2
Clarke-Stewart, K. A., 384, 385, 392n
Clarkson, F. E., 96
Class. *See* Social class
Clay, R., 384
Clayton, S. D., 136, 309
Clinchy, B., 249–50, 252, 255, 264–65
Cline, V., 159
Clinical fallacy, and domestic violence statistics, 215–16
Clover, W. H., 317
Coates, J., 81, 86
Cody, M. J., 81
Cognitive abilities: cross-cultural patterns on, 21; early research on, 2; mathematical achievement, 19, 30, 271–87; Perry's theory of intellectual and ethical development, 266; reflective judgment theory, 266–67; spatial cognitive performance, 20–21; theories of adult intellectual development, 265–67; verbal performance, 21; Women's Ways of Knowing (WWK) model, 249–68
Cognitive tunnel vision, 129
Cohen, C., 341
Cohen, J., 46, 284, 327
Cohen, K. M., 45
Cohen, P., 49
Colby, A., 263
Cole, J. B., 57
Cole, P. M., 48
Coleman, D. H., 218
Coleman, E., 189, 190
Colen, S., 67
College Board, 271, 275
Collins, B., 236n
Collins, P. H., xxi, 56, 59, 60, 67, 69, 73–75, 156, 256–57
Coltrane, S., 415n

Columbia University, 9, 241
Comas-Diaz, L., 5, 56, 309, 360
Coming out process, 190, 198–99
Command-and-control model of leadership, 294
Committee on Pornography and Obscenity, 155
Committee on Women in Psychology, 338
Common language effect size statistic, 29–30
Communication: conversational style, 79–99; gender stereo-types and perception of speech, 95–97; at home, 88–89; length of interaction, 95; magnitude of gender differences in, 91–92; negotiation strategies, 135–51; and new concep-tualization of gender, 97–99; nonverbal behavior, 101–31; overlap in men's and women's styles of communication, 91–99; public versus private speaking, 87–90, 95; report-talk versus rapport-talk, 80, 87–90, 95; ritual nature of talk, 85–86; situational context of interaction, 93–95; and social roles, 93; and status, 89–90, 92–93; tag questions and qualifiers, 96; two-cultures approach to gender differ-ences in, 98
Communication of Affect Receiving Ability Test (CARAT), 123
Complex Post-traumatic Stress Disorder, 344
Compulsory heterosexuality, 192–93
Conduct Disorders, 344, 345, 349
Conflict Tactics Scales (CTS), 211, 217–18, 225, 226
Congenital adrenal hyperplasia (CAH), 185–86
Connected knowing, 255
Connell, R. W., 62, 342, 413n
Connors, D., 193
Conrad, P., 341
Constructed knowing, 255–56
Conversational style: amount of talking done by women ver-sus men, 86–88; cross-cultural patterns in, 85–86; gender differences as important in, 79–80, 82–90; gender stereo-types and perception of speech, 95–97; at home, 88–89; in-teractional sociolinguistic approach to, 82–90; interruptions, 65n; and length of interaction, 95; magni-tude of gender differences in, 91–92; and new conceptuali-zation of gender, 97–99; overlap in men's and women's styles of communication, 91–99; overview of issues on, 79–80; politeness, 94; public versus private speaking, 87–90, 95; and race, 79, 94; report-talk versus rapport-talk, 80, 87–90, 95; ritual nature of talk, 85–86; situational con-text of interaction, 93–95; and social roles, 93; and status, 89–90, 92–93; stereotype on women talking a lot, 86–89; tag questions and qualifiers, 96; two-cultures approach to gender differences in, 98
Conwell, J., 416
Cook, S. L., 233, 235, 237, 238, 239, 240
Cook, S. W., 246
Cooper, H., 25
Copeland, P., 183
Copenhagen Consecutive Perinatal Cohort, 37–42
Cornell, C., 222
Cornell, D., 157
Corner, M. A., 37, 40
Costanzo, M., 114, 120, 123
Costello, N., 40
Costrich, N., 311, 316

Cowan, G., 156, 157
Cox, S. L., 243
Cox, T., Jr., 303n
Cramer, P., 51
Crawford, M., 4n, 7, 10, 80, 116, 250, 263, 272, 309
Cronbach, L. J., 28
Crosby, F. J., 136, 309
Cross, S., 8
Cross-cultural patterns: attachment, 395; cognitive abilities, 21; conversational style, 85–86; cross-sex behavior, 51; day-care, 389; dearth of women in science, 286–87; develop-mental milestones in first year of life, 44–45; maternal deprivation, 393; men's movement, 407; men's rituals, 415; nonverbal behavior, 102; pornography, 174–75
Cross-sex behavior, prohibition against, for boys, 51
Crow, E. L., 327
Crowell, D., 40
Crowley, M., 348
CTS. See Conflict Tactics Scales
Cultural diversity. See Ethnicity; and specific racial and ethnic groups
"Cultural feminism," 145
Culver, C., 48
Cummins, A. G., 126, 127n
Cummins, K. R., 41

Daggett, W. R., 135
Daglish, L., 34
Daly, M., 222, 223
Danaher, D., 48
Danoff-Burg, S., 235
Darley, J. M., 130
Darling, J. F., 40
Darwin, C., 104
Date rape, 233, 244, 417. See also Rape
Davidson, C. V., 348
Davidson, L. A., 120n
Davis, A., 69
Dawis, R. V., 274, 275, 275–76
Day, D. R., 317
Daycare: and attachment theory, 391–97; benefits of, for in-fants and toddlers, 391–97; in Great Britain, 389; as in-sufficient for infant needs, 384, 386–90; overview of issues on, 383–84; teachers' salaries in, 391–92, 392n
De Beauvoir, S., 59
De Bruin, J. P. C., 37, 40
De Grazia, E., 179
De Koster, K., 209
De Laurentis, T., 252
De Vries, G. J., 37, 40
Deaux, K., xxi, 128, 314, 315, 317, 321–32, 328n, 348
DeCecco, J. P., 196
Decoding: definition of, 128; subordination-power hypothe-sis of nonverbal decoding ability, 102, 104–17, 120–31
Defries, Z., 190, 196
DeKeseredy, W. S., 222
Del Boca, F. K., 299n
Delk, J. L., 34
Delpit, L., 268

Demarest, J., 35
DeMaris, A., 226
DeMille, C. B., 176
Democratic leadership, 300
DeMonteflores, C., 189, 194, 195
DeMott, B., 68
Dempster, A. P., 38
Denham, S., 48
Denmark, 37–42, 174, 174–75
Denmark, F. L., 4
Dependent Personality Disorder, 338, 344, 345, 348
Depression, 344, 348
Desaulniers, J., 20
Descriptive gender stereotypes, 322
Deutsch, C., 3
Deutsch, F. M., 20, 21, 101, 120n
Deutsch, H., 3
Deutsch, M., 316
Developmental milestones, in first year of life, 37–42, 44–48
Diagnostic and Statistical Manual (DSM-I), 337, 340
Diagnostic and Statistical Manual (DSM-II), 181, 337, 340, 343, 345
Diagnostic and Statistical Manual (DSM-III/III-R), 337, 338, 340, 342, 349–52
Diagnostic and Statistical Manual (DSM-IV), 337–56; childhood disorders in, 345–46; Dissociative Disorders, 354–55; gender bias in, 337–55; homosexuality in, 181, 342–43, 346; men's disorders in, 344–45; overview of issues on, 337–39; personality disorders in, 338, 344, 345, 348–50; Premenstrual Dysphoria Disorder, 338, 343, 351–54; Sadistic Personality Disorder, 351; Self-defeating Personality Disorder, 338, 343, 350–51; size of, 340–42; women's disorders in, 338, 343–44, 351–54
Dialogue, problem solving through, 140–41
Diethystilbestrol, 182
Difference: different voice theory, 258, 262–65; "different-and-inferior" argument, 145, 258; "different-but-superior" argument, 145; feminist controversy on psychology of, 14, 257–58; problem of, 69–70, 75
Different voice theory, 258, 262–65
Difficult children, 49–50
Dill, B. T., 57, 69–70
DiMatteo, M. R., 120
Dimen, M., 97
Dindia, K., 95
Dinero, T. E., 243
Dinnerstein, D., 413
Dino, G. A., 20, 24
Dipboye, R. L., 313, 316, 317
Discrimination. *See* Sex discrimination
Dissociative amnesia, 354–55
Dissociative Disorders, 344, 354–55
Dissociative Identity Disorder, 344, 354–55
Dittmann, R. W., 185
Diversity issues (race, class, and gender), 55–75. *See also* Gender; Race; Social class
Divorce American Style, 89
Dobash, R. E., 213, 222, 223, 224, 226
Dobash, R. P., 213, 222, 223, 224, 226

Dobkin, A., 195
Doctors. *See* Physicians
"Doctors Wanted: No Women Need Apply" (Walsh), 1
Doering, C. H., 37
Doherty, M. E., 317
Domestic violence: battered husband syndrome, 225, 229; battered woman syndrome, 208; behaviors included in, 208; and child abuse, 225; chronicity of assault, 215; and clinical fallacy, 215–16; criticisms of research on female violence against males, 217–18, 222, 225–29; cycle of battering, 208; among dating couples, 212; among divorcing couples, 223; excusing assaults by women, 218; family-violence perspective on, 225–29; female violence against males, 208, 210–19, 222, 225–29; female violence and increase in probability of woman beating, 216–17; and homicide rates, 213; among married and cohabiting couples, 211–12, 223–24; overview of issues on, 207–08; and posttraumatic stress disorder, 208; reasons women remain in abusive situation, 207–08; and representative sample fallacy, 215–16; self-defense and assaults by women partners, 213–15; statistics on, 210–13; violence-against-women perspective on, 223–29
Domestic violence shelters, 207, 212
Domhoff, G. W., 417n
Dominance: and conversational style, 94–96; and nonverbal sensitivity, 122; pornography and sexualizing dominance, 163, 167; and power, 149–50; as stable and enduring condition, 125. *See also* Power and influence; Status
Dominance Scale, of California Psychological Inventory, 94
Donald, J., 57
Donnell, S. M., 300n
Donnerstein, E., 156, 159, 166–68, 168n, 172, 173, 177, 178n
Donovan, J., 3
Dostoyevsky, F., 175
"Double" and "triple jeopardy," 56
Douglas, W. O., 175
Dovidio, J. F., 102, 120, 120n, 125, 148
Doyle, J. A., 4n, 6
Drakich, J., 86n
Draper, R. D., 253
Dresselhaus, M. D., 286–87
Driscoll, D. M., 292
Drucker, J., 314
DSM. *See Diagnostic and Statistical Manual*
DuBois, C. L. Z., 325
Dunn, J., 48
Dunwoody-Miller, V., 136
Durham, R. L., 266
Dusky, L., 303n
Dutton, D. G., 209, 210
Dutton, M. A., 209
Duveen, G., 51
Dworkin, A., 155, 156, 170, 176–77, 239

Eagly, A. H., xxi, 15–20, 24–30, 44, 92, 95, 108, 112, 127, 128, 216, 291, 300n, 301n, 330, 348
Eakins, B., 87, 92
Eakins, G., 87, 92
Earls, F., 348

Easterbrook, J. A., 129
Eating Disorders, 344
Eaton, W. O., 49
Eble, C., 86
Eccles, J. S., 272, 273, 283, 284, 287
Eckert, E. D., 184
Eckholm, E., 351
Economic class. *See* Social class
Economy and Society (Eliade), 411
Edelsky, C., 88n
Edleson, J. L., 210
Education: beginning of coeducation, 399; of children of
   Color, 268; and mathematics achievement, 271; opposi-
   tion to higher education for women, 1–2; Virginia Military
   Institute's refusal to admit women, 9–10
EEC. *See* European Community
EEOC. *See* Equal Employment Opportunity Commission
Effect size, 26–27
Eggebeen, D., 384
Ego-Dystonic Homosexuality, 181, 342
Ehrenreich, B., 34, 419
Ehrhardt, A. A., 37, 185
Eibl-Eibesfeldt, I., 104
Einsiedel, E., 160, 163, 172
Eisenberg, E., 94
Eisenberg, M., 384
Eisenberg, N., 34
Eisler, R., 363
Ekman, P., 104
Elgin, S. H., 101
Eliade, M., 411
Elliot, L. B., ix
Elliott, A. G. P., 313
Elliott, R., 310, 316
Ellis, D., 222, 223
Ellis, H., 285
Ellis, L., 185, 188
Ellyson, S. L., 102, 107, 120, 120n, 125, 148
Elshtain, J. B., 363
Embedded view of agency, 139–40
Emerson, P., 395
Emery, B., 226
Empathy, 19–20, 115, 141–42, 360, 375
Employment. *See* Workplace
Empowerment, control through, and negotiation strategies,
   140
Emswiller, T., 315, 317, 328n
Encoding, definition of, 128
Engel, R., 40
Engineering, 271, 286–87
English, P. W., 109
Enguidanos, G. M., 57, 361
Enns, L. R., 49
Epistemological perspectives, on knowing, 253–56
Epstein, C. F., 18
Equal Employment Opportunity Commission (EEOC), 8–9,
   307–08
Equal rights litigation: *Price Waterhouse v. Hopkins,* 307–32;
   sex discrimination at Sears Roebuck & Company, 8–9;

Virginia Military Institute's refusal to admit women,
   9–10
Eskilson, A., 97, 316
Espin, O. M., 57
Essed, P., 62, 66
Essentialism, 181–88, 412
Estrich, S., 178n, 243, 244
Ethnicity: Asian Americans as category, 65; Black feminist
   thought, 59; categorization of, 65–66; and childhood psychiatric disorders, 346; and conversational style, 79–80, 94;
   and *Diagnostic and Statistical Manual* (DSM-IV), 337; and
   discrimination in workplace, 308–09; and domestic violence, 207; and "double" and "triple jeopardy," 56; and
   education, 268; ethnomethodological perspective on,
   65–67, 73; exclusion of women of Color from research, 5,
   21, 55–56, 79; family expectations of women, 5; identity
   based on, 66–67; increased research on, 5; and knowing,
   256–57; and learning styles, 83n; mathematical metaphors
   for relationship between gender and, 58, 59–60, 69, 74;
   and men's movement, 408; mothering and child care
   meaning based on, 69–70; and negotiation strategies, 135;
   and nonverbal behavior, 102; and nonverbal decoding ability, 113–14; oppression of Black men, 56; and pornography, 156; psychotherapy with African-American women,
   56; racism and sexism against Black women, 66; and rape,
   233; and relational theory, 360; relationships with gender
   and class, 5–6, 55–75; scientific arguments for inferiority
   based on, 1; and Senate hearings on Clarence Thomas's
   nomination to Supreme Court, 70; and smiling behavior,
   102; subordination of women of Color through rejection,
   21; West Indian immigrants as maids, 67; White middle-
   class bias in feminist thought on, 59–60; and Women's
   Ways of Knowing (WWK) model, 250; and working moth-
   ers, 383–84. *See also* Social class; *and specific ethnic groups*
Ethnomethodological inquiry, 62–68, 73
Ethology, 395
European Childcare Network, 389n
European Community (EEC), 389
Everywoman, 155
Exline, R. V., 104, 105
Eyer, D., xxi, 384, 391–97
Ezell, H. F., 301n

Fadden, T. F., 148
Faderman, L., 190
Fagenson, E. A., 147
Fagot, B. I., 48, 49, 50, 51
Fairfield, M. L., 315, 326
Faludi, S., 9
Family violence. *See* Domestic violence
Farrell, W., 400, 402
Father wound, 410–11, 418n
Fathers: and attachment, 395; influence of, on gender devel-
   opment, 34, 48–49; men's movement and search for lost
   fathers, 408–11, 418, 418n; relationship with infants, 386;
   single fathers' similarity to mothers, 93. *See also* Parents
Fathers for Equal Rights Organization, 229
Fausto-Sterling, A., 36
Favero, J. L., 317

FBI. *See* Federal Bureau of Investigation
Fear of failure, 291
Fear of success, 291
Federal Bureau of Investigation (FBI), 210, 213, 233, 234, 241
Federal Express, 304
Feingold, A., 21, 285–86
Feiring, C., 50
Feld, S. L., 215, 216, 218
Feldman, M., 112
Feldman-Summers, S., 314
Feminine Leadership (Loden), 298
"Feminine mystique," 3
Feminism and Psychology, 4
Feminist thought: definition of, 374; on difference, 14, 257–58; on gender differences versus similarities, 7–8, 15–17; on mythopoetic men's movement, 400, 403; on psychology of men, 6; White middle-class bias in, 59–60; of women of Color, 59. *See also specific topics*
Feminists for Free Expression, 156
Fennema, E., 145
Fenstermaker, S., xxi, 56, 58–70, 73, 74
Ferber, M. A., 303n
Ferguson, T., 360
Fernandez, L. C., 4
Ferraro, K., 224
Ferris, S. R., 101
Fiedler, L., 417
Fields, M. D., 223
Fiester, S. J., 350, 351
Filipczak, B., 135
Filliozat, A. M., 38
Fine, M., 255
Finkelhor, D., 158
Fire in the Belly (Keen), 402
Firestone, S., 69, 109
First, M. B., 339
Fischer, K. W., 266
Fisek, M. H., 147
Fisher, R., 135, 140, 151
Fisher, S., 189
Fiske, S. T., xxi, 131, 307–10, 316, 321–32
Fitzgerald, L. F., 235, 286
Fitzgerald, L. M., 385
Fivush, R., 48
Fliegel, Z. O., 2, 3
Flitcraft, A., 223, 225, 226
Fogel, A., 20
Forbes, D., 48
Forbes, K., 241
Ford, M., 349
Ford, R. S., 96
Ford, T. W., 96
Forgas, J. P., 128
Foucault, M., 125, 341
Fournet, G. P., 122
Fox, L. H., 278
France, 286
Frances, A., xxii, 338, 339, 348–56
Frank, F. D., 314

Freedman, G., 37
Freire, P., 256
French, J. R. P., Jr., 125, 146
French, M., 189
Freud, S., 2–3, 360, 374, 394n, 399
Frey, K. S., 50
Fried, N. E., 309
Friedan, B., 3, 69, 109
Friedman, B. L., 145
Friedman, D. E., 303n
Friedman, G. B., 120n, 132
Friedman, H. S., 112n
Friedman, L., 233
Friedman, W. J., 145
Frieze, I. H., 24, 105, 106, 109, 120
Fromkin, H. L., 317
Frye, M., 63
Fryer, M. M., 101
Fulkerson, K. F., 50
Fundamental attribution error, 92
Furr, S., 50
Furumoto, L., 3
Fusilier, M. R., 313
Futrelle, D., 170n

Gabriel, T., 420
Gagnon, J. H., 188
Galinsky, E., 303n
Gallant, S. J. A., 351
Gambling, Pathological, 344
Gandelman, R., 41
Gaquin, D. A., 212, 223
Garai, J. E., 40
Garb, H. N., 339
Garber, L., 250
Garcia-Preto, N., 360
Gardner, H., 253
Gardner, W., 310, 316
Garfinkel, H., 63
Garland, H., 315
Garnets, L. D., 183
Gaskell, J., 251
Gawelek, M. A., 57
Gay, M., 351
Geary, D. C., 273
Gebhard, P. H., 188
Geis, F. L., 292
Geller, J. A., 209
Gelles, R. J., 174n, 210–12, 215, 216, 222, 227–29
Gelman, D., 353
Gender: definitions of, 7, 62, 64; ethnomethodological perspective on, 63–65, 73; feminist approaches to gender differences versus similarities, 7–8; history of scientific study of, 1–3, 15; journals on, 4; mathematical metaphors for relationship between race and, 58, 59–60, 69, 74; media reporting on, 8, 16, 33, 83, 283–84; new conceptualization of, 97–99; normative conceptions of, 63; overview of current research on, 7–10; paradox of gender, 296–97; relationships with ethnicity and class, 5–6, 55–75; research on, and equal

rights litigation, 8–10; research on, and social change, 8–10; scientific arguments for inferiority of women, 1–3; sex distinguished from, 7; sex-roles approach to, 61–62; textbooks on, 4–5, 4n; traditional conceptualizations of, 60–62; traditional stereotypes, 6–7, 96; White middle-class bias in feminist thought on, 59–60. *See also* Gender differences; Gender stereotypes; Psychology of men; Psychology of women; *and specific topics pertaining to gender*

Gender Advertisements (Goffman), 106

Gender and Discourse (Tannen), 80

Gender and Society, 4

Gender differences: biological causation of, 33–52; emergence of, in first year of life, 37–42, 44–48; feminist approaches to gender differences versus similarities, 7–8, 15–17; and generalizations, 83–84; magnitude issues concerning, 28–30; media reporting of, 8, 16, 33, 83, 283–84; methods used to draw conclusions from research on, 24–28; opposition to continuing research on, 16–17, 19–22, 24; overview of issues surrounding study of, 15–17; parental influence on, 34–35, 48–51; and perpetuation of women's disadvantaged status, 19, 30; problems associated with research on, 16; socialization explanation of, 34–35, 48–52; in status, 50–52; support for continuing research on, 16, 24–30; and traditional conceptualization of gender, 60–61; within-self variability, 21–22

Gender Identity Disorder, 345

Gender: Psychological Perspectives (Brannon), 4n

Gender-Related Differences: Origins and Outcomes (Hoyenga), 4n

Gender-role strain, of men, 399–400

Gender roles. *See* Sex roles

Gender schema, 35

Gender stereotypes: American Psychological Association amicus brief in *Price Waterhouse v. Hopkins,* 310–32; descriptive gender stereotypes, 322; and discrimination in workplace, 307–32; Iron Maiden stereotype, 312, 324; lack-of-fit model of, 311; and leadership, 97; methods for reducing, 316, 328; and normative stereotype model, 311; and perception of speech, 95–97; prescriptive gender stereotypes, 322; and psychiatric diagnoses, 344–45; and tokenism, 312–13, 324; traditional stereotypes, 6–7, 96, 299, 363, 391, 403–04; of working women, 312–13

Gender Stereotypes and Roles (Basow), 4n

Genderism, 86

General Mills, 305

Generalizations, uses and dangers of, 83–84

Gentry, C., 173

Gergen, K. J., 190, 200, 256

Gerhart, B., 136

Germany, 174, 175

Gerson, J., 61, 69

Gerson, K., 401

Geschwind, N., 279–80, 285

Gesell, A., 38

Gesell, Judge, 323, 331, 332

Getting Past No (Ury), 135

Getting to Yes (Fisher and Ury), 135

Gianetto, R. M., 101, 128

Gidycz, C., 236–37, 238, 243

Gifford, D. G., 146, 147

Gilbert, N., xxii, 234, 236–45

Gilder, G., 410

Giles-Sims, J., 212

Gillespie, D. L., 106

Gillette, D., 409, 410, 412, 414, 416

Gilligan, C., 7, 9, 10, 16, 56, 57, 139, 145, 249, 258, 262–63, 265, 295n, 361–63, 374–75, 377

Gilroy, F. D., 47, 337

Ginorio, A. B., 5, 337

Girls Lean Back Everywhere: The Law of Obscenity and the Assault on Genius (de Grazia), 179

Gitter, A. G., 109, 113

Giusti, L. M., 244

Glaberson, W., 307

Glass ceiling, 291–92

Glazer, N., 61

Gleason, J. B., 48

Glenn, E. N., 59, 67

Glucksmann, A., 37, 40

Goddard, M., 102

Goffman, E., 63, 69, 86, 104, 106, 109, 120

Golant, S. K., 209, 292

Gold, J. H., 352, 353

Goldberg, C., 292

Goldberg, H., 402

Goldberger, N., xxii, 57, 249–59, 261–65, 267, 268

Golden, C., 188, 360

Goldstein, D., 208

Golombok, S., 183

Gonsiorek, J. C., 190

Gonyea, J., 385

Goodman, J., 309

Gordon, M. E., 317

Gordon, R. A., 313

Gorman, C., 16, 33

Gorman, C. D., 317

Gorski, R., 186

Gossett, H., 416n

Gossett, T., 61, 65, 68

Gottlieb, F., 343

Gould, S. J., 1, 34

Grady, K. E., 95

Graham, S., 5, 57

Grant, J., 298, 299, 302, 303

Graves, L. M., 313

Graves, R., 416

Gray, B., 137

Gray, J., 295n

Greater Male Variability Hypothesis, 285–86

Green, J. A., 49

Green, K. C., 274

Green, R., 182

Greenblat, C. S., 216

Greene, B., 5, 56, 183, 309, 360

Greeno, J. G., 253

Greer, G., 359

Gregor, T., 415

Gregware, P., 213, 214–15

Grellert, E. A., 185
Griffin, C., 401
Griffin, G., 251
Griffin, T. J., 135
Griscom, J. L., 125
Grisso, T., 310, 316
Grotevant, H. D., 218
Gruber, C. P., 385
Gruchy, C. D. G., 103
Gryl, F. E., 214
Guild, D., 160
Guinier, L., 255
Guloien, T., 163
Gunew, S., 251
Gustafson, G. E., 49
Gutek, B. A., 136, 286, 313, 314, 325
Guzzo, R. A., 314, 326
Gwartney-Gibbs, P. A., 137, 226

Haas, A., 79
Haber, L., 188
Haberfeld, Y., 313
Hacker, A., 83n, 88n
Hagan, K. L., 400
Hagan, R., 48, 49
Hagen, R. L., 316
Haigh, J. G., 176
Hakel, M. D., 313
Halberstadt, A., xxii, 101, 102, 108, 109, 110–12, 113–14,
    115, 116, 120–31, 120n
Halderman, D. C., 188
Hale-Benson, J., 83n
Haley, A., 175
Half the Human Experience (Hyde), 4n
Hall, D. T., 314
Hall, E. T., 104
Hall, F. S., 314
Hall, J., 300n
Hall, J. A., xxii, 29, 79, 101–03, 106, 108–16, 120–32, 120n
Hall, R., 195
Hall, R. L., 37, 40
Hall, S., 74
Hall-McCorquodale, I., 383
Halpern, D., 16, 279
Hamer, D. H., 183
Hamilton, S., 348, 349, 351
Hammersmith, S. K., 188
Hancock, E., 291
Hanmer, J., 227
Hanmer, R., 225
Hanmer, T., 258
Hannah, J. S., 291
Harding, S., 250
Hare-Mustin, R., 7, 16, 17, 258, 360
Harlow, H., 394
Harmony, and negotiation strategies, 141–42
Harney, P. A., 243
Harragan, B. L., 295n
Harriman, A., 295n

Harris, S. L., 315
Harrop, J. W., 210
Harry, J., 185
Hart, B., 217
Hart, J., 189
Hartel, C. E. J., 137
Harvard Law School, 135
Haskett, R., 37
Haslett, B. J., 292
Haste, H., 264, 265
Haugaard, J., 173n
Hayes, C. W., 128
Hays, J., 266
Hazards of Being Male   (Goldberg), 402
Hazelwood, R., 222, 225
Head Start, 391–92, 392n
Hecht, M. A., 120n, 124
Hedges, L. V., 25, 284, 286
Hegel, G. W. F., 341
Heifetz, R. A., 292
Heilman, M. E., xxii, 311–15, 317, 321–32
Heim, P., 292
Helgeson, S., 295n
Hellman, P., 241
Helmreich, R., 316
Heltman, K., 120n, 148
Hendrick, J., 48
Henley, N. M., xxii, 5, 16, 79–80, 102, 104–17, 120, 124, 125,
    128, 130, 131
Hennig, M., 295n
Henton, J., 214
Henwood, K., 57
Herek, G., 193
Heritage, J., 64, 65
Herman, J., 344
Hersch, P., 182
Hertzberger, S. D., 218
Heterosexuality: compulsory heterosexuality, 192–92, 244;
    transitions from heterosexuality to lesbianism, 188–201.
    See also Sexuality
Hewitt Associates, 305
Highby, B. J., xxiii, 243–46
Higher education: and mathematics achievement, 271; oppo-
    sition to, for women, 1–2; Virginia Military Institute's re-
    fusal to admit women, 9–10
Hill, A., 70, 86n
Hill, J. N., 294
Hinde, R. A., 49
Hindley, C. B., 38
Hines, M., 37, 185
Hiring decisions, 313
Hirsch, M., 258
Hirschfeld, R. M. A., 348
Hispanics: conversational style of, 80; and Diagnostic and Sta-
    tistical Manual (DSM-IV), 337; and discrimination in
    workplace, 308; and domestic violence, 207; family expec-
    tations of, 5; feminist thought of, 59; increased research
    on, 5, 55; and relational theory, 360
Histrionic Personality Disorder, 338, 344, 345, 348–49

Hite, S., 160
Hitt, M. A., 313, 317
Ho, C. K., 207
Hobson, J. R., 40
Hocevar, D., 38
Hochschild, A., 60–61, 295n
Hodgson, R. J., 159
Hoffman, L. R., 148, 149, 150
Hoffman, L. W., 383, 392
Holland, J. L., 276, 278
Hollander, J., 188
Hollingworth, L. S., 2, 15
Holloway, M., 286
Holloway, W., 18
Holmes, J., 98
Holtzman, E., 351
Homicide rates, and domestic violence, 213
Homophobia, 342, 344
Homosexuality: biological causation of, 181–88; and brain re-
    search, 181, 182, 185–86; coming out process, 190; and Di-
    agnostic and Statistical Manual (DSM), 181, 342–43, 346;
    essentialist idea of, 181–88; genetic studies on, 184, 187;
    and hormones, 181, 185; labeling of, as abnormal, 181;
    models of identity development, 189–201
Hong Kong, 102
hooks, b., 59, 69
Hooyman, N. R., 385
Hopkins, A., 307–17, 321–32
Hormones: and mathematics achievement, 279–80; prenatal
    hormones and sex differences in first year of life, 33, 41;
    and sexual orientation, 181, 182, 185
Horner, A., 291
Horner, M. S., 7, 291
Horney, K., 3, 362, 368–70
Hornung, C. A., 212
Hotaling, G., 212, 229
Howard, A., 299n, 300
Howard, J. A., 20, 24, 256
Hoyenga, K. B., 4n
Hoyenga, K. T., 4n
Hughes, C. C., 337
Hughes, E. C., 61
Hughes, F. P., 49
Hughes, J. S., 341
Hull, G. T., 61
Humphreys, L. G., 275–80
Hungary, 286–87
Hunter, W. J., 399
Hurd, T., 263
Hurt, S. W., 352
Hurtado, A., 21, 69
Huston, A., 49
Hutchins, L., 191
Hwang, C., P., 385
Hyde, J. S., xxiii, 4n, 5, 6, 16, 92, 105, 145, 272, 283–87, 384,
    385
Hymowitz, C., 291–92
Hyperactivity, 345–46
Hysteria, 343–44

I Never Called It Rape (Warshaw), 240–41
Iacocca, L., 294
Ilgen, D. R., 313, 317
Immigrants as maids, 67
In a Different Voice (Gilligan), 9, 249
In Search of Excellence (Peters), 296
INAH-3. See Interstitial nucleus of anterior hypothalamus
Independence, during childhood, 35
Indians. See American Indians
Infancy: and attachment theory, 49–50, 391–97; continuous
    individual care needed during, 386–88; daycare as unable
    to meet needs during, 384, 386–90; developmental mile-
    stones during first year of life, 37–42, 44–48; gender differ-
    ences in, 37–42; and maternal deprivation, 393–94;
    mother's relationship with infants, 386–90; parents'
    influence on gender development during, 34. See also
    Childhood
Inferential accuracy, 129
Influence. See Power and influence
Ingegno, A., 7
Initiation ritual, in men's movement, 411–12
Innes, C. A., 212
Instone, D., 301n
Integrative, definition of, 141
Intellectual abilities. See Cognitive abilities
Interactive leadership model, 294–97
Intermittent Explosive Disorder, 344, 345
International Council of Women Psychologists, 3
International perspectives. See Cross-cultural patterns; and
    specific countries
Interpersonal Perception Task (IPT), 123
Interpersonal style of leadership, 300
Interstitial nucleus of anterior hypothalamus (INAH-3), 185
IPT. See Interpersonal Perception Task
Iran, 174
Irish, J. T., 120n, 132
Iron John: A Book About Men (Bly), 400, 406, 408–09
Iron John story, 409, 418
Iron Maiden stereotype, 312, 324
Isay, R., 343
Island, D., 209
Israel, 102
Italy, 286
Itzin, C., 155
Iwaniszek, J., 148
Izard, C. E., 122
Izraeli, D., 315
Izraeli, D. N., 315

Jacklin, C., 7, 8, 15, 33, 34, 36, 37, 49–51, 272
Jackson, A., 392
Jackson, L. A., 316
Jacobi, M. P., 2
Jacobs, J., 272, 283
Jaffe, P. G., 219
Jaggar, A., 253
Jago, A. G., 316
James, D., 86n

James, S. M., 57
Jamieson, K. H., 293
Japan, 86, 174, 175
Jardim, A., 295n
Jaschik, M. P., 9
Jaskir, J., 50
Jerdee, T. H., 312, 315, 317
Jewel Companies, 304
Jo, B., 189
Jobs. *See* Workplace
Johannsen, W., 148
Johns Hopkins University, 274, 283
Johnson, A., 239
Johnson, B. T., 27, 28, 127, 291, 300n
Johnson, C., 93, 120n
Johnson, J. B., 301n
Johnson, K., 360
Johnson, L. B., 155
Jones, A., 222
Jones, C., 196
Jones, E. E., 145
Jones, J. M., 243, 245
Jones, T. S., 148, 150
Jordan, J., xxiii, 60, 258, 262, 344, 359–61, 364–66, 368, 370, 373–79
Joslyn, M., 109
Jouriles, E. N., 210
Journal of Men's Studies, 6
Journal of Nonverbal Behavior, 104
Journals: on nonverbal communication, 104; on psychology of men, 6; on psychology of women, 4
Jurik, N. C., 213, 214–15

Kaahumanu, L., 191
Kagan, J., 40, 40–41
Kahn, A. S., 8, 17, 125, 234, 244, 316
Kahn, S. E., 291
Kaiser, G., 273
Kalafat, J., 40, 40–41
Kalbfleisch, P. J., 81
Kaman, V. S., 137
Kanin, E., 225
Kanter, R., 147, 312, 324, 324n
Kanuha, V., 209
Kaplan, A., 258, 344, 359, 365
Kaplan, M., 348
Karau, S., 95, 301n
Karen, R., 385
Karraker, M. K., 34
Karten, S., 96
Kaschak, E., 361
Kasmar, G., 176–77
Kasten, B., 141
Kaufman, B., 343
Kaufman, M., xxiii, 401, 406–20
Kaufman Kantor, G., 212
Kavanagh, K., 50
Kawamoto, J. Y., 360
Keating, C. F., 120n, 148

Keen, S., 402
Keller, E. F., 139, 258
Kelley, H. H., 146
Kelley, K., 155
Kelly, E., 55
Kendrick, W., 179
Keniston, K., 417
Kennedy, T., 233
Kentucky Commission on Women, 211–12
Kenyon, F. E., 189
Kerkstra, A., 120
Kernberg, O., 342–43
Kessler, S. J., 63
Kilmartin, C. T., 4n, 6
Kimball, M. M., ix, 7, 8, 272
Kimbrell, A., 401
Kimmel, D. C., 183
Kimmel, M. S., ix, xxiii, 6, 156, 400, 401, 406–20, 417n
Kimura, D., 33
Kincaid, P. J., 223
King, L. M., 20, 24
King, M., 184
King, P. M., 253, 261, 265–67
Kinnear, L., 102
Kinsey, A. C., 181, 188, 189
Kipnis, A., 402
Kirk, S. A., 339
Kirkpatrick, M., 198
Kirts, D., 241
Kitchener, K. S., 253, 261, 265–67
Kite, M. E., 128
Kitzinger, C., xxiii, 7, 18, 182, 188–201
Kitzinger, S., 192–93
Klakenberg, G., 38
Klein, R., 365
Kleptomania, 344
Klonsky, B. G., 291, 330
Knapp, M. L., 103
Knights Without Armor (Kipnis), 402
Knorr-Cetina, K., 190
Knowing: and childhood, 253; connected knowing, 255; constructed knowing, 255–56; epistemological perspectives on, 253–56; and feminist controversy on psychology of difference, 257–58; gender differences in, 267–68; and metaphor of voice, 257; moral reasoning, 249, 263, 362–63; Perry's theory of intellectual and ethical development, 266; and personal epistemology, 253; procedural knowing, 254–55; received knowing, 254; reflective judgment theory, 266–67; "right" way to know, 256–57; separate knowing, 255; and silence, 254, 257, 262; and social context of meaning-making, 252–53; subjective knowing, 254; theories of adult intellectual development, 265–67; Women's Ways of Knowing (WWK) model, 249–68
Koeske, R. D., 24
Kohlberg, L., 249, 263, 265, 363, 374
Kohut, H., 375
Kolb, D. M., xxiii–xxiv, 136, 138–44
Kolb, S., 45
Kolb, T. M., 218

Koller, A., 255
Komarovsky, M., 61
Kombos, N. A., 122
Koop, C. E., 172, 207
Kopecky, G., 401
Korabik, K., 151
Korner, A. F., 37, 40
Kortenhaus, C. M., 35
Koshland, D. E., 286
Koss, M., 4, 136, 207, 222, 233–34, 236–41, 237n, 238n,
    243–45
Koval, J., 214
Kovel, J., 341
Kraemer, H., 37
Krafka, C., 173
Kram, K. E., 304n
Kramarae, C., 86n, 94, 98, 108
Kramer, B. M., 57, 339
Kramer, C., 106
Krauth, B., 402
Kravitz, D., 148
Krieger, S., 142
Kroll, J. K., 338
Kronsberg, S., 48, 49
Krutetskii, V. A., 274
Kryger, B. R., 313
Kuczynski, L., 48
Kuebli, J., 48
Kuhn, T. S., 256, 274
Kupers, T., xxiv, 181, 339–46, 399–401
Kurz, D., xxiv, 208, 219, 222–29
Kutchins, H., 339
Kutchinsky, B., 174–75

Labouvie-Vief, G., 266
Lacayo, R., 307
Lach, D. H., 137
Lack-of-fit model, 311
Lafayette College, 241
LaFrance, M., xxiv, 102, 104–17, 120, 124, 128, 130, 131
LaFromboise, T. D., 102
Laird, N., 38
Lakoff, R., 79, 80, 84n, 106
Lamb, M., 385, 396
Lamb, S., 209, 338
Lamon, S., 145
Lampl-de Groot, J., 3
Lander, P. S., 189, 194, 200
Landrine, H., 5
Lane, D. M., 29
Lane, K. E., 226
Lang-Takac, E., 264
Langan, P. A., 212
Langston, D., 68
Language. *See* Communication
Language and Women's Place (Lakoff), 79
Lappin, M., 314
Larned, A. G., xxiv, 250, 261–68
LaRussa, G. W., 96

Latane, B., 130
Late Luteal Phase Dysphoric Disorder, 343, 351–53
Latinas: conversational style of, 80; and *Diagnostic and Statis-
    tical Manual* (DSM-IV), 337; and discrimination in work-
    place, 308; and domestic violence, 207; family expectations
    of, 5; feminist thought of, 59; increased research on, 5, 55;
    and relational theory, 360
LaViolette, A. D., 207
Law students, 84, 255, 258
Lazur, R. F., 400
Leach, P., xxiv, 384, 386–90, 393, 397
Leadership: AT&T study of managers, 299–302; autocratic
    leadership, 300; command-and-control model of, 294; and
    conversational style, 94–95; democratic leadership, 300; ef-
    fectiveness of managers not different due to gender differ-
    ences, 298–305; and gender stereotypes, 97; interactive
    leadership model, 294–97; interpersonal style of, 300; and
    mentoring programs, 304; and negotiation strategies, 146;
    overview of issues on, 291–92; and paradox of gender,
    296–97; reasons for small number of women leaders, 291;
    task style of, 300; training and development programs for
    managers, 304–05; women as better managers than men,
    292, 294–99; women in top management, 291–92
Leadership (Burns), 296
Leaper, C., 36
Learning styles, 83n
LeBaron, D., 101
Leder, G. C., 273
Lee, D. M., 315
Leffler, A., 108
Leiderman, P. H., 37
Leinbach, M. D., 48, 49
Lensky, H., 188
Leone, B., 209
Lesbianism: barriers and resistance to identifying as lesbian,
    192–96; and blocking out earlier experiences of, 193–96;
    and coming out process, 198–99; and compulsory hetero-
    sexuality, 192–92, 244; making and describing transition
    to lesbian identity, 196–98; model of identity develop-
    ment, 190–201; and multiple oppressions, 193; and psy-
    chological adjustment, 181; transitions from
    heterosexuality to lesbianism, 188–201
Levant, R. F., ix, 6, 7, 399, 401
LeVay, S., 182, 185–86, 188
Levine, E., 172
Levinson, D., 363
Levy, N., 40
Lewicki, R. J., 135
Lewin, T., 229
Lewine, R., 348
Lewis, D. M., 40
Lewis, M., 35, 40–41, 48, 50
Lewis, S., 56
Lewis, S. G., 197
Lewis, V. G., 182
Liden, R. C., 313
Lightdale, J. R., 21, 24
Lincoln, A., 229
Lindzey, G., 278

Linn, M. C., 92, 145, 286
Linton, R., 61
Linz, D., 156, 157, 167–68, 172, 173, 178n
Lips, H. M., 4n
Lipsett, L. P., 40
Lloyd, B., 103
Lloyd, B. B., 51
Lloyd, S., 214
Loden, M., 294n, 298, 299, 302
Loevinger, J., 253
Lofquist, L. H., 275–76
Logan, J., 374
London, M., 314
Lonsway, K. A., 235
Lopata, H. Z., 61, 62
Lopez, S. R., 19, 57
Lorber, J., 36, 55–56
Lorenz, K., 395
Loring, M., 348
Los Angeles Epidemiology Catchment Area study, 211
Loseke, D., 222
Lott, B., xxiv, 4n, 17, 19–22, 24, 25, 27, 28, 30, 233, 309
Love, L. R., 101, 128
Lu, F. G., 337
Lubinski, D., xxiv, 272, 274–80, 283–86
Lucca, J., 222, 225
Lupri, E., 222, 225
Luszcz, M., 264, 265
Luttrell, W., 257
Lyons, N., 258
Lytton, H., 34, 48, 279

Maccoby, E. E., 7, 8, 15, 34, 37, 44, 49–51
Macdonald, B., 193
Machung, A., 295n
Mackenzie, G. O., 416n
MacKinnon, C., 155–57, 170–71, 175–79
MacKinnon, D. W., 274, 276
MacPherson, G. M., 145
Magolda, M. B., 253
Mahony, R., 208
Mai-Dalton, R. R., 314
Major, B., 128, 136
Majors, R., 400
Makhijani, M. G., 291, 330
Malamuth, N., 157, 159–60, 162, 164–66, 207, 233
Malatesta, C. Z., 48
Male Experience, The (Doyle), 4n, 6
Male role, traditional values attached to, 6–7
Male-bashing, 400
Malone, J., 211
Maltz, D., 98
Maluso, D., 22, 309
Managers. *See* Leadership
Manhood. *See* Gender stereotypes; Mythopoetic men's movement
Manhood Wrecked and Rescued (Hunter), 399
Mann, C., 213, 222, 225
Mannion, K., 181

Maple, T. L., 121
Marecek, J., 7, 16–18, 250, 258, 263, 360
Margolin, L., 225
Markus, H., 8
Marshall, W., 177–78
Martell, R. F., 29, 315, 317, 327
Martin, C. E., 188
Martin, J. R., 258
Martin, P. Y., 225
Martinez, R., 266
Marvel, L., 2
Mary Baldwin College, 9
Masculine Self, The (Kilmartin), 4n, 6
Masculinists, 417n
masculinities, 6
Master/slave dialectic, 341
Masters, P., 188
Masturbatory conditioning, 159
Maternal. *See* Mothers
Maternal Care and Mental Health (Bowlby), 393
Maternal deprivation, 393–94
Mathematical metaphors, for gender, race, and class, 58, 59–60, 69, 74
Mathematics achievement: abilities concerning, and sex differences, 277–78, 279; biological causation of gender differences in, 271–87; and brain research, 280, 283; gender differences in, 19, 30, 271–87; Greater Male Variability Hypothesis, 285–86; and hormones, 279–80; lack of evidence for gender differences in, 283–87; media reporting of, 283–84; overview of issues on, 271–72; preferences concerning, and sex differences, 278–79; psychological profiles of mathematically talented, 274–80; reasons for few women in high-math-ability careers, 286–87; and Theory of Work Adjustment, 275–79
Mathie, V. A., 234
Matlin, M. W., 4n, 5, 6, 108, 207, 272
Maxwell, K., 162, 165–66
Mayo, C., 105, 106
McAlinden, F., 98
McAuslan, P., 235
McCartney, K., 384
McCormack, T., 178
McCullough, B. C., 212
McDonald, E., 184
McDonald, G. J., 190
McDonald, T., 313
McDuffie, D., 235
McElroy, W., 157
McEvoy, G. M., 301n
McEvoy, J., III, 216
McFerron, J. R., 224
McGrath, E., 4
McGraw, K. O., 29–30, 327
McGuffog, C., 50
McGuinness, D., 273
McGuire, R. J., 159
McHugh, M. C., 24, 208
McIntosh, M., 188–89
McKenna, W., 63

McKenzie-Mohr, D., 164–65
McKinley, N. M., 385
McLeer, S., 223
McLeod, M., 223
McNeely, R., 222, 225, 229
Meaney, M. J., 37, 40
Medea, A., 164
Mederos, F., 224
Media reporting: gender differences, 8, 16, 33, 83, 283–84; mathematics achievement, 283–84; on men's movement, 402; premenstrual dysphoric disorder, 353; sexuality, 178
Medical Economics (Ingegno), 7
Medical profession. *See* Physicians
Mednick, B. R., 38
Mednick, M. T., 24, 258, 272
Meeker, B. F., 147
Meese, E., 155
Meese Pornography Commission, 155, 156, 172, 173
Megargee, E., 94
Mehinaku, 415
Mehrabian, A., 101
Meigs, C., 1
Melhuish, E., 389n
Melling, L., 255, 258
Melson, G. F., 20
Memoirs v. Massachusetts, 175n
Men and Women of the Corporation (Kanter), 312
Men of Color, and men's movement, 408
Meng, X. L., 38
Men's movement: mythopoetic men's movement, 399–420; American Men's Studies Association, 6; Men's Studies Association of the National Organization for Men Against Sexism, 6; Society for the Psychological Study of Men and Masculinity, 6. *See also* Mythopoetic men's movement
Men's psychology. *See* Psychology of men
Men's Studies Association, 6
Menstruation, 2. *See also* Premenstrual Dysphoria Disorder
Mental disorders. *See Diagnostic and Statistical Manual*; Psychotherapy; *and specific disorders*
Mentoring programs, 304
Mericle, M. F., 313, 317
Merrill Lynch, 304
Messner, M., 225
Meta-analysis: benefits of, 330; description of, 25–27, 284; and mathematics, 284
Mexican-Americans, conversational style of, 80
Mexico, 102
Meyer, C., 178
Meyer-Bahlburg, H. F. L., 182, 185
Milgram, S., 145
Millar, K. U., 106
Millar, M. G., 106
Miller, A., 367, 368n
Miller, C. L., 126, 127n, 133
Miller, J. B., 55, 109, 120, 128, 130, 137, 139, 256, 258, 262–63, 341, 344, 359, 361–68, 364n, 370, 374–75, 377
Miller, N., 27, 328
Miller, P., 48
Millet, K., 109

Mills, C. J., 277
Mindell, P., 81
Minor, L. L., 277, 278
Minority people: and childhood psychiatric disorders, 346; conversational style of, 79–80, 94; and *Diagnostic and Statistical Manual* (DSM-IV), 337; and discrimination in workplace, 307–08; and domestic violence, 207; education of, 268; exclusion of, from research, 5, 21, 55–56, 79; feminist thought of, 59; impact of ethnicity and gender on, 5–6; increased research on, 5, 55–56; and knowing, 256–57; learning styles of, 83n; and men's movement, 408; mothering and child care meaning for, 69–70; negotiation strategies of, 135; nonverbal behavior of, 102; and nonverbal decoding ability, 113–14; and pornography, 156; racism and sexism against, 66; and rape, 233; and relational theory, 360; scientific arguments for inferiority of, 1; and Senate hearings on Clarence Thomas's nomination to Supreme Court, 70; and smiling behavior, 102; subordination of, through rejection, 21; West Indian immigrants as maids, 67; and *Women's Ways of Knowing* (WWK) model, 250; working mothers, 383–84. *See also specific racial and ethnic groups*
Minstrel shows, 416
Minton, H. L., 190
Mintzberg, H., 146, 295
MIT, 272
Mitchell, G., 121
Mitchell, T. R., 314
Mittelman, M., 163
Mobley, W. H., 314
Mohin, L., 199
Molm, L. D., 149
Molnar, P., 103
"Momism," 383
Mommy track in workplace, 303–04
Money, J., 37, 177, 182, 185, 188
Montagu, A., 61, 65
Moore, D. P., 314
Moore, L. L., 295n
Moore, M., 101
Moore, R., 409, 410, 412, 414, 416
Moraga, C., 59, 60
Moral reasoning, 249, 263, 362–63
Morawski, J., 56
Morey, L. C., 337
Morgan, R., 233
Morning After, The (Roiphe), 243
Morris, S. B., xxv, 309, 310–17, 321–23, 325–31
Morrison, A. M., 293
Morrison, T., 70
Moser, C., 313
Moses, J. L., 315, 326
Moshman, D., 266
Moskowitz, D. S., 20, 93
Moss, H. A., 41
Moss, P., 389n
Mother-blaming, 383, 400
Motherhood mandate, 2

Mothers: and attachment theory, 391–397; early work on motherhood mandate, 2; influence of, on gender development, 34–35, 48–49; maternal deprivation, 393–94; and mathematics ability of children, 283; men's movement and mother-son relationship, 410, 412–14; mommy track in workplace, 303–04; relational theory and mother-child relationship, 364–67, 375–76; relationship with infants, 386–90; relationships with daughters versus sons, 362, 365–66; single fathers' similarity to, 93; Victorian motherhood, 391; working mothers and children's well being, 383–97. *See also* Parents

Mottaz, C., 301n

Mrs. Pilgrim's Progress, 2

Ms. Campus Project on Sexual Assault, 236–38, 238n, 239, 240, 243–45

Muchinsky, P. M., 315, 328

Muehlenhard, C. L., xxv, 234, 235, 243–46

Mulkay, M., 190

Mullen, B., 324

Multiple causation, definition of, 158–59

Multiple Personality Disorder, 344, 354

Mulvey, E., 173n

Munn, P., 48

Murphy, E. F., 175–76

Murray, M., 304n

Mutual empathy, 375–77

Mutual empowerment, 376

Mutuality, 364–66, 375–76

Myth of Male Power, The (Farrell), 402

Myth of Masculinity, The (Pleck), 6

Mythopoetic men's movement: and anthropological androcentrism, 414–17; benefits of, 400–04; criticisms of, 400–01, 412–20; and essentialism, 412; and father wound, 410–11, 418, 418n; feminist criticism of, 400, 403; and flight from feminism, 419–20; historical and political context of, 407–08; and initiation ritual, 411–12; and mother wound, 412–14; and mother-son relationship, 410, 412–14; and new man as wimp, 409–10; overview of issues on, 399–401; philosophy underlying, 6, 400, 403–04, 406–12; and search for the deep masculine, 408–12; and search for lost boyhood, 417–19; and search for lost father, 408–11, 418, 418n; social composition of, 402–03, 408; and sociology of regression, 417–18; and stages of manhood, 410

Nagle, K. J., 49

Naked at the Gender Gap (Baber), 402

Narcissistic Personality Disorders, 344

Narrative reviewing, 25

National Council for Research on Women, 309

National Council of Women Psychologists, 3

National Crime Panel Report, 210

National Crime Surveys, 223, 244

National Crime Victimization Survey (NCVS), 211, 212, 234

National Family Violence Surveys (NFVS), 210–11, 212, 213–14, 215, 216, 226

National Institute of Mental Health, 236

National Organization for Men Against Sexism, 6

National Organization for Women, Task Force on Battered Women/Household Violence, 207

National Research Council, 172

National Survey of Families and Households (NSFH), 211, 213, 223

National Victim Center, 240, 240n

National Women's Political Caucus, 22

Native Americans: increased research on, 5; in law school, 84–85; nonverbal behavior of, 102; rituals of, used in men's movement, 416; and Women's Ways of Knowing (WWK) model, 250

Nature of Managerial Work, The (Mintzberg), 295

NCVS. *See* National Crime Victimization Survey

Negotiating for Your Life (Schapiro), 135

Negotiation strategies: and control through empowerment, 140; and cooperative women, competitive men, 145–48; differences based on gender, 136, 138–48; differences based on status and power considerations, 136, 145–51; and embedded view of agency, 139–40; and empathy, 141; and expectations, 143, 147–48; explanations for gender differences in, 147–48; gender-plus-power explanation of, 147; and gender-role socialization, 147; overview of issues on, 135–36; and preserving harmony, 141–42; problem solving through dialogue, 140–41; and relational view of others, 139; situational power explanation of, 147; woman's voice in formal, public negotiation, 141–44

Neiman-Marcus, 305

"Nervios," 337

Neuberg, S. L., 316

Neustadtl, S., 250

New Psychology of Men, A (Levant and Pollack), 6

Newcombe, N., 96

NFVS. *See* National Family Violence Surveys

Niemela, P., 36

Nierenberg, J., 135

Nietzel, M., 348

Nieva, V. F., 313, 325

Nisbett, R. E., 40, 145

Nishijima, S., 40

Nisonoff, L., 225

Noble, B. P., 292

Noddings, N., 258, 363

Noe, A. W., 325

Nonverbal behavior: and accommodativeness, 108; cross-cultural patterns in, 102; decoding ability for, 102, 104–17; definition of, 104–05; early interest and research on, 104; explanations for sex differences in nonverbal sensitivity, 115–16; journal on, 104; motivation and nonverbal sensitivity, 130–31; "oppression hypothesis" of nonverbal decoding ability, 104–10; overview of issues on, 101–02; and power, 104–05; and race, 102; readability of, 107–08; sensitivity to, 108; smiling, 20, 101–02, 105, 120n; and submissiveness, 108; subordination-power hypothesis of nonverbal decoding ability, 102, 104–17, 120–31

Nonverbal sensitivity: and motivation, 130–31; nature of, 129–30; subordination-power hypothesis of, 102, 104–17, 120–31

Norman, M., 8

Norman, R. Z., 147

Normative conceptions, of gender, 63

Normative stereotype model, 311
Northwestern Bell, 304
Novello, A., 222
Nowell, A., 284, 286
NSFH. *See* National Survey of Families and Households
Nurseries. *See* Childcare

O'Barr, W., 93
Oberklaid, F., 49
Object relations model of adult development, 366
O'Boyle, M. W., 280
O'Brien, C., 122, 123
O'Brien, M., 49
Obscenity. *See* Pornography
Obsessive-Compulsive Disorder (OCD), 344
Obsessive-Compulsive Personality Disorder, 344, 345, 348
OCD. *See* Obsessive-Compulsive Disorder
Odewahn, C. A., 301n
O'Farrell, B., 303n
Offen, K., 258
Ogbu, J. U., 253
O'Leary, K., 98, 210
Olian, J. D., 313
Oliphant, V. N., 313
Olley, J. G., 40
Olson, J. P., 37
Omark, 189
Omi, M., 61, 65, 66
O'Neil, S. M., 189, 198
Only Words (MacKinnon), 175
Oppositional Defiant Disorder, 345
Oppressed status, definition of, 111
"Oppression hypothesis" of nonverbal decoding ability, 104–10
Organizational Dynamics (Grant), 298
Orne, H., 214
Oros, C., 238n, 239
Orr, R., 264, 265
Ortho Pharmaceuticals, 303
Ortman, P. E., 264, 267
Osterwell, Z., 264
Otto, L., 392
Overcoming Math Anxiety (Tobias), 271
Owen, M. A., 304n
Owens, S. D., 313

Packard, E., 341
Page, S., 168n
Pagelow, M. D., 212, 224
Pally, M., 156, 171–72, 174, 176
Paludi, M. A., 4n
Panic disorder, 344
Paradox of gender, 296–97
Paraphilias, 344
"Parent tracks" in workplace, 303–04
Parental leave, 384
Parental Leave Bill, 384
Parents: and attachment theory, 49–50, 391–97; influence of, on gender development, 34–35, 48–51; and mathematics

ability of children, 283; men's movement and parent-child relationship, 410–14; mother-daughter versus mother-son relationships, 362, 365–66; parenting in dual-earner heterosexual couples, 21; relational theory and mother-child relationship, 362, 364–67, 375–76, relationship with infants, 386–90; self-reports of child's developmental milestones, 47; single fathers' similarity to mothers, 93. *See also* Fathers; Mothers
Parker, B., 223, 301n
Parrot, A., 234
Parsons, B., 182, 184–86
Parsons, C. K., 313
Parsons, T., 40, 61
"Pathological arrhythmicity," 343, 344
Pathological Gambling, 344
Patriarchal theory, compared with relational theory, 373–75
Patterson, M. L., 128
Patterson, O., 56
Pearson, J., 81
Peay, P., 360
Pendergrass, M. L., 253
Penelope, J., 189n
Penis envy, 394, 394n
Penrod, S., 156, 167, 172, 173, 178n
People of Color. *See* Men of Color; Women of Color
PepsiCo, 305
Perceptual sensitivity, 129
Performance appraisal, 313–14, 325
Perkins, R., 200
Perot, R., 294
Perry, W. G., 249, 252, 253, 256, 261, 265–67
Personality disorders, 338, 344, 345, 348–50
Peters, L. H., 314
Peters, T., 296
Pfaff, P. L., 122
Pfeffer, J., 146
Pfohl, B., 348
Phelps, J. L., xxv, 243–46
Philipson, I. J., 361
Phillips, D., 384
Phillips, R. D., 337
Physical Abuse of Adult, in DSM, 343
Physical assaults. *See* Domestic violence
Physicians, opposition to women as, 1, 7, 15
Piaget, J., 262
Pickens, B. A., 313, 317
Pike, K. M., 128
Pillard, R. C., xxv, 182, 184–87
Pincus, H. A., 339
Pinderhughes, E., 5
Pirog-Good, M. A., 212
Pizzey, E., 207
Plant, E., 16
Plant, W. T., 276
Play, during childhood, 34, 49, 51
Pleck, J., 6, 399–400
Ploutz-Snyder, R. J., 124
Plummer, K., 188
PMS, 343, 353–54

Pogrebin, L. C., 6
Politeness, 94
Political office seekers, 22
Pollack, W. S., ix, 6, 7, 399, 401
Pollitt, K., 250
Pollner, M., 200
Pollock, V. E., 27
Polokow, V., 392n
Pomerleau, A., 34
Pomeroy, W. B., 188
Pommerenke, H., 176
PONS. See Profile of Nonverbal Sensitivity
Ponse, B., 195, 198
Pool, R. E., 183
Poor: and Head Start, 391–92; scientific arguments for inferi-
    ority of, 1; stereotypes of, 68; working mothers, 383–84
Poor, M., 194
Pornography: and acceptance of interpersonal violence, 166;
    and African Americans, 156; anecdotes and suspicions con-
    cerning, 175–77; antipornography laws, 155–56, 170,
    176–77; Butler decision on, in Canada, 171; and callous at-
    titudes toward female sexuality, 167; censorship of, as inef-
    fective in reducing violence against women, 155–56,
    170–79; children's and adolescents' access to, 162–63; cor-
    relational data concerning, 173–75; and creation of appe-
    tite for increasingly stronger material, 163–64; and
    desensitizing males to rape, 167–68; and First Amendment
    rights, 175; as harmful to women, 156–68, 170–71; labora-
    tory experiments concerning, 171–73; and masturbatory
    conditioning, 159; and objectifying women, 164–65; over-
    view of issues on, 155–56; and rape fantasies, 159–63; and
    rape myths, 165–66; and sex offenders, 177–78; and sexual-
    izing dominance and submission, 163, 167; and trivializa-
    tion of rape, 166–67; as undermining males' internal
    inhibitions against rape, 164–68
Porterfield, W. D., 266
Positivist model, of mental disorders, 341
Posner, B. Z., 147
Posner, R., 175
Post, R., 315
Posttraumatic stress disorder, 208, 344
Potter, E., 256, 262
Potter, J., 191, 192
Powch, I. G., 235, 244
Powell, B., 348
Powell, C., 294
Powell, G. N., xxv, 145–47, 291, 292, 298–305, 313, 315, 317
Power and influence: conversational style, 79–99; definitions
    of power and related concepts, 125–28, 140; and domi-
    nance, 149–50; location of power, 126; negotiation strate-
    gies, 135–51; nonverbal behavior, 101–31; process of
    power, 125–26; quality of power, 126–27; subordination-
    power hypothesis of nonverbal decoding ability, 102,
    104–17, 120–31; and temporal relations, 128. See also
    Status
Power-over, 126–27, 140, 374
Power-to, 127n
Power-with, 127, 140
Power-within, 127n

Powlishta, K. K., 51
Premenstrual Dysphoria Disorder, 338, 343, 351–54
Premenstrual syndrome (PMS), 343, 353–54
Prentice, D. A., 21, 24
Prescriptive gender stereotypes, 322
President's Commission on Obscenity and Pornography,
    155, 179
Price, J. L., 20–21
Price, K. H., 315
Price Waterhouse, 307, 310–17, 321–32
Price Waterhouse v. Hopkins, 307–08, 310–17, 321–32
Prior, M. R., 49
Problem solving through dialogue, 140–41
Profile of Nonverbal Sensitivity (PONS), 110–12, 112n,
    121–23
Promise Keepers, 400
Promotions in the workplace, 314–15, 325–26
Prosapio, D., 402
Pruitt, D., 146, 147
Psychiatry. See Diagnostic and Statistical Manual; Psychother-
    apy; and specific disorders
Psychoanalysis, 2, 3, 412–14
Psychology: feminist effort for improving standing of women
    psychologists, 3–6; marginalization of women psycholo-
    gists, 3; "womanless psychology," 7, 55
Psychology of men: emergence of, as field of study, 6–7;
    feminist objections to emphasis on, 6; journals on, 6; my-
    thopoetic men's movement, 6, 399–420; organizations on,
    6; overview of issues on, 399–400; textbooks on, 6
Psychology of Sex Differences (Maccoby and Jacklin), 7, 8, 15
Psychology of women: exclusion of ethnicity and class from,
    5, 21, 55–56; feminist approaches to gender differences ver-
    sus similarities, 7–8; history of, 1–3, 15; journals on, 4;
    overview of current research on, 7–10; recognition of, as
    field of study, 3–6; Stone Center relational theory, 359–79;
    textbooks on, 4–5, 4n
Psychology of Women (Bardwick), 4–5, 4n
Psychology of Women Quarterly, 4, 363
Psychology of Women, The (Matlin), 4n, 5
Psychology of Women, The (Paludi), 4n
Psychosexual development, 2–3, 374, 394, 394n
Psychotherapy: with African-American women, 56; gender
    bias in Diagnostic and Statistical Manual (DSM), 337–55;
    relational theory, 359–79; White middle-class women as
    norm in, 56. See also specific disorders
Ptacek, J., 224, 227
Puerto Ricans, 80
Pugh, M. D., 96
Pulakos, E. D., 314
Putnam, L. L., 148, 150
Pye, L. W., 135

Quantitative synthesis, 25–27
Quarm, D., 223
Quina, K., 235

Rabinowitz, V. R., 15
Race: Asian Americans as category, 65; Black feminist
    thought, 59; categorization of, 65–66; and childhood psy-

chiatric disorders, 346; and conversational style, 79–80, 94; and *Diagnostic and Statistical Manual* (DSM-IV), 337; and discrimination in workplace, 308–09; and domestic violence, 207; and "double" and "triple jeopardy," 56; and education, 268; ethnomethodological perspective on, 65–67, 73; exclusion of women of Color from research, 5, 21, 55–56, 79; family expectations of women, 5; identity based on, 66–67; increased research on, 5; and knowing, 256–57; and learning styles, 83n; mathematical metaphors for relationship between gender and, 58, 59–60, 69, 74; and men's movement, 408; mothering and child care meaning based on, 69–70; and negotiation strategies, 135; and nonverbal behavior, 102; and nonverbal decoding ability, 113–14; oppression of Black men, 56; and pornography, 156; psychotherapy with African-American women, 56; racism and sexism against Black women, 66; and rape, 233; and relational theory, 360; relationships with gender and class, 5–6, 55–75; scientific arguments for inferiority based on, 1; and Senate hearings on Clarence Thomas's nomination to Supreme Court, 70; and smiling behavior, 102; subordination of women of Color through rejection, 21; West Indian immigrants as maids, 67; White middle-class bias in feminist thought on, 59–60; and Women's Ways of Knowing (WWK) model, 250; and working mothers, 383–84. *See also* Social class; *and specific racial groups*
Rachman, S., 159
Radke-Yarrow, M., 48, 49
Radtke, H. L., 125
Rafter, N. H., 67
Ragins, B. R., 304n
Ramsey, S. J., 105, 106, 109, 120
Randall, M., 188
Rape: advocacy research and rape statistics, 236–46; and alcohol use, 237, 245; causative factors for, 158; date rape, 233, 244, 417; definitions of, 233–34, 237, 244–46; false reports of, 237n; *Ms.* study on, 236–40, 238n, 244, 245; pornography as causative factor for, 156–68; pornography's role in desensitizing males to rape, 167–68; pornography's role in undermining males' internal inhibitions against, 164–68; prevention programs concerning, 241, 241n; rape fantasies, 159–63; rape myths, 165–66; Russell's study on, 238–39, 243, 244; Senate Judiciary Committee Hearings on Violence Against Women act, 237–38, 240–41; statistics on, 233–46; trivialization of, by pornography, 166–67; and verbal sexual coercion, 239–40, 244, 245–46; women's confusion about what constitutes rape, 233–34, 236–37, 244
Rape crisis movement, 236, 236n, 241, 241n
Rape fantasies, 159–63
Rape myths, 165–66
Rape statistics, 233–46
Raphael, R., 420
Rapoport, A., 146
Rapport-talk versus report-talk, 80, 87–90, 95
Rashbaum, B., 385
Rattansi, A., 57
Raven, B. H., 125, 146
Raymond, J. G., 366
Raza, S. M., 313

Reagan, R., 412
Reason, J., 189
Received knowing, 254
Records, 399
Reflective judgment theory, 266–67
Reid, P. T., 5, 55
Reid, R. L., 351
Reinisch, J. M., xxv, 35, 37–43, 44–48, 51
Reis, H., 95
Reiss, A. J., Jr., 172n
Relational authenticity, 376–77
Relational development, 378–79
Relational feminism, 258
Relational theory: authenticity and relational self, 376–77; autonomous functioning, 377–78; description of, 363–67; and empowerment for women, 360, 373–79; and moral reasoning, 249, 263, 362–63; and mother-child relationship, 362, 364–67, 375–76; and mutuality, 364–66, 375–76; and needs of the self, 364; overview of issues on, 359–60; patriarchal theory compared with, 373–75; and perpetuation of male privilege, 360, 367–70, 373; relational development versus self-development in, 376–77; self-in-relation, 364, 366–70, 374
Relational view of others, 139
Renwick, P. A., 313
Renzetti, C., 209
Renzulli, J. S., 274
Report-talk versus rapport-talk, 80, 87–90, 95
Representative sample fallacy, and domestic violence statistics, 215–16
Reproduction of Mothering (Chodorow), 9
Research on gender, 1–10. *See also specific topics*
Rest, J. R., 263
Reynolds, D., 89
Rice, R., 97, 301n
Rich, A., 59, 188, 193, 197
Rich, C., 193
Richardson, D., 189
Richters, J., 49, 392n
Ridgeway, D., 48
Riegel, K. F., 266
Rieker, P. P., 339
Risman, B., 93
Robertson, J., 393
Robertson, P., 176
Robins, E., 189
Robinson, A. B., 145
Robinson-Simpson, G., 222, 225, 229
Roche, G. R., 304n
Roe, A., 276
Roe, S., 237n
Rogers, P., 273
Rogers, P. L., 120
Roiphe, K., 234, 243–45
Rollins, J. H., 4n, 383
Rollman, S. A., 113, 129
Romney, D. M., 34, 48, 279
Roots (Haley), 175
Rose, G. L., 315

Rosen, B., 312, 313, 315, 317
Rosenberg, B. G., 5
Rosenberg, R., 2, 9
Rosenblith, J. F., 44, 47
Rosenblum, L. A., xxv, 37–42
Rosener, J. B., xxv–xxvi, 145, 291–92, 294–99, 294n, 302
Rosenholtz, S. J., 128
Rosenkrantz, P. S., 96
Rosenthal, R., 29, 106, 109, 110, 112, 112n, 120, 122, 123, 327
Rosewater, L. B., 350
Rosnow, R. L., 327
Ross, E. M., 37
Ross, I., 135
Ross, L., 92
Ross, L. T., 235
Ross, R., xxvi, 339, 348–56
Rossi, A. S., 189
Roth, J. A., 172n
Rothbaum, F., 49
Rothblum, E. D., 183
Rotundo, E. A., 401
Rozelle, R. M., 317
Rubin, D. B., xxvi, 29, 37–42, 38
Rubin, G., 412, 413
Rubin, J. Z., 135, 146
Rubin, L., 93, 413n
Rubin, Z., 109
Ruble, D. N., 50, 325
Ruble, T. L., 325
Rubner, M. B., 301n
Ruddick, S., 255, 258
Rudenstine, N., ix
Rudolph, J. R., 190
Russell, D., 348
Russell, D. E. H., xxvi, 156, 158–68, 225, 236, 238–39, 243–45
Russo, N. F., 2
Ruston, 189
Rynes, S., 136

Sabatelli, R., 106
Sachs, J., 48
Sackett, P. R., 325
Sadistic Personality Disorder, 351
Sadker, D., 88n, 273
Sadker, M., 88n, 273
Safilios-Rothschild, C., 106
Saghir, M. T., 189
Saitta, M. B., 102, 120
Saks, M. J., 310, 316
Salaries: of Head Start teachers, 391–92, 392n; male-female salary differences, 136
Sampson, E. E., 256
Sand, E. A., 38
Sanday, P. R., 225, 235, 374
Sanders, C. E., 278, 279
Sanson, A. V., 49
Sansonetti, D. M., 326
Sargent, A. G., 295n
SAT, 271, 272, 275, 277–79

Saudi Arabia, 174
Saunders, D., 214, 222, 226, 227
Saunders, S., 227
Savage, G. T., 149, 150
Saxon, S., 21
Scanzoni, J., 211
Scarborough, E., 3
Scarr, S., 310, 384
Schaffer, H., 395, 397
Schafran, L. H., 234
Schapiro, N., 135
Schein, V. E., 312
Scheinfeld, A., 40
Schellhardt, T., 291–92
Schizophrenia, 348
Schlenker, B. R., 146
Schmidt, W. H., 147
Schmitt, N., 314, 317
Schoenberg, N., 237n
Scholastic Aptitude Test (SAT), 271, 272, 275, 277–79
Schrag, J., 243–44, 245
Schulman, M., 211
Schulsinger, M. F. xxvi, 37–42
Schultz, S. J., 189, 194, 195
Schumacher, D., 223
Schwab, D. P., 313
Schwalm, L., 173
Schwartz, F., 291, 298
Schwartz, M., 182, 223
Schwarzkopf, N., 294
Science and engineering careers, 271, 286–87
Scientific arguments on gender, 1–3
Scotland, 395
Scott, J., 173
Scream Quietly or the Neighbors Will Hear (Pizzey), 207
Scudder, J. N., 148
Scully, D., 165
Sears Roebuck & Company, 8–9
Sebald, H., 383
Secada, W. G., 272
Sechzer, J. A., 15
Secret Museum: Pornography in Modern Culture, The (Kendrick), 179
Sedgwick, P., 342
Segerstrale, U., 103
Segura, D. A., 60
Seibel, C. A., 243
Sekulow, J., 176
Self-defeating Personality Disorder, 338, 343, 350–51
Self-empowerment, 127n
Self-in-relation, 364, 366–70, 374
Seligman, J., 353
Sells, L., 271, 272
Senchak, M., 95
Separate knowing, 255
Separate self model of personal development, 373–74
Settle, S. A., 337
Severino, S. K., 352
Sex: definition of, 7. *See also headings beginning with* Gender

Sex and Education; Or, A Fair Chance for the Girls (Clarke), 1–2

Sex and Gender: An Introduction (Lips), 4n

Sex and Gender: The Human Experience (Doyle and Paludi), 4n

Sex and Sensibility (Pally), 171–72, 176

Sex assignment, 63

Sex categorization, 63–64

Sex differences. *See* Gender differences

Sex discrimination: American Psychological Association amicus brief in *Price Waterhouse v. Hopkins,* 307–32; bias against working women, 313–15, 325–27; in hiring decisions, 313; and lack-of-fit model, 311; and normative stereotype model, 311; and penalties for out-of-role behavior, 315–16, 327–28; in performance appraisal, 313–14, 325; in promotions, 314–15, 325–26; relationship with racism, 5–6, 59–60; at Sears Roebuck & Company, 8–9; and stereotyping of working women, 312–13, 324–25; Virginia Military Institute's refusal to admit women, 9–10; in workplace, 8–9, 307–32

Sex-gender system, 412

Sex offenders, and pornography, 177–78

Sex Roles, 4

Sex-roles approach to gender, 61–62

Sex stereotypes. *See* Gender stereotypes

Sexual Abuse of Adult category, in DSM, 343

Sexual assault. *See* Rape

Sexual Exploitation (Russell), 158

Sexual harassment, 70

Sexual orientation: biological causation of, 181–88; coming out process, 190, 198–99; and *Diagnostic and Statistical Manual* (DSM), 181; genetic studies on, 184, 187; and hormones, 181, 182, 185; models of homosexual identity development, 189–201; overview of issues, 181–82; transitions from heterosexuality to lesbianism, 188–201

Sexuality: biological causation of sexual orientation, 181–88; callous attitudes toward female sexuality due to pornography, 167; compulsory heterosexuality, 192–92; media portrayal of, 178; pornography, 155–79; sexual orientation, 181–201; transitions from heterosexuality to lesbianism, 188–201

Shainess, N., 208

Shame, 50

Shapiro, L., 16

Sharp, C., 315

Sharps, M. J., 20–21

Shea, C., 272

Sheldon, A., 48

Shepard, B., 48

Sherer, D., 310

Sherif, C. W., 128, 316

Sherif, M., 130n, 316

Sherman, J. A., 348

Sherman, J. D., 301n

Shields, A. A., 2

Shields, S. A., 285

Shikiar, R., 313

Shively, M. G., 196

Shotter, J., 190, 200, 374

Shucard, D. W., 41

Shupe, A., 222, 225, 229

Shweder, R., 253

Siderits, M., 148

Sigman, M., 396

Silence, and knowing, 254, 257, 262

Sillen, S., 341

Silverman, J., 41

Silverstein, L., 207, 384, 395, 400

Silverstein, O., 385

Simon, H. A., 297n

Simon, M. C., 315, 317, 327

Simon, W. S., 188

Simons, H. W., 190

Simple causation, definition of, 158

Simpson, D., 266

Sims-Knight, J. E., 44, 47

Singapore, 175

Sinnott, J., 265, 266

Skidd, J. E., 51

Slade, L. A., 317

Slavery, 21, 69, 121, 341

Smiling, 20, 101–02, 105, 120n

Smith, A., 16, 101

Smith, B., 193

Smith, C., 51

Smith, M. L., 348

Smith, P. K., 34

Smith, P. M., 96

Smith, W. K., 233

Smollar, J., 92

SMPY. *See* Study of Mathematically Precocious Youth

Snodgrass, S., 93, 106, 108, 109, 114, 115, 122, 124, 128, 129

Snow, M. E., 37, 49

Snyder, E., 33

Snyder, S., 348

Socarides, C. W., 190, 343, 383

Social class: assumptions based on, 67–68; and childhood psychiatric disorders, 346; and "double" and "triple jeopardy," 56; ethnomethodological perspective on, 67–68, 73; and knowing, 256–57; mathematical metaphors for relationship between race and, 58, 59–60, 69, 74; mothering and child care meaning based on, 69–70; and nonverbal decoding ability, 113–14; relationships with ethnicity and gender, 5–6, 55–75; scientific arguments for inferiority based on, 1. *See also* Race

Social constructionism, 190

Social Psychology of Gender, The (Burn), 4n

Social roles, and conversational style, 93

Social status. *See* Status

Social/historical model, of mental disorders, 341

Socialization: of Asian Americans, 5; and gender differences, 34–35, 48–52; of Latinas, 5; as life-long process, 21–22; and negotiation strategies, 147; and nonverbal sensitivity, 115; parents' influence on, 34–35, 48–51

Society for the Psychological Study of Men and Masculinity, 6

Solicitor General of Canada, 223

Solomon, B., 95

Somatization Disorder, 344

Sommer, R., 104
Sonenstein, F. L., 384
Sorenson, R. L., 149
Sorenson, S. B., 211
Southern, M. L., 276
Spain, D., 415
Spam, P., 353
Spatial cognitive performance, 20–21
Spelman, E. V., 59, 60, 61, 66, 258
Spence, J. T., 111, 316
Spencer, 195
Spender, D., 88, 88n
Spiegel, F. S., 41
Spitz, R., 383, 393
Spitzer, R. L., 343, 348, 351
Spousal abuse. See Domestic violence
Sprecher, S., 106
Sprock, J., 348
SST. See Strange Situation Test
Stacey, J., 61
Stacey, W., 222, 225
Stake, J. E., 149
Stake, M. N., 149
Stam, H. J., 125
Standard score, 26
Stange, T., 48
Stanko, E., 222
Stanley, J. C., 271, 274, 277, 278, 283
Stanton, E. C., 109
Stapp, J., 316
Starhawk, 125, 126, 127n
Stark, E., 223, 225, 226
Stark, R., 216
Status: and conversational style, 89–90, 92–93; "diffuse status," 128; and gender differences, 50–52; and negotiation styles, 136, 145–51; and nonverbal sensitivity, 102, 104–17, 120–31; oppressed status, 111; sex roles as "master statuses," 61; and smiling, 120n. See also Power and influence
Stead, B. A., 295n
Steffen, V. J., 216, 348
Stein, E., 188, 190
Stein, R. M., 156
Steinbacher, R., 47
Steinmetz, S. K., 208, 211, 222, 225, 227, 229
Stephans, N., 61, 65
Stereotypes. See Gender stereotypes
Stern, D., 366
Stern, M., 34
Stern, N., 193
Sternberg, K. J., 385
Stets, J. E., 210–12, 218, 219, 222, 225
Stevens, C. K., 136, 137
Stevens, G. E., 301n
Stevenson-Hinde, J., 49
Stewart, J., 37, 40
Stewart, L. P., 79
Stier, D. S., 108, 109
Stimpson, C. R., ix

Stitt, C., 94
Stiver, I. P., 258, 344, 359, 361, 364, 365, 368, 370
Stogdill, R. M., 317
Stone Center, 258, 262, 344, 359–79, 364n
Stopeck, M. H., 314, 317, 325–26
Stoppard, J. M., 103
Storer, H., 1
Strahan, R. F., 327
Strange Situation Test (SST), 395–96, 396n
Straton, J. C., 208
Straus, M. A., xxvi, 173–74, 208, 210–19, 222, 224–29
Strega, L., 189
Strickland, B., 181
Strober, M., 292
Strossen, N., xxvi, 156, 170–79
Stuckless, N., 223
Study of Mathematically Precocious Youth (SMPY), 274–79, 283
Stumpf, S. A., 314
Subjective knowing, 254
Submissiveness: and conversational style, 96; and nonverbal behavior, 108; and nonverbal sensitivity, 122–23; pornography and sexualizing submission, 163. See also Power and influence; Status
Subordination: as stable and enduring condition, 125; state approach to, 122, 124; trait approach to, 121–24
Subordination-power hypothesis: definitions of power and related concepts, 125–28; modifying factors concerning, 128–29; motivation's role in, 130–31; of nonverbal decoding ability, 102, 104–17, 120–31; psychological mechanisms implicated in, 129–31; state approach to testing, 122, 124; and temporal relations, 128; trait approach to testing, 121–24
Success, attributions for, 315
Sugarman, D. B., 212
Sugimoto, T., 212
Suh, E. J., 20
Sullivan, A. M., 57
Sullivan, M. W., 50
Super, C. M., 44, 45
Suppe, F., 190
Surrey, J. L., 140, 144, 258, 344, 359, 361, 364–67, 370, 375
Swacker, M., 87
Sweden, 175
Swift, C. F., 364
Swim, J., 330
Swisher, K. L., 209
Sympson, S. C., xxvi, 243–46
Szinovacz, M. E., 210
Szumski, B., 209

Tag questions and qualifiers, 96
Tajfel, H., 114
Talbot, D., 420
Talking Nine to Five (Tannen), 80, 94
Tamplin, A., 49
Tannen, D., xxvi–xxvii, 80–91, 94, 95, 97–99, 291, 295n
Tannenbaum, A., 275, 277
Tannenbaum, P. H., 179n

Tarule, J., 249–50, 252, 255
Task style of leadership, 300
Tasker, F., 183
Tatum, B. D., 361
Tavris, C., 8, 17, 145, 338
Taylor, A., 137
Taylor, B., 307, 308
Taylor, J. M., 57, 258, 262
Taylor, S. E., 312–14, 324, 325
Taynor, J., 315, 327
Teachers, influence on gender development, 49–50
Teasdale, T. W., 38
Tedeschi, J. T., 146
Telles, C. A., 211
Terborg, J., 147, 313
Terhune, 146
Terpstra, D. E., 313, 317
Tesman, J. R., 48
Tester, M., 310
Textbooks: on psychology of men, 6; on psychology of
    women, 4–5, 4n
Thacker, R. A., 137
That's Not What I Meant! (Tannen), 81
Thayer, S., 112n
Thelen, E., 44
Theodorson, A., 158–59
Theodorson, G., 158–59
Theory of Work Adjustment, 275–79
Therapy. *See* Psychotherapy
Thoma, S., 263
Thoman, E. B., 37
Thomas, A., 341, 383
Thomas, C., 70
Thomas, D. L., 109
Thomas, M. C., 1
Thomas, V. G., 272
Thomas, W. I., 2
Thompson, C. A., 198
Thompson, D. E., 314
Thompson, K., 164
Thompson, T., 276
Thompson, T. A., 314
Thorndike, E. L., 278
Thorne, B., 36, 61, 62, 98, 106
Tiefer, L., 4
Tifft, L. L., 209
Timmons, M., 266
Tobias, S., 271
Tobin, P., 145
Tokenism, 308–09, 312–13, 324
Tong, R., 251
Torgler, C., 234
Tosi, H., 313
Tracy, D. M., 34
Tracy, K., 94
"Triple jeopardy," 56
Troemel-Ploetz, S., 80
Troiden, R. R., 189
Truth, S., 21

Tsui, A. S., 314
Tunnel vision, cognitive, 129
Turkey, 286
Turner, P. J., 50
Tyree, A., 211
Tyson, M., 233

Ulrich, B. D., 44
Unger, R., 4n, 8, 10, 116, 128, 253, 272, 309
Ungerer, J., 396
Uniform Crime Reports, 234, 239
U.S. Bureau of the Census, 212, 239
U.S. Bureau of Justice Statistics, 174, 241
U.S. Department of Justice, 9–10, 210, 212, 223, 234
U.S. Department of Labor, 136
U.S. General Accounting Office, 304
U.S. Glass Ceiling Commission, 292
U.S. Senate Judiciary Committee hearings on Violence
    Against Women Act, 237–38, 240
University of California, Berkeley, 241n, 271
University of California, Irvine, 291
University of Michigan, 155
University of New Hampshire, 208
Ury, W., 135, 151
Usher, B., 48
Ussher, J. M., 339
Uylings, H. B. M., 37, 40

Van Dyke, D., 89
Van Nostrand, C. H., 293
Van White, 167
Verbal performance, cross-cultural patterns, 21
Verdi, A., 95
Vernon, P. E., 278
Veroff, J., 57, 251, 253
Vetere, V. A., 191, 194
Vidal, G., 170
Villanova, P., 317
Vinacke, 146
Violence: child abuse, 225; domestic violence, 207–29; por-
    nography as causative factor for rape, 156–68; rape statis-
    tics, 233–46
Violence Against Women Act, 237–38, 240–41
Virginia Military Institute (VMI), 9–10
Vissing, Y. M., 210
Vobejda, B., 234
Vogel, S. R., 96
Voice, as metaphor, 257
Voight, N. L., 50
Vonk, R., 22
Vroom, V. H., 316
Vrugt, A., 120

Wagner, D. G., 96
Wahrman, R., 96
Walberg, H. J., 274
Walker, L. E., 208, 212, 224, 348, 350, 351
Walker, L. J., 263
Wall, S., 396n

Wallach, M. A., 274
Wallston, B., 108
Walsh, J. P., 315, 326
Walsh, M. R., ix, x, xxvii, 1–10, 15–17, 33–35, 55–56, 79–80, 101–02, 135–36, 155–56, 181–82, 207–08, 233–34, 249–50, 271–72, 291–92, 307–09, 337–39, 359–60, 383–84, 399–401
Walton, A. L., 20–21
Ward, J. W., 258, 262
Wardell, L., 228
Ware, W. B., 50
Warshaw, R., 237, 240–41
Waters, E., 396n
Watson, C., xxvii, 136, 141, 145–51
Watson, J. S., 41
Watzlawick, P., 256
Weeks, J., 188
Weinberg, M. S., 188, 189, 199
Weinberg, R. M., 315, 326
Weinberg, T. S., 189
Weinrich, J. D., 184, 190
Weinstock, J., 257
Weiss, C., 255, 258
Weisstein, N., ix, 7, 55
Weisz, J. R., 49
Weitz, S., 106, 109, 120
Weitzel-O'Neill, P. A., 147
Wekesser, C., 209
Well of Loneliness, The (Hall), 195
Wellesley College, Stone Center, 258, 262, 344, 359–79
Werner, P. D., 96
Wertheim, M., 273
West, C., xxvii, 56, 58–70, 73, 74, 97
West, M. J., 49
West Germany, 175
West Indian immigrants, as maids, 67
West Point, 97
Western Europe, 407, 489. *See also specific countries*
Westkott, M., xxvii, 3, 360, 362–70, 373, 375, 377
Wetherell, M., 191, 192, 401
Wex, M., 106
Wexley, K. N., 314
Whalen, M., 236n
Wheelan, S., 95
Whitam, F. L., 184, 185
White, B., 384
Whites: bias in feminist thought on gender and race, 59–60; conversational style of, 79, 94; and discrimination in workplace, 307–32; and domestic violence, 207; learning styles of, 83n; and men's movement, 402–03, 408; mothering and child care as constitutive of oppression, 69–70; negotiation strategies of, 135; poor families, 383; predominance of research on, and exclusion of women of Color, 5, 21, 55–56, 62, 79; privileged position of, 21; and relational theory, 360; and Senate hearings on Clarence Thomas's nomination to Supreme Court, 70; subordination of, through seduction, 21; and Women's Ways of Knowing (WWK) model, 250
Whyte, W. H., 406
Widick, C., 266

Widiger, T. A., xxvii, 337, 348–56
Widom, C. W., 348
Wiener, J., 9
Wiener, M., 101
Wilback, K., 317
Wildman Gatherings, 402, 404, 411–12, 417–18
Wiley, J. W., 316, 317
Wiley, M. G., 96, 97, 316
Wilhem, S., 163
Wilkinson, S., xxvii, 182, 188–201
Williams, D. A., 271
Williams, J. B. W., 348
Williams, J. E., 96
Williams, K. R., 213
Williams, P., 73
Williams Committee, 175n
Williamson, N. E., 47
Willie, C. V., 57, 339
Willinsky, J., 251
Willis, C. E., 29
Willis, E., 175
Willson, A., 103
Wilson, A. E., 102
Wilson, D. M., 272
Wilson, E. O., 41
Wilson, M., 222, 223
Wilson, S. K., 219
Wilson, W. E., 49
Wilton, T., 198
Winant, H., 61, 65, 66
Wingfield, L., 264, 265
Winnicott, D. W., 375
Wintrob, R. M., 337
Wisniewski, N., 236–37, 238n, 243
Witt, C., 256
Wittig, M., 55
Wohlers, A. J., 299n
Wolf, D. A., 384
Wolf, K., 393
Wolf, N., 360
Wolfe, D. A., 219
Wolff, P. H., 40
Wolfgang, M. E., 213
Women and Gender: A Feminist Psychology (Unger and Crawford), 4n
Women and Madness (Chesler), 359
Women and the Art of Negotiating (Nierenberg and Ross), 135
Women of Color: and childhood psychiatric disorders, 346; conversational style of, 79–80, 94; and *Diagnostic and Statistical Manual* (DSM-IV), 337; and discrimination in workplace, 308–09; and domestic violence, 207; education of, 268; exclusion of, from research, 5, 21, 55–56, 79; feminist thought of, 59; impact of ethnicity and gender on, 5–6; increased research on, 5, 55–56; and knowing, 256–57; learning styles of, 83n; mothering and child care meaning for, 69–70; negotiation strategies of, 135; nonverbal behavior of, 102; and nonverbal decoding ability, 113–14; and pornography, 156; racism and sexism against, 66; and rape, 233; and relational theory, 360; scientific ar-

guments for inferiority of, 1; and Senate hearings on Clarence Thomas's nomination to Supreme Court, 70; and smiling behavior, 102; subordination of, through rejection, 21; West Indian immigrants as maids, 67; and Women's Ways of Knowing (WWK) model, 250; working mothers, 383–84. *See also specific ethnic and racial groups*

Women's Growth in Connection (Jordan et al.), 360

Women's Lives: Themes and Variation in Gender Learning (Lott), 4n

Women's Minds Women's Bodies: The Psychology of Women in a Biosocial Context (Rollins), 4n

Women's psychology. *See* Psychology of women

Women's Ways of Knowing (Belenky et al.), 249–50, 252–58

Women's Ways of Knowing (WWK) model: definitions of construct of, 261–62; and different ways of knowing, 253–56; empirical studies of, 258, 262–65; and feminist controversy on psychology of difference, 257–58; insufficient evidence for, 261–68; and metaphors of voice and silence, 257; overview of issues, 249–50; and personal epistemology, 253; proponents of, 252–59; and "right" way to know, 256–57; and social context of meaning-making, 252–53

Wong, S. P., 29–30

Wood, J. T., 81, 103

Wood, P. K., 265, 267

Wood, W., 27, 30, 96

Woodward, C. V., xi

Wooley, D. E., 96

Woolf, V., xi, 109

Woolley, H. T., 2, 3, 15

Work Adjustment Theory, 275–79

Workplace: agreeable behavior versus quarrelsomeness in, 20; American Psychological Association amicus brief in *Price Waterhouse v. Hopkins*, 307–32; AT&T study of managers, 299–302; attributions given for women's success, 315; bias against working women, 313–15, 325–27; command-and-control model of leadership, 294; devaluation of masculine women, 315–16, 307–32; effectiveness of managers not based on gender differences, 298–305; females devalued when performing masculine jobs, 315; "glass ceiling" in, 291–92; hiring decisions, 313; interactive leadership model, 294–97; Iron Maiden stereotype, 312, 324; leadership, 291–305; male-female salary differences, 136; mentoring programs in, 304; negotiation strategies in, 135–51; nonverbal sensitivity and

"boss-employee" relationship, 115, 121, 124; nonverbal sensitivity and salary differences, 123; "parent tracks" in, 303–04; parental leave, 384; and penalties for out-of-role behavior, 315–16, 327–28; performance appraisal, 313–14, 325; power and managerial role, 150; power relationships in, 127; promotions, 314–15, 325–26; reasons for few women in high-math-ability careers, 286–87; sex discrimination at Sears Roebuck & Company, 8–9; stereotyping of working women, 312–13, 324–25; tokenism in, 308–09, 312–13, 324; training and development programs for managers, 304–05; women as better managers than men, 292, 294–99; women in top management, 291–92; working mothers and children's well being, 383–97

Wyatt, G. E., 235

Wylie, P., 383

Yee, D. K., 272

Yegidis, B., 240

Yllö, K. A., 218, 222, 224, 226

Yoder, J. D., 8, 17, 125

You Just Don't Understand (Tannen), 80, 91

Young, B. G., 159

Young, I. M., 57

Young, K., 389n

Youniss, J., 92

Zachau-Christiansen, B., 37

Zahn-Waxler, C., 48, 392n

Zanna, M., 164–65

Zavella, P., 69

Zeitz, B., 303n

Zelazo, N. A., 45

Zelazo, P. D., 45

Zelazo, P. R., 45, 47

Zelditch, M., Jr., 128, 147

Zeldow, P. B., 348

Zeus energy, 416

Zigler, E., 384, 389n

Zikmund, W. G., 313, 317

Zillmann, D., 163–64, 166, 167, 168n

Zimmerman, D. H., 58, 61–64, 66, 68, 97

Zinn, M. B., 57

Zucker, K. J., 182, 185

Zuckerman, H., 275, 277

Zuger, B., 182